Active Defense

A Comprehensive Guide to Network Security

Active Defense

A Comprehensive Guide to Network Security

Chris Brenton
with Cameron Hunt

SYBEX®

San Francisco • Paris • Düsseldorf • Soest • Paris

Associate Publisher: Richard J. Staron

Contracts and Licensing Manager: Kristine O'Callaghan

Acquisitions and Developmental Editor: Maureen Adams

Editor: Colleen Wheeler Strand

Production Editor: Elizabeth Campbell

Technical Editor: Scott Warmbrand

Book Designer: Kris Warrenburg

Graphic Illustrator: Tony Jonick

Electronic Publishing Specialist: Maureen Forys, Happenstance Type-O-Rama

Proofreaders: Nanette Duffy, Emily Hsuan, Nelson Kim, Laurie O'Connell, Nancy Riddiough

Indexer: Rebecca Plunkett

CD Coordinator: Christine Harris

CD Technician: Kevin Ly

Cover Designer: Richard Miller, Calyx Design

Cover Illustrator: Richard Miller, Calyx Design

*This book is dedicated to my son,
Skylar Griffin Brenton. May the joy you have
brought into my life be returned to you threefold.*

—Chris Brenton

*This book is dedicated to security professionals
everywhere—only the truly paranoid know peace!*

—Cameron Hunt

ACKNOWLEDGMENTS

I would like to thank all the Sybex people who took part in pulling this book together. This includes Guy Hart-Davis (a.k.a. "The Text Butcher") for getting me started on the right track. Yet again I owe you a bottle of home-brewed mead. I also want to say thank you to Maureen Adams for kicking in on the initial development and CD-ROM work. I also wish to thank my technical editor, Jim Polizzi, whose up-front and challenging style helped to keep me on my toes.

I also wish to thank a few people over at Alpine Computers in Holliston, Mass., for giving input, making suggestions, and just being a cool crew. This includes Cheryl "I Was the Evil Queen but Now I'm Just the Witch Who Lives in the Basement" Gordon for her years of experience and mentoring. Thanks to Chuckles Ahern, Dana Gelinas, Gene Garceau, Phil Sointu, Ron Hallam, Gerry Fowley, the guys in the ARMOC, Bob Sowers, Steve Howard, Alice Peal, and all the members of the firewall and security group for keeping me challenged technically (or technically challenged, whichever the case may be).

On a more personal note, I would like to thank Sean Tangney, Deb Tuttle, Al "That Was Me behind You with the BFG" Goodniss, Maria Goodniss, Chris Tuttle, Toby Miller, Lynn Catterson, and all the Babylonian honeys for being such an excellent group of friends. Thanks to Morgan Stern, who is one of the smartest computer geeks I know and is more than happy to share his knowledge with anyone who asks. Thanks also to Fred Tuttle for being a cool old-time Vermonter and for showing that people can still run for political office and keep a sense of humor.

I also wish to thank my parents Albert and Carolee, as well as my sister Kym. The happiness I have today comes from the love, guidance, and nurturing I have received from you over many years. I could not have wished for a better group of people to call my family.

Finally, I would like to thank my wonderful wife and soul mate Andrea for being the best thing ever to walk into my life. My life would not be complete without you in it, and this book would not have been possible without your support. Thank you for making me the luckiest man alive.

—Chris Brenton

I'd like to thank my friends for their patience, my family for their tolerance, and of course, Nikka, whose knowledge of all my vices and vulnerabilities allowed her to use an astonishing array of incentives to force my timely completion of this book.

I owe an incredible debt to the many security professionals—who have shared their nuanced understanding of current security technologies and the issues surrounding their use—for the preparation of this book. This revision is as much yours as mine.

I owe Jill Schlessinger a tremendous debt for giving me this opportunity in the first place. She patiently listened to my radical revision plan, ignored it, and forced me to follow common sense. She was right all along. Maureen Adams accomplished institutional miracles, while Elizabeth Campbell and Colleen Strand employed the most ingenius good cop-bad cop routine to keep me properly motivated, and more importantly—on schedule! Thank you ladies, the pleasure has been all mine!

—Cameron Hunt

CONTENTS AT A GLANCE

CONTENTS

Introduction

Some of us can remember a time when securing a network environment was a far easier task than it seems to be today. As long as every user had a password and the correct levels of file permissions had been set, we could go to sleep at night confident that our network environment was relatively secure. This confidence may or may not have been justified, but at least we *felt* secure.

Then along came the Internet and everything changed. The Internet has accelerated at an amazing rate the pace at which information is disseminated. In the early 1990s, most of us would not hear about a security vulnerability unless it made it into a major magazine or newspaper. Even then, the news release typically applied to an old version of software that most of us no longer used anyway. These days, hundreds of thousands of people can be made privy to the details of a specific vulnerability in less than an hour.

This is not to say that all this discussion of product vulnerabilities is a bad thing. Actually, quite the opposite is true. Individuals with malicious intent have always had places to exchange ideas. Pirate bulletin boards have been around since the 1980s. Typically, it was the rest of us who were left out in the cold with no means of dispersing this information to the people who needed it most: the network administrators attempting to maintain a secure environment. The Internet has become an excellent means to get vulnerability information into the hands of the people responsible for securing their environments.

Increased awareness also brings increased responsibility. This is not only true for the software company that is expected to fix the vulnerability; it is also true for the network administrator or security specialist who is expected to deploy the fix. Any end user with a subscription to a mailing list can find out about vulnerabilities as quickly as the networking staff. This greatly increases the urgency of deploying security-related fixes as soon as they are developed. (As if we didn't have enough on our plates already!)

So, along with all of our other responsibilities, we need to maintain a good security posture. The first problem is where to begin. Should you purchase a book on firewalls or on securing your network servers? Maybe you need to learn more about network communications in order to be able to understand how these vulnerabilities can even exist. Should you be worried about running backups or redundant servers?

One lesson that has been driven home since the publication of the first edition of this book is the need to view security not as a static package, but rather as a constant process incorporating all facets of networking and information technology. You cannot focus on one single aspect of your network and expect your environment to remain secure. Nor can this process be done in isolation from other networking activities. This book provides system and network administrators with the information they will need to run a network with multiple layers of security protection, while considering issues of usability, privacy, and manageability.

What This Book Covers

Chapter 1 starts you off with a look at why someone might attack an organization's network resources. You will learn about the different kinds of attacks and what an attacker stands to gain by launching them. At the end of the chapter, you'll find a worksheet to help you gauge the level of potential threat to your network.

Chapter 2 introduces risk analysis and security policies. The purpose of a risk analysis is to quantify the level of security your network environment requires. A security policy defines your organization's approach to maintaining a secure environment. These two documents create the foundation you will use when selecting and implementing security precautions.

In Chapter 3, you'll get an overview of how systems communicate across a network. The chapter looks at how the information is packaged and describes the use of protocols. You'll read about vulnerabilities in routing protocols and which protocols help to create the most secure environment. Finally, the chapter covers services such as FTP, HTTP, and SMTP, with tips on how to use them securely.

Chapter 4 gets into topology security. In this chapter, you'll learn about the security strengths and weaknesses of different types of wiring, as well as different types of logical topologies, such as Ethernet and Frame Relay. Finally, you'll look at different types of networking hardware, such as switches, routers, and layer-3 switching, to see how these devices can be used to maintain a more secure environment.

Chapter 5 discusses perimeter security devices such as packet filters and firewalls. You will create an access control policy (based on the security policy created in Chapter 2) and examine the strengths and weaknesses of different firewalling methods. Also included are some helpful tables for developing your access control policy, such as a description of all of the TCP flags as well as descriptions of ICMP type code.

In Chapter 6, we'll discuss creating access control lists on a Cisco router. The chapter begins with securing the Cisco router itself and then goes on to describe both standard and extended access lists. You'll see what can and cannot be blocked using packet filters and take a look at a number of access list samples. The end of the chapter looks at Cisco's new reflexive filtering, which allows the router to act as a dynamic packet filter.

You'll see how to deploy a firewall in your environment in Chapter 7. Specifically, you'll walk through the setup and configuration of Check Point's FireWall-1: securing the underlying operating system, installing the software, and implementing an access control policy.

Chapter 8 discusses intrusion detection systems (IDS). You'll look at the traffic patterns an IDS can monitor, as well as some of the technology's limitations. As a specific IDS example, you will take a look at Internet Security Systems' RealSecure. This includes operating system preparation, software installation, and how to configure RealSecure to check for specific types of vulnerabilities.

Chapter 9 looks at authentication and encryption. You will learn why strong authentication is important and what kinds of attacks exploit weak authentication methods. You'll also read about different kinds of encryption and how to select the right algorithm and key size for your encryption needs.

Read Chapter 10 to learn about virtual private networking (VPN), including when the deployment of a VPN makes sense and what options are available for deployment. As a specific example, you will see how to use two FireWall-1 firewalls to create a VPN. You will also see before and after traces, so you will know exactly what a VPN does to your data stream.

Chapter 11 discusses viruses, Trojan horses, and worms. This chapter illustrates the differences between these applications and shows exactly what they can and cannot do to your systems. You will see different methods of protection and some design examples for deploying prevention software.

Chapter 12 is all about disaster prevention and recovery, peeling away the different layers of your network to see where disasters can occur. The discussion starts with network cabling and works its way inside your network servers. You'll even look at creating redundant links for your WAN. The chapter ends by discussing the setup and use of Qualix Group's clustering product OctopusHA+.

Novell's NetWare operating system is featured in Chapter 13. In this chapter, you'll learn about ways to secure a NetWare environment through user account settings, file permissions, and NDS design. We'll discuss the auditing features that are available with the operating system. Finally, you'll look at what vulnerabilities exist in NetWare and how you can work around them.

Chapter 14 discusses Microsoft Windows networking technologies, specifically NT server and Windows 2000 Server. You'll look at designing a domain structure that will enhance your security posture, as well as how to use policies. We'll discuss working with user accounts' logging and file permissions, as well as some of the password insecurities with Windows NT/2000. Finally, you'll read about the IP services available with NT and some of the security caveats in deploying them.

Chapter 15 is all about UNIX (and the UNIX clones, Linux and FreeBSD). Specifically, you'll see how to lock down a system running the Linux operating system. You'll look at user accounts, file permissions, and IP services. This chapter includes a detailed description of how to rebuild the operating system kernel to enhance security even further.

Ever wonder how an evil villain might go about attacking your network resources? Read Chapter 16, which discusses how attackers collect information, how they may go about probing for vulnerabilities, and what types of exploits are available. You'll also look at some of the canned software tools that are available to attackers.

Chapter 17 shows you how you can stay informed about security vulnerabilities. This chapter describes the information available from both product vendors and a number of third-party resources. Vulnerability databases, Web sites, and mailing lists are discussed. Finally, the chapter ends with a look at auditing your environment using Kane Security analyst, a tool that helps you to verify that all of your systems are in compliance with your security policy.

Who Should Read This Book

The book is specifically geared toward the individual who does not have ten years of experience in the security field—but is still expected to run a tight ship. If you are a security guru who is looking to fill in that last five percent of your knowledge base, this may not be the book for you.

If, however, you are looking for a practical guide that will help you to identify your areas of greatest weakness, you have come to the right place. This book was written with the typical network or system administrator in mind, those administrators who have a pretty good handle on networking and the servers they are expected to manage, but who need to find out what they can do to avoid being victimized by a security breach.

Network security would be a far easier task if we could all afford to bring in a $350-per-hour security wizard to audit and fix our computer environment. For most of us, however, this is well beyond our budget constraints. A strong security posture does not have to be expensive—but it does take time and attention to detail. The more holes you can patch within your networking environment, the harder it will be for someone to ruin your day by launching a network-based attack.

If you have any questions or comments regarding any of the material in this book, feel free to e-mail us at cbrenton@sover.net or cam@cameronhunt.com.

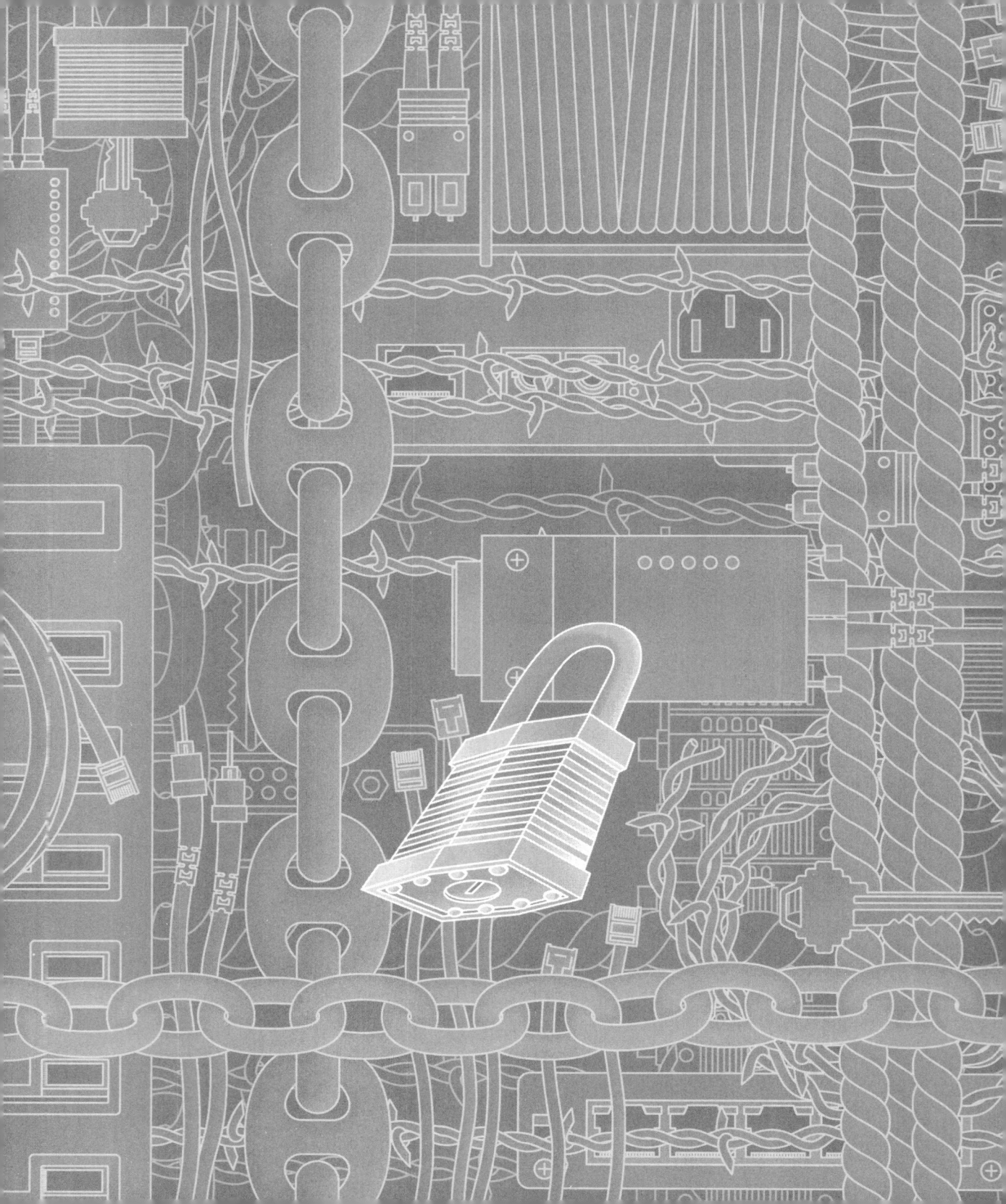

Why Secure Your Network?

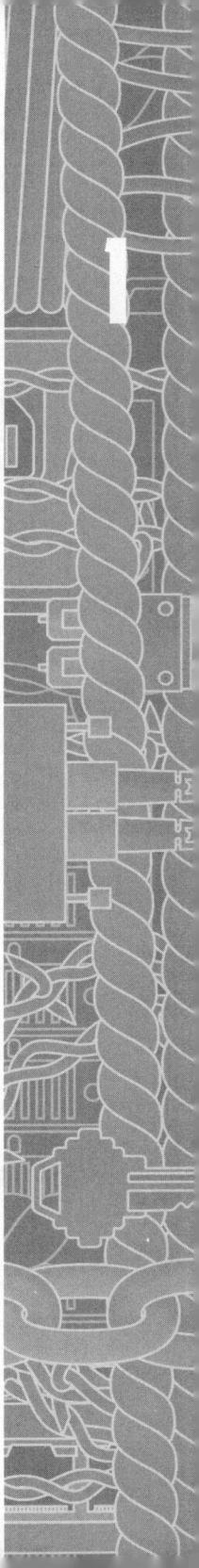

You only have to look at the daily newspaper to see that computer-based attacks are on the rise. Nearly every day, we hear that systems run by government and private organizations have been disrupted or penetrated. Even high-profile entities like the U.S. military and Microsoft have been hacked. You might wonder what you can do to protect your company, when organizations like these can fall prey to attack.

To make matters worse, not all attacks are well publicized. While attacks against the FBI may make the front page, many lower-profile attacks never even reach the public eye. Revealing to the public that a company has had its financial information or latest product designs stolen can cause serious economic effects. For example, consider what would happen if a bank announced that its computer security had been breached and a large sum of money stolen. If you had accounts with this bank, what would you do? Clearly, the bank would want to keep this incident quiet.

Finally, there may well be a large number of attacks that go completely undocumented. The most common are insider attacks: in such cases, an organization may not wish to push the issue beyond terminating the employee. For example, a well-known museum once asked me to evaluate its current network setup. The museum director suspected that the networking staff may have been involved in some underhanded activities.

I found that the networking staff had infiltrated every user's mailbox (including the director's), the payroll database, and the contributors' database. They were also using the museum's resources to run their own business and to distribute software tools that could be used to attack other networks. Despite all these infractions, the museum chose to terminate the employees without pursuing any legal action. Once terminated, these ex-employees attempted to utilize a number of "back doors" that they had set up for themselves into the network. Even in light of this continued activity, the museum still chose not to pursue criminal charges, because it did not wish to make the incident public.

There are no clear statistics on how many security incidents go undocumented. My own experience suggests that most, in fact, are not documented. Clearly, security breaches are on the rise, and every network needs strategies to prevent attack.

TIP   You can report security intrusions to the Computer Emergency Response Team (CERT) Coordination Center at `cert@cert.org`. CERT issues security bulletins and can also facilitate the release of required vendor patches.

Before we get into the meat of how to best secure your environment, we need to do a little homework. To start, we will look at who might attack your network—and why.

Thinking Like an Attacker

In order to determine how to best guard your resources, you must identify who would want to disrupt them. Most attacks are not considered random; the person staging the attack usually believes there is something to gain by disrupting your assets. For example, a crook is more likely to rob someone who appears wealthy, because the appearance of wealth suggests larger financial gain. Identifying who stands to gain from stealing or disrupting your resources is the first step toward protecting them.

Attacker, Hacker, and Cracker

People, from trade magazine writers to Hollywood moviemakers, often use the words *attacker*, *hacker*, and *cracker* interchangeably. The phrase "we got hacked" has come to mean "we were attacked."

However, there are some strong distinctions between the three terms, and understanding the differences will help you to understand who is trying to help reinforce your security posture—and who is trying to infiltrate it. An *attacker* is someone who looks to steal or disrupt your assets. An attacker may be technically adept or a rank amateur. An attacker best resembles a spy or a crook.

The original meaning of a *hacker* was someone with a deep understanding of computers and/or networking. Hackers are not satisfied with simply executing a program; they need to understand all the nuances of how it works. A hacker is someone who feels the need to go beyond the obvious. The art of hacking can be either positive or negative, depending on the personalities and motivations involved.

Hacking has become its own subculture, with its own language and accepted social practices. It is probably human nature that motivates people outside of this subculture to identify hackers as attackers or even anarchists. In my opinion, however, hackers are more like revolutionaries.

History teems with individuals whose motivation was beyond the understanding of the mainstream culture of their time. Da Vinci, Galileo, Byron, Mozart, Tesla—all were considered quite odd and out of step with the accepted social norm. In the information age, this revolutionary role is being filled by the individuals we call hackers.

Hackers tend not to take statements at face value. For example, when a vendor claims, "Our product is 100 percent secure," a hacker may take this statement as a personal challenge. What a hacker chooses to do with the information uncovered, however, is what determines what color hat a particular hacker wears.

To distinguish between hackers who are simply attempting to further their understanding of any information system and those who use that knowledge to illegally or unethically penetrate systems, some in the computer industry use the term *cracker* to refer to the latter. This was an attempt to preserve the traditional meaning of the term "hacker," but this effort has mostly been unsuccessful. Occasionally publications still use the term. The law, however, does not recognize the difference in intent, only the similar behavior of unauthorized system penetration.

White Hat, Grey Hat, and Black Hat Hackers

A hacker who finds a method of exploiting a security loophole in a program, and who tries to publish or make known the vulnerability, is called a *white hat* hacker. If, however, a hacker finds a security loophole and chooses to use it against unsuspecting victims for personal gain, that hacker wears a *black hat*. A *grey hat* hacker is someone who is a "white hat by day, black hat by night." In other words, hackers who are usually employed as legitimate security consultants, but continue their illegal activity on their own time.

Let's look at an example of someone who might be considered a grey hat. Imagine Jane, a security consultant who finds an insecure back door to an operating system. Although Jane does not use the exploit to attack unsuspecting victims, she does charge a healthy fee in order to secure her client's systems against this attack. In other words, Jane is not exploiting the deficiency *per se*, but she is using this deficiency for her own personal gain. In effect, she is extorting money from organizations in order to prevent them from being left vulnerable. Jane does not work with the manufacturer towards creating a public fix for this problem, because it is clearly within her best interests to insure that the manufacturer does not release a free patch.

To cloud the issue even further, many people mistake the motivation of those who post the details of known bugs to public forums. People often assume that these individuals are announcing such vulnerabilities in order to educate other attackers. This could not be further from the truth—releasing vulnerability information to the public alerts vendors and system administrators to a problem and the need to address it. Many times, publicly announcing a vulnerability is done out of frustration or necessity.

For example, back when the Pentium was the newest Intel chip in town, users found a bug that caused computation errors in the math coprocessor portion of the chip. When this problem was first discovered, a number of people did try to contact Intel directly in order to report the problem. I spoke with a few, and all stated that their claims were met with denial or indifference.

It was not until details of the bug were broadcast throughout the Internet and discussed in open forums that Intel took steps to rectify the problem. While Intel did finally stand by its product with a free chip replacement program, people had to air Intel's dirty laundry in public to get the problem fixed. Making bugs and deficiencies public knowledge can be a great way to force a resolution.

NOTE It is proper etiquette to inform a product's vendor of a problem first and not make a public announcement until a patch has been created. The general guideline is to give a vendor at least two weeks to create a patch before announcing a vulnerability in a public forum.

Most manufacturers have become quite responsive to this type of reporting. For example, Microsoft will typically issue fixes to security-related problems within a few days of their initial announcement. Once the deficiency is public knowledge, most vendors will want to rectify the problem as quickly as possible.

Public airing of such problems has given some observers the wrong idea. When someone finds a security-related problem and reports it to the community at large, others may think that the reporter is an attacker who is exploiting the security deficiency for personal gain. This openness in discussing security-related issues, however, has led to an increase in software integrity.

Why Would Someone Want to Ruin My Day?

So what motivates a person to stage an attack against your network? As stated, it is extremely rare for these attacks to be random. They almost always require that something be gained by the attack. What provokes the attack depends on your organization and on the individual staging the attack.

Attacks from Within

Case studies have shown that a vast majority of attacks originate from within an organization. In fact, some studies state that as much as 70 percent of all attacks come from someone within an organization or from someone with inside information (such as an ex-employee). While using firewalls to protect assets from external attacks is all the rage, it is still the employees—who have an insider's view of how your network operates—who are responsible for the greatest amount of damage to, or compromise of, your data. This damage can be accidental (as in user error), or in some cases, intentional.

The most typical cause of a true attack is a disgruntled employee or ex-employee. I once responded to an emergency call from a new client who had completely lost Internet connectivity. Because this was a research firm, Internet access was essential.

Apparently the firm had decided to let an employee "move on to other opportunities," despite the fact that the employee did not wish to leave. Evidently the employee had been quietly asked to pack his personal belongings and leave the building. Being a small organization, the company did not see the need to escort this individual out the door.

On his way out, the former employee made a brief stop at the UNIX system running the company's firewall software. The system was left out in the open and did not use any form of console password. He decided to do a little farewell "housekeeping" and clean up all those pesky program files cluttering up the system. For good measure, he also removed the router's V.34 cable and hid it in a nearby desk. As you can imagine, it cost the organization quite a bit in lost revenue to recover from this disaster. The incident could have been avoided had the equipment been stored in a locked area.

While most administrators take great care in protecting their network from external attacks, they often overlook the greater threat of an internal attack. A person does not even have to be an attacker in order to damage company resources. Sometimes the damage is done out of ignorance.

For example, one company owner insisted on having full supervisor privileges on the company's NetWare server. While he was not particularly computer literate and did not actually require this level of access, he insisted on it simply because he owned the company.

I'm sure you can guess what happened. While doing some housekeeping on his system, he inadvertently deleted the CCDATA directory on his M: drive. If you have ever administered cc:Mail, you know that this directory is the repository for the postoffice, which contains all mail messages and public folders.

In cc:Mail, the main mail files are almost always open and are difficult to back up by normal means. The company lost all mail messages except for personal folders, which most employees did not use. Approximately two years' worth of data just disappeared. While this was not a willful attack, it certainly cost the company money.

An ever-increasing threat is not the destruction of data, but its theft and compromise. This is usually referred to as *industrial* (or *corporate*) *espionage*, and, although not considered as common as internal data destruction, it is still a viable threat to any organization that has proprietary or confidential information—especially when the compromise of that data would leave the organization legally liable. An example of this would be any organization involved with health care that falls under the jurisdiction of the Health Insurance Portability and Accountability Act (1996—USA). Under the Administrative Simplification provisions of HIPAA, security standards are mandated to protect an individual's health information, while permitting appropriate access and use of that information. Any breach of confidentiality could lead to legal action on behalf of the federal government.

External Attacks

External attacks can come from many diverse sources. While these attacks can still come from disgruntled employees, the range of possible attackers increases dramatically. The only common thread is that usually someone gains by staging the attack.

Competitors

If you are in a highly competitive business, an ambitious competitor may see a benefit in attacking your network. This can take the form of stealing designs or financial statements, or just making your network resources unusable.

The benefit of stealing a competitive design is obvious. Armed with this information, a thieving organization can use your design to shorten its own development time or to equip its own product release with better features. If a competitor knows what products your organization will release in the near future, that competitor can beat you to market with a more attractive product.

The theft of financial information can be just as detrimental. A competitor can gain a complete fiscal overview of your organization—and an unfair advantage in the marketplace. This unfair advantage can come from having an insider's view of your organization's financial health, or just from understanding your sources of income.

For example, I once heard of a computer consulting firm that infiltrated the network of a competitor, stealing a fiscal spreadsheet that showed sources of the company's revenue. The attacker was particularly interested to learn that over 60 percent of revenue came from the sale of fax machines, printers, and copiers. I'm told that this allowed the thieves to walk into a client site and ask, "Are you sure you want to rely on Company X for your networking needs? They are, after all, primarily an office supply company. Most of their business is from selling faxes and copiers." This tactic won over more than one client.

Sometimes, however, an attacker does not need to remove anything in order to benefit. For example, let's assume that you work for a distribution firm that generates sales through your Web site. You have your catalog online, and customers can place orders using secure forms. For your specific market niche, you have the lowest prices available.

Now, let's assume that I am your largest competitor but that my prices are slightly higher. It would help my business if I could stop your Web site from accepting inbound connections. It would appear to a potential customer that your Web site is offline. Customers who could not reach your Web site might next decide to check out mine instead. Since your site is not available, customers cannot compare prices—and they may go ahead and order the product from my site.

No actual theft has taken place, but this denial of service is now directly responsible for lost revenue. Not only is this type of attack difficult to prove, it can be even more difficult to quantify. If your site is offline for eight hours, how do you know how many sales were lost?

How prone you may be to competitors' attacks relates directly to how competitive your business is. For example, a high school need not worry about a competitive school stealing a copy of next year's curriculum. A high school does, however, have a higher than average potential for internal attacks.

Militant Viewpoints

If your business can be considered controversial, you may be prone to threats from others who take a different point of view.

For example, I was once called in by an organization that published information on medical research. The organization's Web site included documentation on abortions. Someone searching the site e-mailed the Webmaster, suggesting that some of the information on the site was not what the company intended. The administrator found that all pages discussing abortion issues had been replaced by pro-life slogans and biblical quotations.

Again, such attacks fall into a gray area. Since no information was stolen, it would be difficult to prosecute the attacker. The most relevant laws at the time would have labeled this attack as graffiti or vandalism.

But times are changing. The high-profile nature of security breaches has made them newsworthy, and activists from around the world are using them to further their own goals. The first type is the truly militant hacker, carrying military or violent conflicts into the cyber world. There are four well-known examples:

- During the spring of 1998, in what many observers saw as saber-rattling, Pakistan and India tested nuclear weapons and engaged in a war of words. Pakistani and Indian hackers each launched an assault on the Web sites that were controlled by the other group.

- Serbian and Albanian hackers penetrated each other's sites during the NATO bombing of Serbia in the spring of 1999.

- Palestinian and Israeli hackers (both groups mostly based in the United States) waged a fierce cyberwar that matched the intense real-world hostility that occurred after an Israeli government official visited a Palestinian holy site in late 2000. Even Ehud Tenebaum, the Israeli hacker known as "The Analyzer," who achieved fame in 1998 as the mastermind of the biggest Pentagon attacks in history, joined the fray.

- At a lower level, Taiwanese and Chinese hackers have attempted to deface and discredit each other in the cyber arena for years—all over which side has legitimate claim to the island of Taiwan

The other type is usually motivated by something other than greed or violence. Often called "hacktivists," these individuals attack systems with the goal of stopping services, defacing Web sites, or generally drawing attention to their cause. Recent examples include:

- On November 7, 2000 (the day of the U.S. Presidential Election in the United States), a hacker penetrated the Republican National Committee page and replaced its text with an endorsement of Vice President Al Gore.

- In June 2000, S11, an Australian group, hijacked Nike.com and sent Nike's intended visitors to S11's anti-Nike site (protesting worker conditions in Nike factories).

- During the World Trade Organization meeting in 1999, the Electrohippies, a group based in Britain, temporarily shut down the WTO's web site.

High Profile

Organizations that are well known or frequently in the public eye can become subjects of attack simply due to their level of visibility. A would-be attacker may attempt to infiltrate a well-known site with the hope that a successful attack will bring with it some level of notoriety. Examples of high-profile attacks over the past few years include:

- In March 1997, a group called H4G1S compromised one of NASA's Web pages and used it as a forum to warn of future attacks on organizations responsible for commercializing the Internet. The attack had nothing to do with NASA directly—except for providing some high visibility for the group.

- During May of 1999, major U.S. government sites—including Whitehouse.gov, FBI.gov, and Senate.gov—were defaced.

- In February 2000, some of the most high-profile Internet companies suffered from denial-of-service attacks, including: Amazon.com, Buy.com, CNN.com, eBay, E*Trade, Yahoo!, and ZDNet.

- Microsoft revealed in late October 2000 that hackers had penetrated their site over a series of weeks. Although Microsoft claimed to have been aware of the hackers from the beginning, it was nonetheless a humbling moment for the organization.

Determining whether or not your organization is high profile can be difficult. Most organizations tend to overestimate their visibility or presence on the Internet. Unless you are part of a multinational organization, or your site counts daily Web hits in the six-figure range, you are probably not a visible enough target to be attacked simply for the notoriety factor.

Bouncing Mail

Arguably, the most offensive type of attack is to have your domain's mail system used as a spam relay. *Spam* is unsolicited advertising. Spammers deliver these unsolicited ads in hopes that sheer volume will generate some interest in the product or service advertised. Typically, when a spammer sends an advertisement, it reaches thousands or tens of thousands of e-mail addresses and mailing lists. When a spammer uses your mail system as a spam relay, your mail system becomes the host that tries to deliver all these messages.

The result is a denial of service. While your mail server spends its time processing this spam mail, it is prevented from handling legitimate inbound and outbound mail for your domain.

TIP   Most modern mail systems now include anti-spam settings. While these settings will not prevent you from receiving spam messages, they will prevent your system from being used as a spam relay, by accepting only messages going to or coming from your domain.

Fearing retribution, most spammers would rather use your mail system than their own. The typical spammer will attempt to hide the actual return address, so that anyone trying to trace the message assumes that it was delivered from your domain.

Spammers go to all this trouble because many Internet users do not appreciate receiving spam mail. "Do not appreciate" is an understatement: spam mail can downright infuriate many people, who will take it upon themselves to retaliate by launching a counterattack with mail bombs and denial-of-service attacks.

Such counterattacks can quickly produce devastating results for your business. For example, I once consulted for a small manufacturer of networking products. Shortly after its Internet connection was brought online, one of the aggressive salespeople got the bright idea of sending out a mass mailing to every mailing list and newsgroup that had even a remote association with computer networking.

As you might guess, the mailing generated quite a few responses—but not of the type that the salesperson had hoped for. Within hours of the mailing, literally tens of thousands of messages were attempting delivery into the domain. These messages contained quite colorful descriptions of what each sender thought of the advertisement, the company, and its product line. The volume of mail soon caused both the mail server and the mail relay to run out of disk space. It became impossible to sort through the thousands of messages to determine which were legitimate and which were part of the attack. As a result, all inbound mail had to be purged and the mail relay shut down for about a week until the attacks subsided.

While this particular attack was due to the shortsightedness of a single employee, external spam routed through *your* system can create the same headaches and costs.

Chapter Worksheet

In the sidebar below, you can assess your own network's current susceptibility to attack.

Assessing Your Attack Potential

The following questions will help you evaluate potential threats to your network. Rate each question on a scale of 1 to 5. A 1 signifies that the question does not apply to your organization's networking environment; a 5 means the question is directly applicable.

1. Is your network physically accessible to the public, such as a library or government office?

2. Is your network accessible by users not employed by your organization, such as a school or university?

3. Do you offer a public networking service, such as an Internet service provider?

4. Are there users outside the networking staff who have been granted root or administrator privileges?

5. Are users allowed to share common logon names such as Guest?

6. Can your organization's line of business be considered controversial?

7. Does a portion of your organization's business deal with financial or monetary information?

8. Is any portion of your network electronically accessible by the public (Web server, mail server, and so on)?

9. Does your organization produce a product or provide a highly skilled service?

10. Is your organization experiencing aggressive growth?

11. Do news stories about your organization regularly appear in newspapers or trade magazines?

12. Does your organization do business over public networking channels, such as the Internet or frame relay?

For questions 1–6, if your organization scored between 8 and 12, you should take steps to secure your internal network. If your organization scored above 12, you should lock down your internal environment just as aggressively as you would secure your network's parameter.

Continued on next page

For questions 6–11, if your score was between 7 and 10, t may be most cost effective to utilize only a minimal amount of security around the parameter of your network. If your score was between 11 and 16, you should be utilizing some solid firewall technology. If you scored above 16, consider using multiple firewall solutions.

If question 12 applies to your organization, you shou d investigate extending your defenses beyond the physical limits of your network. Once data leaves the confines of your network, it is that much more difficult to insure that it is not compromised.

In later chapters, we'll examine in detail the technology required by each of the above situations. This checklist is designed to give you an early feel for how security conscious you should be when securing your networking environment. Keep in mind that this list is simply a guide; each network has its own individual nuances. Your mileage may vary.

NOTE   Along with the results of this worksheet, you should also take a close look at the level of computer expertise within your organization. A "power user" environment is less likely to cause damage inadvertently—but is more likely to have the knowledge required to launch an attack. Conversely an uneducated user environment is less likely to launch an attack but more likely to cause accidental damage.

Summary

In this chapter, we saw that the number of security incidents is increasing and that most of these go undocumented. We looked at the differences between a hacker and an attacker and covered the benefits of discussing security vulnerability in a public forum. We also explored who might try to attack your network and why, as well as how to assess your likelihood of being the target of an attack.

Now that you understand who may wish to attack you and why, you can evaluate the different levels of risk to your organization. By performing a risk analysis, you will see more clearly how much protection your organization truly needs.

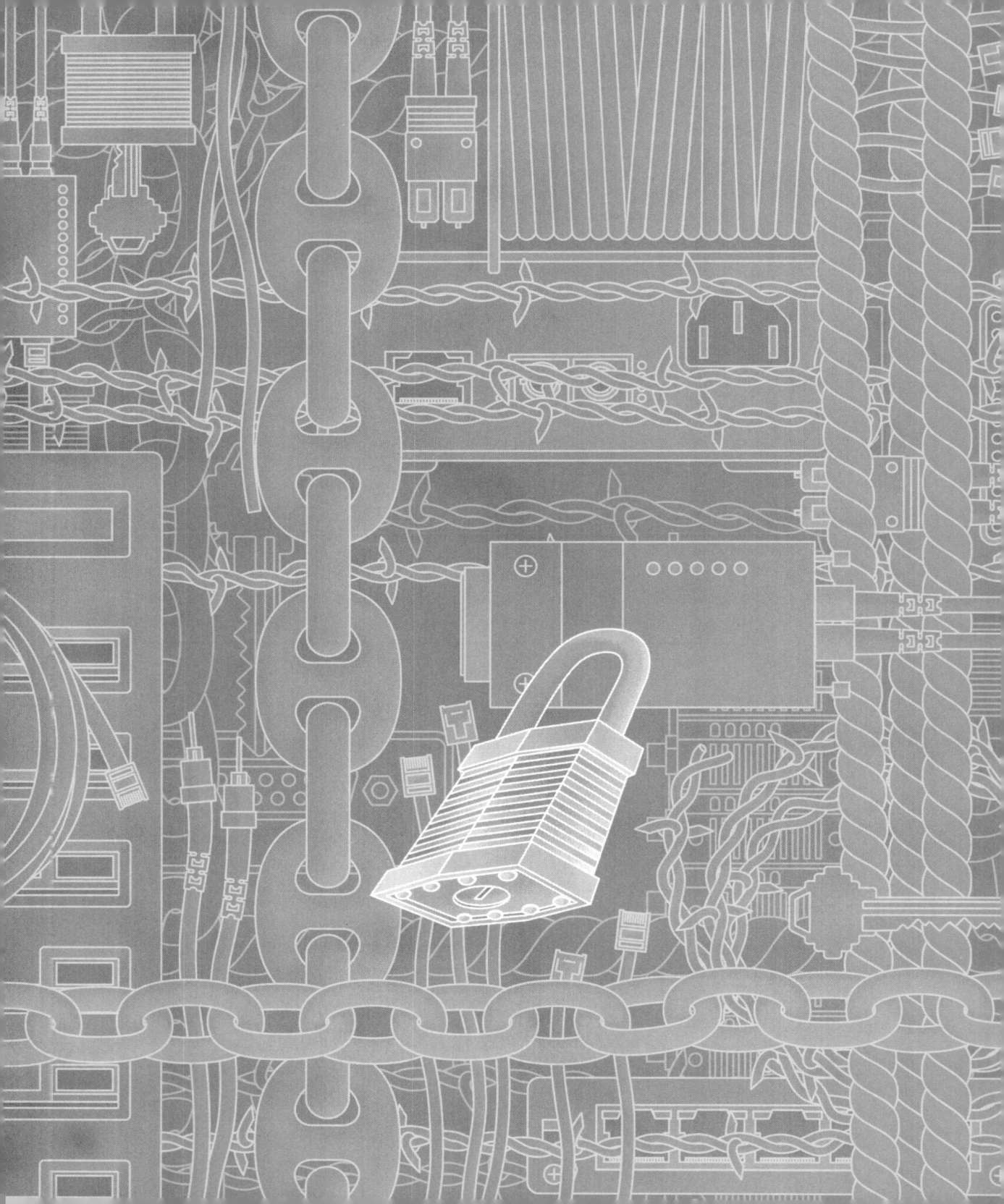

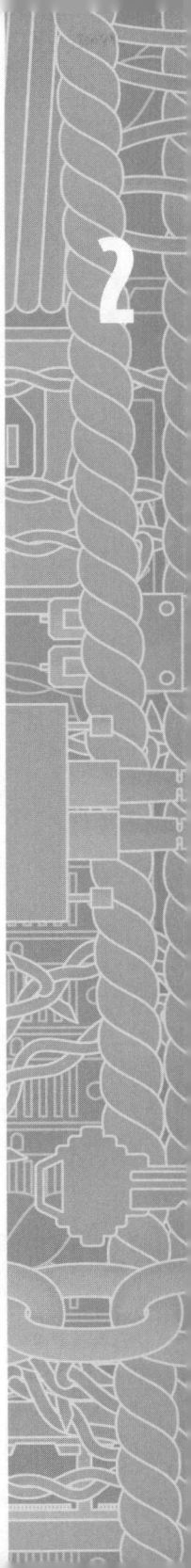

CHAPTER

TWO

How Much Security
Do You Need?

2

Before you decide how to best safeguard your network, you should identify the level of protection you wish to achieve. Begin by analyzing your network to determine what level of fortification you actually require. You can then use this information to develop your security policy. Once you are armed with this information, you are in a good position to start making intelligent decisions about your security structure.

Performing a Risk Analysis

A *risk analysis* is the process of identifying the assets you wish to protect and the potential threats against them. Performing an accurate risk analysis is a vital step in securing your network environment.

A formal risk analysis answers the following questions:

- What assets do I need to protect?
- From what sources am I trying to protect these assets?
- Who may wish to compromise my network and to what gain?
- How likely is it that a threat will violate my assets?
- What is the immediate cost if an asset is compromised?
- What is the cost of recovering from an attack or failure?
- How can these assets be protected in a cost-effective manner?
- Am I governed by a regulatory body that dictates the required level of security for my environment?

What Assets Do I Need to Protect?

Any effective risk analysis must begin by identifying the assets and resources you wish to protect. Assets typically fall into one of four categories:

- Physical resources
- Intellectual resources
- Time resources
- Perception resources

Physical Resources

Physical resources are assets that have a physical form. These include workstations, servers, terminals, network hubs, and even peripherals. Basically, any computing resource that has a physical form can be considered a physical resource.

When performing a risk analysis, don't forget physical resources. I once worked at an organization whose security policies were loose—to say the least. One day, an individual walked in the front door and identified himself as the printer repairman. The receptionist, a trusting soul, waved him through, giving him directions on how to find the office of the company's network administrator. A few minutes later, the "repairman" returned to the front desk, claiming that the printer needed repair and that he was taking it back to the shop.

The printer, of course, did not need repair. The "repairman" never sought out the network administrator; he disconnected the first high-end printer he came across and walked right out the door with it. The network administrator discovered the theft later when employees complained that they could not print (difficult to do when you do not actually have a printer!).

The final objective of a risk analysis is to formulate a cost-effective plan for guarding your assets. In the course of your analysis, do not overlook the most obvious problem areas and solutions. For example, the printer theft just described could have been completely avoided if the organization had required all non-employees to have an escort. Implementing this precaution would have had a zero cost impact—and would have saved the company the cost of replacing a top-end network printer.

Intellectual Resources

Intellectual resources can be harder to identify than physical resources, because they typically exist in electronic format only. An intellectual resource would be any form of information that plays a part in your organization's business. This can include software, financial information, and database records, as well as schematic or part drawings.

Take your time when listing intellectual resources. It can be easy to overlook the most obvious targets. For example, if your company exchanges information via e-mail, the storage files for these e-mail messages should be considered intellectual assets.

Time Resources

Time is an important organizational resource, yet one sometimes overlooked in a risk analysis. Time, however, can be one of an organization's most valued assets. When evaluating what lost time could cost your organization, make sure that you include *all* the consequences of lost time.

Time Is Money

How much is lost time worth? As an example, let's say that you identify one of your Engineering servers as an organizational resource. You identify the physical resource (the server itself) and the intellectual resources (the data stored on the server's hard drive). How do you factor time resources into your risk analysis?

Let's assume that although the server is backed up nightly, the server has no built-in fault tolerance. There is just a single disk holding all of the Engineering data. What if the server experiences a hard drive crash? What is lost in physical, intellectual, and time resources due to this crash?

The physical loss would be the drive itself. Given the cost of hard drive space these days, the dollar value of the drive would be minimal.

As for intellectual loss, any data saved to the server since the last backup would be gone. Since you have nightly backups, the loss should be no greater than one day's worth of information. This, of course, brings us back to time, because it will take time for the engineers to rebuild the lost information.

In determining the actual time loss, consider the cleanup job for the server administrator, who must

- Locate and procure a suitable replacement drive for the server.

- Install the new drive in the system.

- Completely reinstall the network operating system, any required patches, and the back-up software, if necessary.

- Restore all required backup tapes. If a full backup is not performed every night, there may be multiple tapes to restore.

- Address disk space issues, if multiple tapes are required for restoration. (Backup software typically does not record file deletions. Therefore, you may end up restoring files that were previously deleted to create additional disk space.)

Continued on next page

Also, since the server administrator is focusing on recovering the server, her other duties must wait.

Keep in mind that while the server administrator is doing all this work, the Engineering staff may be sitting idle or playing Quake, waiting for the server to come back online. It is not just the server administrator who is losing time, but the entire Engineering staff, as well.

To quantify this loss, let's add some dollars to the equation. Let's assume that your server administrator is proficient enough to recover from this loss in one work day. Let's also assume that she earns a modest salary of $50,000 per year, while the average salary for the 30 programmers who use this system is $60,000 per year.

- Administrator's time recovering the server = $192
- Engineering time to recover one day's worth of data = $6,923
- Engineering time lost due to offline server = $6,923
- Total cost impact of one-day outage = $14,038

Clearly, the cost of a one-day server outage can easily justify the cost of redundant disks, a RAID array, or even a standby server. Our calculations do not even include the possibility of lost revenue or reputation if your Engineering staff now fails to meet a scheduled shipment date.

As you attempt to quantify time as a resource within your organization, make sure you identify its full impact. Very rarely does the loss or compromise of a resource affect the productivity of only a single individual.

Perception Resources

After the denial-of-service attacks in February of 2000, most of the companies (including Yahoo, Amazon, eBay, and Buy.com, among others) involved saw their stock price fall. Although this loss was not long term, it was still had a real, measurable impact on the trust of consumers and stockholders. With the publicity surrounding the penetration of Microsoft's systems in October of 2000, some wondered if valuable source code had been unknowingly altered. Although Microsoft denied damage, the sheer fact of penetration has been enough to damage the credibility and trust of not only the company but also its products.

NOTE

For a publicly-traded company, reputation can translate into a tangible asset. Even for privately held companies or governmental departments, every organization survives on its reputation. In many cases, organizations might be tempted to put more emphasis maintaining a perception of trust and capability than on maintaining true data integrity.

The risk of damage to perception has been the cause of significant trouble for those working in the security industry (including law enforcement entities) who rely on the information and experience of their peers to design better protection systems or to pursue legal actions. In an attempt to encourage the free exchange of valuable technical details of hacking attacks, while preserving the perception of the contributing company, the Federal Bureau of Investigations (FBI) has established the Infrastructure Protection and Computer Intrusion Squad (IPCIS), which functions as an anonymous clearinghouse of hacker techniques and procedures.

NOTE

A *denial-of-service (DoS)* attack attempts to prevent a system from carrying on network communications. A DoS attack may try to make a single service on a target system inoperable, or the goal of the attack may be to deny all network connectivity.

From What Sources Am I Trying to Protect These Assets?

Potential network attacks can come from any source that has access into your network. These sources can vary greatly, depending on your organization's size and the type of network access provided. While performing a risk analysis, insure that you identify all potential sources of attack. Some of these sources could include

- Internal systems
- Access from field office locations
- Access through a WAN link to a business partner
- Access through the Internet
- Access through modem pools

Keep in mind that you are not yet evaluating who may attack your network. You are strictly looking at what media are available to gain access to network resources.

Who May Wish to Compromise Our Network?

In the last chapter, we discussed who in theory might be motivated to compromise your network. You should now put pen to paper and identify these potential threats. To review, potential threats could be

- Employees

- Temporary or consulting personnel

- Competitors

- Individuals with viewpoints or objectives radically different from those of your organization

- Individuals with a vendetta against your organization or one of its employees

- Individuals who wish to gain notoriety due to your organization's public visibility

Depending on your organization, there may be other potential threats you wish to add to this list. The important things to determine are what each threat stands to gain by staging a successful attack, and what this attack may be worth to a potential attacker.

What Is the Likelihood of an Attack?

Now that you have identified your resources and who might attack them, you can assess your organization's level of potential risk to attacks. Do you have an isolated network, or does your network have many points of entry such as a WAN, modem pool, or an inbound VPN via the Internet? Do all of these connection points use strong authentication and some form of firewalling device, or were rattles and incense used to set up a protective aura around your network? Could an attacker find value in exploiting one of these access points in order to gain access to your network resources? Clearly, a typical would-be attacker would prefer to attack a bank rather than a small architectural firm.

Appraising the attack value of your network is highly subjective. Two different people within the same organization could have completely different opinions about the likelihood of an attack. For this reason, consider soliciting input from a few different departments within your organization. You may even want to bring in a trained consultant who has hands-on experience in determining risk assessment. It is important that you define and understand the likelihood of attack as clearly as possible—it will guide you when you cost justify the security precautions required to safeguard your network.

What Is the Immediate Cost?

For each asset listed, record the immediate cost impact of having that resource compromised or destroyed. Do not include long-term effects (such as failure to meet shipment deadlines); simply calculate the cost of having this asset inaccessible as a network resource.

For example, given the hard-drive failure we looked at earlier, the immediate cost impact of the failure would be defined as the lost productivity of the Engineering staff for each minute that the server remains offline—roughly $14.50 per minute.

Sometimes immediate cost can be more difficult to quantify. For example, what if the compromise leads to a competitor gaining access to all schematics, drawings, and parts lists for a new product line? This could allow your competitor to develop a better product and beat your release to market. The loss in such a case could be disastrous. Even more difficult to quantify, but no less real, is the loss of trust, or the perception of weakness. Usually reflected by lower stock prices, compromised investor and consumer confidence (not to mention lowered employee morale) are all immediate reactions that can affect the bottom line.

Sometimes, however, monetary cost is not the main factor in determining losses. For example, while a hospital may suffer little financial loss if an attacker accesses its medical records, the destruction of these records could cause a catastrophic loss of life. When determining the immediate cost of a loss, look beyond the raw dollar value.

What Are the Long-Term Recovery Costs?

Now that you have quantified the cost of the initial failure, you should evaluate the costs incurred when recovering from a failure or compromise. Do this by identifying the financial impact of various levels of loss.

For example, given a server that holds corporate information,

- What is the cost of a momentary glitch that disconnects all users?

- What is the cost of a denial-of-service attack, which makes the resource unreachable for a specific period of time?

- What is the cost of recovering critical files that have been damaged or deleted?

- What is the cost of recovering from the failure of a single hardware component?

- What is the cost of recovering from a complete server failure?

- What is the cost of recovery when information has been stolen and the theft goes undetected?

The cost of various levels of failure, combined with the expectation of how frequently a failure or attempted attack may occur, provides metrics to determine the financial impact of disaster recovery for your organization's network. Based on these figures, you now have a guide to determine what should be reasonably spent in order to secure your assets. Remember that some assets (like reputation or consumer and investor confidence) can be difficult to quantify, but are real nonetheless.

How Can I Protect My Assets Cost-Effectively?

You must consider how much security will cost when determining what level of protection is appropriate for your networking environment. For example, it would probably be overkill for a five-user architectural firm with no remote access to hire a full-time security expert. Likewise, it would be unthinkable for a bank to allow outside network access without regard to any form of security measures or policies.

Most of us, however, fall somewhere in between these two networking examples—so we face some difficult security choices. Is packet filtering sufficient for protecting my Internet connection, or should I invest in a firewall? Is one firewall sufficient, or is it worthwhile to invest in two? These are some of the decisions that plague security experts on a daily basis.

TIP The general guideline is that the cost of all security measures taken to protect a particular asset should be less than the cost of recovering that asset from a disaster. This is why it is important to quantify potential threats as well as the cost of recovery. While security precautions are necessary in the modern networking environment, many of us are still required to justify the cost of these precautions.

Cost justification may not be as difficult as it sounds. For example, we noted that a one-day server outage in our Engineering environment could cost a company well over $14,000. Clearly, this is sufficient cost justification to invest in a high-end server complete with RAID array.

There can be hidden costs involved in securing an environment, and these costs must also be taken into account. For example, logging all network activity to guard against compromise is useless unless someone dedicates the time required to review all the logs generated. Clearly, this could be a full-time job all by itself, depending on the size of the environment. By increasing the level of detail being recorded about your network, you may create a need for a new security person.

Also, with increased security there is typically a reduction in ease of use or access to network resources, which can make it more cumbersome and time-consuming for end users to perform their job functions. This does not mean that you must avoid this reduction in ease of use; it can be a necessary evil when securing an environment and must be identified as a potential cost in lost productivity.

To summarize, before you solicit funds for security precautions, you should outline the ramifications of not putting those precautions into place. You should also accurately identify what the true cost of these precautions may be.

Am I Governed by a Regulatory Body?

Even though you have created a painstakingly accurate risk analysis of your network, there may be some form of regulatory or overview body that dictates your minimum level of security requirements. In these situations, it may not be sufficient to simply cost justify your security precautions. You may be required to meet certain minimum security requirements, regardless of the cost outlay to your organization.

For example, in order to be considered for military contract work, your organization must strictly adhere to many specific security requirements. Typically, the defined security precautions are not the only acceptable security measures, but they are the accepted minimum. You are always welcome to improve on these precautions if your organization sees fit.

When working with the government, many contractors are required to use a computer system that has received a specific Trusted Product rating by the National Security Agency. For a list of which products have received each rating, check out `http://www.radium.ncsc.mil/tpep/epl/epl-by-class.html`.

Other examples of government regulation that dictate security requirements include the Children's Online Privacy and Protection Act (COPPA—see `www.ftc.gov/bcp/conline/pubs/buspubs/coppa.htm`) and the Health Insurance Portability and Accountability Act (HIPAA—see `www.nationalpartnership.org/healthcare/hipaa/guide.htm`). Although the U.S. has yet to pass any privacy laws concerning e-commerce, other countries (most notably in Europe) strictly control what data can be collected and stored by companies.

If your organization's security is subject to some form of regulatory agency, you will be required to modify the cost-justification portion of your risk analysis in order to bring your recommendations in line with dictated policy.

Budgeting Your Security Precautions

You should now have a pretty good idea about what level of security you will be able to cost justify. This should include depreciable items (server hardware, firewalls, and construction of secured areas), as well as recurring costs (security personnel, audits, and system maintenance).

Remember the old saying, "Do not place all of your eggs in one basket"? This wisdom definitely applies to budgeting security. Do not spend all of your budget on one mode of protection. For example, it does little good to invest $15,000 in firewall technology if someone can simply walk through the front door and walk away with your corporate server.

TIP
It may be possible, however, to combine budget expenditures with other groups within your organization. For example, while it may be difficult to cost justify a secure, controlled environment for your networking hardware and servers, you might justify this cost if the room will also house all PBX, voicemail, and telephone equipment.

Another example could be the Engineering server we discussed earlier in this chapter. Engineers always require additional server storage space (it's in the job description). During the next upgrade of server storage, it may be possible to justify a redundant disk system and charge part of the cost to the Engineering department.

A new addition to the security budget at some companies is security insurance. Although this might seem unusual at first glance, most IT professionals can readily see the dollar value of their data and how the corruption or loss of that data justifies taking such a precaution.

The bottom line is to be creative. The further you can stretch your security budget, the more precautions you can take. Security is a proactive expenditure, meaning that we invest money in security precautions and procedures with the hope that we will realize a return on our investment by not having to spend additional money later playing cleanup to a network disaster. The more precautions that can be taken, the less likely disaster is to strike.

Documenting Your Findings

You've now identified all your assets, analyzed their worth to your day-to-day operations, and estimated the cost of recovery for each. Now take some time to formalize and document your findings. There are a number of reasons why this is worth your time.

First, having some sort of document—whether electronic or hard copy—gives you some backup when you begin the tedious process of justifying each of your countermeasures. It is far more difficult to argue with documented numbers and figures than it is to argue with an oral statement. By getting all your ducks in a row up front, you will be less likely to have to perform damage control later.

This document should be considered fluid; expect to have to adjust it over time. No one is ever 100 percent accurate when estimating the cost of intrusion or failures. If you are unfortunate enough to have your inaccuracy demonstrated, consider it an opportunity to update and improve your documentation.

Network environments change over time, as well. What happens when your boss walks into your office and announces, "We need to set up a new field office. What equipment do we need and how much will it cost us?" By having formal documentation that identifies your current costs, you can easily extrapolate these numbers to include the new equipment.

This information is also extremely useful as you begin the process of formalizing a security policy. Many people have an extremely deficient understanding of the impact of network security. Unfortunately, this can include certain managerial types who hold the purse strings on your budget (just look for the pointy hair—it's a dead giveaway).

As you begin to generate your security policy, it is much easier to justify each policy item when you can place a dollar value on the cost of an intrusion or attack. For example, your manager may not see the need for encrypting all inbound data until she realizes that the loss of this information could rival the cost of her salary. The last thing she wants to hear is that someone above her may realize that the company can recoup this loss by simply removing the one person who made a very bad business decision.

Developing a Security Policy

The first question most administrators ask is, "Why do I even need a formal security policy?" A security policy serves many functions. It is a central document that describes in detail acceptable network activity and penalties for misuse.

A security policy also provides a forum for identifying and clarifying security goals and objectives to the organization as a whole. A good security policy shows each employee how she is responsible for helping to maintain a secure environment.

NOTE   For an example of a security policy, see Appendix B.

Security Policy Basics

Security policies tend to be issue driven. A focus on individual issues is the easiest way to identify—and clarify—each point you wish to cover. While it may be acceptable in some environments to simply state, "Non–work-related use of the Internet is bad," those who must adhere to this policy need to know what "non–work-related use" and "bad" actually *mean*.

In order for a policy to be enforceable, it needs to be

- Consistent with other corporate policies

- Accepted by the network support staff as well as the appropriate levels of management

- Enforceable using existing network equipment and procedures

- Compliant with local, state, and federal laws

Consistency Is Key

Consistency insures that users will not consider the policies unreasonable or irrational. The overall theme of your security policy should reflect your organization's views on security and acceptable corporate practices in general.

If your organization has a very relaxed stance towards physical security or use of company assets, it may be difficult or pointless to enforce a strict network usage policy. For example, I once consulted for a firm whose owner insisted that all remote connections to the network be encrypted using the largest cipher key possible. Remote users were required to maintain different logon names and passwords for remote access, and these accounts had be provided with only a minimal amount of access. Also, remote access was left disabled unless someone could justify a specific need for accessing the network remotely.

While this may not seem all that far-fetched, the facility where this network was housed was protected by only a single cipher lock with a three-digit code. The facility had no alarm system and was in a prime physical location to be looted undetected. The combination for the cipher lock had not been changed in over seven years. Also, employees frequently gave out the combination to anyone they felt needed it (this included friends and even the local UPS guy!).

As if all this were not bad enough, there was no password requirement for any of the internal accounts. Many users (including the owner) had no passwords assigned to their accounts. This included two servers that were left in an easily accessible location.

The firm was probably right to be concerned with remote-access security. The measures taken bordered on absurd, however, when compared to the organization's other security policies. Clearly, there were other issues that should have had a higher priority than remote network access. The owner may very well have found this remote-access policy difficult to enforce, because it was inconsistent with the organization's other security practices. If the employees see little regard being shown for physical access to the facility, why should Internet access be any different?

Acceptance within the Organization

For a policy to be enforceable, it must be accepted by the appropriate authorities within the organization. It can be frustrating at best to attempt to enforce a security policy if management does not identify and acknowledge the benefits your policy provides.

A good example of what can happen without management acceptance is the legal case of Randal Schwartz (a major contributor to the Perl programming language) versus Intel. While he was working as a private contractor for Intel, Schwartz was accused of accessing information which, according to Intel's security policy, he should not have been viewing. Although Intel won its controversial case against Schwartz, that case was severely weakened when it came to light that Intel's full-time employees were not bound to the same security policy they were attempting to use to convict Schwartz.

While testifying in the trial, Ed Masi, Intel's corporate vice president and general manager, freely admitted to not following Intel's security policy. What made the case even more murky was that Intel never filed charges against Masi for failing to adhere to the policy. This left the impression that Intel's security policy was fluid at best and that Schwartz was being singled out.

NOTE   You can read all about Randal Schwartz versus Intel at www.lightlink.com/ spacenka/fors/.

An organization's security policy must be accepted and followed at all levels of management. In order to be successful, it must be understood that these policies are equally applicable to *all network users*.

Enforceability

In order for a security policy to have merit, it must be enforceable. Stating that "each network user is required to change his or her password every 90 days" will have little effect if your network operating system does not expire and lock accounts that exceed this 90-day limit.

While you can legally create policies that cannot be enforced, doing so as a matter of practice is not a wise choice. You do not want to leave your users with the impression that ignoring corporate policy is OK because adherence is not verified. If there is no verification, then there are no ramifications for noncompliance. If there were no state troopers, how many of us would drive at the speed limit on the highway?

TIP

Noncompliance with one network usage policy can quickly lead to a domino effect of employees ignoring *all* network usage policies. Choose your battles wisely. This is particularly true if you are establishing a network usage policy for the first time. You do not have to verify usage compliance 100 percent of the time—but make sure that you have some method of reporting or monitoring usage if enforcement of your policy becomes an issue.

Sometimes it is not even sufficient to actively monitor all aspects of a specific policy issue. Take care to disseminate such issues in an appropriate manner. For example, a security policy is typically considered to be company private. However, there may be policy issues that affect individuals outside of the organization. These policy issues must be made public in order to insure that they are enforceable.

There is a story floating around the Internet (it may be truth or it may be lore) that describes how an organization monitored, tracked, and then identified a remote attacker who had broken into one of its systems. As the story goes, the police arrested the suspect, and the accused was brought to trial.

During the trial, the accused freely admitted to accessing the network resource in question. His stated defense was that he had no idea that he was doing anything wrong, since upon accessing the resource he was presented with a "welcome" screen.

The defense argued that it was beyond the accused's ability to determine that he should not have been accessing this specific resource. As a precedent, defense lawyers cited a local property law requiring landowners to post notices to keep trespassers off their land. The judge, who found it easier to relate to local property laws than to high-tech computer crimes, accepted the defense's argument and released the suspect.

As part of enforcing your network security policy, make sure you disseminate it properly. Do not overlook some of the more obvious places to state this policy, such as logon scripts and terminal messages.

Compliance with Local, State, and Federal Laws

You might want to have your organization's legal counsel review any policies before you implement them. If any portion of a specific policy issue is found to be unlawful, the entire issue—or even the policy itself—may be disregarded.

For example, a policy stating that "noncompliance will result in a severe flogging" will be thrown out by a court of law if flogging has been outlawed in your locale. You may truly wish to flog the attacker for compromising your network, but by specifying an illegal reprisal, you may surrender all chances of recourse. *Appropriate wording is crucial.* Insure that all policies are written in a precise, accurate, and legal manner.

A legal review will also help to identify the impact of each policy item. Without precise wording, a well-intentioned policy may have an extremely negative effect.

In a recent court case, an employee won a $175,000 settlement because she accidentally viewed what she considered to be a pornographic Web site while on the job. How did she get away with holding her employer accountable? Was the questionable site located on a company-owned Web server?

The answer should scare you. The company had a corporate policy stating that "pornographic sites will be blocked, and they cannot be accessed from the corporate network." The company was filtering out access to sites that contained what it considered to be questionable subject matter. Unfortunately, there are so many "questionable" sites on the Internet that there is no way to block them all.

The court ruled that the company was liable for breach of contract because it did not hold up its end of the bargain by blocking all so-called questionable sites. By instituting a policy stating that it would filter out these sites, the company was "accepting responsibility for the successful execution of this activity"—and was therefore accountable. The damage award, as well as reimbursement for the employee's "distress," was based on this finding.

How should this policy item have been written? Consider the following statement:

> Accessing Internet-based Web sites with company-owned assets, for purposes other than executing responsibilities within an employee's job function, is considered grounds for dismissal. We reserve the right to monitor and filter all employee network activity in order to insure compliance.

This statement still enforces the same policy spirit by banning undesirable sites. It removes the word "questionable," which is wide open to interpretation, and specifically forbids all Web site access that is not related to an employee's job function. Also, it puts the burden of compliance on the employee, *not* the employer, while still allowing the organization to attempt to filter out these sites.

TIP   Proper wording can make all the difference in the world between a good and a bad security policy.

What Makes a Good Security Usage Policy?

At a minimum, a good security usage policy should

- Be readily accessible to all members of the organization.
- Define a clear set of security goals.
- Accurately define each issue discussed in the policy.
- Clearly show the organization's position on each issue.
- Describe the justification of the policy regarding each issue.
- Define under what circumstances the issue is applicable.
- State the roles and responsibilities of organizational members with regard to the described issue.
- Spell out the consequences of noncompliance with the described policy.
- Provide contact information for further details or clarification regarding the described issue.
- Define the user's expected level of privacy.
- Include the organization's stance on issues not specifically defined.

Accessibility

Making your security policy public within the organization is paramount to its effectiveness. As mentioned earlier, logon scripts and terminal messages are a good start.

If your organization has an employee handbook, see about incorporating your security policy into this document. If your organization maintains an intranet Web site for organizational information, have your document added to this site, as well.

Defining Security Goals

While it may seem like simple common sense, a statement of purpose, which defines why security is important to your organization, can be extremely beneficial. This statement can go a long way toward insuring that policy issues are not deemed frivolous or unnecessary.

As part of this statement, feel free to specify your organization's goals for its security precautions. People are far more accepting of additional standards and guidelines when they understand the benefits these can provide.

TIP A sample security policy has been included in Appendix B. Use this as a guide when creating a security policy for your organization.

Defining Each Issue

Be as clear and precise as possible when describing each policy issue. Insure that all language and terminology are as accurate as possible.

For example, do not refer to Internet access in general; instead, identify the specific services the issue addresses (e-mail, file transfers, and so on). If it becomes necessary later to enforce the policy issue, your organization will have a precise description to fall back on. All too often, general descriptions are open to interpretation—and misinterpretation.

TIP An accurate description becomes even more important if your company uses VPN technology over the Internet. Be precise in defining the difference between public hosts on the Internet and hosts located on the other end of a VPN connection.

Your Organization's Position

Use clear, concise language to state your organization's views on the described policy issue. For example, adjectives such as "unacceptable" contain many shades of gray. A worker's performance might be "unacceptable"—but not necessarily in violation of any specific policy.

When describing matters of policy, stick to words that convey clear and precise meanings. Negative examples of such include "violation," "breach of contract," "offense," and "abuse." Positive examples include "permissible," "legitimate," "sanctioned," and "authorized." By avoiding ambiguous terms, you can be certain that the policy meanings—as well as the ramifications of noncompliance—are clear and enforceable.

Justifying the Policy

We have already discussed a general statement of purpose, which defines an overall set of security goals; you should also justify each policy issue. This shows your network users why each point in the policy is important.

For example, the statement, "Since e-mail is considered to be an unsecured medium, it is not permissible to use it for conveying company private information," simultaneously states the policy issue and justifies the policy.

When Does the Issue Apply?

Be sure to make clear under what circumstances the policy is considered to be in effect. Does the policy affect all users equally, or only certain work groups? Does it remain in effect after business hours? Does it affect the main office only, or field offices as well?

When you set forth clearly how the policy will be applied, you also clarify its expected impact. This insures that there is no uncertainty about whom this policy applies to. You want to eliminate the possibility that any employee will assume that the policy must apply to everyone but himself or herself.

Roles and Responsibilities

Any chain is only as strong as its weakest link, so be sure to make it clear that *all* members of the organization are responsible for asset security. Security is everyone's concern, not just a part of a particular person's job description.

Be sure to identify who is responsible for enforcing security policies and what type of authorization this person has from the organization. If a user is asked to surrender access to the system, it is crucial that a clear policy be in place identifying who has the authority to make such a request.

Consequences of Noncompliance

What if an employee fails to follow or simply ignores a specific security policy issue? Your organization must have a reaction or remedy in place if this occurs. Be sure your policy includes a description of possible reprisals for noncompliance.

It is important that this statement be both legal and clearly defined. Stating that "appropriate action will be taken" does not describe the severity of possible repercussions. Many times a reprisal is left vague because the people writing a policy cannot agree on a proper response. It is extremely important that a proper remedy be assigned, however, because the severity of the penalty can help convey just how seriously your organization views the issue. For example, sending harassing e-mail may be considered grounds for dismissal, while cruising the Web in order to find the best price for a home computer may only warrant a verbal warning. When you identify consequences of noncompliance, be specific about what actions your organization may take.

For More Information

It is difficult to formulate a policy that clearly defines all potential aspects of a specific issue. For this reason, you should identify a resource responsible for providing additional information.

Since individuals' responsibilities can change, identify this resource by job function rather than by name. It's better to write, "Consult your direct supervisor for more information" or "Direct all queries regarding this issue to the network security administrator" than "Forward all questions to Billy Bob Smith."

Level of Privacy

Privacy is always a hot topic: your organization should clearly state its views on privacy with regard to information stored on organizational resources. If an organization does not *expressly* claim all ownership of stored information, this information may be construed the property of the employee.

Don't assume that company private information is private—spell it out. There was a well-publicized case a number of years ago in which a high-level executive left his job for a position with a major competitor. Suspecting that this person may have walked off with some private information, the company retrieved and reviewed all of his e-mail messages. They found evidence that this ex-employee had in fact left with some information that the company considered vital to maintaining its competitive edge.

When the case went to trial, however, the e-mail was considered inadmissible because there was no clear policy identifying e-mail as a company-owned resource. The defense argued that e-mail is identical to postal mail and as such enjoys the same level of privacy.

The judge in the case was well aware that the U.S. Post Office is not allowed to open personal letters without a court order. The defense argued that, in this situation, the company should be held to the same standard as the Post Office, since its resources were responsible for delivering the mail. As a result, the e-mail was declared inadmissible and the company lost its case due to lack of evidence.

The moral of this story is that it is *extremely* important to assert ownership of network resources, and to spell out the measures that can be taken to enforce described policy issues.

Issues Not Specifically Defined

When implementing a firewall, two potential stances are possible with regards to network traffic. The first is "that which is not expressly permitted is denied;" the second is "that which is not expressly denied is permitted." The first takes a firm stance with regard to security, while the latter is a more liberal approach.

These same principles apply to your security policy. You can design your policy to be restrictive ("That which is not expressly permitted is denied") or open ("That which is not expressly denied is permitted") with regard to matters that are not clearly defined. This provides a fallback position if an issue arises that is not specifically described by your security policy. This is a good idea, as you will inevitably forget to mention something.

Include a statement outlining the organization's stance on issues not explicitly addressed within the security policy itself. Which approach is more appropriate will depend on how strict a security policy you are trying to create. Typically, however, it is easier to begin with a tighter stance on security and then open up additional policies as the need arises.

Example of a Good Policy Statement

Now that we have covered the individual points of a good security policy, let's look at a specific example to see how to tie these points together. You will find more examples in Appendix B.

The following is an example of a policy statement excerpt:

> Access to Internet-based Web server resources shall only be allowed for the express purpose of performing work-related duties. This policy is to insure the effective use of networking resources and shall apply equally to all

employees. This policy shall be enforced during both production and non-production time periods. All Web server access can be monitored by networking personnel, and employees may be required to justify Web server access to their direct supervisor. Failure to comply with this policy will result in the issuance of a written warning. For more information regarding what is considered appropriate Web server access of Internet resources, please consult your direct supervisor.

Now let's see if this statement includes everything we have discussed.

Define Each Issue   This policy specifically addresses "access to Internet-based Web server resources." The statement clearly defines the issue to which it pertains.

Your Organization's Position   The statement goes on to declare that Internet access "shall only be allowed for the express purpose of performing work-related duties." The organization's stance is clear. Web browsing is for performing work-related activities *only*.

Justifying the Policy   To justify restriction of Internet access, the policy states, "This policy is to insure the effective use of networking resources." Again, the wording is clear and to the point. The organization is looking to minimize Internet traffic by restricting Internet use to work-related functions only.

When Does the Issue Apply?   The policy specifies that Internet access restrictions "shall apply equally to all employees. This policy shall be enforced during both production and non-production time periods." This spells out that the policy is in effect at all times and that all employees are subject to its guidelines.

Roles and Responsibilities   The policy goes on to state that networking personnel are responsible for monitoring proper Web server access and adds that "employees may be required to justify Web server access to their direct supervisor." This requires each employee to justify all Internet Web server access. It also shows that supervisors are responsible for approving these justifications. The document assumes that some mechanism is in place to notify the supervisor when her subordinates access Internet Web servers.

Consequences of Noncompliance   The policy goes on to state, "Failure to comply with this policy will result in the issuance of a written warning."

Short, sweet, and to the point, this sentence shows what may happen if an employee violates this portion of the security policy.

Contact Information for Further Details   Finally, the policy directs, "For more information regarding what is considered appropriate Web server access of Internet resources, please consult your direct supervisor." The policy tells readers what information is available and where to get it. (The policy does assume here that the supervisor knows the answers or where to get them.)

Level of Privacy   Privacy is mentioned only briefly in our sample policy excerpt, but the policy still goes straight to the point: "All Web server access can be monitored by networking personnel." This implies that the user can expect zero privacy when accessing Internet-based Web servers.

This statement does not, however, define the level of monitoring that may be performed. For example, it does not specify whether network personnel will review the servers visited, the URLs, or the actual page content. In this case, lack of specificity should not be considered a bad thing, because it allows the network administrator some flexibility in the level of audits.

Summary

You should now have a sound understanding of how to evaluate the level of security your environment requires. You should know which assets you need to protect and their inherent value to your organization. This risk analysis will be the cornerstone for each of the security precautions discussed in this book.

You should also know how to write an effective security policy, understanding the importance of a precise security policy to securing your environment.

In the next chapter, we will take a look at how systems communicate. Many security exploits involve "bending" the communication rules, so comprehending how network information is exchanged is vital to securing against such attacks.

CHAPTER

THREE

3

Understanding How Network Systems Communicate

In this chapter, we will review how networked systems move data from point A to point B. I am assuming that you already understand the basics of networking, such as how to assign a valid network address to a device. This chapter will focus on exactly what is going on behind the scenes and along your network cabling. This knowledge is critical in order to give context to the security concepts covered in subsequent chapters.

The Anatomy of a Frame of Data

When data is moved along a network, it is packaged inside a delivery envelope called a *frame*. Frames are topology-specific. An Ethernet frame needs to convey different information than a Token Ring or an ATM frame. Since Ethernet is by far the most popular topology, we will cover it in detail here.

Ethernet Frames

An Ethernet frame is a set of digital pulses transmitted onto the transmission media in order to convey information. An Ethernet frame can be anywhere from 64 to 1,518 bytes (a byte being 8 digital pulses or bits) in size and is organized into four sections:

- Preamble
- Header
- Date
- Frame check sequence

Preamble   A *preamble* is a defined series of communication pulses that tells all receiving stations, "Get ready—I've got something to say." The standard preamble is eight bytes long.

NOTE   Because the preamble is considered part of the communication process and not part of the actual information being transferred, it is not usually included when measuring a frame's size.

Header   A *header* always contains information about who sent the frame and where it is going. It may also contain other information, such as how many bytes the frame contains; this is referred to as the *length field* and is used for error correction. If the receiving station measures the frame to be a different size than indicated in the length field, it asks the transmitting system to send a new frame. If the length field is not used, the header may instead contain a *type field* that describes what type of Ethernet frame it is.

NOTE   The header size is always 14 bytes.

Data   The *data* section of the frame contains the actual data the station needs to transmit, as well as any protocol information, such as source and destination IP address. The data field can be anywhere from 46 to 1,500 bytes in size. If a station has more than 1,500 bytes of information to transfer, it will break up the information over multiple frames and identify the proper order by using *sequence numbers*. Sequence numbers identify the order in which the destination system should reassemble the data. This sequence information is also stored in the data portion of the frame.

If the frame does not have 46 bytes' worth of information to convey, the station pads the end of this section by filling it in with 1 (remember that digital connections use binary numbers). Depending on the frame type, this section may also contain additional information describing what protocol or method of communication the systems are using.

Frame Check Sequence (FCS)   The *frame check sequence* is used to insure that the data received is actually the data sent. The transmitting system processes the FCS portion of the frame through an algorithm called a *cyclic redundancy check* or *CRC*. This CRC takes the values of the above fields and creates a 4-byte number. When the destination system receives the frame, it runs the same CRC and compares it to the value within this field. If the destination system finds a match, it assumes the frame is free of errors and processes the information. If the comparison fails, the destination station assumes that something happened to the frame in its travels and requests that another copy of the frame be sent by the transmitting system.

NOTE   The FCS size is always 4 bytes.

The Frame Header Section

Now that we have a better understanding of what an Ethernet frame is, let's take a closer look at the header section. The header information is ultimately responsible for identifying who sent the data and where the sender wanted it to go.

The header contains two fields to identify the source and destination of the transmission. These are the *node addresses* of both the source and destination systems. This number is also referred to as the *media access control* (MAC) address. The node address is a unique number that is used to serialize network devices (like network cards or networking hardware) and is a unique identifier that distinguishes it from any other networking device in the world. No two networking devices should ever be assigned the same number. Think of this number as equivalent to a telephone number. Every home with a telephone has a unique phone number so that the phone company knows where to direct the call. In this same fashion, a system will use the destination system's MAC address to send the frame to the proper system.

NOTE   The MAC address has nothing specifically to do with Apple's computers and is always represented in all capital letters. It is the number used by all the systems attached to the network (PCs and Macs included) to uniquely identify themselves.

This 6-byte, 12-digit hexadecimal number is broken up into two parts. The first half of the address is the manufacturer's identifier. A manufacturer is assigned a range of MAC addresses to use when serializing its devices. Some of the more prominent MAC addresses appear in Table 3.1.

TABLE 3.1:   Common MAC Addresses

First Three Bytes of MAC Address	Manufacturer
00000C	Cisco
0000A2	Bay Networks
0080D3	Shiva
00AA00	Intel
02608C	3Com
080009	Hewlett-Packard
080020	Sun
08005A	IBM

The first three bytes of the MAC address can be a good troubleshooting aid. If you are investigating a problem, try to determine the source MAC address. Knowing who made the device may put you a little closer to determining which system is giving you trouble. For example, if the first three bytes are **0000A2**, you know you need to focus your attention on any Bay Networks device on your network.

The second half of the MAC address is the serial number the manufacturer has assigned to the device.

One address worthy of note is FF-FF-FF-FF-FF-FF. This is referred to as a *broadcast address*. A broadcast address is special: it means all systems receiving this packet should read the included data. If a system sees a frame that has been sent to the broadcast address, it will read the frame and process the data if it can.

You should never encounter a frame that has a broadcast address in the source node field. The Ethernet specifications do not include any conditions where the broadcast address should be placed in the source node field.

The Address Resolution Protocol

How do you find out what the destination node address is so that you can send data to a system? After all, network cards do not ship with phone books. Finding a node address is done with a special frame referred to as an *address resolution protocol* (ARP) frame. ARP functions differently depending on which protocol you're using (such as IPX, IP, NetBEUI, and so on).

For an example, see Figure 3.1. This is a decode of the initial packet from a system that wishes to send information to another system on the same network. Notice the information included within the decode. The transmitting system knows the IP address of the destination system, but it does not know the destination node address. Without this address, local delivery of data is not possible. ARP is used when a system needs to discover the destination system's node address.

A frame *decode* is the process of converting a binary frame transmission to a format that can be understood by a human being. Typically, this is done using a network analyzer.

FIGURE 3.1:

A transmitting system attempting to discover the destination system's node address

No.	Source	Destination	Layer	Summary	Size	Interpacke	Absolute Time
1	Herne	Broadcast	arp	Req by 10.1.1.132 for 10.1.1.10	64	0 μs	10:17:42 AM
2	Skylar	Herne	arp	Reply 10.1.1.10=0000C0A7F49A	64	575 μs	10:17:42 AM
3	Herne	Skylar	icmp	Type=Echo Request	78	269 μs	10:17:42 AM
4	Skylar	Herne	icmp	Type=Echo Reply	78	2 ms	10:17:42 AM

```
Packet Number : 1               10:17:42 AM
Length : 64 bytes
ether: ================== Ethernet Datalink Layer ==================
       Station: Herne ----> Broadcast
       Type: 0x0806 (ARP)
  arp: ================== Address Resolution Protocol ==================
       Hardware: Ethernet
       Protocol: 0x0800 (IP)
       Operation: ARP Request
       Hardware adress length: 6
       Protocol address length: 4
       Sender Hardware Address: 00-00-E8-2F-77-2A
       Sender Protocol Address: 10.1.1.132
       Target Hardware Address: 00-00-00-00-00-00
       Target Protocol Address: 10.1.1.10
```

Keep in mind that ARP is only for local communications. When a packet of data crosses a router, the Ethernet header will be rewritten so that the source node address is that of the router, not the transmitting system. This means that a new ARP request may need to be generated.

Figure 3.2 shows how this works. Our transmitting system (Fritz) needs to deliver some information to the destination system (Wren). Since Wren is not on the same subnet as Fritz, it transmits an ARP in order to discover the node address of Port A on the local router. Once Fritz knows this address, Fritz transmits its data to the router.

FIGURE 3.2:

Node addresses are used for local communications only.

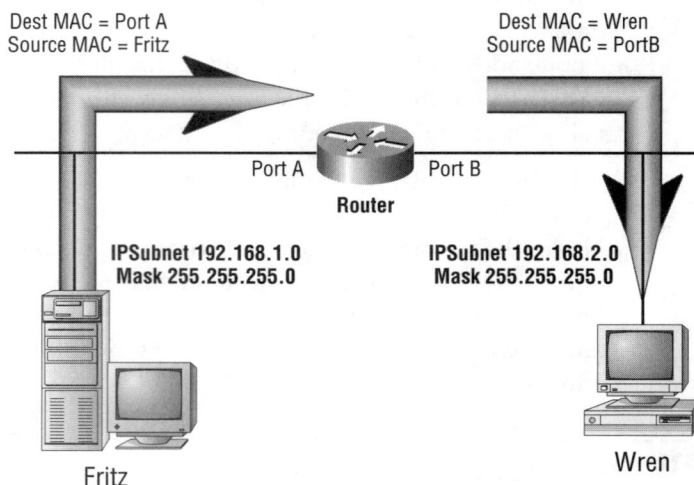

Dest MAC = Port A
Source MAC = Fritz

Dest MAC = Wren
Source MAC = PortB

Port A   Port B
Router

**IPSubnet 192.168.1.0
Mask 255.255.255.0**

**IPSubnet 192.168.2.0
Mask 255.255.255.0**

Fritz

Wren

Our router will then need to send an ARP out of Port B in order to discover the node address of Wren. Once Wren replies to this ARP request, the router will strip off the Ethernet frame from the data and create a new one. The router replaces the source node address (originally Fritz's node address) with the node address of Port B. It will also replace the destination node address (originally Port A) with the node address of Wren.

> **NOTE**
>
> In order for the router to communicate on both subnets, it needed two unique node addresses, one for each port. If Fritz were launching an attack against Wren, you could not use the source node address within the frame on Wren's subnet in order to identify the transmitting system. While the source node address will tell you where the data entered this subnet, it will not identify the original transmitting system.

When Fritz realized that Wren was not on the same subnet, he went looking for a router. A system will run through a process similar to that shown in Figure 3.3 when determining how best to deliver data. Once a system knows where it needs to send the information, it transmits the appropriate ARP request.

FIGURE 3.3:

ARP decision process

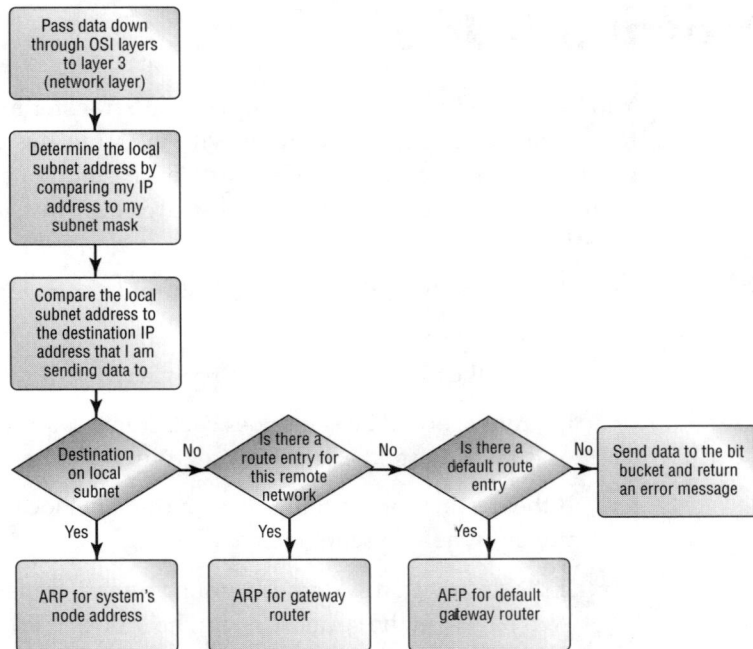

All systems are capable of caching information learned through ARP requests. For example, if Fritz wished a few seconds later to send another packet of data to Wren, he would not have to transmit a new ARP request for the router's node address since this value would be saved in memory. This memory area is referred to as the *ARP cache*.

ARP cache entries are retained for up to 60 seconds. After that, they are typically flushed out and must be learned again through a new ARP request. It is also possible to create static ARP entries, which creates a permanent entry in the ARP cache table. This way, a system is no longer required to transmit ARP requests for nodes with a static entry.

For example, you could create a static ARP entry for the router on Fritz's machine so that it would no longer have to transmit an ARP request when looking for this device. The only problem would occur if the router's node address changed. If the router were to fail and you had to replace it with a new one, you would also have to go back to Fritz's system and modify the static ARP entry because the new router would have a different node address.

A Protocol's Job

You have seen that when a system wants to transfer information to another system, it does so by creating a frame with the target system's node address in the destination field of the frame header. This method of communication is part of your topology's communication rules. This transmission raises the following questions:

- Should the transmitting system simply assume the frame was received in one piece?

- Should the destination system reply, saying, "I received your frame, thanks!"?

- If a reply should be sent, does each frame require its own acknowledgment, or is it OK to send just one for a group of frames?

- If the destination system is not on the same local network, how do you figure out where to send your data?

- If the destination system is running e-mail, transferring a file, and browsing Web pages on the source system, how does it know which application this data is for?

This is where a protocol comes in. A protocol's job is to answer these questions—as well as any others that may pop up in the course of the communication. When we talk about IP, IPX, AppleTalk, or NetBEUI, we are talking about protocols. So why are the specifications that characterize a protocol not simply defined by the topology?

The answer is: diversity. If the communication properties of IP were tied into the Ethernet topology, everyone would be required to use Ethernet for all network segments; this includes wide-area network links. You could not choose to use Token Ring or ATM, because these services would only be available on Ethernet. By defining a separate set of communication rules (protocols), these rules can now be applied over any OSI-compliant topology. This was not the case with legacy systems, which is why the OSI model was developed.

The OSI Model

In 1977 the International Standards Organization (ISO) developed the *Open Systems Interconnection Reference Model* (OSI model) to help improve communications between different vendors' systems. The ISO was a committee representing many different organizations, whose goal was not to favor a specific method of communication but to develop a set of guidelines that would allow vendors to insure that their products would interoperate.

The ISO was setting out to simplify communications between systems. There are many events that must take place in order to insure that data first reaches the correct system and is then passed along to the correct application in a useable format. A set of rules was required to break down the communication process into a simple set of building blocks.

The OSI model consists of seven layers. Each layer describes how its portion of the communication process should function, as well as how it will interface with the layers directly above it, below it, and adjacent to it on other systems. This allows a vendor to create a product that operates on a certain level and to be sure it will operate in the widest range of applications. If the vendor's product follows a specific layer's guidelines, it should be able to communicate with products created by other vendors that operate at adjacent layers.

To use the analogy of a house for just a moment, think of the lumber yard that supplies main support beams used in house construction. As long as the yard follows the guidelines for thickness and material, builders can expect beams to function correctly in any house that has a proper foundation structure.

Simplifying a Complex Process

An analogy to the OSI model would be the process of building a house. While the final product may seem a complex piece of work, it is much simpler when it is broken down into manageable sections.

A good house starts with a foundation. There are rules that define how wide the foundation wall must be, as well as how far below the frost line it needs to sit. After that, the house is framed off or *packaged*. Again, there are rules to define how thick the lumber must be and how far each piece of framing can span without support.

Once the house is framed, there is a defined process for putting on a roof, adding walls, and even connecting the electrical system and plumbing. By breaking down this complicated process into small, manageable sections, building a house becomes easier. This breakdown also makes it easier to define who is responsible for which section. For example, the electrical contractor's responsibilities include running wires and adding electrical outlets, but not shingling the roof.

The entire structure becomes an interwoven tapestry with each piece relying on the others. For example, the frame of our house requires a solid foundation. Without it, the frame will eventually buckle and fall. The frame may also require that load-bearing walls be placed in certain areas of the house in order to insure that the frame does not fall in on itself.

The OSI model strives to set up these same kinds of definitions and dependencies. Each portion of the communication process becomes a separate building block. This makes it easier to determine what each portion of the communication process is required to do. It also helps to define how each piece will be connected to the others.

Figure 3.4 is a representation of the OSI model in all its glory. Let's take the layers one at a time to determine the functionality expected of each.

Physical Layer   The *physical layer* describes the specifications of our transmission media, connectors, and signal pulses. A repeater or a hub is a physical layer device because it is frame-stupid and simply amplifies the electrical signal on the wire and passes it along.

Data-Link Layer   The *data-link layer* describes the specifications for topology and communication between local systems. Ethernet is a good example of a data-link layer specification, as it works with multiple physical layer specifications (twisted-pair cable, fiber) and multiple network layer specifications (IPX, IP). The data-link layer is the "door between worlds," connecting the physical aspects of the network (cables and digital pulses) with the abstract world of software and data streams. Bridges and switches are considered to be data-link devices because they are frame-aware. Both use information specific to the frame header to regulate traffic.

Network Layer   The *network layer* describes how systems on different network segments find each other; it also defines network addresses. A network address is a name or number assigned to a group of physically connected systems.

NOTE

The network address is assigned by the network administrator and should not be confused with the MAC address assigned to each network card. The purpose of a network address is to facilitate data delivery over long distances. Its functionality is similar to the zip code used when mailing a regular letter.

IP, IPX, and AppleTalk's Datagram Delivery Protocol (DDP) are all examples of network-layer functionality. Service and application availability are based on functionality prescribed at this level.

FIGURE 3.4:

The OSI model

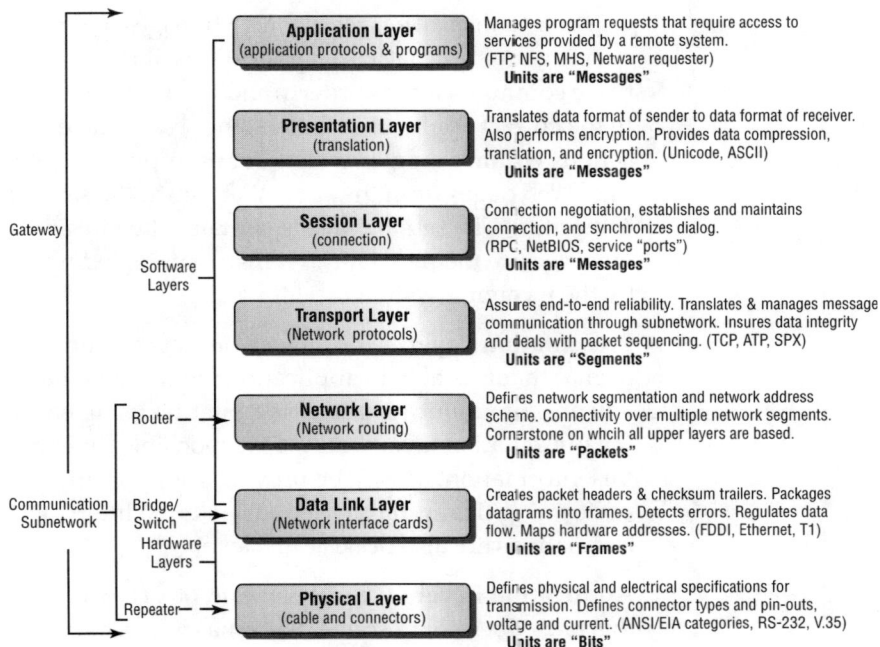

Application Layer (application protocols & programs)	Manages program requests that require access to services provided by a remote system. (FTP, NFS, MHS, Netware requester) **Units are "Messages"**
Presentation Layer (translation)	Translates data format of sender to data format of receiver. Also performs encryption. Provides data compression, translation, and encryption. (Unicode, ASCII) **Units are "Messages"**
Session Layer (connection)	Connection negotiation, establishes and maintains connection, and synchronizes dialog. (RPC, NetBIOS, service "ports") **Units are "Messages"**
Transport Layer (Network protocols)	Assures end-to-end reliability. Translates & manages message communication through subnetwork. Insures data integrity and deals with packet sequencing. (TCP, ATP, SPX) **Units are "Segments"**
Network Layer (Network routing)	Defines network segmentation and network address scheme. Connectivity over multiple network segments. Cornerstone on whcih all upper layers are based. **Units are "Packets"**
Data Link Layer (Network interface cards)	Creates packet headers & checksum trailers. Packages datagrams into frames. Detects errors. Regulates data flow. Maps hardware addresses. (FDDI, Ethernet, T1) **Units are "Frames"**
Physical Layer (cable and connectors)	Defines physical and electrical specifications for transmission. Defines connector types and pin-outs, voltage and current. (ANSI/EIA categories, RS-232, V.35) **Units are "Bits"**

Gateway — Software Layers — Router — Communication Subnetwork — Bridge/Switch — Hardware Layers — Repeater

NOTE   For more detail about network layer functionality, see "More on the Network Layer" later in this chapter.

Transport Layer   The *transport layer* deals with the actual manipulation of your data and prepares it for delivery through the network. If your data is too large for a single frame, the transport layer breaks it up into smaller pieces and assigns sequence numbers. Sequence numbers allow the transport layer on the other receiving system to reassemble the data into its original content. While the data link layer performs a CRC check on all frames, the transport layer can act as a backup check to insure that all the data was received and is usable. Examples of transport layer functionality are IP's Transmission Control Protocol (TCP), User Datagram Protocol (UDP), IPX's Sequence Packet Exchange (SPX), and AppleTalk's AppleTalk Transaction Protocol (ATP).

Session Layer   The *session layer* deals with establishing and maintaining a connection between two or more systems. It insures that a query for a specific type of service is made correctly. For example, if you try to access a system with your Web browser, the session layers on both systems work together to insure you receive HTML pages and not e-mail. If a system is running multiple network applications, it is up to the session layer to keep these communications orderly and to insure that incoming data is directed to the correct application. In fact, the session layer maintains unique conversations within a single service. For example, imagine downloading two distinct Web pages from the same Web site at the same time (from the same computer). The session layer maintains the integrity of each file transfer—making sure the two data streams aren't mixed up or otherwise confused by the receiving system.

Presentation Layer   The *presentation layer* insures that data is received in a format that is usable to applications running on the system. For example, if you are communicating over the Internet using encrypted communications, the presentation layer would be responsible for encrypting and decrypting this information. Most Web browsers support this kind of functionality for performing financial transactions over the Internet. Data and language translations are also done at this level.

Application Layer   The label *application layer* is a bit misleading, because this term does not describe the actual program that a user may be running on a system. Rather, this is the layer that is responsible for determining when access to network resources is required. For example, Microsoft Word does not function at the application layer of the OSI model. If a user tries to retrieve a document from her home directory on a server, however, the application layer networking software is responsible for delivering her request to the remote system.

NOTE   In geek lingo, the layers are *numbered* in the order I've described them. If I were to state that switches function at layer 2 of the OSI model, you would interpret this to mean that switches work within the guidelines provided by the data-link layer of the OSI model.

How the OSI Model Works

Let's look at an example to see how these layers work together. Assume you're using your word processing program, and you want to retrieve a file called `resume.txt` from your home directory on a remote server. The networking software running on your system would react similarly to the description that follows.

Formulating a File Request

The application layer detects that you are requesting information from a remote file system. It formulates a request to that system that `resume.txt` should be read from disk. Once it has created this request, the application layer passes the request off to the presentation layer for further processing.

The presentation layer determines if it needs to encrypt this request or perform any type of data translation. Once this has been determined and completed, the presentation layer then adds any information it needs to pass along to the presentation layer on the remote system and forwards the packet down to the session layer.

The session layer checks which application is requesting the information and verifies what service is being requested from the remote system (file access). The session layer adds information to the request to ensure that the remote system knows how to handle this request. Then it passes all this information along to the transport layer.

The transport layer ensures that it has a reliable connection to the remote system and begins the process of breaking down all the information so that it can be packaged into frames. If more than one frame is required, the information is split up and each block of information is assigned a sequence number. These sequenced chunks of information are passed one at a time down to the network layer.

The network layer receives the blocks of information from the transport layer and adds the network address for both this and the remote system. This is done to each block before it is passed down to the data-link layer.

At the data-link layer, the blocks are packaged into individual frames. As shown in Figure 3.5, all the information added by each of the previous layers (as well as the actual file request) must fit into the 46- to 1,500-byte data field of the Ethernet frame. The data-link layer then adds a frame header, which consists of the source and destination MAC addresses, and uses this information (along with the contents of the data field) to create a CRC trailer. The data-link layer is then responsible for transmitting the frame according to the topology rules in use on the network. Depending on the topology, this could mean listening for a quiet moment on the network, waiting for a token, or waiting for a specific time division before transmitting the frame.

NOTE   The physical layer does not add any information to the frame.

FIGURE 3.5:

The location of each layer's information within our frame

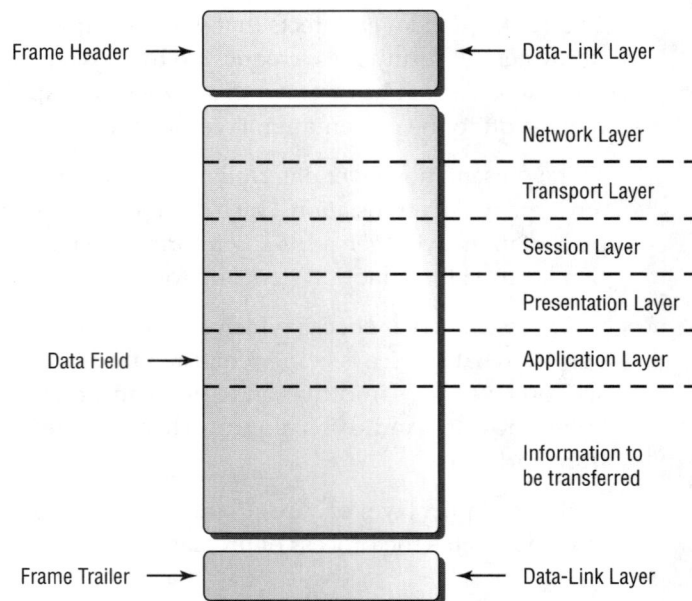

Frame Header → [ ] ← Data-Link Layer

Network Layer

Transport Layer

Session Layer

Presentation Layer

Data Field → Application Layer

Information to be transferred

Frame Trailer → [ ] ← Data-Link Layer

The physical layer is responsible for carrying the information from the source system to its destination. Because the physical layer has no knowledge of frames, it is simply passing along the digital signal pulses transmitted by the data-link layer. The physical layer is the medium by which a connection is made between the two systems; it is responsible for carrying the signal to the data-link layer on the remote system.

Your workstation has successfully formulated your data request ("Send me a copy of resume.txt.") and transmitted it to the remote system. At this point, the remote system follows a similar process, but in reverse.

Receiving Data on the Remote System

The data-link layer on the remote system reads in the transmitted frame. It notes that the MAC address in the destination field of the header is its own and recognizes that it needs to process this request. It performs a CRC check on the frame and compares the results to the value stored in the frame trailer. If these values match, the data-link layer strips off the header and trailer and passes the data field up to the networking layer. If the values do not match, the data-link layer sends a request to the source system asking that another frame be sent.

The network layer on the remote system analyzes the information recorded by the network layer on the source system. It notes that the destination software address is its own. Once this analysis is complete, the network layer removes information related to this level and passes the remainder up to the transport layer.

The transport layer receives the information and analyzes the information recorded by the transport layer on the source system. If it finds that packet sequencing was used, it queues any information it receives until all the data has been received. If any of the data is missing, the transport layer uses the sequence information to formulate a reply to the source system, requesting that this piece of data be resent. Once all the data has been received, the transport layer strips out any transport information and passes the full request up to the session layer.

The session layer receives the information and verifies that it is from a valid connection. If the check is positive, the session layer strips out any session information and passes the request up to the presentation layer.

The presentation layer receives the frame and analyzes the information recorded by the presentation layer on the source system. It then performs any translation or decryption required. Once translation or decryption has been completed, it strips out the presentation layer information and passes the request up to the application layer.

The application layer insures that the correct process running on the system receives the request for data. Because this is a file request, it is passed to whichever process is responsible for access to the file system.

This process then reads the requested file and passes the information back to the application layer. At this point, the entire process of passing the information through each of the layers would repeat. If you're amazed that the requested file is retrievable in anything less than a standard coffee break, then you have a pretty good idea of the magnitude of what happens when you request a simple file.

More on the Network Layer

As I mentioned earlier, the network layer is used for delivery of information between *logical networks*.

NOTE   A logical network is simply a group of systems assigned a common network address by the network administrator. These systems may be grouped together because they share a common geographical area or a central point of wiring.

Network Addresses

The terminology used for network addresses is different depending on the protocol in use. If the protocol in use is IPX, the logical network is simply referred to as a network address. With IP it is a *subnet* and with AppleTalk it is called a *zone*.

NOTE   NetBIOS and NetBEUI are non-routable protocols, although NetBEUI can be thought of as overlapping the transport, network, and (the LLC portion of the) data-link layer. They do not use network numbers and do not have the ability to propagate information between logical network segments. A *non-routable protocol* is a set of communication rules that expects all systems to be connected locally. A non-routable protocol has no direct method of traveling between logical networks. A NetBIOS frame is incapable of crossing a router without some form of help.

Routers

Routers are used to connect logical networks, which is why they are sometimes referred to in the IP world as *gateways*. Figure 3.6 shows the effect of adding a router to a network. Notice that protocols on either side of the device must now use a unique logical network address. Information destined for a non-local system must be routed to the logical network on which the system resides. The act of traversing a router from one logical network to another is referred to as a *hop*. When a protocol hops a router, it must use a unique logical network address on both sides.

FIGURE 3.6:

The effects of adding a router to the network

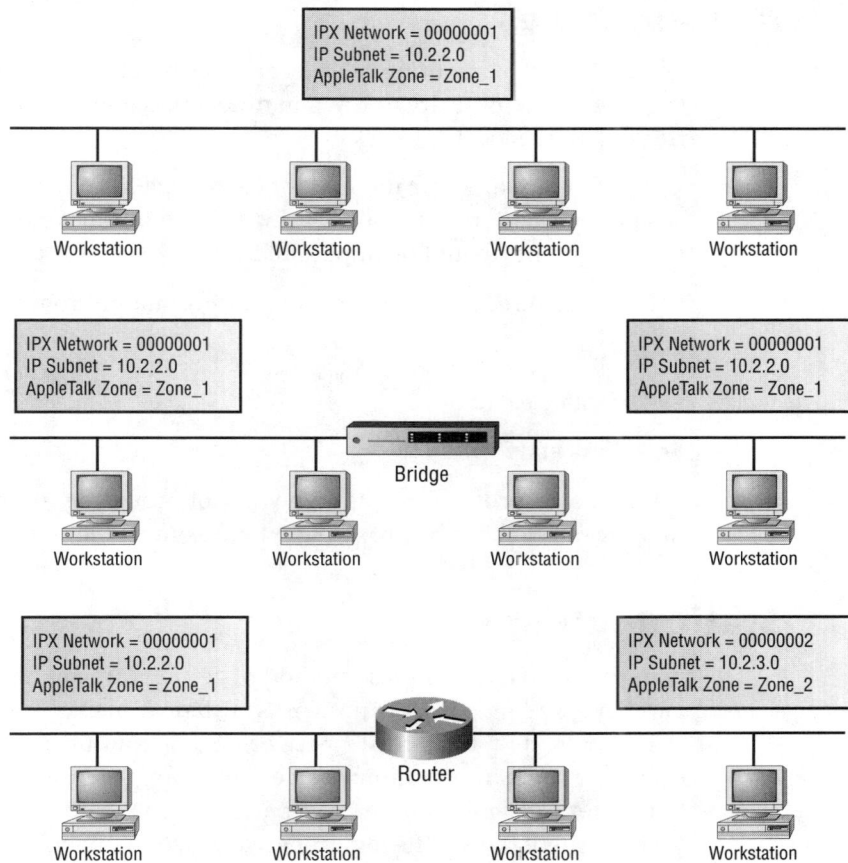

IPX Network = 00000001
IP Subnet = 10.2.2.0
AppleTalk Zone = Zone_1

Workstation   Workstation   Workstation   Workstation

IPX Network = 00000001
IP Subnet = 10.2.2.0
AppleTalk Zone = Zone_1

IPX Network = 00000001
IP Subnet = 10.2.2.0
AppleTalk Zone = Zone_1

Bridge

Workstation   Workstation   Workstation   Workstation

IPX Network = 00000001
IP Subnet = 10.2.2.0
AppleTalk Zone = Zone_1

IPX Network = 00000002
IP Subnet = 10.2.3.0
AppleTalk Zone = Zone_2

Router

Workstation   Workstation   Workstation   Workstation

So how do systems on one logical network segment find out what other logical segments exist on the network? Routers can either be statically programmed with information describing the path to follow in order to find remote networks, or they can use a special type of maintenance frame such as the routing information protocol (RIP) to relay information about known networks. Routers use these frames and static entries to create a blueprint of the network known as a *routing table*.

NOTE   Routing tables tell the router which logical networks are available to deliver information to and which routers are capable of forwarding information to that network.

Routing Tables

You can think of a routing table as being like a road map. A road map shows all the streets in a local city or town in much the same way a routing table keeps track of all the local networks.

Without having some method for each of these routers to communicate and let each other know who is connected where, communication between logical network segments would be impossible.

There are three methods for routing information from one network to another:

- Static
- Distance vector
- Link state

While each protocol has its own ways of providing routing functionality, each implementation can be broken down into one of these three categories.

Static Routing

Static routing is the simplest method of getting information from one system to another. Used mostly in IP networks, a static route defines a specific router to be the point leading to a specific network. Static routing does not require routers to exchange route information: it relies on a configuration file that directs all traffic bound for a specific network to a particular router. This, of course, assumes that you can predefine all the logical networks you will wish to communicate with. When this is not feasible (for example, when you are communicating on the

Internet), a single router may be designated as a default to receive all traffic destined for networks that have not been predefined. When static routing is used, most workstations receive an entry for the default router only.

For example, let's assume I configure my system to have a default route that points to the router Galifrey. As my system passes information through the network layer, it will analyze the logical network of the destination system. If the system is located on the same logical network, the data-link layer adds the MAC address of that system and transmits the frame onto the wire. If the system is located on some other logical network, the data-link layer will use the MAC address for Galifrey and transmit the frame to it. Galifrey would then be responsible for insuring that the frame gets to its final destination.

The benefits of this type of routing are simplicity and low overhead. My workstation is not required to know or care about what other logical networks may be available and how to get to them. It has only two possibilities to worry about—deliver locally or deliver to Galifrey. This can be useful when there is only one possible route to a final destination. For example, most organizations have only one Internet connection. Setting up a static route that points all IP traffic to the router that borders this connection may be the easiest way to insure that all frames are delivered properly. Because all my routing information is configured at startup, my routers do not need to share route information with other routers. Each system is only concerned with forwarding information to its next default route. I do not need to have any dynamic routing frames propagated through my network, because each router has been preset as to where it should forward information.

While static routing is easy to use, it does suffer from some major drawbacks that severely limit its application. When redundant paths are provided, or even when multiple routers are used on the same logical network, you may find it more effective to use a routing method that is capable of exchanging dynamic routing information. Dynamic routing allows routing tables to be developed on the fly, which can compensate for hardware failures. Both distance vector and link state routing use dynamic routing information to insure routing tables stay up to date.

Static Routing Security

While static routing requires a high level of maintenance, it is also the most secure method of building your routing tables. Dynamic routing allows routing tables to be updated dynamically by devices on the network. An attacker can exploit this feature in order to feed your routers incorrect routing information, thus preventing your network from functioning properly. In fact, depending on the dynamic routing protocol you use, an attacker may only need to feed this bogus information to a single router. The compromised router would then take care of propagating this bogus information throughout the rest of the network.

Each static router is responsible for maintaining its own routing table. This means that if one router is compromised, the effects of the attack are not automatically spread to every other router. A router using static routing can still be vulnerable to ICMP redirect attacks, but its routing tables cannot be corrupted through the propagation of bad route information.

NOTE   For more information on ICMP, see the "Packet Filtering ICMP" section of Chapter 5.

Distance Vector Routing

Distance vector is the oldest and most popular form of creating routing tables. This is primarily due to the routing information protocol (RIP), which is based on distance vector. For many years, distance vector routing was the only dynamic routing option available, so it has found its way onto many networks.

Distance vector routers build their tables on secondhand information. A router will look at the tables being advertised by other routers and simply add 1 to the advertised hop values to create its own table. With distance vector, every router will broadcast its routing table once per minute.

Propagating Network Information with Distance Vector

Figure 3.7 shows how propagation of network information works with distance vector.

Router A has just come online. Because the two attached networks (1 and 2) have been programmed into it, Router A immediately adds these to its routing table, assigning a hop value of 1 to each. The hop value is 1 instead of 0 because this information is relative to other attached networks, not the router. For example, if the router is advertising the route to Network 1 on Network 2, then one hop is appropriate because any system sending information to Network 1 from Network 2 would have to travel one hop (the router itself) to get there. A router usually does not advertise routing information about a directly attached network on that network itself. This means that the router should not transmit a RIP frame stating, "I can reach Network 1 in one hop," on Network 1 itself.

FIGURE 3.7:

A routed network about to build its routing tables dynamically

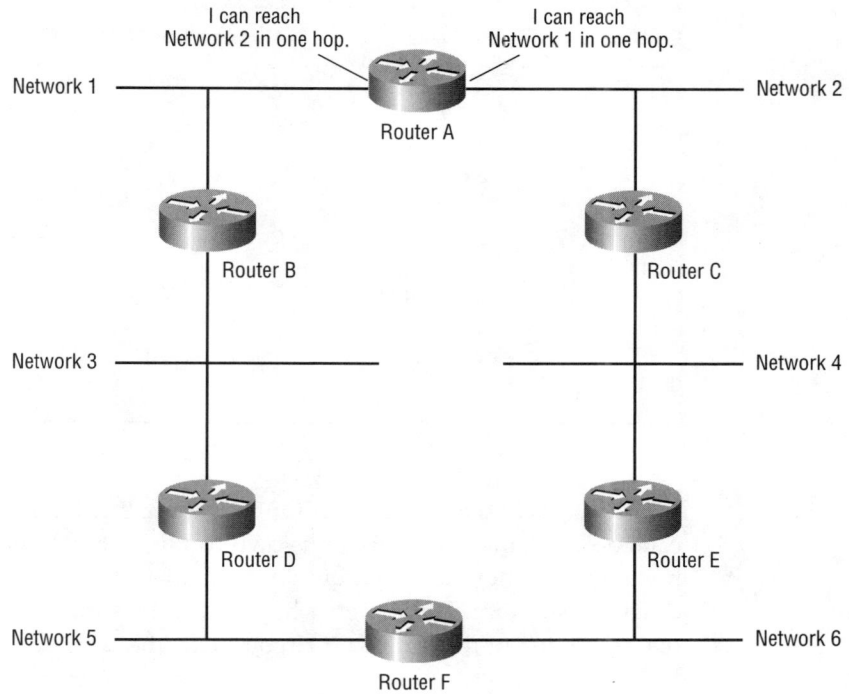

So Router A sends out two RIP packets, one on each network, to let any other devices know about the connectivity it can provide. When Routers B and C receive these packets, they reply with RIP packets of their own. Remember that the network was already up and running. This means that all the other routers have already had an opportunity to build their tables. From these other RIP packets, Router A collects the information shown in Table 3.2.

TABLE 3.2:   Routing Information Received by Router A

Router	Network	Hops to Get There
B	3	1
B	5	2
B	6	3

Continued on next page

TABLE 3.2 CONTINUED: Routing Information Received by Router A

Router	Network	Hops to Get There
B	4	4
B	2	5
C	4	1
C	6	2
C	5	3
C	3	4
C	1	5

Router A will then analyze this information, picking the lowest hop count to each network in order to build its own routing table. Routes that require a larger hop count are not discarded but are retained in case an alternate route is required due to link failure. These higher hop values are simply ignored during the normal operation of the router. Once complete, the table appears similar to Table 3.3.

TABLE 3.3:   Router A's Routing Table

Network	Hops to Get There	Next Router
1	1	Direct connection
2	1	Direct connection
3	2	B
4	2	C
5	3	B
6	3	C

All we've done is to pick the lowest hop count to each network and added 1 to the advertised value. Once the table is complete, Router A will again broadcast two RIP packets, incorporating this new information.

Now that Routers B and C have noted that there is a new router on the network, they must reevaluate their routing tables, as well. Before Router A came online, the table for Router B would have looked like Table 3.4.

TABLE 3.4:   Router B's Routing Table before Router A Initializes

Network	Hops to Get There	Next Router
1	1	Direct connection
2	5	D
3	1	Direct connection
4	4	D
5	2	D
6	3	D

Now that Router A is online, Router B will modify its table to reflect the information shown in Table 3.5.

TABLE 3.5:   Router B's Routing Table after Router A Initializes

Network	Hops to Get There	Next Router
1	1	Direct connection
2	2	A
3	1	Direct connection
4	3	A
5	2	D
6	3	D

It takes us two RIPs on the same logical network to get to this point. The first time Router A sent a RIP to Router B it only knew about Network 2, as you could see in Figure 3.7. It was not until Router C sent a reply RIP that Router A had to send a second RIP frame to Router B, incorporating this new information. Table 3.5 would be broadcast with only the direct common network information being removed (Network 1). This means that while Router A was updating Router B with the information it had learned from Router C, it was also relaying back the route information originally sent to it by that router (Router B). The only difference is that Router A has increased by 1 each hop count reported by Router B.

Because the hop value is larger than what Router B currently has in its tables, Router B would simply ignore this information.

Router C would go through a similar process, adjusting its table according to the information it receives from Router A. Again, it will require two RIP frames on the same logical network to yield a complete view of our entire network so that Router C can complete the changes to its tables.

These changes would then begin to propagate down through our network. Router B would update Router D when A first comes online and then again when it completes its tables. This activity would continue until all the routers have an accurate view of our new network layout. The amount of time that is required for all our routers to complete their table changes is known as the time to *convergence*. The convergence time is important, because our routing table is in a state of flux until all our routers become stabilized with their new tables.

WARNING   Keep in mind that in a large network, convergence time can be quite long, as RIP updates are only sent once or twice per minute.

Distance Vector Routing Problems

It's important to note that our distance vector routing table has been almost completely built on secondhand information. Any route that a router reports with a hop count greater than 1 is based upon what it has learned from another router. When Router B tells Router A that it can reach Network 5 in two hops or Network 6 in three, it is fully trusting the accuracy of the information it has received from Router D. If, as a child, l you ever played the telephone game (where each person in a line receives a whispered message and tries to convey it exactly to the next), you quickly realize that secondhand information is not always as accurate as it appears to be.

Figure 3.8 shows a pretty simple network layout. It consists of four logical networks separated by three routers. Once the point of convergence is reached, each router will have created a routing table, as shown in the diagram.

FIGURE 3.8:

Given the diagrammed network, each router would construct its routing table.

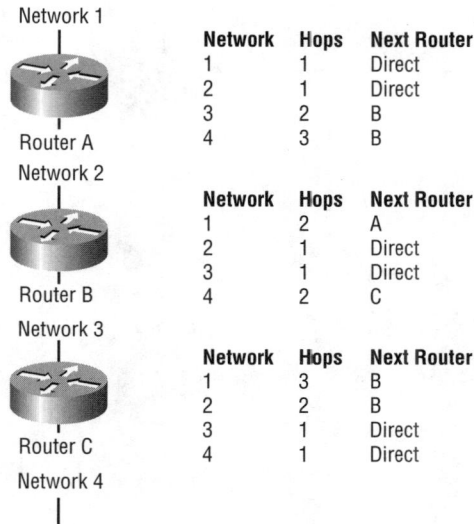

Network 1

Router A

Network	Hops	Next Router
1	1	Direct
2	1	Direct
3	2	B
4	3	B

Network 2

Router B

Network	Hops	Next Router
1	2	A
2	1	Direct
3	1	Direct
4	2	C

Network 3

Router C

Network	Hops	Next Router
1	3	B
2	2	B
3	1	Direct
4	1	Direct

Network 4

Now, let's assume that Router C dies a fiery death and drops offline. This will make Network 4 unreachable by all other network segments. Once Router B realizes that Router C is offline, it will review the RIP information it has received in the past, looking for an alternate route. This is where distance vector routing starts to break down. Because Router A has been advertising that it can get to Network 4 in three hops, Router B simply adds 1 to this value and assumes it can now reach Network 4 through Router A. Relying on secondhand information clearly causes problems: Router B cannot reach Network 4 through Router A, now that Router C is offline.

As you can see in Figure 3.9, Router B would now begin to advertise that it can now reach Network 4 in four hops. Remember that RIP frames do not identify *how* a router will get to a remote network, only that it *can* and how many hops it will take to get there. Without knowing how Router A plans to reach Network 4, Router B has no idea that Router A is basing its route information on the tables it originally received from Router B.

So Router A would receive a RIP update from Router B and realize that it has increased the hop count to Network 4 from two to four. Router A would then adjust its table accordingly and begin to advertise that it now takes five hops to reach Network 4. It would again RIP and Router B would again increase the hop count to Network 4 by one.

FIGURE 3.9:

Router B incorrectly believes that it can now reach Network 4 through Router A and updates its tables accordingly.

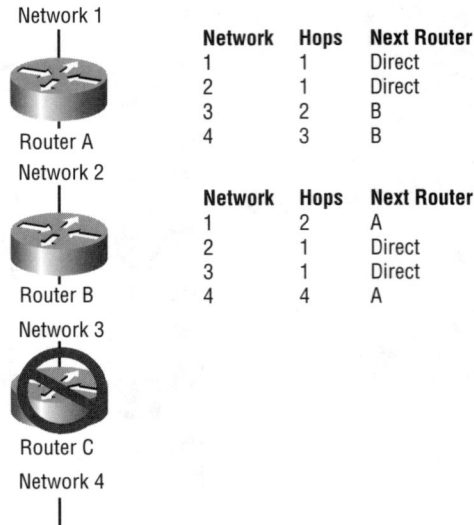

Network 1

Network	Hops	Next Router
1	1	Direct
2	1	Direct
3	2	B
4	3	B

Router A

Network 2

Network	Hops	Next Router
1	2	A
2	1	Direct
3	1	Direct
4	4	A

Router B

Network 3

Router C

Network 4

NOTE

This phenomenon is called *count to infinity* because both routers would continue to increase their hop counts forever. Because of this problem, distance vector routing limits the maximum hop count to 15. Any route that is 16 or more hops away is considered unreachable and is subsequently removed from the routing table. This allows our two routers to figure out in a reasonable amount of time that Network 4 can no longer be reached.

Reasonable is a subjective term, however. Remember that RIP updates are only sent out once or twice per minute. This means that it may be a minute or more before our routers buy a clue and realize that Network 4 is gone. With a technology that measures frame transmissions in the micro-second range, a minute or more is plenty of time to wreak havoc on communications. For example, let's look at what is taking place on Network 2 while the routers are trying to converge.

Once Router C has dropped offline, Router B assumes that it has an alternative route to Network 4 through Router A. Any packets it receives are checked for errors and passed along to Router A. When Router A receives the frame, it performs an error check again. It then references its tables and realizes it needs to forward the frame to Router B in order to reach Network 4. Router B would again receive the frame and send it back to Router A.

This is called a *routing loop*. Each router plays hot potato with the frame, assuming the other is responsible for its delivery and passing it back and forth. While our example describes only one frame, imagine the amount of bandwidth lost if there is a considerable amount of traffic destined for Network 4. With all these frames looping between the two routers, there would be very little bandwidth available on Network 2 for any other systems that may need to transmit information.

Fortunately, the network layer has a method for eliminating this problem, as well. As each router handles the frame, it is required to decrease a hop counter within the frame by 1. The hop counter is responsible for recording how many routers the information has crossed. As with RIP frames, this counter has a maximum value of 15. As the information is handled for the 16th time (the counter drops to 0) the router realizes that the information is undeliverable and simply drops the information.

While this 16-hop limitation is not a problem for the average corporate network, it can be a severe limitation in larger networks. For example, consider the vast size of the Internet. If RIP were used throughout the Internet, certain areas of the Internet could not reach many resources.

Security Concerns with RIP

Besides our RIP routing tables being built upon secondhand information, note that this information is never actually verified. For example, if Router B claims to have the best route to a given network, none of the other routers will verify this information. In fact, they do not even verify that this information was sent from Router B or that Router B even exists!

Needless to say, this lack of verification can be a gaping security hole. It is not all that difficult to propagate bogus routing information and bring an entire network to its knees. This is a clear example of how one savvy but malicious user can interrupt communications for an entire network.

Because of this security concern and the other problems we've noted, many organizations use static routing or have deployed link state routing protocols such as OSPF (Open Shortest Path First). Besides eliminating many of the convergence problems found in RIP, OSPF also brings authentication to the table, requiring routers to supply a password in order to participate in routing updates. While not infallible, this method does dramatically increase the security in a dynamic routing environment.

Link State Routing

Link state routers function in a similar fashion to distance vector, but with a few notable exceptions. Most importantly, link state routers use only firsthand information when developing their routing tables. Not only does this help to eliminate routing errors, it drops the time to convergence to nearly zero. Imagine that our network from Figure 3.7 has been upgraded to using a link state routing protocol. Now let's bring Router A online and watch what happens.

Propagating Network Information with Link State

As Router A powers up, it sends out a type of RIP packet referred to as a *hello*. The hello packet is simply an introduction that states, "Greetings! I am a new router on this network; is there anybody out there?" This packet is transmitted on both of its ports and will be responded to by Routers B and C.

Once Router A receives a reply from Routers B and C, it creates a *link state protocol* (LSP) frame and transmits it to Routers B and C. An LSP frame is a routing maintenance frame that contains the following information:

- The router's name or identification
- The networks it is attached to
- The hop count or cost of getting to each network
- Any other routers on each network that responded to its hello frame

Routers B and C would then make a copy of Router A's LSP frame and forward the frame in its entirety along through the network. Each router receiving Router A's LSP frame would then copy the information and pass it along. With link state routing, each router maintains a copy of every other router's LSP frame. The router can use this information to diagram the network and thus build routing tables. Because each LSP frame contains only the route information that is local to each router that sent it, this network map is created strictly from firsthand information. A router will simply fit the LSP puzzle pieces together until its network picture is complete.

Router A would then make an LSP frame request from either Router B or C. An LSP frame request is a query requesting that the router forward a copy of all known LSP frames. Because each router has a copy of all LSP frames, either router is capable of supplying a copy from every router on the network. This avoids making Router A request this information from each router individually, thus saving bandwidth. Once an LSP network is up and running, updates are only transmitted every two hours or whenever a change takes place (such as a router going offline).

Convergence Time with Link State

Our link state network is up and running. Note that Routers B and C were not required to recompute their routing tables. They simply added the new piece from Router A and continued to pass traffic. This is why convergence time is nearly zero. The only change required of each router is to add the new piece to its tables. Unlike distance vector, updates were not required in order to normalize the routing table. Router B did not need a second packet from Router A, telling it what networks were available through Router C. Router B simply added Router A's LSP information to its existing table and was already aware of the links.

Recovering from a Router Failure in a Link State Environment

Let's revisit Figure 3.9 to look at how link state routing reacts when a router goes offline. Again, for the purpose of this example let's assume that our routing protocol has been upgraded from distance vector to link state. Let's also assume that our routing tables have been created and that traffic is passing normally.

If Router C is shut down normally, it will transmit a maintenance frame (known as a *dying gasp*) to Router B, informing it that it is about to go offline. Router B would then delete the copy of Router C's LSP frame that it has been maintaining and forward this information along to Router A. Both routers now have a valid copy of the new network layout and realize that Network 4 is no longer reachable. If Router C is not brought down gracefully but again dies a fiery death, there would be a short delay before Router B realizes that Router C is no longer acknowledging packets sent to it. At this point Router B would realize that Router C is offline. It would then delete Router C's LSP frame from its table and forward the change along to Router A. Again, both systems have a valid copy of the new network layout. Because we are dealing with strictly firsthand information, there are none of the pesky count-to-infinity problems that we experienced with distance vector. Our router tables are accurate, and our network is functioning with a minimal amount of updating. This allows link state to traverse a larger number of network segments. The maximum is 127 hops, but this can be fewer, depending on the implementation.

Security with Link State Routing

Most link state routing protocols support some level of authenticating the source of dynamic route updates. While it is not impossible to incorporate this functionality into distance vector routing, most distance vector routing protocols predate the need to authenticate routing table updates. Authentication is an excellent means of insuring that each router only accepts routing table updates from a trusted host. While authentication is not 100 percent secure, it is a far cry from trusting every host on the wire.

For example, OSPF supports two levels of authentication: password and message digest. *Password authentication* requires each router that will be exchanging route table information to be preprogrammed with a password. When a router attempts to send OSPF routing information to another router, it includes the password string as verification. Routers using OSPF will not accept route table updates unless the password string is included in the transmission. This helps to insure that table updates are only accepted from trusted hosts.The drawback to this authentication method is that the password is transmitted as clear text. This means that an attacker who is monitoring the network with a packet analyzer can capture the OSPF table updates and discover the password. An attacker who knows the password can use it to pose as a trusted OSPF router and transmit bogus routing table information.

Message digest is far more secure in that it does not exchange password information over the wire. Each OSPF router is programmed with a password and a key-ID. Prior to transmitting an OSPF table update, a router will process the OSPF table information, password, and key-ID through an algorithm in order to generate a unique message digest, which is attached to the end of the packet. The message digest provides an encrypted method of verifying that the router transmitting the table can be considered a trusted host. When the destination router receives the transmission, the destination router uses the password and key-ID it has been programmed with to validate the message digest. If the message is authentic, the routing table update is accepted.

TIP

While it is possible to crack the encryption used by OSPF, doing so takes time and lots of processing power. This makes OSPF with message digest authentication an excellent choice for updating dynamic routing information over insecure networks.

Connectionless and Connection-Oriented Communications

We can now get our information from Point A to Point B, regardless of whether the systems are located on the same logical network. This raises the question, "Once we get there, how do we carry on a proper conversation?" This is where the transport layer comes in.

The transport layer is where we begin to set down the rules of communication etiquette. It's not enough that we can get this information from one system to another; we also have to insure that both systems are operating at the same level of decorum.

As an analogy, let's say you pull up to the finest restaurant in the city in your GMC Pacer and proceed to the front door sporting your best set of leather chaps, Harley jacket, and bandanna. Once inside, you greet the maitre d' with "Yo wimp, gimme a table and some grub, NOW!" Surprisingly, you're escorted out of the restaurant at gunpoint. What went wrong? Why, you employed improper etiquette, of course—everyone knows the correct term is not "grub" but "escargot."

You can avoid such verbal breakdown, as well as those in network communications, by insuring that all parties involved are communicating at the same level of etiquette. There are two forms of network communication etiquette:

- Connection-oriented
- Connectionless

Connection-Oriented Communications

A *connection-oriented* communication exchanges control information referred to as a *handshake* prior to transmitting data. The transport layer uses the handshake to insure that the destination system is ready to receive information. A connection-oriented exchange will also insure that data is transmitted and received in its original order.

Modems are heavy users of connection-oriented communications, as they need to negotiate a connection speed prior to sending any information. In networking, this functionality is accomplished through the use of a transport layer field referred to as a *flag* in the IP and AppleTalk world or as a *connection control field* under IPX. Only connection-oriented communications use these fields. When IP is the underlying routing protocol, TCP is used to create connection-oriented communications. IPX uses SPX, and AppleTalk uses ATP to provide this functionality. As a communication session is started, the application layer (not necessarily the program you are using) will specify if it needs to use a connection-oriented protocol. Telnet is just such an application. When a telnet session is started, the application layer will request TCP as its transport service in order to better insure reliability of the connection. Let's look at how this session is established to see how a handshake works.

The TCP Three-Packet Handshake

At your workstation you type in **telnet thor.foobar.com** to establish a remote connection to that system. As the request is passed down through the transport layer, TCP is selected to connect the two systems so that a connection-oriented communication can be established. The transport layer sets the synchronization (SYN) flag to 1 and leaves all other flags at 0. IP uses multiple flag fields and uses the binary system to set values. This means that the only possible values of an IP flag are 1 and 0. IPX and AT use a hexadecimal value, as their frames only contain one flag field. This allows the one field to contain more than two values.

By setting SYN to 1 and all other fields to 0, we let the system on the other end (thor.foobar.com) know that we wish to establish a new communication session with the system. This request would then be passed down the remaining layers, across the wire to the remote system, and then up through its OSI layers.

If the service is available on the remote system (more on services in a moment), the request is acknowledged and sent back down the stack until it reaches the transport layer. The transport layer would then set the SYN flag to 1, as did the originating system, but it will also set the acknowledgment (ACK) flag to 1. This lets the originating system know that its transmission was received and that it's OK to send data. The request is then passed down the stack and over the wire back to the original system.

The original system would then set the SYN flag to 0 and the ACK flag to 1 and transfer this frame back to Thor. This lets Thor know, "I'm acknowledging your acknowledgment and I'm about to send data." At this point, data would be transferred, with each system being required to transmit an acknowledgment for each packet it receives.

Figure 3.10 shows a telnet session from the system Loki to the system Thor. Each line represents a different frame that has been transmitted from one system to the other. Source and destination systems are identified, as well as some summary information about the frame. Notice that the first three frames are identified as TCP frames, not telnet, and that they perform the handshaking just described. Once TCP establishes the connection-oriented connection, then telnet can step in to transfer the data required. The TCP frames that appear later in the conversation are for acknowledgment purposes. As stated, with a connection-oriented protocol every frame must be acknowledged. If the frame was a request for information, the reply can be in the form of delivering the requested information. If a frame is sent that does not require a reply, however, the destination system is still required to acknowledge that the frame was received.

FIGURE 3.10:

An example of a connection-oriented communication

No.	Siz	Source	Destination	Layer	Summary
1	64	LOKI.FOOBAR.COM	THOR.FOOBAR.COM	tcp	Port:1042 ---> TELNET SYN
2	64	THOR.FOOBAR.COM	LOKI.FOOBAR.COM	tcp	Port:TELNET ---> 1042 ACK SYN
3	64	LOKI.FOOBAR.COM	THOR.FOOBAR.COM	tcp	Port:1042 ---> TELNET ACK
4	82	LOKI.FOOBAR.COM	THOR.FOOBAR.COM	telnt	Cmd=Do; Code=Suppress Go Ahead; Cmd=Will; Code=Termin
5	64	THOR.FOOBAR.COM	LOKI.FOOBAR.COM	tcp	Port:TELNET ---> 1042 ACK
6	70	THOR.FOOBAR.COM	LOKI.FOOBAR.COM	telnt	Cmd=Do; Code=Terminal Type; Cmd=Do; Code=Terminal Spe
7	64	LOKI.FOOBAR.COM	THOR.FOOBAR.COM	telnt	Cmd=Won't; Code=; Cmd=Will; Code=Terminal Type;
8	73	THOR.FOOBAR.COM	LOKI.FOOBAR.COM	telnt	Cmd=Will; Code=Suppress Go Ahead; Cmd=Do; Code=; Cmd=
9	64	THOR.FOOBAR.COM	LOKI.FOOBAR.COM	tcp	Port:TELNET ---> 1042 ACK
10	67	LOKI.FOOBAR.COM	THOR.FOOBAR.COM	telnt	Cmd=Subnegotiation Begin; Code=; Data=..P....
11	76	THOR.FOOBAR.COM	LOKI.FOOBAR.COM	telnt	Cmd=Subnegotiation Begin; Code=Terminal Speed; Data= .....
12	64	LOKI.FOOBAR.COM	THOR.FOOBAR.COM	tcp	Port:1042 ---> TELNET ACK
13	64	THOR.FOOBAR.COM	LOKI.FOOBAR.COM	tcp	Port:TELNET ---> 1042 ACK
14	92	LOKI.FOOBAR.COM	THOR.FOOBAR.COM	telnt	Cmd=Subnegotiation Begin; Code=Terminal Speed; Data= .38
15	64	THOR.FOOBAR.COM	LOKI.FOOBAR.COM	telnt	Cmd=Do; Code=Echo;
16	64	LOKI.FOOBAR.COM	THOR.FOOBAR.COM	telnt	Cmd=Won't; Code=Echo;
17	129	THOR.FOOBAR.COM	LOKI.FOOBAR.COM	telnt	Cmd=Will; Code=Echo; Data=..Red Hat Linux release 4.1 (Var
18	64	LOKI.FOOBAR.COM	THOR.FOOBAR.COM	telnt	Cmd=Do; Code=Echo;
19	64	THOR.FOOBAR.COM	LOKI.FOOBAR.COM	tcp	Port:TELNET ---> 1042 ACK
20	65	THOR.FOOBAR.COM	LOKI.FOOBAR.COM	telnt	Data=login:
21	64	LOKI.FOOBAR.COM	THOR.FOOBAR.COM	tcp	Port:1042 ---> TELNET ACK

If you're still a bit fuzzy on handshaking and connection-oriented communications, let's look at an analogy. Let's say you call a friend to inform him you'll be having a network Quake party on Saturday night and that he should come by with his laptop. You follow these steps:

- You dial your friend's phone number (SYN=1, ACK=0).

- Your friend answers the phone and says, "Hello" (SYN=1, ACK=1).

- You reply by saying, "Hi, Fred, this is Dave" (SYN=0, ACK=1).

You would then proceed to transfer your data about your upcoming party. Every time you pause, Fred would either transfer back information ("Yes, I'm free Saturday night.") or send some form of acknowledgment (ACK) to let you know he has not yet hung up.

When the conversation is complete, you would both tear down the connection by saying goodbye, which is a handshake to let each other know that the conversation is complete and that it's OK to hang up the phone. Once you hang up, your connection-oriented communication session is complete.

The purpose of connection-oriented communications is simple. They provide a reliable communication session when the underlying layers may be considered less than stable. Insuring reliable connectivity at the transport layer helps to speed up communication when data becomes lost. This is because the data does not have to be passed all the way up to the application layer before a retransmission frame is created and sent. While this is important in modem communications, where a small amount of noise or a crossed line can kill a communication session, it is not as useful with network-based communication. TCP and SPX originate from the days when the physical and data-link layers could not always be relied on to successfully transmit information. These days, this is less of a concern because reliability has increased dramatically from the earlier years of networking.

Connectionless Communications

A *connectionless* protocol does not require an initial handshake or acknowledgments to be sent for every packet. When you use a connectionless transport, it makes its best effort to deliver the data but relies on the stability of the underlying layers, as well as application layer acknowledgments, to insure that the data is delivered reliably. IP's User Datagram Protocol (UDP) and IPX's NetWare Core Protocol (NCP) are examples of connectionless transports. Both protocols rely on connectionless communications to transfer routing and server information, as well. While AppleTalk does not utilize connectionless communication for creating data sessions, AppleTalk does use it when advertising servers with its name binding protocol (NBP). Broadcasts are always transmitted using a connectionless transport.

As an example of connectionless communications, check out the network file system (NFS) session in Figure 3.11. NFS is a service that allows file sharing over IP. It uses UDP as its underlying transport protocol. Notice that all data acknowledgments are in the form of a request for additional information. The destination system (Thor) assumes that the last packet was received if the source system (Loki) requests additional information. Conversely, if Loki does not receive a reply from Thor, NFS takes care of requesting the information again. As long as we have a stable connection that does not require a large number of retransmissions, allowing NFS to provide error correction is a very efficient method of communicating because it does not generate unnecessary acknowledgments.

FIGURE 3.11:

NFS uses UDP to create a connectionless session.

No.	Size	Source	Destination	Layer	Summary
1	198	LOKI.FOOBAR.COM	THOR.FOOBAR.COM	nfs	Call Lookup ???/games.tar.gz
2	174	THOR.FOOBAR.COM	LOKI.FOOBAR.COM	nfs	Reply Lookup for games.tar.gz
3	182	LOKI.FOOBAR.COM	THOR.FOOBAR.COM	nfs	Call Get File Attributes for games.tar.gz
4	142	THOR.FOOBAR.COM	LOKI.FOOBAR.COM	nfs	Reply Get File Attributes
5	194	LOKI.FOOBAR.COM	THOR.FOOBAR.COM	nfs	Call Read From File games.tar.gz; Offset 0; 1024 bytes
6	1,170	THOR.FOOBAR.COM	LOKI.FOOBAR.COM	nfs	Reply Read From File; 1024 bytes
7	194	LOKI.FOOBAR.COM	THOR.FOOBAR.COM	nfs	Call Read From File games.tar.gz; Offset 1024; 1024 bytes
8	1,170	THOR.FOOBAR.COM	LOKI.FOOBAR.COM	nfs	Reply Read From File; 1024 bytes
9	194	LOKI.FOOBAR.COM	THOR.FOOBAR.COM	nfs	Call Read From File games.tar.gz; Offset 2048; 1024 bytes
10	1,170	THOR.FOOBAR.COM	LOKI.FOOBAR.COM	nfs	Reply Read From File; 1024 bytes
11	194	LOKI.FOOBAR.COM	THOR.FOOBAR.COM	nfs	Call Read From File games.tar.gz; Offset 3072; 1024 bytes
12	1,170	THOR.FOOBAR.COM	LOKI.FOOBAR.COM	nfs	Reply Read From File; 1024 bytes
13	194	LOKI.FOOBAR.COM	THOR.FOOBAR.COM	nfs	Call Read From File games.tar.gz; Offset 4096; 1024 bytes
14	1,170	THOR.FOOBAR.COM	LOKI.FOOBAR.COM	nfs	Reply Read From File; 1024 bytes
15	194	LOKI.FOOBAR.COM	THOR.FOOBAR.COM	nfs	Call Read From File games.tar.gz; Offset 5120; 1024 bytes
16	1,170	THOR.FOOBAR.COM	LOKI.FOOBAR.COM	nfs	Reply Read From File; 1024 bytes
17	194	LOKI.FOOBAR.COM	THOR.FOOBAR.COM	nfs	Call Read From File games.tar.gz; Offset 6144; 1024 bytes
18	1,170	THOR.FOOBAR.COM	LOKI.FOOBAR.COM	nfs	Reply Read From File; 1024 bytes
19	194	LOKI.FOOBAR.COM	THOR.FOOBAR.COM	nfs	Call Read From File games.tar.gz; Offset 7168; 1024 bytes
20	1,170	THOR.FOOBAR.COM	LOKI.FOOBAR.COM	nfs	Reply Read From File; 1024 bytes
21	194	LOKI.FOOBAR.COM	THOR.FOOBAR.COM	nfs	Call Read From File games.tar.gz; Offset 8192; 1024 bytes
22	1,170	THOR.FOOBAR.COM	LOKI.FOOBAR.COM	nfs	Reply Read From File; 1024 bytes
23	194	LOKI.FOOBAR.COM	THOR.FOOBAR.COM	nfs	Call Read From File games.tar.gz; Offset 9216; 1024 bytes

Let's look at another analogy to see how this type of communication differs from the connection-oriented one described earlier. Again, let's say you call Fred to invite him and his laptop to your network Quake party on Saturday night. You call Fred's number but this time get his answering machine. You leave a detailed message indicating when the party will take place and what he should bring. Unlike the first call, which Fred answered, you are now relying on

- Your ability to dial the correct phone number, as you did not reach your friend to confirm that this number was in fact his

- The fact that the phone company did not drop your phone connection in the middle of your message (answering machines do not ACK—unless, of course, you talk until the beep cuts you off)

- The answering machine's proper recording of the message—without eating the tape

- The ability of Fred's cat to discern between the tape and a ball of yarn

- The absence of a power failure (which would cause the machine to lose the message)

- Fred's retrieval of this message between now and the date of the party

As you can see, you have no real confirmation that your friend will actually receive the message. You are counting on the power company, the answering machine, and so on, to enable Fred to get your message in a timely manner. If you wanted to insure the reliability of this data transmission you could send an application layer acknowledgment request in the form of "Please RSVP by Thursday." If you did not get a response by then, you could try transmitting the data again.

So, which is a better transport to use: connectionless or connection-oriented? Unfortunately, the answer is whichever one your application layer specifies. If telnet wants TCP, you cannot force it to use UDP.

Security Implications

One technology that has made good use of the flag field of connection-oriented communications is firewalls. A firewall will use the information in the flag field to determine if a connection is inbound or outbound and, based on its rule table, either accept or deny the connection.

For example, let's say our firewall rules allow internal users access to the Internet but block external users from accessing internal systems. This is a pretty common security policy. How do we accomplish this?

We cannot simply block all inbound traffic, because this would prohibit our internal users from ever receiving a reply to their data requests. We need some method of allowing replies back in while denying external systems the ability to establish connections with internal systems. The secret to this is our TCP flags.

Remember that a TCP-based session needs to handshake prior to sending data. If we block all inbound frames that have the SYN field set to 1 and all other fields set to 0, we can prevent any external user from establishing a connection with our internal system. Because these settings are only used during the initial handshake and do not appear in any other part of the transmission, it is an effective way of blocking external users. If external users cannot connect to an internal system, they cannot transmit data to or pull data from that system.

NOTE   Many firewalls will deny all UDP connections—UDP does not have a flag field, and most firewalls have no effective way of determining if the data is a connection request or a reply. This is what has made *dynamic packet filtering* firewalls so popular: they monitor and remember all connection sessions. With dynamic packet filtering you can create a filter rule that accepts UDP packets from an external host only when that host has been previously queried for information using UDP. This insures that only UDP replies are allowed back in past the firewall. While a packet filter or some proxy firewalls can only effectively work with TCP connections, a dynamic packet filtering firewall can safely pass UDP as well.

Network Services

We can now find our remote system and insure that both systems are using the same level of communications. Now, how do we tell the server what we want? While computers are powerful tools—capable of processing many requests per second—they still have a problem with the phrase, "You know what I mean?" This is why we need a way to let a system know exactly what we want from it. It would be a real bummer to connect to a slick new Web site only to have the server start spewing e-mail or routing information at you because it had no idea which of its data you're looking for.

To make sure the computer knows what you want from it, you need to look to the session layer.

NOTE   You may remember from our discussion of the session layer that it is the layer responsible for insuring that requests for service are formulated properly.

A *service* is a process or application that runs on a server and provides some benefit to a network user. E-mail is a good example of a value-added service. A system may queue your mail messages until you connect to the system with a mail client in order to read them. File and print sharing are two other common examples of network services.

Services are accessed by connecting to a specific port or socket. Think of ports as virtual mail slots on the system and you'll get the idea. A separate mail slot (port number) is designated for each service or application running on the system. When a user wishes to access a service, the session layer is responsible for insuring that the request reaches the correct mail slot or port number.

On a UNIX or NT system, IP port numbers are mapped to services in a file called (oddly enough) services. An abbreviated output of a services file is shown in Table 3.6. The first column identifies the service by name, while the second column identifies the port and transport to be used. The third column is a brief description of the functionality provided by the service. Table 3.6 is only a brief listing of IP services. More information can be found in request for comment (RFC) 1700.

TABLE 3.6: An Abbreviated Services File

Name of Service	Port and Transport	Functionality
ftp-data	20/tcp	Used to transfer actual file information
ftp	21/tcp	Used to transfer session commands
telnet	23/tcp	Creates a remote session
smtp	25/tcp	E-mail delivery
whois	43/tcp	Internic domain name lookup
domain	53/tcp	Domain name queries
domain	53/udp	DNS zone transfers
bootps	67/udp	bootp server
bootpc	68/udp	bootp client
pop3	110/tcp	PostOffice V.3
nntp	119/tcp	Network News Transfer
ntp	123/tcp	Network Time Protocol
ntp	123/udp	Network Time Protocol
netbios-ns	137/tcp	nbns
netbios-ns	137/udp	nbns
netbios-dgm	138/tcp	nbdgm
netbios-dgm	138/udp	nbdgm
netbios-ssn	139/tcp	nbssn
snmp	161/udp	Simple Network Management protocol
snmp-trap	162/udp	Simple Network Management protocol

NOTE   These port numbers are not UNIX-specific. For example, any operating system using SMTP should use port 25.

According to the file summarized in Table 3.6, any TCP request received on port 23 is assumed to be a telnet session and is passed up to the application that handles remote access. If the requested port is 25, it is assumed that mail services are required and the session is passed up to the mail program.

The file in Table 3.6 is used on UNIX systems by a process called the *Internet daemon* (inetd). Inetd monitors each of the listed ports on a UNIX system and is responsible for *waking up* the application that provides services to that port. This is an efficient means of managing the system for infrequently accessed ports. The process is only active and using system resources (memory, CPU time, and so on) when the service is actually needed. When the service is shut down, the process returns to a sleep mode, waiting for inetd to call on it again.

Applications that receive heavy use should be left running in a constant listening mode. For example, Web server access usually uses port 80. Note that it is not listed in the services file in Table 3.6 as a process to be handled by inetd. This is because a Web server may be called upon to service many requests in the course of a day. It is more efficient to leave the process running all the time than to bother inetd every time you receive a page request.

All of these port numbers are referred to as *well-known ports*. Well-known ports are de facto standards used to insure that everyone can access services on other machines without needing to guess which port number is used by the service. For example, there is nothing stopping you from setting up a Web server on port 573, provided that the port is not in use by some other service. The problem is that most users will expect the service to be available on port 80 and may be unable to find it. Sometimes, however, switching ports may be done on purpose—we will look at that in just a minute.

NOTE   *De facto standard* means that it is a standard by popularity; it is not a rule or law.

Ports 0–1023 are defined by the Internet Assigned Numbers Authority (IANA) for most well-known services. While ports have been assigned up to 7200, the ports below 1024 make up the bulk of Internet communications. These assignments are not hard-and-fast rules; rather, they are guides to insure that everyone offers public services on the same port. For example, if you want to access Microsoft's Web page you can assume it offers the service on port 80, because this is the well-known port for that service.

When a system requests information, it not only specifies the port it wishes to access but also which port should be used when returning the requested information. Port numbers for this task are selected from 1024 to 65535 and are referred to as *upper port numbers.*

To illustrate how this works, let's revisit our telnet session in Figure 3.10. When Loki attempts to set up a telnet session with Thor, it will do so by accessing port 23 on Thor (port 23 is the well-known service port for telnet). If we look at frame number 2, we see that Thor is sending the acknowledgment (ACK) back on port 1042. This is because the session information in the original frame that Loki sent Thor specified a source port of 1042 and a destination port of 23. The destination port identified where the frame was going (port 23 on Thor), while the source port identified which port should be used when sending replies (port 1042 on Loki). Port 23 is our well-known service port, while port 1042 is our upper port number used for the reply.

Upper reply ports are assigned on the fly. It is nearly impossible to predict which upper port a system will request information to be received on, as the ports are assigned based on availability. It is for this reason that packet filters used for firewalling purposes are sometimes incorrectly set up to leave ports above 1023 open all the time in order to accept replies.

This leads to one of the reasons why a port other than a well-known port may be used to offer a service. A savvy end user who realizes that a packet filter will block access to the Web server running on her system may assign the service to some upper port number like 8001. Because the connection will be made above port 1023, it may not be blocked. The result is that despite your corporate policy banning internal Web sites and a packet filter to help enforce it, this user can successfully advertise her Web site provided she supplies the port number (8001) along with the universal resource locator (URL). The URL would look similar to this:

```
http://thor.foobar.com:8001
```

The :8001 tells your Web browser to access the server using port 8001 instead of 80. Because most packet filters have poor logging facilities, the network administrator responsible for enforcing the policy of "no internal Web sites" would probably never realize it exists unless he stumbles across it.

TIP

The next time your boss accuses you of wasting time by cruising the Web, correct her by replying, "I am performing a security audit by attempting to pursue links to renegade internal sites which do not conform to our corporate security policy. This activity is required due to inefficiencies in our firewalling mechanism." If you're not fired on the spot, quickly submit a PO for a new firewall while the event is fresh in the boss' mind.

Speaking of switching port numbers, try to identify the session in Figure 3.12. While the session is identified as a Simple Mail Transfer Protocol (SMTP), it is actually a telnet session redirected to port 25 (the well-known port for SMTP). We've fooled the analyzer recording this session into thinking that we simply have one mail system transferring mail to another. Most firewalls will be duped in the same fashion because they use the destination port to identify the session in progress—they do not look at the actual applications involved. This type of activity is usually analogous to someone *spoofing* or faking a mail message. Once I've connected to the remote mail system, I'm free to pretend the message came from anywhere. Unless the routing information in the mail header is checked (most user-friendly mail programs simply discard this information), the actual origin of this information cannot be traced.

FIGURE 3.12:

While this looks like a normal transfer of mail, it is actually someone spoofing a mail message to the destination system.

No.	Source	Destination	Layer	Summary	Size	Interpacket	Absolute Time
1	Loki	Thor	tcp	Port:1051 ---> SMTP SYN	64	0 µs	9:40:09 AM
2	Thor	Loki	tcp	Port:SMTP ---> 1051 ACK SYN	64	960 µs	9:40:09 AM
3	Loki	Thor	tcp	Port:1051 ---> SMTP ACK	64	857 µs	9:40:09 AM
4	Thor	Loki	tcp	Port:SMTP ---> 1051 ACK PUSH	138	103 ms	9:40:10 AM
5	Loki	Thor	tcp	Port:1051 ---> SMTP ACK	64	12 ms	9:40:10 AM
6	Loki	Thor	tcp	Port:1051 ---> SMTP ACK PUSH	80	9 s	9:40:19 AM
7	Thor	Loki	tcp	Port:SMTP ---> 1051 ACK PUSH	134	1 ms	9:40:19 AM
8	Loki	Thor	tcp	Port:1051 ---> SMTP ACK	64	17 ms	9:40:19 AM
9	Loki	Thor	tcp	Port:1051 ---> SMTP ACK PUSH	91	18 s	9:40:36 AM
10	Thor	Loki	tcp	Port:SMTP ---> 1051 ACK	64	19 ms	9:40:36 AM
11	Thor	Loki	tcp	Port:SMTP ---> 1051 ACK PUSH	97	9 ms	9:40:36 AM
12	Loki	Thor	tcp	Port:1051 ---> SMTP ACK	64	20 ms	9:40:36 AM
15	Loki	Thor	tcp	Port:1051 ---> SMTP ACK PUSH	93	21 s	9:40:57 AM
16	Thor	Loki	tcp	Port:SMTP ---> 1051 ACK	64	11 ms	9:40:57 AM
17	Thor	Loki	tcp	Port:SMTP ---> 1051 ACK PUSH	104	303 ms	9:40:57 AM
18	Loki	Thor	tcp	Port:1051 ---> SMTP ACK	64	15 ms	9:40:57 AM
19	Loki	Thor	tcp	Port:1051 ---> SMTP ACK PUSH	64	2 s	9:41:00 AM
20	Thor	Loki	tcp	Port:SMTP ---> 1051 ACK PUSH	108	2 ms	9:41:00 AM
21	Loki	Thor	tcp	Port:1051 ---> SMTP ACK	64	17 ms	9:41:00 AM
22	Loki	Thor	tcp	Port:1051 ---> SMTP ACK	80	12 s	9:41:12 AM
23	Thor	Loki	tcp	Port:SMTP ---> 1051 ACK	64	12 ms	9:41:12 AM
24	Loki	Thor	tcp	Port:1051 ---> SMTP ACK PUSH	122	28 s	9:41:40 AM
25	Thor	Loki	tcp	Port:SMTP ---> 1051 ACK	64	15 ms	9:41:40 AM
26	Loki	Thor	tcp	Port:1051 ---> SMTP ACK PUSH	68	5 s	9:41:45 AM
27	Thor	Loki	tcp	Port:SMTP ---> 1051 ACK	64	16 ms	9:41:45 AM
28	Loki	Thor	tcp	Port:1051 ---> SMTP ACK PUSH	64	6 s	9:41:50 AM
29	Thor	Loki	tcp	Port:SMTP ---> 1051 ACK	64	17 ms	9:41:50 AM
30	Loki	Thor	tcp	Port:SMTP ---> 1051 ACK PUSH	102	275 ms	9:41:51 AM
31	Loki	Thor	tcp	Port:1051 ---> SMTP ACK	64	18 ms	9:41:51 AM
32	Loki	Thor	tcp	Port:1051 ---> SMTP ACK	64	3 s	9:41:53 AM
33	Thor	Loki	tcp	Port:SMTP ---> 1051 ACK PUSH	98	2 ms	9:41:53 AM
34	Thor	Loki	tcp	Port:SMTP ---> 1051 ACK FIN	64	953 µs	9:41:53 AM

Such spoofing is what has made *intrusion detection systems* (IDS) so popular—they can be programmed to catch this type of activity. Look at Figure 3.12 again, but this time check out the frame size used by the transmitting system. Notice that the largest frame sent is 122 bytes. This indicates a telnet session, as telnet requires that each character typed be acknowledged. Had this been an actual mail system transferring data, we would have seen packet sizes closer to 1,500 bytes, because SMTP does not require that only a single character be sent in every frame. A good IDS can be tuned to identify such inconsistencies.

Figure 3.13 shows the final output of this spoofing session. Without the header information, I might actually believe this message came from bgates@microsoft.com. The fact that the message was never touched by a mail system within the Microsoft domain indicates that it is a phony. I've used this example in the past when instructing Internet and security classes. Do not believe everything you read, especially if it comes from the Internet!

FIGURE 3.13:

The output from our spoofed mail message

```
From bgates@microsoft.com  Wed Feb  5 16:42:21 1997
Return-Path: <bgates@microsoft.com>
Received: from loki.foobar.com (loki.foobar.com [10.2.2.20])
        by thor.foobar.com (8.8.4/8.8.4) with SMTP
        id QAA00887 for cbrenton@thor.foobar.com; Wed, 5 Feb 1997 16:41:04 -0500
Date: Wed, 5 Feb 1997 16:41:04 -0500
From: bgates@microsoft.com (Bill Gates)
Message-Id: <199702052141.QAA00887@thor.foobar.com>
Subject: Quake Party
Status: R

The party sounds cool! I'll bring the P5's and the cheeze wiz!

Later...
```

Port numbers are also used to distinctly identify similar sessions between systems. For example, let's build on Figure 3.10. We already have one telnet session running from Loki to Thor. What happens if four or five more sessions are created? All sessions have the following information in common:

Source IP address: 10.2.2.20 (loki.foobar.com)

Destination IP address: 10.2.2.10 (thor.foobar.com)

Destination port: 23 (well-known port for telnet)

The source ports will be the only distinctive information that can be used to identify each individual session. Our first connection has already specified a source port of 1042 for its connection. Each sequential telnet session that is established after that would be assigned some other upper port number to uniquely identify it. The actual numbers assigned would be based upon what was not currently being used by the source system. For example, ports 1118, 1398, 4023, and 6025 may be used as source ports for the next four sessions. The actual reply port number does not really matter; what matters is that it can uniquely identify that specific session between the two systems. If we were to monitor a number of concurrent sessions taking place, the transaction would look similar to Figure 3.14. Now we see multiple reply ports in use to identify each session.

FIGURE 3.14:

Multiple telnet sessions
in progress between Loki
and Thor

No.	Source	Destination	Layer	Summary	Size
1	LOKI.FOOBAR.COM	THOR.FOOBAR.COM	telnt	Data=l	64
2	THOR.FOOBAR.COM	LOKI.FOOBAR.COM	telnt	Data=l	64
3	LOKI.FOOBAR.COM	THOR.FOOBAR.COM	tcp	Port:1036 ---> TELNET ACK	64
4	LOKI.FOOBAR.COM	THOR.FOOBAR.COM	telnt	Data=s	64
5	THOR.FOOBAR.COM	LOKI.FOOBAR.COM	telnt	Data=s	64
6	LOKI.FOOBAR.COM	THOR.FOOBAR.COM	tcp	Port:1036 ---> TELNET ACK	64
7	LOKI.FOOBAR.COM	THOR.FOOBAR.COM	telnt	Data=.	64
8	THOR.FOOBAR.COM	LOKI.FOOBAR.COM	telnt	Data=..	64
9	LOKI.FOOBAR.COM	THOR.FOOBAR.COM	tcp	Port:1036 ---> TELNET ACK	64
10	THOR.FOOBAR.COM	LOKI.FOOBAR.COM	telnt	Data=install.log .	71
11	LOKI.FOOBAR.COM	THOR.FOOBAR.COM	tcp	Port:1036 ---> TELNET ACK	64
12	THOR.FOOBAR.COM	LOKI.FOOBAR.COM	telnt	Data=[cbrentor@thor /tmp]$	80
13	LOKI.FOOBAR.COM	THOR.FOOBAR.COM	tcp	Port:1036 ---> TELNET ACK	64
14	LOKI.FOOBAR.COM	THOR.FOOBAR.COM	telnt	Data=l	64
15	THOR.FOOBAR.COM	LOKI.FOOBAR.COM	telnt	Data=l	64
16	LOKI.FOOBAR.COM	THOR.FOOBAR.COM	tcp	Port:1038 ---> TELNET ACK	64
17	LOKI.FOOBAR.COM	THOR.FOOBAR.COM	telnt	Data=s	64
18	THOR.FOOBAR.COM	LOKI.FOOBAR.COM	telnt	Data=s	64
19	LOKI.FOOBAR.COM	THOR.FOOBAR.COM	tcp	Port:1038 ---> TELNET ACK	64
20	LOKI.FOOBAR.COM	THOR.FOOBAR.COM	telnt	Data=..	64
21	THOR.FOOBAR.COM	LOKI.FOOBAR.COM	telnt	Data=..	64
22	LOKI.FOOBAR.COM	THOR.FOOBAR.COM	tcp	Port:1038 ---> TELNET ACK	64
23	THOR.FOOBAR.COM	LOKI.FOOBAR.COM	telnt	Data=install.log .	71
24	LOKI.FOOBAR.COM	THOR.FOOBAR.COM	tcp	Port:1038 ---> TELNET ACK	64
25	LOKI.FOOBAR.COM	THOR.FOOBAR.COM	telnt	Data=[cbrentor@thor /tmp]$	80
26	LOKI.FOOBAR.COM	THOR.FOOBAR.COM	tcp	Port:1038 ---> TELNET ACK	64
27	LOKI.FOOBAR.COM	THOR.FOOBAR.COM	telnt	Data=l	64
28	THOR.FOOBAR.COM	LOKI.FOOBAR.COM	telnt	Data=l	64
29	LOKI.FOOBAR.COM	THOR.FOOBAR.COM	tcp	Port:1039 ---> TELNET ACK	64
30	LOKI.FOOBAR.COM	THOR.FOOBAR.COM	telnt	Data=s	64
31	THOR.FOOBAR.COM	LOKI.FOOBAR.COM	telnt	Data=s	64
32	LOKI.FOOBAR.COM	THOR.FOOBAR.COM	tcp	Port:1039 ---> TELNET ACK	64

IP is not the only protocol to use ports. AppleTalk and IPX also use ports, which are referred to as *sockets*. Unlike IP and AT, which use decimal numbers to identify different ports, IPX uses hexadecimal numbers. Well-known and upper ports function the same with AppleTalk and IPX as they do with IP. AppleTalk and IPX simply do not have as many services defined.

File Transfer Protocol (FTP): The Special Case

In all of our examples so far, the source system would create a single service connection to the destination system when accessing a specific service. Unless multiple users requested this service, only a single connection session was required.

FTP is used to transfer file information from one system to another. FTP uses TCP as its transport and ports 20 and 21 for communication. Port 21 is used to transfer session information (username, password, commands), while port 20 is referred to as the *data port* and is used to transfer the actual file.

Figure 3.15 shows an FTP command session between two systems (Loki is connecting to Thor). Notice the three-packet TCP handshake at the beginning of the session, which was described in the discussion on connection-oriented communications earlier in this chapter. All communications are using a destination port of 21, which is simply referred to as the FTP port. Port 1038 is the random upper port used by Loki when receiving replies. This connection was initiated by Loki at port 1038 to Thor at port 21.

FIGURE 3.15:

An FTP command session between two systems

No.	Size	Source	Destination	Layer	Summary
1	64	LOKI.FOOBAR.COM	THOR.FOOBAR.COM	tcp	Port:1038 ---> FTP SYN
2	64	THOR.FOOBAR.COM	LOKI.FOOBAR.COM	tcp	Port:FTP ---> 1038 ACK SYN
3	64	LOKI.FOOBAR.COM	THOR.FOOBAR.COM	tcp	Port:1038 ---> FTP ACK
4	164	THOR.FOOBAR.COM	LOKI.FOOBAR.COM	ftp	Reply:(Service ready for new user.)
5	64	LOKI.FOOBAR.COM	THOR.FOOBAR.COM	tcp	Port:1038 ---> FTP ACK
6	73	LOKI.FOOBAR.COM	THOR.FOOBAR.COM	ftp	Command=USER(User Name)
7	64	THOR.FOOBAR.COM	LOKI.FOOBAR.COM	tcp	Port:FTP ---> 1038 ACK
8	95	THOR.FOOBAR.COM	LOKI.FOOBAR.COM	ftp	Reply:(User name okay, need password.)
9	64	LOKI.FOOBAR.COM	THOR.FOOBAR.COM	tcp	Port:1038 ---> FTP ACK
10	71	LOKI.FOOBAR.COM	THOR.FOOBAR.COM	ftp	Command=PASS(Password)
11	64	THOR.FOOBAR.COM	LOKI.FOOBAR.COM	tcp	Port:FTP ---> 1038 ACK
12	88	THOR.FOOBAR.COM	LOKI.FOOBAR.COM	ftp	Reply:(User logged in, proceed.)
13	64	LOKI.FOOBAR.COM	THOR.FOOBAR.COM	ftp	Command=SYST(System Operating System Type)
14	77	THOR.FOOBAR.COM	LOKI.FOOBAR.COM	ftp	Reply:(Name system type.)
15	64	LOKI.FOOBAR.COM	THOR.FOOBAR.COM	tcp	Port:1038 ---> FTP ACK
16	66	LOKI.FOOBAR.COM	THOR.FOOBAR.COM	ftp	Command=TYPE(Representation Type)
17	66	LOKI.FOOBAR.COM	THOR.FOOBAR.COM	ftp	Command=TYPE(Representation Type)
18	78	THOR.FOOBAR.COM	LOKI.FOOBAR.COM	ftp	Reply:(Command okay.)
19	64	LOKI.FOOBAR.COM	THOR.FOOBAR.COM	tcp	Port:1038 ---> FTP ACK

Figure 3.16 shows Loki initiating a file transfer from Thor. Lines 7, 8, and 9 show the TCP three-packet handshake. Lines 10 through 24 show the actual data transfer.

This is where things get a bit weird. Loki and Thor still have an active session on ports 1038 and 21, as indicated in Figure 3.15. Figure 3.16 is a second, separate session running parallel to the one shown in Figure 3.15. This second session is initiated in order to transfer the actual file or data.

FIGURE 3.16:

An FTP data session

No.	Size	Source	Destination	Layer	Summary
2	66	LOKI.FOOBAR.COM	THOR.FOOBAR.COM	ftp	Command=TYPE(Representation Type)
3	78	THOR.FOOBAR.COM	LOKI.FOOBAR.COM	ftp	Reply:(Command okay.)
4	79	LOKI.FOOBAR.COM	THOR.FOOBAR.COM	ftp	Command=PORT(Data Port)
5	88	THOR.FOOBAR.COM	LOKI.FOOBAR.COM	ftp	Reply:(Command okay.)
6	77	LOKI.FOOBAR.COM	THOR.FOOBAR.COM	ftp	Command=RETR(Retrieve File)
7	64	THOR.FOOBAR.COM	LOKI.FOOBAR.COM	tcp	Port:FTP-DATA ---> 1037 SYN
8	64	LOKI.FOOBAR.COM	THOR.FOOBAR.COM	tcp	Port:1037 ---> FTP-DATA ACK SYN
9	64	THOR.FOOBAR.COM	LOKI.FOOBAR.COM	tcp	Port:FTP-DATA ---> 1037 ACK
10	132	THOR.FOOBAR.COM	LOKI.FOOBAR.COM	ftp	Reply:(File status okay; about to open data connection.)
11	1,518	THOR.FOOBAR.COM	LOKI.FOOBAR.COM	tcp	Port:FTP-DATA ---> 1037 ACK
12	1,518	THOR.FOOBAR.COM	LOKI.FOOBAR.COM	tcp	Port:FTP-DATA ---> 1037 ACK
13	64	LOKI.FOOBAR.COM	THOR.FOOBAR.COM	tcp	Port:1037 ---> FTP-DATA ACK
14	1,518	THOR.FOOBAR.COM	LOKI.FOOBAR.COM	tcp	Port:FTP-DATA ---> 1037 ACK
15	1,518	THOR.FOOBAR.COM	LOKI.FOOBAR.COM	tcp	Port:FTP-DATA ---> 1037 ACK
16	1,518	THOR.FOOBAR.COM	LOKI.FOOBAR.COM	tcp	Port:FTP-DATA ---> 1037 ACK
17	64	LOKI.FOOBAR.COM	THOR.FOOBAR.COM	tcp	Port:1037 ---> FTP-DATA ACK
18	64	LOKI.FOOBAR.COM	THOR.FOOBAR.COM	tcp	Port:1034 ---> FTP ACK
19	1,518	THOR.FOOBAR.COM	LOKI.FOOBAR.COM	tcp	Port:FTP-DATA ---> 1037 ACK PUSH
20	1,518	THOR.FOOBAR.COM	LOKI.FOOBAR.COM	tcp	Port:FTP-DATA ---> 1037 ACK
21	1,518	THOR.FOOBAR.COM	LOKI.FOOBAR.COM	tcp	Port:FTP-DATA ---> 1037 ACK
22	1,518	THOR.FOOBAR.COM	LOKI.FOOBAR.COM	tcp	Port:FTP-DATA ---> 1037 ACK
23	64	LOKI.FOOBAR.COM	THOR.FOOBAR.COM	tcp	Port:1037 ---> FTP-DATA ACK
24	1,518	THOR.FOOBAR.COM	LOKI.FOOBAR.COM	tcp	Port:FTP-DATA ---> 1037 ACK

There is something else a bit odd about this connection: look closely at line number 7. Thor—not Loki—is actually initiating the TCP three-packet handshake in order to transfer the file information. While Loki was responsible for initiating the original FTP command session to port 21, Thor is actually the one initiating the FTP data session.

This means that in order to support FTP sessions to the Internet, we must allow connections to be established from Internet hosts on port 20 to our internal network. If our firewall device does not allow us to define a source port for inbound traffic (which some do not), we must leave all ports above 1023 completely open! Not exactly the most secure security stance.

Passive FTP

There is also a second type of FTP transfer known as *passive FTP* (PASV FTP). Passive FTP is identical to standard FTP in terms of sending commands over port 21. The difference between PASV FTP and standard FTP lies in how the data session gets initiated. PASV FTP is the mode supported by most Web browsers.

Before transferring data, a client can request PASV mode transmission. If the FTP server acknowledges this request, the client is allowed to initiate the TCP three-packet handshake, instead of the server. Figure 3.17 shows a capture of two systems using PASV FTP. Packet 21 shows "This workstation" (or FTP client) requesting that PASV FTP be used. In packet 22, the FTP server responds, stating that PASV mode is supported.

FIGURE 3.17:

A passive mode FTP session

No.	Source	Destination	Layer	Summary	Size	Interpacke	Absolute Time
5	00A0C9898D21	This_Workstation	tcp	Port:FTP ---> 1138 ACK SYN	64	176 ms	11:17:52 AM
6	This_Workstation	00A0C9898D21	tcp	Port:1138 ---> FTP ACK	64	529 µs	11:17:52 AM
7	00A0C9898D21	This_Workstation	ftp	Reply:(Service ready for new user.)	104	96 ms	11:17:53 AM
8	This_Workstation	00A0C9898D21	ftp	Command=USER(User Name)	74	34 ms	11:17:53 AM
9	00A0C9898D21	This_Workstation	ftp	Reply:(User name okay, need password.)	130	94 ms	11:17:53 AM
10	This_Workstation	00A0C9898D21	tcp	Port:1138 ---> FTP ACK	64	129 ms	11:17:53 AM
11	This_Workstation	00A0C9898D21	ftp	Command=PASS(Password)	73	61 ms	11:17:53 AM
12	00A0C9898D21	This_Workstation	ftp		89	90 ms	11:17:53 AM
13	This_Workstation	00A0C9898D21	tcp	Port:1138 ---> FTP ACK	64	142 ms	11:17:53 AM
14	00A0C9898D21	This_Workstation	ftp	Unknown FTP Code	266	84 ms	11:17:53 AM
15	This_Workstation	00A0C9898D21	ftp	Command=REST(Restart at Marker)	66	29 ms	11:17:53 AM
16	00A0C9898D21	This_Workstation	ftp	Reply:(Requested file action pending further information.)	80	83 ms	11:17:53 AM
17	This_Workstation	00A0C9898D21	ftp	Command=SYST(System Operating System Type)	64	17 ms	11:17:53 AM
18	00A0C9898D21	This_Workstation	ftp	Reply:(Name system type.)	86	84 ms	11:17:53 AM
19	This_Workstation	00A0C9898D21	ftp	Command=PWD(Print Working Directory)	64	26 ms	11:17:53 AM
20	00A0C9898D21	This_Workstation	ftp	Reply:(PATHNAME created.)	89	82 ms	11:17:53 AM
21	This_Workstation	00A0C9898D21	ftp	Command=PASV(Passive Listen)	64	39 ms	11:17:54 AM
22	00A0C9898D21	This_Workstation	ftp	Reply:(Entering passive mode (h1,h2,h3,h4,p1,p2).)	109	86 ms	11:17:54 AM
23	This_Workstation	00A0C9898D21	tcp	Port:1139 ---> 3323 SYN	64	101 ms	11:17:54 AM
24	This_Workstation	00A0C9898D21	tcp	Port:1138 ---> FTP ACK	64	52 ms	11:17:54 AM
25	00A0C9898D21	This_Workstation	tcp	Port:3323 ---> 1139 ACK SYN	64	30 ms	11:17:54 AM
26	This_Workstation	00A0C9898D21	tcp	Port:1139 ---> 3323 ACK	64	469 µs	11:17:54 AM
27	This_Workstation	00A0C9898D21	ftp	Command=TYPE(Representation Type)	66	36 ms	11:17:54 AM
28	00A0C9898D21	This_Workstation	ftp	Reply:(Command okay.)	78	95 ms	11:17:54 AM
29	This_Workstation	00A0C9898D21	ftp	Command=Unknown Command	66	22 ms	11:17:54 AM
30	00A0C9898D21	This_Workstation	ftp	Reply:(Syntax error, command unrecognized or too long.)	96	81 ms	11:17:54 AM
31	This_Workstation	00A0C9898D21	ftp	Command=Unknown Command	66	38 ms	11:17:54 AM
32	00A0C9898D21	This_Workstation	ftp	Reply:(Syntax error, command unrecognized or too long.)	96	83 ms	11:17:54 AM
33	This_Workstation	00A0C9898D21	ftp	Command=CWD(Change to Working Directory)	65	23 ms	11:17:54 AM
34	00A0C9898D21	This_Workstation	ftp	Reply:(Requested file action okay, completed.)	87	87 ms	11:17:54 AM
35	This_Workstation	00A0C9898D21	ftp	Command=LIST(List Information of)	64	18 ms	11:17:54 AM
36	00A0C9898D21	This_Workstation	ftp	Reply:(Data connection already open; transfer starting.)	112	85 ms	11:17:54 AM
37	This_Workstation	00A0C9898D21	tcp	Port:3323 ---> 1139 ACK PUSH	1,312	51 ms	11:17:54 AM
38	00A0C9898D21	This_Workstation	tcp	Port:3323 ---> 1139 ACK FIN	64	381 µs	11:17:54 AM

Notice what occurs in packet 23. Our FTP client initiates the TCP three-packet handshake in order to transfer data. This fixes one problem but causes another. Since the client initiates the session, we can now close inbound access from port 20. This lets us tighten up our inbound security policy a bit. Note that to initiate this passive session, however, the client is using a random upper port number for the source and destination. This means that the port the client will use to transfer data can and will change from session to session. This also means that in order to support PASV FTP, I must allow outbound sessions to be established on all ports above 1023. Not a very good security stance if you are looking to control outbound Internet access (such as a policy forbidding Internet Quake games).

As if all this were not enough to deal with, administrators can run into another problem with FTP when they use a firewall or network translation (NAT) device. The problem revolves around the fact that FTP uses two separate sessions.

NOTE   NAT allows you to translate IP addresses from private numbers to legal numbers. This is useful when the IP addresses you are using on your network were not assigned to you by your ISP. We will talk more about NAT when we discuss firewalls in Chapter 5.

While I am transferring a large file over the Internet (let's say the latest 60MB patch file from Microsoft), my control session to port 21 stays quiet. This session is not required to transmit any information during a file transfer until the transfer is complete. Once it is complete, the systems acknowledge over the control session that the file was in fact received in its entirety.

If it has taken a long time to transfer the file (say, over an hour), the firewall or NAT device may assume that the control session is no longer valid. Since it has seen no data pass between the two systems for a long period of time, the device assumes that the connection is gone and purges the session entry from its tables. This is a bad thing—once the file transfer is complete, the systems have no means to handshake to insure the file was received. The typical symptom of this problem is that the client transferring or receiving the file hangs at 99 percent complete.

Luckily, most vendors make this timeout setting adjustable. If you are experiencing such symptoms, check your firewall or NAT device to see if it has a TCP timeout setting. If so, simply increase the listed value. Most systems default to a timeout value of one hour.

Other IP Services

Many application services are designed to use IP as a transport. Some are designed to aid the end user in transferring information, while others have been created to support the functionality of IP itself. Some of the most common services are described below, including the transport used for data delivery and the well-known port number assigned to the service.

Boot Protocol *(bootp)* and Dynamic Host Configuration Protocol (DHCP)

There are three methods of assigning IP addresses to host systems:

Manual   The user manually configures an IP host to use a specific address.

Automatic   A server automatically assigns a specific address to a host during startup.

Dynamic   A server dynamically assigns free addresses from a pool to hosts during startup.

Manual is the most time-consuming but the most fault tolerant. It requires that each IP host be configured with all the information the system requires to communicate using IP. Manual is the most appropriate method to use for systems that must maintain the same IP address or systems that must be accessible even when the IP address server may be down. Web servers, mail servers, and any other servers providing IP services are usually manually configured for IP communications.

Bootp supports automatic address assignment. A table is maintained on the bootp server that lists each host's MAC number. Each entry also contains the IP address to be used by the system. When the bootp server receives a request for an IP address, it references its table and looks for the sending system's MAC number, returning the appropriate IP address for that system. While this makes management a little simpler, because all administration can be performed from a central system, the process is still time-consuming, because each MAC address must be recorded. It also does nothing to free up IP address space that may not be in use.

DHCP supports both automatic and dynamic IP address assignments. When addresses are dynamically assigned, the server issues IP addresses to host systems from a pool of available numbers. The benefit of a dynamic assignment over an automatic one is that only the hosts that require an IP address have one assigned. Once complete, the IP addresses can be returned to the pool to be issued to another host.

NOTE

The amount of time a host retains a specific IP address is referred to as the *lease period*. A short lease period insures that only systems requiring an IP address have one assigned. When IP is only occasionally used, a small pool of addresses can be used to support a large number of hosts.

The other benefit of DHCP is that the server can send more than just address information. The remote host can also be configured with its host name, default router, domain name, local DNS server, and so on. This allows an administrator to remotely configure IP services to a large number of hosts with a minimal amount of work. A single DHCP server is capable of servicing multiple subnets.

The only drawbacks with DHCP are

- Increased broadcast traffic (clients send an all-networks broadcast when they need an address)

- Address space stability if the DHCP server is shut down

On many systems, the tables that track who has been assigned which addresses are saved in memory only. When the system goes down, this table is lost. When you restart the system, IP addresses may be assigned to systems that were already leased to another system prior to the shutdown. If this occurs, you may need to renew the lease on all systems or wait until the lease time expires.

NOTE

Both **bootp** and DHCP use UDP as their communication transport. Clients transmit address requests from a source port of 68 to a destination port of 67.

Domain Name Services (DNS)

DNS is responsible for mapping host names to IP addresses and vice versa. It is the service that allows you to connect to Novell's Web server by entering www.novell.com, instead of having to remember the system's IP address. All IP routing is done with addresses, not names. While IP systems do not use names when transferring information, names are easier for people to remember; DNS was developed to make reaching remote systems that much easier. DNS allows a person to enter an easy-to-remember name while allowing the computer to translate this into the address information it needs to route the requested data.

DNS follows a hierarchical, distributed structure. No single DNS server is responsible for keeping track of every host name on the Internet. Each system is responsible for only a portion of the framework.

Figure 3.18 shows an example of how DNS is structured. Visually it resembles a number of trees strapped to a pole and hanging upside down. The *pole* is not meant to represent the backbone of the Internet; it simply indicates that there is DNS connectivity between the different domains. The systems located just below the pole are referred to as the root name servers. Each root name server is responsible for one or more top-level domains. Examples of top-level domains are the .com, .edu, .org, .mil, or .gov found at the end of a domain name. Every domain that ends in .com is said to be part of the same top-level domain.

FIGURE 3.18:

A visual representation of the hierarchical structure of DNS

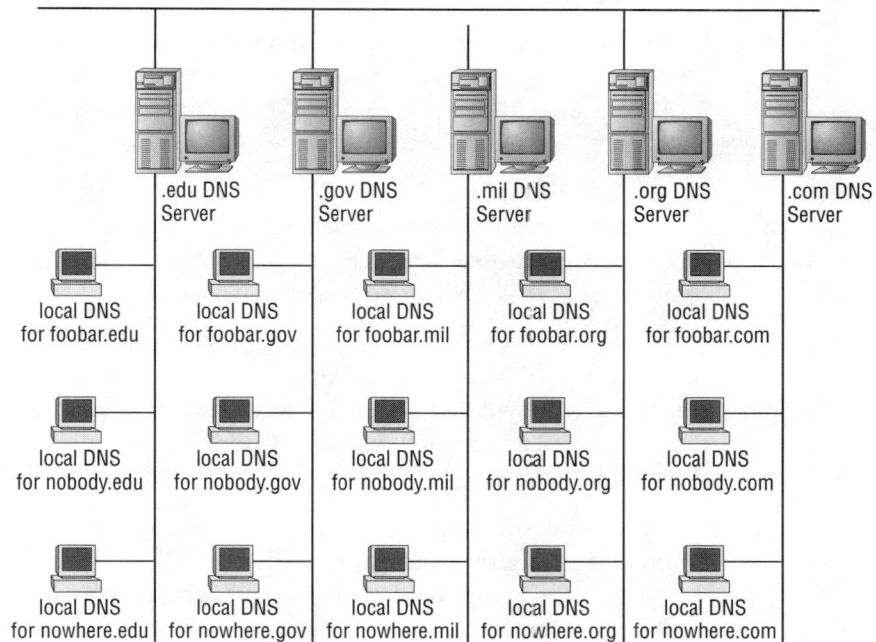

The root name servers are responsible for keeping track of the DNS servers for each subdomain within a top-level domain. They do not know about individual systems within each subdomain, only the DNS servers that are responsible for them. Each subdomain DNS server is responsible for tracking the IP addresses for all the hosts within its domain.

Let's walk through an example to see how it works. Let's say you're part of the foobar.com domain. You are running a Web browser and have entered the following URL:

```
http://www.sun.com
```

Your system will first check its DNS cache (if it has one) to see if it knows the IP address for www.sun.com. If it does not, it forms a DNS query (a DNS query is simply a request for IP information) and asks one of the DNS servers within the foobar.com domain for the address. Let's assume the system it queries is ns .foobar.com.

If ns.foobar.com does not have this information cached, it also forms a DNS query and forwards the request to the root name server responsible for the top-level domain .com, because this is where the Sun domain is located.

The root name server will consult its tables and form a reply similar to this: "I do not know the IP address for www.sun.com. I do, however, know that ns.sun .com is responsible for all the hosts within the sun.com domain. Its IP address is 10.5.5.1. Please forward your query to that system." This reply is then sent to ns.foobar.com.

Ns.foobar.com now knows that if it needs to find a system with the sun.com domain, it needs to ask ns.sun.com. Ns.foobar.com caches this name server information and forwards the request to ns.sun.com.

Ns.sun.com will in turn consult its tables and look up the IP address for www.sun.com. Ns.sun.com will then forward the IP address to ns.foobar.com. Ns.foobar.com will then cache this address and forward the answer to your system. Your system can now use this IP address information to reach the remote Web server.

If you think that there is a whole lot of querying going on, then you have a good understanding of the process. The additional traffic is highly preferable, however, to the amount of overhead that would be required to allow a single system to maintain the DNS information for every system on the Internet.

As you may have noticed, DNS makes effective use of caching information during queries. This helps to reduce traffic when looking up popular sites. For example, if someone else within foobar.com now attempted to reach www.sun.com, the IP address for this system has been cached by ns.foobar.com. It can now answer this query directly.

The amount of time that ns.foobar.com remembers this information is determined by the *time to live* (TTL) set for this address. The TTL is set by the administrator responsible for managing the remote name server (in this case ns.sun.com). If www.sun.com is a stable system, this value may be set at a high value, such as 30 days. If it is expected that the IP address for www.sun.com is likely to change frequently, the TTL may be set to a lower value, such as a few hours.

Caveats about the TTL Settings

Let's look at an example to see why it is important to properly manage your TTL settings. Let's say the mail relay for foobar.com is run from the system mail.foobar.com. Let's also assume that a high TTL value of 30 days has been set in order to reduce the number of DNS queries entering the network from the Internet. Finally, let's assume that your network has changed ISPs and you have been assigned a new set of IP numbers to use when communicating with the Internet.

The network is readdressed, and the changeover takes place. Immediately users begin to receive phone calls from people saying that mail sent to their address is being returned with a delivery failure notice. The failure is intermittent—some mail gets through, while other messages fail.

What went wrong? Since the TTL value has been set for 30 days, remote DNS servers will remember the old IP address until the TTL expires. If someone sent mail to the foobar.com domain the day before the changeover, it may be 30 days before their DNS server creates another query and realizes that the IP address has changed! Unfortunately, the domains most likely affected by this change are the ones you exchange mail with the most.

There are two ways to resolve this failure:

1. Ignore it and hide under your desk. Once the TTL expires, mail delivery will return to normal.

2. Contact the DNS administrator for each domain you exchange mail with and ask them to reset their DNS cache. This will force the remote system to look up the address the next time a mail message must be sent. This option is not only embarrassing—it may be impossible when dealing with large domains such as AOL or CompuServe.

Avoiding this type of failure takes some fundamental planning. Simply turn down the TTL value to an extremely short period of time (like one hour) at least 30 days prior to the changeover. This forces remote systems to cache the information for only a brief amount of time. Once the changeover is complete, the TTL can be adjusted back up to 30 days to help reduce traffic. Thirty days is a good TTL value for systems that are not expected to change their host name or address.

NOTE   DNS uses TCP and UDP transports when communicating. Both use a destination port of 53.

Hypertext Transfer Protocol (HTTP)

HTTP is used in communications between Web browsers and Web servers. It differs from most services in that it does not create and maintain a single session while a user is retrieving information from a server. Every request for information—text, graphics, or sound—creates a separate session, which is terminated once that request is completed. A Web page with lots of graphics needs to have multiple simultaneous connections created in order to be loaded onto a browser. It is not uncommon for a Web browser to create 10, 20, or even 50 sessions with a Web server just to read a single page.

Since version 1.0, HTTP has included Multimedia Internet Mail Extensions (MIME) to support the negotiation of data types. This has helped HTTP to become a truly cross-platform service, since MIME allows the Web browser to inform the server what type of file formats it can support. MIME also allows the server to alert the Web browser as to what type of data it is about to receive. This allows the browser to select the correct, platform-specific viewing or playing software for the data it is about to receive.

NOTE   HTTP uses the TCP transport and a destination port of 80 when communicating.

Post Office Protocol (POP)

Post Office Protocol is typically used when retrieving mail from a UNIX shell account. It allows a user to read her mail without creating a telnet connection to the system. When you dial in to your ISP in order to retrieve your mail, you are typically using the POP protocol in order to retrieve mail from a UNIX system.

When a UNIX user receives an e-mail message, it is typically stored in the /var/spool/mail directory. Normally this message could be retrieved remotely by telnetting to the system and running the mail command. While it is a useful utility, mail does not have much of a user interface. To the inexperienced user, the commands can seem cryptic and hard to remember.

POP allows a user to connect to the system and retrieve her mail using her username and password. POP does not provide shell access; it simply retrieves any mail messages the user may have pending on the system.

There are a variety of mail clients available that support POP (POP3 is the latest version), so the user has a good amount of freedom to choose the e-mail client she likes best.

When using POP3, the user has the option to either leave her messages up on the POP server and view them remotely (*online mail*) or download the messages to the local system and read them offline (*offline mail*). Leaving the messages on the server allows the system administrator to centrally back up everyone's mail when backing up the server. The drawback, however, is that if the user never deletes her messages (I've seen mailboxes with over 12,000 messages), the load time for the client can be excruciatingly long. Because a copy of each message is left up on the server, all messages must be downloaded every time the client connects.

The benefit of using the POP client in offline mode is that local folders can be created to organize old messages. Because messages are stored locally, the load time for many messages is relatively short. This can provide a dramatic improvement in speed when the POP server is accessed over a dial-up connection. Note that only local folders can be used. POP3 does not support the use of global or shared folders. The downside to offline mode is that each local system must be backed up to insure recovery in the event of a drive failure. Most POP clients operate in offline mode.

One of POP3's biggest drawbacks is that it does not support the automatic creation of global address books. Only personal address books can be used. For example, if your organization is using a POP3 mail system, you have no way of automatically viewing the addresses of other users on the system. This leaves you with two options:

- You can manually discover the other addresses through some other means and add them to your personal address book.

- You can require that the system administrator generate a list of e-mail addresses on the system and e-mail this list to all users. Each user can then use the file to update his or her personal address book.

Neither option is particularly appealing, so POP is best suited for the home Internet user who does not need sharable address books or folders. For business use, the IMAP4 protocol (discussed in the next section) is more appropriate.

When a message is delivered by a POP3 client, the client forwards the message either back to the POP server or on to a central mail relay. Which of these is performed depends on how the POP client is configured. In either case, the POP client uses Simple Mail Transfer Protocol (SMTP, discussed in an upcoming section) when delivering new messages or replies. This forwarding system, not the POP client, is ultimately responsible for the delivery of the message.

By using a forwarding mail relay, the POP client can disconnect from the network before the message is delivered to its final destination. While most SMTP messages are delivered very quickly (in less than one second), a busy mail system can take 10 minutes or more to accept a message. Using a forwarding system helps to reduce the amount of time a remote POP client is required to remain dialed in.

If the mail relay encounters a problem (such as a typo in the recipient's e-mail address) and the message cannot be delivered, the POP client will receive a delivery failure notice the next time it connects to the POP server.

NOTE   POP3 uses TCP as a transport and communicates using a destination port of 110.

Internet Message Access Protocol, Version 4 (IMAP4)

IMAP was designed to be the next evolutionary step from the Post Office Protocol. While it has the same features as POP, it includes many more, which allow it to scale more easily in a workgroup environment.

As with POP3, the user has the option to either leave messages up on the server and view them remotely (*online mail*) or download the messages to the local system and read them offline (*offline mail*). IMAP, however, supports a third connection mode referred to as *disconnected*.

In online mode, all messages are stored on the IMAP server. While it can be time-consuming to start up a POP mail client in online mode if many messages are involved, IMAP avoids this problem through the use of *flags*.

As you've seen, when a POP client connects to a POP server, the client will simply authenticate and begin to download messages. All messages on the server are considered to be new and unread, which means that the user's entire inbox must be transferred before messages can be viewed or read. When an IMAP client connects to an IMAP server, however, it authenticates and checks the flag status on existing messages. Flagging allows a message to be marked as "seen," "deleted," or "answered." This means that an IMAP client can be configured to collect only messages that have not been seen, avoiding the transfer of the entire mailbox.

In offline mode, connection time can be reduced through the use of *previewing*. Previewing allows the user to scan the header information of all new messages without actually transferring them to her local system. If the user is looking to remotely retrieve only a specific message, she can choose which messages to receive and which messages to leave on the server as unread. The user can also delete messages based upon the header information or file size without having to transfer them to the local system first. This can be a real time-saver if you usually retrieve your mail remotely and you receive a lot of unsolicited advertisements.

IMAP includes a third connection mode not supported by POP, referred to as *disconnected*. (Someone *certainly* had a twisted sense of humor when they called it that—you can just see the poor support people pulling their hair out over this one: "I disconnected my computer just like the instructions said, so how come I can't see my mail?") When a remote IMAP client is operating in disconnected mode, it retrieves only a copy of all new messages. The originals are left up on the IMAP server. The next time the client connects to the system, the server is synchronized with any changes made to the cached information. This mode has a few major benefits:

- Connection time is minimized, reducing network traffic and/or dial-in time.

- Messages are centrally located so they can be backed up easily.

- Because all messages are server-based, mail can be retrieved from multiple clients and/or multiple computers.

The last benefit is extremely useful in an environment where people do not always work from the same computer. For example, an engineer who works from home a few days a week can easily keep his mail synchronized between his home and work computers. When working in offline mode, as most POP clients do, mail retrieved by the engineer's work system would not be viewable on his home system. An IMAP client does not have this limitation.

Another improvement over POP is that IMAP supports the writing of messages up to the server. This allows a user to have server-based folders instead of just local ones. These folders can be synchronized in disconnect mode, as well.

IMAP also supports group folders. This allows mail users to have *bulletin board* areas where messages can be posted and viewed by multiple people. This functionality is similar to news under NNTP (a description of NNTP and news follows).

Group folders provide an excellent means of sharing information. For example, the Human Resources department could set up a group folder for corporate policy information. This would reduce the need to create printed manuals.

TIP

If you are using IMAP or if your current e-mail system supports group folders, create one entitled `computer support` or something similar. In it you can post messages providing support for some of your most common support calls. This can help reduce the number of support calls received and provide the user with written directions about how to work through a problem. You can even add screen captures, which can make resolving the problem much easier than walking through it over the phone would.

IMAP has been designed to integrate with the Application Configuration Access Protocol (ACAP). ACAP is an independent service that allows a client to access configuration information and preferences from a central location. Support for ACAP enhances the portability of IMAP even further.

For example, our engineer who works from home a few days a week could also store his personal address book and configuration information up on the server, as well. If he is at work and adds a new name and e-mail address to his address book, that name would be available when he is using his home system. This would not be true with POP where each client has a separate address book saved on each local system. ACAP also insures that any configuration changes would take effect on both systems.

ACAP provides mail administrators some control to set up corporate standards for users when accessing mail. For example, the administrator can set up a global address book that everyone could access.

NOTE

IMAP uses TCP as a transport with a destination port of 143.

Network File System (NFS)

NFS provides access to remote file systems. The user can access the remote file system as if the files were located on the local system. NFS provides file access only. This means that other functionality such as processor time or printing must be provided by the local system.

NFS requires configuration changes on both the server and the client. On the server, the file system to be shared must first be *exported*. This is done by defining which files are to be made sharable. This can be a single directory or an entire disk. You must also define who has access to this file system.

On the client side, the system must be configured to *mount* the remote file system. On a UNIX machine this is done by creating an entry in the system's /etc/fstab file, indicating the name of the remote system, the file system to be mounted, and where it should be placed on the local system. In the UNIX world, this is typically a directory structure located under a directory. In the DOS world, the remote file system may be assigned a unique drive letter. DOS and Windows require third-party software in order to use NFS.

While it offers a convenient way to share files, NFS suffers from a number of functional deficiencies. File transfer times are slow when compared to FTP or NetWare's NCP protocol. NFS has no file-locking capability to insure that only one user can write to a file. As if this were not bad enough, NFS makes no assurances that the information has been received intact. I've seen situations where entire directories have been copied to a remote system using NFS and have become corrupted in transit. Because NFS does not check data integrity, the errors were not found until the files were processed.

NOTE   NFS uses the UDP transport and communicates using port 2049.

Network News Transfer Protocol (NNTP)

NNTP is used in the delivery of *news*. News is very similar in functionality to e-mail, except messages are delivered to *newsgroups*, not end users. Each newsgroup is a storage area for messages that follow a common thread or subject. Instead of a mail client, a news client is used to read messages that have been posted to different subject areas.

For example, let's say you are having trouble configuring networking on your NetWare server. You could check out the messages that have been posted to the newsgroup comp.os.netware.connectivity to see if anyone else has found a solution to the same problem. There are literally tens of thousands of newsgroups on a wide range of subjects. My own personal favorites are

```
comp.protocols

alt.clueless

alt.barney.dinosaur.die.die.die
```

In order to read news postings, you must have access to a *news server*. News servers exchange messages by relaying any new messages they receive to other servers. The process is a bit slow: it can take three to five days for a new message to be circulated to every news server.

News is very resource intensive. It's not uncommon for a news server to receive several gigabits of information per week. The processes required to send, receive, and clean up old messages can eat up a lot of CPU time, as well.

News has dwindled in appeal over the last few years due to an activity known as *spamming*. Spamming is the activity of posting unsolicited or off-subject messages. For example, at the time of this writing comp.os.netware.connectivity contains 383 messages. Of these, 11 percent are advertisements for get-rich-quick schemes, 8 percent are ads for computer-related hardware or services, 6 percent are postings describing the sender's opinion on someone or something using many superlatives, and another 23 percent are NetWare-related but have nothing to do with connectivity. This means that only slightly more than half the postings are actually on-topic. For some groups the percentages are even worse.

NOTE   NNTP uses TCP as a transport and port 119 for all communications.

NetBIOS over IP

NetBIOS over IP is not a service *per se*, but it does add session layer support to enable the encapsulation of NetBIOS traffic within an IP packet. This is required when using Windows NT or Samba, which use NetBIOS for file and printer sharing. If IP is the only protocol bound to an NT server, it is still using NetBIOS for file sharing via encapsulation.

Samba is a suite of programs that allows UNIX file systems and printers to be accessed as shares. In effect, this makes the UNIX system appear to be an NT server. Clients can be other UNIX systems (running the Samba client) or Windows 95/98/NT/2000 systems. The Windows clients do not require any additional software, because they use the same configuration as when they are communicating with an NT/2000 server.

The source code for Samba is available as freeware on the Internet. More than 15 different flavors of UNIX are supported.

NOTE

When NetBIOS is encapsulated within IP, both TCP and UDP are used as a transport. All communications are conducted on ports 137–139.

Simple Mail Transfer Protocol (SMTP)

SMTP is used to transfer mail messages between systems. SMTP uses a message-switched type of connection: each mail message is processed in its entirety before the session between two systems is terminated. If more than one message must be transferred, a separate session must be established for each mail message.

SMTP is capable of transferring ASCII text only. It does not have the ability to support rich text or transfer binary files and attachments. When these types of transfers are required, an external program is needed to first translate the attachment into an ASCII format.

The original programs used to provide this functionality were uuencode and uudecode. A binary file would first be processed by uuencode to translate it into an ASCII format. The file could then be attached to a mail message and sent. Once received, the file would be processed through uudecode to return it to its original binary format.

Uuencode/uudecode has been replaced by the use of MIME. While MIME performs the same translating duties, it also compresses the resulting ASCII information. The result is smaller attachments, which produce faster message transfers with reduced overhead. Apple computers use an application called Binhex, which has the same functionality as MIME. MIME is now supported by most UNIX and PC mail systems.

Uuencode/uudecode, Binhex, and MIME are not compatible. If you can exchange text messages with a remote mail system but attachments end up unusable, you are probably using different translation formats. Many modern mail gateways provide support for both uuencode/uudecode and MIME to eliminate such communication problems. Some even include support for Binhex.

NOTE

SMTP uses the TCP transport and destination port 25 when creating a communication session.

Simple Network Management Protocol (SNMP)

SNMP is used to monitor and control network devices. The monitoring or controlling station is referred to as the *SNMP management station*. The network devices to be controlled are required to run SNMP *agents*. The agents and the management station work together to give the network administrator a central point of control over the network.

NOTE

The SNMP agent provides the link into the networking device. The device can be a manageable hub, a router, or even a server. The agent uses both static and dynamic information when reporting to the management station.

The *static information* is data stored within the device in order to identify it uniquely. For example, the administrator may choose to store the device's physical location and serial number as part of the SNMP static information. This makes it easier to identify which device you're working with from the SNMP management station.

The *dynamic information* is data that pertains to the current state of the device. For example, port status on a hub would be considered dynamic information, as the port may be enabled or disabled depending on whether it is functioning properly.

The SNMP management station is the central console used to control all network devices that have SNMP agents. The management station first learns about a network device through the use of a *management information base* (MIB). The MIB is a piece of software supplied by the network device vendor, usually on floppy disk. When the MIB is added to the management station, it teaches the management station about the network device. This helps to insure that SNMP management stations created by one vendor will operate properly with network devices produced by another.

Information is usually collected by the SNMP management station through *polling*. The SNMP management station will issue queries at predetermined intervals in order to check the status of each network device. SNMP only supports two commands for collecting information: get and getnext. The get command allows the management station to retrieve information on a specific operating parameter. For example, the management station may query a router to report on the current status of one of its ports. The getnext command is used when a complete status will be collected from a device. Instead of forcing the SNMP management station to issue a series of specific get commands, getnext can be used to sequentially retrieve each piece of information a device can report on.

SNMP also allows for the controlling of network devices through the command set. The set command can be used to alter some of the operational parameters on a network device. For example, if your get command reported that port 2 on the router was disabled, you could issue a set command to the router to enable the port.

SNMP typically does not offer the same range of control as a network device's management utility. For example, while you may be able to turn ports on and off on our router, you would probably be unable to initialize IP networking and assign an IP address to the port. The amount of control available through SNMP is limited by which commands are included in the vendor's MIB, as well as the command structure of SNMP itself. The operative word in SNMP is "simple." SNMP provides only a minimal amount of control over network devices.

While most reporting is done by having the SNMP management station poll network devices, SNMP does allow network devices to report critical events immediately back to the management station. These messages are called *traps*. Traps are sent when an event occurs that is important enough to not wait until the device is again polled. For example, your router may send a trap to the SNMP management console if it has just been power cycled. Because this event will have a grave impact on network connectivity, it is reported to the SNMP management station immediately instead of waiting until the device is again polled.

NOTE   SNMP uses the UDP transport and destination ports 161 and 162 when communicating.

Telnet

Telnet is used when a remote communication session is required with some other system on the network. Its functionality is similar to a mainframe terminal or remote control session. The local system becomes little more than a dumb terminal providing screen updates only. The remote system supplies the file system and all processing time required when running programs.

NOTE   Telnet uses the TCP transport and destination port 23 when creating a communication session.

WHOIS

WHOIS is a utility used to gather information about a specific domain. The utility usually connects to the system rs.internic.net and displays administrative contact information as well as the root servers for a domain.

This is useful when you wish to find out what organization is using a particular domain name. For example, typing the command

```
whois sun.com
```

will produce the following information regarding the domain:

```
Sun Microsystems Inc. (SUN)       SUN.COM       192.9.9.1
Sun Microsystems, Inc. (SUN-DOM)     SUN.COM
```

If you performed a further search by entering the command

```
whois sun-dom
```

additional information would be produced:

```
Sun Microsystems, Inc. (SUN-DOM)
2550 Garcia Avenue
Mountain View, CA 94043
Domain Name: SUN.COM
Administrative Contact, Technical Contact, Zone Contact:
Lowe, Fredrick (FL59) Fred.Lowe@SUN.COM
408-276-4199
Record last updated on 21-Nov-96.
Record created on 19-Mar-86.
Database last updated on 16-Jun-97 05:26:09 EDT.
Domain servers in listed order:
NS.SUN.COM   192.9.9.3
VGR.ARL.MIL  128.63.2.6, 128.63.16.6, 128.63.4.4
The InterNIC Registration Services Host contains ONLY Internet
Information
(Networks, ASN's, Domains, and POC's).
Please use the whois server at nic.ddn.mil for MILNET Information.
```

WHOIS can be an extremely powerful troubleshooting tool: you now know who is responsible for maintaining the domain, how to contact them, and which systems are considered to be primary name servers. You could then use a DNS tool such as nslookup to find the IP addresses of Sun's mail systems or even their Web server.

NOTE WHOIS uses the TCP transport and destination port 43 when creating a communication session.

IRC

IRC (Internet Relay Chat) protocol allows clients to communicate in real time. It is made up of various separate networks (known as *nets*) of IRC servers. Users run a client that connects them to a server on one of the nets. The server relays information to and from other servers on the same net. Once connected to an IRC server, a user will be presented with a list of one or more topical *channels*. Channel names usually being with a #, such as #irchelp, and since all servers on a given net share the same list of channels, users connected to any server on that net can communicate with one another.

NOTE Channels that begin with a & instead of a # are local to a given server only, and are not shared with other servers on the net.

Each IRC client is distinguished from other clients by a unique nickname (or *nick*). Servers store additional information about each client, including the real name of the host that the client is running on, the username of the client on that host, and the server to which the client is connected.

Operators are those clients that have been given the ability to perform maintenance on the IRC nets, such as disconnecting and reconnecting servers as needed to correct for any network routing problems. Operators can also forcibly remove other clients from the network by terminating their connection. Operators can be assigned to a server, or just to a channel, and they are identified by @ symbol next to their nick.

NOTE IRC can use both TCP and UDP as transports, and most modern IRC servers listen on ports 6667–7000.

Upper Layer Communications

Once we get above the session layer, our communications become pretty specific to the program we're using. The responsibilities of the presentation and application layers are more a function of the type of service requested than the underlying protocol in use. Data translation and encryption are considered *portable features*.

NOTE   Portable means that these features can be applied easily to different services without regard for the underlying protocol. It does not matter if I'm using IP or IPX to transfer my data, the ability to leverage these features will depend on the application in use.

For example, Lotus has the ability to encrypt mail messages prior to transmission. This activity is performed at the presentation layer of the program. It does not matter if I'm connecting to my mail system via TCP, SPX, or a modem. The encryption functionality is available with all three protocols, because the functionality is made available by the program itself. Lotus Notes is not dependent on the underlying protocol.

Summary

In this chapter, we began by discussing the anatomy of an Ethernet frame and how systems on a local Ethernet segment communicate. We also covered how routing is used to assist communication in large networking environments. From there we looked at the different methods of connection establishment and finished off the chapter by discussing IP services. For a more in-depth look at any of these technologies, you might want to refer to *Multiprotocol Network Design and Troubleshooting* (Sybex, 1997).

In the next chapter, we will begin to look at some of the insecurities involved in everyday communications. We will look at how building security into your core network design can not only improve performance (always a good thing)—it can make your data less susceptible to attack, as well.

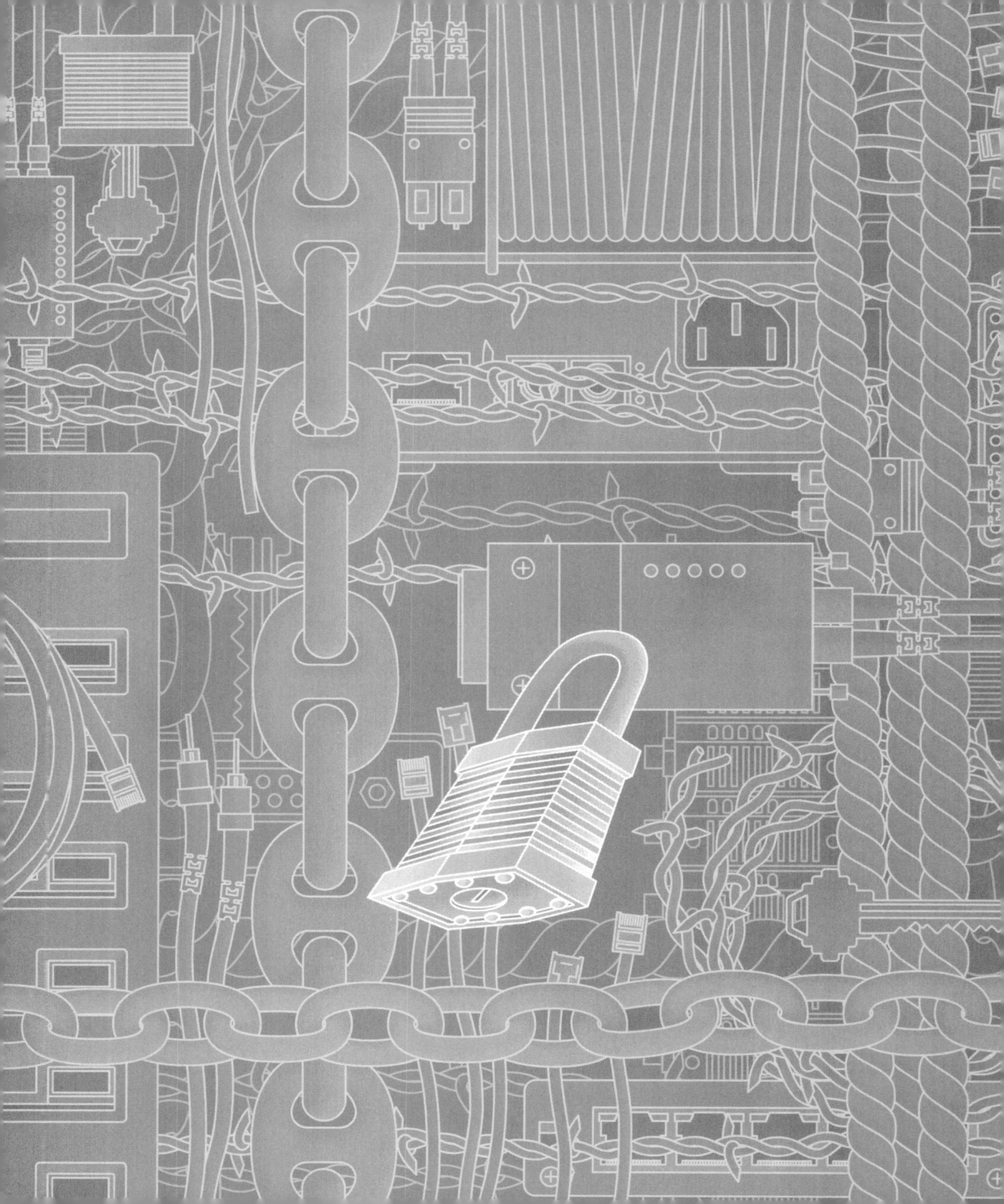

CHAPTER
FOUR

Topology Security

In this chapter, we will look at the communication properties of network transmissions. You will also see what insecurities exist in everyday network communications—and how you can develop a network infrastructure that alleviates some of these problems.

Understanding Network Transmissions

It is no accident that the National Security Agency, which is responsible for setting the encryption standards for the U.S. government, is also responsible for monitoring and cracking encrypted transmissions that are of interest to the government. In order to know how to make something more secure, you must understand what vulnerabilities exist and how these can be exploited.

This same idea applies to network communications. In order to be able to design security into your network infrastructure, you must understand how networked systems communicate with each other. Many exploits leverage basic communication properties. If you are aware of these communication properties, you can take steps to insure that they are not exploited.

Digital Communications

Digital communication is analogous to Morse code or the early telegraph system: certain patterns of pulses are used to represent different characters during transmission. If you examine Figure 4.1, you'll see an example of a digital transmission. When a voltage is placed on the transmission medium, this is considered a binary 1. The absence of a signal is interpreted as a binary 0.

FIGURE 4.1:

A digital transmission plotted over time

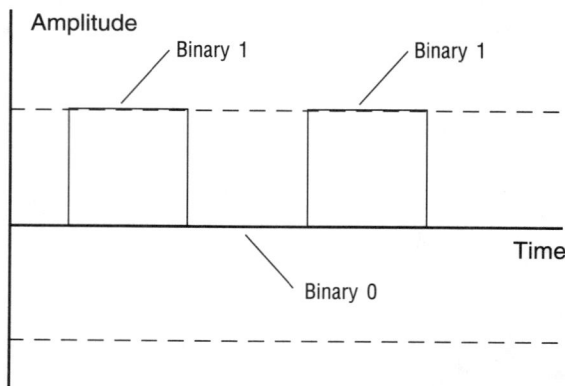

Because this waveform is so predictable and the variation between acceptable values is so great, it is easy to determine the state of the transmission. This is important if the signal is electrical, because the introduction of noise to a circuit can skew voltage values slightly. As shown in Figure 4.2, even when there is noise in the circuit, you can still see what part of the signal is a binary 1 and which is a 0.

FIGURE 4.2:

A digital transmission on a noisy circuit

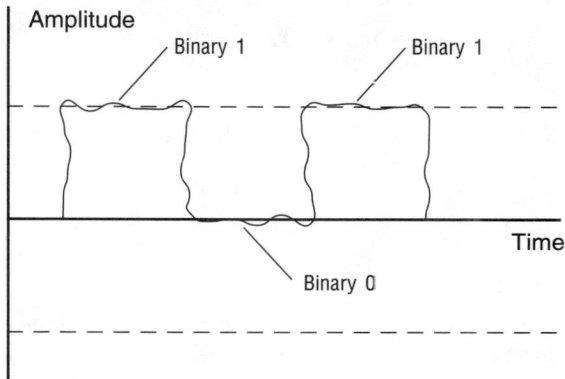

This simple format, which allows digital communication to be so noise-resistant, can also be its biggest drawback. The information for the ASCII character *A* can be transmitted with a single analog wave or vibration, but transmitting the binary or digital equivalent requires eight separate waves or vibrations (to transmit 01000001). Despite this inherent drawback, digital communication is usually much more efficient than analog circuits, which require a larger amount of overhead in order to detect and correct noisy transmissions.

NOTE   *Overhead* is the amount of additional information that must be transmitted on a circuit to insure that the receiving system gets the correct data and that the data is free of errors. Typically, when a circuit requires more overhead, less bandwidth is available to transmit the actual data. This is like the packaging used for shipping. You didn't want hundreds of little Styrofoam acorns, but they're there in the box taking up space to insure your item is delivered safely.

When you have an electric circuit (such as an Ethernet network that uses twisted-pair wiring), you need to pulsate your voltage in order to transmit information. This means your voltage state is constantly changing, which introduces your first insecurity: electromagnetic interference.

Electromagnetic Interference (EMI)

EMI is produced by circuits that use an alternating signal, like analog or digital communications (referred to as an *alternating current* or an *AC circuit*). EMI is not produced by circuits that contain a consistent power level (referred to as a *direct current* or a *DC circuit*).

For example, if you could slice one of the wires coming from a car battery and watch the electrons moving down the wire (kids: don't try this at home), you would see a steady stream of power moving evenly and uniformly down the cable. The power level would never change: it would stay at a constant 12 volts. A car battery is an example of a DC circuit, because the power level remains stable.

Now, let's say you could slice the wire to a household lamp and try the same experiment (kids: *definitely* do not try this at home!). You would now see that, depending on the point in time when you measured the voltage on the wire, the measurement would read anywhere between –120 volts and +120 volts. The voltage level of the circuit is constantly changing. Plotted over time, the voltage level would resemble an analog signal.

As you watched the flow of electrons in the AC wire, you would notice something very interesting. As the voltage changes and the current flows down the wire, the electrons tend to ride predominantly on the surface of the wire. The center point of the wire would show almost no electron movement at all. If you increased the frequency of the power cycle, more and more of the electrons would travel on the surface of the wire, instead of at the core. This effect is somewhat similar to what happens to a water skier—the faster the boat travels, the closer to the top of the water the skier rides.

As the frequency of the power cycle increases, energy begins to radiate at a 90° angle to the flow of current. In the same way that water will ripple out when a rock breaks its surface, energy will move out from the center core of the wire. This radiation is in a direct relationship with the signal on the wire; if the voltage level or the frequency is increased, the amount of energy radiated will also increase (see Figure 4.3).

This energy has magnetic properties to it and is the basis of how electromagnets and transformers operate. The downside to all of this is that the electromagnetic radiation can be measured in order to "sniff" the signal traveling down the wire. Electricians have had tools for this purpose for many years. Most electricians carry a device that they can simply connect around a wire in order to measure the signal traveling through the center conductor.

FIGURE 4.3:

A conductor carrying an AC
signal radiating EMI

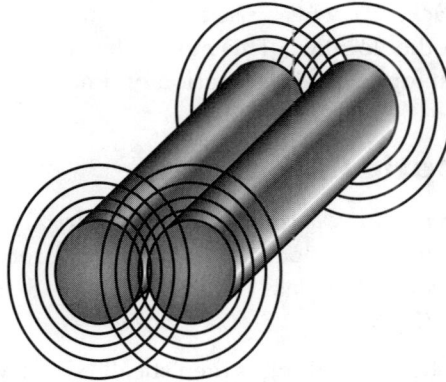

Copper wire conducting AC signal

There are more sophisticated devices that can measure the EMI radiation coming off an electrical network cable and actually record the digital pulses traveling down the wire. Once a record of these pulses has been made, it is a simple matter to convert them from a binary format to a format readable by humans (although a serious geek is just as happy reading the information in binary format, we did specifically say "humans").

NOTE   While twisted-pair cabling has become very popular due to its low cost, it is also extremely insecure. Most modern networks are wired using unshielded twisted pair. Since twisted pair is used for the transmission of electrical signals, EMI is produced. Because the cable does not use any shielding, it is extremely easy to detect the EMI radiating from each of the conductors. So while twisted pair is an excellent choice for general network use, it is not a very good selection if the information traveling along the wire needs to remain 100 percent secure.

So your first point of vulnerability is your actual network cables. These are typically overlooked when people evaluate the security of a network. While an organization may go to great lengths to secure its computer room, there may be a web of cabling running through the ceilings. This can be even more of a problem if your organization is located in shared office space and you have cabling running through common areas.

This means that a would-be attacker would never have to go near a computer room or wiring closet to collect sensitive information. A stepladder and a popped ceiling tile are all that's needed to create an access point to your network. A savvy attacker may even use a radio transmitter to relay the captured information to another location. This means the attacker can safely continue to collect information for an extended period of time.

Fiber Optic Cable

Fiber optic cable consists of a cylindrical glass thread center core 62.5 microns in diameter wrapped in cladding that protects the central core and reflects the light back into the glass conductor. This is then encapsulated in a jacket of tough KEVLAR fiber.

The whole thing is then sheathed in PVC or Plenum. The diameter of this outer sheath is 125 microns. The diameter measurements are why this cabling is sometimes referred to as 62.5/125 cable. While the glass core is breakable, the KEVLAR fiber jacket helps fiber optic cable stand up to a fair amount of abuse. Figure 4.4 shows a fiber optic cable.

FIGURE 4.4:

A stripped-back fiber optic cable

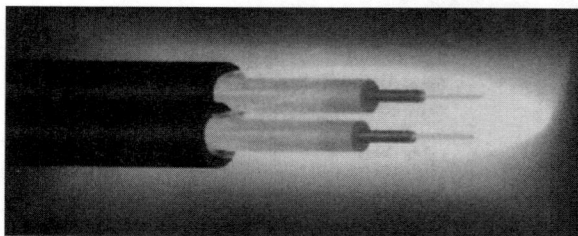

Unlike twisted-pair cable, fiber uses a light source for data transmission. This light source is typically a light-emitting diode (LED) that produces a signal in the visible infrared range. On the other end of the cable is another diode that receives the LED signals. The type of light transmission can take one of two forms: single mode or multimode.

WARNING   Never look into the beam of an active fiber optic cable! The light intensity is strong enough to cause permanent blindness. If you must visually inspect a cable, first make sure that it is completely disconnected from the network. Just because a cable is dark for a moment does not mean it is inactive. The risk of blindness or visual "dead spots" is too high to take risks—unless you know the cable is *completely* disconnected.

Light Dispersion

You'll see light dispersion if you shine a flashlight against a nearby wall: the light pattern on the wall will have a larger diameter than the flashlight lens. If you hold two flashlights together and shine them both against the wall, you'll get a fuzzy area in the middle where it's difficult to determine which light source is responsible for which portion of the illumination. The farther away from the wall you move, the larger this fuzzy area gets. This is, in effect, what limits the distance on multimode fiber (that is, if you can call 1.2 miles a distance limitation for a single cable run). As the length of the cable increases, it becomes more difficult for the diode on the receiving end to distinguish between the different light frequencies.

Single-mode fiber consists of an LED that produces a single frequency of light. This single frequency is pulsed in a digital format to transmit data from one end of the cable to another. The benefit of single-mode fiber over multimode is that it is faster and will travel longer distances (in the tens-of-miles range). The drawbacks are that the hardware is extremely expensive and installation can be tedious at best. Unless your company name ends with the word "Telephone" or "Utility," single-mode fiber would be overkill.

Multimode transmissions consist of multiple light frequencies. Because the light range does not need to be quite so precise as single-mode, the hardware costs for multimode are dramatically less than for single-mode. The drawback of multimode fiber is *light dispersion*, the tendency of light rays to spread out as they travel.

Because multimode transmissions are light-based instead of electrical, fiber benefits from being completely immune to all types of EMI monitoring. There is no radiation to monitor as a signal passes down the conductor. While it may be possible to cut away part of the sheath in order to get at the glass conductor, this might cause the system to fail thus foiling the attacker. However, newer fiber optic systems are more resilient, and ironically, more susceptible to monitoring from this kind of attack.

Fiber cable has one other major benefit: it is capable of supporting large bandwidth connections. 10MB, 100MB, and even gigabit Ethernet are all capable of supporting fiber cable. So along with security improvements, there are performance improvements. This is extremely helpful in justifying the use of fiber cable within your network—it allows you to satisfy both bandwidth and security concerns. If Woolly Attacker is going to attempt to tap into your network in order to monitor transmissions, he will to want to pick a network segment with a lot of traffic so that he can collect the largest amount of data. Coincidentally, these are also the segments where you would want to use fiber cable in order to support the large amount of data flowing though this point in the network. By using fiber cable on these segments, you can help to protect the integrity of your cabling infrastructure.

Bound and Unbound Transmissions

The atmosphere is what is referred to as an *unbound medium*—a circuit with no formal boundaries. It has no constraints to force a signal to flow within a certain path. Twisted-pair cable and fiber optic cable are examples of bound media, as they restrain the signal to within the wire. An unbound transmission is free to travel anywhere.

Unbound transmissions bring a host of security problems. Since a signal has no constraints that confine it within a specific area, it becomes that much more susceptible to interception and monitoring. The atmosphere is capable of transmitting a variety of signal types. The most commonly used are light and radio waves.

Light Transmissions

Light transmissions through the atmosphere use lasers to transmit and receive network signals. These devices operate similarly to a fiber cable circuit, except without the glass media.

Because laser transmissions use a focused beam of light, they require a clear line of sight and precise alignment between the devices. This helps to enhance system security, because it severely limits the physical area from which a signal can be monitored. The atmosphere limits the light transmission's effective distance, however, as well as the number of situations in which it can be used.

Unbound light transmissions are also sensitive to environmental conditions—a heavy mist or snowfall can interfere with their transmission properties. This means that it is very easy to interrupt a light-based circuit—thus denying users service. Still, light transmissions through the atmosphere make for a relatively secure transmission medium when physical cabling cannot be used.

Radio Waves

Radio waves used for networking purposes are typically transmitted in the 1–20GHz range and are referred to as *microwave* signals. These signals can be fixed frequency or spread spectrum in nature.

Fixed Frequency Signals   A *fixed frequency signal* is a single frequency used as a carrier wave for the information you wish to transmit. A radio station is a good example of a single frequency transmission. When you tune in to a station's carrier wave frequency on your FM dial, you can hear the signal that is riding on it.

A *carrier wave* is a signal that is used to carry other information. This information is superimposed onto the signal (in much the same way as noise) and the resultant wave is transmitted into the atmosphere. This signal is then received by a device called a *demodulator* (in effect, your car radio is a demodulator that can be set for different frequencies), which removes the carrier signal and passes along the remaining information. A carrier wave is used to boost a signal's power and to extend the receiving range of the signal.

Fixed frequency signals are very easy to monitor. Once an attacker knows the carrier frequency, he has all the information he needs to start receiving your transmitted signals. He also has all the information he needs to jam your signal, thus blocking all transmissions.

Spread Spectrum Signals   A *spread spectrum signal* is identical to a fixed frequency signal, except multiple frequencies are transmitted. The reason multiple frequencies are transmitted is the reduction of interference through noise. Spread spectrum technology arose during wartime, when an enemy would jam a fixed frequency signal by transmitting on an identical frequency. Because spread spectrum uses multiple frequencies, it is much more difficult to disrupt.

Notice the operative words "more difficult." It is still possible to jam or monitor spread spectrum signals. While the signal varies through a range of frequencies, this range is typically a repeated pattern. Once an attacker determines the timing and pattern of the frequency changes, she is in a position to jam or monitor transmissions.

NOTE   Because it is so easy to monitor or jam radio signals, most transmissions rely on encryption to scramble the signal so that it cannot be monitored by outside parties. We cover encryption in Chapter 9.

Terrestrial vs. Space-Based Transmissions   There are two methods that can be used to transmit both fixed frequency and spread spectrum signals. These are referred to as *terrestrial* and *space-based* transmissions.

> **Terrestrial Transmissions**   *Terrestrial transmissions* are completely land-based radio signals. The sending stations are typically transmission towers located on top of mountains or tall buildings. The range of these systems is usually line of sight, although an unobstructed view is not required. Depending on the signal strength, 50 miles is about the maximum range achievable with a terrestrial transmission system. Local TV and radio stations are good examples of industries that rely on terrestrial-based broadcasts. Their signals can only be received locally.
>
> **Space-Based Transmissions**   *Space-based transmissions* are signals that originate from a land-based system but are then bounced off one or more satellites that orbit the earth in the upper atmosphere. The greatest benefit of space-based communications is range. Signals can be received from almost every corner of the world. The space-based satellites can be tuned to increase or decrease the effective broadcast area.

Of course, the larger the broadcast range of a signal, the more susceptible it is to being monitored. As the signal range increases, so does the possibility that someone knowledgeable enough to monitor your signals will be within your broadcast area.

Choosing a Transmission Medium

You should consider a number of security issues when choosing a medium for transferring data across your network.

How Valuable Is My Data?

As you saw in earlier chapters, the typical attacker must feel like he or she has something to gain by assaulting your network. Do you maintain databases that contain financial information? If so, someone might find the payoff high enough to make it worth the risk of staging a physical attack.

Which Network Segments Carry Sensitive Data?

Your networks carry sensitive information on a daily basis. In order to protect this information, you need to understand the workflow of how it is used. For example, if you identify your organization's accounting information as sensitive, you should know where the information is stored and who has access to it. A small workgroup with its own local server will be far more secure than an accounting database that is accessed from a remote facility using an unbound transmission medium.

TIP

Be very careful when analyzing the types of services that will be passing between your facilities. For example, e-mail is typically given little consideration, yet it usually contains more information about your organization than any other business service. Considering that most e-mail systems pass messages in the clear (if an attacker captures this traffic, it appears as plain text), e-mail should be one of your best-guarded network services.

Will an Intruder Be Noticed?

It's easy to spot an intruder when an organization consists of three of four people. Scale this to three or four thousand, and the task becomes proportionately difficult. If you are the network administrator, you may have no say in the physical security practices of your organization. You can, however, strive to make eavesdropping on your network a bit more difficult.

When you select a physical medium, keep in mind that you may need to make your network more resilient to attacks if other security precautions are lacking.

Are Backbone Segments Accessible?

If a would-be attacker is going to monitor your network, he is going to look for central nodes where he can collect the most information. Wiring closets and server rooms are prime targets because these areas tend to be junction points for many communication sessions. When laying out your network, pay special attention to these areas and consider using a more secure medium (such as fiber cable) when possible.

Consider these issues carefully when choosing a method of data transmission. Use the risk analysis information you collected in Chapter 2 to cost justify your choices. While increasing the level of topology security may appear to be an expensive proposition, the cost may be more than justified when compared to the cost of recovering from an intrusion.

Topology Security

Now that you have a good understanding of the transmission media available for carrying your data, we will discuss how these media are configured to function as a network. *Topology* is defined as the rules for physically connecting and communicating on given network media. Each topology has its own set of rules for connecting your network systems and even specifies how these systems must "speak" to each other on the wire. By far the most popular local area network (LAN) topology is Ethernet.

Ethernet Communications

In Chapter 3, you saw what type of information is included within an Ethernet frame. Now we will examine how Ethernet moves this information from one system to another across a network. The better you understand network communication properties, the easier it will be to secure your network.

NOTE   Ethernet was developed in the late 1970s by Xerox; it later evolved into the IEEE specification 802.3 (pronounced "eight-oh-two-dot-three"). Its flexibility, high transmission rate (at the time, anyway), and nonproprietary nature quickly made it the networking topology of choice for many network administrators.

Ethernet is by far the most popular networking topology. Its ability to support a wide range of cable types, low-cost hardware, and plug-and-play connectivity has caused it to find its way into more corporate (as well as home) networks than any other topology.

Ethernet's communication rules are called *Carrier Sense Multiple Access with Collision Detection* (CSMA/CD). This is a mouthful, but it's simple enough to understand when you break it down:

- *Carrier sense* means that all Ethernet stations are required to listen to the wire at all times (even when transmitting). By "listen," I mean that the station should be constantly monitoring the network to see if any other stations are currently sending data. By monitoring the transmissions of other stations, a station can tell if the network is open or in use. This way, the station does not just blindly transfer information and interfere with other stations. Being in a constant listening mode also means that the station is ready when another station wants to send it data.

- *Multiple access* simply means that more than two stations can be connected to the same network, and that all stations are allowed to transmit whenever the network is free. It is far more efficient to allow stations to transmit only when they need to than it is to assign each system a time block in which it is allowed to transmit. Multiple access also scales much more easily as you add more stations to the network.

- *Collision detection* answers the question: "What happens if two systems think the circuit is free and try to transmit data at the same time?" When two stations transmit simultaneously, a *collision* takes place. A collision is similar to interference, and the resulting transmission becomes mangled and useless for carrying data. As a station transmits data, it watches for this condition; if it detects such a condition, the workstation assumes that a collision has taken place. The station will back off, wait for a random period of time, and then retransmit.

NOTE   Each station is responsible for determining its own random waiting period before retransmission. This helps to insure that each station is waiting for a different period of time, avoiding another collision. In the unlikely event that a second collision does occur (the station backs off but is again involved in a collision), each station is required to double its waiting period before trying again. When two or more consecutive collisions take place, it is referred to as a *multiple collision*.

If you were to chart CSMA/CD, it would look something like Figure 4.5. This process takes place after the ARP decision process discussed in Chapter 3.

Promiscuous Mode

An integral part of Ethernet communications is that each system is constantly monitoring the transmissions of all the other stations on the wire. Unfortunately, this is also Ethernet's biggest security flaw. It is possible to configure a system to read all of this information it receives. This is commonly referred to as a *promiscuous mode* system.

Promiscuous mode can be leveraged by a network administrator to monitor a network from one central station so that errors and network statistics can be gathered. A network analyzer is effectively a computer operating in promiscuous mode. Since a station is listening to all network traffic anyway, a simple software change allows a system to actually record all the information it sees.

FIGURE 4.5:

Flow chart of Ethernet
communication rules

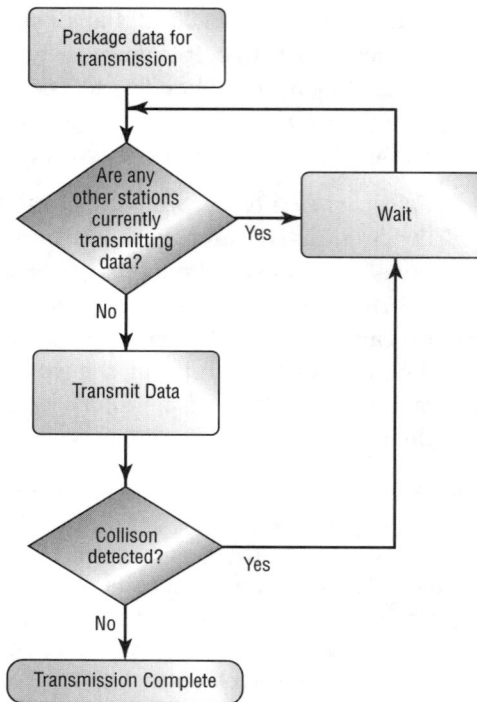

Unfortunately, the existence of promiscuous mode also means that a not-so-honest person may be able to eavesdrop on network communications or steal sensitive information. This is particularly a problem because most information passed along a computer network is transmitted as clear text. See Figure 4.6 for an example of this output.

In order to minimize the amount of information that can be collected with a network monitor or analyzer, you must segment network traffic to isolate network communications. This is best accomplished with a bridge, switch, or router. These devices are discussed in the "Basic Networking Hardware" section of this chapter.

Wide Area Network Topologies

Wide area network (WAN) topologies are network configurations that are designed to carry data over a great distance. Unlike LANs, which are designed to deliver data between many systems, WAN topologies are usually point to point.

Point to point means that the technology was developed to support only two nodes sending and receiving data. If multiple nodes need access to the WAN, a LAN will be placed behind it to accommodate this functionality.

Private Circuit Topologies

Leased lines are dedicated analog or digital circuits that are paid for on a flat-rate basis. This means that whether you use the circuit or not, you are paying a fixed monthly fee. Leased lines are point-to-point connections—they are used to connect one geographical location to another. The maximum throughput on a leased line is 56Kbps.

A *T1* is a full-duplex signal (each end of the connection can transmit and receive simultaneously) over two-pair wire cabling. This wire pair terminates in a receptacle that resembles the square phone jacks used in older homes. T1s are used for dedicated point-to-point connections in the same way that leased lines are. Bandwidth on a T1 is available in increments from 64Kb up to 1.544Mb. T1s use time division to break the two wire pairs into 24 separate channels. *Time division* is the allotment of available bandwidth based on time increments. This is extremely useful, as a T1 is capable of carrying both voice and data at the same time.

FIGURE 4.6:

A packet capture of a network file

```
Packet Number : 13          3:52:02 PM
Length : 66 bytes
ether: =================== Ethernet Datalink Layer ===================
       Station: Skylar ----> This_Workstation
       Type: 0x0800 (IP)
   ip: =================== Internet Protocol ===================
       Station:10.1.1.100 ---->10.1.1.25
       Protocol: TCP
       Version: 4
       Header Length (32 bit words): 5
       Precedence: Routine
              Normal Delay, Normal Throughput, Normal Reliability
       Total length: 48
       Identification: 21249
       Fragmentation not allowed, Last fragment
       Fragment Offset: 0
       Time to Live: 128 seconds
       Checksum: 0x9148(Valid)
  tcp: ================= Transmission Control Protocol =================
       Source Port: 258
       Destination Port: 1027
       Sequence Number: 417610
       Acknowledgement Number: 898472
       Data Offset (32-bit words): 5
       Window: 8510
       Control Bits: Acknowledgement Field is Valid (ACK)
              Push Function Requested (PSH)
       Checksum: 0x5DB5(Valid)
       Urgent Pointer: 0
```

There are two common ways to deploy leased lines or T1s:

- The circuit constitutes the entire length of the connection between the two organizational facilities (such as a branch office and a main office).

- The leased line is used for the connection from each location to its local exchange carrier. Connectivity between the two exchange carriers is then provided by some other technology, like frame relay (discussed in the next section).

The first of these two options creates the more secure connection, but at a much higher cost. Using a private circuit for end-to-end connectivity between two geographically separated sites is the best way to insure that your data is not monitored. While it is still possible to sniff one of these circuits, an attacker would need to gain physical access to some point along its path. The attacker would also need to be able to identify the specific circuit to monitor. Telephone carriers are not known for using attacker-friendly labels like "Bank XYZ's financial data: monitor here."

The second option is simply used to get your signal to the local exchange carrier. From there, your data would travel over a public network, such as frame relay or X.25.

Frame Relay and X.25

Frame relay and X.25 are *packet-switched* technologies. Because data on a packet-switched network is capable of following any available circuit path, such networks are represented by clouds in graphical presentations such as Figure 4.7.

Both X.25 and frame relay must be configured as *permanent virtual circuits* (PVCs), meaning that all data entering the cloud at point A is automatically forwarded to point B. These end points are defined at the time the service is leased. For large WAN environments, frame relay can be far more cost effective than dedicated circuits. This is because you can run multiple PVCs through a single WAN connection.

For example, let's say you have four remote sites that require a 56Kb connection to the home office. If you were to construct this network out of dedicated circuits, you would require a 56Kb leased line connection at each of the remote sites, as well as four 56Kb leased line connections running into the main office.

With frame relay, however, you could replace the four dedicated connections at the main office with one fractional T1 connection and simply activate four channels of the T1 circuit to accept the data. By requiring only a single circuit at the main site, you can reduce your WAN costs.

In fact, there is nothing that says the CIR at the main office must equal the CIR value of all your remote sites. For example, let's assume that the connections to your remote site are used strictly for transferring e-mail. If bandwidth requirements are low, you may be able to drop the CIR at the main office from 256Kb to 128Kb. As long as the combined traffic to your four remote sites never exceeds 128Kb, you would not even notice a drop in performance. This would reduce your WAN costs even further.

NOTE   The packet-switched network is a shared medium. Your exchange carrier uses the same network for all PVCs it leases out. In effect, you are sharing available bandwidth with every other client.

FIGURE 4.7:

A WAN frame relay cloud connecting three remote networks to a corporate office

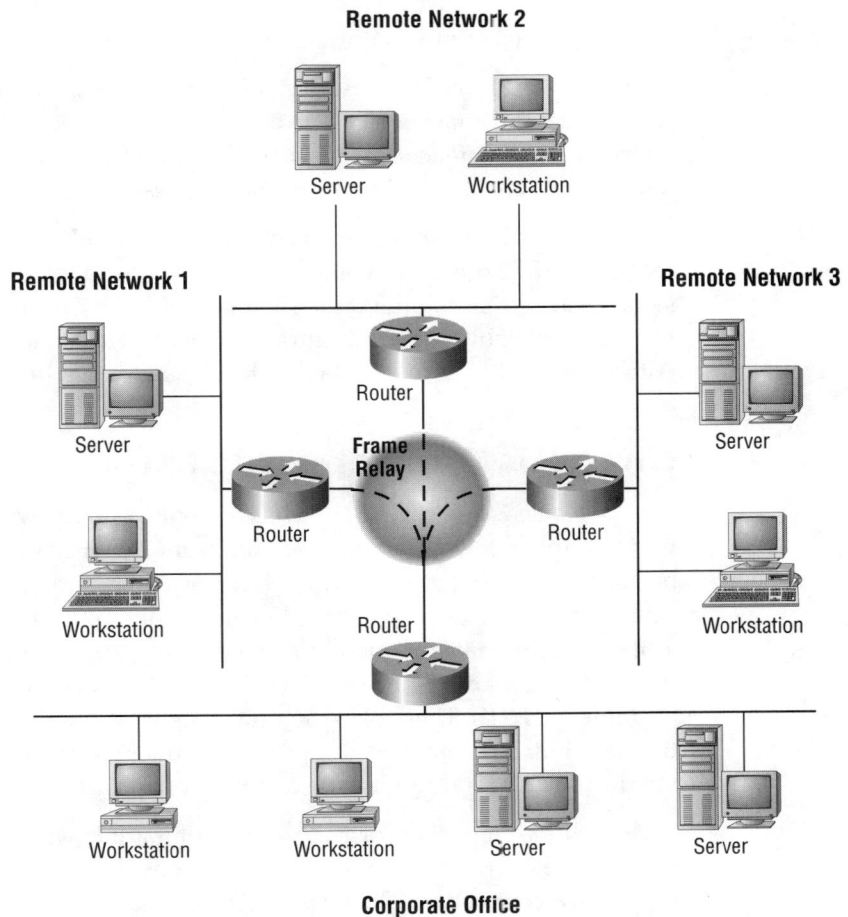

Your connection point into the cloud is defined through the use of a *Data Link Connection Identifier* (DLCI). A unique DLCI is assigned to each router that connects to the cloud. The DLCI lets the local exchange carrier know which PVC it should map to your connection.

As long as everyone uses their assigned DLCI, life is happy. The problem is when someone incorrectly, or with malicious intent, assigns his or her router the same DLCI as your circuit. This can cause traffic to be diverted to their network. In order for this to occur, the following conditions must be met:

1. The attacker must be connected to the same local exchange carrier.

2. The attacker must be connected to the same physical switch.

3. The attacker must know your DLCI.

Clearly, this is not the most difficult attack to stage. While it would be expensive (unless the attacker can gain access to another organization's network and "borrow" that connection), this attack may be well worth the effort if the attacker knows that sensitive information will be passing across the link.

Also, a would-be attacker can actually redirect a PVC to another geographical location. While doing so would eliminate the need to be connected through the same local carrier and the same switch in order to capture data, it also means that the attacker would have to infiltrate the exchange carrier's management system. Although this is not an easy task, it has been done in the past.

Asynchronous Transfer Mode (ATM)

Asynchronous Transfer Mode (ATM) is a point-to-point WAN technology most commonly implemented at speeds ranging from 25 to 622Mbps. Although ATM has become very popular as a cost-effective, scalable, and reliable alternative to traditional leased lines, it also has significant vulnerabilities when it comes to user authentication, data integrity, data availability, and data privacy. ATM works differently than Frame Relay or X.25 because it breaks up data into fixed-size packets known as *cells*. These cells are quite small (53 bytes), which allows them to transmit video, audio, and computer data over the same network, all the while making sure that no single type of data monopolizes the bandwidth.

The cell-based packets of ATM aren't compatible with packet-filtering firewalls, because these firewalls would have to be considered the endpoint of a point-to-point ATM connection. The overhead of *segmentation and reassembly (SAR)* of ATM packets simply wouldn't be efficient. Also, because ATM services can transfer non-IP traffic, there are vulnerabilities not associated with IP traffic (and therefore not covered by traditional IP-based network security mechanisms).

So how would a hacker get access to your ATM data? The first method depends on your transport media. Although most ATM is run on fiber optic cables, this is not necessarily the hacker-showstopper you would think. Hackers have eavesdropped on fiber by pulling away the insulation, and then bending the fiber optic enough to force some of the light out of the transmission path (but not enough to completely terminate the session and thus alerting someone to their actions).

The second method takes advantage of the virtual circuit running on a network: switched (SVC) or permanent (PVC). Most SVC management systems have an "Add to Call" feature that allows any system to join a session currently in progress. If the SVC administrator has not predefined and closed a session, any person has the ability to join in and eavesdrop. PVC's are also vulnerable through their management systems, especially if their interfaces are telnet- or web-based—where a hacker can take advantage of sniffing passwords (in the case of telnet) or in exploiting weaknesses in implementation (web-based utilities).

Once a hacker had access to your network (and could create their own PVC or SVC) they could use the Interim Local Management Interface (ILMI) or Private Network-to-Network Interface (PNNI) to change the routing of your ATM network, and send the data directly to a system on the Internet they control.

Basic Networking Hardware

These days there is a plethora of networking products to consider when planning your network infrastructure. There are devices for everything from connecting computer systems to the network to extending a topology's specifications to controlling network traffic. Sometimes your choices are limited. For example, to connect an office computer to the network, you must have a network card.

Many of these devices, when used correctly, can also help to improve your network security. In this section, we will take a look at some common networking hardware and discuss which can be used to reinforce your security posture.

Repeaters

Repeaters are simple two-port signal amplifiers. They are used in a bus topology to extend the maximum distance that can be spanned on a cable run. The strength of the signal is boosted as it travels down the wire. A repeater will receive a digital signal on one of its ports, amplify it, and transmit it out the other side.

A repeater is like a typical home stereo amplifier. The amp takes the signal it receives from the CD or tape deck, amplifies the signal, and sends it on its way to the speakers. If the signal is a brand-new Radiohead CD, it simply boosts the signal and sends it on its way. If you're playing an old Grateful Dead concert tape that is inaudible because of the amount of background hiss, the amp happily boosts this signal, as well, and sends it on its way.

Repeaters function similarly to a stereo amplifier: they simply boost whatever they receive and send it on its way. Unfortunately, the signal a repeater receives could be a good frame of data, a bad frame of data, or even background noise. A repeater does not discern data quality; it simply looks at each of the individual digital pulses and amplifies them.

A repeater provides no data segmentation. All communications that take place on one side of a repeater are passed along to the other side, whether the receiving system is on the other end of the wire or not. Again, think of a repeater as a dumb amplifier and you will get the idea.

Hubs

Hubs are probably the most common piece of network hardware next to network interface cards. Physically, they are boxes of varying sizes that have multiple female RJ45 connectors. Each connector is designed to accept one twisted-pair cable outfitted with a male RJ45 connector. This twisted-pair cable is then used to connect a single server or workstation to the hub.

Hubs are essentially multiport repeaters that support twisted-pair cables in a star typology. Each node communicates with the hub, which in turn amplifies the signal and transmits it out each of the ports (including back out to the transmitting system). As with repeaters, hubs work at the electrical level. When you design your network typology, think of hubs, which provide zero traffic control, as functionally identical to repeaters.

Wireless Hubs

A new variation of the traditional hub is the *wireless* hub. Using radio transmissions instead of twisted-pair cable, these hubs allow computers with wireless NICs to communicate with each other through the hub. Concerns about security have led most of the wireless hub manufactures to include basic encryption in the wireless system.

Bridges

A *bridge* looks a lot like a repeater; it is a small box with two network connectors that attach to two separate portions of the network. A bridge incorporates the functionality of a repeater (signal amplification), but it actually looks at the frames of data, which is a great benefit. A common bridge is nearly identical to a repeater except for the indicator lights, as shown in Figure 4.8. A forward light flashes whenever the bridge needs to pass traffic from one collision domain to another.

FIGURE 4.8:

A common bridge

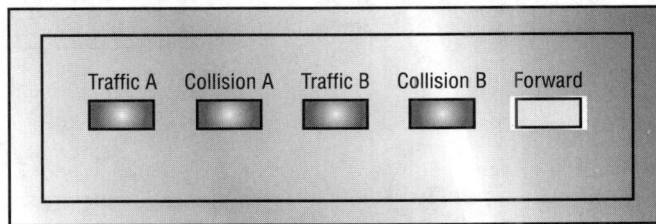

Bridge

In our discussion of Ethernet in Chapter 3, we introduced the concept of a data frame and described the information contained within the frame header. Bridges put this header information to use by monitoring the source and destination MAC address on each frame of data. By monitoring the source address, the bridge learns where all the network systems are located. It constructs a table, listing which MAC addresses are directly accessible by each of its ports. It then uses that information to play traffic cop and regulate the flow of data on the network. Let's look at an example.

A Bridge Example

Look at the network in Figure 4.9. Betty needs to send data to the server Thoth. Because everyone on the network is required to monitor the network, Betty first listens for the transmissions of other stations. If the wire is free, Betty will then transmit a frame of data. The bridge is also watching for traffic and will look at the destination address in the header of Betty's frame. Because the bridge is unsure of which port the system with MAC address 00C08BBE0052 (Thoth) is connected to, it amplifies the signal and retransmits it out Port B. Note that until now the bridge functionality is very similar to that of a repeater. The bridge does a little extra, however; it has learned that Betty is attached to Port A and creates a table entry with her MAC address.

FIGURE 4.9:

Betty transmits data to the server Thoth by putting Thoth's MAC address into the destination field of the frame.

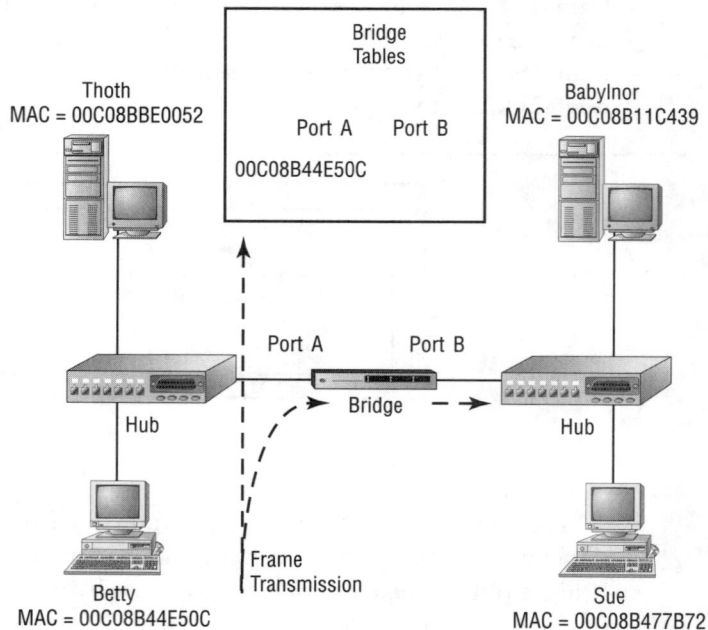

When Thoth replies to Betty's request, as shown in Figure 4.10, the bridge will look at the destination address in the frame of data again. This time, however, it finds a match in its table, noting that Betty is also attached to Port A. Because it knows Betty can receive this information directly, it drops the frame and blocks it from being transmitted from Port B. The bridge will also make a new table entry for Thoth, recording the MAC address as being off of Port A.

For as long as the bridge remembers each station's MAC address, all communications between Betty and Thoth will be isolated from Sue and Babylnor. *Traffic isolation* is a powerful feature, because it means that systems on both sides of the bridge can be carrying on conversations at the same time, effectively doubling the available bandwidth. The bridge insures that communications on both sides stay isolated, as if they were not even connected together. Because stations cannot see transmissions on the other side of the bridge, they assume the network is free and send their data.

FIGURE 4.10:

Thoth's reply to Betty's message

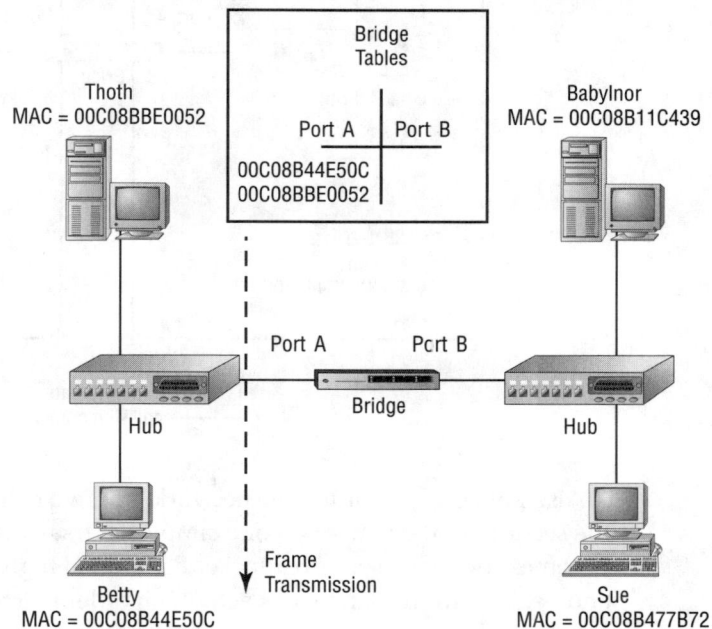

Each system only needs to contend for bandwidth with systems on its own segment. This means that there is no way for a station to have a collision outside of its segment. Thus these segments are referred to as *collision domains*, as shown in Figure 4.11. Notice that one port on each side of the bridge is part of each collision domain. This is because each of its ports will contend for bandwidth with the systems it is directly connected to. Because the bridge isolates traffic within each collision domain, there is no way for separated systems to collide their signals. The effect is a doubling of potential bandwidth.

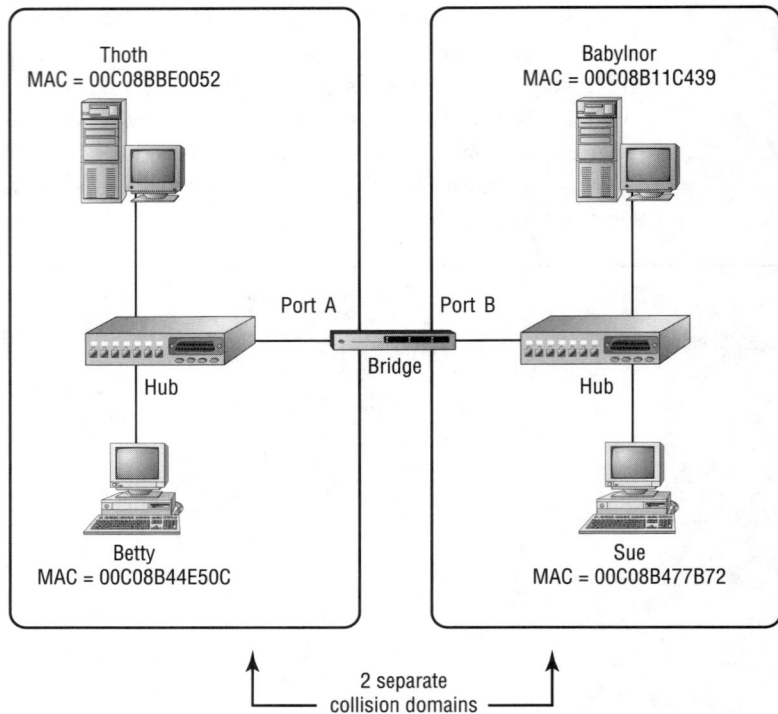

Also notice that splitting the network into two collision domains has increased the security of the network. For example, let's say that the system named Babylnor becomes compromised. An attacker has gained high-level access to this system and begins capturing network activity in order to look for sensitive information.

Given the above network design, Thoth and Betty would be able to carry on a conversation with relative security. The only traffic that will find its way onto Babylnor's collision domain is broadcast traffic. You may remember from Chapter 3 that a broadcast frame needs to be delivered to all local systems. For this reason, a bridge will also forward broadcast traffic.

By using a bridge in this situation, you get a double bonus light. You have not only increased performance, but security as well.

So what happens when traffic needs to traverse the bridge? As mentioned, when a bridge is unsure of the location of a system it will always pass the packet along just in case. Once the bridge learns that the system is in fact located off of its other port, it will continue to pass the frame along as required.

If Betty begins communicating with Sue, for example, this data will cross the bridge and be transmitted onto the same collision domain as Babylnor. This means that Babylnor is capable of capturing this data stream. While the bridge helped to secure Betty's communications with Thoth, it provides no additional security when Betty begins communicating with Sue.

In order to secure both of these sessions, you would need a bridge capable of dedicating a single port to each system. This type of functionality is provided in a device referred to as a *switch*.

Switches

Switches are the marriage of hub and bridge technology. They resemble hubs in appearance, having multiple RJ45 connectors for connecting network systems. Instead of being a dumb amplifier like a hub, however, a switch functions as though it has a little miniature bridge built into each port. A switch will keep track of the MAC addresses attached to each of its ports and route traffic destined for a certain address only to the port to which it is attached.

Figure 4.12 shows a switched environment in which each device is connected to a dedicated port. The switch will learn the MAC identification of each station once a single frame transmission occurs (identical to a bridge). Assuming that this has already happened, you now find that at exactly the same instant Station 1 needs to send data to Server 1, Station 2 needs to send data to Server 2, and Station 3 needs to send data to Server 3.

FIGURE 4.12:

A switch installation showing three workstations and three servers that need to communicate

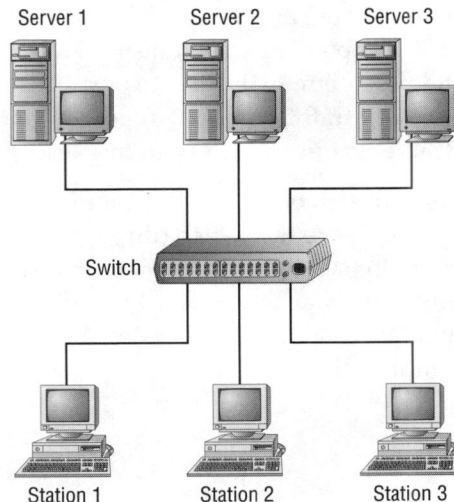

There are some interesting things about this situation. The first is that each wire run involves only the switch and the station attached to it. This means that each collision domain is limited to only these two devices, because each port of the switch is acting like a bridge. The only traffic seen by the workstations and servers is any frame specifically sent to them or to the broadcast address. As a result, all three stations will see very little network traffic and will be able to transmit immediately. This is a powerful feature that goes a long way toward increasing potential bandwidth. Given our example, if this is a 10Mbps topology, the effective throughput has just increased by a factor of 3. This is because all three sets of systems can carry on their conversations simultaneously, as the switch isolates them from each other. While it is still technically 10Mbps Ethernet, potential throughput has increased to 30Mbps.

Besides increasing performance dramatically, you have also increased security. If any one of these systems becomes compromised, the only sessions that can be monitored are sessions with the compromised system. For example, if an attacker gains access to Server 2, she will not be able to monitor communication sessions with Servers 1 or 3, only Server 2.

This is because monitoring devices can only collect traffic that is transmitting within their collision domain. Since Server 2's collision domain consists of itself and the switch port it is connected to, the switch does an effective job of isolating System 2 from the communication sessions being held with the other servers.

While this is a wonderful security feature, it does make legitimate monitoring of your network somewhat cumbersome. This is why many switches include a *monitoring port*.

A monitoring port is simply a port on the switch that can be configured to receive a copy of all data transmitted to one or more ports. For example, you could plug your analyzer into port 10 of the switch and configure the device to listen to all traffic on port 3. If port 3 is one of your servers, you can now analyze all traffic flowing to and from this system.

This can also be a potential security hole. If an attacker is able to gain administrative access to the switch (through telnet, HTTP, SNMP, or the console port), she would have free rein to monitor any system connected to, or communicating through, the switch. To return to our example, if the attacker could access Server 2 and the switch itself, she is now in a perfect position to monitor all network communications.

NOTE   Keep in mind that bridges, switches, and similar networking devices are designed primarily to improve network performance, not to improve security. Increased security is just a secondary benefit. This means that they have not received the same type of abusive, real-world testing as, say, a firewall or router product. A switch can augment your security policy, but it should not be the core device to implement it.

VLAN Technology

Switching introduces a new technology referred to as the *virtual local area network* (VLAN). Software running on the switch allows you to set up connectivity parameters for connected systems by workgroup (referred to as VLAN groups) instead of by geographical location. The switch's administrator is allowed to organize port transmissions logically so that connectivity is grouped according to each user's requirements. The "virtual" part is that these VLAN groups can span over multiple physical network segments, as well as multiple switches. By assigning all switch ports that connect to PCs used by accounting personnel to the same VLAN group, you can create a virtual accounting network.

Think of VLANs as being the virtual equivalent of taking an ax to a switch with many ports in order to create multiple switches. If you have a 24-port switch and you divide the ports equally into three separate VLANs, you essentially have three 8-port switches.

"Essentially" is the key word here, as you still have one physical device. While this makes for simpler administration, from a security perspective it is not nearly as good as having three physical switches. If an attacker is able to compromise a switch using VLANs, he might be able to configure his connection to monitor any of the other VLANs on the device.

This can be an extremely bad thing if you have one large switch providing connectivity on both sides of a traffic-control device such as a firewall. An attacker may not need to penetrate your firewall—he may find the switch to be a far easier target. At the very least, the attacker now has two potential ways into the network instead of just one.

Routers

A *router* is a multiport device that decides how to handle the contents of a frame, based on protocol and network information. To truly understand what this means, we must first look at what a protocol is and how it works.

Until now, we've been happily communicating using the Media Access Control address assigned to our networking devices. Our systems have used this number to contact other systems and transmit information as required.

The problem with this scheme is that it does not scale very well. For example, what if you have 2,000 systems that need to communicate with each other? You would now have 2,000 systems fighting each other for bandwidth on a single Ethernet network. Even if you employ switching, the number of broadcast frames will eventually reach a point where network performance will degrade and you cannot add any more systems. This is where protocols such as IP and IPX come in.

Network Protocols

At its lowest levels, a *network protocol* is a set of communication rules that provide the means for networking systems to be grouped by geographical area and common wiring. To indicate it is part of a specific group, each of these systems is assigned an identical protocol network address.

Network addresses are kind of like zip codes. Let's assume someone mails a letter and the front of the envelope simply reads: Fritz & Wren, 7 Spring Road. If this happens in a very small town, the letter will probably get through (as if you'd used a MAC address on a LAN).

If the letter were mailed in a city like Boston or New York, however, the Post Office would have no clue where to send it (although postal workers would probably get a good laugh). Without a zip code, they may not even attempt delivery. The zip code provides a way to specify the general area where this letter needs to be delivered. The postal worker processing the letter is not required to know exactly where Spring Road is located. She simply looks at the zip code and forwards the letter to the Post Office responsible for this code. It is up to the local Post Office to know the location of Spring Road and to use this knowledge to deliver the letter.

Protocol network addresses operate in a similar fashion. A protocol-aware device will add the network address of the destination device to the data field of a frame. It will also record its own network address, in case the remote system needs to send a reply.

This is where a router comes in. A router is a protocol-aware device that maintains a table of all known networks. It uses this table to help forward information to its final destination. Let's walk through an example to see how a routed network operates.

A Routed Network Example

Let's assume you have a network similar to that shown in Figure 4.13 and that System B needs to transmit information to System F.

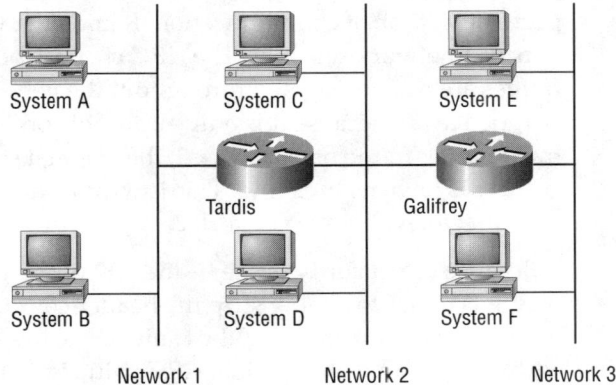

FIGURE 4.13:

An example of a routed network

System B will begin by comparing its network address to that of System F. If there is a match, System B will assume the system is local and attempt to deliver the information directly. If the network addresses are different (as they are in our example), System B will refer to its routing table. If it does not have a specific entry for Network 3, it will fall back on its default router, which in this case is Tardis. In order to deliver the information to Tardis, System B would ARP for Tardis's MAC address.

System B would then add the network protocol delivery information for System F (the source and destination network numbers) to the data and create a frame using Tardis's MAC address as the destination. It does this because System B assumes that Tardis will take care of forwarding the information to the destination network.

Once Tardis receives the frame, it performs a CRC check to insure the integrity of the data. If the frame checks out, Tardis will then completely strip off the header and trailer. Tardis then analyzes the destination network address listed in the frame (in this case Network 3) to see if it is locally connected to this network. Since Tardis is not directly connected to Network 3, it consults its routing table in order to find the best route to get there. Tardis then discovers that Galifrey is capable of reaching Network 3.

Tardis now ARPs to discover the local MAC address being used by Galifrey. Tardis then creates a new frame around the data packet by creating a header consisting of its MAC address to the source address field and Galifrey's MAC address in the destination field. Finally, Tardis generates a new CRC value for the trailer.

While all this stripping and recreating seems like a lot of work, it is a necessary part of this type of communication. Remember that routers are placed at the borders of a network segment. The CRC check is performed to insure that bad frames are not propagated throughout the network. The header information is stripped away because it is only applicable on Network 1. When Tardis goes to transmit the frame on Network 2, the original source and destination MAC addresses have no meaning. This is why Tardis must replace these values with ones that are valid for Network 2.

Because the majority of the header (12 of the 14 bytes) needs to be replaced anyway, it is easier to simply strip the header completely away and create it from scratch. As for stripping off the trailer, once the source and destination MAC addresses change, the original CRC value is no longer valid. This is why the router must strip it off and create a new one.

NOTE
A data field that contains protocol information is referred to as a *packet*. While this term is sometimes used interchangeably with the term *frame*, a packet in fact only describes a portion of a frame.

So Tardis has created a new frame around the packet and is ready to transmit it. Tardis will now transmit the frame out onto Network 2 so that the frame will be received by Galifrey. Galifrey receives the frame and processes it in a similar fashion to Tardis. It checks the CRC and strips off the header and trailer.

At this point, however, Galifrey realizes that it has a local connection to System F, because they are both connected to Network 3. Galifrey builds a new frame around the packet and, instead of needing to reference a table, it simply delivers the frame directly.

Protocol Specificity

In order for a router to provide this type of functionality, it needs to understand the rules for the protocol being used. This means that a router is *protocol specific*. Unlike a bridge, which will handle any valid topology traffic you throw at it, a router has to be specifically designed to support both the topology and the protocol being used. For example, if your network contains Banyan Vines systems, make sure that your router supports VinesIP.

Routers can be a powerful tool for controlling the flow of traffic on your network. If you have a network segment that is using IPX and IP but only IP is approved for use on the company backbone, simply enable IP support only on your router. The router will ignore any IPX traffic it receives.

A wonderful feature of routers is their ability to block broadcasts. (As I mentioned in Chapter 3, broadcasts are frames that contain all Fs for the destination MAC address.) Because any point on the other side of the router is a new network, these frames are blocked.

NOTE   There is a counterpart to this called an *all-networks broadcast* that contains all Fs in both the network and MAC address fields. These frames are used to broadcast to local networks when the network address is not known. Most routers will still block these all-networks broadcasts by default.

Most routers also have the ability to filter out certain traffic. For example, let's say your company enters a partnership with another organization. You need to access services on this new network but do not want to allow your partner to access your servers. To accomplish this, simply install a router between the two networks and configure it to filter out any communication sessions originating from the other organization's network.

Most routers use static packet filtering to control traffic flow. The specifics of how this works will be covered in Chapter 6. For now, just keep in mind that routers cannot provide the same level of traffic control that may be found in the average firewall. Still, if your security requirements are minimal, packet filtering may be a good choice—chances are you will need a router to connect your networks, anyway.

A Comparison of Bridging/Switching and Routing

Table 4.1 represents a summary of the information discussed in the preceding sections. It provides a quick reference to the differences between controlling traffic at the datalink layer (bridges and switches) and controlling traffic at the network layer (routers).

TABLE 4.1:   Bridging/Switching versus Routing

A Bridge (Switch):	A Router:
Uses the same network address off all ports	Uses different network addresses off all ports
Builds tables based on MAC address	Builds tables based on network address
Filters traffic based on MAC information	Filters traffic based on network or host information
Forwards broadcast traffic	Blocks broadcast traffic
Forwards traffic to unknown addresses	Blocks traffic to unknown addresses
Does not modify frame	Creates a new header and trailer
Can forward traffic based on the frame header	Must always queue traffic before forwarding

Layer-3 Switching

Now that you have a clear understanding of the differences between a switch and a router, let's look at a technology that, on the surface, appears to mesh the two. *Layer-3 switching*, *switch routing*, and *router switching* all are used interchangeably to describe the same devices.

So what exactly is a switch router? The device is not quite as revolutionary as you might think. In fact, these devices are more an evolution of existing router technology. The association with the word "switch" is more for marketing appeal to emphasize the increase in raw throughput these devices can provide.

These devices typically (but not always) perform the same functions as a standard router. When a frame of data is received, it is buffered into memory and a CRC check is performed. Then, the topology frame is stripped off the data packet. Just like a regular router, a switch router will reference its routing table to determine the best route of delivery, repackage the data packet into a frame, and send it on its merry way.

How does a switch router differ from a standard router? The answer lies under the hood of the device. Processing is provided by application-specific integrated circuit (ASIC) hardware. With a standard router, all processing was typically performed by a single RISC (Reduced Instruction Set Computer) processor. In a switch router, components are dedicated to performing specific tasks within the routing process. The result is a dramatic increase in throughput.

Keep in mind that the real goal of these devices is to pass information along faster than the standard router. In order to accomplish this, a vendor may choose to do things slightly differently than the average router implementation in order to increase throughput (after all, raw throughput is everything, right?). For example, a specific vendor implementation may not buffer inbound traffic in order to perform a CRC check on the frame. Once enough of the frame has been read in order to make a routing decision, the device may immediately begin transmitting information out the other end.

From a security perspective, this may not always be a good thing. Certainly performance is a concern—but not at the cost of accidentally passing traffic that should have been blocked. Since the real goal of a switch router is performance, it may not be as nitpicky as the typical router about what it passes along.

Layer-3 switching has some growing up to do before it can be considered a viable replacement for the time-tested router. Most modern routers have progressed to the point where they are capable of processing more than one million packets per second. Typically, higher traffic rates are required only on a network backbone. To date, this is why switches have dominated this area of the network.

Switch routing may make good security sense as a replacement for regular switches, however. The ability to segregate traffic into true subnets instead of just collision domains brings a whole new level of control to this area of the network.

Like their router counterparts, some switch routers support access control lists, which allow the network administrator to manipulate which systems can communicate between each of the subnets and what services they can access. This is a much higher level of granular control than is provided with a regular switch. Switch routing can help to fortify the security of your internal network without the typical degradation in performance. If your security requirements are light, a switch router may be just the thing to augment your security policy.

NOTE   We will look at some examples of implementing an access control list (ACL) on a Cisco router in Chapter 6.

Summary

We've covered a lot of ground in this chapter. We discussed the basics of communication properties and looked at transmission media and hardware from a security perspective. We also discussed what traffic control options are available with typical network hardware.

In the next few chapters, we'll look at systems that are specifically designed to implement security policies. We will start by discussing firewalls and then work our way into intrusion-detection systems.

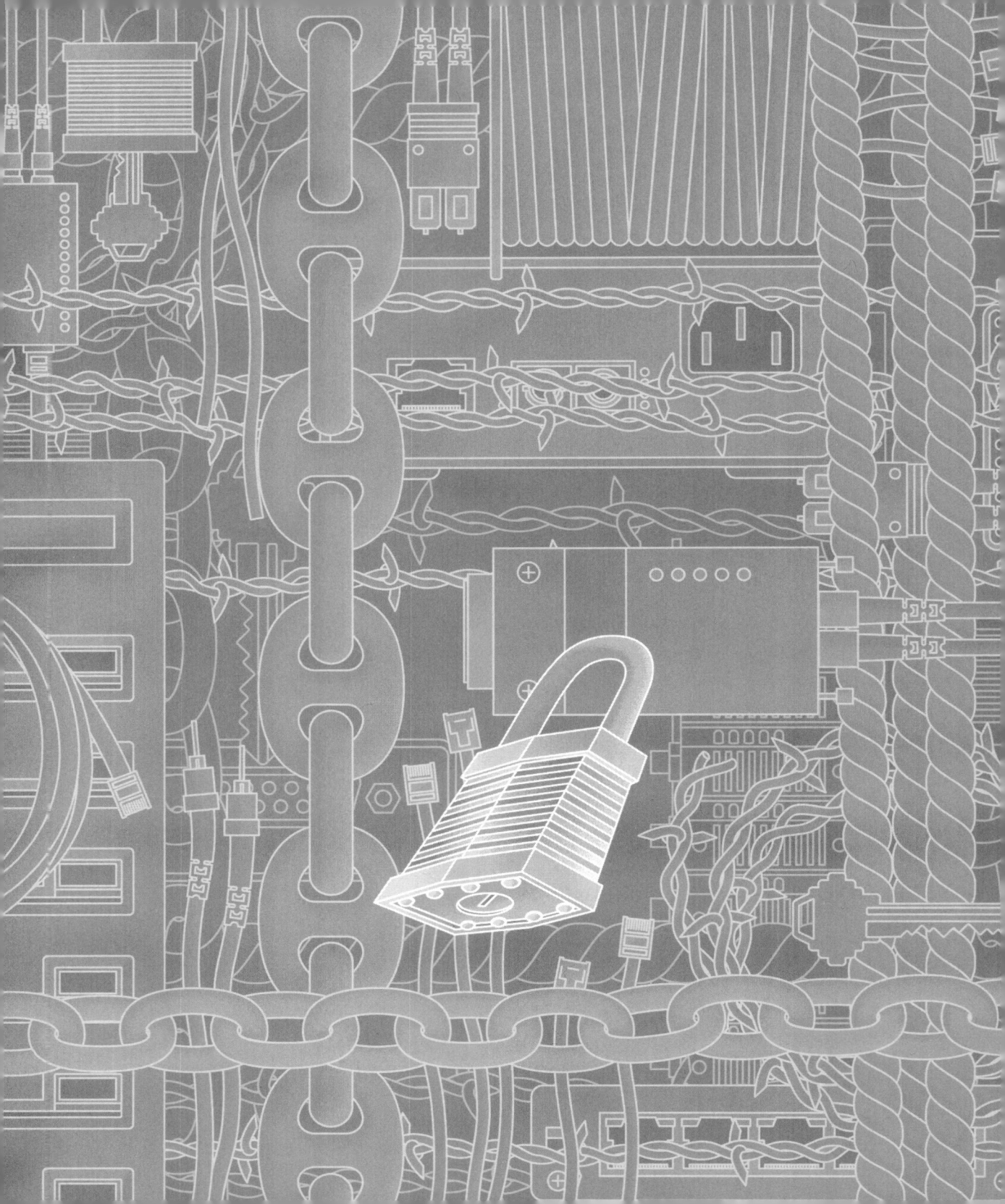

CHAPTER

FIVE

Firewalls

In this chapter, we will discuss firewalls and their implementation. Not all firewalls operate in the same way, so you should select a firewall based upon the security it provides, while insuring that it is a proper fit for your business requirements. For example, if the firewall you chose will not support AOL's Instant Messenger and IM is a critical business function, it may have been cheaper to simply buy a pair of wire cutters. Before we discuss firewalls, we will review what information you need to collect in order to make an informed purchase decision.

Defining an Access Control Policy

Before you can choose the type or brand of firewall to purchase, you have to ask yourself a very simple question (one that can be very time consuming to answer): What are (or should be) the rules that deal with the flow of data traffic in and out of your network? The answers to this question will form your access control policy. An *access control policy* is simply a corporate policy that states which type of access is allowed across an organization's network perimeters. For example, your organization may have a policy that states, "Our internal users can access Internet Web sites and FTP sites or send SMTP mail, but we will only allow inbound SMTP mail from the Internet to our internal network."

An access control policy may also apply to different areas within an internal network. For example, your organization may have WAN links to supporting business partners. In this case, you might want to define a limited scope of access across this link to insure that it is only used for its intended purpose.

An access control policy simply defines the directions of data flow to and from different parts of the network. It will also specify what type of traffic is acceptable, assuming that all other data types will be blocked. When defining an access control policy, you can use a number of different parameters to describe traffic flow. Some common descriptors that can be implemented with a firewall are listed in Table 5.1.

TIP

If you do not have an access control policy, you should create one. A clearly defined access control policy helps to insure that you select the correct firewall product or products. There is nothing worse than spending $10,000 on new firewall software, only to find it does not do everything you need it to.

TABLE 5.1:   Access Control Descriptors

Description	Definition
Direction	A description of acceptable traffic flow based on direction. For example, traffic from the Internet to the internal network (inbound) or traffic from the internal network heading towards the Internet (outbound).
Service	The type of server application that will be accessed. For example, Web access (HTTP), File Transfer Protocol (FTP), Simple Mail Transfer Protocol (SMTP).
Specific Host	Sometimes more granularity is required than simply specifying direction. For example, an organization may wish to allow inbound HTTP access, but to only a specific computer. Conversely, the organization may only have one business unit to which it wishes to grant Internet Web server access.
Individual Users	Many organizations have a business need to let certain individuals perform specific activities but do not want to open up this type of access to everyone. For example, the company CFO may need to be able to access internal resources from the Internet because she does a lot of traveling. In this case, the device enforcing the access control policy would attempt to authenticate anyone trying to gain access, to insure that only the CFO can get through.
Time of Day	Sometimes an organization may wish to restrict access during certain hours of the day. For example, an access control policy may state, "Internal users can access Web servers on the Internet only between the hours of 5:00 PM and 7:00 AM."
Public or Private	At times it may be beneficial to use a public network (such as Frame Relay or the Internet) to transmit private data. An access control policy may define that one or more types of information should be encrypted as that information passes between two specific hosts or over entire network segments.
Quality of Service	An organization may wish to restrict access based on the amount of available bandwidth. For example, let's assume that an organization has a Web server that is accessible from the Internet and wants to insure that access to this system is always responsive. The organization may have an access control policy that allows internal users to access the Internet at a restricted level of bandwidth when a potential client is currently accessing the Web server. When the client is done accessing the server, the internal users would have 100 percent of the bandwidth available to access Internet resources.
Role	Similar to restricting access to individual users, administrators use roles to group individuals with similar access needs. This grouping simplifies the complexity of access control and eases administrative workloads.

Be creative and try to envision what type of access control your organization may require in the future. This will help to insure that you will not quickly outgrow your firewall solution. I have had quite a few organizations tell me that they had zero interest in accessing their local network from the Internet. Many of these same clients came back within six months, looking for an Internet-based remote access solution. Always try to think in scale—not just according to today's requirements.

Definition of a Firewall

A *firewall* (unlike a simple router that merely directs network traffic) is a system or group of systems that enforces an access control policy on network traffic as it passes through access points. Once you have determined the levels of connectivity you wish to provide, it is the firewall's job to insure that no additional access beyond this scope is allowed. It is up to your firewall to insure that your access control policy is followed by all users on the network.

Firewalls are similar to other network devices in that their purpose is to control the flow of traffic. Unlike other network devices, however, a firewall must control this traffic while taking into account that not all the packets of data it sees may be what they appear to be.

For example, a bridge filters traffic based on the destination MAC address. If a host incorrectly labels the destination MAC address and the bridge inadvertently passes the packet to the wrong destination, the bridge is not seen as being faulty or inadequate. It is expected that the host will follow certain network rules, and if it fails to follow these rules, then the host is at fault, not the bridge.

A firewall, however, must assume that hosts may try to fool it in order to sneak information past it. A firewall cannot use communication rules as a crutch; rather, it should expect that the rules will *not* be followed. This places a lot of pressure on the firewall design, which must plan for every contingency.

When Is a Firewall Required?

Typically, access is controlled between the internal network and the Internet, but there are many other situations in which a firewall may be required.

Dial-In Modem Pool

A firewall can be used to control access from a dial-in modem pool. For example, an organization may have an access control policy that specifies that dial-in users may only access a single mail system. The organization does not want to allow access to other internal servers or to the Internet. A firewall can be used to implement this policy.

External Connections to Business Partners

Many organizations have permanent connections to remote business partners. This can create a difficult situation—the connection is required for business, but now someone has access to the internal network from an area where security is not controlled by the organization. A firewall can be used to regulate and document access from these links.

Between Departments

Some organizations (such as trading companies) are required to maintain internal firewalls between different areas of the network. This is to ensure that internal users only have access to the information they require. A firewall at the point of connection between these two networks enforces access control.

Firewall Types

Not all firewalls are built the same. A number of different technologies have been employed in order to control access across a network perimeter. The most popular are

- Static packet filtering
- Dynamic packet filtering
- Stateful filtering
- Proxy

Static Packet Filtering

Static packet filtering controls traffic by using information stored within the packet headers. As packets are received by the filtering device, the attributes of the data stored within the packet headers are compared against the access control policy (referred to as an *access control list* or ACL). Depending on how this header information compares to the ACL, the traffic is either allowed to pass or dropped.

A static packet filter can use the following information when regulating traffic flow:

- Destination IP address or subnet

- Source IP address or subnet

- Destination service port

- Source service port

- Flag (TCP only)

The TCP Flag Field

When the TCP transport is used, static packet filtering can use the flag field in the TCP header when making traffic control decisions. Figure 5.1 shows a packet decode of a TCP/IP packet. The Control Bits field identifies which flags have been set. Flags can be either turned on (binary value of 1) or turned off (binary value of 0).

FIGURE 5.1:

A TCP/IP packet decode

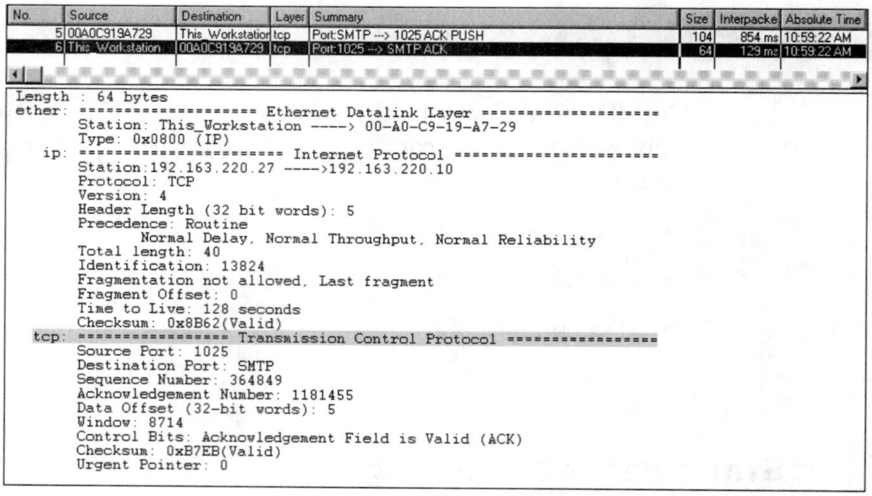

```
No.   Source          Destination      Layer Summary                              Size  Interpacke Absolute Time
   5  00A0C919A729    This_Workstation tcp  Port:SMTP ---> 1025 ACK PUSH          104   854 ms 10:59:22 AM
   6  This_Workstation 00A0C919A729    tcp  Port:1025 ---> SMTP ACK               64    129 ms 10:59:22 AM

Length : 64 bytes
ether: ==================== Ethernet Datalink Layer ====================
       Station: This_Workstation ----> 00-A0-C9-19-A7-29
       Type: 0x0800 (IP)
   ip: ==================== Internet Protocol ====================
       Station:192.163.220.27 ---->192.163.220.10
       Protocol: TCP
       Version: 4
       Header Length (32 bit words): 5
       Precedence: Routine
            Normal Delay, Normal Throughput, Normal Reliability
       Total length: 40
       Identification: 13824
       Fragmentation not allowed, Last fragment
       Fragment Offset: 0
       Time to Live: 128 seconds
       Checksum: 0x8B62(Valid)
  tcp: ================ Transmission Control Protocol ================
       Source Port: 1025
       Destination Port: SMTP
       Sequence Number: 364849
       Acknowledgement Number: 1181455
       Data Offset (32-bit words): 5
       Window: 8714
       Control Bits: Acknowledgement Field is Valid (ACK)
       Checksum: 0xB7EB(Valid)
       Urgent Pointer: 0
```

So what does the flag field tell us? You may remember from our discussion of the TCP three-packet handshake in Chapter 3 that different flag values are used to identify different aspects of a communication session. The flag field gives the recipient hosts some additional information regarding the data the packet is carrying. Table 5.2 lists the valid flags and their uses.

TABLE 5.2: Valid TCP/IP Flags

TCP Flag	Flag Description
ACK (Acknowledgement)	Indicates that this data is a response to a data request and that there is useful information within the Acknowledgment Number field.
FIN (Final)	Indicates that the transmitting system wishes to terminate the current session. Typically, each system in a communication session issues a FIN before the connection is actually closed.
PSH (Push)	Prevents the transmitting system from queuing data prior to transmission. In many cases it is more efficient to let a transmitting system queue small chunks of data prior to transmission so that fewer packets are created. On the receiving side, Push tells the remote system not to queue the data, but to immediately push the information to the upper protocol levels.
RST (Reset)	Resets the state of a current communication session. Reset is used when a non-recoverable transmission failure occurs. It is a transmitting system's way of stating, "Were you listening to me? Do I have to say it again?" This is typically caused by a non-responsive host or by a spouse enthralled by an afternoon sporting event.
SYN (Synchronize)	Used while initializing a communication session. This flag should not be set during any other portion of the communication process.
URG (Urgent)	Indicates that the transmitting system has some high-priority information to pass along and that there is useful information within the Urgent Pointer field. When a system receives a packet with the Urgent flag set, it processes the information before any other data that may be waiting in queue. This is referred to as processing the data *out-of-band*.

The flag field plays an important part in helping a static packet filter regulate traffic. This is because a firewall is rarely told to block all traffic originating off of a specific port or going to a particular host.

For example, you may have an access control policy that states, "Our internal users can access any service out on the Internet, but all Internet traffic headed to the internal network should be blocked." While this sounds like the ACL should be blocking all traffic coming from the Internet, this is in fact not the case.

Remember that all communications represent a two-step process. When you access a Web site, you make a data request (step 1) to which the Web site replies by returning the data you requested (step 2). This means that during step 2 you are expecting data to be returned from the Internet-based host to the internal system. If the second half of our statement were taken verbatim ("…all Internet traffic headed to the internal network should be blocked."), our replies would never make it back to the requesting host. We are back to the "wire cutters as an effective security device" model: our firewall would not allow a complete communication session.

This is where our flag field comes into play. Remember that during the TCP three-packet handshake, the originating system issues a packet with SYN=1 and all other flags equal to 0. The only time this sequence is true is when one system wishes to establish a connection to another. A packet filter will use this unique flag setting in order to control TCP sessions. By blocking the initial connection request, a data session between the two systems cannot be established.

So to make our access control policy more technically correct, we would state, "all Internet traffic headed to the internal network with SYN=1 and all other flags equal to 0 should be blocked." This means that any other flag sequence is assumed to be part of a previously established connection and would be allowed to pass through.

This is clearly not the most secure method of locking down your network perimeter. By playing with the flag values, a would-be attacker can fool a static packet filter into allowing malicious traffic through. In this way, these predators stay one step ahead of these security devices.

FIN Scanners

Because a simple packet filter is capable of blocking port scans, some people decided to become creative. The simple port scanner eventually evolved into the *FIN scanner*. A FIN scanner operates under a similar principle to the port scanner, except that the transmitted packets have FIN=1, ACK=1 and all other flags set to 0.

Now, since our packet filter is only looking to block packets which have SYN=1 and all other flags set to 0, these packets are happily passed along. The result is that an attacker can analyze the returning data stream to determine which hosts are offering what services. If the destination host returns an ACK=1, RST=1 (a generic system response for nonexistent services), the software knows that this is an unused port. If, however, the destination host returns an ACK=1, FIN=1 (the service's agreeing to close the connect), the FIN scanner knows that there is a service monitoring that port. This means that our packet filter is unable to deter these scanning probes.

For example, there are software programs called *port scanners* that can probe a destination host to see if any service ports are open. The port scanner sends a connection request (SYN=1) to all the service ports within a specified range. If any of these connection requests causes the destination host to return a connection request acknowledgment (SYN=1, ACK=1), the software knows that there is a service monitoring that port.

Packet Filtering UDP Traffic

As if TCP traffic were not hard enough to control, UDP traffic is actually worse. This is because UDP provides even less information regarding a connection's state than TCP does. Figure 5.2 shows a packet decode of a UDP header.

FIGURE 5.2:

A UDP header decode

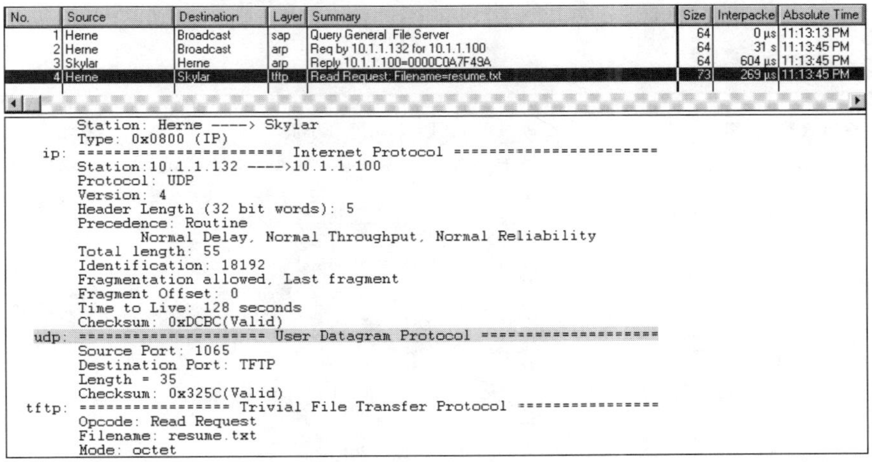

```
No.    Source    Destination   Layer  Summary                                    Size  Interpacke  Absolute Time
    1  Herne     Broadcast     sap    Query General File Server                   64    0 µs       11:13:13 PM
    2  Herne     Broadcast     arp    Req by 10.1.1.132 for 10.1.1.100            64    31 s       11:13:45 PM
    3  Skylar    Herne         arp    Reply 10.1.1.100=0000C0A7F49A              64    604 µs     11:13:45 PM
    4  Herne     Skylar        tftp   Read Request; Filename=resume.txt          73    269 µs     11:13:45 PM

           Station: Herne ----> Skylar
           Type: 0x0800 (IP)
     ip:   ======================= Internet Protocol =======================
           Station:10.1.1.132 ---->10.1.1.100
           Protocol: UDP
           Version: 4
           Header Length (32 bit words): 5
           Precedence: Routine
                 Normal Delay, Normal Throughput, Normal Reliability
           Total length: 55
           Identification: 18192
           Fragmentation allowed, Last fragment
           Fragment Offset: 0
           Time to Live: 128 seconds
           Checksum: 0xDCBC(Valid)
     udp:  ==================== User Datagram Protocol ====================
           Source Port: 1065
           Destination Port: TFTP
           Length = 35
           Checksum: 0x325C(Valid)
     tftp: ================ Trivial File Transfer Protocol ================
           Opcode: Read Request
           Filename: resume.txt
           Mode: octet
```

Notice that our UDP header does not use flags for indicating a session's state. This means that there is no way to determine if a packet is a data request or a reply to a previous request. The only information that can be used to regulate traffic is the source and destination port number. Even this information is of little use in many situations, because some services use the same source and destination port number.

For example, when two Domain Name Servers (DNS) are exchanging information, they use a source and destination port number of 53. Unlike many other services, they do not use a reply port of greater than 1023. This means that a static packet filter has no effective means of limiting DNS traffic to only a single direction.

You cannot block inbound traffic to port 53, because that would block data replies as well as data requests.

This is why, in many cases, the only effective means of controlling UDP traffic with a static packet filter is either to block the port or to let it through and hope for the best. Most people tend to stick with the former solution, unless they have an extremely pressing need to allow through UDP traffic (such as running networked Quake games, which use UDP port 26000).

Packet Filtering ICMP

The *Internet Control Message Protocol* (ICMP) provides background support for the IP protocol. It is not used to transmit user data, but is used for maintenance duty to insure that all is running smoothly. For example, Ping uses ICMP to insure that there is connectivity between two hosts. Figure 5.3 shows a packet decode of an ICMP header.

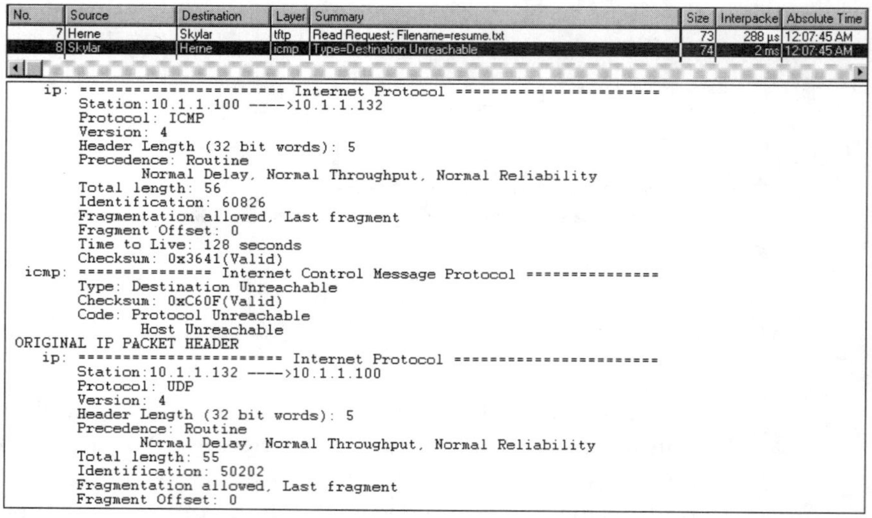

FIGURE 5.3:

An ICMP header

```
No.   Source      Destination   Layer  Summary                               Size  Interpacke  Absolute Time
  7  Herne       Skylar        tftp   Read Request; Filename=resume.txt       73   288 µs     12:07:45 AM
  8  Skylar      Herne         icmp   Type=Destination Unreachable            74    2 ms      12:07:45 AM

  ip: ======================= Internet Protocol =======================
       Station:10.1.1.100 ---->10.1.1.132
       Protocol: ICMP
       Version: 4
       Header Length (32 bit words): 5
       Precedence: Routine
              Normal Delay, Normal Throughput, Normal Reliability
       Total length: 56
       Identification: 60826
       Fragmentation allowed, Last fragment
       Fragment Offset: 0
       Time to Live: 128 seconds
       Checksum: 0x3641(Valid)
 icmp: =============== Internet Control Message Protocol ===============
       Type: Destination Unreachable
       Checksum: 0xC60F(Valid)
       Code: Protocol Unreachable
             Host Unreachable
ORIGINAL IP PACKET HEADER
   ip: ======================= Internet Protocol =======================
       Station:10.1.1.132 ---->10.1.1.100
       Protocol: UDP
       Version: 4
       Header Length (32 bit words): 5
       Precedence: Routine
              Normal Delay, Normal Throughput, Normal Reliability
       Total length: 55
       Identification: 50202
       Fragmentation allowed, Last fragment
       Fragment Offset: 0
```

NOTE   ICMP does not use service ports. There is a Type field to identify the ICMP packet type as well as a Code field to provide even more granular information about the current session.

The Code field can be a bit confusing. For example, in Figure 5.3 the code states `Protocol Unreachable; Host Unreachable`. This could lead you to think that the destination system is not responding. If you compare the source IP address for this ICMP packet to the destination IP address in the section after `Original IP Packet Header`, you will notice that they are the same (`10.1.1.100`). So if the destination was in fact "unreachable," how could it have possibly sent this reply?

The combination of these two codes actually means that the requested service was not available. If you look at the top of Figure 5.3, you will see that the transmission that prompted this reply was a Trivial File Transfer Protocol (TFTP) request for `resume.txt`. Only a destination host will generate a protocol unreachable error. Table 5.3 identifies the different type field values for ICMP packets.

NOTE Remember that UDP does not use a flag field. This makes UDP incapable of letting the transmitting system know that a service is not available. To rectify this problem, ICMP is used to notify the transmitting system.

TABLE 5.3:   ICMP Type Field Values

Type	Name	Description
0	Echo Reply	Responds to an echo request.
3	Destination Unreachable	Indicates that the destination subnet, host, or service cannot be reached.
4	Source Quench	Indicates that the receiving system or a routing device along the route is having trouble keeping up with the inbound data flow. Hosts that receive a source quench are required to reduce their transmission rate. This is to insure that the receiving system will not begin to discard data due to an overload inbound queue.
5	Redirect	Informs a local host that there is another router or gateway device that is better able to forward the data the host is transmitting. A redirect is sent by local routers.
8	Echo	Requests that the target system return an echo reply. Echo is used to verify end-to-end connectivity as well as measure response time.
9	Router Advertisement	Is used by routers to identify themselves on a subnet. This is not a true routing protocol, as no route information is conveyed. It is simply used to let hosts on the subnet know the IP addresses of their local routers.

Continued on next page

TABLE 5.3 CONTINUED: ICMP Type Field Values

Type	Name	Description
10	Router Selection	Allows a host to query for router advertisements without having to wait for the next periodic update. Also referred to as a *router solicitation.*
11	Time Exceeded	Informs the transmitting systems that the Time To Live (TTL) value within the packet header has expired and the information never reached its intended host.
12	Parameter Problem	Is a catchall response returned to a transmitting system when a problem occurs that is not identified by one of the other ICMP types.
13	Timestamp	Is used when you are looking to quantify link speed more than system responsiveness. Timestamp is similar to an Echo request, except that a quick reply to a Timestamp request is considered more critical.
14	Timestamp Reply	Is a response to a Timestamp request.
15	Information Request	Has been superseded by the use of bootp and DHCP. This request was originally used by self-configuring systems in order to discover their IP address.
16	Information Reply	Is a response to an information request.
17	Address Mask Request	Allows a system to dynamically query the local subnet as to what is the proper subnet mask to be used. If no response is received, a host should assume a subnet mask appropriate to its address class.
18	Address Mask Reply	Is a response to an address mask request.
30	Traceroute	Provides a more efficient means of tracing a route from one IP host to another than using the legacy Traceroute command. This option can only be used when all intermediary routers have been programmed to recognize this ICMP type. Implementation is via a switch setting using the `ping` command.

Table 5.4 identifies valid codes that may be used when the ICMP type is Destination Unreachable (Type=3).

TABLE 5.4:   ICMP Type 3 Code Field Values

Code	Name	Description
0	Net Unreachable	The destination network cannot be reached due to a routing error (such as no route information) or an insufficient TTL value.
1	Host Unreachable	The destination host cannot be reached due to a routing error (such as no route information) or an insufficient TTL value.
2	Protocol Unreachable	The destination host you contacted does not offer the service you requested. This code is typically returned from a host while all others are returned from routers along the path.
4	Fragmentation Needed and Don't Fragment Was Set	The data you are attempting to deliver needs to cross a network that uses a smaller packet size, but the "don't fragment" bit is set.
5	Source Route Failed	The transmitted packet specified the route that should be followed to the destination host, but the routing information was incorrect.

Table 5.5 identifies valid codes that may be used when the ICMP type is redirect (Type=5).

TABLE 5.5:   ICMP Type 5 Code Field Values

Code	Name	Description
0	Redirect Datagram for the Network (or Subnet)	Indicates that another router on the local subnet has a better route to the destination subnet.
1	Redirect Datagram for the Host	Indicates that another router on the local subnet has a better route to the destination host.

Employing filtering on the values of the Type and the Code fields, we have a bit more granular control than simply looking at source and destination IP addresses. Not all packet filters are capable of filtering on all Types and Codes. For example, many will filter out Type=3, which is destination unreachable, without regard to the Code value. This limitation can cause some serious communication problems.

Let's assume you have a network configuration similar to the one shown in Figure 5.4. Your local network uses a Token Ring topology, while your remote business partner uses Ethernet. You wish to give your business partner access to your local Web server in order to receive the latest product updates and development information.

FIGURE 5.4:

Problems blocking destination unreachable messages

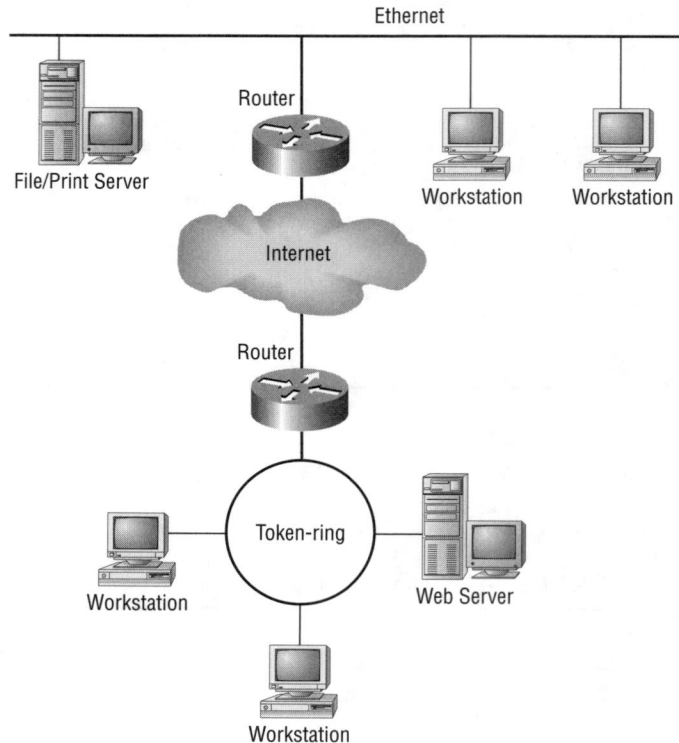

Now, let's also assume that your router is blocking inbound ICMP destination unreachable messages. You have done this in an effort to block Denial of Service (DoS) attacks by preventing external attackers from sending false host unreachable (Type=5, Code=1) messages. Since your router has limited packet filtering ability, you must block all ICMP Type=5 traffic.

This can present you with some problems, however. When your business partner's employees try to access your local Web server, they may not be able to view any HTML pages. This problem has the following symptoms—and can be quite confusing:

- The browser on the workstation located on the Ethernet segment appears to resolve the destination host name to an IP address.

- The browser appears to connect to the destination Web server.

- If either router provides session logging, traffic appears to flow between the two systems.

- The log on the local Web server indicates that the workstation connected to the Web server and that a number of files were returned.

So what has gone wrong? Unfortunately, by blocking all Type=3 traffic you have blocked the Fragmentation Needed (Type=3, Code=4) error messages, as well. This prevents the router from adjusting the *Mean Transfer Unit* (MTU) of the traffic being delivered.

MTU describes the maximum payload size that can be delivered by a packet of data. In an Ethernet environment, the MTU is 1.5Kb. In a Token Ring environment, the MTU can be as large as 16Kb. When a router receives packets that are too large for a destination network, it will send a request to the transmitting system asking it to break the data into smaller chunks (IMCP Type=3, Code=4). If the router tries to fragment this data itself, it might run into queuing problems if its buffers become full. For this reason, it is easier to have the remote system send smaller packets.

So if we watch the flow of data in Figure 5.4

1. An Ethernet workstation forms an HTML data request.

2. This request is delivered to the destination Web server.

3. The two systems perform a TCP three-packet handshake using 64-byte packets.

4. Once the handshake is complete, the Web server responds to the data request using a 16Kb MTU.

5. This reply reaches the router on the remote Ethernet network.

6. The Ethernet router issues a fragmentation request (IMCP Type=3, Code=4) back to the Web server asking that it use a 1.5Kb MTU.

7. The request makes it back to the border router at the Token Ring network.

8. This router checks its ACL, determines that it is supposed to drop all destination unreachable messages (ICMP Type=3), and drops the packet.

The fragmentation request never makes it back to your local network, and your remote business partner is unable to view your Web pages. When using static packet filtering, always make sure that you fully understand the ramifications of the traffic you are blocking or allowing to pass through.

Static Packet Filtering Summary

Static packet filters are non-intelligent filtering devices. They offer little protection against advanced types of attack. They look at a minimal amount of information in order to determine which traffic should be allowed to pass and which traffic should be blocked. Many routers have the ability to perform static packet filtering.

Dynamic Packet Filtering

Dynamic filtering takes static packet filtering one step further by maintaining a connection table in order to monitor the state of a communication session. It does not simply rely on the flag settings. This is a powerful feature that can be used to better control traffic flow.

For example, let's assume that an attacker sends your system a packet of data with a payload designed to crash your system. The attacker may perform some packet trickery in order to make this packet look like a reply to information requested by the internal system. A regular packet filter would analyze this packet, see that the ACK bit is set, and be fooled into thinking that this was a reply to a data request. It would then happily pass the information along to the internal system.

A dynamic packet filter would not be so easily fooled, however. When the information was received, the dynamic packet filter would reference its connection table (sometimes referred to as a *state table*). When reviewing the table entries, the dynamic packet filter would realize that the internal system never actually connected to this external system to place a data request. Since this information had not been explicitly requested, the dynamic packet filter would throw the packet in the bit bucket.

Dynamic Packet Filtering in Action

Let's take a look at how dynamic packet filtering works, in order to get a better idea of the increased security it can provide. In Figure 5.5, you can see two separate network configurations: one where the internal host is protected by a static packet filter and one where a dynamic packet filter is used.

FIGURE 5.5:

The differences between static and dynamic packet filtering

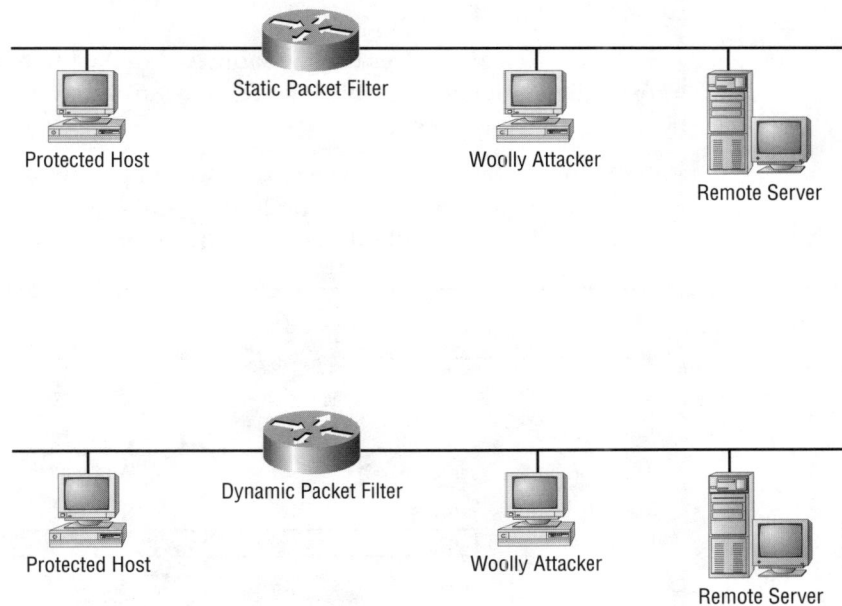

Static Packet Filter

Protected Host

Woolly Attacker

Remote Server

Dynamic Packet Filter

Protected Host

Woolly Attacker

Remote Server

Now, let's look at some access rules to see how each of these two firewall devices would handle traffic control. The ACL on both firewalls may look something like this:

- Allow the protected host to establish any service sessions with the remote server.

- Allow any session that has already been established to pass.

- Drop all other traffic.

The first rule allows the protected host to establish connections to the remote server. This means that the only time a packet with the SYN bit set is allowed to pass is if the source address is from the protected host and the destination is the remote server. When this is true, any service on the remote server may be accessed.

The second rule is a catchall. Basically it says, "If the traffic appears to be part of a previously established connection, let it pass." In other words, all traffic is OK—provided that the SYN bit is not set and all other bits are off.

The third rule states that if any traffic does not fit neatly into one of the first two rules, drop it just to be safe.

Both our firewall devices use the same ACL. The difference is in the amount of information each has available in order to control traffic. Let's transmit some traffic to see what happens.

In Figure 5.6, the internal system tries to set up a communication session with the remote server. Since all passing traffic passes the criteria set up in the access control lists, both firewalls allow this traffic to pass.

FIGURE 5.6:

Connection establishment from the protected host

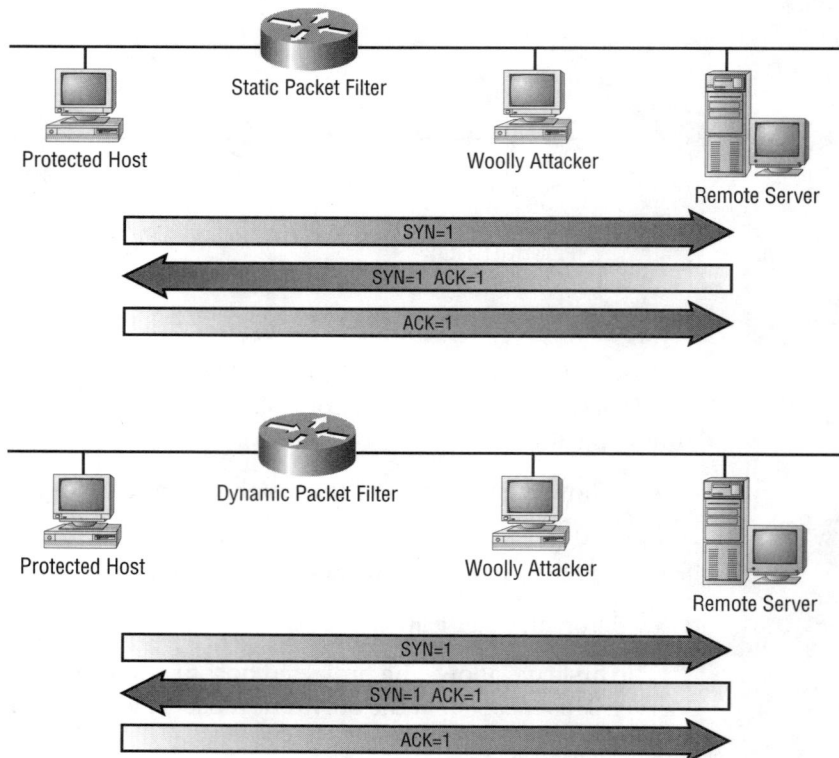

Once the handshake is complete, our protected host makes a data request. This packet will have the ACK bit set, and possibly the PSH bit. When the remote server receives this request, it will also respond with the ACK bit set and possibly the PSH bit, as well. Once the data transfer is complete, the session will be closed, each system transmitting a packet with the FIN bit set.

Figure 5.7 shows this established session passing data. Note that we have no problems passing our firewall devices because of our second rule: "Allow any session that has already been established to pass." Each firewall is making this determination in a slightly different way, however.

FIGURE 5.7:

An established session between the two hosts

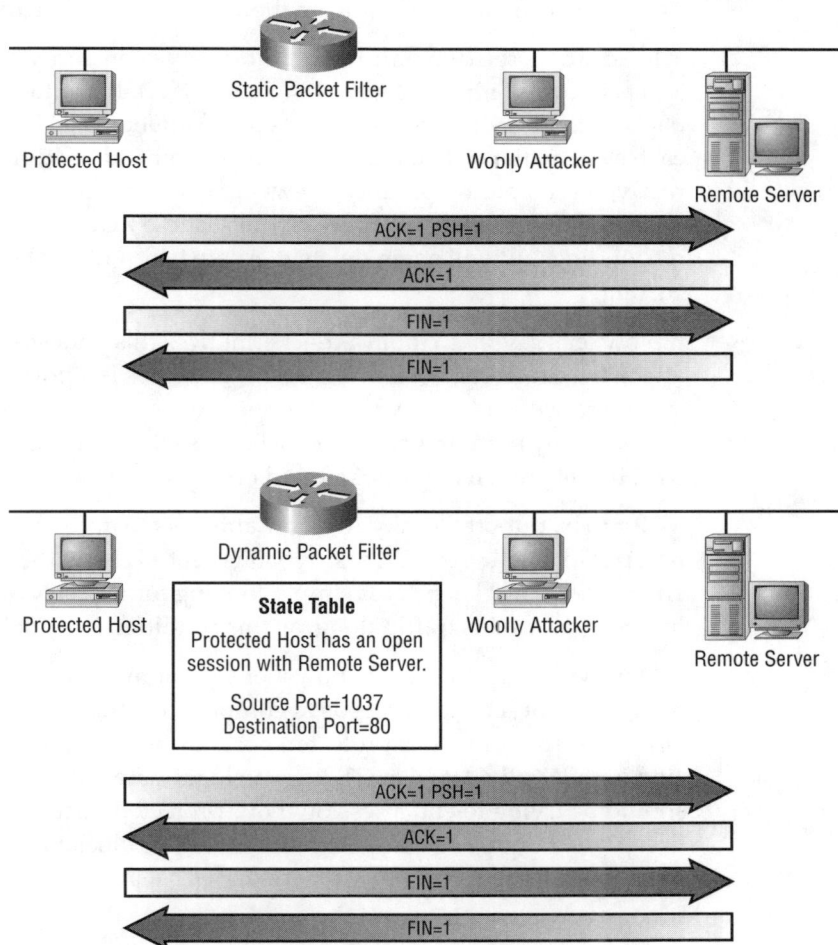

Our static packet filter is simply looking at the flag field to see if the SYN bit is the only bit set. Since this is not true, the static packet filter assumes that this data is part of an established session and lets it pass through.

Our dynamic packet filter is doing the same check, but it also created a state table entry when the connection was first established. Every time the remote server tries to respond to the protected host, the state table is referenced to insure the following:

- The protected host actually made a data request.

- The source port information matches the data request.

- The destination port information matches the data request.

In addition, the dynamic packet filter may even verify that the sequence and acknowledgment numbers all match. If all this data is correct, the dynamic packet filter also allows the packets to pass. Once the FIN packets are sent by each system, the state table entry will be removed. Additionally, if no reply is received for a period of time (anywhere from one minute to one hour, depending on the configuration), the firewall will assume that the remote server is no longer responding and will again delete the state table entry. This keeps the state table current.

Now let's say that Woolly Attacker notices this data stream and decides to attack the protected host. The first thing he tries is a port scan on the protected system to see if it has any listening services. As you can see in Figure 5.8, this scan is blocked by both firewall devices, because the initial scanning packets have the SYN bit set and all other bits turned off.

Not to be put off, Woolly Attacker attempts to perform a FIN scan by transmitting packets with the ACK and FIN bits set to 1. Now the results are a bit different. Since the packet filter is simply looking for the SYN bit being set to 1, it happily passes this traffic along, as this condition has not been met.

Our dynamic packet filter, however, is a bit more fussy. It recognizes that the SYN bit is not set and proceeds to compare this traffic to the state table. At this point, it realizes that our protected host has never set up a communication session with Woolly Attacker. There is no legitimate reason that Woolly Attacker should be trying to end a session if our protected host never created one in the first place. For this reason, the traffic would be blocked. This is shown in Figure 5.9.

FIGURE 5.8:

Both filtering methods can block a port scan.

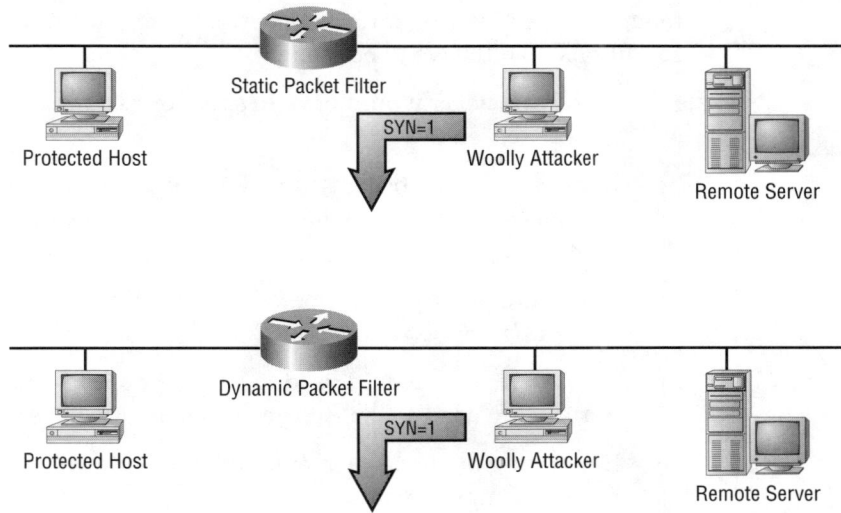

FIGURE 5.9:

The effects of performing a FIN scan

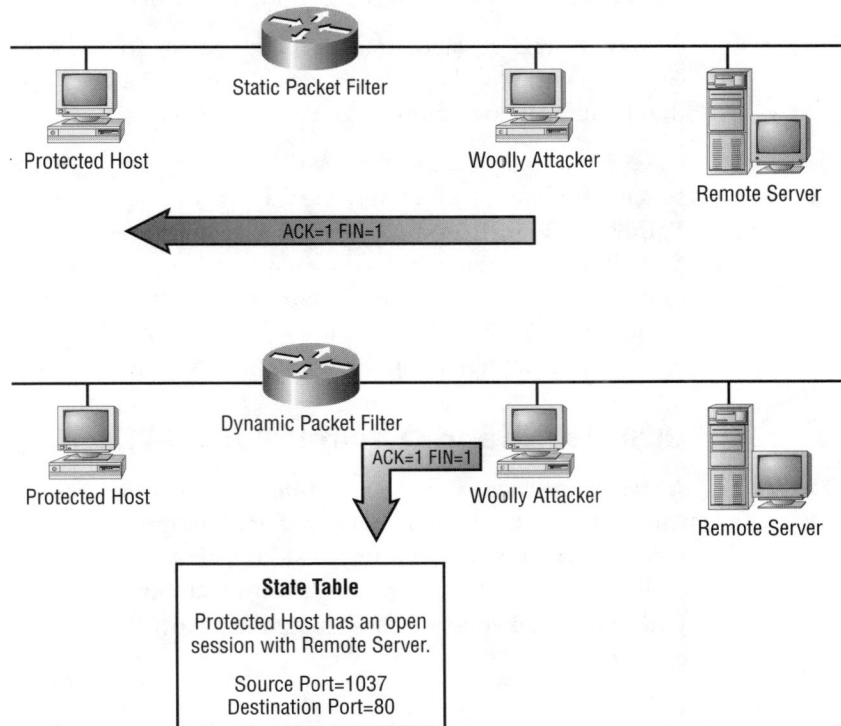

So what if Woolly Attacker tries to spoof the firewall by pretending to be the remote server? In order for him to perform this attack successfully, a number of conditions would have to be met:

- Woolly Attacker would have to spoof or assume the IP address of the remote server.

- If the address has been assumed, Woolly Attacker might have to take further measures to insure that the remote server cannot respond to requests on its own.

- If the address has been spoofed, Woolly Attacker would need some method of reading replies off the wire.

- Woolly Attacker would need to know the source and destination service ports being used so that his traffic will match the entries in the state table.

- Depending on the implementation, the acknowledgment and sequence numbers might have to match, as well.

- Woolly Attacker would have to manipulate the communication session fast enough to avoid timeouts, both on the firewall and on the protected host.

So while it is possible to launch this type of attack, it is not very easy to succeed. Clearly, Woolly Attacker would have to be very knowledgeable and feel that he has much to gain by going to all this effort.

Keep in mind that this discussion is theory only. Your actual mileage with a specific firewall product may vary. For example, at the time of this writing, Check Point's FireWall-1 product (which is a dynamic packet filter) has a touted feature that allows the state table to be maintained even after a rule set change. Unfortunately, this feature also means that state is not always maintained as effectively as it should be. In the FIN scan attack just described, Check Point's FireWall-1 would have passed along the scan packets, as well.

UDP Traffic and Dynamic Packet Filtering

As you have seen, static packet filtering has some real problems handling UDP traffic. This is because the UDP header has zero information regarding connection state. This is where dynamic packet filtering can be extremely useful, as the firewall itself is able to remember state information. It does not rely on information within the packet header but maintains its own tables regarding the state of all sessions.

TIP It is strongly advised that dynamic packet filtering be used instead of static filtering when UDP traffic must be allowed through. The addition of state table information makes this firewall method far more secure with no loss in service.

Is My Transport Supported?

The implementation of dynamic packet filtering is *transport specific*. That means it has to be specifically implemented for each protocol transport, such as TCP, UDP, and ICMP. When choosing a dynamic packet filter, make sure that the firewall is capable of maintaining state for all transports that you wish to use.

For example, with version 1.*x* of FireWall-1, state was only maintained with UDP traffic. While it is true that this is where such traffic control was most needed, TCP and ICMP were regulated in the same manner as a static packet filter. It was not until version 2.*x* that state was maintained for TCP traffic, as well.

Dynamic Packet Filter Summary

Dynamic packet filters are intelligent devices that make traffic-control decisions based on packet attributes and state tables. State tables enable the firewall device to "remember" previous communication packet exchanges and make judgments based on this additional information.

The biggest limitation of a dynamic packet filter is that it cannot make filtering decisions based upon payload, which is the actual data contained within the packet. In order to filter on payload, you must use a proxy-based firewall.

Stateful Filtering

Stateful filtering improves upon the power of dynamic packet filtering. First implemented by Check Point under the name "Stateful Multilevel Inspection," stateful rules are protocol-specific, keeping track of the context of a session (not just its state). This allows filtering rules to differentiate between the various connectionless protocols (like UDP, NFS, and RPC), which—because of their connectionless nature—were previously immune to management by static filtering and were not uniquely identified by dynamic filtering.

The greatest addition that stateful filtering provides to dynamic filtering is the ability to maintain application state, not just connection state. Application state allows a previously authenticated user to create new connections without reauthorizing, whereas connection state just maintains that authorization for the duration of a single session.

An example of this would be a firewall that allows internal access based on per-user authentication. If an authenticated user attempts to open another browser, dynamic filtering router would prompt the user for his password. Stateful filtering, however, would recognize that a pre-existing (and concurrent) connection is being maintained with that same machine, and would automatically authorize the additional session.

Proxies

A *proxy server* (sometimes referred to as an *application gateway* or *forwarder*) is an application that mediates traffic between two network segments. Proxies are often used instead of filtering to prevent traffic from passing directly between networks. With the proxy acting as mediator, the source and destination systems never actually "connect" with each other. The proxy plays middleman in all connection attempts.

How a Proxy Passes Traffic

Unlike its packet-filtering counterparts, a proxy does not route any traffic. In fact, a properly configured proxy will have all routing functionality disabled. As its name implies, the proxy stands in or speaks for each system on each side of the firewall.

For an analogy, think of two people speaking through a language interpreter. While it is true these two people are carrying on a conversation, they never actually speak to one another. All communication passes through the interpreter before being passed on to the other party. The interpreter might have to clean up some of the language used, or filter out comments or statements that might seem hostile.

To see how this relates to network communications, refer to Figure 5.10. Our internal host wishes to request a Web page from the remote server. It formulates the request and transmits the information to the gateway leading to the remote network, which in this case is the proxy server.

Once the proxy receives the request, it identifies what type of service the internal host is trying to access. Since in this case the host has requested a Web page, the proxy passes the request to a special application used only for processing HTTP sessions. This application is simply a program running in memory that has the sole function of dealing with HTTP communications.

A proxy mediating a communication session

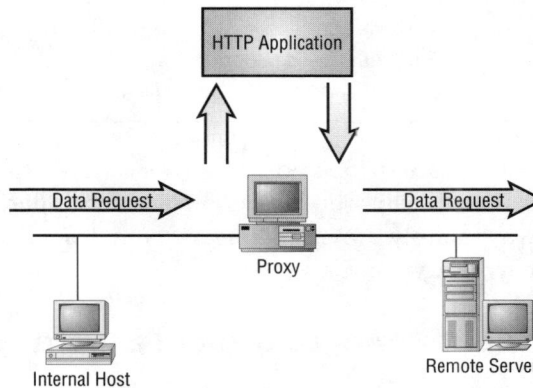

When the HTTP application receives the request, it verifies that the ACL allows this type of traffic. If the traffic is acceptable, the proxy formulates a new request to the remote server—only it uses itself as the source system. In other words, the proxy does not simply pass the request along; it generates a new request for the remote information.

This new request is then sent to the remote server. If the request were checked with a network analyzer, it would look like the proxy had made the HTTP request, not the Internal host. For this reason, when the remote server responds, it responds to the proxy server.

Once the proxy server receives the reply, it again passes the response up to the HTTP application. The HTTP application then scrutinizes the actual data sent by the remote server for abnormalities. If the data is acceptable, the HTTP application creates a new packet and forwards the information to the internal host.

As you can see, the two end systems never actually exchange information directly. The proxy constantly butts into the conversation to make sure that all goes securely.

Since proxies must "understand" the application protocol being utilized, they can also implement protocol-specific security. For example, an inbound FTP proxy can be configured to filter out all put and mput requests received by an external system. This could be used to create a read-only FTP server: people outside the firewall would be unable to send the FTP server the commands required to initiate a file write. They could, however, perform a file get, which would allow them to receive files from the FTP server.

TIP Proxy servers are application specific. In order to support a new protocol via a proxy, a proxy must be developed for that protocol. If you select a proxy firewall, make sure that it supports all the applications you wish to use.

There are stripped-down proxies know as *plug gateways*. These are not true proxies because they do not understand the application they are supporting. Plug gateways simply provide connectivity for a specific service port and offer little benefit beyond dynamic filtering.

Client Configuration in a Proxy Environment

Some proxy servers require all internal hosts to run connection software such as SOCKS or a modified winsock.dll file. Each of these programs serves a single function: to forward all non-local traffic to the proxy. Depending on the environment, this can be extremely beneficial or a complete pain in the rear quarter.

Benefits of a Proxy Client

There are a number of benefits to running proxy client software. The first is ease of configuration. Since the client is designed to forward all non-local data requests to the proxy, the only required configuration information is a valid IP address and subnet mask. Router and DNS parameters can be ignored, because this information only needs to be configured on the proxy.

In fact, many proxies do not even require that you use IP as a protocol. For example, Microsoft Proxy Server 2.0 ships with a replacement winsock.dll file, which allows IPX to be used on the local workstations. Once the traffic reaches the proxy, it is translated to IP and forwarded to the remote server. For an environment that is predominantly IPX-based, this can be a very simple solution that avoids running additional protocols on the network.

Proxy clients can also offer transparent authentication in order to validate outbound connection attempts based on logon name and password. For example, Novell's BorderManager integrates with NetWare Directory Services (NDS) to transparently authenticate users as they access the Internet. As long as a user is authenticated to NDS, that user is not prompted for a password when accessing Internet resources.

NOTE

User authentication of outbound sessions is used for ncreased logging and management. If authentication is not used, a firewall must rely on the source IP address to identify who has accessed which Internet resources. This can be a problem; all a user has to do in order to change her identity is change her IP address. This can be a serious problem in a DHCP or bootp environment if you wish to track all of your users.

Drawbacks to a Proxy Client

Unfortunately, there are a number of drawbacks to using a proxy client. The first is deployment. If you have 1,000 machines that will need to use the proxy server, plan on loading additional software on each of these machines. Software compatibility may also be a problem; some applications may not be compatible with the replacement winsock.dll file. For example, many Winsock replacements are still written to the 1.*x* specification, although there are now applications that require Winsock 2.*x*.

And what if many of your desktop machines do not run Windows? Many proxies do not provide client software for any operating system other than Windows. In this case, you have to be sure that all IP applications you wish to use are SOCKS compliant. While there are SOCKS versions of many IP applications such as telnet and FTP, it's all too often the case that a favorite application is not SOCKS compliant.

Client software can also be a problem for mobile or laptop users. For example, let's say you are a laptop user who connects to the local network during the day and dials in to your Internet Service Provider (ISP) in the evening. In this case, you would have to make sure that your proxy client is enabled during the day, but disabled at night. Not exactly the type of procedure you'd want to have your pointy-haired boss performing on a daily basis.

Finally, a proxy client can be a real problem if you have multiple network segments. This is because the proxy client expects to forward all non-local traffic to the proxy server—not a good solution if you have a large network environment with many subnets. While some configurations do allow you to exempt certain subnets from being forwarded to the proxy, this typically involves modifying a text file stored on the local workstation. Again, if you administer 1,000 desktop machines, plan on putting in quite a few long nights just to update all your desktop machines regarding a subnet address change.

Transparent Proxies

Not all proxies require special client software. Some can operate as a *transparent proxy*, which means that all internal hosts are configured as though the proxy were a regular router leading to the Internet. As the proxy receives traffic, it processes the traffic in a fashion similar to our example in Figure 5.10.

If you decide that a proxy firewall is the best fit for your security requirements, make sure you also decide whether you wish to use a transparent or a non-transparent proxy. The marketing material for many proxy packages can be a bit vague about whether the package requires special client software. Typically, if a product claims to support SOCKS, it is not a transparent proxy. Make sure you know the requirements before investing in a firewall solution.

Filtering Java, ActiveX, and HTML Scripts

As you have seen, proxies can analyze the payload of a packet of data and make decisions as to whether this packet should be passed or dropped. This is a powerful feature, that gives the administrator far more ability to scrutinize what type of data should be allowed into the network. When it comes to content filtering, the first thing most people think about is Java and ActiveX.

Java is a *portable* programming language. Portable means it is designed to be run on any network operating system. Typically, Java support is accomplished through the use of a Java-aware Web browser. Java programs are referred to as *applets*.

ActiveX is a specialized implementation of a Microsoft Object Linking and Embedding (OLE) or Component Object Model (COM) object. With ActiveX, you create a self-sufficient program known as an *ActiveX control*. The benefit to an ActiveX control is that it can be shared across multiple applications. ActiveX is not a programming language. ActiveX controls are created using some other programming language such as C++, PowerBuilder, Visual Basic, or even Microsoft Java.

Java applets and ActiveX controls can be pulled down from a server and run on any compatible Web browser. Functionality for these programs can include anything from dancing icons to shared applications. There are few limits to the types of programs that can be created.

This is where our problems begin. While both Java and ActiveX were developed with security in mind (Java probably more so than ActiveX), quite a few exploits have been discovered in both.

> **NOTE**
>
> To have a look at the kinds of exploits that can be performed, point your Web browser at **www.digicrime.com**. This site contains a number of Java and ActiveX exploits that show just how malicious these programs can be in the wrong hands.

Now that you know why using Java and ActiveX can be a bad thing, the question is, what can you do about it? Many proxy firewalls provide the ability to filter out some or all Java and ActiveX programming code. This allows your users to continue accessing remote Web sites—without fear of running a malicious application.

For example, FireWall-1 includes proxy applications that are referred to as security servers. *Security servers* give the firewall administrator the ability to identify certain program codes that he wishes to filter out. Figure 5.11 shows the URI dialog box that allows the FireWall-1 administrator to pick and choose the types of code he wants to filter out.

FIGURE 5.11:

The URI Definition dialog box allows you to filter programming code.

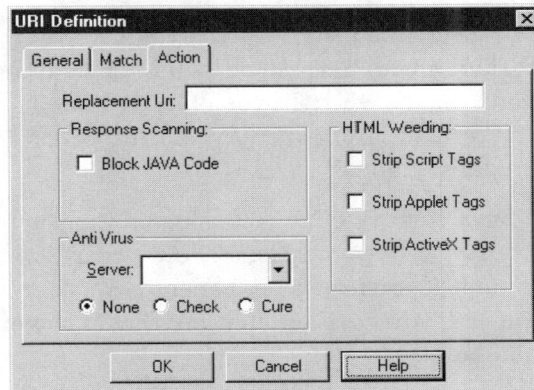

The HTML Weeding check boxes allow the administrator to filter out all tag references to Java scripts, Java applets, or even ActiveX controls. The Block JAVA Code check box causes the firewall to filter out any and all Java programming code. The combination of these options provides some flexibility in determining what types of data are allowed to reach your internal Web browsers.

NOTE   Enabling these features blocks both good and bad code, without distinguishing between the two. In other words, your choices are all or nothing. There are, however, proxies that can selectively filter out only "known to be malicious" programming code. While this allows some Java and/or ActiveX to be passed through the proxy, it does so at a reduced level of security. These proxies can only filter out *known* problems; they cannot help with exploits that have yet to be discovered. Unless you stay on top of the latest exploits, you may still end up letting some malicious code past your firewall.

What Type of Firewall Should I Use?

This section title asks a completely loaded question. Post this question to any firewall discussion list, and you are guaranteed to start a flame war. (For real fun, follow this question up with "Should I run my firewall on Macintosh, UNIX, Linux, NT, Windows 2000 or a vendor-specific platform?")

There are no clear-cut absolutes for choosing a particular type of firewall solution. Anyone who tells you otherwise has a product to push. Cost, business need, and security requirements should all be considered when you are looking for a proper solution.

Since static filtering is considered weak, it is the lowest level of perimeter security. It is also the most basic, however, as static filtering ability is built into most routers. If you have a permanent WAN connection, chances are you are using a router. If you have a router, you should be performing static packet filtering as a minimum.

Dynamic Filtering or Proxy?

Each of these firewalls has its strengths and weaknesses. Dynamic filtering is typically easier to work with than a proxy and has a better ability to meet most business needs, but it is not quite as competent at screening traffic as a proxy server may be. While both a dynamic packet filter and a proxy will block traffic known to be bad, each can act a little differently in the face of dubious traffic.

For example, let's say you have two firewalls: a dynamic packet filter and a proxy. Each receives a packet of data that has the high-priority flag set for a certain application, and neither has been programmed as to how to handle this type of data. Typically (but not always), the dynamic packet filter would pass questionable traffic, while the proxy would drop it. In addition, since the proxy is application aware, it could further check the contents of the actual data, while the dynamic packet filter could not. Again, this is theoretical comparison between two forms of perimeter protection. Your actual mileage may vary, depending on the specific product you choose.

Proxies tend to be a bit more secure, but it can be more difficult to get them to fit a particular business need. For example, many proxies have trouble supporting modern services such as Microsoft's NetMeeting or Real Audio and Video. So while the level of perimeter security is higher, this is of little comfort if a proxy is unable to meet the business requirements of the organization it is protecting.

The most secure perimeter security device is a pair of wire cutters. Since few organizations are willing to use this security device, and want Internet connectivity, some level of risk must be assumed. A proper firewall selection meets all the business needs of connectivity while employing the highest level of security possible. Additionally, a good firewall product will incorporate both dynamic packet filtering and proxy technology in order to provide the highest level of security and flexibility.

Which Platform Should I Choose?

This topic has been the subject of many a religious war. Search the archives of any firewall mailing list and you will find volumes on this specific topic. Just like a religious belief system, the selection of a proper firewall platform is a personal decision that you should make only after proper investigation.

This section is not going to tell you which platform to choose; it will simply point out some of the strengths and weaknesses of each platform and leave the final decision up to you. Just like choosing a proper firewall product, choosing the operating system to run it on is clearly not a one-size-fits-all prospect.

One primary distinction that exists is between server-based and appliance-based firewalls. A *server-based firewall* is an application that runs on top of an operating system. An example is Check Point's Firewall-1, which runs on Windows NT and 2000. An *appliance-based firewall*, or *integrated solution*, is a firewall application that runs on proprietary hardware and software. For example, the

Cisco PIX firewall is an example of an integrated device in which the entire system is not capable of being anything other than a firewall, and does not include a hard drive or other traditional components of a server. Because of its integrated and proprietary nature, these boxes are traditionally faster, more robust, and considered more secure than server-based firewalls. Server-based firewalls, on the other hand, often provide additional configuration and support options, and can be cheaper than the integrated solutions.

Server-Based Firewalls

Server-based firewalls are applications that run on top of an operating system. Firewalls exist for the following platforms:

- Macintosh
- Unix
- Linux
- Microsoft Windows NT
- Microsoft Windows 2000

Macintosh

As unlikely a choice as this might seem to most system administrators, there are firewall products designed for the Macintosh operating system. And although some system administrators might scoff at the idea, there are impressive examples of secure Mac-based Internet systems—including the United States Army, which has been hosting its Web site on a WebSTAR server running the Macintosh OS since the early part of 1999, and that server hasn't been successfully hacked since.

However, the Macintosh operating system is undergoing a radical change, which will culminate in 2001 with the release of the consumer version of OS X (10). OS X is based on the NeXTStep operating system, which itself is based on the Mach kernel and BSD (Berkeley Software Distribution of UNIX). Even though Apple has released the source code of OS X, it has made significant changes to the kernel to adapt it to the Macintosh platform. It has yet to be seen how these changes (along with Apple-specific implementations of DNS and HTTP) will affect the security as whole.

Macintosh Strengths   So what distinguishes the Macintosh as an operating system from other notable server OSs? There is a widespread belief that running a firewall on a Mac will be inherently more secure simply because most hackers are unfamiliar with Mac technology. And while there are some reported vulnerabilities in applications that run on the Mac, very few reports exists about weaknesses of the operating system itself.

There is also the ease of configuration. Because the Macintosh is GUI-only and offers few network services (beyond basic file and print), complexity (the bane of any security system) is greatly reduced.

Finally, a firewall running on the new OS X will see benefits of performance (from a cutting-edge UNIX-based operating system), configuration (each specific service can be turned on or off at will), and support tools (most UNIX-based security support utilities will run on OS X).

Macintosh Weaknesses   There are some significant weaknesses that are actually the flip side of the Macintosh's strengths. Because the system is not well known, the possibility exists that many vulnerabilities are waiting to be discovered by any hacker who might make a serious attempt to penetrate it.

Also, because a Macintosh server has only a limited number of configuration and application choices, administrators may feel that they miss extras—like the ability to highly customize the components on their server.

And although there are firewall products for the Macintosh, most of these are designed to be personal firewalls, not to function as servers to protect an entire network. This, coupled with the lack of many supportive tools for firewalls (such as Macintosh-based analysis and response tools), significantly limits the flexibility of a Macintosh-based firewall.

There is also the issue of performance. Although in recent years Apple hardware has seen very impressive performance, the operating system has not followed suit. As a result, a very busy Macintosh server acting as a firewall and router can potentially become overwhelmed.

Furthermore, OS X will introduce some new weaknesses. Because of its UNIX heritage, the greatest initial security risks on OS X come from the daemons (services) that are installed by default—something that we'll cover more in depth in talking about UNIX (below).

UNIX

UNIX has been around far longer than other operating systems, including Microsoft Windows NT (and NT-based operating systems like Windows 2000), and the first firewalls were designed on Unix systems. This means that the idiosyncrasies of the platform are well understood and documented, and the firewall products that run on it are stable. Although most versions of Unix are sold commercially (such as Sun's Solaris, HP's HP-UX, and IBM's AIX), it is still considered a fairly open system because so much is known about its fundamental structure and services. When security weaknesses are discovered with Unix, they tend not to be with the core operating system, but with services and applications running on top of it.

Unix also has the benefit of outperforming other operating systems. This, combined with the many hardware platforms and configurations that support Unix, makes it a preferred operating system for intensive and large data operations. Good firewall practice dictates that all applications and components not essential to the operation of the firewall are disabled, and this is particularly easy to accomplish in UNIX.

UNIX Strengths   Specific strengths of UNIX are many. It is highly configurable, well understood by many in the security industry, and is the most prominent operating system in existence. Many resources are dedicated to understanding and fixing any security issues that might arise.

UNIX is also considered to be a very stable high-performing operating system. In addition because of its ability to run on multiple hardware platforms (such as the DEC Alpha and the IBM RS/6000), and on multiple-processor versions of these platforms, it can support high data rates required of any firewall supporting a large network. It is also relatively immune from the need to reboot the machine after configuration changes, something that has afflicted Windows NT-based systems.

There are more security and security support products for UNIX than for any other platform (although Windows NT is a close second). This, coupled with its 30-year history, has made UNIX the preferred choice for many large organizations.

UNIX Weaknesses   So what are the negatives? Problems arise when inexperienced Unix administrators place firewalls on "out of the box" installations and don't disable the many vulnerable (but potentially valuable on a non-firewall system) programs and services (*daemons*) that are enabled by default. And because many of these daemons are configured to run in the security context of the root (the all-powerful superuser account) they provide an attacker with complete access to the system once they have exploited vulnerable system components.

Deactivating daemons is relatively simple. Administrators simply remove or rename the scripts that activate the respective daemon at boot time, or comment out the line in the `inetd.conf` configuration file, if the daemon is called by `inetd`. (See the following view of an `inetd.conf` configuration file.)

```
# These are standard services.
#
ftp     stream  tcp     nowait  root    /usr/sbin/tcpd  in.ftpd -l -a
telnet  stream  tcp     nowait  root    /usr/sbin/tcpd  in.telnetd
gopher  stream  tcp     nowait  root    /usr/sbin/tcpd  gn
#smtp   stream  tcp     nowait  root    /usr/bin/smtpd  smtpd
#nntp   stream  tcp     nowait  root    /usr/sbin/tcpd  in.nntpd
#
# Shell, login, exec and talk are BSD protocols.
#
shell   stream  tcp     nowait  root    /usr/sbin/tcpd  in.rshd
login   stream  tcp     nowait  root    /usr/sbin/tcpd  in.rlogind
#exec   stream  tcp     nowait  root    /usr/sbin/tcpd  in.rexecd
talk    dgram   udp     wait    root    /usr/sbin/tcpd  in.talkd
ntalk   dgram   udp     wait    root    /usr/sbin/tcpd  in.ntalkd
#dtalk  stream  tcp     waut    nobody  /usr/sbin/tcpd  in.dtalkd
#
# Pop and imap mail services et al
#
pop-2   stream  tcp     nowait  root    /usr/sbin/tcpd  ipop2d
pop-3   stream  tcp     nowait  root    /usr/sbin/tcpd  ipop3d
imap    stream  tcp     nowait  root    /usr/sbin/tcpd  imapd
#
# Tftp service is provided primarily for booting.  Most sites
# run this only on machines acting as "boot servers." Do not uncomment
# this unless you *need* it.
#
#tftp   dgram   udp     wait    root    /usr/sbin/tcpd  in.tftpd
#bootps dgram   udp     wait    root    /usr/sbin/tcpd  bootpd
#
# Finger, systat and netstat give out user information which may be
# valuable to potential "system crackers."  Many sites choose to
disable
# some or all of these services to improve security.
#
# cfinger is for GNU finger, which is currently not in use in RHS Linux
#
finger   stream  tcp     nowait  root    /usr/sbin/tcpd  in.fingerd
#cfinger stream  tcp     nowait  root    /usr/sbin/tcpd  in.cfingerd
#systat  stream  tcp     nowait  guest   /usr/sbin/tcpd  /bin/ps -auwwx
#netstat stream  tcp     nowait  guest   /usr/sbin/tcpd  /bin/netstat -f
inet
#
```

```
# Time service is used for clock synchronization.
#
time    stream  tcp     nowait  nobody  /usr/sbin/tcpd  in.timed
time    dgram   udp     wait    nobody  /usr/sbin/tcpd  in.timed
#
# Authentication
#
auth    stream  tcp     nowait    nobody /usr/sbin/in.identd in.identd
-l -e -o
#
# End of inetd.conf
```

More weaknesses are exploited in Unix on a weekly basis than on any other operating system. As an example, CERT (the Computer Emergency Response Team at Carnegie Mellon) reported on September 15, 2000 that hackers were using two common vulnerabilities to conduct widespread attacks. The first vulnerability is with the rpc.statd daemon that is used to support NFS (Network File System). The second is with wu-ftpd, an ftp server package provided by Washington University. Because these services are installed and activated on most UNIX (and Linux) systems by default, administrators who install firewalls on default installations are leaving their entire network vulnerable.

Unix is considered to be a more difficult system to learn and administer, and the cost of a Unix system has traditionally been more expensive than other operating systems. And because there are so many documented weaknesses with Unix, an administrator has to invest more time in securing the system; otherwise an attacker with access to the same information on Unix vulnerabilities can take advantage of "so many holes."

OpenBSD: An exception to the UNIX rule   One UNIX variation that minimizes the risk of pre-installed vulnerable daemons is OpenBSD. OpenBSD installs with no accessibility; the administrator is forced to manually choose which services and components will run.

Created and maintained by volunteers and distributed for free, OpenBSD is sometimes confused with Linux. In fact, it is a very tightly controlled collaborative UNIX project with specific goals. While weaknesses can still be found, the response time to correct those weaknesses is considered the best in the industry. That, coupled with a proactive attitude toward locating and correcting software errors, makes OpenBSD a compelling choice for many firewall administrators.

Linux

What about Linux, the most significant challenger in the operating system wars in recent memory? Linux shares many of the strengths and weaknesses of UNIX.

Linux Strengths   Like Unix, the Linux platform is highly configurable, stable, well-understood, and has many available security related products. The greatest attraction to Linux, however, is its open nature. In fact, Linux is more open than OpenBSD, and many in the security industry favor this principle of exposing source code to as many eyes as possible in the search for errors and vulnerabilities. And the communal nature of the Linux community means a ready and willing support group for security specialists with concerns and questions.

Linux Weaknesses   The factors that weigh against Linux are that it's difficult to learn and has many known vulnerabilities.

Microsoft Windows NT

In contrast to Linux, Microsoft brings the power of familiarity. As Cervantes observed in *Don Quixote*, however, familiarity breeds contempt, and that's true of Microsoft Windows NT and Windows 2000.

NT Strengths   Since Windows NT is an extension of the Windows Desktop environment (by far the most popular operating system ever produced), NT is a far more familiar environment to the typical end user. This means that the user is not forced to learn a completely new environment just to run firewall software. Even more important, a company is not required to hire additional resources just to manage its firewall.

In fact, NT-based systems have traditionally been less expensive than their UNIX counterparts, and the fact that the investment in hardware and software (let alone expertise) is usually less for an NT-based system must be taken into account.

It is argued that familiarity augments security. Since people are familiar with NT, they are less likely to configure the platform incorrectly and cause a security problem. While it may or may not be true that UNIX can be configured to be a more secure environment, certainly a secure environment can never be achieved if a user does not understand how to properly manage it.

Finally, the argument can be made for consistency. Since many organizations run NT for file, print, and application services, it makes sense to standardize on this one platform for all required services. This makes administration easier and more harmonious. It also helps to reduce or abolish compatibility problems.

NT Weaknesses   The greatest weakness attributed to NT is one of perception—that Microsoft is slow and reluctant to admit and correct security weaknesses. While there has been an incident where a third party has discovered a weakness, privately notified Microsoft, and then notified the public because they waited for over a month for Microsoft to announce a patch, there is no evidence that this is a pattern. And while significant vulnerabilities have been discovered, they have, for the most part, been limited to services that are not pre-installed on NT and would not be placed on a firewall system (like IIS—Microsoft's Web server).

Because of the proprietary nature of NT, not much is known about the internal workings of the services, and they are not configurable to the same degree as UNIX daemons. This might also provide some uncertainty for security specialists who are looking for the most secure platform with which to run their firewall.

Other negatives include the need to reboot NT servers after configuration changes (or even after several days or weeks of operation due to system instability), and purchase and licensing fees associated with an NT server.

Windows 2000

How does Windows 2000 compare to Windows NT? Windows 2000 shares many common weaknesses with Windows NT, including its proprietary nature, the perceived reluctance on the part of Microsoft to admit (and remedy) vulnerabilities, and the significant costs associated with using a Windows product. Like NT, Windows 2000 also has the strength of user familiarity and consistency throughout the network.

Windows 2000 does have some unique strengths that distinguish it from NT. First is the ability to make configuration changes without needing to restart the server. Second is the increased stability of the server, which lengthens its uptime (and therefore, increases reliability).

Many experts believe that it is too early to determine how secure W2K is compared to NT, and that more time is necessary to expose potential errors and vulnerabilities. Some weaknesses unique to W2K have already been discovered and patched—such as the vulnerability in the Telnet Service that would allow a hacker to take full control of an administrative telnet session, leaving the entire server (and potentially the entire network) exposed and at risk.

Appliance-Based Firewalls

Also called *integrated solutions*, appliance-based firewalls run on proprietary hardware and software, and usually consist of a physically small box with network connections and a power source. Appliance-based firewalls include

- Cisco Pix

- Check Point VPN-1

- eSoft Interceptor

- Progressive Systems Phoenix Adaptive Firewall

- SonicWALL PRO

- WatchGuard LiveSecurity System 4.1

Integrated firewalls provide an all-in-one solution, with the vendor supplying the hardware, software, and operating system. Integrated solutions are quite popular, especially for small businesses that do not have a full-time IT staff and require basic firewall functionality without the need for advanced customization. Larger businesses also rely on more expensive, higher-end integrated firewalls to handle the extreme traffic flow generated by having many computers that require protected access to the Internet, or e-commerce sites that have millions of visitors a day.

Appliance Strengths

The greatest benefit of integrated solutions is their short configuration time. Many firewalls are pre-configured to protect your network literally out of the box. Simply by connecting the Internet into one port, and your internal network into another, the device begins to immediately filter network traffic. Small businesses benefit from this simplicity, especially when they do not have a full-time or experienced IT staff. If configuration is required, administration can be done from a simple Web browser or from the installation of a proprietary administrative utility.

Performance is the other benefit most often cited by large corporations who purchase integrated firewalls. Because these firewalls use programmable hardware (also called *firmware*), they can operate at much higher speeds than those firewalls that have an extra layer of operating system and hardware, (both of which are designed to do general computing tasks, and have not been optimized for firewall tasks).

This focus on dedicated design also has the potential of reducing firewall costs, since there is no requirement to purchase an operating system and licenses in addition to the firewall application; everything is included in a tightly integrated package by the vendor. This monolithic approach (where everything is controlled, designed, and supported by vendor) can actually increase security by minimizing the number of hands in the pie. And simplicity (having one vendor produce everything) is considered the Holy Grail of any security system.

Appliance Weaknesses

On the other hand, such a monolithic approach to a firewall might limit the flexibility of a product or the ability to upgrade the underlying hardware (such as installing more RAM as desired in a server-based firewall). Appliances also limit an organization to one vendor for their entire security system, as opposed to using a modular system that could encourage "best of breed" for all components—the best operating system tied to the best firewall which feeds into the best analysis system, with all three coming from different vendors.

Appliances have also been known to be more expensive than simple software solutions, and depending on the level of complexity needed by your organization, you might be better served by going with a traditional software firewall.

Additional Firewall Considerations

No matter what type of firewall you choose, there are some potential features that you should analyze closely before selecting a specific firewall product. These features are common to all types of firewalls, so we will review them here in a two-part summary.

- Firewall Functionality
  - Address translation
  - Firewall logging and analysis
  - VPNs

- Management

  - Intrusion Detection and Response

  - Integration and deployment

  - Authentication/Access Control/LDAP

  - Third-party tools

We will examine each of these features and the issues you need to consider when choosing a firewall product.

Address Translation

Address translation is considered a basic firewall function. Don't trust a firewall product that doesn't include this option. When an IP address is converted from one value to another, it is called *address translation*. This feature has been implemented in most firewall products and is typically used when you do not wish to let remote systems know the true IP address of your internal systems. Figure 5.12 shows the typical deployment of this configuration.

FIGURE 5.12:

Address translation

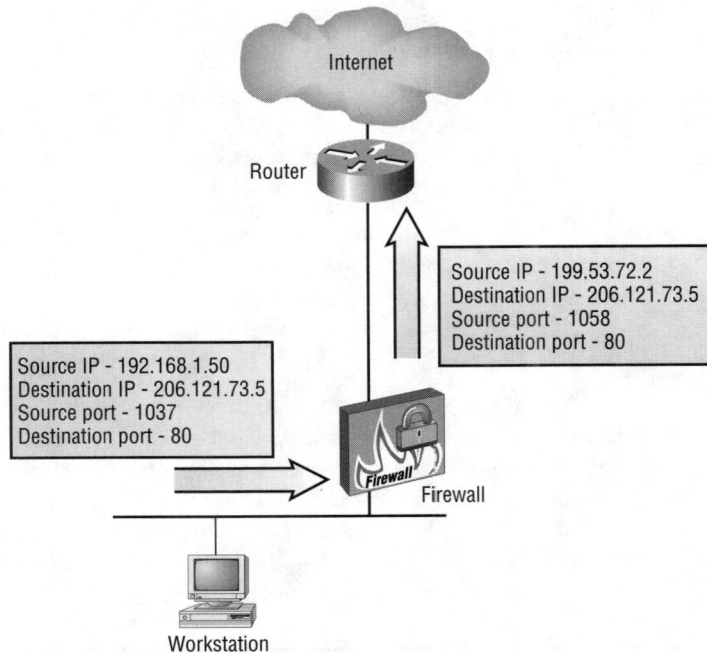

Internet

Router

Source IP - 199.53.72.2
Destination IP - 206.121.73.5
Source port - 1058
Destination port - 80

Source IP - 192.168.1.50
Destination IP - 206.121.73.5
Source port - 1037
Destination port - 80

Firewall

Workstation

Our internal workstation wishes to access an external Web site. It formulates a request and delivers the information to its default gateway, which in this case is the firewall. The desktop system has one minor problem, though: the subnet on which it is located is using private addressing.

Private addressing is the use of IP subnet ranges that can be used by any organization when addressing its internal hosts. This is allowable because these ranges are not permitted to be routed on the Internet. While this means we can use these addresses without fear of conflict, it also means that any request we send out to a remote system will not know which route to take in order to reply. These ranges are

- 10.0.0.0–10.255.255.255

- 172.16.0.0–172.32.255.255

- 192.168.0.0–192.168.255.255

It's All in the Port Numbers

How does the firewall distinguish between replies that are coming back to this workstation and traffic that is destined for other systems or for the firewall itself? If the firewall is translating the address of all desktop machines to match the address of its own interface, how does it tell the difference between different sessions?

Look closely at the two packet headers in Figure 5.12 and you will see that one other value has been changed. Along with the source IP address, the firewall has also changed the source port number. This port number is used to identify which replies go to which system.

Remember that the source port is typically a value dynamically assigned by the transmitting system. This means that any value above 1023 is considered acceptable. There should be no problems with having the firewall change this value for accounting purposes. In the same way that the source port number can be used between systems to distinguish between multiple communication sessions, the firewall can use this source port number to keep track of which replies need to be returned to each of our internal systems.

Our firewall will modify the IP header information on the way out and transmit the packet to its final destination. On the way back, our firewall will again need to modify the IP header in order to forward the data to the internal system. In the reply packet, it will be the destination IP address and service port that will need to be changed. This is because the remote server will have replied to the IP address and source port specified by the firewall. The firewall needs to replace these values with the ones used by the desktop workstation before passing along the information.

So while our workstation could reach the remote server, the remote server would not be able to reply. This is where address translation is useful: we can map the IP address of the workstation to some other legal IP address. In the case of Figure 5.12, we have translated the desktop's IP address of 192.168.1.50 to the same legal address used by the external interface of the firewall, which is 199.53.72.2.

There are three ways of deploying address translation:

- Hiding Network Address Translation (hiding NAT)
- Static Network Address Translation (static NAT)
- Port Address Translation (PAT)

The benefits and limitations of each are reviewed in the following sections.

Hiding NAT

Hiding NAT functions exactly as described in Figure 5.12. All internal IP hosts are hidden behind a single IP address. This can be the IP address of the firewall itself or some other legal number. While hiding NAT can theoretically support thousands of concurrent sessions, multiple hiding addresses can be used if you require additional support.

The biggest limitation of hiding NAT is that it does not allow the creation of any inbound sessions. Since all systems are hidden behind a single address, the firewall has no way of determining which internal system the remote session request is destined for. Since there is no mapping to an internal host, all inbound session requests are dropped.

This limitation can actually be considered a feature, as it can help augment your security policy. If your policy states that internal users are not allowed to run their own servers from their internal desktop machines (Web, FTP, and so on), using hiding NAT for all desktop machines is a quick way to insure that these services cannot be directly accessed from outside the firewall.

Static NAT

Static NAT functions similarly to hiding NAT, except that only a single private IP address is mapped to each public IP address used. This is useful if you have an internal system using private IP addresses, but you wish to make this system accessible from the Internet. Since only one internal host is associated with each legal IP address, the firewall has no problem determining where to forward traffic.

For example, let's assume that you have an internal Exchange server and you wish to enable SMTP functionality so that you can exchange mail over the Internet. The Exchange server has an IP address of 172.25.23.13, which is considered private address space. For this reason, the host cannot communicate with hosts located on the Internet.

You now have two choices:

- You can change the address from a private number to a legal number for the entire subnet on which the Exchange server is located.

- You can perform static NAT at the firewall.

Clearly, the second option is far easier to deploy. It would allow internal systems to continue communicating with the Exchange server using its assigned private address, while translating all Internet-based communications to a virtual legal IP address.

Static NAT is also useful for services that will break if hiding NAT is used. For example, some communications between DNS servers require that the source and destination port both be set to port 53. If you use hiding NAT, the firewall would be required to change the source port to some random upper port number, thus breaking the communication session. By using static NAT, the port number does not need to be changed, and the communication sessions can be carried out normally.

TIP

Most NAT devices will allow you to use both static and hiding NAT simultaneously. This allows you to use static NAT on the systems that need it, while hiding the rest.

Port Address Translation (PAT)

Port address translation is utilized by most proxy firewall products. When PAT is used, all outbound traffic is translated to the external IP address used by the firewall, in a way similar to hiding NAT. Unlike hiding NAT, the external address of the firewall must be used. This cannot be set to some other legal value.

The method for dealing with inbound traffic varies from product to product. In some implementations, ports are mapped to specific systems. For example, all SMTP traffic directed at the firewall's external interface (which has a destination port number of 25) is automatically forwarded to a specific internal system. For a small environment, this limitation is rarely a problem. For large environments that operate multiple systems running the same type of server (such as multiple mail or FTP servers), this deficiency can be a major obstacle.

In order to get around this problem, some proxy servers can analyze data content in order to support multiple internal services. For example, a proxy may be able to forward all inbound SMTP mail addressed as `user@eng.bofh.org` to one internal mail system and mail addressed to `user@hr.bofh.org` to another.

If you have multiple internal servers running the same service, make sure your firewall can distinguish between them. I've seen more than one organization that has been bitten by this limitation and has been forced to place servers outside the firewall. This is like walking to work in a blizzard because the shiny new Corvette you just purchased got stuck in a half-inch of snow.

Firewall Logging and Analysis

While a firewall's primary function is to control traffic across a network perimeter, a close second is its ability to document and analyze all the traffic it encounters. Logging is important because it documents who has been crossing your network perimeter—and who has attempted to cross, but failed. Analysis is important because it might not be readily apparent from a casual view of the log which incidents are attempts to actually cross your perimeter, and which are investigations for openings in the "fence" in preparation for a future attack.

What defines a good firewall log? Obviously, this comes down to personal preference. There are, however, a number of features you should consider:

- The log should present all entries in a clear, easy-to-read format.

- You should be able to view all entries in a single log so that you can better identify traffic patterns, although the ability to export the log data to an analysis tool would be of even greater value.

- The log should clearly identify which traffic was blocked and which traffic was allowed to pass.

- Ideally, you should be able to manipulate the log, using filtering and sorting, to focus on specific types of traffic, although this feature is best suited to an analysis tool.

- The log should not overwrite itself or drop entries based upon a specific size limitation.

- You should be able to securely view logs from a remote location.

- The logging software should have some method of exporting the log to at least one common format, such as ASCII text (preferably with some kind of delimiter). This allows the data to be manipulated further within a reporting tool, spreadsheet, or database program.

Kind of a tall order, but all are important features. It is very rare that an attacker will gain access on the very first try. If you schedule time to scrutinize the logs on a regular basis, you may be able to thwart an attack before it even happens. A good logging tool will help.

For example, look at the log viewer shown in Figure 5.13. This is FireWall-1's log viewer, and it does a very good job of fulfilling the criteria we have listed. The log is easy to read, easy to follow, and can even be reviewed remotely from an alternate workstation through a secure session. The Select menu option even lets you select different filtering and sort options.

FIGURE 5.13:

Firewall-1's log viewer

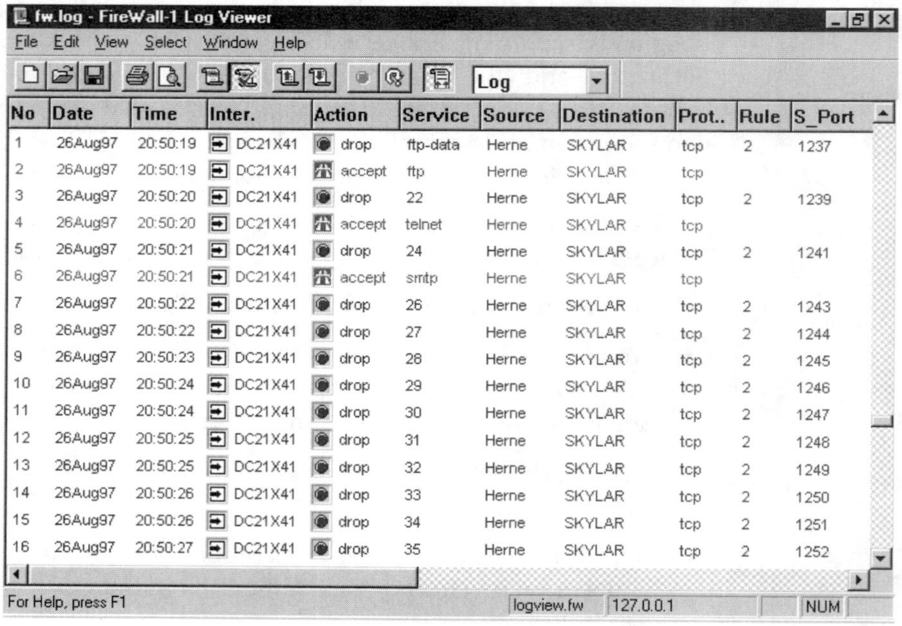

No	Date	Time	Inter.	Action	Service	Source	Destination	Prot..	Rule	S_Port
1	26Aug97	20:50:19	DC21X41	drop	ftp-data	Herne	SKYLAR	tcp	2	1237
2	26Aug97	20:50:19	DC21X41	accept	ftp	Herne	SKYLAR	tcp		
3	26Aug97	20:50:20	DC21X41	drop	22	Herne	SKYLAR	tcp	2	1239
4	26Aug97	20:50:20	DC21X41	accept	telnet	Herne	SKYLAR	tcp		
5	26Aug97	20:50:21	DC21X41	drop	24	Herne	SKYLAR	tcp	2	1241
6	26Aug97	20:50:21	DC21X41	accept	smtp	Herne	SKYLAR	tcp		
7	26Aug97	20:50:22	DC21X41	drop	26	Herne	SKYLAR	tcp	2	1243
8	26Aug97	20:50:22	DC21X41	drop	27	Herne	SKYLAR	tcp	2	1244
9	26Aug97	20:50:23	DC21X41	drop	28	Herne	SKYLAR	tcp	2	1245
10	26Aug97	20:50:24	DC21X41	drop	29	Herne	SKYLAR	tcp	2	1246
11	26Aug97	20:50:24	DC21X41	drop	30	Herne	SKYLAR	tcp	2	1247
12	26Aug97	20:50:25	DC21X41	drop	31	Herne	SKYLAR	tcp	2	1248
13	26Aug97	20:50:25	DC21X41	drop	32	Herne	SKYLAR	tcp	2	1249
14	26Aug97	20:50:26	DC21X41	drop	33	Herne	SKYLAR	tcp	2	1250
15	26Aug97	20:50:26	DC21X41	drop	34	Herne	SKYLAR	tcp	2	1251
16	26Aug97	20:50:27	DC21X41	drop	35	Herne	SKYLAR	tcp	2	1252

Look closely at the services reported in each of the packet entries in Figure 5.13. See anything strange? Our source system Herne appears to be attempting to connect to Skylar on every TCP service port sequentially. Our display starts at service port 20 (FTP-data) and continues one port at a time to port 35. This is an indication that Herne is running a port scanner against Skylar in order to see what services are offered.

In contrast to this would be a log viewer such as the one used with Secure Computing's BorderWare firewall. This firewall maintains no less than six separate logs. While this makes tracking a particular service a bit easier, it makes tracking a specific host far more difficult. You would need to use a third-party program in order to combine the information and get a clear look at what is going on. Also, while the log in Figure 5.13 can be exported and saved using a simple menu option, BorderWare requires you to enable FTP administration and manually transfer the file to your local machine.

TIP   Keep the flexibility of the log interface in mind when you are selecting a firewall product. While the firewall's ACL will typically be set and require very few changes, you should plan on spending quite a bit of time reviewing your firewall logs and analyzing traffic flow.

Virtual Private Networks (VPNs)

Virtual private networks (*VPNs*) are considered a feature that sets a high-end firewall apart from the rest of the crowd. VPNs allow authenticated and encrypted access to an intranet through the public Internet. This means that instead of expensive point-to-point communication, LANs or mobile users can use inexpensive ISPs to communicate with their internal organization's resources.

However, simply providing basic VPN service is not enough. You'll need to determine what configuration, management, and encryption options your firewall provides for VPNs. In some cases a dedicated VPN solution that integrates into your firewall might provide the best results.

Intrusion Detection and Response

The ability of a firewall to notify an administrator while an attack is taking place should also enter the purchase and deployment decision. In the case of the high-profile DoS (Denial of Service) attacks that took place in February of 2000, the ability of the firewall systems to instantly notify the IT staff of unusual network activity allowed several of the sites to return to functionality within the hour.

Future firewall systems promise a degree of cooperation that would allow entire networks to respond to and reconfigure themselves in the event of an attack. While experts feel that the technology for this level of proactive monitoring and response is feasible, challenges remain. To be truly effective, such a system would require the cooperation and communication of all affected parties, even if this involved distinct (or even competitive) businesses and organizations. Assuming such a level of communication and integration existed, the anonymity of an attacker would become much more difficult to maintain, and the effects of an attack would be neutralized much more quickly.

There are already formal and informal groups that monitor and report intrusions, as well as virus, worms, and Trojan horse infections (such as the "I Love You" worm in May of 2000). However, the reporting mechanisms are, more often than not, manual, requiring an "eyes on" approach. Ideally, reporting would be automatic, standardized, and provide intelligent systems with enough information to allow for automatic or proactive defensive actions.

Integration and Access Control

Firewalls are integrating more and more with other network systems and services. This trend promises to simplify administration, reduce complexity, and increase TCO (Total Cost of Ownership), as firewalls no longer have to duplicate pre-existing network infrastructure.

Examples of integration include directory and authentication services that eliminate redundant user account information and allow customizable authentication schemes. Two industry standards that provide these services are LDAP (Lightweight Directory Access Protocol) and RADIUS (Remote Authentication Dial In User Service).

Lightweight Directory Access Protocol (LDAP)

LDAP creates a tunnel between two directory services, or between a directory service and a client. For firewalls, this means that instead of creating user and group/ role accounts redundantly, the system can use accounts and properties stored in a third-party directory service to determine access. This has a direct benefit of reducing the administrative burden of creating and managing duplicate user and group/ role accounts, and it also reduces complexity—the greatest enemy to any security system. Examples of directory services include Microsoft's AD (Active Directory), Novell's NDS (Netware Directory Services), iPlanet's Directory Server.

Remote Authentication Dial In User Service (RADIUS)

RADIUS offers an extensible and independent platform for authentication. Not only does this allow for customized authentication schemes (such as smart cards or biometric devices), RADIUS servers offload the actual authentication workload from the firewall (or LDAP-compliant directory services). By providing an infrastructure dedicated only to authentication, RADIUS simplifies and strengthens the authentication (and as a result, access) process.

Third-Party Tools

Many modern networks are a Frankenstein of multiple technologies from many different vendors; while this may be an optimal collection of technology for your organization, it can be a nightmare to administer. Fortunately, new technologies are emerging that are designed to centrally monitor and manage all of your network devices and applications. An excellent example is HP's OpenView which provides management in the following areas:

- Applications
- Availability
- Networks
- Performance
- Services
- Systems
- Storage and Data

The ability for your firewall to work with third-party management tools could easily be a decisive factor in which product you choose.

But management is not the only area for which you can find third-party products. Check Point's VPN-1 allows other vendors to extend their features to include URL filtering, antivirus scanning, and e-mail spamming protection. These additional benefits might justify the (usually) increased cost of such a product.

You Decide

There are some strong arguments for each choice. In order to make the proper selection for your environment, you will need to review all of these arguments and decide which are more applicable to your particular environment.

Table 5.6 breaks down popular firewall products by price, feature, and platform.

Firewall Deployment

You have selected a firewall product—now the big question is how it should be placed within your network environment. While there are many different opinions on this topic, the most common deployment is shown in Figure 5.14.

In this design, all internal systems are protected by the firewall from Internet-based attacks. Even remote sites connected to the organization via the WAN link are protected. All systems that are accessible from the Internet (such as the Web

TABLE 5.6:   Popular firewall products compared by price, feature, and platform

Name	Services(Static/ Dynamic/State-ful/Proxy)	Operating Systems (or Appliance)	Address translation	Firewall logging and analysis
Check Point VPN-1 Appliance 330	All	Appliance	Yes	Monitoring activity by port, service, protocol, and time of day
Cisco Secure PIX Firewall Model 515-R-BUN	All	Appliance	Yes	Add-on (Cisco Secure Policy Manager)
eSoft Interceptor	All	BSD Unix	Yes	No native support
Progressive Systems Phoenix Adaptive Firewall	All	Appliance	Yes	Export of data only
SonicWALL PRO	All	Appliance	Yes	Limited, no analysis
WatchGuard LiveSecurity System 4.1I	All	Appliance (Linux OS), install and management done from Windows applications	Yes	Real time logging, graphing and analysis

server and the mail relay) are isolated on their own subnet. This subnet is referred to as a *DMZ* or *demilitarized zone,* because while it may be secure from attack, you cannot be 100 percent sure of its safety, as you are allowing inbound connections to these systems.

Using a DMZ provides additional protection from attack. Since some inbound services are open to these hosts, an attacker may be able to gain high-level access to these systems. If this occurs, it is less likely that additional internal systems will be compromised, since these machines are isolated from the rest of the network.

VPNs	Intrusion Detection and Response	Integration and access control	Other services (including integrated third party tools)
Yes (including IPsec)	Can be centrally coordinated	DES and 3DES, IKE, IPSec, RADIUS, Secure ID, S/Key, TACACS, TACACS+, LDAP	URL filtering, antivirus scanning, and e-mail spamming protection
IPSec, PPTP	Cisco Secure Policy Manager	RADIUS, TACACS+	Antivirus, URL blocking
ICPSec (optional), PPTP (standard)	Pager, e-mail, SNMP	CryptoCard, RADIUS, SecurID cards, S/Key	Learning Company's SiteBlocker, AOL, filter rules, NNTP, packet screening, remote shell, Rlogin, RTSP, security scanner, SNMP, Spam filter, VDOlive, X Windows system
Proprietary (IPSec in future)	Reactive anti-attack port scanning (no alert capability)	Entrust, RADIUS, SecurID, Security Dynamics ACE Server, LDAP	None
IPSec, PPTP	Email	56-bit DES, 3DES	AutoUpdate, cookies, hacker prevention attacks, Java, NNTP, proxy blocking
PPTP	Email, pager	RCryptoCard, Internal ACL, Microsoft Windows NT, RADIUS, SecurID	NetMeeting (hardware based on Linux 2.0 kernel), SNMP

FIGURE 5.14:

Where to place your firewall

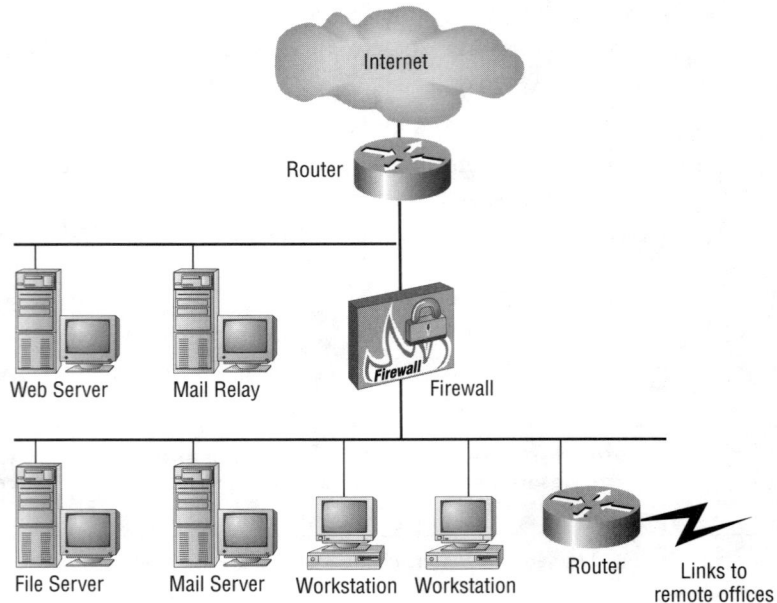

Additional network cards can be added to the firewall in order to control other types of remote access. For example, if the company has WAN links to business partners that are not officially part of the organization, another subnet could be created from an additional NIC card in the firewall. All routers connecting to these remote business partners would then be located on this subnet. The firewall would be able to control traffic between these sites and the internal network.

Additionally, you can use the static packet filtering capability of your router to increase security even further. This provides a multilayered wall of protection at your network perimeter. If an exploit is found in one of your security devices, the second device may be able to patch the leak.

There are many variations of this basic design. For example, you could add an additional type of firewall to the configuration you saw in Figure 5.14 in order to enhance security even more. For instance, if the firewall in the figure is a dynamic packet filter, you could place a proxy firewall behind it in order to better secure your Internet connection.

| TIP | Just remember that it is always a good idea to place your firewall between the Internet and the assets you wish to protect, so that all communication sessions must pass through the firewall. While this may sound like an extremely basic idea, you might be surprised—if not shocked—at the way some organizations attempt to deploy a firewall. |

Summary

This concludes our discussion of firewalls and how they work. Keep in mind the basic types and services that all firewalls offer, including:

- Static/dynamic/stateful/proxy filtering
- VPN capabilities
- Monitoring, logging, and analysis
- Extra services and third-party product integration

You should now be well equipped to select a firewall specifically for your organization's security and business needs.

In the next two chapters, we will look at some examples of how to set up and configure a few specific firewall products.

CHAPTER

SIX

6

Configuring Cisco Router Security Features

In the previous chapter, we discussed firewall theory and how the devices go about filtering traffic. In this chapter, we will look at how to configure a Cisco router in order to secure network perimeters. Cisco has become a staple in providing Internet connectivity, so most likely you are using a Cisco router in order to connect to your Internet Service Provider. Since a router is required equipment for a dedicated WAN connection, knowing how to configure Cisco security features can also be useful for controlling traffic between business partners.

Cisco Routers

Cisco is arguably the number-one supplier of hardware routers. It has a diverse product line, which means it has a router to suit almost every configuration requirement. Whether you are using an analog dial-up, ISDN, leased line, Frame Relay, T1, or even a T3 circuit to connect to your ISP, Cisco has a number of products that can fit your needs.

A unique ability of the Cisco router series is that, as of IOS 11.3, *reflexive filtering* is supported. Reflexive filtering allows a Cisco router to maintain connection session state. This means that while most routers only support static filtering, a Cisco router using IOS 11.3 or higher is capable of performing dynamic packet filtering. This is extremely beneficial for the small shop that does not require a full-featured firewall, or for use on perimeters where a full-featured firewall is not cost effective (such as a WAN link to a business partner or a so-called "Chinese firewall"). This feature set can even be combined with an additional firewall solution to strengthen a perimeter even further. Cisco routers running the newer IOS 12.1 can also filter based on connection time and context, further extending their usefulness as security devices.

When selecting a router for Internet connectivity, most organizations have traditionally gone with a Cisco 2500 series router. However, because the 2500 series routers are not very expandable, companies with newer implementations have started to purchase the 2600 series that is modular, expandable, and has compatible interfaces with other Cisco router families. In addition, businesses have begun to incorporate newer technologies into their networks such as Fast Ethernet (100Mbps), Gigabit Ethernet (1000Mbps), VLANs (Virtual LANs), VPNs, digital telephony, and streaming multimedia. This demand has dramatically increased the variety of router offerings—even from a single vendor.

A summary of the more popular models of the 2500 and 2600 series product lines is shown in Table 6.1. Remember that earlier Cisco models typically used an Attachment Unit Interface (AUI) connection for Ethernet segments, so you may need to purchase a transceiver as well.

NOTE   A transceiver will convert between the DB15 pin connection used by an AUI connection, and the female RJ45 connection used in a twisted-pair environment.

TABLE 6.1:   Popular Models of the Cisco 2500 and 2600 Series

Cisco Model Number	Included Ports	Speed
2503	1 Ethernet, 1 BRI, 2 serial	128K ISDN, 10 Mbps
2520	1 Ethernet (AUI), 1 Ethernet (RJ45), 1 BRI, 1 Serial	128K ISDN, 10 Mbps
2610	1 Ethernet (RJ45), 1 Network Module slot, 2 WAN Interface Card slot, 1 Advanced Integration Module (AIM) slot	Port specific (Maximum = 100 Mbps)
2611	2 Ethernet (RJ45), 1 Network Module slot, 2 WAN Interface Card slot, 1 AIM slot	Port specific (Maximum = 100 Mbps)

Where to Begin

Cisco routers are extremely flexible devices. The number of configurable options can be downright daunting. For example, the online "Cisco IOS Software Command Summary" for IOS 12.1 (the latest major OS release) is hundreds of pages long. Keep in mind this is a "summary," not a fully detailed manual—not exactly something you can toss in your shirt pocket!

A full description of how to configure a Cisco router is beyond the scope of this book. This section will simply focus on how to implement your security policies using this device. We will therefore assume the following:

- IOS 12.0 or higher has been loaded on the router.

- The router is powered up and physically connected to your LAN and WAN.

- Both interfaces have a valid IP address and subnet mask.

- You can ping the router at the other end of the WAN located at your ISP.

- You are reasonably familiar with the Cisco command interface.

Once these requirements have been met, you are ready to start locking down your perimeter.

Basic Security Tips

The place to start in securing your perimeter is to insure that the router itself does not become compromised. The router will be of little use in controlling traffic across your borders if Woolly Attacker can change the configuration. A Cisco router offers various levels of access:

- User EXEC Mode

- Privileged EXEC Mode

User EXEC Mode

User EXEC mode is the first mode of operation you reach when connecting to a Cisco router. If you are running a direct console session, you are placed in user EXEC mode automatically. If you are connecting to the router via a telnet session, you are first prompted for a terminal password.

NOTE   A Cisco router will deny all telnet session attempts if a terminal password has not been set.

A Cisco router changes the terminal prompt, depending on which mode of operation you are currently using. The prompt always starts with the name of the router and ends with some special sequence to let you know where you are. Table 6.2 lists some of the more common prompts.

Don't worry about the meaning of the other prompts for now. We will cover them in the next section.

TABLE 6.2: Cisco Command Prompts

Prompt Appearance	Description
router>	User EXEC mode
router#	Privilege mode
router(config)#	Global configuration mode
router(config-if)#	Interface configuration mode

While in user EXEC mode, a user is allowed to check connectivity and to look at statistics, but not to make any type of configuration changes to the device. This helps to limit the amount of damage that can be done by an attacker if your terminal password is compromised or if the attacker can gain physical access to the device.

Privilege Mode

A user must enter user EXEC mode before entering privilege mode. This means that a remote attacker must be able to compromise two passwords in order to gain full access to the router. *Privilege mode*, by default, is the big kahuna. At this level of access, a user is free to change or even delete any configuration parameters. You enter privilege mode by entering the command

```
enable
password: privilege_password
```

Since you use the command enable to gain privilege access, this mode is sometimes referred to as *enable mode*. In the past, the command given to change the enable password was as follows:

```
enable password new_password
```

However, Cisco now recommends using the following command that uses a stronger encryption algorithm:

```
enable secret new_password
```

You can actually specify up to 16 different levels (0–15) of privilege-level access, each with its own unique password. In this case, the password a user enters when accessing privilege mode would determine what level of privileged access the user receives. This can be useful if you need to allow an administrator access to some privilege-level commands, but not all. To set a password for a specific privilege level, enter the command

```
enable secret level new_password
```

where *level* is replaced by some value between 0 and 15. The lower the value, the lower the level of privilege-level access.

Disabling All Unused Services

A common security practice on any network-enabled device is to disable all unused services. Examples of services that should be disabled if unused include:

- SNMP

- NTP (Network Time Protocol)

- CDP (Cisco Discovery Protocol)

> **NOTE**
>
> NTP and CDP are enabled by default. To turn off CDP, use the `no cdp run` command. For NTP, use the `ntp disable` command on each interface that is not using NTP.

Changing the Login Banner

It's a good idea to change the logon screen banner so a customized message is displayed. If an attacker tries to access your router, the last thing you want him to see is a "welcome" message. Your message should reflect your organization's stance on unauthorized access to network hardware. Change the banner with the following command:

```
banner login # message #
```

where # can actually be an ASCII-delimiting character. This character cannot be used in the message and is simply used to let the command know where the message ends—you can place your message over multiple lines in order to change its appearance. You must be in privilege mode to use this command.

An example of this command would be

```
banner login # Unauthorized access prohibited #
```

Changing the Terminal Password

A Cisco router running under 12.1 can support multiple concurrent telnet sessions. It is a good idea to change these passwords on a regular basis to help insure that the device is not compromised. To change a password for one these connections (the first—labeled '0'), enter privilege mode and enter the following commands:

```
line vty 0
login
password 2SeCret4U
```

TIP   Remember that Cisco passwords are case sensitive, so use a combination of cases to make the password harder to guess.

Since you cannot select which vty you wish to use when connecting remotely, Cisco recommends that you set all vty passwords to the same character string.

Using Stronger Password Authentication

A weakness of the Cisco password system in the past was that there was no accounting capability. Since each administrator was using the same passwords, there was no audit trail to see who made which changes. Beginning with IOS 12.0, Cisco has adopted a new security paradigm called AAA (or Authentication, Authorization, and Accounting) to account for this and other weakness in the password system:

Authentication   This is the method of *identifying users*, whether via login/password, challenge/response, messaging support, and/or encryption. AAA authentication is applied by creating a named list of one or more authentication methods that are then bound to one or more interfaces.

Authorization   This is the method of *controlling access*, including one-time or service based authorization, per-user account and profile, user group, and protocol-based access control (IP, IPX, ARA, and telnet).

Accounting   This is the method of *collecting information* that is then used to bill, audit, and report network activities. Types of information include user identities, start/stop times, commands issued (like FTP get), number of packets and/or bytes. Through accounting, users are associated with resources they have accessed.

Cisco has chosen to implement industry standard technologies along with AAA, including RADIUS, TACACS+ (Terminal Access Controller Access Control System), and Kerberos. Authentication configuration outside of AAA cannot work with these standards. Here is how Cisco implements them in AAA:

RADIUS   Routers are RADIUS clients, transmitting authentication information to a RADIUS server.

TACACS+   The database is maintained by a service running on a UNIX or NT machine. Routers pass requests to the TACACS+ service.

Kerberos   Kerberos is used to verify that users and the network services they use are really who and what they claim to be. Routers can verify this by analyzing the Kerberos ticket assigned to authorized users.

SNMP Support

Simple Network Management Protocol (SNMP) can be used to collect statistics as well as to make configuration changes to a Cisco router. This is done through the use of *community strings*. In brief, a community string is a password system that identifies a specific level of access for a device (either read-only or read-write). For example, most devices come preconfigured to use a community string of `public` for read-only access to the device. Anyone who accesses the router via SNMP using this community string is automatically granted access.

Besides poor authentication, SNMP has another major security flaw: it transmits all information in clear text. Anyone monitoring the network can grab the community name from passing traffic. SNMP also uses UDP as a transport. As you saw in Chapter 5, UDP can be extremely difficult to filter due to its connectionless state.

For these reasons, you should avoid using SNMP on your routers if possible. While the manageability can be a real bonus in a large environment, this backdoor access to your router can be a serious security concern.

TIP

If you must use SNMP, use SNMPv2. The latest version supports MD5 authentication to help improve security. While this security is not foolproof, it is far better than the original SNMP specification. Cisco router versions 10.3 and up support SNMPv2.

Guarding Your Configuration File

The configuration of a Cisco router can be displayed by entering the command

```
write term
```

or

```
show running-config
```

The configuration can even be backed up to a remote server using the TFTP protocol. A sample header from a Cisco router configuration file is shown below:

```
! Cisco router configuration file
hostname lizzybell
enable secret 5 $1$722$CE
enable password SuperSecret
line vty 04
password SortaSecret
!
```

The privilege mode (enable) password is encrypted using a one-way encryption algorithm. This way, anyone who sees your configuration file does not immediately become privy to this password. The enable password string is simply used for backward compatibility. If this configuration file were mistakenly loaded on an older revision router that does not support encrypted passwords, this password would be used instead of the encrypted one.

The telnet session passwords are in clear text, however, so this file should be guarded as closely as possible. If this file is loaded via TFTP, an attacker monitoring the network now has the first password required to access this device. To better safeguard this information, you can encrypt all passwords by typing the following command in global configuration mode:

```
service password-encryption
```

This will encrypt the memory copy of all password strings. In order to make this permanent, you need to save these changes by typing

```
write term
```

or

```
copy running-config startup-config
```

Even though all your password strings are now encrypted, you should still take precautions to safeguard the configuration file. Cracker programs exist that attempt to guess a password's value by comparing the encrypted string to entries located in a dictionary file. If a match is found, the clear text equivalent of the password is returned. The only way to prevent this type of attack is to insure that even your encrypted password strings do not fall into the wrong hands.

Protect Against Spoofing

Woolly Attacker uses *spoofing* to transmit a packet that appears to originate from the secure side of a firewall—when in actuality it comes from an unsecured network. There are several methods to prevent spoofing on Cisco routers:

- Use access lists: configure input access lists on all interfaces to pass traffic only if it comes from known (or expected) source addresses. All other traffic is denied.

- Disable source routing: source routing should be disabled on all interfaces. (See the later section in this chapter for more on "Source Routing.")

- Turn off minor services: also referred to as *small servers*, these services normally aren't critical to most network infrastructures but have the potential of being exploited. The command `no service tcp-small-servers` is an example of how to turn these off for IP communications.

Disable Directed Broadcasts

DoS (denial-of-service) attacks work by flooding a target computer with so much information (or so many connection requests) that the target is unable to service legitimate requests. One of the tools used by hackers to achieve these types of attacks is the capability of routers to forward directed broadcasts. To disable directed broadcasts, enter

```
no ip directed broadcastRouting
```

By default, Cisco routers ship with IP routing enabled, so you won't have to change this functionality. You do, however, need to consider how best to update your router regarding which subnets you are running on your internal network. The router automatically knows about any locally connected networks. In order to reach any subnets beyond these, you must tell a router specifically how to reach them.

Sometimes this is not an issue. For example, take a look at Figure 6.1. Our firewall is performing network address translation (NAT) for our internal network.

All traffic the router sees will appear as though it came from the locally attached segment. In this case, no other route entries are required beyond a default route. The router does not need to know about the 192.168.1.0 network because we are using NAT.

FIGURE 6.1:

Our router does not need a route entry for the internal network because the firewall is performing NAT.

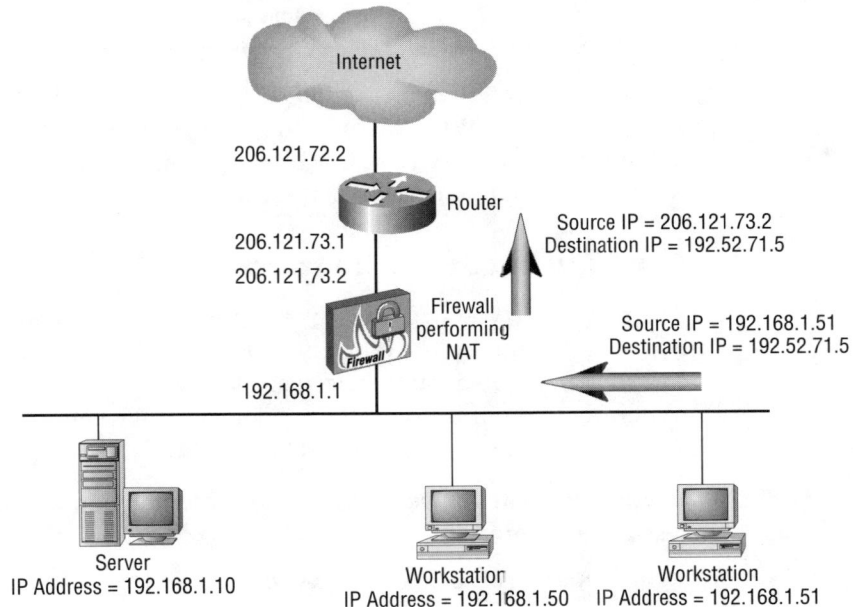

If you do have additional subnets that the router will need to know about, you need to decide between creating static entries on the router (static routing) or using a dynamic protocol such as RIP or OSPF so the router can receive route information automatically (dynamic routing). There are strengths and weaknesses to either choice, depending on your configuration.

Static routing is far more secure from a security perspective. If the router has been programmed with your route configuration, an attacker cannot change this information without compromising the router. If a dynamic protocol is used, an attacker may be able to send false updates to the router, thus corrupting the router table.

Dynamic protocols are useful if you are running multiple paths to the same network. For example, if you had multiple links leading to the Internet, it might be beneficial to use a dynamic routing protocol for redundancy or even load balancing. If you must use a dynamic routing protocol, use one that supports authentication such as OSPF. This will at least afford you some level of security. Routing protocols, such as RIP, simply trust that any host sending them routing information must know what it is talking about.

NOTE   See Chapter 3 for more on dynamic routing protocols.

Most of the Internet connections in use have but a single link between the organization and its ISP. For these environments, static routing is preferred. The slight maintenance increase caused by having to manually configure your routing table will be well worth the additional security.

Configuring Static Routing

At a minimum, you will need to configure your router with a default route setting. The default route setting tells the router, "If you do not have a routing table entry for a particular subnet, forward the data to this other router and let that router figure out how to deliver it." The default route should be configured to use your ISP's router at the other end of the WAN link.

A default route can be configured by entering global configuration mode and typing the command

```
ip default-route xxx.xxx.xxx.xxx
```

where *xxx.xxx.xxx.xxx* is the local IP address of the default router. Once you have created a default route, you will need to enter static routes for each of your internal subnets using legal addresses. While still in global configuration mode, enter the command

```
ip route yyy.yyy.yyy.0 255.255.255.0 xxx.xxx.xxx.xxx 1
```

You must do this once for each subnet you need to add. The command breaks down as follows:

ip route   Add a static IP routing entry.

yyy.yyy.yyy.0   Replace this value with the IP subnet address.

255.255.255.0   Replace this value with a valid subnet mask address.

xxx.xxx.xxx.xxx   Replace this value with the IP address of the next hop router.

1 This is the metric or cost associated with following this path. Use a value of 1 unless you have multiple paths to the same destination. In this case, set the most preferred route to 1 and the alternate route to 2.

Let's walk through an example to see how this would be configured. If you look at Figure 6.2, you will see that you actually have multiple routers within your environment that you need to configure.

FIGURE 6.2:

Defining static routes on multiple routers

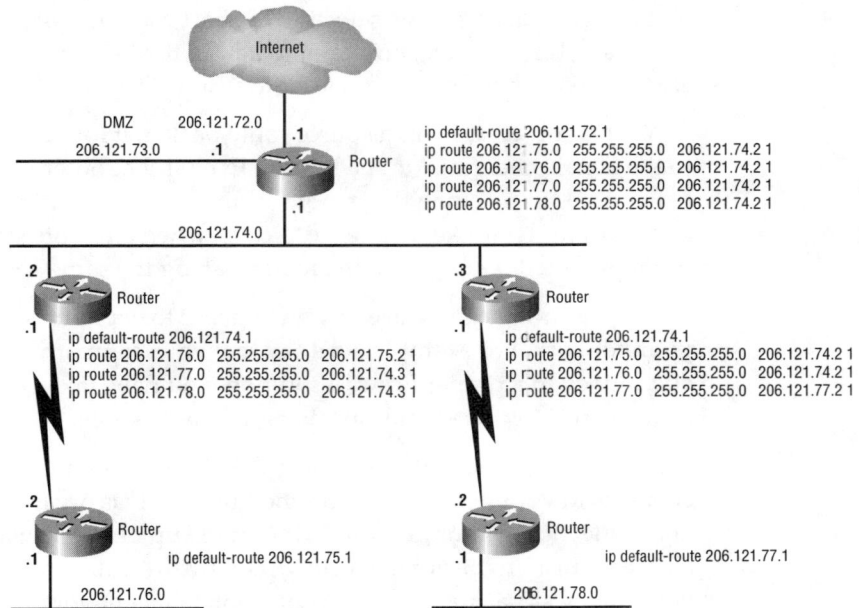

```
                                   Internet

        DMZ      206.121.72.0                ip default-route 206.121.72.1
                              .1             ip route 206.121.75.0   255.255.255.0   206.121.74.2 1
  206.121.73.0        .1                     ip route 206.121.76.0   255.255.255.0   206.121.74.2 1
                              Router         ip route 206.121.77.0   255.255.255.0   206.121.74.2 1
                              .1             ip route 206.121.78.0   255.255.255.0   206.121.74.2 1

             206.121.74.0

   .2                                   .3
        Router                               Router
   .1                                   .1
     ip default-route 206.121.74.1             ip cefault-route 206.121.74.1
     ip route 206.121.76.0  255.255.255.0  206.121.75.2 1   ip route 206.121.75.0  255.255.255.0  206.121.74.2 1
     ip route 206.121.77.0  255.255.255.0  206.121.74.3 1   ip route 206.121.76.0  255.255.255.0  206.121.74.2 1
     ip route 206.121.78.0  255.255.255.0  206.121.74.3 1   ip route 206.121.77.0  255.255.255.0  206.121.77.2 1

   .2                                   .2
        Router                               Router
   .1        ip default-route 206.121.75.1   .1        ip default-route 206.121.77.1

     206.121.76.0                           206.121.78.0
```

Notice that each router has a default route setting. If you start at the very back of the network (206.121.76.0 or 206.121.78.0), you can see that the default route entries lead all the way out to the Internet. This is a good thing, because it is all the subnets out on the Internet that we wish to avoid programming into our routers. The default route acts as a catchall for any undefined routes.

NOTE Our two most distant routers in Figure 6.2 (206.121.75.2 and 206.121.77.2) are only using a default route. There are no static route entries. This is because you need to pass through the default router in order to reach any subnet that is not directly attached to these devices. While you could add static route entries, they would be redundant.

Finally, notice that we did not add a route entry into any of our routers for the DMZ. This is because it is unnecessary. Our Internet router is directly attached to this segment, so it already knows how to get there. As for the other routers, the DMZ can be reached by simply utilizing the default route entry.

Source Routing

We need to make one final routing entry before we are finished. This routing change is to disable source routing. Typically, IP packets contain no routing information. The packets leave selecting the best route up to the network routing hardware. It is possible, however, to add to the header information the route you wish to take when accessing a remote system. This is referred to as *source routing*.

When a router receives a source route packet, it forwards the information along to the next hop defined in the header. Even if the router is sure that it knows a far better path for reaching the remote system, it will comply with the path specifications within the packet header. Typically, when a remote system receives a source route packet, it will reply to the request along the same specified path.

Source routing can be used by an attacker to exploit potential back doors within your network. For example, let's say that your company has invested a lot of time and money in a proper firewall solution. You have taken every effort to lock down your Internet connection as tightly as possible.

Let's also assume that you have a WAN link to a remote business partner that connects to your network behind the firewall. This organization also has an Internet connection, but unlike yours, it is made up of very trusting souls who think all the security hype is a marketing ploy by firewall vendors. For this reason, your business partner has zero protection at its network perimeter.

Using source routed packets, it is possible for a potential attacker to send traffic first to your remote business partner, then have the traffic sent over the WAN link to your network by including source route information within the packets of data. Despite all your security efforts, Woolly Attacker has found an easy access entrance to your networking environment. The only thing missing is valet parking.

Source routing can be a bad thing and should be disabled at all your network perimeters. The only legitimate reason for allowing source-routed packets is if you need to do connectivity diagnostics across specific links on the Internet. Since this is not an activity many of us must do, it is best to leave the feature disabled.

To disable source routing, enter global configuration mode and enter the command

```
no ip source-route
```

Cisco Security Features

Table 6.3 provides a list of all the various security features in the Cisco IOS (some fairly recent):

TABLE 6.3: Cisco IOS Security Features

Features	Description
Standard Access Lists and Static Extended Access Lists	Enables basic filtering by evaluating packets at the network layer (some extended access lists can evaluate information at transport layer).
Dynamic Access Lists (also known as Lock-and-Key)	Provides temporary access to authenticated users.
Reflexive Access Lists	Allows incoming TCP or UDP. packets only if they belong to a session initiated from inside the firewall.
TCP Intercept	Protects against SYN flood attacks (a type of DoS attack).
Context-based Access Control	Examines application layer information to determine not just state, but *context* of all TCP and UDP connections in order to dynamically open or close connections as necessary. Also responsible for alerts and logs.
Intrusion Detection	Compares all network traffic with stored *signatures*, reacting to detected intrusions by sending an alarm, resetting the connection, or dropping the connection.
Authenticating Proxy	Applies user-based access policies (as opposed to group or IP-based policies).
Port/Application Mapping	Enables context-based access controls to work on non-registered (non-standard) or custom ports.
NAT	Hides private IP addresses from the public Internet.
User Authentication and Authorization	Verifies identity and permission level based on user accounts.

At the core of all of these security methods is the access list. Cisco *access lists* (also called *filters*) are used to selectively pass or block traffic received by a Cisco router. The router evaluates each packet received against the criteria defined in an access list, such as the source or destination address of the information, the upper-layer protocol, the time, user identify, or other factors. Access lists are useful for controlling traffic that attempts to pass your network perimeter. Since a router is typically used to segregate or partition network segments anyway (for instance, to separate your network from a business partner or the Internet), you can see why these devices contain some form of advanced filtering capability.

Cisco routers provide two methods of filtering traffic. The simplest is the *standard access list*, while *extended access lists* are used for more granular control. Once an access list is created, it is applied to a specific interface on the router. The access list is then told to screen either inbound network traffic (traffic coming from the attached network to the interface) or outbound network traffic (traffic leaving the router and headed towards the attached network). This ability to filter either inbound or outbound traffic can be a real time-saver in complex configurations.

In Cisco IOS 12.1, IP and IPX extended access lists can also be used with time ranges. *Permit* and *deny* statements are then activated in accordance with their associated time ranges. Other advantages are:

Increased control   Resources (such as IP address/mask pair and port number, policy routing, or on-demand link creation) are linked to available times.

Better integration   Time-based policy can be linked with Cisco's firewall and IPSec products.

Reduced cost   Traffic can be rerouted to less expensive links based on time of day.

Increased efficiency   Access lists don't have to be processed at open times of the day.

To create a time range, use the following command:

```
time-range {name of time range}
```

To define the actual time range, enter this command:

```
periodic {days of the week} {hh:mm} to {days of the week} {hh:mm}
```

Access List Basics

Access lists are generated by creating a number of test conditions that become associated with list identifier numbers. Access lists are created while in global configuration mode and use the following syntax:

```
access-list {list #} permit/deny {test condition} {time range}
```

You would repeat this command for every test condition you wish to use in order to screen traffic (such as allow SMTP, deny HTTP, and so on). The list number you use identifies which protocol you would like to apply these rules to. Table 6.4 shows protocols associated with names, and Table 6.5 shows protocols associated with list numbers.

TABLE 6.4: Cisco Access Control Lists By Name

Protocol
Apollo Domain
IP
IPX
ISO CLNS
NetBios IPX
Soure-route bridging NetBIOS

TABLE 6.5: Sample of Cisco Access Control Lists By Number

Protocol	List Type	Range Identifier
IP	Standard	1–99; 1300–1999
IP	Extended	100–199; 2000–2699
Ethernet Type codes	N/A	200–299
AppleTalk	N/A	600–699
Ethernet Addresses	N/A	700–799
IPX	Standard	800–899
IPX	Extended	1000–1099

NOTE

Some protocols require that their associated access lists are identified only by name, others only by number, and the rest can either/or.

Notice that only one type of filtering is supported for certain protocols. As of Cisco IOS 11.2 and higher, the range identifiers used by IP can be replaced by an alphanumeric name. This name can be up to 64 characters long but must start with an alphabetic character. The name must be unique, and each name can only describe a single set of standard or extended filters. You cannot combine the two. The syntax for creating an access list name is

```
IP access-list standard/extended {name}
```

TIP

Using names instead of access list numbers can be extremely beneficial. Doing so extends the number of unique lists you can create and allows you to associate a descriptive name to a particular set of filters (such as "spoofing"). Also, reflexive filters can only be associated with an access list name. You cannot use an access list identifier number.

Access lists will be processed in the order you create them: if you create five filter conditions and place them in the same access list, the router will evaluate each condition in the order it was created until the first match is found. Conditions are processed as "first fit," not "best fit," so it is important to pay close attention to the order you use. For example, let's say you have an access list that states

- Allow all internal systems full IP access to the Internet.

- Do not let any internal systems telnet to hosts on the Internet.

Since the first rule states, "All outbound traffic is OK," you would never actually make it to the second rule. This means that your internal users would still be able to use telnet.

Once you have created an access list that you wish to apply to your router, enter configuration mode for a specific interface and enter the command

```
{protocol} access-group {list # or name} in/out
```

To remove an access list from an interface (always a good thing to do if you are testing a new filter), simply precede the command with the word *no* as follows:

```
no {protocol} access-group {list # or name} in/out
```

Likewise, to delete an entire access list, enter the command

```
no access-list {list # or name}
```

Keep in mind that this will delete all filter conditions associated with a particular access list number or name. One of the biggest drawbacks of access lists is that you cannot edit entries. This can make data entry a bit tedious. For example, if you have created 15 access list entries and realize that you actually want entry 11 processed after entry 13, you must delete the entire list and recreate it from scratch.

TIP   Create your access lists offline in a text editor. Once you have the filters in the correct order, simply copy the rules to the Windows Clipboard and use the Paste ability of your terminal emulator. This also allows you to keep a local backup of all your filter conditions.

All access filters have an implicit deny at the end. This means that if you do not tell the router to specifically allow a certain type of traffic to pass, it will assume that it should be blocked. For example, if your access list states, "Traffic from the subnet 192.168.1.0 is OK to let through," the router will assume that it should block traffic from all subnets *except* 192.168.1.0. This feature helps to insure that you do not let anything through that you did not mean to.

Standard Access Lists

Standard access lists allow you to filter on source IP address. This is useful when you wish to block all traffic from a specific subnet or host. A standard access list does not look at the destination IP address or even the service; it makes its filtering determination based solely on the source address of the transmitting system.

While this sounds a bit limiting, it can actually be quite useful. Examine Figure 6.3. Here we have a very simple network design. There is only one way in and out of the network, which is through the router. The internal network segment uses an IP subnet address of 206.121.73.0.

In this environment, the router should never see any traffic originating from the Internet that appears to have originated from the IP subnet 206.121.73.0. This is because that segment is directly connected to the Ethernet port of the router. While the router will see traffic originating from this subnet on its Ethernet port, it should never be detected off of the serial (WAN) port.

FIGURE 6.3:

Using standard access lists

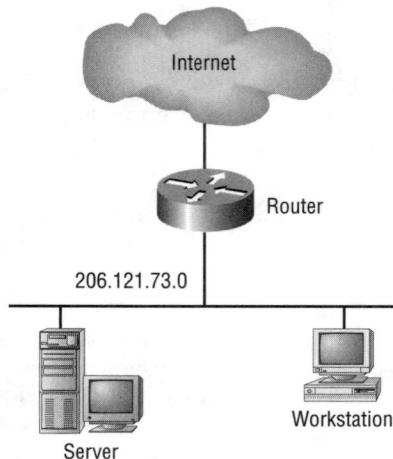

IP spoofing is a process in which an attacker pretends to be a system on your local network transmitting information, even though he is off at some remote location. This can be used to exploit certain system vulnerabilities. For example, Microsoft Windows is vulnerable to a type of attack known as *Land*. A Land attack packet has the following attributes:

Source IP: The IP address of the system under attack

Destination IP: The IP address of the system under attack

Transport: TCP

Source port: 135

Destination port: 135

Flag setting: SYN=1

There are other ports and settings that can be used, but this should give you the general idea. The attack fools the system into thinking it is talking to itself. This will produce a race condition, which will cause the system to eventually hang or lock up.

You may be thinking, "No problem, I plan to block all inbound connection requests, so this packet would never get through because the SYN flag is set high." Not true, Grasshopper: look at the source address. When the router evaluates this packet, it may very well think that the packet was received from the internal network.

While Cisco routers do not have this problem (they maintain the association of the packet with the interface it was received on), many routers do. If your access rules state, "Port 135 from the internal network is OK to let through," the router will approve the packet of data, pass the information along to the routing process, which would then pass the traffic along to the Ethernet segment.

So how do you solve this problem? Since you will never see legitimate traffic originating from the Internet, which uses your internal subnet address, there will be no loss in connectivity if you filter out such traffic. This is called a *spoofing filter*, because you are insuring that no traffic that is trying to spoof your internal address will be allowed to pass.

It is also a good idea to place an inbound filter on your Ethernet port that states, "Only accept traffic from the 206.121.73.0 subnet." This helps to insure that none of your internal users attempts a spoofing attack on some other network. As administrator, it is your job to not only protect your own environment, but also to make sure you do not inadvertently make someone else's life miserable.

You can create spoofing filters using standard access lists. The syntax for a standard access list entry is

```
access-list {list # or name} permit/deny {source} {mask}
```

So you could create the following access list entries in global configuration mode on the router in Figure 6.3:

```
access-list 1 deny 206.121.73.0 0.0.0.255
access-list 2 permit 206.121.73.0 0.0.0.255
```

Access list 1 would be applied by entering configuration mode for the WAN interface and entering the command

```
ip access-group 1 in
```

Likewise, access list 2 would be applied by entering configuration mode for the Ethernet interface and entering the command

```
ip access-group 2 in
```

You may notice that the mask value looks a little strange. This is because this value is a pattern match, not a subnet mask. A pattern match uses the following criteria when evaluating a test condition:

0 The corresponding byte in the defined address must match the test condition exactly.

1 This is a wildcard character: any value in this byte is considered a match.

So in this example our pattern match says, "Any IP address which contains the byte values 206.121.73." As long as the first three bytes match the source IP address, the access list test condition considers it a match.

To match all network traffic, use the following address and mask:

```
0.0.0.0 255.255.255.255
```

This tells the Cisco router that all traffic is to be considered a match. When you write your access rules, this address and mask can simply be replaced by the word "any." This is not very useful for standard access lists (if you do not want to accept any traffic, it's easier to just pull the plug), but it will come in handy when we get into extended access lists in the next section.

Access List Pattern Matching

If you think of the pattern match value as "an anti-subnet mask," you'll be in pretty good shape. The pattern match will always be the exact opposite of what you would use for a subnet mask. This is pretty easy to follow if you are filtering full subnet classes, but it can get a bit confusing if you are working with true subnetting.

For example, let's say that instead of a full class C network, you are only using a portion of this class C address space. Let's assume that the network address is 206.121.73.64 and the subnet mask is 255.255.255.224. In this case, what would you use for a pattern match to insure that you are only filtering on your network space?

All TCP/IP address space is actually created using a binary number system. We use decimals simply because these are easier for human consumption. In order to determine the pattern match you will use, you first have to convert the last byte of the subnet mask to binary:

```
224 = 128 + 64 + 32 = 11100000
```

In the last byte you are using three bits for networking and five bits to identify each unique host. In order to ignore any host on your network, you would use a pattern match that has all the host bits set high, like this:

```
00011111 = 16 + 8 + 4 + 2 + 1 = 31
```

So in order to accommodate your new network address and subnet mask, you would need to change your access to the following:

```
access-list 1 deny 206.121.73.64 0.0.0.31
access-list 2 permit 206.121.73.64 0.0.0.31
```

In effect, you have told your access list, "Filter the packet when you see an address space value 206.121.73.64 – 206.121.73.95 (64 + 31)." This will let you screen for your small chunk of this class C address space—without having to filter or allow more than you need to.

Besides spoofing rules, why else might you use standard access lists? Standard access lists are extremely effective at blocking access from any undesirable remote site. This could be known attackers, mail spammers, or even competitors.

Remember that this connection is yours to manage as you see fit. There is no requirement that once you are connected to the Internet you must accept traffic from all sources. While accepting all traffic is considered the polite thing to do, it may not always make the most business sense.

For example, there are mailing lists and organizations that have dedicated resources to identifying spam sites. Spam, or unsolicited advertising e-mail, can be a waste of organizational resources at best, or it can cause a denial of service at worst. Many administrators now filter traffic from sites known to support (or at the very least fail to prevent) spammers and their activities. All traffic is filtered, because a site that does not control outbound spam mail typically makes no effort to prevent other types of attacks from being launched against your network.

TIP

A Cisco interface can only accept one access list per port, per direction. This means that you should only apply a standard access list when you won't need an extended access list. If you require the increased flexibility of an extended access list, simply incorporate your filters into a single list.

Static Extended Access Lists

Extended access lists take the concept of standard access lists one step further. Instead of simply filtering on source IP address, extended access lists can also filter on

- Destination IP address
- Transport (IP, TCP, UDP, ICMP, GRE, IGRP)
- Destination port number
- Packet type or code in the case of ICMP
- Established connects (verifies that either the ACK or RST bits have been set)

Clearly, this can give you a much more granular level of control over your perimeter traffic. Extended access lists are created in global configuration mode using the following syntax:

```
access-list {list # or name} permit/deny {protocol} {source} {mask}
{destination} {mask} {operator} {port} est (short for establish if
applicable)
```

Valid operators are

lt   Less than

gt   Greater than

eq   Equal to

neq   Not equal to

As an example, let's say you wish to create a set of extended access rules allowing open access to HTTP on the host 206.121.73.10 and allowing telnet access, as well—but only from hosts on the subnet 199.52.24.0. These rules would look similar to the following:

```
access-list 101 permit any 206.121.73.10 0.0.0.0 eq 80
access-list 101 permit 199.52.24.0 0.0.0.255 206.121.73.10 0.0.0.0 eq 23
```

You would then install these rules on the serial port by entering configuration mode for that interface and entering the command

```
ip access-group 101 in
```

Problems with FTP

As you saw in the section on FTP in Chapter 3, this protocol can be a real pain to support through a firewall. This is because the protocol actually uses two ports while transferring files. To review, you are stuck with the following:

- **Standard FTP:** All inbound service ports above 1023 must be left open to support data connection.

- **Passive FTP:** All outbound service ports above 1023 must be left open to support data connection.

In a world of the lesser of two evils, it is usually better to support only passive FTP. This is supported by all Web browsers and most graphic FTP programs. It is typically not supported by command-line FTP programs.

In order to support passive FTP, you must allow all internal hosts to access any TCP ports above 1023 on systems located out on the Internet. Not the best security stance, but it is certainly far better than the standard FTP alternative.

If there are specific services you wish to block, you can create these access list entries before the entry that opens all outbound ports. Since the rules are processed in order, the deny rules would be processed first, and the traffic would be dropped. For example, let's say you wish to block access to X11 and Open Windows servers, but you want to open the remaining upper ports for passive FTP use. In this case you would create the following rules:

```
access-list 101 deny any any eq 2001
access-list 101 deny any any eq 2002
access-list 101 deny any any eq 6001
access-list 101 deny any any eq 6002
access-list 101 permit any any gt 1023
```

The only problem here is that you would receive random FTP file transfer failures when the client attempted to use ports 2001, 2002, 6001, or 6002. This would probably not happen often, but intermittent failures are usually the most annoying.

Creating a Set of Access Lists

Let's go through an example to see how this would all pull together. Let's assume that you have a network configuration similar to the one in Figure 6.4. You need to allow HTTP to the Web server and SMTP access to the mail server. The mail server also runs the local DNS process. Additionally, you would like to provide unrestricted outbound access to all TCP services.

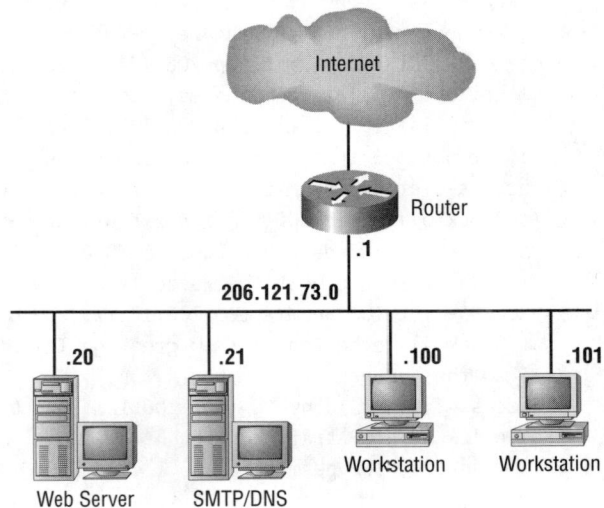

FIGURE 6.4:

Using access lists on a simple network

Your access list rules would look something like those that follow. Lines starting with an exclamation point (!) are considered comments or remarks by the Cisco IOS.

```
! Stop any inbound spoofing
access-list 1 deny 206.121.73.0 0.0.0.255
! Let in replies to established connection
access-list 101 permit tcp any 206.121.73.0 0.0.0.255 gt 1023 est
! Look for port scanning
access-list 101 deny tcp any any eq 19 log
! Allow in SMTP mail to the mail server
access-list 101 permit tcp any 206.121.73.21 0.0.0.0 eq 25
! Allow in DNS traffic
access-list 101 permit tcp any 206.121.73.21 0.0.0.0 eq 53
access-list 101 permit udp any 206.121.73.21 0.0.0.0 eq 53
! Allow in HTTP to the web server
access-list 101 permit tcp any 206.121.73.20 0.0.0.0 eq 80
! Let in replies if an internal user pings an external host
access-list 101 permit icmp any any echo-reply
! Allow for flow control
access-list 101 permit icmp any any source-quench
! Let in replies if an internal user runs traceroute
access-list 101 permit icmp any any time-exceeded
! Insure that our internal users do not spoof
access-list 2 permit 206.121.73.0 0.0.0.255
! Let out replies from the web server
access-list 102 permit tcp 206.121.73.20 0.0.0.0 any gt 1023 est
! Let out replies from the mail/DNS server
access-list 102 permit tcp 206.121.73.21 0.0.0.0 any gt 1023 est
! Let out DNS traffic from the DNS server
access-list 102 permit udp 206.121.73.21 0.0.0.0 any eq 53
! Block all other UDP traffic except for DNS permitted above
access-list 102 deny udp 206.121.73.0 0.0.0.255 any
! Allow a single host to create Telnet sessions to the router
access-list 102 permit tcp 206.121.73.200 0.0.0.0 206.121.73.1 0.0.0.0 eq 23
! Block all other hosts from creating Telnet sessions
! to the router
access-list 102 deny tcp any 206.121.73.1 0.0.0.0 eq 23
! Allow all TCP traffic through
access-list 102 permit ip 206.121.73.0 0.0.0.255 any
```

Once this list has been entered (or pasted) in global configuration mode, you would first go to configuration mode for the serial interface and enter the commands

```
ip access-group 1 in
ip access-group 101 in
```

You would then go to configuration mode for the Ethernet interface and enter the commands

```
ip access-group 2 in
ip access-group 102 in
```

When you're finished, your access lists will be active and your router should begin filtering traffic. You should test your configuration immediately to make sure that all is working as you expect.

A Few Comments on Our Sample Access Lists

The third access list is labeled "look for port scanning." This is accomplished by logging a specific port so that any activity is displayed on the console terminal. As mentioned, routers typically have very poor logging capability. You do not want to log too much information—it may scroll off the screen before you catch it. By monitoring a port that you know an attacker will check (port 19 is `chargen`, or Character Generator, which has quite a few vulnerabilities), you can strike a good balance between not logging too much information and still catching suspect traffic.

Lines 12 and 13 limit outbound replies to only the Web and mail servers. Since these are the only two systems offering services, they are the only two that should be sending replies back to Internet hosts. Lines 14 and 15 limit UDP traffic to DNS and only from the DNS server. Since UDP is unreliable, it is also insecure. These filters limit your vulnerability to a single system. Of course, this means that all internal hosts will need to use the mail system for DNS resolution.

Lines 16 and 17 specify that only a single host can gain remote access to the router. This will help to strengthen the device's protection even further. Remember that when you use telnet to manage the router (without enabling any router-to-router encryption), all information (including passwords) is sent clear text. These filters help to insure that even if someone does compromise the passwords, they are only useful from a single remote system (unless of course the attacker fakes his IP address, but we will not go there).

Finally, the access rules end by stating, "Let out any TCP traffic we have not explicitly denied." If there are TCP services you wish to filter, you could enter these test conditions prior to this last rule.

TIP
Do not save your changes right away. Perform your testing with the changes in active memory only. If you have inadvertently locked yourself out of the device, you can simply power cycle it to return to the last saved configuration. Just remember to save the new configuration once you know the changes are acceptable!

Dynamic Access Lists

Exceptions can arise for any security policy, and *dynamic access lists* are a reflection of that necessity. Also called *lock-and-key*, this feature creates dynamic extended access lists. However, it can also be used with standard and static extended access lists.

If activated, lock-and-key changes the existing access list for a given interface to allow a designated user to access a given resource. Lock-and-key then alters the access list again, reverting it to its previous state.

Lock-and-key provides benefits beyond that of traditional standard and static extended access lists:

- Users are authenticated through a challenge mechanism.

- In larger networks lock-and-key provides a simplified method for management.

- Router processing of access lists is decreased.

- Fewer exploitable openings occur in the router infrastructure.

Here is an example of how lock-and-key works:

1. Let's say a vacationing administrator must remotely connect to the network to perform troubleshooting. The administrator opens a telnet session to the router.

2. The router performs a user authentication process (either by itself or through a separate security system like TACACS+ or RADIUS).

3. Upon successful authentication, the administrator is logged out of the telnet session, and the router makes a temporary entry in the dynamic access list.

4. The administrator now has access into the internal network and makes the required changes.

5. Once finished, the administrator initiates a new telnet session and manually clears the temporary entry. The administrator could have also specified an idle or absolute timeout value for the entry; in which case the router would have automatically cleared the entry after it had expired.

For example, consider the following code, starting with the command to configure a dynamic access list:

```
access-list {access-list-number} dynamic {dynamic-name} {deny or permit}
telnet {source} {source-wildcard} {destination} {destination-wildcard}
precedence {precedence} tos {tos} established log
```

In practice, even if administrative policy is to manually clear the entry, a timeout value is an easily configurable reassurance that a potential security hole is closed.

Spoofing

The temporary entry in the dynamic access list created by lock-and-key is an opening that makes the router susceptible to spoofing. One method of countering this threat is to enable encryption on the router and on the remote router servicing the remote host (in our example, the router acting as the administrator's immediate gateway). With an encrypted connection, the host IP address is hidden from any potential hackers within the encrypted traffic, and therefore can't be spoofed.

Reflexive Access Lists

As of IOS 11.3, Cisco routers support *reflexive access lists*. Reflexive access lists are made to be a replacement for the static `establish` command. When reflexive access lists are used, the router creates a dynamic state table of all active sessions.

The ability to generate a state table pushes the Cisco router into the realm of a true firewall. By monitoring state, the router is in a far better position to make filter determinations than equivalent devices that only support static filtering.

In order to use reflexive access lists, you must use access list names, not range identifier numbers. This is not a big deal, as using a name allows you to be far more descriptive in labeling your access lists.

The syntax for creating a reflexive access list is

```
permit {protocol} {source} {mask} {destination} {mask} reflect {name}
```

So you could create a reflexive access list using the following parameters:

```
permit ip any any reflect ipfilter
```

Let's assume that you only wish to allow in SMTP to a single internal host, as well as any replies to active sessions that were established by any system on your internal network. In this situation, you could create the following in global configuration mode:

```
ip access-list extended inboundfilters
permit tcp any 206.121.73.21 0.0.0.0 eq 25
evaluate tcptraffic
```

This would allow inbound replies to active sessions and inbound SMTP sessions to be established.

The only caveat with reflexive access lists is that entries are purged from the table after 300 seconds of inactivity. While this is not a problem for most protocols, the FTP control session (port 21) can sit idle for a far longer period of time during a file transfer. You can increase this timeout value using the following command:

```
ip reflexive-list timeout {timeout in seconds}
```

TCP Intercept

DoS (denial-of-service) attacks have become quite prevalent recently. The most popular way to implement this attack is using the SYN flood. A hacker creates a SYN flood by initiating a large quantity of connection requests in a short amount of time. Because the connection requests don't come from valid addresses, the server can't complete the connection. The result is that the server is so tied up in attempting to respond to invalid requests that it has no resources left to answer legitimate requests for services (such as Web, FTP, and e-mail).

Cisco's *TCP intercept* component resolves this problem by answering all incoming connection requests itself. If successful, it opens a connection with the server and links the two connections together. If the connection request is not legitimate, the connection request is dropped—and a threshold counter is incremented. Once the limit on this counter is reached, all additional connection requests from that particular address are automatically dropped.

Activating TCP Intercept

Before TCP intercept can be enabled, an extended access list has to be created:

```
access-list {access-list-number} {deny or permit} tcp {destination}
```

Following this, enter the command to activate TCP intercept:

```
ip tcp intercept list {access-list-number}
```

TCP intercept can operate in two modes: intercept or passive watch. In default *intercept* mode, TCP intercept intercedes and responds to every incoming SYN with a SYN-ACK. Only after receiving an ACK from the remote host does the router pass along the original SYN request to the server, completing a three-way TCP handshake. Finally, the router joins both connections together.

If TCP intercept is configured in *passive watch* mode, the router does not intercept communications unless a connection request goes unanswered after a period of time (default to 30 seconds). Passive watch mode is configured with the following command:

```
ip tcp intecept mode {intercept or watch}
```

Context-Based Access Control

Context-Based Access Control (CBAC) uses information at the application layer of the OSI model to filter TCP and UDP network traffic and analyze and permit traffic going through both sides of a router. Because of its ability to look at application data, CBAC allows filtering for protocols that open up multiple channels (such as RPC, FTP, and most multimedia protocols), as well as Java applets (providing they are not compressed or archived).

Because CBAC opens connections dynamically (limiting data to those sessions that were initiated from within a firewall), it provides a defense against DoS attacks. CBAC also verifies that TCP sequence numbers are within expected ranges, and will also watch and respond to abnormally elevated rates of connection requests.

Application-based logging and alerts are another benefit of CBAC. By tracking time stamps, source and destination addresses, ports, and data transferred, CBAC gives centralized reporting and management systems enough information to match network patterns against hacking "signatures," allowing the system to automate some of its defense against known penetration and DoS methods.

While CBAC can evaluate any generic TCP or UDP session, it can also analyze the following popular application protocols:

- FTP
- TFTP
- H.323 (protocol used by Microsoft Netmeeting)
- HTTP (including Java applets)

- Microsoft Netshow
- rexec, rsh, rlogin
- RealMedia
- RTSP (Real Time Streaming Protocol)
- SMTP

CBAC Example

Let's use a sample FTP session to walk through the CBAC process in detail:

1. The external interface of a router receives a packet originating on the internal (secure) side of the network.

2. The router uses the outbound access list defined on the external interface to determine if the packet is allowed. Non-allowed packets are automatically denied.

3. If the packet is allowed, CBAC creates a new connection state table and stores the packet's information in it.

4. CBAC then temporarily modifies the incoming access list on the external interface to allow the returning session data into the internal network (packets that match the same state data that was taken from the outgoing packet and stored in the connection state table). Only after the access list is modified does CBAC forward the outgoing packet from the external interface.

5. As data returns to the external interface, all packets are compared to the incoming access control list. If the valid connection data matches the temporary changes made by CBAC to the access control list, those packets are forwarded into the internal network, completing the connection.

6. When a connection terminates (or if it times out), CBAC removes the connection state table and the temporary changes to the access control list, returning the router to its previous state.

Configuring CBAC

There are several steps to configuring CBAC:

1. **Select the interface.** For networks with a DMZ (Demilitarized Zone), the evaluation will take place on the internal interface. For simple networks, packets are screened on the external interface.

2. **Implement an IP access list.** After creating a basic access list, all CBAC-evaluated traffic is permitted out, but all incoming CBAC traffic is denied. (CBAC will make its own dynamic and temporary exceptions to these rules.)

3. **Set timeouts and thresholds.** These settings determine how long connection state tables are maintained and how long to wait before incomplete connections are terminated, which provides a defense against DoS attacks. To activate this last feature, enter the following at the console:

```
ip inspect tcp synwait-time {seconds}
```

4. **Create an inspection rule.** This determines what application layer protocols will be evaluated at the interface. Options include alerting, auditing, and whether the rule checks for IP fragmentation. This example establishes an FTP inspection rule:

```
ip inspect name ftprule ftp alert on audit-trail on timeout 30
```

5. **Apply the inspection rule.** The rule is applied to outbound traffic if it is set at the external interface, and to inbound traffic if it is set at the internal interface. Continuing our example,

```
ip inspect ftprule out
```

6. **Establish logging.** This helps determine unauthorized access attempts as well as creating a record of legitimate traffic and services. Global auditing would be enabled like this:

```
ip inspect audit-trail
```

Firewall Intrusion Detection System

Cisco's *Intrusion Detection System (IDS)* uses 59 attack signatures to recognize and react to hacking attempts. IDS is designed to recognize, record, and react to an attack before a breach can occur. IDS signatures are broken into two categories: info and attack. An *info signature* looks for attempts to collect information about the network, (like a port scan). The *attack signature* looks for actual breach attempts. Each of these two categories is further subdivided into atomic and compound signatures. *Atomic signatures* look for tiny details, such as a request for a specific port. *Compound signatures* look for overall patterns.

IDS Process

The IDS system works as follows:

Audit rule is created.   Any number of signatures (from one to all) can be associated with a rule.

Audit rule is applied.   When the rule is applied to incoming traffic, IDS has an opportunity to evaluate them *before* the ACL does, thereby providing attack details that would normally be lost by ACL denial. If the rule is applied to outgoing traffic on an interface, IDS analyzes that data only after it has entered the router from another port.

Packets are audited.   Various modules analyze the packet, starting with IP, then moving on to either ICMP, TCP, or UDP, and ending with the application layer.

Signature is matched.   If a packet matches a signature at any of the models, then the appropriate action takes over:

- **Alarm**: sends an alarm to a central monitoring system.

- **Drop**: the packet is not forwarded.

- **Reset**: the packet has its reset flag set. These packets are then sent to each party in the connection.

Configuring IDS

The steps to configure IDS include:

- Activate IDS

- Activate the Post Office

- Create and activate audit rules

Activating IDS   Activating IDS requires two commands to be issued at the console in global configuration mode. The first establishes auditing:

```
ip audit {protocol} {signature} {options}
```

The second command establishes a limit to how many stored events matching a particular signature are sent to the IDS Director (the centralized alert monitoring system for IDS):

```
ip audit po max-events {quantity of events}
```

Activating the Post Office The Post Office is a proprietary Cisco protocol that creates point-to-point connections between the IDS central management system and IDS hosts (routers configured with IDS features). Alarms are transferred along the Post Office to either a log, or to the IDS Director.

```
ip audit notify nr-director/log
```

All hosts are assigned a number between 1 and 65535 (the host-id). The Director, along with all participating IDS routers, are assigned a common organization number also between 1 and 65535 (the org-id).

```
ip audit po local hostid {host-id} orgid {org-id}
```

Post Office parameters for the Director also have to be set, including the following:

rmtaddress: the IP address of the Director

localaddress: the IP address of the host interface

port: 45000 by default, this is the port number through which the Director expects to hear alarms

preference: if more than one route is configured to the Director, this number (either 1 or 2) determines the priority for this particular connection

timeout: how long until the Post Office determines a connection has timed out (in seconds)

application: what type of system is handling the events (log or Director)

```
ip audit po remote hosted {host-id} orgid {org-id} rmtaddress
{ipaddress} localaddress {ipaddress} port {port-number} preference
{number} timeout {seconds} application {type}
```

Creating and Activating Audit Rules The first two commands determine what default actions are taken when packets match an info signature or an attack signature (alarm, drop, or reset):

```
ip audit info alarm/drop/reset
ip audit attack alarm/drop/reset
```

Once default actions are specified, a user-supplied audit-name (which can be used later to assign signatures to the rule) is assigned to a particular rule along with a signature type (info or attack), standard ACL, and action (alarm, drop, reset):

```
Ip audit name {audit-name} info/attack list {standard ACL} action
alarm/drop/reset
```

Once defined, a rule is then applied to an interface along with a direction (in or out). This command is issued in interface mode:

```
ip audit {audit-name} in/out
```

Finally, the IP address of the network to be protected is configured (in global configuration mode):

```
ip audit po protected {ip address}
```

Authentication Proxy

Cisco's *authentication proxy* associates security policies with user profiles, allowing control over how individuals access network resources. User profiles come from a RADIUS or TACACS+ server, but only when the user is actively engaging in data transfers. Cisco has integrated the authentication proxy with other security services like NAT, CBAC, VPN, and IPSec, which provides a consistent integration of all access control policies.

The authentication proxy works by intercepting a user's HTTP requests. If the user has already been authenticated, the proxy forwards that packet (and any subsequent packets from the same connection). If the authentication proxy determines that they haven't been authorized, the router's HTTP server provides the user with a prompt to provide a username and password. If the user doesn't provide correct information after five attempts, the proxy ceases to respond (denying even a login prompt) for two minutes.

When the authentication proxy determines that the user has provided a valid username and password, it obtains the user profile from the AAA server. Based on this profile, the authentication proxy makes a dynamic entry to the ACL of both the inbound and outbound interfaces required to complete the connection. If the user continues to use the connection within the timeout limit, she is not prompted to re-enter her credentials. The authentication proxy removes the dynamic ACL changes after the end of the timeout period.

Configuring Application Proxy

There are three required steps to configure the application proxy:

- Configure AAA
- Configure the HTTP server
- Configure the application proxy

Configuring AAA   The following command enables the router for AAA:

```
aaa new-model
```

The next two commands define which authentication service is to be offered to the user by default at login (RADIUS or TACACS+), and then allow those services:

```
aaa authentication login default RADIUS/TACACS+
aaa authorization auth-proxy default {1st method} {2nd method}…
```

To specify the RADIUS or TACACS+ server, use

```
radius/tacacs-server server host {hostname}
```

To specify the service key used for encryption and authentication between the router and the server, use

```
radius/tacacs-server key {key}
```

Finally, an ACL permits traffic back from the authentication server:

```
access-list {number of access list}
permit tcp host {source} eq {tacacs} host {destination}
```

Configuring the HTTP Server   These commands are entered in global configuration mode. The first enables the HTTP server on the router:

```
ip http server
```

The second command sets AAA as the authentication mode:

```
ip http authentication aaa
```

The third and final command specifies which access list is bound to the HTTP server:

```
ip http access-class {number of access list}
```

Configuring the Authentication Proxy   Finally, the authentication proxy is itself configured. The first command sets the timeout, after which the authentication proxy removes the dynamic changes to the ACL (along with user authentication entries):

```
ip auth-proxy auth-cache-time {minutes}
```

The next command actually creates the authentication proxy rule and associates it with the HTTP protocol:

```
Ip auth-proxy name {rule name} http
```

The final command is issued in interface mode, and activates the rule by associating it with an interface:

```
ip auth-proxy {rule name}
```

Application Mapping

Cisco uses *port-to-application mapping (PAM)* to allow organizations to create CBAC-enforced filtering policies around non-standard (non-registered) TCP and UDP ports. The PAM feature does this by creating a table map associating applications with specific ports. Using standard ACLs, PAM can also be applied to an entire subnet, or a single host. There are three different types of entries in the PAM table:

System-defined   These entries cannot be edited or deleted, and consist of the registered (or well-known) port-to-application mappings (such as TCP 21=FTP).

User-defined   Custom entries of port-to-application mappings, with the limitation that applications can't be mapped to well-known ports (i.e., HTTP can't be mapped to TCP 21, which is already assigned to FTP by a system-defined entry).

Host-defined   This option allows mappings to be created specifically for an IP host or subnet. This creates additional security by only allowing HTTP traffic destined for a custom (and therefore hidden) port on a Web server if it originates from an internal subnet. Host-defined entries are also the only way to override system-defined mappings.

Configuring PAM

PAM is enabled on a router by specifying the application name and the port number, along with the option of associating PAM with a standard ACL (in order to apply a mapping to a subnet or host):

```
ip port-map {application name} port {port number} list {ACL number}
```

Delete a mapping by using a variant of the previous command:

```
no ip port-map {application name} port {port number} list {ACL number}
```

Overriding a standard port-to-application mapping requires two commands, the first to create a standard ACL that is applied to a specific host; the second to create the port mapping override:

```
access-list {ACL number} permit {IP address of host}
ip port-map {application name} port {port number} list {ACL from
access-list command}
```

Network Address Translation

Originally conceived as a technique to preserve IP addresses, *Network Address Translation (NAT)* provides an additional layer of network security by hiding your network IP addresses from the Internet. NAT allows organizations to use private IP address ranges (private because no public router will recognize or route packets with a source or destination address that belongs to a private range), yet still have connectivity with the Internet.

Cisco uses the following terms to make understanding NAT concepts and configuration clearer:

Inside local address   The private IP address assigned to a host on the internal network.

Inside global address   The public IP address that is assigned to outgoing data originating from an inside local address (assigned to a host on the private network) as it crosses the NAT router. This address is unique on the public Internet, hence global.

Outside global address   The host IP address as assigned by the owner of the host (and a valid public Internet address).

Outside local address   The IP address of a host on the outside network *as it appears to the inside network*. Because NAT can work both ways, the outside global address of a host can also be hidden from the internal private network.

A router performing NAT works on the border between the private network of an organization and the public Internet. When a host on the internal network requests a connection to a host with an outside global address (such as a public Web server), it sends the packet to a NAT router. NAT changes the source IP address (the host's inside local address) on the packet to an outside global address (assigned to the NAT interface connected to the Internet), and then forwards the packet to the Internet host. As the Internet host returns the packet, it sets its own outside global address as the source address and the NAT-assigned outside global address as the destination address. When the packet reaches NAT, NAT replaces the destination outside global address with the inside local address of the host that originated the session, and forwards the packet to the internal host. NAT repeats this process for the duration of the session.

Static Address Translation

NAT can perform both static and dynamic address translation. *Static translation* associates a single inside local address to a single inside global address (which is not shared with any other sessions originating from the internal network). Static translation allows an outside global address to *initiate* a communication session with a host on the internal network, while keeping the assigned inside local address secret. For example, you would use static address translation if you had a Web server that was located on the internal network that still needed to be able to receive HTTP sessions originating from an outside global address.

The first step to configuring static address translation is associating an inside local address with an inside global address:

```
ip nat inside source static
```

The final four commands define the private and public interfaces as being either inside or outside in relation to NAT:

```
interface {type} {number}
ip nat inside
interface {type} {number}
ip nat outside
```

Dynamic Address Translation

Dynamic address translation associates an inside local address with an internal global address chosen from a pool of addresses. This is the most common configuration for hosts on the internal network that act as clients for Internet services. It is also the least taxing administratively.

The first command to enable dynamic address translation creates a range of IP addresses (the address pool):

```
ip nat pool {name of pool} {starting IP address} {ending IP address}
```

Then an ACL is created that defines which inside local addresses are allowed to be translated:

```
access list {access list number} permit {source}
```

Dynamic address translation is enabled while specifying the access list created in the previous command:

```
ip nat inside source list {access list number} pool {name of pool}
```

The final four commands define the private and public interfaces as being either inside or outside in relation to NAT:

```
interface {type} {number}
ip nat inside
interface {type} {number}
ip nat outside
```

User Authentication and Authorization

Cisco routers use user-based authentication and authorization for access to network resources, (including access to the router itself). *Authentication* is the process that verifies the identity of the user. *Authorization* generally follows immediately after authentication and ensures that a user actually has the permissions necessary to access a resource. In both instances, separate security services are commonly used (RADIUS, Kerberos, and less common, TACACS and TACACS+). There are three steps to enable authentication and authorization services on a router:

- Activate AAA
- Activate authentication
- Activate authorization

Activating AAA

Activating AAA on a router is quite simple. Keep in mind, however, that TACACS and TACACS+ are older protocols and not compatible with AAA (which was designed for the newer RADIUS and Kerberos protocols). Enter the following command in global configuration mode:

```
aaa new-model
```

Deactivating AAA is just as easy as activating it:

```
no aaa new-model
```

Activating Authentication

Authentication (like authorization) relies on a method list. A *method list* contains one or more ways a user can be authenticated (or authorized) on a router. In case one of the services is unavailable (perhaps your RADIUS server goes down), the router can use a backup method (another RADIUS server or a locally-stored user database) to authenticate the user. Instead of defining individual authentication services, the method list is defined on groups. A single group can have more than one instance of the same type of service (i.e., one or more RADIUS services in the RADIUS group).

The first command defines the group name and the IP addresses of its members:

```
aaa group server radius {group name} server {ip address}
```

The next command defines a method list titled "default" and applies the list to all router logins. All users will be authenticated by the RADIUS group unless all servers within that group are unreachable, in which case the router will look to the local user database:

```
aaa authentication login default group radius local
```

Activating Authorization

Method lists are also used to define where the system finds and retrieves the system profiles that define user access. Configured in a manner similar to authentication method lists, authorization method lists also define which network services are controlled by the various methods. These network services are combined into five categories:

Auth-proxy   part of the Authentication Proxy system, used to associate policies on a per-user basis

Commands   defines access on specific commands given in the EXEC mode on the router

EXEC   specifies characteristics of the router terminal session in general

Network   all network sessions including PPP

Reverse Access   pertains to reverse telnet sessions

The first command creates a method list:

```
aaa authorization auth-proxy/network/exec/commands {level}/reverse-access
{list name} {method}
```

The second command (performed in interface mode) links the authorization method list with an interface:

```
login authorization  {list name}
```

Additional Security Precautions

Along with all the security precautions we have looked at so far, there is one more worth adding to the list. Our final task is to help prevent *Smurf attacks*. Named after the original program that would launch this attack, Smurf uses a combination of IP spoofing and ICMP replies in order to saturate a host with traffic, causing a denial of service.

The attack goes like this: Woolly Attacker sends a spoofed ping packet (echo request) to the broadcast address of a network with a large number of hosts and a high-bandwidth Internet connection. This is known as the *bounce site*. The spoofed ping packet has a source address of the system Woolly wishes to attack.

The premise of the attack is that when a router receives a packet sent to an IP broadcast address (such as 206.121.73.255), it recognizes this as a network broadcast and will map the address to an Ethernet broadcast address of FF:FF:FF: FF:FF:FF. So when your router receives this packet from the Internet, it will broadcast it to all hosts on the local segment.

I'm sure you can see what happens next. All the hosts on that segment respond with an echo reply to the spoofed IP address. If this is a large Ethernet segment, there may be 500 or more hosts responding to each echo request they receive.

Since most systems try to handle ICMP traffic as quickly as possible, the target system whose address Woolly Attacker spoofed quickly becomes saturated with echo replies. This can easily prevent the system from being able to handle any other traffic, thus causing a denial of service.

This not only affects the target system, but your organization's Internet link, as well. If the bounce site has a T3 link (45Mbps) but the target system's organization is hooked up to a leased line (56Kbps), all communication to and from your organization will grind to a halt.

So how can you prevent this type of attack? You can take steps at the source site, bounce site, and target site to help limit the effects of a Smurf attack.

Blocking Smurf at the Source

Smurf relies on the attacker's ability to transmit an echo request with a spoofed source address. You can stop this attack at its source by using the standard access list described earlier in this chapter. This will insure that all traffic originating from your network does in fact have a proper source address—stopping the attack at its source.

Blocking Smurf at the Bounce Site

In order to block Smurf at the bounce site, you have two options. The first is to simply block all inbound echo requests. This will prevent these packets from ever reaching your network.

If blocking all inbound echo requests is not an option, then you need to stop your routers from mapping traffic destined for the network broadcast address to the LAN broadcast address. By preventing this mapping, your systems will no longer receive these echo requests.

To prevent a Cisco router from mapping network broadcasts to LAN broadcasts, enter configuration mode for the LAN interface and enter the command

```
no ip directed-broadcast
```

WARNING   This must be performed on every LAN interface on every router. This command will not be effective if it is performed only on your perimeter router.

Blocking Smurf at the Target Site

Unless your ISP is willing to help you out, there is little you can do to prevent the effects of Smurf on your WAN link. While you can block this traffic at the network perimeter, this is too late to prevent the attack from eating up all of your WAN bandwidth.

You can, however, minimize the effects of Smurf by at least blocking it at the perimeter. By using reflexive access lists or some other firewalling device that can maintain state, you can prevent these packets from entering. Since your state table would be aware that the attack session did not originate on the local network (it would not have a table entry showing the original echo request), this attack would be handled like any other spoof attack and promptly dropped.

Summary

You should now have a good idea of how to configure basic connectivity on a Cisco router. We discussed how to create standard and extended access lists in order to control traffic flow. This knowledge can be extremely useful because most network perimeters are bordered by a router. Knowing how to configure filtering allows you to control traffic at these points.

When you need a higher level of protection, you should use a fully featured firewall. In the next chapter, we will look at how to set up and configure Check Point's FireWall-1.

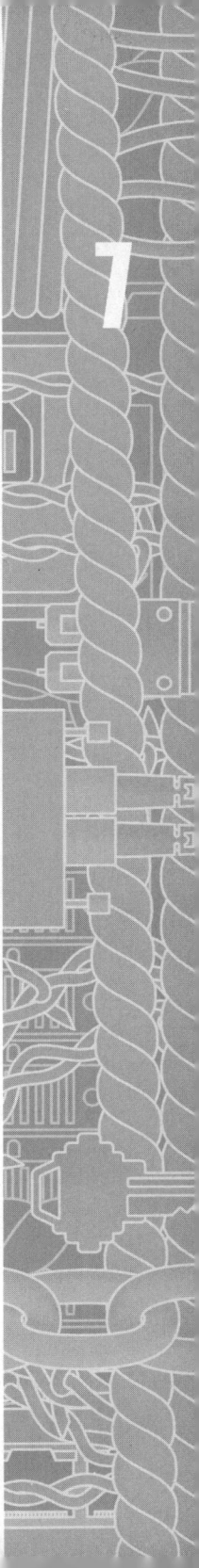

Check Point's FireWall-1

Choosing which firewall to cover in this chapter was difficult. There are many firewall products on the market, with a wide range of features. I chose FireWall-1 because it is by far the most popular firewall on the market today. It has enjoyed a larger deployment than any other firewall solution, barring the Cisco router that we covered in Chapter 6.

FireWall-1 Overview

FireWall-1 supports a wide range of features, but uses three primary components to create and enforce security policies:

- GUI management interface
- Management Server
- FireWall Module

GUI Management Interface

A GUI client is used to define a network (or enterprise) Security Policy (along with Address Translation and Bandwidth policies), which in turn is defined by using network objects (hosts, gateways, etc.) and security rules. The GUI includes the Log Viewer and System Status Viewer.

FireWall-1 creates an INSPECT script from the policies (Security, Address Translation, and/or Bandwidth) that are defined at the GUI. INSPECT is an object-oriented, high-level scripting language that is proprietary to Check Point. The INSPECT script is then compiled to create the Inspection Code, which is then loaded into the various Inspection Modules (discussed later in this chapter) on the network. Because the original INSPECT scripts are text files, they can be customized by security administrators to meet specific needs.

Management Server

Although the various policies are created using the GUI client, they are actually stored on the Management Server. The Management Server is responsible for storing and maintaining all FireWall-1 databases, (including those for network object and user definitions), policies, and log files for all network enforcement points.

FireWall Module

A FireWall Module is a software component that is installed on any network enforcement point (usually a gateway). FireWall Modules receive the policies from the Management Server and implement them, thereby securing the network.

Inspection Module

The Inspection Module is loaded in the OS, below the network layer (*below* in reference to the OSI model) but above the data-link layer. Packets are analyzed by the Inspection Module and compared to the policies.

IP addresses, port numbers, and state information from previous communications are all analyzed by the Inspection Module to determine if the policies will permit the packets. All state and context information for all sessions are stored in dynamic connection tables. Continually updated, these tables provide the Inspection Module with cumulative data with which it checks follow-on communications.

Security Servers

Security Servers are responsible for user authentication and content security. Authentication and can work with FTP, HTTP, Rlogin, and telnet. Some of the authentication schemes (or vendor technologies) that can be used with FireWall-1 include:

- FireWall-1 Password
- OS Password
- S/Key
- SecurID Tokens
- RADIUS
- Axent Pathways Defender
- TACACS/TACACS+
- Digital Certificates

There are three different authentication methods that can be used with the above schemes:

User Authentication   Conducted transparently (the user does not connect explicitly to the FireWall-1 gateway), User Authentication allows access from any IP address.

Client Authentication   Available for any service, Client Authentication is associated with a particular IP address, and may or may not be transparent.

Session Authentication   User connection requests are intercepted by Fire-Wall-1, which then activates the Session Authentication Agent (installed on the client). Upon successful receipt of credentials, FireWall-1 completes the connection request.

Security Servers are also responsible for Content Security, which is available for the following protocols:

HTTP   controls content based on schemes (HTTP, FTP, etc), methods (GET and POST), hosts (*.com), paths, and queries.

FTP   controls content based on anti-virus checks on the files, as well as file name restrictions, and FTP commands (GET and PUT).

SMTP   controls content based on address fields ("From" and "To"), as well as header and attachment types (*.VBS). Address translation is also available, hiding real user names from the outside world while still preserving the ability to restore correct address in a response.

Security and Management Services

In addition to authentication and content filtering, FireWall-1 provides the following security and management services:

- NAT (Network Address Translation)
- VPN (Virtual Private Networks)
- LDAP (Lightweight Directory Access Protocol) Account Management
- Third-party device management (Open Security Extension)

- Fault-tolerance (High Availability)
- Load balancing (ConnectControl)

Network Address Translation (NAT)

NAT maps private IP addresses to one or more public IP addresses. FireWall-1 provides both dynamic and static address mapping through two methods:

Graphical Address Translation Rule Base   An Address Translation Rule Base can be used to specify objects by name rather than by IP address (the objects having been assigned an IP address previously). Rules can then be applied to specific destination and source IP addresses or services.

Automatic Configuration   With Automatic Configuration, translation properties are assigned to network objects (such as networks or workstations), and then rules are automatically generated for these properties.

Virtual Private Networks (VPN)

Check Point's VPN-1 Gateway is a combination of FireWall-1 and an optional VPN module. VPN-1 provides site-to-site and remote user VPN access while supporting industry standard protocols:

- DES
- Triple DES
- IPSec/IKE
- Digital certificates

For more on VPN, see Chapter 10, "Virtual Private Networking."

Lightweight Directory Access Protocol (LDAP)

FireWall-1 uses an Account Management module to pull user data from any LDAP-compliant server. As a result, LDAP users (and even servers) can be used by rules like any other network object. A simple example would be a user outside the firewall requesting access to resources behind the gateway. Because the FireWall Module can query the LDAP database stored on a third-party

LDAP-compliant server to verify the credentials offered by a user, the importation of large user databases is not needed.

The Account Management Client can be launched from the FireWall-1 GUI or as a stand-alone application. Templates can be used to apply configuration properties to multiple users at once. Any change in a template is automatically made to all users who are associated with the template. Because all the components involved (FireWall-1, Account Management Client, and LDAP servers) use SSL, the communication is secure.

Third-Party Device Management

The Open Security Extension is an optional component that takes a network-wide policy and applies it to third-party security devices from vendors like 3Com, Microsoft, Cisco, and Nortel. Once a Security Policy is defined, FireWall-1 creates an ACL (Access Control List) and sends it to each router and device in the network.

The Open Security Extension also has the ability to import pre-existing Access Lists as Security Policy objects, along with log messages, allowing for centralized management of policies in conjunction with logging and reporting.

Fault Tolerance

Because all FireWall Modules on a network share connection and state information, each individual FireWall Module has a complete awareness of all network communications. If a FireWall Module fails, another FireWall Module takes control and maintains the connection in its place.

Because the state tables of each connection are continually synchronized between FireWall Modules, the system can support asymmetric routing. Without this information, packets that are part of the same session but travel through different routes and different gateways might be interpreted differently, and some might be dropped.

Load Balancing

ConnectControl is an optional module that creates a Logical Server object (multiple physical servers providing the same service). Rules can be defined that direct all connections of a particular server to a given Logical Server. Clients are only aware of one Logical Server, although in reality they are connected to any of the physical servers making up the Logical Server. There are five load-balancing algorithms:

Server load   Only available when a server has a load-measuring agent installed, FireWall-1 uses the information from the various agents to determine which server is best able to handle the incoming connection.

Round trip   PING data determines which server has the shortest round-trip time and therefore should handle a connection.

Round robin   The next server in the list is assigned the connection.

Random   A server is selected based on a random algorithm.

Domain   The closest server as determined by domain names is chosen.

Finding Good FireWall-1 Support

The best technical information on FireWall-1 outside of Check Point comes from Phoneboy—specifically www.phoneboy.com. In addition to one of the best FAQ sites on the product, the site hosts a moderated list dedicated to FireWall-1 at www.phoneboy.com/fw1/wizards/index.html

Of course, you can still subscribe to the official Check Point FireWall-1 mailing list by sending a message to

```
<Majordomo@us.checkpoint.com>
```

with the words

```
subscribe fw-1-mailinglist
```

in the body of the message. Although this list is operated by Check Point, it is truly an unmoderated list. Subscribers discuss problems and complaints quite openly, and only rarely do you see someone from Check Point posting to the list. This means that you receive advice and help from neighborly people within the end-user community. This is always a good thing—you are far more likely to receive straight advice, not marketing hype.

Choosing a Platform

One of FireWall-1's strengths is the diversity of platforms it supports. FireWall-1 components work with various operating systems as illustrated in Table 7.1.

TABLE 7.1:   Operating Systems support by FireWall-1

FireWall-1 Modules	Operating Systems
Management Server and Enforcement Module	Microsoft Windows NT 4.0 (SP4–SP6a)
	Sun Solaris 2.6, Solaris 7 (32-bit mode only)
	Red Hat Linux 6.1 (with kernel 2.2.*x*)
	HP-UX 10.20, 11.0 (32-bit mode only)
	IBM AIX 4.2.1, 4.3.2, 4.3.3
GUI Client	Microsoft Windows 9*x*, NT, 2000
	Sun Solaris SPARC
	HP-UX 10.20
	IBM AIX

We will use the NT 4.0 version as a model for our discussion. There are a number of reasons for this selection:

- The information required to secure a UNIX system for firewall use has been widely distributed. Techniques for securing NT are less common.

- NT and NT product versions are less mature than their UNIX counterparts, so there are a number of caveats to watch out for during an installation.'

- Running a firewall on NT is becoming extremely popular.

For these reasons, our discussion will be limited to the NT version of the product. While there are many interface similarities between the NT and UNIX versions (you can even run the firewall on a UNIX platform and the control software from NT), the installation process does vary greatly between versions.

Prepping NT for Firewall Installation

First let's look at getting NT ready for the firewall product installation. There are a number of tweaks you can perform in order to increase security and optimize performance.

Hardware Requirements

A production NT server that will be used as a firewall should meet or exceed the following criteria (I am assuming that you will have a T1-speed connection or less and that the server will be dedicated to firewall functionality):

- Pentium 200 processor
- 1GB of disk storage
- RAID III or higher redundancy
- 128MB of RAM (minimum for FireWall-1 per Check Point's recommendation)
- 2 PCI network cards

While FireWall-1 will run on a lesser platform, Internet performance and availability have quickly become critical functions. If you are just bringing up an Internet connection for the first time, you will be amazed how quickly your organization relies on it, just like any other business service.

Installing NT

FireWall-1 will run on NT server or workstation. Since this system should be dedicated to firewall functionality, the license count difference between these two products should not be an issue. Therefore, you can use either product. It is recommended, however, that NT server be used, because the permission setting on the Registry makes this platform a bit more secure.

NOTE The Windows NT Registry, which stores all the configuration information for the system, varies slightly between NT Server and Workstation. NT Server has a stricter access control policy with regard to Registry keys. This insures that only the system administrator is able to change the values stored within the database keys, thus increasing the integrity of the Registry information.

When installing NT server, observe the following guidelines:

- Install all required network cards before loading NT.
- Create an NTFS C partition of at least 800MB which will hold the NT operating system and swap file.
- Create an NTFS D partition of the remaining drive space (200MB minimum) to hold the firewall software as well as the firewall logs.

- Load TCP/IP as the only protocol. Make sure IP forwarding is enabled.

- Remove all services unless you plan to have this server join a domain in order to use OS authentication for inbound access. If you do wish to use OS authentication, you will need to run the Computer Browser, NetBIOS Interface, RPC Configuration, Server, and Workstation services.

- Install the SNMP service if you choose to use it (see the "Installing FireWall-1" section for some caveats).

- Configure the system as a stand-alone workgroup, not a domain, whenever possible.

- If the server will be part of a domain, disable all WINS bindings on the external interface.

- Disable the guest account and create a new Administrator-equivalent account for performing firewall management. When you are ready to install the firewall software, log off as Administrator, log on as the new account name, and disable the Administrator account.

- Enable auditing and track logon failures in User Manager. Under User Rights, remove the right for all users to log on from the network. Modify the Logon Locally right to include only the user name you created as an Administrator equivalent.

- Install Service Pack 6a. This is considered the most stable service pack and has the most comprehensive security fixes to date.

- Change the boost to the foreground application to None under the Performance tab in System Properties.

- If you are running the server service (for domain authentication), go to the Server Properties dialog box and change Optimization to Maximize throughput for network applications.

TIP

NT has a problem where it associates driver names with the NIC card loading order in the Registry. If the card settings are changed in any way (IRQ change, cards added or removed, and so on), this Registry setting may become corrupt. You can check this by running the `ipconfig` command, which will return incorrect card information or an error message that states, "The Registry has become corrupt." This is why it is important to install the NICs *before* installing NT. The only sure fix is to reload the operating system and all patches from scratch (not as an upgrade).

Once you have followed these guidelines, you are ready to make an emergency recovery disk and begin the FireWall-1 product install. Remember that if you load any new software from the NT server CD after this point, you will have to reinstall

- SP6a
- All hotfixes
- The firewall software (as an update)
- The firewall patch

Make sure you have your system exactly the way you want it before you install the firewall software.

Pre-install Flight Check

At this point, you should verify that the firewall platform has IP connectivity. Create a default route that points to the local router interface leading to the Internet. Create required route table entries for any internal network segments that are not directly connected to the firewall. The correct syntax to use when creating route table entries is

```
route add -p {remote IP} mask {subnet mask} {gateway address}
```

So to create a route entry to the network 192.168.2.0, which is on the other side of a local router at IP address 192.168.1.5, you would type

```
route add -p 192.168.2.0 mask 255.255.255.0 192.168.1.5
```

Likewise, if the route entry was only for the host 192.168.2.10, you would type

```
route add -p 192.168.2.10 mask 255.255.255.255 192.168.1.5
```

NOTE   The -p switch tells the operating system to make this route entry permanent, allowing the route entry to remain persistent over operating system reboots.

Once you have created your route table, you should test connectivity. This can be done using ping and traceroute. At this point, the firewall platform should have connectivity to all internal and external hosts. If it does not, you need to troubleshoot the problem before going any further.

You should also make sure that you can ping external IP addresses from internal hosts. This will not be possible, however, if you are using private address space for your internal hosts. If you are using private address space, pinging the external interface of the firewall should suffice.

You should also run the `ipconfig` command and record the adapter drive name associated with the external IP address. This name will be similar to `Elnk32`. This information will be required later during the firewall software installation if you have purchased a single gateway product. Make sure you record the name exactly, because the entry is case sensitive.

TIP

If you are worried about someone trying to break in to your network while you are testing for connectivity, simply disconnect the WAN connection to your router. You can then test connectivity as far as the IP address on the router's serial interface.

Generating a License

Once you have verified connectivity, you are ready to generate a firewall license. This is done by pointing your Web browser at

    http://license.checkpoint.com/

By filling in the online forms, you can register the product and generate a valid license key. The information you will be prompted for includes

- Who you are

- Your e-mail address

- Who sold you the software

- The certificate key number on the inside jacket of the CD case

- The platform and operating system you plan to use

- The external IP address of the firewall

Once you complete the forms, you will be presented with a valid host ID, feature set, and license key. This information will also be sent to the e-mail address that you specified on the form. Once you have this information in hand, you are ready to begin your firewall installation.

NOTE

The firewall software ships with a 30-day evaluation license that will expire on a specific date (not 30 days after the software is installed). You can use this license to get your firewall up and running if you need it, but the evaluation may not support all the options you require.

Installing FireWall-1

The FireWall-1 CD contains program files for all NOS versions, as well as Adobe Acrobat versions of the manuals. Under the Windows directory, you will find directories for the firewall server software along many additional components:

FloodGate-1   Check Point's bandwidth management solution, this module works to ensure bandwidth for specific types of network traffic.

Meta IP   This module, responsible for user-to-address mapping is Check Point's method of automatically linking user identity to IP addresses in order to implement and log user-based security policies.

Reporting   By providing pre-defined templates, this module consolidates and reports information from Check Point logs.

High Availability   This module provides service redundancy (one service fails, another takes over performing the same task) and chaining (one service providing checks for executables, the next verifying that no unauthorized ActiveX script is passed, and so on) for content security services.

VPN-1 SecuRemote   Check Point's VPN client, this software encrypts all communication between the client and a secured network.

VPN-1 Secure Client   As an add-on to SecuRemote, the Secure Client functions as a workstation firewall.

Session Authentication Agent   This component allows Windows clients to authenticate to FireWall-1 modules and use any allowed IP service.

The FireWall-1 installation is fairly intuitive. First, install the CD in your NT server (which should autoplay). Then you will be prompted to agree to the License Agreement, after which you are provided with a product menu allowing you to choose the Server/Gateway components or Mobile/Desktop Components. After selecting the Server/Gateway option, you are given the option to select which specific Server/Gateway components to install (the default is all of them).

You are then prompted to determine if this will be a stand-alone or distributed installation. Finally, the actual FireWall-1 installation begins, and you are asked where to install the firewall software. For ease of administration, you should install the software to the D partition specified earlier. Next, as shown in Figure 7.1, you will select which product version you wish to install. Typically this will be either the FireWall-1 Enterprise Product (an unlimited license firewall) or the FireWall-1 Single Gateway Product (a version that can be licensed for up to 250 hosts). Make sure you select the correct product: selecting the Single Gateway Product will later prompt you to identify the external interface of the firewall while the Enterprise version will not.

FIGURE 7.1:

The Select Product Type dialog box

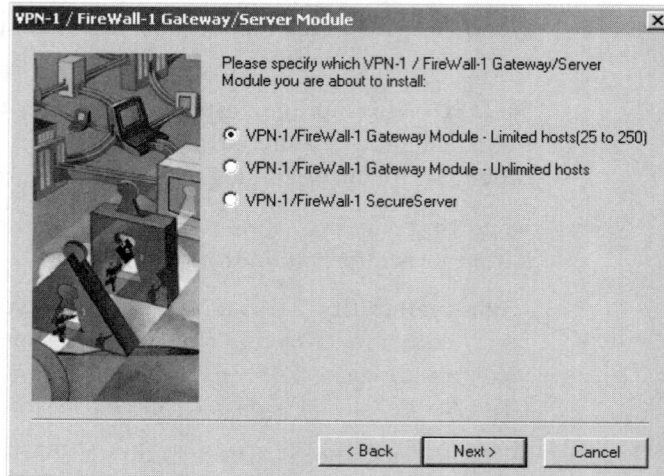

NOTE   The FireWall-1 license is based on the number of protected nodes, *not* on the number of concurrent Internet connections. The reasoning is that a firewall's job is to protect IP hosts, a benefit you get whether the system accesses the Internet or not. Make sure your license will cover all of your IP nodes that will sit behind the firewall.

Once you select the proper product, the Setup program will then ask if the installation should be backwards-compatible with previous versions of FireWall-1, as shown in Figure 7.2.

The Setup program will then perform some additional configuration changes and prompt you to enter your license information. If you have this information in hand, it is a good idea to remove the evaluation license before installing your permanent license. The evaluation license will eventually generate error messages in Event Viewer once the license expires. Also, you cannot remove a single license. You must remove all of them and then re-enter the ones you wish to keep. For these reasons, it is just easier to do it right the first time. This screen is followed by one that prompts you for where to install the program files.

FIGURE 7.2:

The Backwards compatibility screen

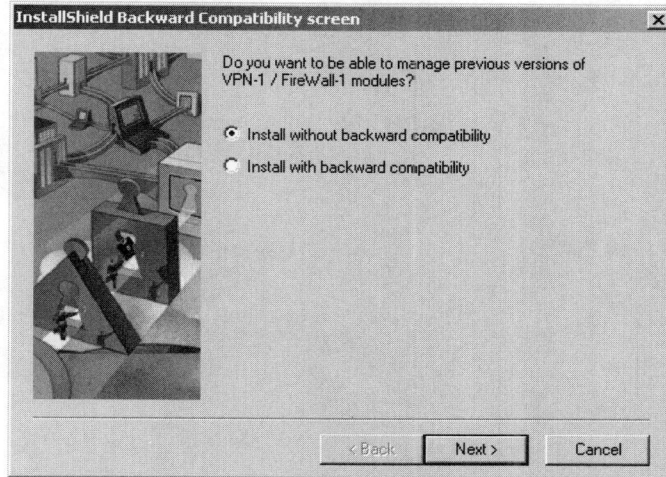

Next you will be asked to create a firewall administrator as shown in Figure 7.3. The firewall administrator account information is maintained separately from Windows NT. The administrator name does not have to match the logon name you use to gain access to Windows NT.

You can set the level of access allowed for each administrator. Your choices are

Read/Write All   User is allowed full access to all firewall utilities, and is the only option that allows the editing of security policies.

Customized   Except for Edit Users and System Status, all of the following customized options can be Read Only or Read/Write:

- Edit Users databases
- Security Rules
- Bandwidth Rules
- Compression Rules
- Log Viewer
- System Status

FIGURE 7.3:

The Administrators dialog box

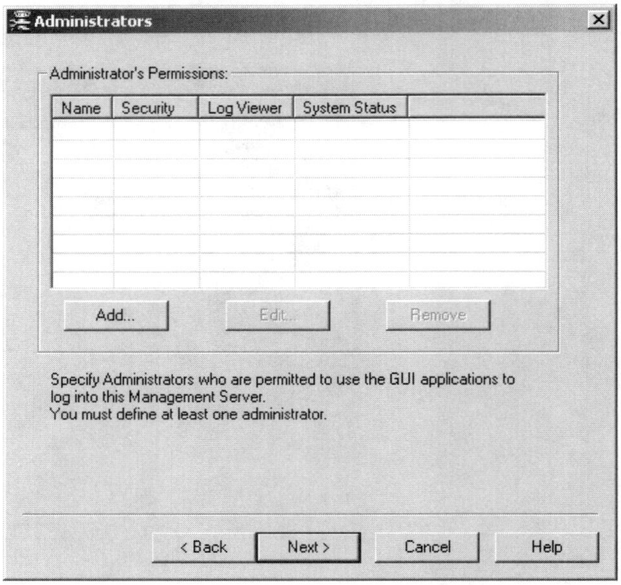

No permissions User has no permission (but still might be allowed to utilize the reporting client) objects.

Reporting Clients Permissions Determines if the user is allowed to run the Reporting Tool (also specified to be Read Only or Read/Write) and the Log Consolidator.

Once you have created at least one firewall administrator, the next screen verifies that the IP address found in the `hosts` file of the computer is correct. If no IP address is present, you must enter the IP address of your external interface. After this window, click Next to move on to the GUI client configuration.

The GUI client configuration allows you to define remote hosts that are allowed to remotely manage the firewall. Remote users are still prompted for a logon name and password. This setting simply limits the number of source IP addresses that will be able to receive a logon prompt. By default, administration is only allowed from the firewall itself.

A typical configuration will create a user with Monitor Only rights and will use the GUI client setting to limit the points of access. The combination of these two settings will allow you to remotely monitor your firewall's activities in a secure manner.

If you are installing a single gateway, you will next be prompted for the name of the adapter for the external interface. This information can be retrieved by typing **ipconfig** at a command prompt. Enter the character string exactly, as this entry is case sensitive.

You will then be prompted to choose whether FireWall-1 should control IP forwarding. If you tell the firewall to control IP forwarding, the server will be unable to pass traffic if the firewall process becomes disabled. If you tell it not to control IP forwarding, disabling the firewall process leaves the connection wide open. Obviously, for increased security, you want the firewall to control the flow of IP traffic. After this, the next screen offers Security Server protocol settings, followed by a screen prompting you to enter random data for the generation of encryption keys used in authentication and VPN operations.

Once the installation is complete, you will be prompted to reboot your server. When the server comes back up, you can log on and go to the FireWall-1 program group and select the FireWall-1 Configuration icon in order to change any of the settings configured during the FireWall-1 installation process.

Installing the FireWall-1 GUI Client

The FireWall-1 GUI client is located on the CD under the same Windows directory as the FireWall-1 server software, and is installed by default with the FireWall-1 Server/Gateway modules. The GUI client is made up of four separate components:

- The Policy Editor for managing your firewall rules

- The Log Viewer for monitoring firewall activity

- The System Status Viewer for reporting summary traffic statistics and whether the firewall is up or down

- The Real Time Monitor for viewing activity statistic as they happen

These components can be installed on the firewall itself or on any remote Windows 9x or NT/2000 system. You can also selectively install each of the four components.

When you launch any of the client components, you will be presented with the FireWall-1 logon screen. Simply enter the logon name and password you created as a FireWall-1 administrator, along with the hostname of the firewall server. For faster access, identify the firewall server by IP address instead of by host name. When you are running the client from the firewall itself, use the Loopback address (127.0.0.1).

The FireWall-1 Configuration Utility

Now that the FireWall-1 software is installed, you can add any administrator accounts you require. Launch the FireWall-1 Configuration utility and click the Administrators tab. This screen is shown in Figure 7.4.

FIGURE 7.4:

The Administrators tab of the FireWall-1 Configuration utility

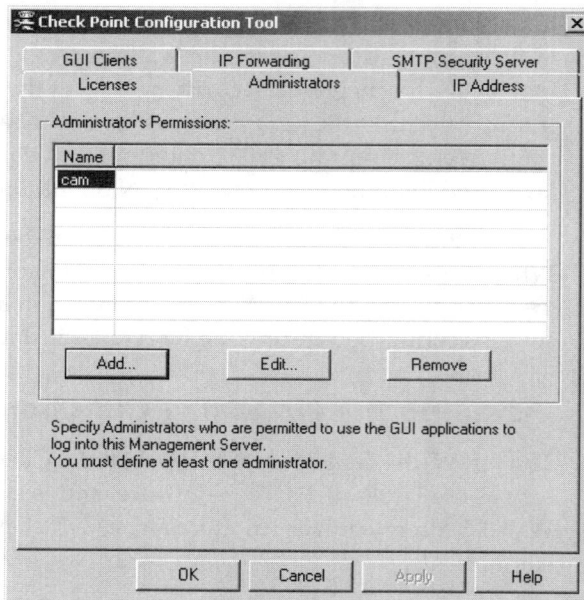

FIGURE 7.4:

The Administrators tab of the FireWall-1 Configuration utility

As you can see in Figure 7.4, the tab options are identical to the options that were available when you were prompted to create administrator accounts during the FireWall-1 server installation.

From the FireWall-1 Configuration utility you can also configure the SMTP Security Server you wish to use. This screen is shown in Figure 7.5.

The SMTP security server is the only security server that adds another tab to the FireWall-1 Configuration utility. This tab lets you define parameters for the SMTP process, such as timeout values, which directory to use for spooling mail messages, where to send error messages. Since NT has no built-in mail ability, you must have error messages forwarded to a remote mail system by specifying the system's name and a valid mail account.

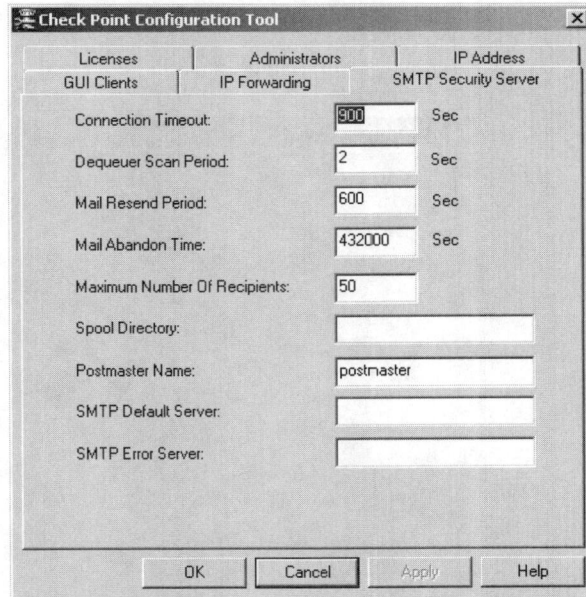

Once you have completed the configuration, you can close the FireWall-1 Configuration utility. Now you can launch the Policy Editor and create your firewall rules.

FireWall-1 Security Management

Managing a security policy through FireWall-1 is a multistep process. First, you must define objects you wish to control, and then you must define users, after which you apply these objects to the rule base. While this configuration may seem a bit complex, it is actually quite straightforward and allows for extremely granular security control. All security management is performed through the Security Policy-1 tab of the Policy Editor as shown in Figure 7.6.

Begin by defining your network objects. Select Manage ➢ Network Objects from the Security Policy-1 menu (the available menu options change depending on which policy tab is selected), which will produce the Network Object management screen as shown in Figure 7.7. When you start this screen for the first time, there will be no entries.

FIGURE 7.6:

The FireWall-1 Policy Editor (with the Security Policy 1 tab selected)

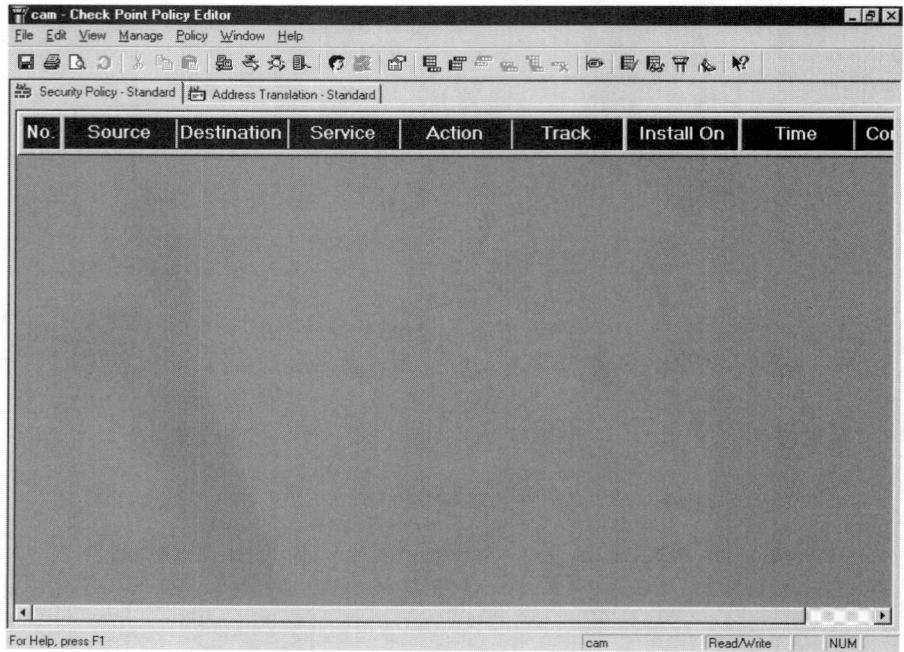

FIGURE 7.7:

The Network Objects management screen

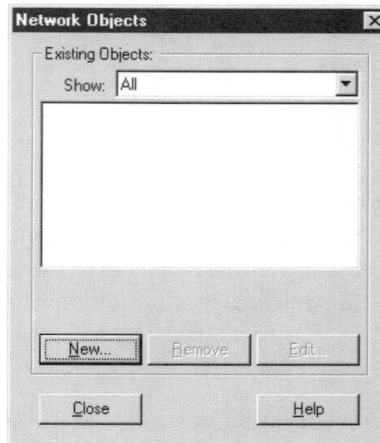

There a number of different object types that can be created. These include

Workstation   This is a generic object used to create any computer host. This includes hosts with multiple NIC cards, such as the firewall.

Network   This object is used to define an entire IP subnet. This is useful when you wish to apply the same security policy to an entire subnet.

Domain   This object is used to define all hosts within a specific DNS domain name. It is recommended that you do not use this object, because it relies on accurate DNS information and slows down the processing speed of the firewall.

Router   This object is used to define network routers. FireWall-1 has the ability to convert policies created through the Policy Editor to access lists and to update defined routers automatically.

Switch   This object allows you to define network switches.

Integrated Firewall   This object represents an installed FireWall-1 module (also known as an enforcement point).

Group   This object allows you to collect multiple objects under one. For example, you could create a group of all network objects and refer to them as the group local net.

Logical Server   A grouping of two or more modules providing the same service, this object is used to enable load balancing.

Address Range   Instead of an entire IP subnet, this object allows a security policy to be applied to a collection of addresses.

Creating an Object for the Firewall

The first object you should create is one representing the firewall. This is done by selecting New ➢ Workstation from the Network Objects management screen. The will produce the Workstation Properties screen shown in Figure 7.8.

First, assign a name and an IP address. The system name should be the same as the computer's DNS host name and the Microsoft computer name. Also, it is beneficial to standardize on a single address when referring to the firewall, even though it has multiple interfaces. Typically, the external interface is used. This should be consistent with your local DNS. You may even want to create a hosts file entry on the firewall that includes the system's name and external IP address.

FIGURE 7.8:

The Workstation Properties
screen

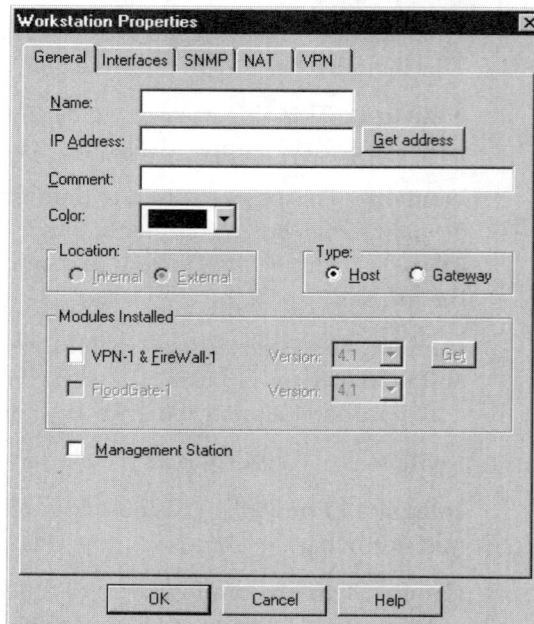

Workstation Properties ☒

General | Interfaces | SNMP | NAT | VPN

N̲ame: [　　　　　　　]

IP A̲ddress: [　　　　　　] G̲et address

C̲omment: [　　　　　　　　]

Color: [■　 ▼]

Location:
○ I̲nternal ○ E̲xternal

Type:
● H̲ost ○ Gate̲way

Modules Installed
☐ VPN-1 & F̲ireWall-1   Version: [4.1 ▼] Get
☐ Flo̲odGate-1   Version: [4.1 ▼]

☐ M̲anagement Station

[OK] [Cancel] [Help]

TIP FireWall-1 will run faster if the NT server has an entry for itself in the local `hosts` file stored in `C:\winnt\system32\drivers\etc`.

The firewall and any system that sits behind it are considered to be on the internal network. The only systems considered external are the ones sitting outside the external interface of the firewall. Also, since this system has multiple NIC cards, it is considered a gateway, not a host. Finally, you should indicate that FireWall-1 is installed on this machine.

If you click the Interfaces tab, you will be presented with a list of system interfaces. Since you have not created any entries yet, the list will be blank. To create an entry, click the Add button. This will produce the Interface Properties screen shown in Figure 7.9.

Here is where you will define your IP spoofing rules. By configuring each of your interfaces, you can insure that the firewall only accepts traffic from a valid IP address. This will help to prevent Smurf and other attacks that rely on using a spoofed address.

FIGURE 7.9:

The Interface Properties
screen

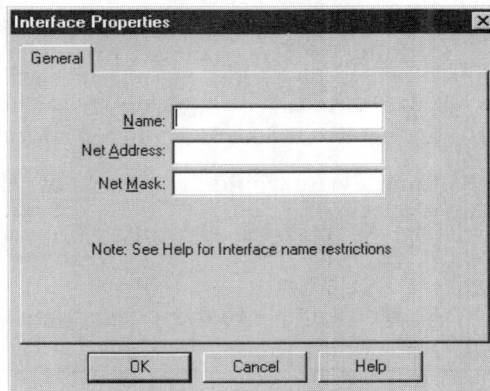

The name you use for each interface should match the adapter name used
by Windows NT. This will insure that the spoofing rules are applied to the correct interface. You also need to enter the locally attached network address (not
the IP address of the NIC but the network subnet address), as well as a valid
subnet mask.

Next you will define what traffic source addresses are valid. To do this, select
one of the options under Valid Addresses. Here's what each option means:

Any   This option, the default, assumes that life is happy and we trust
everyone. No screening takes place for any spoofed IP traffic.

No security policy!   This option is the same as the Any option. No spoof
detection is performed.

Others   This option is used in combination with the spoofing filters
defined for the other interfaces. In effect, this options states, "All traffic is
acceptable except for what has been defined on another interface." This is
the option you would typically select for your external interface.

Others +   This option is the same as Others, except that you have the
option to define an additional host, network, or group whose traffic would
be considered acceptable, as well.

This net   This option states that only traffic from the locally connected subnet will be accepted. This is useful for defining a DMZ or an internal network segment that has no routed links leading to other subnets.

Specific   This option allows you to specify a particular host, network, or group whose traffic would be considered acceptable. This is useful for defining your internal network when you have multiple subnets.

Once you specify which addresses are valid, you must then tell the firewall what to do when it detects a spoofed address. Your options are

None   Why would I want to know about spoofed packets?

Log   Create a log entry in the firewall log indicating a spoofed packet was detected.

Alert   Log the event and take some form of pre-configured action.

NOTE   You can configure alerts from the Security Policy-1 menu by selecting Policy ➤ Properties and clicking the Log and Alert tab.

At a minimum, you should log any attempts to use spoofed packets against your network. The Alert option is useful because it allows you to define some other method of notification that may be able to get your attention more quickly. For example, you could have the firewall send you an e-mail message stating that an alert condition has been encountered.

Repeat this process for each interface that has been installed in your firewall. Once you've done so, you are ready to click OK and save your firewall network object.

Working with NAT

Let's create a few more network objects—only we will assume that the internal network is using private address space. This means that your firewall will need to perform network address translation between your internal network and the Internet.

As an example, let's set up an internal host that will be acting as a mail relay. Since this host needs to be reachable from the Internet, you will need to use static NAT. Repeat the initial steps you used to configure the firewall object. The only configuration difference is under the General tab of the Workstation Properties screen: leave the FireWall-1 installed check box unchecked. You may also wish to set a different color for this object in order to distinguish it from other objects.

Once you have filled out all the general information, instead of selecting the Interfaces tab, select the Address Translation tab. The screen should appear similar to Figure 7.10.

FIGURE 7.10:

The Address Translation tab of the Workstation Properties screen

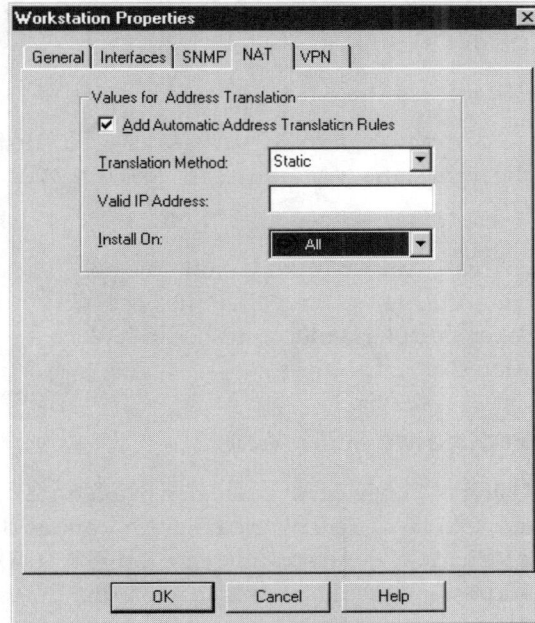

Configuring the workstation object to use NAT is pretty straightforward. Once you select the Add Automatic Address Translation Rules check box, the other options become active. For a translation method, you can select

Hide   Hide the system behind a legal address.

Static   Map this private address to a legal address.

Since this system needs to be reachable, define the Translation Method as Static. Next, enter a legal IP address to use in the Valid IP Address field. The Install On option lets you choose which firewalled object enforces address translation rules. Choosing All installs the rules on all firewalled objects. Finally, click OK and install this entry into your rule base.

Creating Route Entries on the Firewall

You need to perform one more step in order to have this translated address handled correctly. Since NT is actually providing the routing functionality, not Fire-Wall-1, you need to fool NT by creating a static route entry at the command prompt which associates the static NAT address with the host's legal IP address. Do this by typing the command

```
route add -p {legal IP address} mask 255.255.255.255 {private IP address}
```

For example, if the IP address assigned to the mail relay is 192.168.1.10, and the legal static NAT address is 206.121.73.10, the entry would appear as follows:

```
route add -p 206.121.73.10 mask 255.255.255.255 192.168.1.10
```

This is correct, provided that the host is attached to a segment that is locally connected to the firewall. If the host is located on a remote segment that is on the other side of a router, you should replace the private IP address entry with the router's local address.

Problems with ARP

Using NAT can cause problems when translating between OSI layer 2 (data link) and OSI layer 3 (network) communications. To see how this problem occurs, take a look at the network shown in Figure 7.11. The internal network is using private address space. This means that in order for the mail relay to have full Internet connectivity, static NAT must be used.

Now let's assume that your ISP issues you a single class C address space of 206.121.73.0. You assign 206.121.73.1 to the Ethernet interface on the router, 206.121.73.2 to the external interface on the firewall, and you wish to use 206.121.73.10 as the static NAT address for the mail relay. This creates an interesting problem. Let's follow the communication session when you try to send an outbound e-mail message to see what happens. For simplicity, let's assume that your mail relay already knows the IP address of the external host to which it needs to deliver a message.

Your mail relay identifies that it needs to deliver a message to an external host. It creates an IP header using its assigned IP address as the source address (192.168.1.10), and the IP address of the remote mail system as the destination IP address (192.52.71.4). The mail relay sets SYN=1 on this initial packet in order to establish a new session. Your mail relay would then ARP for the MAC address of 192.168.1.1 (its default gateway setting) and forward this first packet to the firewall.

FIGURE 7.11:

A network using private
address space

FIGURE 7.11:

A network using private
address space

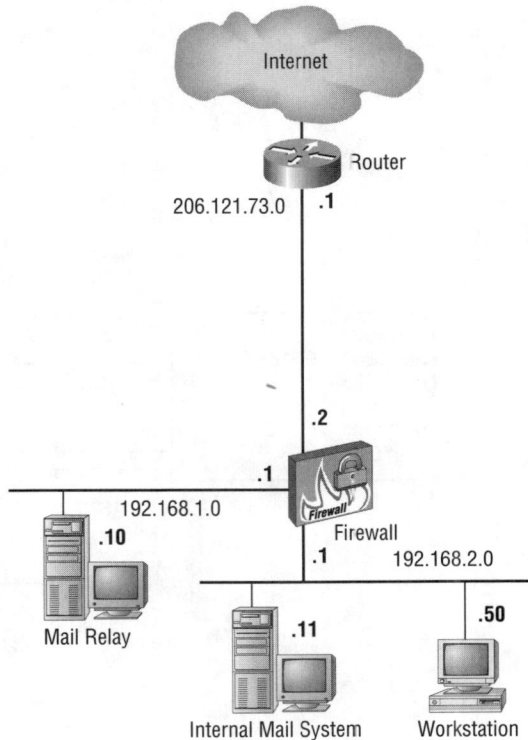

Your firewall reviews the NAT table and realizes that this host address needs to be statically mapped. The firewall then changes the source IP address to 206.121.73.10, and ARP for its default gateway setting, which is the Ethernet interface of the router (206.121.73.1). The firewall then transmits this initial connection request. This process is shown in Figure 7.12.

Through the magic of the Internet, this initial packet of data is routed to the destination host. Let's assume that the remote host is in fact a mail system and that your connection request is accepted. The remote host creates an IP header using its IP address as the source address (192.52.71.4) and the legal IP address of your mail system as the destination IP address (206.121.73.10). The mail system sets SYN=1 and ACK=1 to acknowledge your request to establish a new session. Let's assume that this reply makes it all the way back to your router without error.

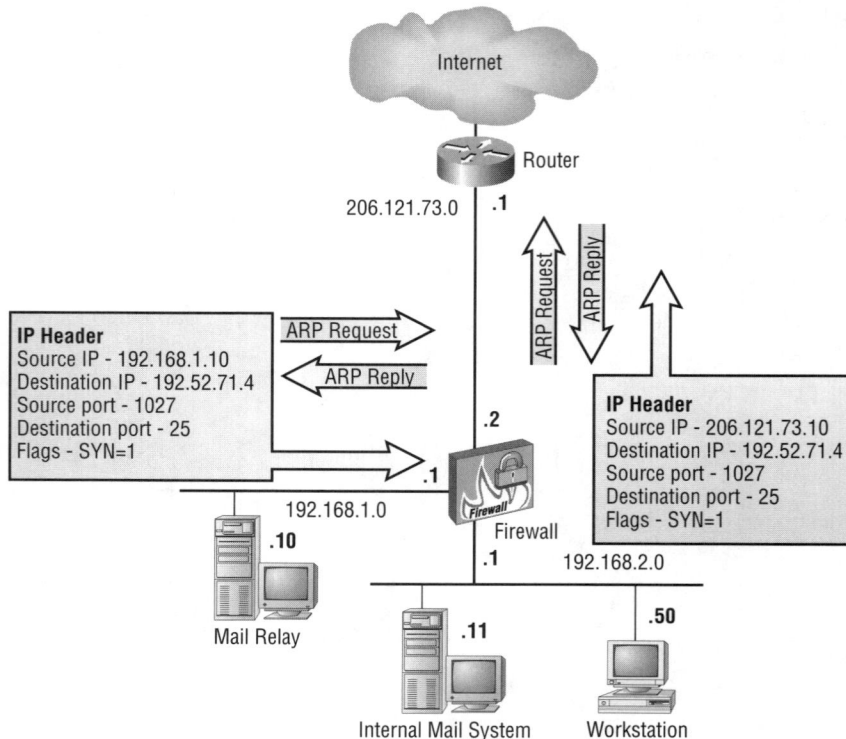

At this point, an interesting problem arises. Your router receives this acknowledgment in its WAN port and consults its routing table. The router realizes that the 206.121.73.0 network is directly connected to its Ethernet port. Not realizing that this system is on the other side of the firewall, it attempts local delivery by transmitting an ARP to 206.121.73.10. Since no actual system is using this address, the ARP request fails. The router assumes that the host is down and returns an error to the remote mail system.

How do you get around this ARP problem and get the router to deliver the reply directly to the firewall? Luckily, you have a few options available to remedy this situation.

Fixing ARP at the Router

If the router supports static ARP entries, you could create a phony entry on the router that maps the MAC address of the firewall's external interface to the IP address you are translating. When the firewall receives a packet for 206.121.73.10, it will no longer need to transmit an ARP broadcast. The router would consult its ARP cache, find the static entry you created, and deliver the packet directly to the firewall.

If the router is a Cisco, you could create this entry with the following command in global configuration mode:

```
arp {ip address} {hardware address}
```

TIP
To find the external MAC address of the firewall, you can ping the firewall's external address and then view the ARP cache entry on the router. This will display the MAC address entry in the format the router expects you to use when creating the static entry.

Not all routers support the creation of static ARP entries. If you are stuck using one of these routers, you will have to try one of the other options that follow. The only drawback to configuring static ARP entries on the router is that if you have multiple devices on the segment between the firewall and the router (such as other routers or an unprotected server), each device will need a static ARP entry in order to reach this translated address.

Fixing ARP at the Firewall

You can also fix this problem on the firewall by telling the NT server to respond to an ARP request for the translated address when it sees one. This is referred to as proxy ARP and is a common feature on UNIX platforms. Unfortunately, NT has no built-in method for performing proxy ARP for other IP addresses. Fortunately, we can configure proxy ARP through the FireWall-1 software.

NOTE
Most UNIX machines support static ARP entries with a -p switch. This switch tells the UNIX machine to "publish," or act as a proxy for, the specified IP address. If your firewall is running on UNIX, this will fix the ARP problem with NAT addresses.

To our ARP problem, you will need to create a file in the \%fw1%\state directory. Name the file local.arp. In this file, create one entry per line that associates each statically mapped IP address with the MAC address of the firewall's external interface. The format of each line should be

```
206.121.73.10        00-00-0C-34-A5-27
```

Once you have rebooted the system, the firewall will begin responding to ARP requests for the listed entries.

The only drawback to this method is that it does not work consistently if you create 10 or more entries. How often the system replies will depend on how busy it is at the time. If you have many IP addresses that will need to be translated, you should look at fixing proxy ARP for NT through one of the other listed methods.

Fixing ARP through Routing Changes

Of course, the easiest way to fix ARP for NAT addresses would be to make sure that ARP is never an issue. You can do this by changing your subnet address scheme and your routing tables so that the router no longer thinks that the static NAT address is local.

For example, let's say that you went back to your ISP and asked it to issue you a new legal subnet address, in addition to the one already supplied. Instead of asking for a full class C address space, you ask for one that uses a 255.255.255.252 subnet mask. Most ISPs will be receptive to this request, because it only supports two hosts and ISPs usually have address space broken down into this increment for use on point-to-point WAN links.

TIP

If your ISP will not issue you additional address space, you can subnet the address space you have already received.

Once you have obtained this address space, use it to address the network between the router and the firewall. For example, if your ISP issued you the network address 206.121.50.64, you could use 206.121.50.65 for the Ethernet interface on the router and 206.121.50.66 for the external interface on the firewall. You would then need to create a route entry on the router, telling it that the best route to the 206.121.73.0 network is through the firewall's external interface (206.121.50.66).

TIP

Remember that if you change the external IP address on the firewall, you will need to generate a new license key.

So your router no longer thinks it is local to your statically mapped addresses and will no longer send an ARP request for this address when attempting delivery. The router will defer to its routing table and realize that this is not a local host, so it must transmit the packet to the next hop, which is the firewall.

Working with the FireWall-1 Rules

Now that you have created your required network objects, it is time to employ them in your firewall rules and implement your security policy. A sample policy is shown in Figure 7.13.

FIGURE 7.13:

Sample FireWall-1 rules

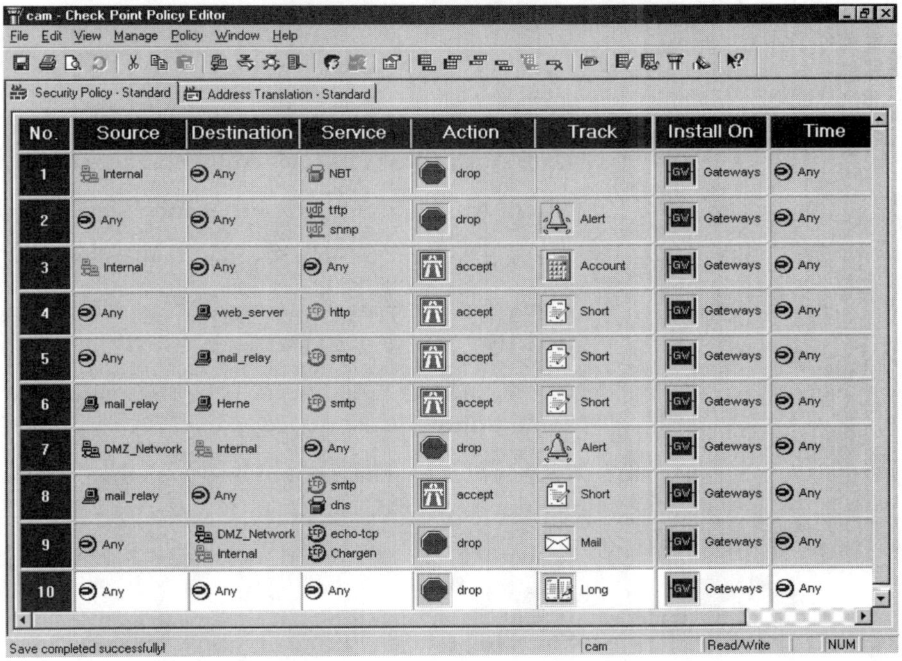

cam - Check Point Policy Editor
File Edit View Manage Policy Window Help
Security Policy - Standard
Address Translation - Standard
No. Source Destination Service Action Track Install On Time
1 Internal Any NBT drop Gateways Any
2 Any Any tftp snmp drop Alert Gateways Any
3 Internal Any Any accept Account Gateways Any
4 Any web_server http accept Short Gateways Any
5 Any mail_relay smtp accept Short Gateways Any
6 mail_relay Herne smtp accept Short Gateways Any
7 DMZ_Network Internal Any drop Alert Gateways Any
8 mail_relay Any smtp dns accept Short Gateways Any
9 Any DMZ_Network Internal echo-tcp Chargen drop Mail Gateways Any
10 Any Any Any drop Long Gateways Any
Save completed successfully!
cam
Read/Write
NUM

The rules read from left to right. For example, Rule 4 states, "Any IP host connecting to the system `web_server` on port 80 should be allowed through the firewall." Port 80 is the well-known port for HTTP. Remember that FireWall-1 is simply going to screen the packet headers. It has no way to know for sure if the remote system is actually transmitting HTTP requests. The service column employs service names, instead of port numbers, for improved ease of use. Here's a description of each column:

No.   Identifies each rule by number in order to provide a reference

Source   Identifies the source hosts or networks affected by this rule

Destination   Identifies the destination hosts or networks affected by this rule

Service   Identifies the service port numbers affected by this rule

Action   Determines what should be done with a packet if the source, destination, and service are a match. Options are

> **Accept**   Lets it through
>
> **Drop**   Discards the packet with no notification to the source
>
> **Reject**   Sends an RST=1 packet to the source
>
> **User Auth**   Invokes User Authentication for the connection
>
> **Client Auth**   Invokes Client Authentication for the connection
>
> **Session Auth**   Invokes Session Authentication for the connection
>
> **Encrypt**   Encrypts outgoing packets, accepts and decrypts incoming packets
>
> **Client Encrypt**   Accepts only SecuRemote (Check Point's VPN client) communications

Track   Determines what should be done when this rule finds a match. Options are

> **Ignore**   Not represented by an icon, leaving Track blank does not create a log entry
>
> **Short log entry**   Records the source IP address and destination IP and port address
>
> **Long log entry**   Records the short entries plus source port and packet size
>
> **Account**   Writes entry to an accounting log
>
> **Alert**   Takes special predefined action

Mail   Sends an e-mail which includes the log entry

SNMP Trap   Issues an SNMP trap (defined in SNMP Trap Alert field on the Log and Alert tab of the Properties Setup Window)

User defined   Performs a user-customizable action

Install On   Defines on which systems the rule entry should be enforced. The default is Gateways, which includes all NetworkObjects defined as Gateways. You can also selectively install each rule on:

Dst   Represents inbound traffic on Network Objects defined as Destination (usually servers)

Src   Similar to Dst, but represents outbound traffic (that is client-initiated)

Routers   Rules are enforced on all routers

Integrated FireWalls   Rules are enforced on all integrated FireWalls

Targets   Rules are applied to a specific target, on both in and outbound traffic (called *eitherbound* by Check Point)

Time   Determines what time of day, day of the week, or day of the month this rule should be enforced. For example, if Time on rule 3 were changed to read 5:00 PM to 8:00 AM, users could only access the Internet during non-business hours. A new Group object can also be created that can hold multiple Time objects, which are applied collectively (as the Group) to a particular rule.

Comments   Allows you to add text describing the purpose of the rule. (This column is only partially shown in Figure 7.13.)

Understanding the Rule Set

Let's look briefly at each of the rules shown in Figure 7.13. Feel free to adapt these rules to your environment as you see fit.

Rule 1 tells the firewall to drop, but not log, all NetBIOS traffic originating from the internal network. Windows machines broadcast name information once per minute. These entries can quickly fill up your log and make it difficult to weed out the information you are actually interested in. When you leave the Track column blank, the log does not record this traffic.

Rule 2 is used to block any services that you absolutely do not want to let past your firewall. This can be used to minimize the effects of a break-in. For example, let's say that your Web server is attacked and compromised. The attacker may try to transmit SNMP information to a remote location in order to gain additional information on the internal environment. Since most organizations typically have a fairly loose policy regarding Internet access, this information would be allowed to leave the network. Rule 2 not only blocks this traffic, it also notifies the administrator that something fishy is going on.

Rule 3 lets your internal systems perform any type of communication they desire, except for services blocked by earlier rules. Like a router access list, FireWall-1 processes rules in order so traffic is evaluated on a first fit basis, not a best fit basis.

Rules 4 and 5 allow in acceptable traffic to your Web server and mail relay, respectively. Because these systems are located on an isolated DMZ, Rule 6 is required to let your mail relay deliver SMTP messages to your internal mail system. When this rule is combined with Rule 7, no other traffic is permitted from the DMZ to the internal network. Again, this helps to protect your internal systems if one of your public servers becomes compromised. Rule 8 is then used to allow your mail relay to deliver messages to hosts out on the Internet.

Rule 9 looks for suspicious activity: specifically, for traffic trying to connect to TCP echo and/or the Character Generator service. These services have many known exploits. None of your internal systems actually offers these services. Rule 9 is set up specifically to see if someone is probing your network, perhaps with a scanner. If such traffic is detected, you want the firewall to take additional action beyond simply creating a log entry. So why not monitor all unused ports? If the attacker is using a port scanner, this rule may be evaluated hundreds—even thousands—of times. The last thing you want is to cause a denial of service on your mail system as the firewall tries to warn you of an attack in progress (kind of defeats the whole purpose, doesn't it?).

Rule 10 is your implicit denial. This rules states, "Deny all traffic that does not fit neatly into one of the above-mentioned rules."

Modifying the Rules

To add a row and create a new rule entry, select the Edit menu option. Each new row will be created with the default rule: "Deny all traffic." To change the parameters, simply right-click in each box and select Add.

To change the Source entry for a rule, for example, you would simply right-click in the Source box and select Add from the drop-down menu. You would then see a list of valid objects you could add to specify the source parameter for this new rule. Continue this process until you have created all the rules required to implement your security policy.

Modifying the Firewall Properties

The rule base is not the only place where you need to configure traffic parameters. You also need to modify the properties of the firewall itself. To do this, select Policy ➢ Properties from the Security Policy-1 menu. The Properties Setup screen is shown in Figure 7.14.

FIGURE 7.14:

The Properties Setup screen

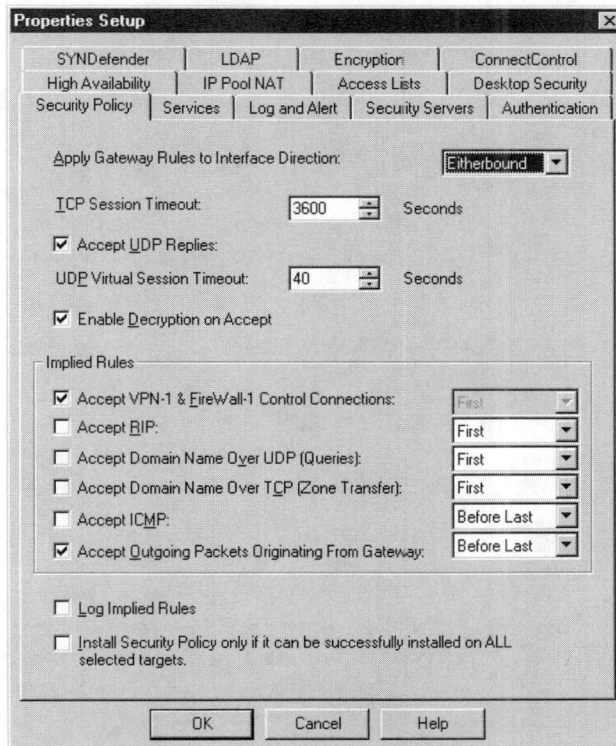

NOTE   This screen is a bit disturbing, as it defines traffic that should be processed *outside* of the rule base. In other words, this screen defines services that should be processed even if they have not been specifically defined within the Rule Base Editor.

Notice that the Accept RIP option is not selected by default. This option tells the firewall, "Accept RIP traffic before you even process the rule base." Even if you do not have a rule telling the firewall to accept RIP updates, the firewall will do so, anyway. If Woolly Attacker knows you are using FireWall-1, he may attempt to transmit false RIP updates to your firewall in an effort to corrupt your routing table. This is another one of the reasons that static routing should be used whenever possible.

There are also services that you can enable or disable on other Properties Setup tabs, as well. Make sure you check the Services and Access Lists tab to insure that they match your access control policy.

When Properties Are Processed

This is a major security hole if you do not configure these properties to match your security policy. You can specify when to process each of these properties by using these settings:

First   Accept this traffic before processing the rule base.

Before Last   Accept this traffic, unless the rule base specifically blocks it from taking place.

Last   Process this traffic after the last rule in the rule base. If it is not specifically blocked, let it pass. If the last rule is "Drop all traffic from any source to any destination," this property is not evaluated.

So why this major lapse in security? As with many things in life, security was compromised in an effort to make the firewall easier to use, appealing to the lowest common denominator. For example, the firewall administrator may not be able to figure out that she needs to accept RIP traffic in order to process route updates. The administrator may be a little slow on the uptake and not realize that she needs to pass DNS queries in order to allow internal systems to resolve host names to IP addresses. These properties are enabled by default in order to cover for this kind of mistake. Rather than improving consumer education, companies compensate by decreasing the level of security their products offer.

The SYNDefender Tab

The final Properties Setup tab you should evaluate is the SYNDefender tab. SYN-Defender allows the firewall to protect internal systems from SYN-based attacks.

You may remember from our discussion of TCP-based communications in Chapter 3 that two hosts will exchange a TCP handshake before initializing the session. During this handshake

1. Source sends a packet to the destination with SYN=1.

2. Destination replies to source with SYN=1, ACK=1.

3. Source sends a packet to the destination with ACK=1.

4. Source starts transmitting data.

NOTE   A TCP host uses two separate communication queues: a small one for sessions that still have the TCP handshake taking place, and a larger one for sessions that have been fully established. It is the smaller queue that is the target of a SYN attack.

When the destination host receives the first SYN=1 packet, it stores this connection request in a small "in process" queue. Since sessions tend to be established rather quickly, this queue is small and only able to store a relatively low number of connection requests. This was done for memory optimization, in the belief that the session would be moved to the larger queue rather quickly, thus making room for more connection requests.

A SYN attack floods this smaller queue with connection requests. When the destination system issues a reply, the attacking system does not respond. This leaves the connection request in the smaller queue until the timer expires and the entry is purged. By filling up this queue with bogus connection requests, the attacking system can prevent the system from accepting legitimate connection requests. Thus a SYN attack is considered a denial of service.

The SYNDefender tab offers two ways to combat this problem. You can configure the firewall to act as

- A passive SYN gateway

- A SYN gateway

As a *passive SYN gateway*, the firewall queues inbound connection requests and spoofs the reply SYN=1, ACK=1 packet back to the transmitting host. This prevents the connection request from ever reaching the internal system. If a proper ACK=1 is received from the transmitting system, the firewall then handshakes with the internal system and begins passing traffic between the two hosts. In effect, the firewall is acting like a SYN proxy.

The only drawback to this method is that it adds a slight delay to the initial session establishment. It also adds a lot more processing on the firewall as it attempts to mediate all of these connection requests. For example, a Web browser will create multiple sessions when it downloads a Web page. A separate session is established for each graphic, piece of text, or icon. Most popular Web sites will create a minimum of 50 sessions, and some graphically rich sites will top 300 simultaneous connections. As an added protection, the passive SYN gateway allows you to specify a timeout (the default is 10 seconds) and the Maximum Sessions allowed (the default is 5000).

The other option is to set up the firewall as a *SYN gateway*. In this mode, the firewall lets the SYN=1 request and the SYN=1, ACK=1 reply simply pass through the firewall. At this point, however, the firewall will spoof an ACK=1 back into the internal system in order to complete the connection request and move the session to the larger queue. When the remote system responds with an ACK=1 of its own, the firewall blocks this one packet but allows the rest of the session to take place normally.

If the remote host does not reply within a configurable amount of time, the firewall will send an RST=1 to the internal system, thus terminating the session. The only problem here is that you may end up creating sessions on the internal system that are not required if an attack is taking place. This is typically not a problem, because the active session queue is in a far better position to handle multiple sessions then the connection queue would be. This method also helps to remove the establishment delay caused by the SYN relay method.

Working with Security Servers

Security servers allow the firewall to proxy connections for a specific service, allowing for better traffic control: you can now make decisions based on payload content. This is useful when you want to make filtering decisions based on the content of the data rather than on the service being used.

For example, let's assume that you have three different domain names registered with the InterNIC: foobar.com, fubar.com, and bofh.com. Foobar.com is the primary domain name, but you want to receive mail for all three domains. This applies to every user: mail for ftuttle@foobar.com, ftuttle@fubar.com, and ftuttle@bofh.com should all be routed to the same person. Outbound mail, however, should always appear to originate from the foobar.com domain.

If you try to configure your mail server to handle multiple domains, you might be in for a lot of work. Many mail systems would require you to configure three different mail addresses for each user. Typically, the first one would be automatically created (such as ftuttle@foobar.com), and you would have to manually create an e-mail alias for the other two entries (ftuttle@fubar.com and ftuttle@bofh.com). These additional aliases would increase administration time and introduce the possibility of errors through typing mistakes or missing entries.

If you were really unlucky, your mail system might not even have the ability to host multiple mail domains. This is especially true of older mail servers. As mail administrator, you are only allowed to configure a single mail domain on these older mail servers. This would cause mail addressed to the additional domains to be rejected.

A simpler solution would be to configure the SMTP security server so that you can screen inbound mail for the destination domain name. If the domain name fubar.com or bofh.com was detected, you could have the security server replace either with the domain name foobar.com. Mail that is addressed to foobar.com would be allowed through without alteration. This would mean that all inbound mail messages reaching your mail server would always have a destination domain address of foobar.com. Since your mail server only sees a single domain name, you won't have to create alias e-mail addresses for each user.

Configuring the SMTP Security Server

In order to use the SMTP security server, you first need to enable it through the FireWall-1 Configuration utility. We discussed how to enable this server in the section on the FireWall-1 Configuration utility and even showed this feature enabled in Figure 7.5. Once the SMTP security server is enabled, you will need to define SMTP resources with the Security Policy-1 tab.

For the main menu of the Security Policy-1 tab, select Manage ➤ Resources. This will produce the Resource Management screen. If this is the first time you have run the Resource Manager, it will contain no entries. Click New and select SMTP. You should now be looking at the SMTP Definition box, as shown in Figure 7.15.

FIGURE 7.15:

The SMTP Definition box
General tab

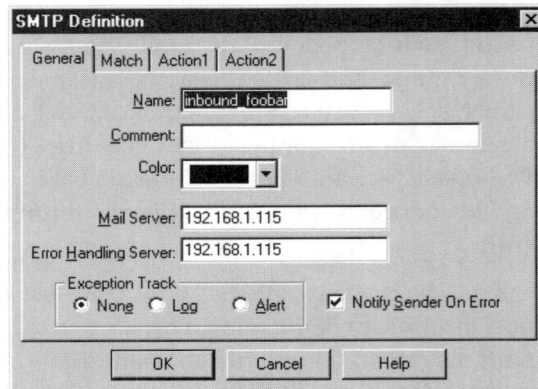

FIGURE 7.15: The SMTP Definition box General tab

Start by configuring the resource to handle inbound mail that has been sent to foobar.com. You could use a descriptive name, such as inbound_foobar, so that this definition would be easy to recognize once it has been added to the security policy. Within the mail server field, enter the IP address of the mail server to which you want to forward mail. (Use the IP address to expedite mail delivery: the firewall does not have to resolve the host name.) Within the Error Handling Server field, enter the IP address of the mail system to which you want to forward error messages. This can be the same IP address you defined in the Mail Server field.

Exception tracking defines whether you wish to log all e-mail messages that this resource processes. You also have the option of sending an alert. Finally, you have the option to select the Notify Sender On Error check box. If the resource matches an inbound mail message, but the security server is unable to deliver the message, checking this box means an error message will be returned to the original sender.

You can now configure the Match tab, as shown in Figure 7.16.

FIGURE 7.16:

The Match tab of the SMTP Definition box

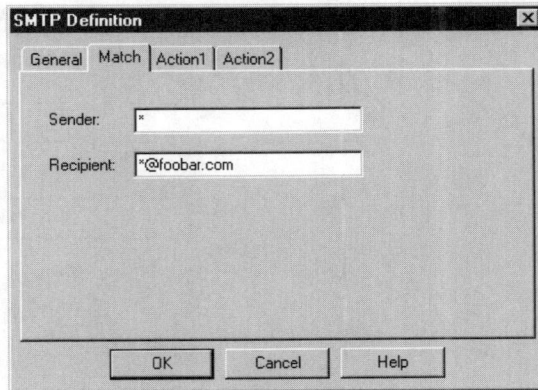

The configuration of the Match tab is pretty straightforward. Enter the text you wish this resource to match within either the Sender or the Recipient field. An asterisk (*) acts as a wildcard and will match any character string. Note that you have told the resource to match any sender, but the Recipient field within the e-mail message must end in @foobar.com. This will match all inbound mail for the foobar.com domain.

Since you are not looking to rewrite any of your e-mail headers, you are done configuring this particular resource. Simply click OK to save this entry.

You must now create entries for the domains you wish to alias. From the Resource Management screen, again click New and select SMTP. This will create a new SMTP Definition box, like the one shown in Figure 7.17.

Select the General tab and give this resource a descriptive name (such as inbound-fubar.com). Since mail addressed to fubar.com will be delivered to the same mail system as foobar.com, enter the same Mail Server and Error Handling Server IP address that you used for the foobar.com entry.

Under the Match tab, you will again use an asterisk to pattern match the Sender field, but the Recipient field will contain the entry *@fubar.com. This will allow you to pattern-match inbound e-mail addresses sent to this alternative domain name. Since this is one of the domain names that you want to rewrite, you must modify the Action1 tab, shown in Figure 7.17.

FIGURE 7.17:

The Action1 tab of the
SMTP Definition box

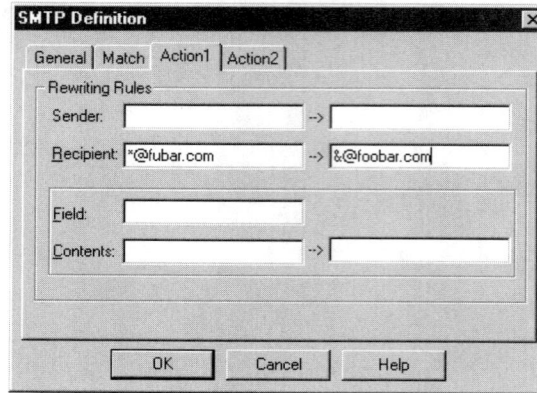

The only fields you need to fill in on the Action1 tab are the fields you wish to have rewritten. Any field left blank will remain untouched. The fields on the left attempt to match text within the specified portion of the e-mail header. The fields on the right contain what this text should be changed to if a pattern match occurs.

The first Recipient field contains the character string *@fubar.com. This is the portion of the address that you want to rewrite. The right-hand Recipient field contains the character string &@foobar.com. The ampersand (&) tells the resource, "Copy the value of the asterisk in the previous field and paste it here." This allows you to maintain the same user name in your new recipient header. The remaining text simply tells the resource to replace fubar.com with foobar.com.

This completes the configuration of the SMTP resource for inbound fubar.com mail. You can click OK and return to the Resource Management screen. You also need to create an SMTP resource for bofh.com. Follow the same steps you took for the fubar.com resource, but replace the name and pattern match information with bofh.com. Once you have finished, you can close the Resource Management screen and return to the Security Policy-1 tab in order to incorporate these resources into your security policy.

Figure 7.18 shows your SMTP resources added to a very simple security policy. Row 1 blocks all traffic that you do not want passing the firewall in either direction. Row 2 defines a very loose security policy, which allows all internal systems to access any services located on the Internet (except for those explicitly dropped in row 1).

FIGURE 7.18:

A security policy using SMTP resources

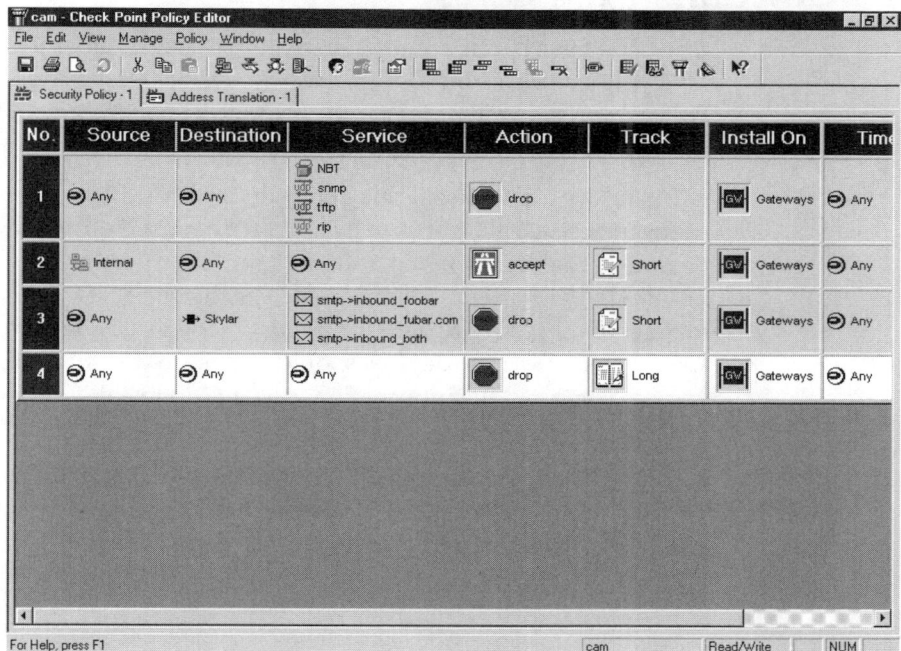

Row 3 is the entry which includes the SMTP resources. The rule states that any system can connect to Skylar (the firewall) and attempt to deliver SMTP messages. All SMTP messages will then be processed by the three SMTP resources you created. Each resource was added to this rule by right-clicking in row 3's Service box and selecting Add With Resource ➤ SMTP, then selecting the name of the resource, which is shown in the Resource drop-down list.

Since your mail server has full Internet access per row 2, you do not need to configure an outbound SMTP resource. The mail system should be fully capable of delivering all outbound mail directly.

TIP
A side benefit of the current rule base is that it prevents your mail systems from being used as spam relays. The firewall will only accept messages going to one of your three domains. The internal mail system cannot be reached directly from the Internet. This means that neither of your mail systems could be used by a spammer to relay advertisements to multiple recipients.

Installing the Rules

Once you have configured the firewall to reflect your security policy, you should save your settings. You should always do a File ➤ Save As from the Security Policy-1 tab menu in order to create a unique policy name. This will provide you with some revision control in case you later need to restore an older policy.

You now need to install this policy on the firewall in order to activate your changes. Select Policy ➤ Install from the Security Policy-1 tab menu. This will produce a dialog box that displays all the hosts where your firewall policy will be installed. At a minimum, you should see the object for your firewall. If you are managing multiple firewalls, or if you will be installing access control lists on specific routers, these devices should appear in this dialog box, as well. When you have verified the information, click OK to install your policy on the selected hosts.

This will bring up the Install Security Policy dialog box shown in Figure 7.19. The information in this dialog box should report that a policy script was compiled without errors and that it was installed successfully to the firewall. If no errors occurred, click Close. Your firewall should be ready for use.

FIGURE 7.19:

The Install Security Policy dialog box

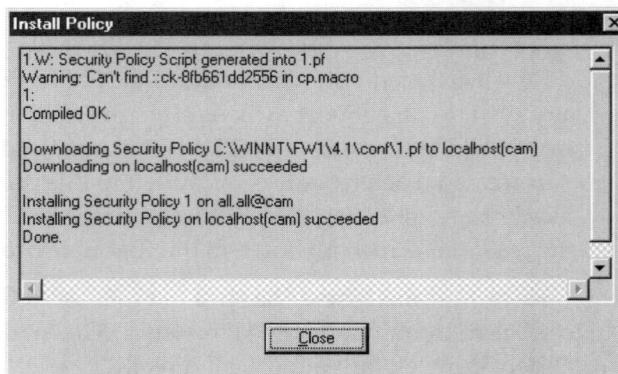

If errors were reported, look at the error messages closely. Typically, errors are due to conflicts in the rules. For example, you may have created one rule stating that a particular system has full Internet access, only to later define that the same system is not allowed to use FTP.

When you install your rule base, the firewall first checks that there are no conflicts. If you wish to verify that there are no rule conflicts before you attempt to install your rules, you can select the Policy ➢ Verify option instead. In my experience, however, this check is not exhaustive. It is possible for a rule set to pass the Verify check, only to show problems during installation.

Summary

This completes our review of Check Point FireWall-1. In this chapter, you saw why FireWall-1 is one of the most popular firewalling products and became aware of a number of caveats. You also went through the installation and setup procedure on a Windows NT server. You should now have a good idea of how to deploy this product within your network environment.

In the next chapter, we will evaluate methods of controlling security within your network perimeters. We will look at intrusion detection systems that can be combined with a firewall solution to produce an extremely secure environment.

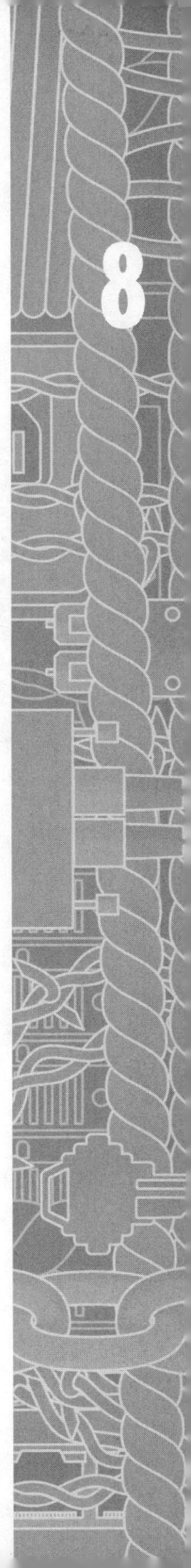

CHAPTER

EIGHT

8

Intrusion Detection Systems

Intrusion detection systems (IDS) (as a generic term) represent a fairly new technology that has been receiving a lot of recent press. While the technology is only three or four years old, it brings vendors' promises of revolutionizing the network security market. In fact, one vendor has ventured to say that its IDS completely removes the need for a firewall. Clearly, someone in marketing must be writing this company's technical documents, because IDS is a way to augment—not replace—your existing security mechanisms.

The FAQs about IDS

To understand an intrusion detection system, think about having one or more network protocol experts (affectionately known as "bit weenies") armed with a network analyzer and watching passing traffic. These specialists know about all the latest exploits that an attacker may attempt to launch, and they diligently check every packet to see if any suspicious traffic is passing on the wire. If they find suspicious traffic, they immediately contact the network administrator and inform her of their findings.

Take out the human element from this scenario, and you have an intrusion detection system. An IDS captures all passing traffic on the network, just like a network analyzer. Once this information has been read into memory, the system compares the packets to a number of known attack patterns. For example, if the IDS notices that a particular host is repeatedly sending SYN packets to another host without ever attempting to complete the connection, the IDS would identify this as a SYN attack and take appropriate action. A good IDS may have well over 100 attack patterns saved in its database.

The action taken depends on the particular IDS system you are using and how you have it configured. All IDS systems are capable of logging suspicious events. Some will even save a raw packet capture of the traffic so that it can be analyzed later by the network administrator. Others can be configured to send out an alert, such as an e-mail message or a page. Many IDS systems can attempt to interfere with the suspicious transmission by resetting both ends of the connection. Finally, there are a few that can interact with a firewall or router in order to modify the filter rules and block the attacking host. The benefits and drawbacks to each of these actions will be discussed in detail later in this chapter.

An IDS has traditionally been broken up into two parts:

- The *sensor*, which is responsible for capturing and analyzing the traffic

- The *console*, from which the sensor can be managed and all reports are run

Intrusion detection systems are extreme resource hogs. Vendors typically recommend that you run the sensor on a dedicated system with 256MB of RAM and an Intel 300MHz Pentium III or Pro processor (or RISC equivalent if the sensor is running on UNIX). Since an IDS logs all traffic, copious amounts of disk space are required for its databases. While about 100MB of disk space is usually recommended, plan on using a whole lot more unless you will frequently purge the database or your network sees very little traffic. The requirements for the dedicated system running the console are about the same, except you must reserve enough disk space to store a copy of each sensor's database.

IDS Limitations

So far, an IDS sounds like a wonderful security device—but these systems are not perfect and do have their limitations. In fact, the authors of a popular column in the trade magazine *Infoworld* declared IDS dead at the end of the year 2000 because of switched network technologies, imperfect one-size-fits-all attack signatures, high-volume network traffic overloading IDS systems, and encrypted network data hiding pertinent attack information from the IDS system, while leaving Web servers vulnerable. Many times IDS systems simply cannot respond in time to prevent an attack. Let's look at a common denial of service (DoS) attack to see how this can occur.

Teardrop Attacks

In order to understand how a teardrop attack is used against a system, you must first understand the purpose of the fragmentation offset field and the length field within the IP header. A decode of an IP header is shown in Figure 8.1. The fragmentation offset field is typically used by routers. If a router receives a packet that is too large for the next segment, the router will need to fragment the data before passing it along. The fragmentation offset field is used along with the length field so that the receiving system can reassemble the datagram in the correct order. When a fragmentation offset value of 0 is received, the receiving system assumes either that this is the first packet of fragmented information or that fragmentation has not been used.

FIGURE 8.1:

A decode of an IP header

```
Packet Number : 13              3:52:02 PM
Length : 66 bytes
ether: ==================== Ethernet Datalink Layer ====================
       Station: Skylar ----> This_Workstation
       Type: 0x0800 (IP)
   ip: ====================== Internet Protocol ======================
       Station:10.1.1.100 ---->10.1.1.25
       Protocol: TCP
       Version: 4
       Header Length (32 bit words): 5
       Precedence: Routine
              Normal Delay, Normal Throughput, Normal Reliability
       Total length: 48
       Identification: 21249
       Fragmentation not allowed, Last fragment
       Fragment Offset: 0
       Time to Live: 128 seconds
       Checksum: 0x9148(Valid)
  tcp: ================= Transmission Control Protocol =================
       Source Port: 258
       Destination Port: 1027
       Sequence Number: 417610
       Acknowledgement Number: 898472
       Data Offset (32-bit words): 5
       Window: 8510
       Control Bits: Acknowledgement Field is Valid (ACK)
              Push Function Requested (PSH)
       Checksum: 0x5DB5(Valid)
       Urgent Pointer: 0
```

If fragmentation has occurred, the receiving system will use the offset to determine where the data within each packet should be placed when rebuilding the datagram. For an analogy, think of a child's set of numbered building blocks. As long as the child follows the numbering plan and puts the blocks together in the right order, he can build a house, a car, or even a plane. In fact, he does not even need to know what he is trying to build. He simply has to assemble the blocks in the specified order.

The IP fragmentation offset works in much the same manner. The offset tells the receiving system how far away from the front of the datagram the included payload should be placed. If all goes well, this schema allows the datagram to be reassembled in the correct order. The length field is used as a verification check to insure that there is no overlap and that data has not been corrupted in transit. For example, if you place fragments 1 and 3 within the datagram and then try to place fragment 2, but you find that fragment 2 is too large and will overwrite some of fragment 3, you know you have a problem.

At this point, the system will try to realign the datagrams to see if it can make them fit. If it cannot, the receiving system will send out a request that the data be resent. Most IP stacks are capable of dealing with overlaps or payloads that are too large for their segment.

Launching a Teardrop Attack

A *teardrop attack* starts by sending a normal packet of data with a normal-size payload and a fragmentation offset of 0. From the initial packet of data, a teardrop attack is indistinguishable from a normal data transfer. Subsequent packets, however, have modified fragmentation offset and length fields. This ensuing traffic is responsible for crashing the target system.

When the second packet of data is received, the fragmentation offset is consulted to see where within the datagram this information should be placed. In a teardrop attack, the offset on the second packet claims that this information should be placed somewhere within the first fragment. When the payload field is checked, the receiving system finds that this data is not even large enough to extend past the end of the first fragment. In other words, this second fragment does not overlap the first fragment; it is actually fully contained inside of it. Since this was not an error condition that anyone expected, there is no routine to handle it and this information causes a buffer overflow—crashing the receiving system. For some operating systems, only one malformed packet is required. Others will not crash unless multiple malformed packets are received.

IDS versus Teardrop

How would a typical IDS deal with this attack? When the teardrop attack is launched, the initial packet resembles a normal data transfer. From just looking at this first packet of information, an IDS has no way of knowing that an attack is about to occur.

When the second packet is transmitted, the IDS would be able to put together the datagram fragments and identify that this is a classic example of a teardrop attack. Your IDS could then alert the networking staff and take preventive measures to stop the attack.

You only have one tiny little problem: if your attacker was lucky enough to identify an operating system that will crash with only one malformed packet, it is too late to prevent the attack from occurring. While it is true that your networking staff will have the benefit of knowing that their server has just crashed, they have probably already figured that out from the number of calls from irate users.

So while your intrusion detection system was able to tell you why the server crashed, it was unable to prevent the attack from occurring in the first place. In order to prevent future occurrences, you would need to patch the system before an attacker strikes again.

Why not simply block the attacking IP address? Your attacker is probably savvy enough to use IP spoofing, making it look like the attack came from somewhere other than his or her real IP address. Unless your IDS is on the same collision domain as the attacking system, it will be unable to detect that a spoofed address is being used. This means that your attacker could continue to randomly change the source IP address and launch successful attacks.

Other Known IDS Limitations

In February 1998, Secure Networks, Inc. released a white paper about testing it had performed on a number of intrusion detection systems. This testing discovered a number of vulnerabilities in IDS that would allow an attacker to launch an attack and go completely undetected.

While some of the conclusions of the study are a bit melodramatic, the actual testing raises some valid points. In short, the study focused on two problem areas: IDS detection of manipulated data and direct attacks on the IDS itself. The conclusion of the study was that sniffer-based intrusion detection would never be capable of reliably detecting attacks.

Data Manipulation

This conclusion was based on the fact that virtually none of the intrusion detection systems in the study reassembled the IP packets in an identical manner to systems communicating via IP. This resulted in some inconsistencies between what the IDS perceived was occurring within the packet stream and what the receiving system was able to process.

One of the problems was that some of the intrusion detection systems did not verify the checksum field with the IP header (refer to Figure 8.1). This would most certainly be done by the receiving system, and manipulating this field would cause the IDS to record a different payload than the receiving system would process.

The example cited in the study was the PHF CGI attack. An IDS would attempt to detect this attack by looking for the character string phf within the payload portion of all HTTP requests. If this pattern was detected, the IDS would assume that this attack was taking place. A savvy attacker could attempt to send a series of packets, each with one character that produced the string phoof. The attacker could then manipulate the checksum field so that each packet that contained the letter o had an invalid checksum. The result would be that while the receiving system (which would verify the checksum) would only process the character string phf, the IDS (which does not verify the checksum) would read this transmission as phoof.

While this inconsistency in how traffic is processed is certainly a valid concern, it is not insurmountable. For example ISS RealSecure, one of the packages that exhibited this problem, was fixed by the next product release. Such problems are typical in an infant technology. Firewall vendors have gone through a similar learning process and continue to make improvements even today. There is no reason to assume that network security will ever become a stagnant field.

Attacks against the IDS

Another issue raised by the Secure Networks study was the vulnerability of the IDS to direct attacks. This is a valid concern, because a direct attack against the IDS may inhibit its ability to detect intrusions. By shutting down the IDS, an attacker could launch an attack against the network without fear of detection.

IDS versus Firewall

This highlights a major difference between a firewall and an IDS. A firewall acts as a perimeter guard. This means that all traffic must pass through it in order to move from one section of a network to another. If the firewall is attacked and services are disrupted, it will typically *fail open*, meaning that it will be unable to pass traffic. While this disrupts all transmissions, it prevents an attacker from disabling the firewall and using this opportunity to launch an attack on an internal host.

An IDS, on the other hand, does not sit between network segments. It is designed to run unobtrusively within a single collision domain. If the IDS is disabled, it technically *fails closed* because traffic flow is not disrupted. An attacker may be able to disable the IDS while still gaining access to network resources. This means that all attacks launched while the IDS is offline will go undocumented.

Again, this problem is not as insurmountable as the Secure Network study would make it seem. There is no legitimate reason to have the intrusion detection system directly addressable by every network host. The act of sniffing network traffic does not require a valid IP address. The only systems requiring connectivity are

- The sensor
- The console

- A DNS system (if you wish to resolve IP addresses to host names)

- The firewall or router (if you wish to let the IDS modify filtering rules)

Segregating IDS communications from the public network can easily be accomplished using a separate private network along with private IP address space. In fact, it can even be done in-band, as long as routing to this subnet is disabled. While the sensor requires an IP protocol stack and thus an IP address on the main network, there is no reason why this address has to be valid. An example of this configuration is shown in Figure 8.2.

FIGURE 8.2:

Managing IDS through a separate subnet

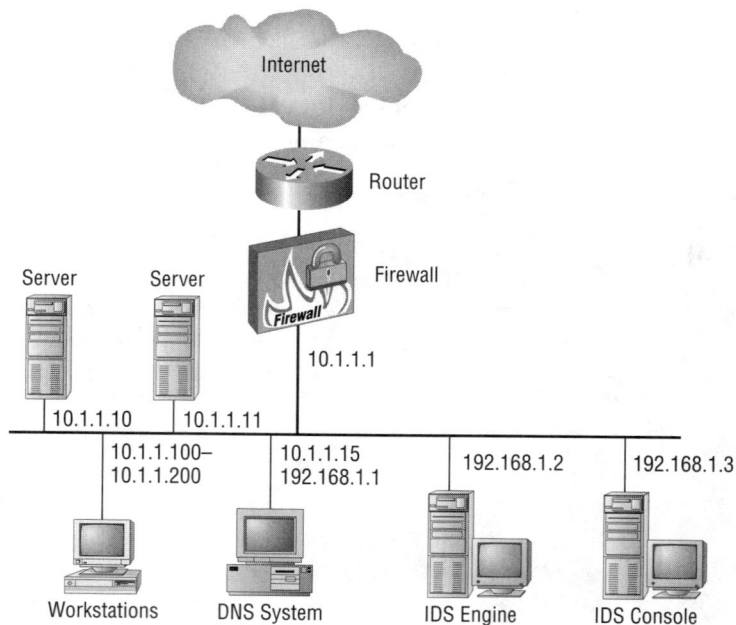

In Figure 8.2, your regular network systems have been assigned address space from the 10.1.1.0 subnet. All systems within this subnet are allowed some level of Internet access, and your firewall has been configured to use NAT with these addresses. As far as the firewall is concerned, only the 10.1.1.0 network exists internally.

If you look closely at the figure, you will notice that the DNS system has two IP addresses: one for the 10.1.1.0 network and one for the 192.168.1.0 network. This device has been specifically configured not to route any traffic between these two subnets. IP forwarding has been disabled: while it is able to communicate with systems on both subnets, it is unable to act as a router and forward traffic between them.

Your IDS sensor and monitor are using address space from the 192.168.1.0 subnet. While they will be able to communicate with each other and the DNS system, they will not be able to communicate with any system using a 10.1.1.0 address. This is because there are no devices routing between the two network segments. Your IDS is also unable to send to or receive any data from systems outside the firewall.

What happens when your IDS sensor tries to monitor traffic? As mentioned, the IDS sensor will capture all traffic on the network, not just traffic on its own subnet. This means that it is perfectly capable of recording all traffic on the local network, including communications between systems on the 10.1.1.0 subnet and the Internet. It can then report these findings to the console via the 192.168.1.0 subnet.

What happens when either system needs to resolve an IP address to a host name? We did, after all, mention that the DNS system was incapable of routing information. While this is a true statement, it does not prohibit you from using the DNS system as a proxy in order to resolve address queries.

In Chapter 3, you saw that DNS is simply an application layer service that is responsible for translating host names to IP addresses and vice versa. When your sensor sends a DNS query to the DNS server, it will attempt to respond to the request with information stored locally (either through local domain files or via cached entries). If this is not possible, the DNS server will attempt to contact one of the root name servers.

If the best route to the root name server has been configured to be through the 10.1.1.15 IP address, such as by creating a default route that points to 10.1.1.1 on the firewall, the DNS server will transmit the request using the source IP address 10.1.1.15. The DNS server is not routing your query; it is acting as a proxy in order to resolve the query for you.

When it receives a reply to the query, the DNS server will then forward the response back to the sensor using the best route it knows. This would require the system to transmit using the 192.168.1.1 address. Again, the information is not being routed; it is being proxied by the DNS service. This means that your IDS is fully capable of resolving DNS queries without using the same subnet address as the rest of the network.

The result is a hidden subnet that is not directly addressable from the Internet. An attacker would need to penetrate the firewall and compromise the DNS server in order to gain connectivity to either the IDS sensor or console. If the IDS cannot be directly addressed, it obviously cannot be attacked.

TIP

Just like a firewall, an IDS sensor that will be using IP on the public network should be hardened before use. This includes insuring that it has all the latest security patches installed and that the system is not running any unnecessary services. A hardened system will be far more resistant to attack—and therefore a much better platform for running a security monitoring process.

IDS Countermeasures

Along with logging and alerting, an intrusion detection system has two other active countermeasures at its disposal:

- Session disruption
- Filter rule manipulation

These vary with each specific product, but let's look at the general strengths and weaknesses of each method.

Internal Attacks against the IDS

The IDS sensor and console are vulnerable to internal attack, however. If someone on the `10.1.1.0` network discovers the IP address of the IDS, it would be a simple matter of changing or spoofing the local address in order to address these systems directly on the `192.168.1.0` subnet. This is referred to as "security through obscurity"—the systems will only remain secure as long as no one knows where they are hidden. Still, by making these systems completely inaccessible from the Internet, you have dramatically limited the scope of potential attack origination points and simplified the process of discovering the attacker.

When internal attacks are a concern, you can go with an IDS that does not require an IP stack. For example, RealSecure supports network monitoring from a system that does not have IP bound to the monitored network. With no IP address, the system is invulnerable to any form of IP-based attack. Of course, this also means that you will have to make special considerations for the monitoring console. You will either need to run the IDS console on the same system as the sensor or install a second network card in the sensor so that it can communicate with the console through a private subnet.

Session Disruption

Session disruption is the easiest kind of countermeasure to implement. While there are some variations on its implementation, in its most basic form session disruption is produced by having the IDS reset or close each end of an attack session. This may not prevent the attacker from launching further attacks, but it does prevent the attacker from causing any further damage during the current session.

For example, let's say that your IDS sensor detects a would-be attacker attempting to send the character string CWD ~root during an FTP session. If formulated correctly, this exploit would provide the attacker with root-level FTP access on some older systems. This level of access is granted without any password authentication, and the attacker would now be able to read or write to any file on the system.

If session disruption is enabled, your IDS sensor would first identify and log this potential attack, then spoof ACK-FIN packets to both ends of the session in order to tear down the connection. The IDS sensor would do this, pretending to be the system on the other end of the connection. For example, it would transmit an ACK-FIN to the attacker using the source IP address, port numbers, and sequence numbers of the FTP server. This would effectively close the communication session, preventing the attacker from accessing the file system. Depending on the IDS sensor in use, it may then attempt to block all communications from the attacking host indefinitely or for a user-configurable period of time.

While session disruption is a powerful feature, it is not without its limitations. For example, the teardrop example given earlier in this chapter showed that the intrusion detection system would be unable to block the attack. While the IDS has enough time to react to the FTP exploit, it could never react quickly enough to save a system from teardrop if only one malformed IP header is enough to crash the system.

Filter Rule Manipulation

Some IDS sensors have the ability to modify the filter rules of a router or firewall in order to prevent continued attacks. This stops the attacking system from transmitting additional traffic to the target host; the IDS adds a new filter rule to the firewall that blocks all inbound traffic from the suspect IP address. While filter rule manipulation is a powerful novelty, it is not without its limitations. You should fully understand the implications of this feature before you enable it.

On the positive side, filter rule manipulation can prevent an attack with far less network traffic than session disruption. Once the IDS modifies the filter rules, attack traffic ceases. With session disruption, the IDS must continually attempt to close every attack session. If you have a persistent attacker, this could add quite a bit of extra traffic to the wire.

On the negative side, filter rule manipulation is not always 100 percent effective. For example, what if the source IP address of the attack is inside the firewall? In this case, modifying the filter rules will have no effect. Since the attacking traffic never actually passes through the firewall, it is not subject to the filter rules. This means that a filter change will have no effect on the attack.

Also, a savvy attacker may use a spoofed IP address rather than a real one. While the firewall may begin blocking the initial attack, all the attacker has to do is select another spoofed address in order to circumvent this new rule change. With session disruption, the IDS reacts based on attack signature, not source IP address. This means that session disruption would be able to continually fend off the attack, while filter rule manipulation would not. The IDS could make successive rule changes, thus attempting to block all spoofed addresses as they are detected. If the attacker quickly varies the source IP address, however, the IDS would never be able to keep up. Remember that it takes a certain amount of time (typically 10–30 seconds) for the IDS and the firewall to complete the filter change.

WARNING   The ability to perform live filter rule changes could be exploited for a DoS attack. If the attacker purposely varies the source IP address in order to trigger multiple filter rule changes, the firewall may become so busy that it stops passing traffic. Any active sessions during the filter rule change may be terminated, as well.

Clearly, the ability to modify filter rules should be used sparingly and only for attacks that would be considered extremely detrimental. For example, just about every unpatched IP device or system produced before 1996 is vulnerable to the *Ping of death*, an exploit that breaks the IP protocol stack on a target system by sending it an oversized ICMP datagram. If you are running an environment with many older systems that have not been patched, modifying the filter rules to block these attacks makes a lot of sense. While frequent rule changes could potentially cause a Denial of Service, letting this traffic onto your network most certainly would interrupt all IP communications.

TIP   The *Ping of death* affects networking hardware as well as computer systems. Make sure that all of your IP devices are patched against this form of attack.

NOTE   Not all intrusion detection systems are compatible with all firewalls and routers. For example, ISS RealSecure can only modify Check Point FireWall-1. At the time of this writing, it is not compatible with any other firewall product, although there are plans to add Cisco routers to a future release. So, while session disruption can be used by any IDS that supports this feature, you can only use filter manipulation if you are using a compatible system that performs firewall functions.

Host-Based IDS

Until now we have focused on intrusion detection systems that run on a dedicated server and monitor all passing network traffic. These devices are used to control traffic within an entire collision domain. There are, however, host-based IDS products, which are designed to protect only a single system.

Host-based IDS functions similarly to a virus scanner. The software runs as a background process on the system you wish to protect as it attempts to detect suspicious activity. Suspicious activity can include an attempt to pass unknown commands though an HTTP request or even modification to the file system. When suspicious activity is detected, the IDS can then attempt to terminate the attacking session and send an alert to the system administrator.

Some Drawbacks

Host-based intrusion detection systems have quite a few drawbacks, which make them impractical for many environments. For starters, most can monitor only specific types of systems. For example, CyberCop Server by Network Associates is only capable of protecting Web servers. If the server is running multiple services (such as DNS, file sharing, POP3, and so on), the host-based IDS system may not be able to detect an intrusion. While most do watch core server functions, such as modifications to a user's access rights, an attacker may find a way to disable the IDS before attempting any changes to the system. If the IDS becomes disabled, the attacker is free to wreak havoc on the system.

Another problem is that host-based intrusion detection systems simply run as a background process and do not have access to the core communication functionality of the system. This means that the IDS is incapable of fending off attacks against the protocol stack itself. For example, it takes 10 or more teardrop packets to crash an unpatched NT server. While this is more than ample time for a network-based IDS to react and take countermeasures, a host-based IDS would be left helpless because it would never even see this traffic.

It can also be argued that there is a logistical flaw in running your intrusion detection software on the system you wish to protect. If an attacker can infiltrate the system, the attacker may compromise the IDS, as well. This is an extremely bad thing: the attacker has just punched through your last line of security defense.

TIP

Only sloppy attackers fail to clean up after themselves by not purging logs and suspected processes. This is why many security experts suggest that system administrators forward all log entries to a remote system. If the system is compromised by an attacker, the logs cannot be altered. This same principle should be extended to your intrusion detection systems, as well.

When Is Host-Based IDS Effective?

Despite all these drawbacks, host-based intrusion detection systems do have their place. For example, let's assume you have a Web server you wish to protect that is located on a DMZ network segment. This DMZ is behind your firewall but in an isolated segment that only contains the Web server. The firewall is configured to only allow in HTTP traffic to the Web server.

In this situation, a host-based IDS product may be sufficient to protect the Web server, because the firewall is providing most of your protection. The firewall should insure that the only traffic allowed to reach the Web server is HTTP requests. This means that you should not have to worry about any other services being compromised on the Web server.

Your host-based intrusion detection system only has to insure that no suspect file access requests or CGI and Java exploits are included in these HTTP requests and passed along to the Web server process running on the system. While this is still no small feat, it does limit the scope of the kinds of exploits the IDS will be expected to handle.

Host-based IDS can also be extremely useful in a fully switched environment. The reasoning behind this is shown in Figure 8.3. In this figure, all systems are directly connected to a backbone switch. This, in effect, gives every system its own collision domain: the switch will isolate all unicast traffic so that only the two systems involved in the communication will see the traffic.

FIGURE 8.3:

A network-based IDS is incapable of seeing all traffic in a fully switched environment.

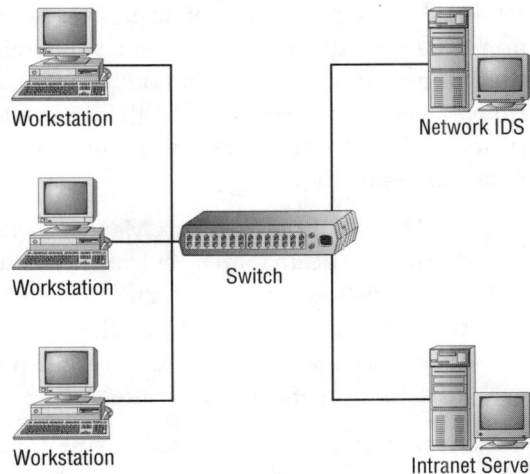

Since the switch is isolating communication sessions, your network-based IDS will be unable to see all of the passing network traffic. If a workstation launches an attack against the intranet Web server, the IDS will be completely unaware that the attack is taking place and thus unable to take countermeasures. This also means that the attack would not appear in the IDS logs, so no record will be made of the event.

A host-based IDS would be in a much better position to protect the intranet Web server. Since it runs on the system you wish to protect, it is unaffected by the traffic isolation properties of the switch. It will see all the traffic that the Web server sees, so it can protect the system from HTTP-based attacks.

TIP Most switch vendors allow you to configure one of the switch's ports as a monitoring port. This allows the switch to send a copy of all passing traffic to any system connected to this port. If you will be using a network-based IDS in a switched environment, connect it to this monitoring port in order to insure that the IDS can verify all passing traffic.

IDS Fusion

In an attempt to not only overcome the limitations of traditional IDS, but also allow for more proactive defense, IDS research is pushing toward the integration—or to use the more common term of military origin, the *fusion*—of data. By combining the packet information (the actual information being communicated) from servers and hosts, along with information of other types and sources, IDS systems can more accurately determine information about an attack. Additional data sources include:

SNMP   Simple Network Management Protocol enables network devices to communicate with a centralized monitoring system and report *how* they are operating, not just what data is being transferred. An example would be a router that updates a network monitoring system with the amount of traffic per second passing through a given interface, (which can be used by IDS to determine if a hacker is attempting a DoS attack).

System logs   Most operating systems can be configured to record an extensive amount of detail concerning their overall state at any given moment, along with the specifics from each operating system component. Consider an e-mail server that logs not just the arrival time of e-mail, but also the IP address of the originating server. This information could be used by IDS to trace the path of worm-carrying e-mails and to tell all e-mail servers in a system to filter out any e-mail originating from the offending server.

System messages   While most pertinent system data is usually logged, this is not always the case—either through the fault of misconfiguration or simply because of an operating system weakness. IDS uses system messages to create a greater overall picture of an entire network, which allows for combing the data (fusion) and retrieving meaning (pattern analysis) from the network's state.

Commands   Most operating systems are not designed or configured to record every single command issued by all users. IDS fusion is designed to overcome just that limitation—illuminating patterns that might be missed by system logs themselves (which only report information of a direct system or security nature). An example would be a command designed to delete proprietary company information—though extremely damaging to an organization, does not violate or affect system integrity.

User Behavior   A corollary to monitoring user commands, normal user behavior over time creates its own patterns, and by constantly analyzing user account activity against that account's own profile, IDS systems can determine if that account has been hijacked—before any greater violation or penetration of systems has yet appeared.

While the concept of analyzing all user, system, and network data and behavior seems straightforward enough, in reality IDS fusion is very difficult; it relies on complicated mathematical formulas and requires some intense back-end resources to operate effectively—and even then it is still highly subjective and experimental. Nonetheless, IDS Fusion promises to revolutionize network defense through cooperative data-sharing and response by all networks affected by an attack.

IDS Setup

For the purpose of discussing how you would set up an IDS, we will look at Internet Security Systems (ISS) RealSecure. RealSecure sensor is actually several separate products consisting of

RealSecure Console (Workgroup Manager)   controls the entire RealSecure system, including all network and server sensors. Also stores the master database (used to generate reports).

RealSecure Network Sensor   records all network traffic on a given segment and compares it against attack signatures.

RealSecure Server (OS) Sensor   monitors system logs and interface traffic, looking for attacks directed at a particular system.

Before You Begin

For this walk-through, we will focus on the Windows NT version of RealSecure. As mentioned, you can choose to run the sensors and the console on the same system or on separate platforms (although you cannot run both the Network and Server/OS sensors on the same platform). The factors governing this decision are cost, performance, and whether or not you operate a switched network. The RealSecure software costs the same whether you want to use one platform or two. For two platforms, however, you will obviously need to purchase two server-class systems, as well as two Windows NT server licenses.

If the system will be monitoring a low-bandwidth connection (T1 speeds or less), you will probably be better off running a single "killer" machine rather than two lower-quality computers. If you plan to monitor a network backbone or other high-traffic area, you may wish to consider purchasing two appropriately outfitted systems. Receiving and processing every packet on the wire takes a lot of CPU horsepower. RealSecure checks each packet for more than 130 different suspect conditions. Combine this with making log entries and launching countermeasures when required, and you have a very busy system.

Where to Place Your IDS

In order to decide where to best place your IDS, you must ask yourself, "Which systems do I wish to protect and from which sources?" It's good to clarify this point up front—you may find you actually need more than one IDS sensor. You should have a solid security objective in mind before you fill out a purchase request for hardware or software.

One potential deployment is shown in Figure 8.4. In this configuration, both the DMZ and the internal connection of the firewall are being monitored. This allows you to verify all inbound traffic from the Internet. It also allows you to reinforce the existing firewall. Both IDS sensors are running without IP being bound to the public network segment. IP is only running on a network card that connects the sensors back to the console. This allows your IDS sensors to be completely invisible to all systems on the public network segment.

There are a few limitations to this configuration, however. First, you will be unable to monitor attack traffic from the Internet that is targeted at the firewall. While your firewall should be capable of logging such activity, you may not have the benefits of raw packet captures, dynamic filter rule manipulation, or any of the other features that an IDS can offer. If your link to the Internet is a T1 or less, and you want to monitor Internet traffic only, you may be better off buying one really good server and running all IDS functions outside the firewall. Since IP will not be needed on this system, it should be safe from attack.

Another limitation of the design in Figure 8.4 is that it does not allow you to monitor any of the unicast traffic generated between internal systems. If your goal is to monitor all network traffic, you may wish to move your internal IDS sensor to its own port on the switch and configure this switch port for monitoring. This would allow you to see all traffic activity inside the firewall.

FIGURE 8.4:

A potential deployment of
two IDS sensors

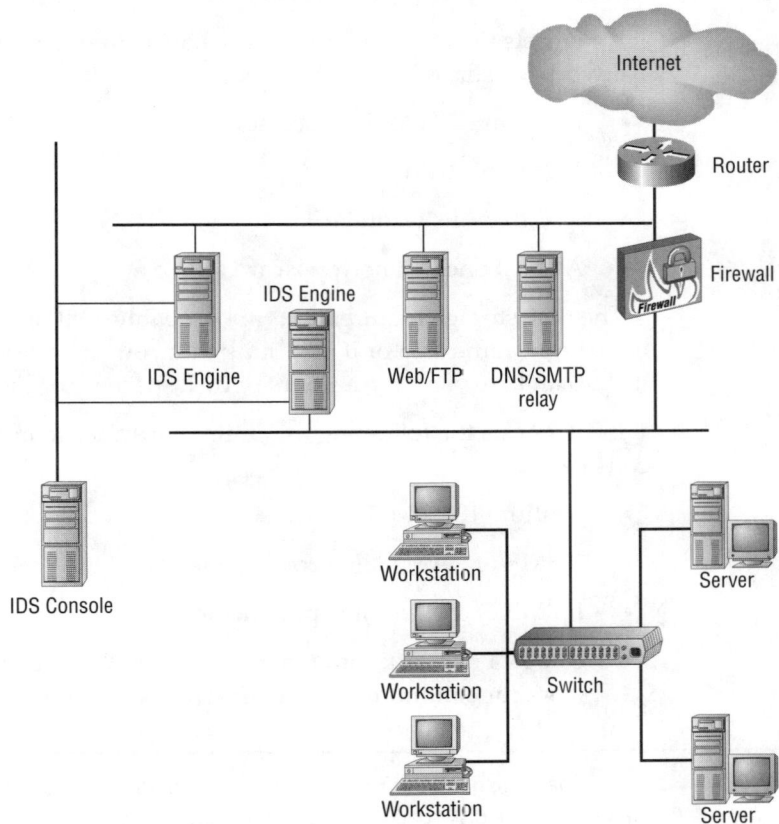

If your goal is to lock down the network as much as possible, you may wish to combine these solutions: placing one IDS sensor outside the firewall and another IDS sensor off a monitoring switch port, and having both sensors communicate with the console through a private subnet. This would allow you to monitor all passing traffic within your network while still maintaining control from a central console.

Once you have selected the areas you wish to monitor, you can select the number of IDS sensors required, as well as the appropriate hardware.

Hardware Requirements

ISS suggests the following minimum hardware requirements for the RealSecure Network Sensor

- Pentium II 300MHz processor

- 128MB of RAM

- 110MB of disk storage

- At least one PCI network card

The disk storage requirements are probably a bit light. If you will be monitoring a high-traffic area or if you think that you may wish to capture a lot of raw data, plan to expand the amount of disk space accordingly.

ISS suggests the following minimum hardware requirements for the RealSecure console:

- Pentium II 300MHz processor

- 128MB of RAM (256 recommended)

- 100MB of disk storage per sensor

- One PCI network card (an additional NIC can be used to create a secure network for communicating with sensors on remote machines)

TIP   Again, be generous with disk space. It is better to have too much than not enough. The more disk space available, the longer you will be able to retain your logs. This is important if you want to look at any long-term trends. If you will be running the sensor and the console on the same system, consider increasing the processor requirements to a 400MHz Pentium II and the memory requirements to 192MB.

Installing NT

RealSecure should be run on a Windows NT server that has been dedicated to IDS functions.

When installing NT server, observe the following guidelines:

- Install all required network cards before loading NT.

- Create an NTFS C partition of 800MB, which will hold the NT operating system and swap file.

- Create an NTFS D partition of the remaining drive space (200MB minimum) to hold the IDS program files and logs.

- Remove all protocols except TCP/IP.

- In the Control Panel, open the Services dialog box and disable all services except the Event Log service and the Net Logon service.

- Install the 128-bit version of Service Pack 5 (or greater).

- At a minimum, install the hotfixes `getadmin-fix`, `ndis-fix`, `pent-fix`, `srvr-fix`, and `teardrop2-fix`. Other hotfixes, such as `scsi-fix`, can be installed as you require.

- Under the Performance tab in System Properties, change the Boost to the foreground application to None.

- If you are running the server service, go to the Server Properties dialog box and change Optimization to Maximize throughput for network applications.

Once you have followed these guidelines, you are ready to make an emergency recovery disk and install RealSecure.

RealSecure Installation

Installing RealSecure is straightforward. You can download a demo of the various installation files if you contact ISS via e-mail. The demo is simply a copy of the full product that will expire in 15 days. For more information, visit the ISS Web site at

```
www.iss.net
```

The first component to install is the RealSecure Workgroup Manager (Console). The self-extracting executable will start by copying some files to a temporary directory and launching the Setup program. If you do not have at least Service Pack 5 installed (Service Pack 6a is preferred), the Setup program will warn you that it is required and terminate execution.

As shown in Figure 8.5, you are first asked to select which portions of the program you wish to install. You can choose to install the console, restore private keys, or export the public keys of the console. Installing either the Network or OS/Server Sensors are separate installation procedures. The latter two options are useful after the IDS software has been installed. These options are provided so that you can manage the encryption keys used by the console and the sensors when they are located on different systems. RealSecure uses a public/private key pair for all communications between the console and the sensor. Once you have made your selection, click Next.

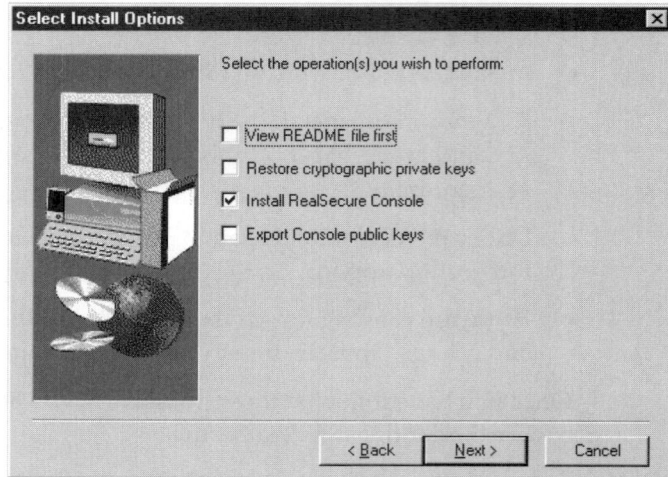

You will then be prompted to choose the destination for the RealSecure files. The default is to place them under the Program Files directory on the C drive. It is strongly recommended that you change this path to D so that all RealSecure files are stored on their own partition. This will help to insure that system functionality is not affected if the log files grow large enough to fill the entire drive. Once you have specified a new path, click Next to continue.

Once you have selected a location for your files, if the system detects that you have not installed the high encryption version of a service pack, it will give you the following message:

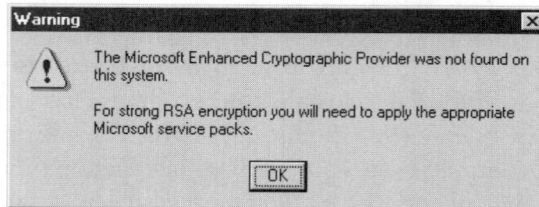

After you acknowledge the warning, you will be presented with the Select Cryptographic Setup screen as shown in Figure 8.6. This screen allows you to select a *cryptographic services provider (CSP)*. The CSP is the component responsible for encrypting and decrypting all traffic between the console and the sensors. The Microsoft Base Cryptographic Provider is installed as part of Service Pack 3 or later, so it is available on all patched systems. If you have a third-party CSP installed on the system, that should appear in this window, as well.

FIGURE 8.6:

The Cryptographic Setup screen

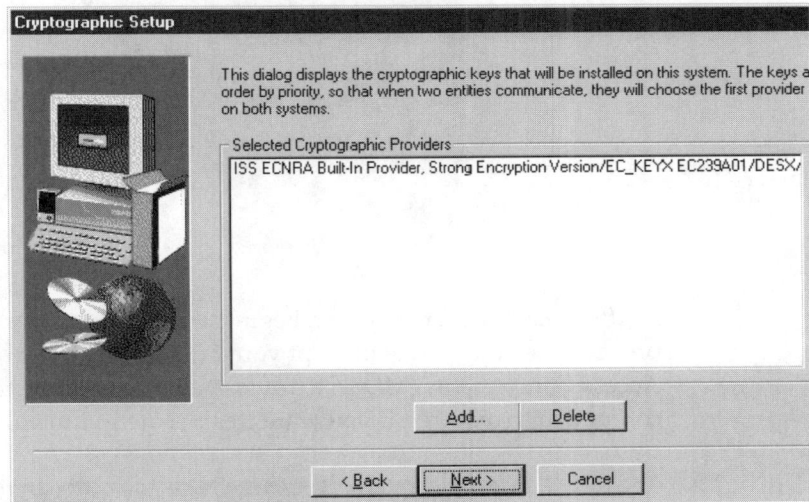

At this point, the installation utility will prompt you to name the program group and begin installing files to the system. Once this process is complete, you will be presented with the dialog box in Figure 8.7, which offers you the opportunity to archive your private keys, (securing them with a pass-phrase in the process).

You should use the 128-bit version of Service Pack 6a if you wish to use strong encryption. If you have installed the 40-bit version of any Service Pack, you will only be able to use weak encryption. If you select strong encryption with only the 40-bit version of any Service Pack installed, the installation utility will warn you that only weak encryption can be used. Weak encryption is usually sufficient for use behind a firewall. If you will be communicating on a public network, however, you should seriously consider using strong encryption. As with strong authentication, there is a slight performance degradation when you use strong instead of weak encryption. It is far more secure, however.

At this point, the installation utility will prompt you to name the program group and begin installing files to the system. Once this process is complete, you will be presented with the dialog box in Figure 8.7, which offers you the opportunity to archive your private keys, (securing them with a pass-phrase in the process).

FIGURE 8.7:

RealSecure can archive
your private keys.

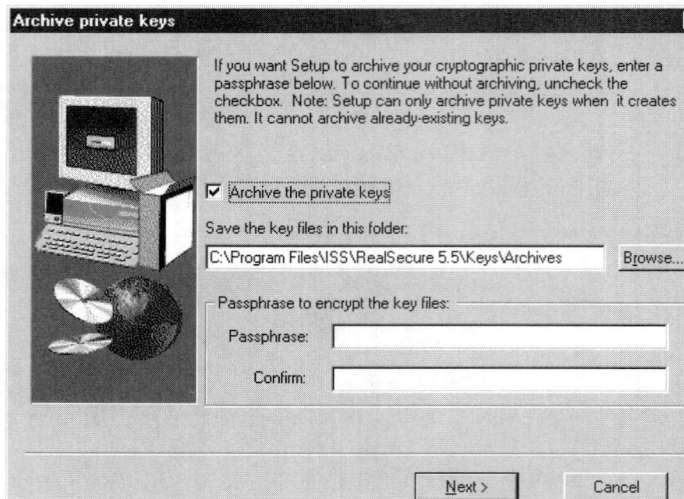

After this screen, the system begins to copy files. Near the end of the copy process, the system will prompt you if it detects that you lack Microsoft's Data Access Components (MDAC). You can choose to allow the system to install the components (required if you want RealSecure to function properly).

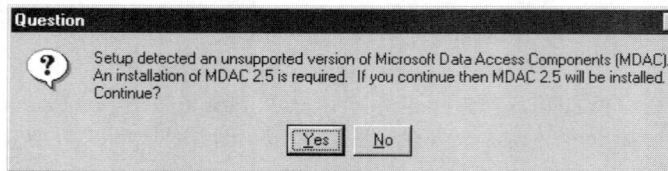

After RealSecure installs the update MDAC (if required), the installation program prompts you to harden security by checking the permission levels set on the Registry keys and directories used by RealSecure. This is done in order to insure that they can only be accessed by the system administrator or an equivalent account.

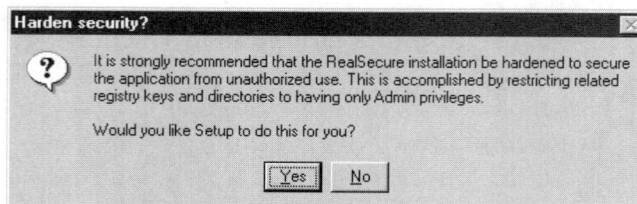

You can only set directory permissions on an NT server if you have partitioned your drives to use NTFS.

Now the installation is complete. You will be prompted to reboot the server so that Registry changes can take effect and the IDS sensor service can start. The sensor starts automatically during system initialization, but the console must be launched from the RealSecure program group. Once the system restarts, copy your ISS.KEY file to the RealSecure program directory.

Configuring RealSecure

To launch the RealSecure console, select the RealSecure icon from within the RealSecure program group. This will produce the screen shown in Figure 8.8. The top of your screen is the RealSecure menu. All functions are available via pull-down menu options or from the toolbar. On the bottom of the screen is the Sensor view. This window displays all sensors that are currently being monitored. An unmonitored sensor will still collect data; it simply cannot report this information back to the console. To select a console to monitor, click Sensor ➤ Monitor Sensor from the Sensor menu.

FIGURE 8.8:

The RealSecure Console screen

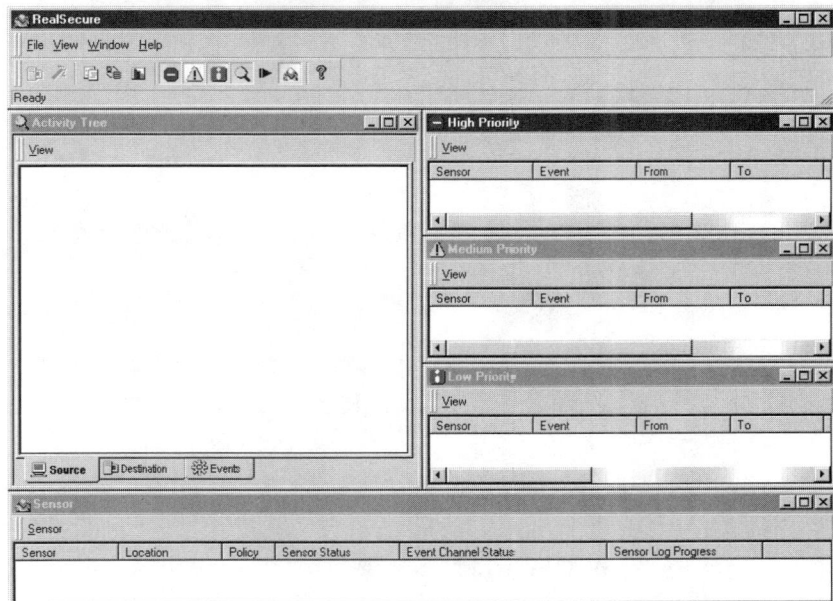

TIP

In order to see all the information screens, you should use a screen resolution of 800 x 600 or higher.

Selecting Monitor Sensor will produce the Add Sensor dialog box. Use this box to select all the sensors you wish to monitor. If you have installed the console and the OS or Network Sensor on the same computer, you should see an entry for the localhost sensor. If the sensor is on a remote computer, you will need to click Add and fill in the IP address of the IDS sensor. Do this for each sensor on your network. Then highlight each sensor you want and click OK to begin monitoring them.

When the sensor appears on the Sensor View, you can right-click a particular sensor entry to produce a Maintenance menu. From this menu, select the Properties option in order to configure the specific characteristics of this sensor. If you have selected a Network Sensor, this will produce the Sensor Properties screen shown in Figure 8.9.

FIGURE 8.9:

The Policies tab of the Network Sensor screen

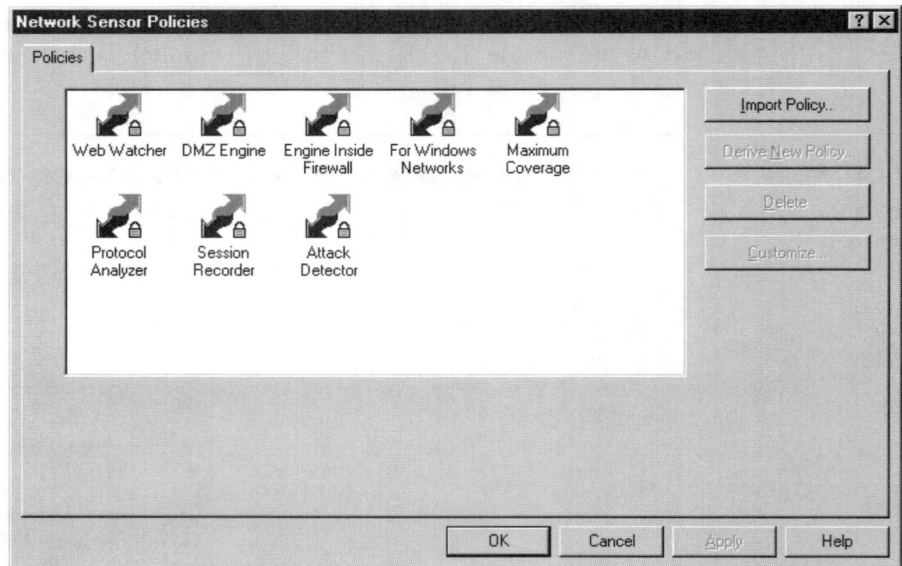

The Policies tab of the Network Sensor Properties screen allows you to customize the type of security policy your IDS will use. You can select the following options:

Web Watcher   applies HTTP-based attack signatures to all Web traffic.

DMZ Engine   analyzes traffic inside of a DMZ (Demilitarized Zone), searching for attempts to cross the DMZ into the internal network.

Engine Inside Firewall   scans traffic on the internal network looking for anomalies.

For Windows Networks   applies only Windows-based signatures to data on a network, optimizing the IDS system by screening out all non-Windows data.

Maximum Coverage   enables all signatures and all protocol profiles and sends all results to the console. While not a good idea on heavily used networks, this policy is good for evaluation purposes.

Protocol Analyzer   used to view the actual network data. No signatures are activated with this policy—it is used primarily to give administrators an idea of the data flowing across a network.

Session Recorder   provides default connection information for NNTP, FTP, SMTP traffic. These defaults are then modified to create a custom policy.

Attack Detector   only processes the most intense data; this policy does no decoding of network data and doesn't record regular connection information.

NOTE   Remember—the more verification the IDS sensor must perform, the more horsepower it is going to require. The different policies are designed to help you check for only the specific vulnerabilities you need to worry about.

Of course, no policy is ever going to be an exact fit. For this reason, you should consider using one of the policies as a template and customizing it to fit your needs. Instead of editing any of the default policies directly, you should highlight the closest fit and click the Derive New Policy button. This will clone the policy you have highlighted and allow you to give it a name. Once you have completed this task, you can click Customize in order to critique the settings. This will produce the Policy Editor window for your new custom policy. The Policy Editor allows you to alter security and connection events, create user-defined events, and establish filters. As seen in Figure 8.10, on the left side of the window is the tree view of a particular tab, on the upper right-hand side is a detailed list, while the bottom right-hand section displays an explanation of whatever is selected on the left pane of the window.

FIGURE 8.10:

The Security Events tab of the Policy Editor screen allows you to customize your IDS policy settings.

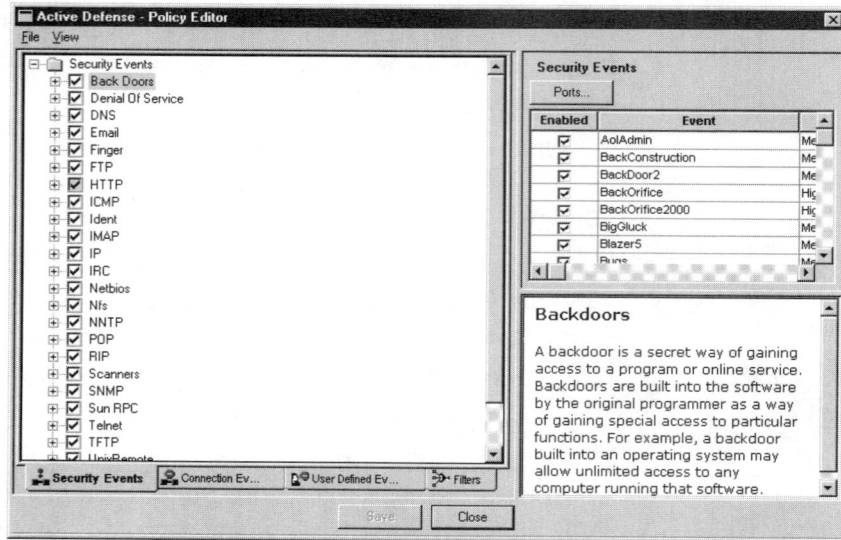

The Security Events tab allows you to configure which attacks your IDS should look for and what type of action should be taken if a particular exploit is detected. The IDS sensor will look for every item that is checked off in the Enabled column. If you know for sure that you are immune to a particular type of exploit, you can conserve resources by not inspecting for it. For example, if none of your hosts is running Finger as a service, there should be no need to check for any of the Finger exploits.

TIP

If you are ever unsure whether you need to worry about a particular exploit, online Help has an excellent description of each exploit listed. If you are still unsure whether you need to worry about a particular exploit, it is better to err on the side of caution and let the IDS check for the vulnerability.

The Priority column allows you to select the level of urgency you wish to associate with each event. If you refer back to Figure 8.8, you will see that each of these priority levels is displayed in its own window. This allows you to quickly distinguish between traffic you wish to investigate later and traffic that requires your immediate attention. It also helps to sort these items for later reports. Regardless of the priority you set for an item, the Display box (under the Response column) must be checked in order to have detected events reported in one of the three console windows.

If you click on the Response column, the Action dialog box shown in Figure 8.11 appears. From here you can select how you want the IDS sensor to react when a specific event is detected. This can be as benign as simply logging the event or as reactive as killing the connection, modifying the firewall rules, and sending notification of the event via e-mail or an SNMP trap message. You can even record the raw data of the packets in order to completely document the attack.

FIGURE 8.11:

The Response dialog box

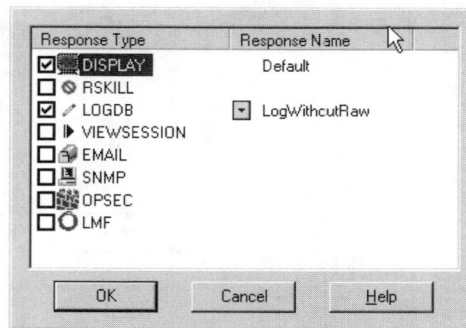

If you click the Connection Events tab of the Policy Editor menu, you will be presented with a screen similar to the one shown in Figure 8.12. Use the Connection Events screen when you require a bit more granularity. For example, let's assume you have a Web server sitting on a DMZ network. While you expect the Web server to receive connections from the outside world, this system should never try to establish any kind of connection with any other system. If this occurs, it is possible that the Web server has been compromised by an attacker who is now trying to probe or attack other systems.

Using the Connection Events settings, you can easily set up three policy rules to monitor all source traffic that originates from your Web server. Three are required because you need to set up one rule for TCP, one rule for UDP, and another for ICMP. For the source address, use the IP address of the Web server. Set Destination Address, Source Port, and Destination Port to Any, because you want to be informed of all traffic originating from this system.

NOTE   This is a powerful tool, which allows you to monitor more than just events that seem suspicious. The Connection Events settings can also be used to monitor specific services, even if no exploits are detected.

FIGURE 8.12:

The Connection Events tab
of the Policy Editor menu

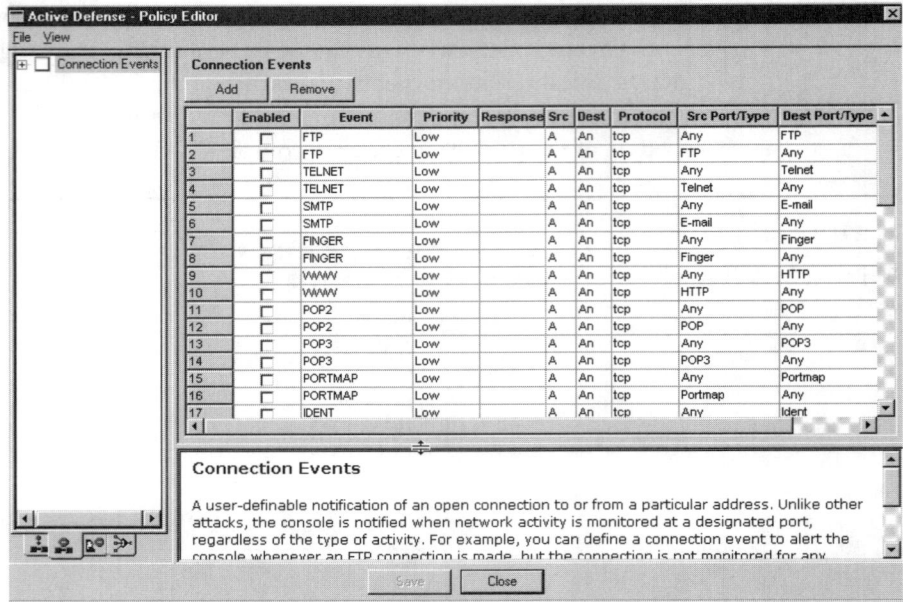

The User-Specified Filters tab of the Edit Policy menu allows you to configure specific services or systems that the IDS should not monitor. This is useful if you wish to insure that specific types of traffic are not recorded in the IDS logs. For example, you could filter out all HTTP traffic from your desktop system's IP address so that your pointy-haired boss does not find out just how much time you spend surfing the Dilbert Zone. (There *may* even be a few useful security-related reasons for this feature.)

Finally, the Filters tab lets you ignore any protocol, connection type, or traffic on your network. This is can be beneficial, especially if you suspect a hacker is exploiting services beyond the common ones (DNS, FTP, HTTP, etc.) By defining a comprehensive policy, and then ignoring the common protocols, unusual traffic patterns can stand out.

When you have finished editing your sensor policy, click OK to return to the Policies tab of the Sensor Properties screen. You will be informed that you have made policy changes and that they need to be applied using the Apply to Sensor button. You can do this now or go on to the General tab to customize the sensor even further.

The General tab (oddly enough) displays general information about the sensor configuration. From here you can see what software version the sensor is running and the system's IP address. You can also view or change the port numbers used to communicate with the console, which NIC the sensor is monitoring, and even the directory where the RealSecure software is located. Typically, you will not need to change any of these settings.

The Alerts tab defines three levels of alerts that the sensor can write to the NT Event Log: Error, Warning, and Informative. Each level can be enabled or disabled, and if enabled, can be configured to notify the console and/or send an SNMP trap to a third-party management system. The Encryption tab shows the current cryptographic provider (the system used to encrypt communication between the sensor and the console) along with all available providers. If you are configuring an OS sensor, the next tab is used to define connection and audit policy settings for the sensor. And finally, the Event Log tab pulls all sensor entries from the NT Event log and displays them in the window, allowing an administrator to quickly see how the sensor is interacting with the operating system, or if the sensor itself is having a problem.

While responses can be configured for each individual sensor policy, global responses can be used to simplify administration. By selecting the Global Responses option under the View menu, you will be presented with the screen shown in Figure 8.13. There are some important configuration options on this screen that you may wish to modify. The most important is the RSKILL item, which displays the Tag RealSecure Kills check box. When this box is checked, RealSecure adds information to all packets used for session disruption, which helps the person on the other end detect the reason for the dropped connection. While the traffic would have to be inspected with either an analyzer or a tool specifically designed to look for this type of traffic, broadcasting that RealSecure disrupted the connection may be more information than you wish to hand out. If you want your IDS sensor to be truly invisible, you should deselect this option.

Also on this tab are text boxes where you can enter the information required to use the associated action item. For example, you must supply a mail gateway and a destination e-mail address if you wish to receive e-mail notification of certain events. Other examples include the Lucent and Check Point firewalls. If you click on the LMF icon on the left pane of the window, the Lucent Firewall options are presented in the right pane, as shown in Figure 8.14. From this screen you can specify the IP address of the firewall that should be notified during certain events and which key should be used to contact it.

FIGURE 8.13:

The Responses tab of the Sensor Properties screen

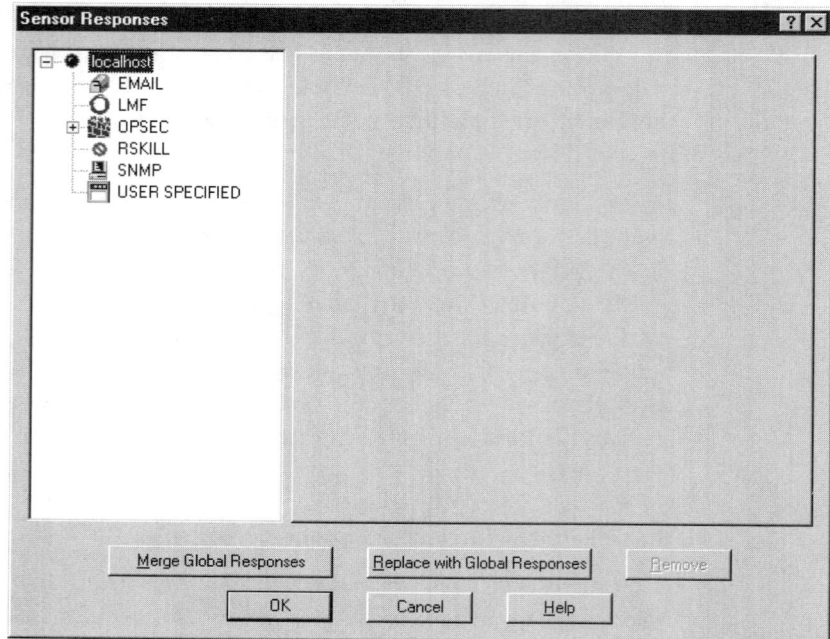

FIGURE 8.13:

The Responses tab of the Sensor Properties screen

The option below LMF is OPSEC, which refers to FireWall-1 from Check Point. Options on this tab include Notify, which specifies how FireWall-1 should log the recorded event. The Action item specifies how the firewall responds to an event, whether to simply notify, to inhibit the event, or to inhibit and close the connection. The FireWall Host specifies which firewall routers are affected—all of them, just the gateway devices, or others as specified by the administrator. The Inhibit Expiration option allows you to specify whether the rule change should be permanent or removed after a specific period of time. And finally, the Initialization Settings and Event Port options specify the IP address and port number of the FireWall-1 Management Server.

Once you have finished making configuration changes to the sensor, you should apply your changes to the system (if the changes were made to the Global Responses page), or to the sensor from its own Responses window. Click OK, and your changes are applied to the system or sensor, and all further traffic inspection is performed using these new policies.

FIGURE 8.14:

The Lucent Firewall screen of the Global Responses window

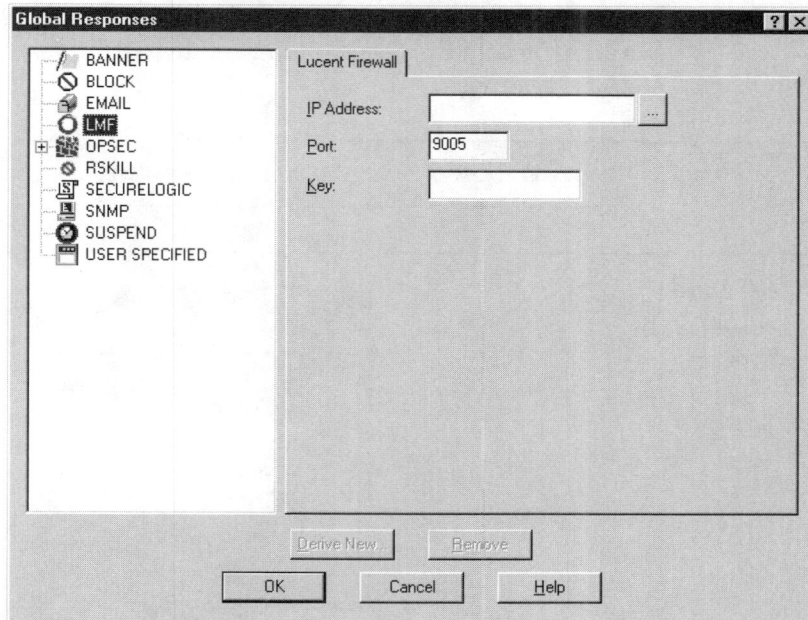

The Lucent Firewall screen of the Global Responses window

NOTE   If you have multiple sensors, you should consider using the Global Responses instead of configuring steps for each one.

Monitoring Events

You can now monitor events from the RealSecure console. The Priority windows on the right-hand side of the screen should begin to display selected events once they are detected. You can even try to trigger one of the events by launching an attack against one of your protected systems. You do not have to try anything destructive; a simple port scan should suffice to insure that the IDS sensor is doing its job.

On the left-hand side of the screen is the RealSecure console is the Activity Tree. This window is shown in Figure 8.15 with the Events tab selected. The Activity Tree allows you to quickly sort through all recent activity by source IP address, destination IP address, or even specific event. This can be an extremely powerful tool for determining what traffic is traversing your network. For example, a quick review of Figure 8.15 shows you that someone from an IP address of 24.6.91.205 has attempted gain access to this NT system (IP address 24.92.184.100) through a NetBIOS session.

TIP   You can access an exploit description of each detected vulnerability by right-clicking it.

FIGURE 8.15:

The Events tab of the Activity Tree window

The amount of detailed information that you can collect with a good IDS is downright scary. For example, let's say you want to further investigate the attempt at system access as illustrated in Figure 8.16. You could click the Source Tab in order to get a better look at what these users are doing. By expanding the tree you can continue down one of the branches until you can see exactly where each host was going.

By right-clicking the individual event at the lowest level of detail in the tree, you can choose the Inspect Event option. This creates the Event Inspector window, which provides a high level of detail—the source and destination IP addresses, the protocols, the source and destination ports, (including the information type and value), along with the actions taken. In fact, you can resolve the IP address of the system that sent the request into a domain name (see Figure 8.16). This can be useful; by knowing the domain name you can contact the owner of the domain name, and eventually trace the activity to a particular system.

While this does not guarantee you'll find the hacker, you can at least eliminate one avenue used to attempt system penetration. In Figure 8.16, you can see that the source of the connection request to the server comes from a computer on the home.com domain, (which just happens to be the name reserved for @Home, AT&T's cable modem ISP. You could now do a WHOIS query to find out the contact information for the owners of the domain name, and contact them with the details of the attempted access. @Home keeps track of which users are assigned particular host names, and they have a strict usage policy prohibiting unauthorized probing of systems by their clients.

FIGURE 8.16:

The Event Inspector window

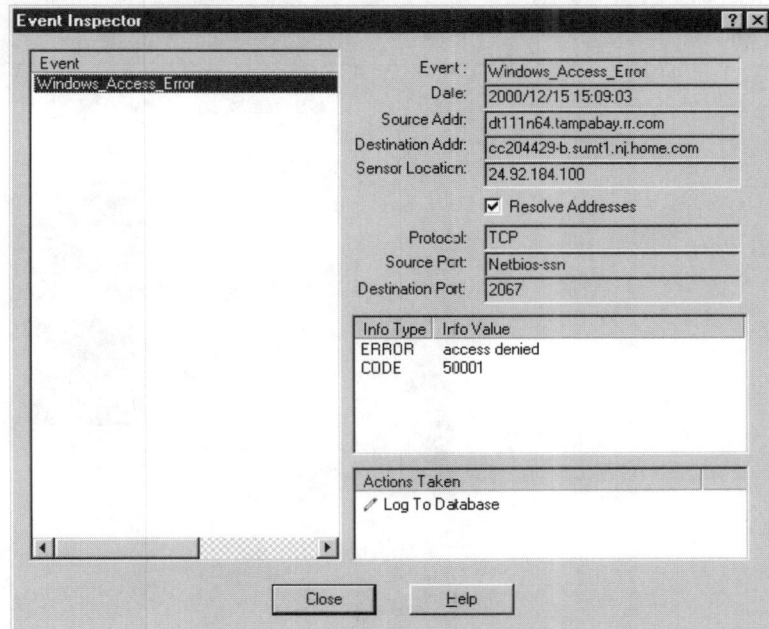

The Destination tab yields much of the same detail. The difference is that the tree is sorted by destination IP address or host name. By navigating down the branches, you can see who has accessed each address and what type of traffic was generated.

Reporting

An intrusion detection system would not be complete without the ability to run detailed, summary management reports. Before you can run reports from the

RealSecure console, you must upload the data stored in each sensor's database. Do this by selecting File ➤ Synchronize All Logs from the RealSecure console menu.

After all the data has been transferred to the console, you can begin to run reports. Select View ➤ Reports from the RealSecure console menu. The system includes a dozen canned reports. The Top 20 Events report is shown in Figure 8.17.

FIGURE 8.17:

A report on the top 20 events

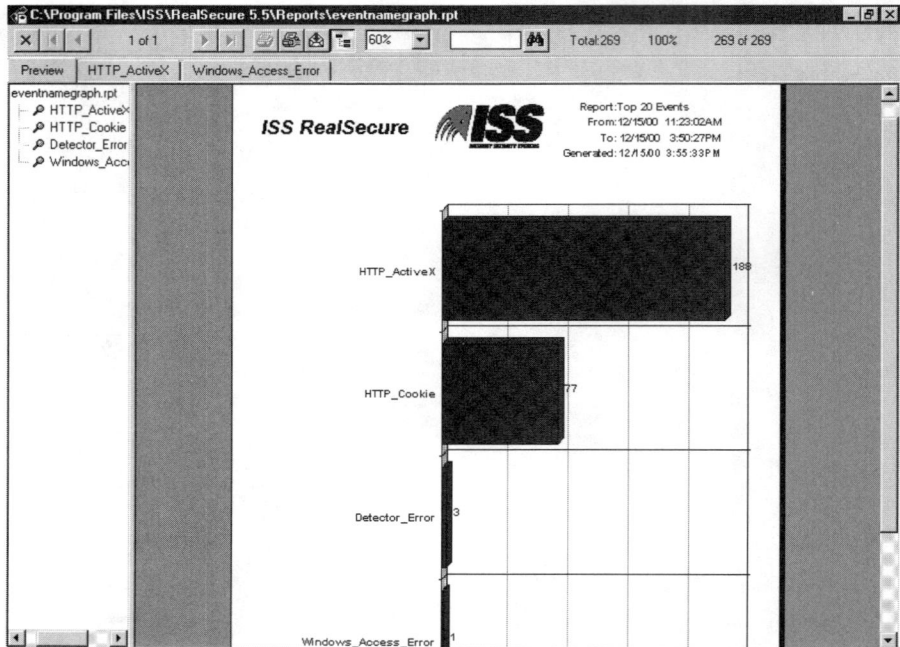

The Top 20 Events report is designed to give you a 20,000-foot view of what has transpired on your network. If you require further detail, you can select one of the events listed in the left-hand column. This will produce an additional text report that identifies every recorded instance of the event. Of course, all reports can be printed if the RealSecure console has access to a local or network printer.

If none of the reports is to your liking, you can customize new reports to fit your requirements. The console database is even ODBC-compliant, so you can read the data file with ODBC-compliant database programs such as Microsoft Access. This provides even more flexibility in analyzing and reporting the information collected by the RealSecure system.

Summary

In this chapter you have learned about the basics of intrusion detection systems and how they can aid in securing a network environment. You have seen some of the strengths and weaknesses of IDS products in general. We even walked through the installation and configuration of RealSecure, one of the top-selling IDS products.

The next chapter looks at authentication and encryption technology. These have become extremely popular subjects as organizations race to provide connectivity over less-than-secure network channels.

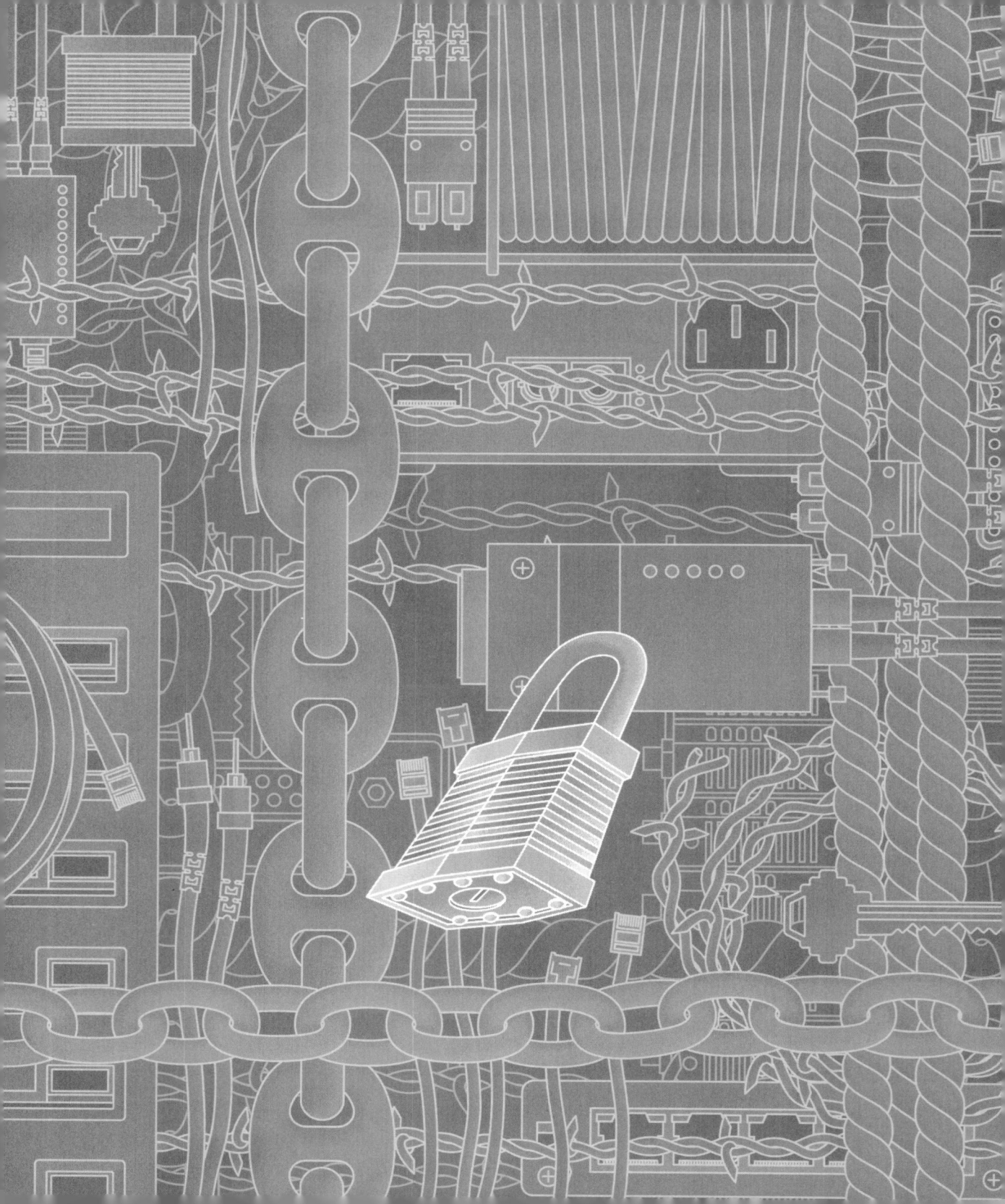

CHAPTER
NINE

Authentication and Encryption

9

Authentication and encryption are two intertwined technologies that help to insure that your data remains secure. *Authentication* is the process of insuring that both ends of the connection are in fact who they say they are. This applies not only to the entity trying to access a service (such as an end user) but to the entity providing the service, as well (such as a file server or Web site). *Encryption* helps to insure that the information within a session is not compromised. "Compromising" could include not only reading the information within a data stream, but altering it, as well.

While authentication and encryption each has its own responsibilities in securing a communication session, maximum protection can only be achieved when the two are combined. For this reason, many security protocols contain both authentication and encryption specifications.

The Need for Improved Security

When IP version 4, the version currently in use on the Internet, was created back in the '70s, network security was not a major concern. While system security was important, little attention was paid to the transport used when exchanging information. When IP was first introduced, it contained no inherent security standards. The specifications for IP do not take into account that you may wish to protect the data that IP is transporting. This will change with IP version 6, but it appears that wide acceptance of this new specification is still many years away.

Clear Text Transmissions

IP currently transmits all data as clear text, which is commonly referred to as *transmitting in the clear*. This means that the data is not scrambled or rearranged; it is simply transmitted in its raw form. This includes data and authentication information. To see how this appears, let's start by looking at Figure 9.1.

Figure 9.1 shows a network analyzer's view of a communication session. We have a user who is in the process of retrieving mail with a POP3 mail client. Packets 3–5 are the TCP three-packet handshake used to initialize the connection. Packets 6 and 7 are the POP3 mail server informing the client that it is online and ready. In packet 8, we start finding some very interesting information. If you look towards the bottom of Figure 9.1, you will see the decoded contents of the data field within packet 8. The command USER is used by a POP3 client to pass the logon name to a POP3 server. Any text following the USER command is the name of the person who is attempting to authenticate with the system.

FIGURE 9.1:

A packet decode of an authentication session initializing

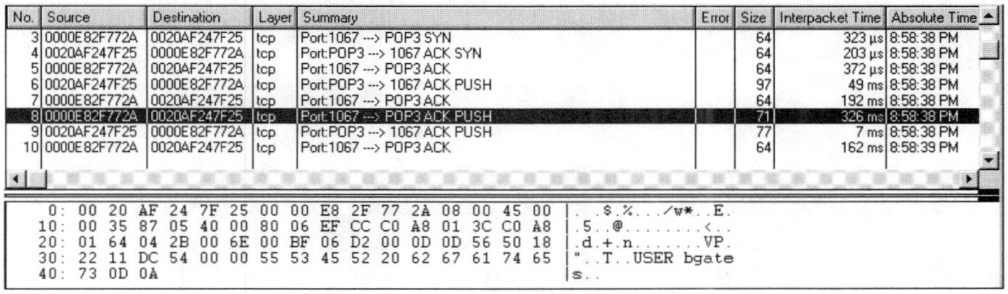

Figure 9.2 shows the POP3 server's response to this logon name. If you look at the decode for packet 9, you can see that the logon name was accepted. This tells us that the logon name you captured in Figure 9.1 is in fact legitimate. If you can discover this user's password, you will have enough information to gain access to the system.

FIGURE 9.2:

The POP3 server accepting the logon name

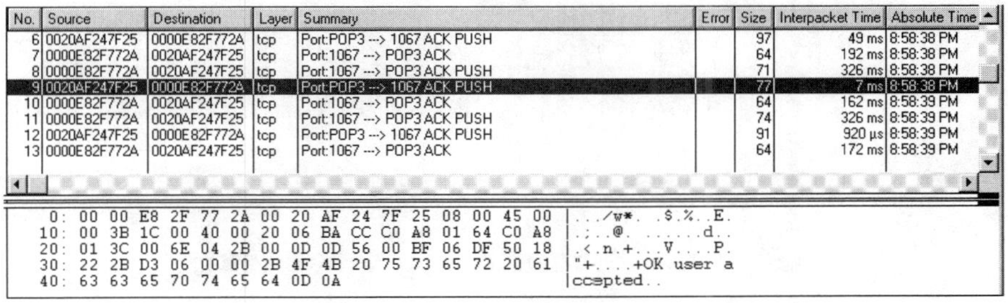

In Figure 9.3, you can see a decode of packet 11. This is the next set of commands sent by the POP3 mail client to the server. The command PASS is used by the client to send the password string. Any text that follows this command is the password for the user attempting to authenticate with the system. As you can see, the password is plainly visible.

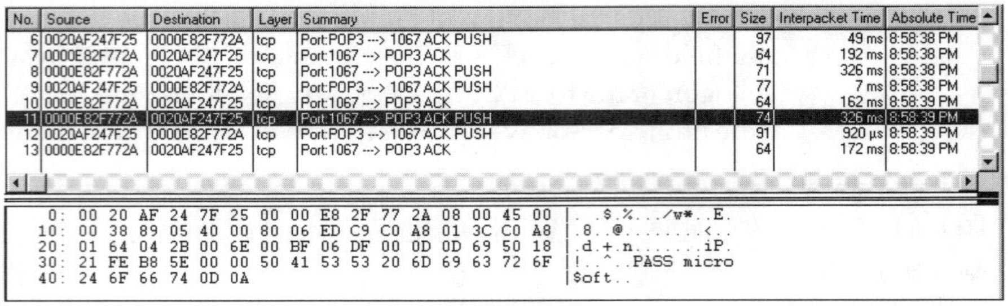

FIGURE 9.3:

The POP3 client sending the user's password

No.	Source	Destination	Layer	Summary	Error	Size	Interpacket Time	Absolute Time
6	0020AF247F25	0000E82F772A	tcp	Port:POP3 ---> 1067 ACK PUSH		97	49 ms	8:58:38 PM
7	0000E82F772A	0020AF247F25	tcp	Port:1067 ---> POP3 ACK		64	192 ms	8:58:38 PM
8	0000E82F772A	0020AF247F25	tcp	Port:1067 ---> POP3 ACK PUSH		71	326 ms	8:58:38 PM
9	0020AF247F25	0000E82F772A	tcp	Port:POP3 ---> 1067 ACK PUSH		77	7 ms	8:58:38 PM
10	0000E82F772A	0020AF247F25	tcp	Port:1067 ---> POP3 ACK		64	162 ms	8:58:39 PM
11	0000E82F772A	0020AF247F25	tcp	Port:1067 ---> POP3 ACK PUSH		74	326 ms	8:58:39 PM
12	0020AF247F25	0000E82F772A	tcp	Port:POP3 ---> 1067 ACK PUSH		91	920 µs	8:58:39 PM
13	0000E82F772A	0020AF247F25	tcp	Port:1067 ---> POP3 ACK		64	172 ms	8:58:39 PM

```
 0:  00 20 AF 24 7F 25 00 00 E8 2F 77 2A 08 00 45 00   . .$.%.../w*..E.
10:  00 38 89 05 40 00 80 06 ED C9 C0 A8 01 3C C0 A8   .8..@........<..
20:  01 64 04 2B 00 6E 00 BF 06 DF 00 0D 0D 69 50 18   .d.+.n.......iP.
30:  21 FE B8 5E 00 00 50 41 53 53 20 6D 69 63 72 6F   !..^..PASS micro
40:  24 6F 66 74 0D 0A                                  $oft..
```

In Figure 9.4 we see a decode of packet 12. This is the server's response to the authentication attempt. Notice that the server has accepted the logon name and password combination. We now know that this was a valid authentication session and that we have a legitimate logon name and password combination in order to gain access to the system. In fact, if we decoded further packets, we would be able to view every e-mail message downloaded by this user.

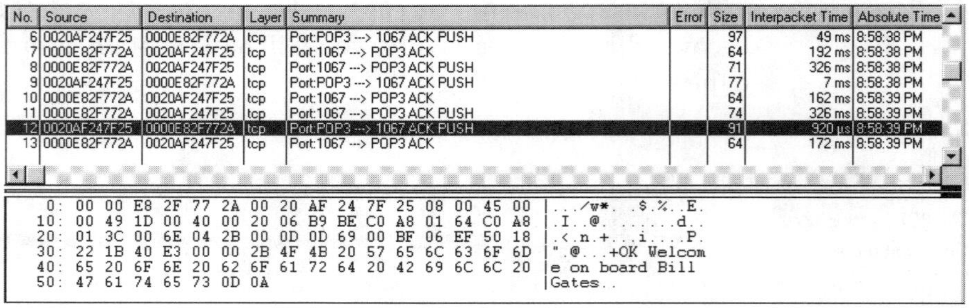

FIGURE 9.4:

The POP3 server accepting the authentication attempt

No.	Source	Destination	Layer	Summary	Error	Size	Interpacket Time	Absolute Time
6	0020AF247F25	0000E82F772A	tcp	Port:POP3 ---> 1067 ACK PUSH		97	49 ms	8:58:38 PM
7	0000E82F772A	0020AF247F25	tcp	Port:1067 ---> POP3 ACK		64	192 ms	8:58:38 PM
8	0000E82F772A	0020AF247F25	tcp	Port:1067 ---> POP3 ACK PUSH		71	326 ms	8:58:38 PM
9	0020AF247F25	0000E82F772A	tcp	Port:POP3 ---> 1067 ACK PUSH		77	7 ms	8:58:38 PM
10	0000E82F772A	0020AF247F25	tcp	Port:1067 ---> POP3 ACK		64	162 ms	8:58:39 PM
11	0000E82F772A	0020AF247F25	tcp	Port:1067 ---> POP3 ACK PUSH		74	326 ms	8:58:39 PM
12	0020AF247F25	0000E82F772A	tcp	Port:POP3 ---> 1067 ACK PUSH		91	920 µs	8:58:39 PM
13	0000E82F772A	0020AF247F25	tcp	Port:1067 ---> POP3 ACK		64	172 ms	8:58:39 PM

```
 0:  00 00 E8 2F 77 2A 00 20 AF 24 7F 25 08 00 45 00   .../w*. .$.%..E.
10:  00 49 1D 00 40 00 20 06 B9 BE C0 A8 01 64 C0 A8   .I..@. ......d..
20:  01 3C 00 6E 04 2B 00 0D 0D 69 00 BF 06 EF 50 18   .<.n.+...i....P.
30:  22 1B 40 E3 00 00 2B 4F 4B 20 57 65 6C 63 6F 6D   ".@...+OK Welcom
40:  65 20 6F 6E 20 62 6F 61 72 64 20 42 69 6C 6C 20   e on board Bill
50:  47 61 74 65 73 0D 0A                               Gates..
```

Passively Monitoring Clear Text

This POP3 authentication session was captured using a network analyzer. A network analyzer can be either a dedicated hardware tool or a software program that runs on an existing system. Network analyzer software can be purchased for less than $1,000 for Windows or Mac platforms and is freely available for UNIX.

Network analyzers operate as truly passive devices, meaning that they do not need to transmit any data on to the network in order to monitor traffic. While some analyzers do transmit traffic (usually in an effort to locate a management station), it is not a requirement. In fact, an analyzer does not even need a valid network address. This means that a network analyzer can be monitoring your network, and you would have no means of detecting its presence without tracing cables and counting hub and switch ports.

It is also possible for an attacker to load network analyzer software onto a compromised system. This means that an attacker does not need physical access to your facility in order to monitor traffic. She can simply use one of your existing systems to capture the traffic for her. This is why it is so important to perform regular audits on your systems. You clearly do not want a passively monitoring attack to go unnoticed.

In order for a network analyzer to capture a communication session, it must be connected somewhere along the session's path. This could be on the network at some point between the system initializing the session and the destination system. This could also be accomplished by compromising one of the systems at either end of the session. This means that an attacker cannot capture your network traffic over the Internet from a remote location. She must place some form of probe or analyzer within your network.

NOTE   As you saw in Chapter 4, you can reduce the amount of traffic that an analyzer can capture using bridges, switches, and routers.

Clear Text Protocols

POP3 is not the only IP service that communicates via clear text. Nearly every nonproprietary IP service that is not specifically designed to provide authentication and encryption services transmits data as clear text. Here is a partial list of clear text services:

FTP   Authentication is clear text.

Telnet   Authentication is clear text.

SMTP   Contents of mail messages are delivered as clear text.

HTTP   Page content and the contents of fields within forms are sent clear text.

IMAP   Authentication is clear text.

SNMPv1   Authentication is clear text.

WARNING The fact that SNMPv1 uses clear text is particularly nasty. SNMP is used to manage and query network devices. This includes switches and routers, as well as servers and even firewalls. If the SMTP password is compromised, an attacker can wreak havoc on your network. SNMPv2 and SNMPv3 include a message algorithm similar to the one used with Open Shortest Path First (OSPF). This provides a much higher level of security and data integrity than the original SNMP specification. Unfortunately, not every networking device supports SNMPv2, let alone SNMPv3. This means that SNMPv1 is still widely used today.

Good Authentication Required

The need for good authentication should by now be obvious. A service that passes logon information as clear text is far too easy to monitor. Easily snooped logons can be an even larger problem in environments that do not require frequent password changes. This gives our attacker plenty of time to launch an attack using the compromised account. Also of concern is that most users try to maintain the same logon name and password for all accounts. This means that if I can capture the authentication credentials from an insecure service (such as POP3), I may now have a valid logon name and passwords to other systems on the network, such as NT and NetWare servers.

Good authentication goes beyond validating the source attempting to access a service during initial logon. You should also validate that the source has not been replaced by an attacking host in the course of the communication session. This type of attack is commonly called *session hijacking*.

Session Hijacking

Consider the simple network drawing in Figure 9.5. A client is communicating with a server over an insecure network connection. The client has already authenticated with the server and has been granted access. Let's make this a fun example and assume that the client has administrator-level privileges. Woolly Attacker is sitting on a network segment between the client and the server and has been quietly monitoring the session. This has given the attacker time to learn what port and sequence numbers are being used to carry on the conversation.

FIGURE 9.5:

An example of a man-in-the-middle attack

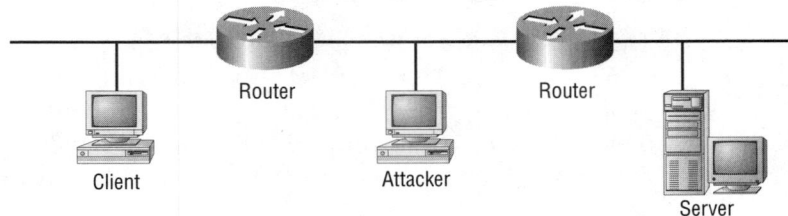

Router   Router

Client   Attacker

Server

Now let's assume that Woolly Attacker wishes to hijack the administrator's session in order to create a new account with administrator-level privileges. The first thing he does is force the client into a state where it can no longer communicate with the server. This can be done by crashing the client by sending it a Ping of death or through a utility such as WinNuke. This can also be done by launching an attack such as an ICMP flood. No matter what type of attack Woolly launches, his goal is to insure that the client cannot respond to traffic sent by the server.

NOTE   When an ICMP flood is launched against a target, the target spends so much time processing ICMP requests that it does not have enough time to respond to any other communications.

Now that the client is out of the way, Woolly Attacker is free to communicate with the server as if he were the client. He can do this by capturing the server's replies as they head back to the client in order to formulate a proper response. If Woolly has an intimate knowledge of IP, he may even be able to completely ignore the server's replies and transmit port and sequence numbers based on what the expected responses from the server will be. In either case, Woolly Attacker is now communicating with the server—except that the server thinks it is still communicating with the original client.

So good authentication should also verify that the source remains constant and has not been replaced by another system. This can be done by having the two systems exchange a secret during the course of the communication session. A secret can be exchanged with each packet transmitted or at random intervals during the course of the session. Obviously, verifying the source of every packet is far more secure than verifying the source at random intervals. The communication session would be even more secure if you could vary the secret with each packet exchange. This would help to insure that your session would not be vulnerable to session hijacking.

Verifying the Destination

The need to authenticate the source both before and during a communication session is apparent. What may not be apparent is the need to verify the server. Many people take for granted that they will either connect to the intended server or that they will receive some form of host unreachable message. It may not dawn on them that what they assume is the server may actually be an attacker attempting to compromise the network.

C2MYAZZ

The C2MYAZZ utility is an excellent example of a server spoofing attack (also known as *session hijacking* or *man in the middle*). When Windows 95 was originally introduced, it included two methods of authenticating with a session message block (SMB) system. The default was to authenticate using an encrypted password. This was the preferred method for authenticating with a Windows NT domain. LANMAN authentication was also included, however, for backwards compatibility with SMB LANMAN server. LANMAN authentication requires that the logon name and password be sent in the clear.

When C2MYAZZ is run, it passively waits for a client to authenticate to the NT server. When a logon is detected, C2MYAZZ transmits a single packet back to the client requesting that LANMAN authentication be used instead. The client, trusting that this is the server sending the request, happily obliges and retransmits the credentials in the clear. The C2MYAZZ utility would then capture and display the logon name and password combination. C2MYAZZ causes no disruption in the client's session, as the user will still be able to logon and gain system access.

What makes this utility even more frightening is that it can be run from a single bootable floppy disk. An attacker only needs to place this disk into the floppy drive of a system, power the system on, and come back later to collect the captured credentials.

NOTE   Microsoft did release a patch for this vulnerability, but you need to install it on every Windows 95 workstation. Newer versions of Windows don't suffer from this vulnerability.

DNS Poisoning

Another exploit which displays the need for authentication is *DNS poisoning*. DNS poisoning, also known as *cache poisoning*, is the process of handing out incorrect IP address information for a specific host with the intent to divert traffic from its true destination. Eugene Kashpureff proved this was possible in the summer of 1997 when he diverted requests for InterNIC hosts to his alternate domain name registry site called AlterNIC. He diverted these requests by exploiting a known vulnerability in DNS services.

When a name server receives a reply to a DNS query, it does not validate the source of the reply or ignore information not specifically requested. Kashpureff capitalized on these vulnerabilities by hiding bogus DNS information inside valid replies. The name server receiving the reply would cache the valid information, as well as the bogus information. The result was that if a user tried to resolve a host within the InterNIC's domain (for example rs.internic.net which is used for whois queries), she would receive an IP address within AlterNIC's domain and be diverted to a system on the AlterNIC network.

While Kashpureff's attack can be considered to be little more than a prank, it does open the door to some far nastier possibilities. In an age when online banking is the norm, consider the ramifications if someone diverted traffic from a bank's Web site. An attacker, using cache poisoning to divert bank traffic to an alternate server, could configure the phony server to appear identical to the bank's legitimate server.

When a bank client attempts to authenticate to the bank's Web server in order to manage his bank account, an attacker could capture the authentication information and simply present the user with a banner screen stating that the system is currently offline. Unless digital certificates are being used, the client would have no way of knowing he'd been diverted to another site unless he happened to notice the discrepancy in IP addresses.

NOTE   Digital certificates are described in the "Digital Certificate Servers" section later in this chapter.

It is just as important that you verify the server you are attempting to authenticate with as it is to verify the client's credentials or the integrity of the session. All three points in the communication process are vulnerable to attack.

Encryption 101

Cryptography is a set of techniques used to transform information into an alternate format that can later be reversed. This alternate format is referred to as the *ciphertext* and is typically created using a crypto algorithm and a crypto key. The *crypto algorithm* is simply a mathematical formula that is applied to the information you wish to encrypt. The *crypto key* is an additional variable injected into the algorithm to insure that the ciphertext is not derived using the same computational operation every time the algorithm processes information.

Let's say the number 42 is extremely important to you and you wish to guard this value from peering eyes. You could create the following crypto algorithm in order to encrypt this data:

```
data / crypto key + (2 x crypto key)
```

This process relies on two important pieces: the crypto algorithm itself and the crypto key. Both are used to create the ciphertext, which would be a new numeric value. In order to reverse the ciphertext and produce an answer of 42, you need to know both the algorithm and the key. There are less secure crypto algorithms known as *Caesar ciphers* which do not use keys, but these are typically not used because they do not have the additional security of a crypto key. You only need to know the algorithm for a Caesar cipher in order to decrypt the ciphertext.

NOTE   Julius Caesar is credited as being one of the first people to use encryption. It is believed that he used a simple form of encryption in order to send messages to his troops.

Since encryption uses mathematical formulas, there is a symbiotic relationship between

- The algorithm
- The key
- The original data
- The ciphertext

This means that knowing any three of these pieces will allow you to derive the fourth. The exception is when you know the combination of the original data and the ciphertext. If you have multiple examples of both, you may be able to discover the algorithm and the key.

Methods of Encryption

The two methods of producing ciphertext are

- The stream cipher
- The block cipher

The two methods are similar except for the amount of data each encrypts on each pass. Most modern encryption schemes use some form of a block cipher.

Stream Cipher

The *stream cipher* is one of the simplest methods of encrypting data. When a stream cipher is employed, each bit of the data is sequentially encrypted using one bit of the key. A classic example of a stream cipher was the Vernam cipher used to encrypt teletype traffic. The crypto key for the Vernam cipher was stored on a loop of paper. As the teletype message was fed through the machine, one bit of the data would be combined with one bit of the key in order to produce the ciphertext. The recipient of the ciphertext would then reverse the process, using an identical loop of paper to decode the original message.

The Vernam cipher used a fixed-length key, which can actually be pretty easy to deduce if you compare the ciphertext from multiple messages. In order to make a stream cipher more difficult to crack, you could use a crypto key which varies in length. This would help to mask any discernible patterns in the resulting cipher-text. In fact, by randomly changing the crypto key used on each bit of data, you can produce ciphertext that is mathematically impossible to crack. This is because using different random keys would not generate any repeating patterns that could give a cracker the clues required to break the crypto key. The process of continually varying the encryption key is known as a *one-time pad*.

Block Cipher

Unlike stream ciphers, which encrypt every single bit, *block ciphers* are designed to encrypt data in chunks of a specific size. A block cipher specification will iden-tify how much data should be encrypted on each pass (called a *block*) as well as what size key should be applied to each block. For example, the Data Encryption Standard (DES) specifies that DES encrypted data should be processed in 64-bit blocks using a 56-bit key.

There are a number of different algorithms that can be used when processing block cipher encryption. The most basic is to simply take the data and break it up

338 Chapter 9 • Authentication and Encryption

into blocks while applying the key to each. While this method is efficient, it can produce repetitive ciphertext. If two blocks of data contain exactly the same information, the two resulting blocks of ciphertext will be identical, as well. As mentioned earlier, a cracker can use ciphertext that repeats in a nonrandom fashion to break the crypto key.

A better solution is to use earlier resultants from the algorithm and combine them with later keys. Figure 9.6 shows one possible variation. The data you wish to encrypt is broken up into blocks labeled DB1–DB4. An *initialization vector* (IV) is added to the beginning of the data to insure that all blocks can be properly ciphered. The IV is simply a random character string to insure that two identical messages will not create the same ciphertext. To create your first block of ciphertext (CT1), you mathematically combine the crypto key, the first block of data (DB1), and the initialization vector (IV).

FIGURE 9.6:

Block cipher encryption

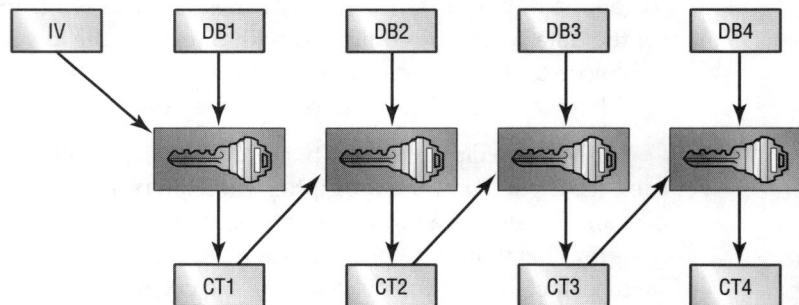

Key + IV + DB1 = CT1
Key + CT1 + DB2 = CT2
Key + CT2 + DB3 = CT3
Key + CT3 + DB4 = CT4

When you create the second block of ciphertext (CT2), you mathematically combine the crypto key, the first block of ciphertext (CT1), and the second block of data (DB2). Because the variables in your algorithm have changed, DB1 and DB2 could be identical, but the resulting ciphertext (CT1 and CT2) will contain different values. This helps to insure that the resulting ciphertext is sufficiently scrambled so that it appears completely random. This process of using resulting ciphertext in order to encrypt additional blocks of data will continue until all the data blocks have been processed.

There are a number of different variations on how to mathematically combine the crypto key, the initialization vector, and previously created ciphertext. All these methods share the same goal, which is to create a seemingly random character string of ciphertext.

Public/Private Crypto Keys

So far, all the encryption techniques we have discussed use *secret key algorithms*. A secret key algorithm relies on the same key to encrypt and to decrypt the ciphertext. This means that the crypto key must remain secret in order to insure the confidentiality of the ciphertext. If an attacker learns your secret key, she would be able to unlock all encrypted messages. This creates an interesting Catch-22, because you now need a secure method of exchanging the secret key in order to use the secret key to create a secure method of exchanging information!

In 1976, Whitfield Diffie and Martin Hellman introduced the concept of public cipher keys in their paper "New Directions in Cryptography." Not only did this paper revolutionize the cryptography industry; the process of generating public keys is now known as *Diffie-Hellman*.

In layman's terms, a *public key* is a crypto key that has been mathematically derived from a private or secret crypto key. Information encrypted with the public key can only be decrypted with the private key; however, information encrypted with the private key cannot be decrypted with the public key. In other words, the keys are not symmetrical. They are specifically designed so that the public key is used to encrypt data, while the private key is used to decrypt ciphertext.

This eliminates the Catch-22 of the symmetrical secret key, because a secure channel is not required in order to exchange key information. Public keys can be exchanged over insecure channels while still maintaining the secrecy of the messages they encrypted. If your friend Fred Tuttle wants to send you a private message, all Fred has to do is encrypt it using your public key. The resulting ciphertext can then only be decrypted using your private key.

Diffie-Hellman can even be used to provide authentication. This is performed by signing a message with your private key before encrypting it with the recipient's public key. *Signing* is simply a mathematical algorithm that processes your private key and the contents of the message. This creates a unique digital signature, which is appended to the end of the message. Since the contents of the message are used to create the signature, your digital signature will be different on every message you send.

For example, let's say you want to send Fred a private message. First you create a digital signature using your private key, then you encrypt the message using Fred's public key. When Fred receives the message, he first decrypts the cipher-text using his private key and then checks the digital signature using your public key. If the signature matches, Fred knows that the message is authentic and that it has not been altered in transit. If the signature does not match, Fred knows that either the message was not signed by your private key or that the ciphertext was altered in transit. In either event, the recipient knows that he should be suspicious of the contents of the message.

Encryption Weaknesses

Encryption weaknesses fall into one of three categories:

- Mishandling or human error
- Deficiencies in the cipher itself
- Brute force attacks

When deciding which encryption method best suits your needs, make sure you are aware of the weaknesses of your choice.

Mishandling or Human Error

While the stupid user syndrome may be an odd topic to bring up when discussing encryption methods, it does play a critical role in insuring that your data remains secure. Some methods of encryption lend themselves better to poor key management practices than others. When selecting a method of encryption, make sure you have the correct infrastructure required to administer the cipher keys in an appropriate manner.

While a one-time pad may be the most secure cipher to use, you must be able to generate enough unique keys to keep up with your data encryption needs. Even if you will use a regular secret key cipher, you must make sure that you have a secure method of exchanging key information between hosts. It does little good to encrypt your data if you are simply going to transmit your secret key over the same insecure channel.

Simple key management is one of the reasons that public/private cipher keys have become so popular. The ability to exchange key information over the same insecure channel that you wish to use for your data has great appeal. This greatly simplifies management: you can keep your private key locked up and secure while transmitting your public key using any method you choose.

Proper Key Management Is Key

Back in the 1940s, the Soviet Union was using a one-time pad in order to encrypt its most sensitive data. As you saw in the section on stream ciphers, it is mathematically impossible to break encryption using a one-time pad. This, of course, assumes that the user understands the definition of "one-time." Apparently, the Soviet Union did not.

Since cipher keys were in short supply, the Soviet Union began reusing some of its existing one-time pad keys by rotating them through different field offices. The assumption was that as long as the same office did not use the same key more than once, the resulting ciphertext would be sufficiently secure (how many of you can see your pointy-haired boss making a similar management decision?).

Apparently, this assumption was off base: the United States was able to identify the duplicate key patterns and decrypt the actual messages within the ciphertext. For more than five years, the United States was able to track Soviet spying activity within the United States. This continued until information regarding the cracking activity was relayed to a double agent.

WARNING   You must make sure that the public keys you use to encrypt data have been received from the legitimate source and not from an attacker who has swapped in a private key of his own. The validity of a public key can easily be authenticated through a phone call or some other means.

Cipher Deficiencies

Determining whether there are any deficiencies in the cipher algorithm of a specific type of encryption is probably the hardest task a non-cryptographer can attempt to perform. There are, however, a few things you can look for to insure that the encryption is secure:

- The mathematical formula that makes up the encryption algorithm should be public knowledge. Algorithms that rely on secrecy may very well have flaws that can be extorted in order to expedite cracking.

- The encryption algorithm should have undergone open public scrutiny. Anyone should be able to evaluate the algorithm and be free to discuss their findings. This means that analysis of the algorithm cannot be restricted by confidentiality agreements or contingent on the cryptographer's signing a nondisclosure agreement.

- The encryption algorithm should have been publicly available for a reasonable amount of time in order to insure that a proper analysis has been performed. An encryption algorithm with no known flaws that has only been publicly available for a few months has not stood the test of time. One of the reasons that many people trust DES encryption is that it has been around for nearly 15 years.

- Public analysis should have produced no useful weaknesses in the algorithm. This can be a gray area because nearly all encryption algorithms have some form of minor flaw. As a rule of thumb, the flaws found within an algorithm should not dramatically reduce the amount of time needed to crack a key beyond what could be achieved by trying all possible key combinations.

By following these simple guidelines, you should be able to make an educated estimation about the relative security of an encryption algorithm.

Brute Force Attacks

A brute force attack is simply an attempt to try all possible cipher key combinations in order to find the one that unlocks the ciphertext. This is why this attack is also known as an *exhaustive key search*. The cracker makes no attempt to actually crack the key, but relies on the ability to try all possible key combinations in a reasonable amount of time. All encryption algorithms are vulnerable to brute force attacks.

There are a couple of key terms in the preceding paragraph. The first is "reasonable." An attacker must feel that launching a brute force attack is worth the time. If an exhaustive key search will produce your VISA platinum card number in a few hours, the attack may be worth the effort. If, however, four weeks of work are required in order to decrypt your father-in-law's chili recipe, a brute force attack may not be worth the attacker's effort.

The other operative word is "vulnerable." While all encryption algorithms are susceptible to a brute force attack, some may take so long to try all possible key combinations that the amount of time spent cannot be considered reasonable. For example, encryption using a one-time pad can be broken using a brute force attack, but the attacker had better plan on having many of his descendants carry on his work long after he is gone. To date, the earth has not existed long enough for an attacker to be able to break a proper one-time pad encryption scheme using existing computing power.

So the amount of time required to perform a brute force attack is contingent on two factors: how long it takes to try a specific key and how many possible key combinations there are. The amount of time required to try each key is dependent on the device providing the processing power. A typical desktop computer is capable of testing approximately five keys per second. A device specifically designed to break encryption keys may be able to process 200 keys or more per second. Of course, greater results can be achieved by combining multiple systems.

As for the number of possible key combinations, this is directly proportional to the size of the cipher key. Size does matter in cryptography: the larger the cipher key the more possible key combinations exist. Table 9.1 shows some common methods of encryption, along with their associated key size. Notice that as the size of the key increases, the number of possible key combinations increases exponentially.

TABLE 9.1:   Methods of Encryption and Their Associated Keys

Encryption	Bits in Key	Number of Possible Keys
Netscape	40	1.1×10^6
DES	56	72.1×10^6
Triple DES (2 keys)	112	5.2×10^{33}
IDEA	128	3.4×10^{38}
RC4 (key bits can vary, commonly uses 128-bit keys)	128	3.4×10^{38}
Triple DES (3 keys)	168	3.7×10^{50}
Blowfish	Up to 448	
AES	128, 192, 256	3.4×10^{38}

Of course, all this leads to the question: how long does it take to perform an exhaustive key search on a particular encryption algorithm? The answer should scare you. DES encryption (discussed in the DES section of this chapter) has become somewhat of an industry standard. Over the past few years, RSA Laboratories has staged a DES challenge in order to see how long it would take for a person or persons to crack a string of ciphertext and discover the message hidden inside.

In 1997, the challenge was completed in approximately five months. In January 1998, the challenge was completed in 39 days. During the final challenge, in January 1999, the Electronic Frontier Foundation (EFF) was able to complete the challenge in just under 22 hours.

The EFF accomplished this task through a device designed specifically for brute forcing DES encryption. The cost of the device was approximately $250,000—well within the price range of organized crime and big business. Just after the challenge, the EFF published a book entitled *Cracking DES* (O'Reilly and Associates), which completely documents the design of the device they used. Obviously, this has put a whole new spin on what key lengths are considered secure.

Government Intervention

As you may know, the federal government regulates the export or use of encryption across U.S. borders. These regulations originated back in World War II, when the use of encryption was thought to be limited to spies and terrorists. These regulations still exist today due in part to the efforts of the National Security Agency (NSA). The NSA is responsible for monitoring and decrypting all communication that can be considered of interest to the security of the United States government.

Originally, the regulations controlled the cipher key size that could be exported or used across U.S. borders. The limitation before the year 2000 was a maximum key size of 40 bits, but there were exceptions to this rule. Organizations that wished to use a larger key size had to apply to the Department of Commerce and obtain a license to do so under the International Traffic in Arms Regulations (ITAR). In order to obtain a usage license for keys larger than 40 bits, you typically had to be a financial institution or a U.S.-based company with foreign subsidiaries.

That all changed in January of 2000, when the U.S. changed its export law to allow any commercial retail encryption product to be sold to overseas, provided it was first reviewed by the government. Other countries are following in the lead of the U.S.—and this entire trend is considered to be a by-product of the explosive growth of e-commerce in the past few years. This decision on the part of the United States points to the threat posed to encryption by evermore powerful computer systems—a cycle which sees no end in sight.

Good Encryption Required

If you are properly verifying your authentication session, why do you even need encryption? Encryption serves two purposes:

- To protect the data from snooping

- To protect the data from being altered

In the section on clear text transmissions earlier in this chapter, you saw how most IP services transmit all information in the clear. This should be sufficient justification for why you need encryption to shield your data from peering eyes.

Encryption can also help to insure that your data is not altered during transmission. This is commonly referred to as a *man-in-the-middle attack*, because it relies on the attacker's ability to disrupt the data transfer. Let's assume you have a Web server configured to accept online catalog orders. Your customer fills out an online form, which is then saved on the Web server in a plain text format. At regular intervals, these files are transferred to another system via FTP or SMTP.

If an attacker can gain access to the Web server's file system, she would be able to modify these text files prior to processing. A malicious attacker could then change quantities or product numbers in order to introduce inaccuracies. The result is a very unhappy client when the wrong order is received. While this example assumes that the attacker has gained access to a file system, it is possible to launch a man-in-the-middle attack while information is in transit on the network, as well.

So while your attacker has not stolen anything, she has altered the data—and disrupted your business. Had this information been saved using a good encryption algorithm, this attack would have been far more difficult to stage, because the attacker would not know which values within the encrypted file to change. Even if she were a good guesser, the algorithm decrypting the cipher would detect the change in data.

Solutions

There are a number of solutions available for providing authentication and encryption services. Some are products produced by a specific vendor, while others are open standards. Which option is the right one for you depends on your specific requirements. The options listed below are the most popular for providing authentication, encryption, or a combination of the two. Most likely, one of these solutions can fill your needs.

Data Encryption Standard (DES)

DES is the encryption standard used by the United States government for protecting sensitive, but not classified, data. The American National Standards Institute (ANSI) and the Internet Engineering Task Force (IETF) have also incorporated DES into security standards. DES is by far the most popular secret key algorithm in use today.

The original standard of DES uses a 40-bit (for export) or 56-bit key for encrypting data. The latest standard, referred to as *Triple DES*, encrypts the plain text three times using two or three different 56-bit keys. This produces ciphertext that is scrambled to the equivalent of a 112-bit or 168-bit key, while still maintaining backwards-compatibility.

DES is designed so that even if someone knows some of the plain text data and the corresponding ciphertext, there is no way to determine the key without trying all possible keys. The strength of DES encryption–based security rests on the size of the key and on the proper protection of the key. While the original DES standard has been broken in brute force attacks of only three days, the new Triple DES standard should remain secure for many years to come.

Advanced Encryption Standard (AES)

Advanced Encryption Standard (AES) is the follow-up to DES. AES is designed to overcome the deficiencies of DES (encryption weakness, key length restrictions, and device-specific application) while providing a framework for future technological advancements. While AES is not set to be a full standard until summer of 2001, NIST (National Institute of Standards and Technology) announced on October 2, 2000 that the Rijndael algorithm would be at the core of the replacement to DES. Rijndael is a variable length block cipher, but its implementation in AES will initially be in key lengths of 128, 192, and 256 bits.

NIST chose Rijndael because it performed well not just on Pentium-class machines, but also on smart cards. Combined with the ability to use variable length keys and other encryption features, NIST has decided that Rijndael is the best of all five standards submitted for final AES evaluation.

Digital Certificate Servers

As you saw in the section on public and private cipher keys, a private key can be used to create a unique digital signature. This signature can then be verified later with the public key in order to insure that the signature is authentic. This process provides a very strong method of authenticating a user's identity. A *digital certificate server* provides a central point of management for multiple public keys. This prevents every user from having to maintain and manage copies of every other user's public cipher key. A Lotus Notes server will act as a digital certificate server, allowing users to sign messages using their private keys. The Notes server will then inform the recipient on delivery whether the Notes server could verify the digital signature.

Digital certificate servers, also known as *certificate authorities* (CA), provide verification of digital signatures. For example, if Toby receives a digitally signed message from Lynn but does not have a copy of Lynn's public cipher key, Toby can obtain a copy of Lynn's public key from the CA in order to verify that the message is authentic. Also, let's assume that Toby wishes to respond to Lynn's e-mail but wants to encrypt the message in order to protect it from prying eyes. Toby can again obtain a copy of Lynn's public key from the CA, so that the message can be encrypted using Lynn's public key.

Certificate servers can even be used to provide single sign-on and access control. Certificates can be mapped to access control lists for files stored on a server in order to restrict access. When a user attempts to access a file, the server verifies that the user's certificate has been granted access. This allows a CA to manage nearly all document security for an organization.

NOTE   Netscape Certificate Server is a good example of a CA that supports file-level access control.

The largest benefit comes from using a CA that supports X.509, an industry standard format for digital certificates. This allows certificates to be verified and information to be encrypted between organizations. If the predominant method of exchanging information between two domains is e-mail, a CA may be far more cost effective than investing in virtual private networking.

IP Security (IPSec)

IP Security (IPSec) is public/private key encryption algorithm that is being spear-headed by Cisco Systems. It is not so much a new specification as a collection of open standards. IPSec uses a Diffie-Hellman exchange in order to perform authentication and establish session keys. IPSec also uses a 40-bit DES algorithm in order to encrypt the data stream. IPSec has been implemented at the session layer, so it does not require direct application support. Use of IPSec is transparent to the end user.

One of the benefits of IPSec is that it is very convenient to use. Since Cisco has integrated IPSec into its router line of products, IPSec becomes an obvious virtual private network (VPN) solution. While IPSec is becoming quite popular for remote network access from the Internet, the use of a 40-bit DES algorithm makes it most suited for general business use. Organizations that need to transmit sensitive or financial data over insecure channels may be prudent to look for a different encryption technology.

Kerberos

Kerberos is another authentication solution, which is designed to provide a single sign-on to a heterogeneous environment. Kerberos allows mutual authentication and encrypted communication between users and services. Unlike security tokens, however, Kerberos relies on each user to remember and maintain a unique password.

When a user authenticates to the local operating system, a local agent sends an authentication request to the Kerberos server. The server responds by sending the encrypted credentials for the user attempting to authenticate to the system. The local agent then tries to decrypt the credentials using the user-supplied password. If the correct password has been supplied, the user is validated and given authentication tickets, which allow the user to access other Kerberos-authenticated services. The user is also given a set of cipher keys that can be used to encrypt all data sessions.

Once the user is validated, she is not required to authenticate with any Kerberos-aware servers or applications. The tickets issued by the Kerberos server provide the credentials required to access additional network resources. This means that while the user is still required to remember her password, she only needs one password to access all systems on the network to which she has been granted access.

One of the biggest benefits of Kerberos is that it is freely available. The source code can be downloaded and used without cost. There are also many commercial applications, such as IBM's Global Sign-On (GSO) product, which are Kerberos-compatible but sport additional features and improved management. A number of security flaws have been discovered in Kerberos over the years, but most, if not all, have been fixed as of Kerberos V.

Point-to-Point Tunneling Protocol vs. Layer Two Tunneling Protocol

A discussion on encryption techniques would not be complete without at least mentioning *PPTP* and *L2TP*. Developed by Microsoft, PPTP uses authentication based on the Point-to-Point Protocol (PPP) and encryption based on a Microsoft algorithm. Microsoft has integrated support for PPTP into both NT Server and Windows 95/98.

Many within the cryptography field refer to PPTP as *kindergarten crypto*. This is due to the relative ease in which people have broken both the authentication mechanism and the encryption algorithm. There are a number of tools available on the Internet that will capture password information within a PPTP session. This is a bit disappointing, considering that PPTP is less than four years old. With so many tools available that will break PPTP, it is of little use as a protocol for protecting your data.

NOTE   For additional information on the insecurities of PPTP, check out `http://underground.org/`

Layer Two Tunneling Protocol (L2TP) was designed by taking the best parts of PPTP and Cisco's L2F (Layer Two Firewall). Most commonly used with IPSec, L2TP focuses on creating the tunnel between two points and leaves encryption tasks to IPSec (or whatever encryption algorithm you've chosen). As a result, L2TP has the following advantages over PPTP:

- LT2P can work over any packet point-to-point network, including Frame Relay, X.25, and ATM.

- L2TP can create multiple tunnels between a single pair of endpoints.

- L2TP can compress its header information.

- L2TP can provide its own tunnel authentication, (not necessary when using L2TP with IPSec).

Remote Access Dial-In User Service (RADIUS)

RADIUS allows multiple remote access devices to share the same authentication database. This provides a central point of management for all remote network access. When a user attempts to connect to a RADIUS client (such as a terminal access server), he is challenged for a logon name and password. The RADIUS client then forwards these credentials to the RADIUS server. If the credentials are valid, the server returns an affirmative reply and the user is granted access to the network. If the credentials do not match, the RADIUS server will reply with a rejection, causing the RADIUS client to drop the user's connection.

RADIUS has been used predominantly for remote modem access to a network. Over the years, it has enjoyed widespread support from such vendors as 3COM, Cisco, and Ascend. RADIUS is also starting to become accepted as a method for authenticating remote users who are attempting to access the local network through a firewall. Support for RADIUS has been added to Check Point's FireWall-1 and Cisco's PIX firewall.

The biggest drawback to using RADIUS for firewall connectivity is that the specification does not include encryption. This means that while RADIUS can perform strong authentication, it has no process for insuring the integrity of your data once the session is established. If you do use RADIUS authentication on the firewall, you will need an additional solution in order to provide encryption.

RSA Encryption

The *RSA encryption algorithm* was created by Ron Rivest, Adi Shamir, and Leonard Adleman in 1977. RSA is considered the de facto standard in public/private key encryption: it has found its way into products from Microsoft, Apple, Novell, Sun, and even Lotus. As a public/private key scheme, it is also capable of performing authentication.

The fact that RSA is widely used is important when considering interoperability. You cannot authenticate or decrypt a message if you are using a different algorithm from the algorithm used to create it. Sticking with a product which supports RSA helps to insure that you are capable of exchanging information with a large base of users. The large installation base also means that RSA has received its share of scrutiny over the years. This is also an important consideration when you are selecting an algorithm to protect your data.

RSA encryption is owned by RSA Laboratories, which in turn is owned by Security Dynamics. The patent for the RSA algorithm was issued in 1983 and will expire in the year 2000. While RSA Labs still holds control of the patent, the company has been quite generous in the number of institutions to which it has made the technology freely available. RSA Labs has even published source code, which is freely available for noncommercial use.

Hashing

Digital signatures typically work by signing the entire message using a private key. This can be cumbersome and time consuming. An alternative is to create a message digest, and then sign (or encrypt) the message digest (sometimes referred to as a hash) with a private key, thus achieving the same effect as signing the entire message.

This all starts with the hashing algorithm, a mathematical process that takes an original file and creates a digital summary known as a message digest. The message digest is then signed (encrypted) by a private key and transmitted. The receiver applies the public key of the signer to the encrypted message digest to verify the identity of the receiver. The receiver then processes the original file using the same hashing algorithm as the sender, and compares the resulting message digest with the original. If they match, the receiver can be assured that the message has not been altered in transit.

SHA-1

Created by NIST (National Institute for Standards and Technology), SHA-1 (Secure Hash Algorithm) is part of the U.S. Government's DSS standard, and works with DES to create digital signatures. Released in 1994, (to correct for an unpublished flaw in the original SHA), SHA-1 produces a 160-bit message digest. On October 12, 2000, NIST announced three new SHA-based algorithms to work with the new AES (Advanced Encryption Standard) that will replace DES in 2001. SHA-256, SHA-384, and SHA-512 will work with the three different AES key sizes (128, 192, and 256 bits).

MD5

Created by Professor Robert Rivest of MIT in 1991, MD5 is the latest in the MD-series of hash algorithms. Explicitly designed to run on 32-bit processors, MD5 produces a 128-bit digest. MD5 is a faster, although not as secure, alternative to SHA-1.

Secure Shell (SSH)

Secure Shell (SSH) is a powerful method of performing client authentication and safeguarding multiple service sessions between two systems. Written by a Finnish student named Tatu Yl nen, SSH has received widespread acceptance within the UNIX world. The protocol has even been ported to Windows and OS/2.

Systems running SSH listen on port 22 for incoming connection requests. When two systems running SSH establish a connection, they validate each other's credentials by performing a digital certificate exchange using RSA. Once the credentials for each system have been validated, triple DES is used to encrypt all information that is exchanged between the two systems. The two hosts will authenticate each other in the course of the communication session and periodically change encryption keys. This helps to insure that brute force or playback attacks are not effective.

SSH is an excellent method of securing protocols that are known to be insecure. For example, telnet and FTP sessions exchange all authentication information in the clear. SSH can encapsulate these sessions to insure that no clear text information is visible.

Secure Sockets Layer (SSL)

Created by Netscape, Secure Sockets Layer *(SSL)* provides RSA encryption at the session layer of the OSI model. By encrypting at the session layer, SSL has the ability to be service independent. Although SSL works equally well with FTP, HTTP, and even telnet, the main use of SSL is in secure Web commerce. Since the RSA encryption is a public/private key encryption, digital certificates are also supported. This allows SSL to authenticate the server and optionally authenticate the client.

Netscape includes SSL in its Web browser and Web server products. Netscape has even provided source code so that SSL can be adapted to other Web server platforms. A Webmaster developing a Web page can flag the page as requiring an SSL connection from all Web browsers. This allows online commerce to be conducted in a relatively secure manner.

The Internet Engineering Task Force (IETF) is considering a standard based on SSL 3.0 known as the Transport Layer Security (TLS) protocol. While the difference between the two will be minimal, TLS will not interoperate with SSL.

Security Tokens

Security tokens, also called token cards (or smart cards), are password-generating devices that can be used to access local clients or network services. Physically, a token is a small device with an LCD display that shows the current password and the amount of time left before the password expires. Once the current password expires, a new one is generated. This provides a high level of authentication security, since a compromised password has a very limited life span. Figure 9.7 shows a number of security tokens produced by Security Dynamics Technologies. These tokens are referred to as SecurID cards.

FIGURE 9.7:

SecurID cards from Security Dynamics Technologies

Security tokens do not directly authenticate with an existing operating system or application. An agent is required in order to redirect the logon request to an authentication server. For example, FireWall-1 supports inbound client authentication via SecurID. When a user out on the Internet wishes to access internal services protected by FireWall-1, she uses her SecurID token to authenticate at the firewall. FireWall-1 does not handle this authentication directly; rather, an agent on the firewall forwards the logon request to a SecurID authentication server, known as an *ACE/Server*. If the credentials are legitimate, validation is returned to the agent via an encrypted session and the user is allowed access to the internal network.

Each security token is identified by a unit ID number. The unit ID number uniquely identifies each security token to the server. The unit ID is also used to modify the algorithm used to generate each password so multiple tokens will not produce the same sequence of passwords. Since passwords expire at regular intervals (usually 60 seconds), the security token needs to be initially synchronized with the authentication server.

There are a number of benefits to this type of authentication. First, users are no longer required to remember their passwords. They simply read the current password from the security token and use this value for authentication. This obviously removes the need to have users change their passwords at regular intervals, because this is done automatically by the security token. Also, it is far less likely that a user will give out his password to another individual because the token is a physical device which needs to be referenced during each authentication attempt. Even if a user does read off his password to another user, the consequences are minimized because the password is only valid for a very short period of time.

Security tokens are an excellent means of providing authentication. Their only drawback is that they do not provide any type of session encryption. They rely on the underlying operating system or application to provide this functionality. For example, this means that authentication information could still be read as clear text if an attacker snoops on a telnet session. Still, the limited life span of any given password makes this information difficult to capitalize on.

Simple Key Management for Internet Protocols (SKIP)

Simple Key Management for Internet Protocols (SKIP) is similar to SSL in that it operates at the session level. As with SSL, this gives SKIP the ability to support IP services regardless of whether the services specifically support encryption. This is extremely useful when you have multiple IP services running between two hosts.

What makes SKIP unique is that it requires no prior communication in order to establish or exchange keys on a session-by-session basis. The Diffie-Hellman public/private algorithm is used to generate a shared secret. This shared secret is used to provide IP packet–based encryption and authentication.

While SKIP is extremely efficient at encrypting data, which improves VPN performance, it relies on the long-term protection of this shared secret in order to maintain the integrity of each session. SKIP does not continually generate new key values, as SSH does. This makes SKIP encryption vulnerable if the keys are not protected properly.

Summary

In this chapter, you saw why good authentication is important and what kinds of attacks can be launched if you do not use it. You also learned about encryption and the differences between secret and public/private algorithms. Finally, we looked at a number of authentication and encryption options that are currently available.

Now that you understand encryption, it is time to put it to use by creating a virtual private network (VPN). Extranets have become quite popular, and the ability to create a secure VPN has become a strong business need.

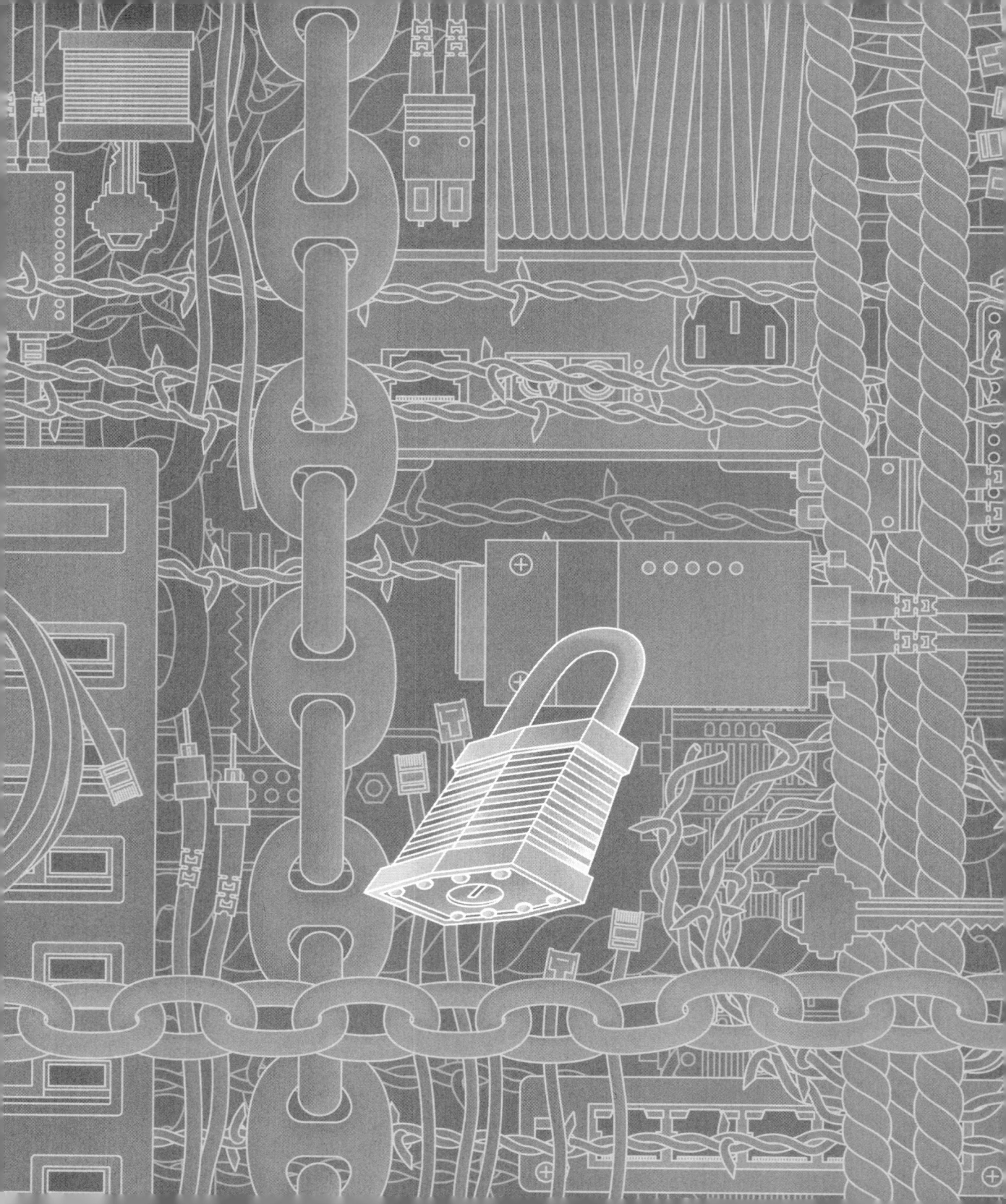

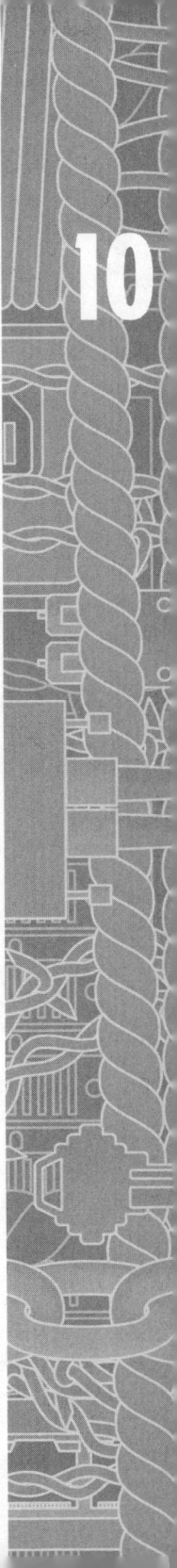

CHAPTER
TEN

10

Virtual Private Networking

Not since the introduction of the Internet has a single technology brought with it so much promise—or so much controversy. Virtual private networking (VPN) has been touted as the cure-all for escalating WAN expenses, and feared for being the Achilles' heel in perimeter security. Obviously, the true classification of VPN technology lies somewhere in the middle.

Interestingly, it has been financial institutions, trading companies, and other organizations at high risk of attack that have spearheaded the deployment of VPN technology. Monetary and economic organizations have embraced VPNs in order to extend their network perimeter.

VPN Basics

A *virtual private network* session is an authenticated and encrypted communication channel across some form of public network, such as the Internet. Since the network is considered to be insecure, encryption and authentication are used to protect the data while it is in transit. Typically, a VPN is *service independent*, meaning that all information exchanged between the two hosts (Web, FTP, SMTP, and so on) is transmitted along this encrypted channel.

Figure 10.1 illustrates a typical example of a VPN configuration. The figure shows two different networks that are both connected to the Internet. These two networks wish to exchange information, but they want to do so in a secure manner, as some of the data they will be exchanging is private. To safeguard this information, a VPN is set up between the two sites.

VPNs require a bit of advance planning. *Before* establishing a VPN, the two networks must do the following:

- Each site must set up a VPN-capable device on the network perimeter. This could be a router, a firewall, or a device dedicated to VPN activity.

- Each site must know the IP subnet addresses used by the other site.

- Both sites must agree on a method of authentication and exchange digital certificates if required.

- Both sites must agree on a method of encryption and exchange encryption keys as required.

FIGURE 10.1:

An example of a VPN between two Internet sites

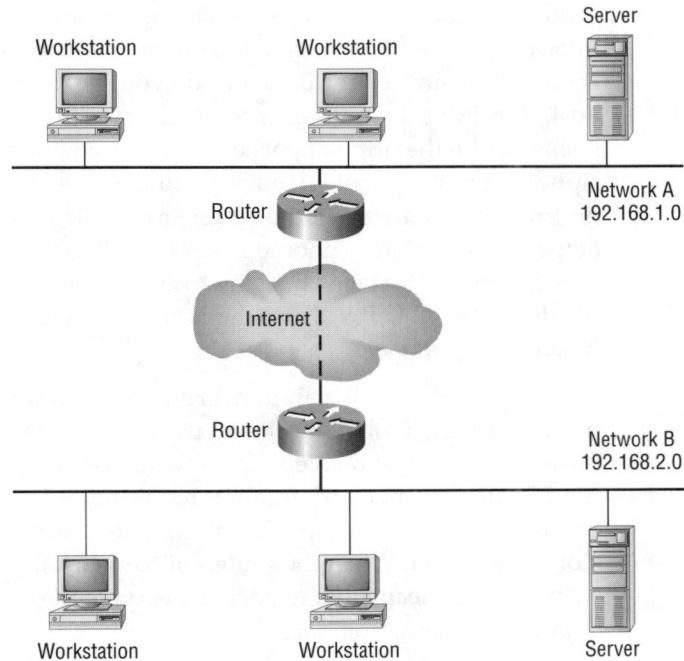

In Figure 10.1, the devices at each end of the VPN tunnel are the routers you are using to connect to the Internet. If these are Cisco routers, they are capable of supporting IPSEC, which provides Diffie-Hellman authentication and 40-bit DES encryption.

The router on Network A must be configured so that all outbound traffic headed for the 192.168.2.0 subnet is encrypted using DES. This is known as the remote *encryption domain*. The router on Network A also must know that any data received from the router on Network B will require decryption. The router on Network B would be configured in a similar fashion, encrypting all traffic headed for the subnet 192.168.1.0 while decrypting any replies received from the router on Network A. Data sent to all other hosts on the Internet is transmitted in the clear. It is only communications between these two subnets that will be encrypted.

NOTE   A VPN only protects communications sessions between the two encryption domains. While it is possible to set up multiple VPNs, you must define multiple encryption domains.

With some VPN configurations, a network analyzer placed between the two routers would display all packets using a source and destination IP address of the interfaces of the two routers. You do not get to see the IP address of the host that actually transmitted the data, nor do you see the IP address of the destination host. This information is encrypted along with the actual data within the original packet. Once the original packet is encrypted, the router will encapsulate this ciphertext within a new IP packet using its own IP address as the source and a destination IP address of the remote router. This is called *tunneling*. Tunneling helps to insure that a snooping attacker will not be able to guess which traffic crossing the VPN is worth trying to crack, since all packets use the two routers' IP addresses. Not all VPN methods support this feature, but it is nice to use when it is available.

Since you have a virtual tunnel running between the two routers, you have the added benefit of being able to use private address space across the Internet. For example, a host on Network A would be able to transmit data to a host on the 192.168.2.0 network without requiring network address translation. This is because the routers encapsulate this header information as the data is delivered along the tunnel. When the router on Network B receives the packet, it simply strips off the encapsulating packet, decrypts the original packet, and delivers the data to the destination host.

Your VPN also has the benefit of being platform and service independent. In order to carry on secure communications, your workstations do not have to use software that supports encryption. This is done automatically as the traffic passes between the two routers. This means that services such as SMTP, which are transmitted in the clear, can be used in a secure fashion—provided the destination host is on the remote encryption domain.

VPN Usage

Although VPNs are beginning to enjoy a wide deployment, there are only two specific applications for which they are being used. These are

- Replacement for dial-in modem pools
- Replacement for dedicated WAN links

A VPN can replace the listed technology completely or only in specific situations. The limited application is greatly due to the amount of manual configuration that is required in order to configure a VPN. As technology evolves, you may see this process become more dynamic. For example, two IPSEC-compatible routers may dynamically handshake and exchange keys before passing SMTP traffic. When the delivery process is complete, the VPN could be torn down. While this technology is currently not on the horizon, it is certainly possible.

Modem Pool Replacement

Modem pools have always been the scourge of the network administrator. While there are stable solutions available, these are usually priced beyond the budget of a small to mid-sized organization. Most of us end up dealing with modems that go off auto-answer, below-grade wiring, incorrectly configured hunt groups, and the salesperson who is having trouble dialing in because little Timmy deleted some files to make room for another game. For anyone who has been responsible for administering a modem pool, the thought of getting rid of such headaches can bring tears of joy.

A VPN solution for remote users can dramatically reduce support costs. There are no more phone lines to maintain or 800 numbers to pay for. You are not required to upgrade your hardware every time a new modem standard is released or to upgrade your phone lines to support new technology, such as ISDN. All inbound access is managed through your Internet connection, a connection your company already maintains in order to do business on the Internet.

Access costs can be cheaper, as well. For example, many organizations maintain an 800 number in order to allow employees remote access to the network free of charge. This can place a large cost burden on the organization, as the per-minute charge for using an 800 number can be double the cost of calling direct. Most ISPs charge $20 per month or less for unlimited access. Large ISPs, such as CompuServe, can even provide local dial-up numbers internationally. For heavy remote access users, it may be far more cost effective for an organization to reimburse the employee for an ISP account than it would be to pay 800-number charges.

Besides reducing infrastructure costs, you can reduce end-user support costs, as well. The most common remote-access Helpdesk problem is helping the end user configure network settings and connect to the network. If the user first needs to dial in to an ISP, this support can be provided by the ISP providing access. Your organization's Helpdesk only needs to get involved when the user can access resources out on the Internet but is having problems connecting to internal resources. This greatly limits the scope of required support.

TIP
When selecting a firewall solution, consider whether you will be providing end users with remote VPN access. Most firewall packages provide special client software so that an end user can create a VPN to the firewall.

There are a few drawbacks to consider when deciding whether to provide end users with remote VPN access. The first is the integrity of the remote workstation. With penetration tools such as L0pht's Netcat and the Cult of the Dead Cow's Back Orifice freely available on the Internet, it is entirely possible that the remote workstation can become compromised. Most ISPs do not provide any type of firewall for dial-in users. This means that dialed-in systems are wide open to attack. The remote client could be infiltrated by an attacker, who could then use the VPN tunnel to attack internal resources.

The other drawback is more theoretical. Allowing VPN access into your network requires that you punch another hole through your firewall. Every open hole gives attackers that much more room to squirm their way in. For example, NT users who relied on PPTP to provide safe encrypted access to their network were caught off guard when a vulnerability was found with the PPTP service running on the NT server. By sending the PPTP server a single PPTP start session request with an invalid packet length value, an attacker could make the server core dump and crash. This would bring down the PPTP server, along with any other service running on that system.

Dedicated WAN Link Replacement

As you saw in Figure 10.1, a VPN can be used to connect two geographically separate networks over the Internet. This is most advantageous when the two sites are separated by large distances, as when your organization has one office in Germany and another in New York. Instead of having to pay for a dedicated circuit halfway around the world, each site would only be required to connect to a local ISP. The Internet could then be used as a backbone to connect these two networks.

A VPN connection may even be advantageous when two sites are relatively close to one another. For example, if you have a business partner that you wish to exchange information with but the expected bandwidth does not justify a dedicated connection, a VPN tunnel across an already existing Internet connection may be just the ticket. In fact, it may even make life a bit easier.

System Capacity Checklist

If you will be providing client VPN access to your network, keep a sharp eye on system capacity. Here are some questions you should ask yourself:

- How many concurrent users will there be? More users means you need more capacity.

- When will VPN clients connect remotely to your network? If most remote VPN access will take place during normal business hours, a faster Internet link and faster hardware may be required.

- What services will the clients be accessing? If remote VPN access will be for bandwidth-intensive applications like file sharing, a faster Internet link and faster hardware may be required, as well.

- What kind of encryption do you plan to use? If remote VPN access will be using a large key algorithm, such as TripleDES, then faster encryption hardware may be required.

Consider the network drawing in Figure 10.2. There is an internal network protected by a firewall. There is also a DMZ segment which holds your Web server and SMTP relay. Additionally, you have an extra network card in the firewall for managing security to a number of dedicated T1 lines. The T1 circuits connect you to multiple business partners and are used so that sensitive information does not cross the Internet. This sensitive information may be transmitted via e-mail or by FTP.

While this setup may appear pretty straightforward on the surface, it could potentially run into a number of problems. The first is routing. Your firewall would need to be programmed with the routing information for each of these remote networks. Otherwise, your firewall would simply refer to its default route setting and send this traffic out to the Internet. While these routing entries can be set in advance, how will you be updated if one of the remote networks makes a routing or subnet change? While you could use RIP, you have already seen in Chapter 3 that this is a very insecure routing protocol. Open Shortest Path First (OSPF) would be a better choice, but depending on the equipment at the other end of the link, you may not have the option of running OSPF.

FIGURE 10.2:

A network using dedicated
links to safeguard sensitive
information

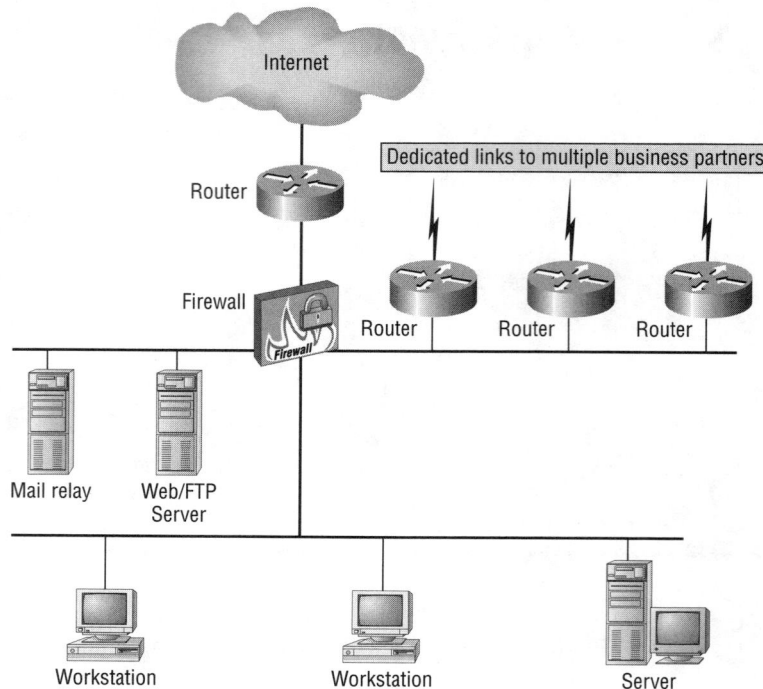

You may also run into IP address issues. What if one of the remote networks is using NAT with private address space? If you perform a DNS lookup on one of these systems, you will receive the public IP address, not the private. This means that you may have additional routing issues or you may be required to run DNS entries for these systems locally. Also, what if two or more of the remote networks are using the same private address space? You now may be forced to run NAT on the router at your end of the connection just so your hosts can distinguish between the two networks.

There is also a liability issue here. What if an attacker located at one of your remote business partners launches an attack against one of the other remote business partners? You have now provided the medium required for this attack to take place. Even if you can legally defend yourself, this would certainly cause a lot of embarrassment and strain your business relationships.

Replacing your dedicated business partner connections with VPNs would resolve each of these problems. As long as you can insure the integrity of the data stream, administering multiple VPNs would be far simpler than managing multiple dedicated circuits.

As with remote client access, you must open a hole through your firewall in order to permit VPN traffic. While strong authentication will dramatically decrease the chances that an attacker will be able to exploit this hole, it is a hole in your perimeter security just the same.

Selecting a VPN Product

When deciding which VPN product to use, you should look for several features:

- Strong authentication
- Adequate encryption
- Adherence to standards
- Integration with other network services

Of course, this assumes that you have a choice when selecting a VPN product. If you are setting up a VPN in order to connect to a specific site, your options may be limited. For example, Novell's firewall product BorderManager supports VPN connectivity. The problem is that the VPN is *proprietary*. This means that the only way to create a VPN with a BorderManager firewall is to place another Border-Manager firewall at the other end of the VPN tunnel. If you are setting up a VPN in order to communicate with a specific remote network, find out what VPN package that network is using. Then you can determine what your product options are.

Strong Authentication

Without strong authentication, you have no way to determine if the system at the other end of the VPN tunnel is who you think it is. Diffie-Hellman, discussed in Chapter 9, is the authentication method of choice when validating the tunnel end points. It allows a shared secret to be created through the exchange of public keys. This removes the need to exchange secret information through some alternative means.

TIP   If you are not using a known and trusted certificate authority when exchanging public keys over the Internet, verify the key values through some other means, such as a phone call or fax.

Adequate Encryption

Note that the word "adequate"—not "strong"—appears in the title of this section. You should determine what level of protection you actually require before selecting a method of encryption. For example, if you will be exchanging interesting but not necessarily private information over the Internet, 40–56-bit DES encryption may be more than sufficient. If you will be moving financial data or equally valuable information, stick with something stronger, like Triple DES.

The reason you want to choose the right level of encryption is performance. The stronger the encryption algorithm you use, the larger the delay that will be introduced from the encryption and decryption processes. For example, two networks connected to the Internet via 56K circuits which are using Triple DES may not be able to pass traffic fast enough in order to prevent application timeouts. While it is always better to err on the side of caution by using a larger key, give some thought to what size key you actually need before assuming bigger is always better.

The type of key you use will also affect performance. Secret key encryption, such as DES, is popular with VPNs because it is fast. Public/private encryption schemes, such as RSA, can be 10 to 100 times slower than secret key algorithms which use the same size key. This is because key management with a public/private scheme requires more processor time. Many VPN products will use a public/private key algorithm in order to initially exchange the secret key, but then use secret key encryption for all future communications.

TIP   Use the brute force attack time estimates discussed in Chapter 9 as a guide in determining what size encryption key to use with your VPN.

Adherence to Standards

You saw in Chapter 9 why it is important to stick with encryption schemes that have survived public scrutiny. The same holds true when selecting a method of encryption for your VPN. Stick with an algorithm that has stood the test of time and has no significant vulnerabilities. For example, the only real deficiency found with DES is the small key size used in the original version. This can easily be rectified by using Triple DES, which increases the number of keys that are used.

You should also make sure that the VPN product is compatible with other VPN solutions. As mentioned earlier in this section, Novell BorderManager is only capable of creating VPN connections with other BorderManager systems. This severely limits the product selection at the other end of the tunnel. If you are using BorderManager as a firewalling solution and later need to create a VPN to a remote business partner, you may find yourself purchasing a separate solution in order to fulfill this need.

Integration with Other Network Services

Newer VPN solutions have the capability to integrate with other services including firewalls, user directories, and monitoring software. Check Point's VPN-1 is completely integrated into the entire Check Point management suite, allowing not just complete security integration, but also address translation and bandwidth allocation. The ability to centrally manage the authentication of VPN connections as well as control how much bandwidth each connection is allowed is a powerful feature.

Of course, the ideal VPN solution would integrate with products from a different vendor. So far, success has been limited—although newer products are including industry standards such as LDAP and Triple DES.

Microsoft is such an example. They have included a VPN solution within their Windows 2000 product. The advantage, of course, is the integration of encryption and authentication technologies with Active Directory. Some vendors (such as Check Point) can mix their own VPN products with Microsoft VPN, allowing one centrally defined VPN policy to be applied equally to Microsoft and vendor-specific VPN access points. Also, because Active Directory is LDAP-compliant, third-party VPN's can base VPN permissions on the user account information stored in Active Directory.

VPN Product Options

There are a number of options available to you when you are selecting what kind of device to use for a VPN connection. These options fall into three categories:

- Firewall-based VPN

- Router-based VPN

- Dedicated software or hardware

The option you choose will depend on your requirements, as well as on the equipment you have already purchased.

Firewall-Based VPN

The most popular VPN solution is *firewall integration*. Since you will probably want to place a firewall on your network perimeter, anyway, it is a natural extension to let this device support your VPN connections, as well. This provides a central point of management as well as direct cohesion between your firewall security policy and the traffic you wish to let through your end of the tunnel.

The only drawback is performance. If you have a busy Internet circuit, and you want to use multiple VPNs with strong encryption on all of them, consolidating all of these services on a single box may overload the system. While this will probably not be an issue for the average installation, you should keep scale and performance in mind while you are deciding where to terminate your VPN tunnel. Some firewalls, such as FireWall-1, do support encryption cards in order to reduce processor load. The encryption card fits in a standard PCI expansion slot and takes care of all traffic encryption and decryption. In order to use one of these cards, however, you must make sure that all of your PCI slots are not currently being used by network cards.

Router-Based VPN

Another choice would be your Internet border router. This is yet another device that you need to have installed in order to connect to the Internet. Terminating the VPN at your border router will allow you to decrypt the traffic stream before it reaches the firewall. While process load is still a concern, many routers now use application-specific integrated circuit (ASIC) hardware. This allows the router to dedicate certain processors for specific tasks, thus preventing any one activity from overloading the router.

The only real drawback to a router-based VPN solution is security. Typically (but not always), routers are extremely poor at providing perimeter security compared to the average firewall. It is possible that an attacker may be able to spoof traffic past the router that the firewall will interpret as originating from the other side of the VPN tunnel. This means that the attacker may be able to gain access to services that are typically not visible from other locations on the Internet.

Dedicated Hardware or Software

If you have already purchased a firewall and router and neither supports VPN ability, all is not lost. You can still go with a hardware or software solution that is dedicated to creating VPN connections. For example, DEC's AltaVista Tunnel is an excellent product which supports tunnels to remote networks and remote-user VPNs. Since this in an independent product, it will work with any existing firewall.

The biggest drawback to a dedicated solution is an additional point of administration and security management. If the device is located outside the firewall, you have the same spoofing issues that you had with the router solution. If you locate the device inside the firewall, you may not be able to manage access using your firewall security policy. Most VPN solutions encrypt the original packet in its entirety. This means that the IP header information is no longer available to the firewall in order to make traffic control decisions. All traffic passing from one end of the tunnel to the other would use the same encapsulating packet headers. This means that the firewall will not be able to distinguish between an SMTP and a telnet session encapsulated within the tunnel. You must rely on the dedicated VPN device to provide tools to control the type of traffic you wish to let through your end of the tunnel.

VPN Alternatives

Not every remote-access solution requires a fully functional VPN. Some applications already provide strong encryption and authentication. For example, if you are a Lotus Notes user, your Notes ID file is actually your private encryption key. This key can be used to create a digital certificate, which, along with password authentication, is used to insure that you are in fact who you claim to be.

Lotus Notes will also encrypt information that it transmits along the network. From the Lotus Notes client main menu, you can select File ➤ Tools ➤ User Preferences ➤ Ports to produce the User Preferences screen shown in Figure 10.3. By selecting the Encrypt network data check box, you can optionally encrypt all data transmitted through the highlighted communication port. In Figure 10.3, all TCP/IP traffic will be encrypted.

If your remote network access will be limited to Lotus Notes replication, you could simply open up a port through your firewall and allow Lotus Notes to take care of all authentication and encryption for you. If you do not want to leave the Lotus Notes server openly exposed to the Internet, you could force all inbound sessions to authenticate at the firewall first (if your firewall supports this ability). This means that until you authenticate at the firewall, the Lotus Notes server remains inaccessible. Once you have passed the firewall authentication, you still need to pass the Notes authentication before you are allowed access to data on the server.

The Lotus Notes User Preferences screen

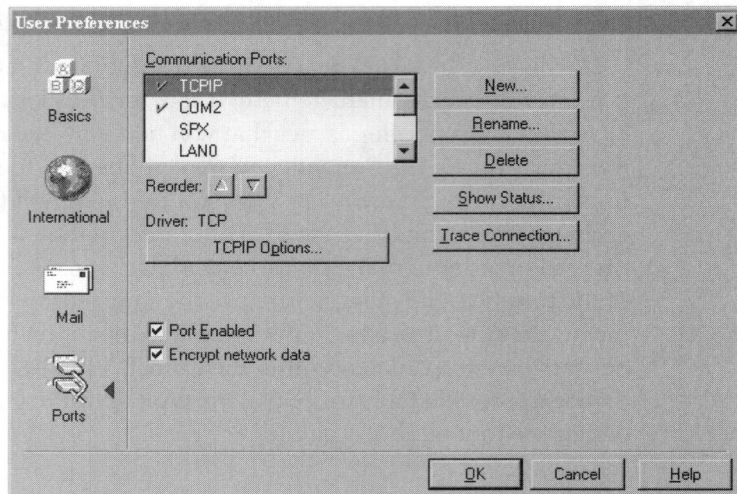

Lotus Notes uses TCP port 1352 for all client-to-server and server-to-server communications.

Quite a few products provide their own authentication and encryption. Some even allow access to additional network resources. For example, Citrix's WinFrame and MetaFrame products provide terminal server capability based on the Windows NT operating system. They also support decent authentication and encryption. This means that users on the Internet can use a Citrix client in order to access the Citrix server through an encrypted session. Once connected to the server, users can access any internal applications to which the system administrator has granted them access.

The biggest drawback to these alternate solutions is that they require special software to be run on the client in order to initiate the connection. You no longer have the service independence of a true VPN solution. This is changing, however, as vendors like Citrix are working to make their products more universally accessible. For example, the latest versions of WinFrame and MetaFrame no longer require the use of a specialized client. You can now use an optional Web browser plug-in which supports the latest versions of Netscape and Internet Explorer.

| TIP | A browser plug-in makes an excellent remote solution: a network administrator simply needs to make the plug-in software and configuration file available via a Web server. Remote users can then download the required software (about 300KB) and connect to the Citrix server using their favorite Web browser. |

Setting up a VPN

Let's return to the FireWall-1 product we discussed in Chapter 7 in order to walk through the configuration of a VPN between two remote networks. While we will specifically be discussing FireWall-1, many of the steps required to set up the VPN are similar to other products' setups. The goal is to give you a firm understanding of what is involved in the configuration process, not to endorse one product over another.

As mentioned in Chapter 7, FireWall-1 supports a number of VPN options. These include SKIP, IPSEC, and a FireWall-1 proprietary algorithm. In our example, we will be working with SKIP since it provides better authentication than IPSEC (although current trends point to the integration of SKIP capabilities in IPSEC) and is an accepted standard. It also supports full tunneling, which allows SKIP to be used in a private address space environment.

Preparing the Firewall

| NOTE | If you are unfamiliar with FireWall-1, please review Chapter 7, which covers how to install and configure the product. |

This section assumes that you have a working firewall which is capable of providing controlled Internet access. In the course of this procedure, you will notice that the firewall policy has a minimal amount of rules. This has been done solely for clarity in our examples. Your rule set will vary and should include all required policies.

| TIP | Place encryption rules at the top of the Policy Editor so they will be processed first. |

Our VPN Diagram

Figure 10.4 shows a network drawing of the VPN you will create. The figure shows two remote network sites. One is behind a firewall named HOLNT200 and the other is behind a firewall named Witchvox. Behind HOLNT200 is an FTP server that holds files containing financial information. The goal is to set up a secure tunnel so that clients on the other side of Witchvox can retrieve the financial files in a secure manner. Since FTP transmits all data in the clear, you want to use a VPN to insure that your financial information is not compromised.

FIGURE 10.4:

An example of a VPN

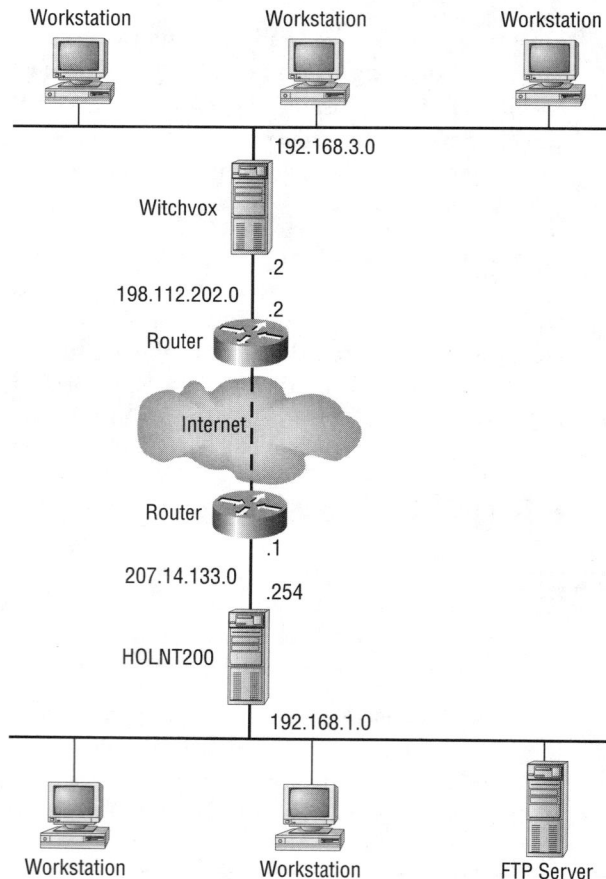

Configure your VPN by defining encryption domains for each end of the VPN tunnel. This identifies which remote networks the firewall will exchange encrypted traffic with. For example, you will configure the firewall Witchvox to encrypt any traffic headed for the 192.168.1.0 network. Conversely, you will also instruct Witchvox to decrypt all traffic received from the 192.168.1.0 network. HOLNT200 will be configured in a similar manner, except the remote encryption domain is defined as 192.168.3.0.

Configuring Required Network Objects

Your first step is to make sure all required network objects are created. Each firewall will need to have the following objects:

- A network object or group for the local encryption domain
- A network object or group for the remote encryption domain
- A workstation object for itself
- A workstation object for the remote firewall

Defining Network Objects

If you do not have a local network object defined, you will need to define one now. This can be accomplished from the Security Policy tab main menu by selecting Manage ➤ Network Objects ➤ New ➤ Network. This will produce the Network Properties screen shown in Figure 10.5. Give this object a name and assign a valid subnet address and mask. Notice that this configuration is being performed on Witchvox, so the Location of the 192.168.3.0 network object is identified as Internal. Click OK to save this entry.

FIGURE 10.5:

The Network Properties screen

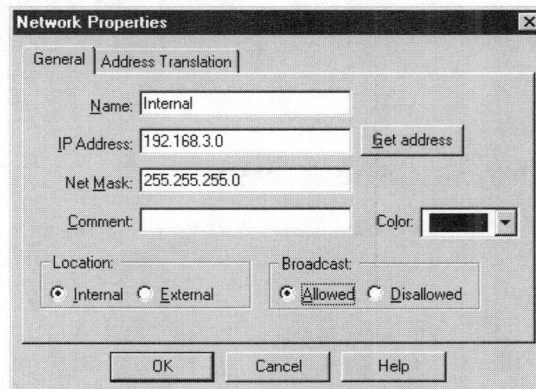

If you have multiple network segments, define each of them now. Once you have defined all of your network objects, you will also need to create a group object and place each of these network objects inside of it. Later on you will need to define an encryption domain. When identifying the domain, you will only be allowed to specify one object. If you need to identify multiple network segments, you can do this by specifying the group of your network objects.

Once you have identified your internal subnets, you must also identify the subnets at the remote encryption domain. Do this by creating additional network objects, just as you did for your local segments. The only difference is that the Location of the object must be defined as External, as shown in Figure 10.6. In Figure 10.6, we are still configuring the Witchvox firewall, so the 192.168.1.0 object is part of the remote network. This is why it is identified as being external to the firewall.

TIP   You may also wish to assign the remote subnets a unique color so you do not confuse them with your local objects.

FIGURE 10.6:

Remote subnets need to be defined as External.

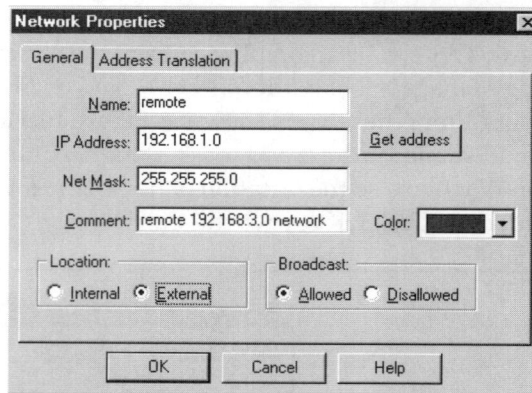

Defining the Firewalls

You now need to configure the firewall objects. If you have not done so already, create a network object for the firewall by selecting Manage ➤ Network Objects ➤ New ➤ Workstation from the Security Policy tab main menu. In Figure 10.7, you are still configuring the Witchvox firewall and creating a workstation object which will represent itself. Notice that the configuration uses the IP address from the external NIC on the firewall and that the Location is identified as Internal.

FIGURE 10.7:

The General tab for the
Witchvox firewall object

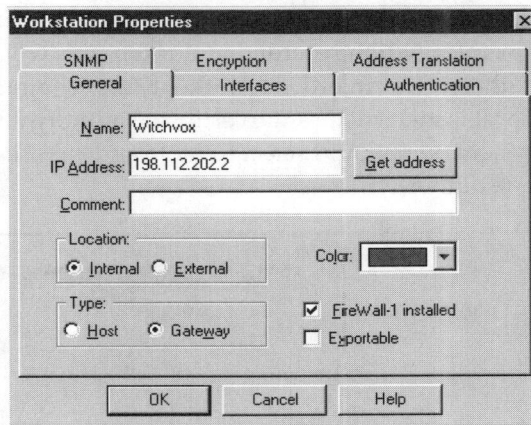

Next click the Encryption tab to define your local encryption domain and select a method of encryption. This is shown in Figure 10.8. Notice that Other is selected under Encryption Domain and the local network object specified. Also notice that SKIP has been selected in the Encryption Schemes Defined.

FIGURE 10.8:

The Encryption tab for the
Witchvox firewall object

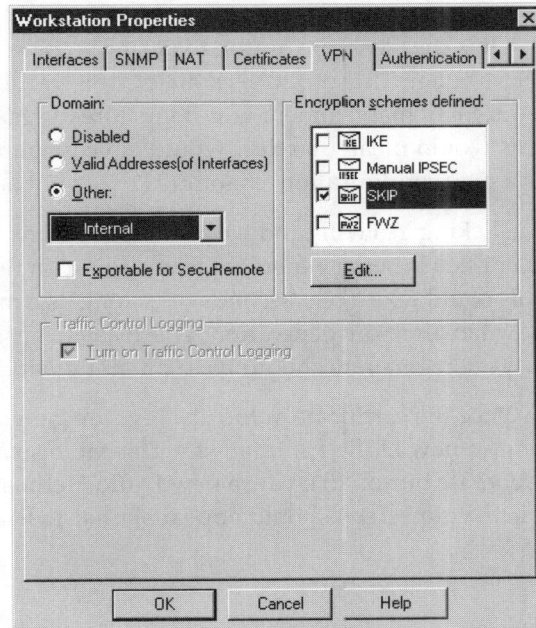

Once you have selected SKIP encryption, click the Edit button. This will produce the SKIP Properties window shown in Figure 10.9. Notice that there is no key information recorded in this tab. You will need to generate a new certificate authority key in order to authenticate with remote systems. In this configuration, Local is identified as the certificate authority. If you wanted to indicate a different system, you would select Remote and choose a predefined object for the certificate authority.

FIGURE 10.9:

The CA Key tab of SKIP Properties

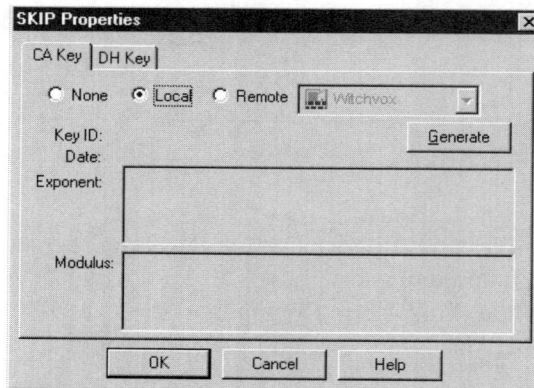

Click the Generate button to create a new certificate authority key (CA key) for this system. This produces a dialog box warning you that you are about to change your SKIP management key. If you already had VPN connections with other sites, this would mean that they would have to manually fetch the new key. Since this is a new configuration, changing keys is not an issue. Click Yes to continue.

Clicking Yes will produce a new dialog box informing you that a new management key is being generated. Depending on the processor speed of your system, this could take a few seconds or as long as a minute. Figure 10.10 shows the CA Key tab after key generation. These keys are unique to this specific system. The keys you generate should have different values.

Once the certificate authority keys are generated, select the DH Key tab to generate a new Diffie-Hellman key. This tab resembles the CA Key tab. Click the Generate button to create a new Diffie-Hellman key. Once key generation is complete, your screen should appear similar to Figure 10.11.

FIGURE 10.10:

The CA Key tab after key generation

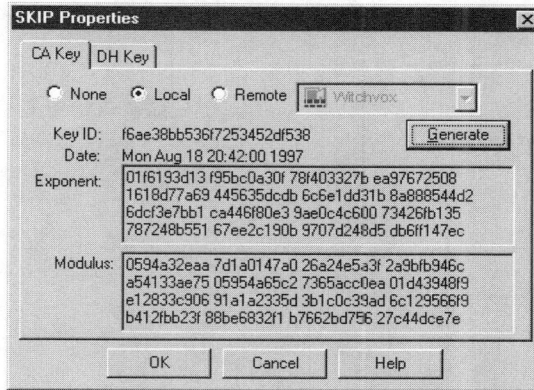

NOTE   Like the certificate authority keys, your Diffie-Hellman key will be unique to your system, so you will not receive an identical key string to the one shown in the figure.

Once you have finished, click the Write button to save this key, then click OK.

FIGURE 10.11:

The DH Key tab for SKIP Properties

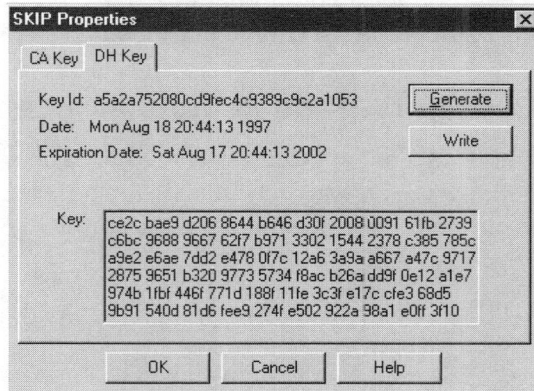

Now that you have configured an object for your local firewall, you also need to define an object for the firewall at the other end of the VPN tunnel. This is shown in Figure 10.12. You are still working on Witchvox, but you are defining an object for the firewall HOLNT200. Notice that the system is being associated with its external IP address and that the Location is identified as External.

Once the General tab is filled out, click OK to save. You will not be working with the Encryption tab on the HOLNT200 object until you have also defined objects on the remote firewall. You can now click Close on the Network Objects screen and install these objects onto the firewall. Do this by selecting Policy ➤ Install from the Security Policy tab main menu.

Configuring the Remote Firewall

Now that you have defined the required objects on Witchvox, you also need to define these objects on HOLNT200. The process is identical to the steps you have taken so far, with the following exceptions:

- The 192.168.1.0 subnet will be defined as Internal, not External.

- The 192.168.3.0 subnet will be defined as External, not Internal.

- The HOLNT200 firewall will be defined as Internal, not External.

- Keys will be generated for the HOLNT200 object, not Witchvox.

- Witchvox will be defined as External, not Internal.

Once these objects are created, install them on HOLNT200 by selecting Policy ≻ Install from HOLNT200's Security Policy tab main menu.

Exchanging Keys

In order to exchange keys, go back to the Witchvox firewall and edit the object you created for HOLNT200. When the Workstation Properties screen for HOLNT200 appears, select the Encryption tab. Under the Encryption Domain option, associate the object you create for the 192.168.1.0 network (the remote network which sits behind HOLNT200). You should also select SKIP under Encryption Schemes Defined. Your dialog box should appear similar to Figure 10.13.

FIGURE 10.13:

Encryption properties
for the remote firewall
HOLNT200

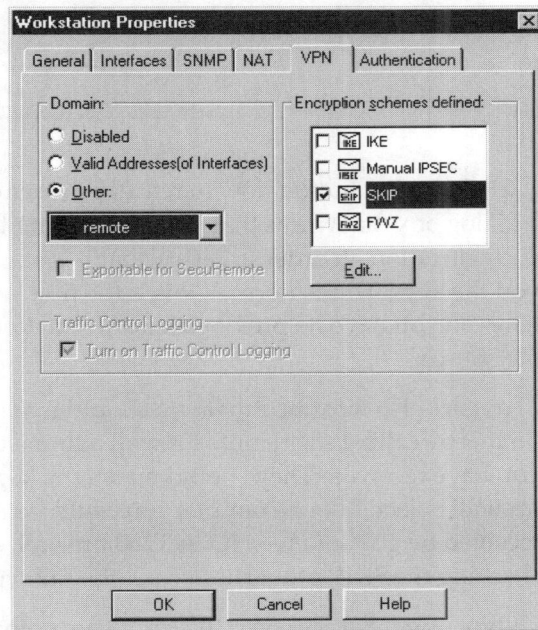

When you click the Edit button in order to manage your SKIP properties, you will notice the screen looks a little different from this same screen on the Witchvox object. This is shown in Figure 10.14. Instead of the certificate authority being defined as a local system, Remote is selected, with the HOLNT200 object selected as the remote system. The Generate button is also missing and has been replaced with a button labeled Get. This is because you will not be generating a new key, but fetching it from HOLNT200.

FIGURE 10.14:

The CA Key tab for HOLNT200's SKIP Properties

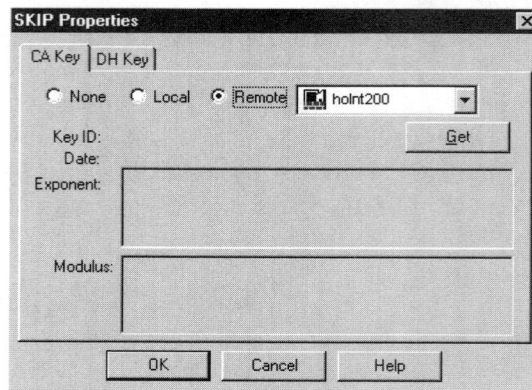

Click the Get button now to retrieve the remote certificate. This will produce a dialog box that warns that you are fetching the keys for HOLNT200 without authentication, in order to certify that it is actually HOLNT200 who is sending you the keys. This is normal: this is the first key exchange between the two systems, so you have no previous key information that can be used to authenticate the source.

You are also informed that you should manually verify the key values. You can do this by calling the remote firewall administrator and reading off the key values you have received. They should match the key values generated for their local firewall object. In our example, you could verify that the correct keys were received by going to the HOLNT200 firewall, editing the HOLNT200 object, and checking the SKIP properties under the Encryption tab.

Once you have retrieved the certificate authority keys, click the DH Key tab to fetch the Diffie-Hellman key. As on the CA Key tab, the Generate button has been replaced with a Get button. Click the Get button now in order to fetch the key from the remote firewall. Your screen should appear similar to Figure 10.15. As with the certificate authority key, you should manually validate the key value by calling the remote firewall administrator. Click the Write button and then click OK to save the changes you have made to this object.

FIGURE 10.15:

FIGURE 10.15:

The DH Key tab for
HOLNT200's SKIP
Properties

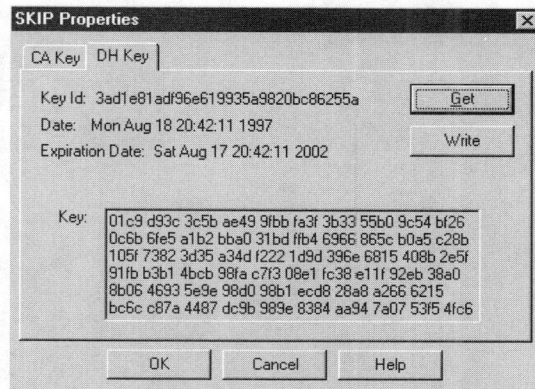

Fetching Keys on the Remote Firewall

Witchvox now has all the key information it needs from HOLNT200. You must
now go to the HOLNT200 firewall and edit the Witchvox object so that HOLNT200
can fetch the key information it requires, as well. The process is identical to what
you've done, except that the Encryption Domain defined under the Encryption
tab on Witchvox must indicate the subnet 192.168.3.0 (the subnet sitting behind
Witchvox). The rest of the steps are identical. Once HOLNT200 fetches the keys it
needs you should manually verify them, as well.

Modifying the Security Policy

You have created all of your required network objects and exchanged keys;
now you must define a set of policy rules so that the firewall knows when to
use your VPN. This is done by creating a new rule at the top of the Policy Editor
and adding both the local and remote networks to the Source and Destination
columns. Under the Services column, you can leave the default of Any (which
will encrypt all traffic between the two encryption domains) or you can select to
only encrypt certain services. In the Action column, right-click within the box and
select Encrypt. Your rules should now appear similar to row 1 in Figure 10.16.

NOTE   Both the local and the remote encryption domains should appear in the Source
and Destination columns.

FIGURE 10.16:

Defining the rules about which traffic should be encrypted

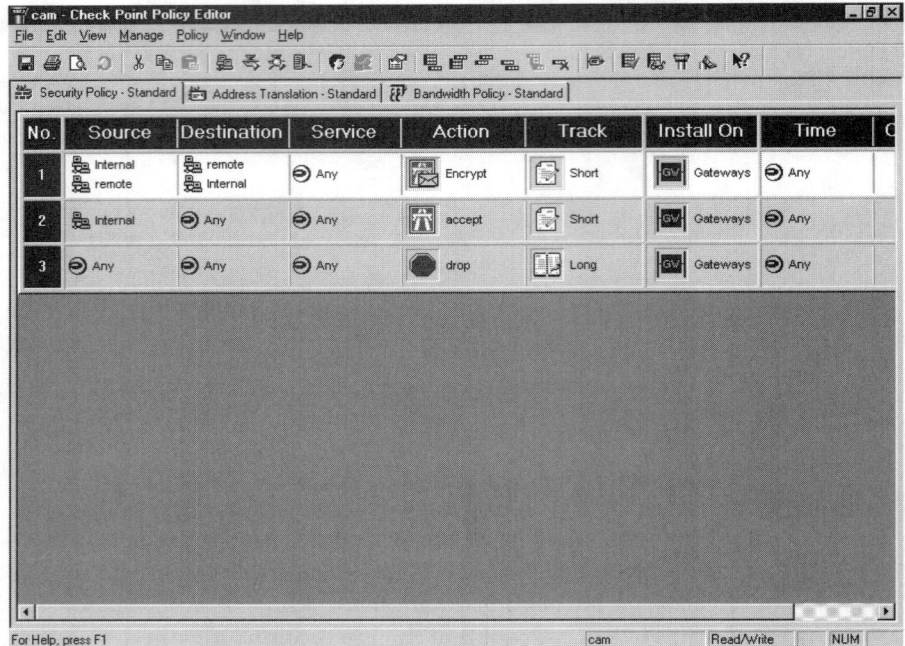

Now you need to define the encryption properties for this specific VPN. This is done by again right-clicking in the Action box, only this time you need to select Edit Properties. This will produce the Encryption Properties window shown in Figure 10.17. Since FireWall-1 supports multiple forms of encryption, it is possible to use different forms of encryption on multiple VPNs. This is why you must specify the type of encryption you wish to use for this VPN tunnel.

In the Encryption Properties windows, select SKIP and click the Edit button. This will produce the SKIP Properties window shown in Figure 10.18. You are allowed to set the following options:

Kij Algorithm   This selects the method of encryption to use when the systems exchange Crypt and MAC keys.

Crypt Algorithm   This selects the method of encryption to use when encrypting and decrypting data.

MAC Algorithm   This selects the method of encryption to use for authenticating the system at the remote end of the VPN tunnel.

FIGURE 10.17:

The Encryption Properties window

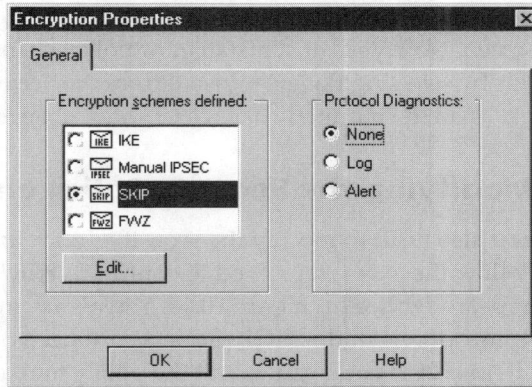

Allowed Peer Gateway   This specifies who is allowed to initiate a VPN transmission. If Any is selected, then either firewall associated with each encryption domain is allowed to transmit encrypted data. If a specific system is indicated, then you will need two separate rules in the Security Policy Editor.

NSID   This selects how the name space IDs are derived. Selecting None includes the NSID information within the encapsulation header.

IPSEC Options   One or both of these options must be selected if SKIP is used with IPSEC. The ESP option selects encryption, and the AH option selects authentication.

FIGURE 10.18:

The SKIP Properties window

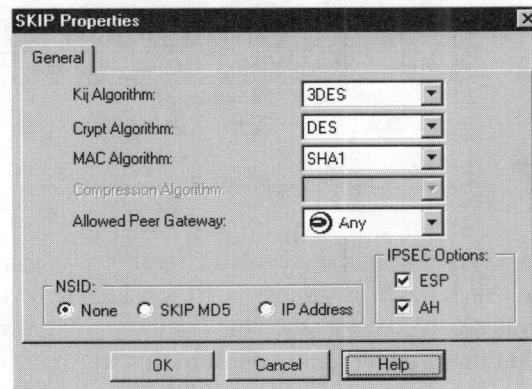

Once you have defined your SKIP options for this specific VPN connection, click OK twice to save any changes. This should return you to the Security Policy main screen. Now you must install your policy changes in order to make them active. Do this by selecting Policy ≻ Install from the Security Policy tab main menu. This completes all the required changes to Witchvox in order to setup your VPN connection.

Modifying the Security Policy on the Remote Firewall

You also need to modify the security policy and SKIP properties on HOLNT200. Follow the exact steps used to configure Witchvox. The policy rules should appear identical to Figure 10.16. You also want to make sure that you select the same options under SKIP properties. Once your policy changes are complete on HOLNT200, you must install the policy to make your changes active.

Testing the VPN

The setup of your VPN should now be complete. All that is left is to test the VPN in order to verify that it is functioning properly. This is accomplished by initiating an FTP session from the 192.168.3.0 network behind Witchvox to the FTP server located behind HOLNT200. If you check the firewall log on Witchvox, you should see an outbound session similar to Figure 10.19. Log entry No. 1 shows an FTP session coming from 192.168.3.10 which is going to 192.168.1.10, which is the IP address of the remote FTP server. Notice that the log indicates that the traffic is being encrypted.

FIGURE 10.19:

The FTP log entry on Witchvox

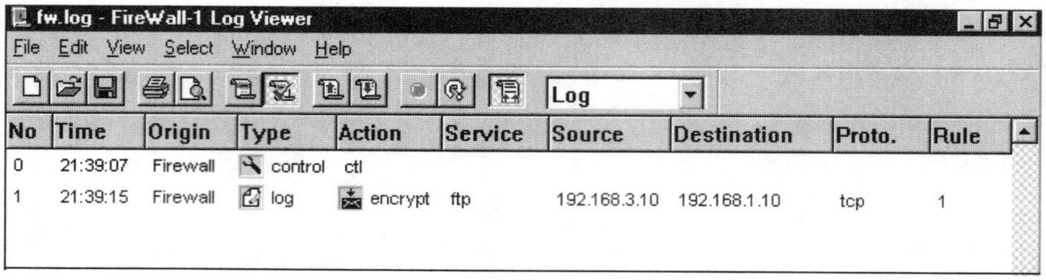

No	Time	Origin	Type	Action	Service	Source	Destination	Proto.	Rule
0	21:39:07	Firewall	control	ctl					
1	21:39:15	Firewall	log	encrypt	ftp	192.168.3.10	192.168.1.10	tcp	1

So you know that your FTP session was transmitted successfully. You also need to check the firewall log on HOLNT200 in order to insure that the transmission was received properly. This is shown in Figure 10.20. Notice that the log indicates that the firewall had to decrypt this traffic. You may also notice that since the firewall knows the true name of the FTP server (LAB31), it has substituted this name for the destination IP address.

FIGURE 10.20:

The FTP log entry on HOLNT200

Verifying the Data Stream

While all of this looks correct, the true test is to break out a network analyzer and decode the traffic being transmitted by the firewalls. While the log entries claim that the traffic is being encrypted and decrypted, it never hurts to check. A network analyzer will show you the contents of the packets being transmitted. If you can read the financial information within the data stream, you know you have a problem.

Figure 10.21 shows a packet decode of the FTP session before it is encrypted by the firewall. Notice that you can clearly distinguish that this is an FTP session. You can also identify the IP addresses of the systems carrying on this conversation. If you review the information in the bottom window, you can even see the data being transferred, which appears to be credit card information.

FIGURE 10.21:

The data stream before it is encrypted

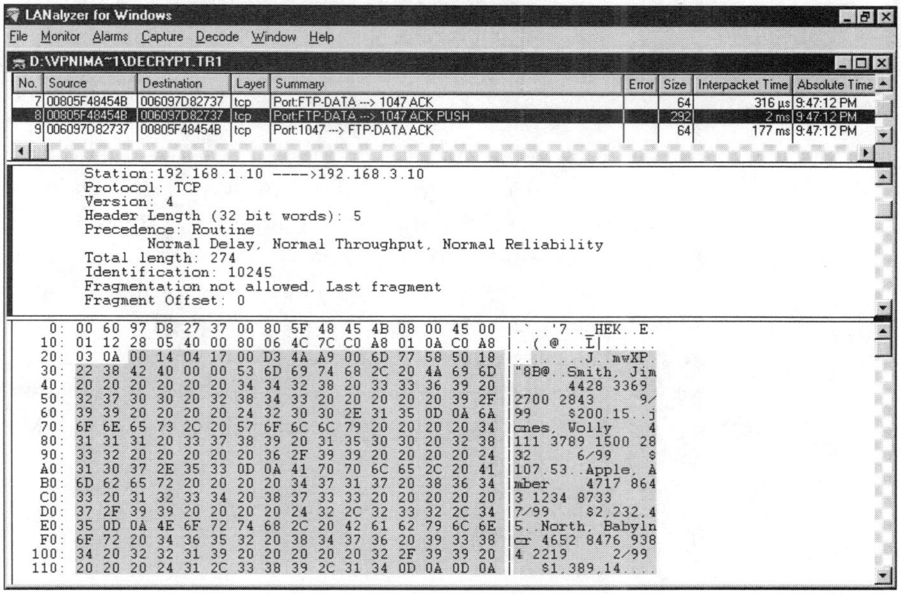

Figure 10.22 shows the same data stream, but from outside the firewall. This is what an attacker would see who was trying to capture data traveling along the VPN. Notice that the transport protocol for each packet is identified as 57. This identifies the transport as being a tunneling protocol and prevents you from seeing the real transport used in the encapsulated packet (in this case TCP) or the service that is riding on that transport (in this case FTP).

FIGURE 10.22:

The data stream after it is encrypted

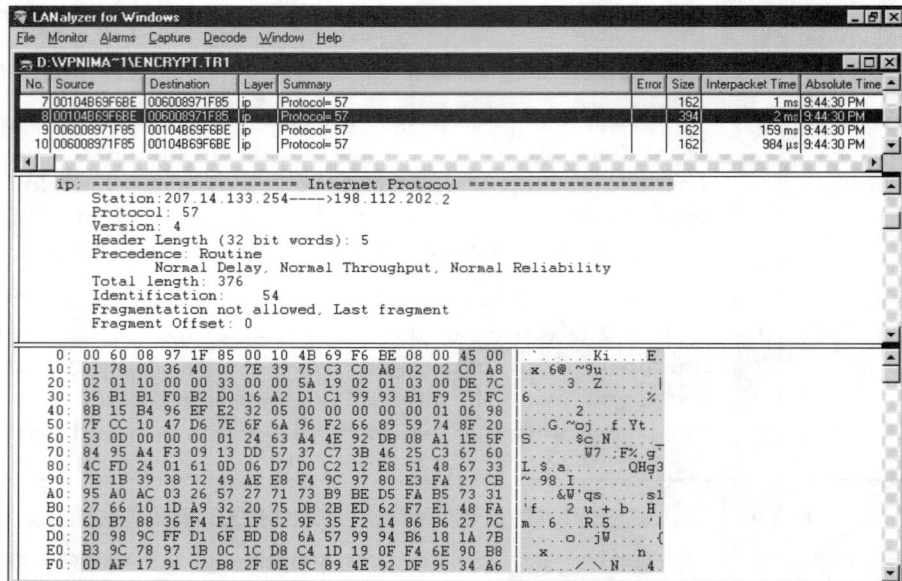

If you look at the middle window, you will see that the source and destination IP addresses are that of HOLNT200 and Witchvox, respectively. You do not see the true source and destination IP addresses of the data stream. This, combined with hiding the transport and service within the encrypted packet, helps to keep any one data transmission from looking more interesting to an attacker than any other. In fact, there is no certain method of verifying that all this captured traffic is from a single session. Each packet listed in the top window may be from different communication sessions that are taking place simultaneously. In order to find the FTP session, an attacker may be forced to decrypt hundreds or even thousands of packets.

The real test is the bottom window. Note that your data is now scrambled into ciphertext and is no longer readable. This prevents an attacker from being able to read the enclosed data, as you could in Figure 10.21. In order to get to this information, an attacker would need to identify which packets contain the financial information and decrypt them with a brute force attack.

Given these two packet traces, it is safe to say that your VPN is functioning properly and encrypting the data that flows between the two encryption domains.

Summary

In this chapter we defined the term virtual private networking and discussed when it is beneficial to use a VPN. We also covered what you should look for in a VPN product and what your options are for deployment. Finally, we walked through the configuration of a VPN between two firewalls and looked at the effect it had on the passing data stream.

In the next chapter, you will look at viruses and how you can go about keeping these little pieces of destructive code off your network.

CHAPTER

## ELEVEN

Viruses, Trojans, and Worms: Oh My!

Just about every system administrator has had to deal with a virus at one time or another. This fact is extremely disheartening, because these tiny pieces of code can cause an immense amount of damage. The loss in productivity and intellectual property can be expensive for any organization. Clearly, the cost of recovering from a virus attack more than justifies the cost of taking preventive measures.

Viruses: The Statistics

While the early 1990's seemed to be an era of relative safety from viruses, the Internet has—and continues to—dramatically increase the threat computer systems face from hostile code. An NCSA (National Center for Supercomputing Applications) study in 1997 illustrated the then-phenomenal statistic that 99.33 percent of the organizations polled had experienced a recent virus episode. In 1996, the monthly infection rate was 10 out of every 1,000 computers. In 1997, this rate more than tripled. In a study released in October 2000, ICSA (now TruSecure) noted that virus incidents per 1,000 machines were at least doubling every year—for five years running—with 160 machines per 1000 having been infected in 2000. Other items noted in the study:

- Annual losses per company due to virus infection were in the hundreds of thousands.

- Of companies surveyed, over 40 percent had experienced data loss due to virus infections.

- Two-thirds of companies had file-related e-mail problems due to incoming viruses.

- Only one of the surveyed companies recorded never having had a virus during the year covered by the survey—illustrating an infection rate of 99.67 percent.

- Major virus infections (25 or more computers infected at once) happened to 51 percent of the companies.

- Of the 51 percent with major infections, 80 percent received the virus by way of e-mail attachments.

- 64 percent of server outages due to virus infections lasted more than an hour, with a median downtime of 21 hours.

- Only 70 percent of PCs were protected with full-time automatic anti-virus protection.

- 76 percent of organizations polled believed the virus problem was worse than the year before (1999).

On an interesting note, the survey noted that reports of boot viruses, or floppy-born viruses, were nearly nonexistent. This seems in direct contrast to the NCSA survey of 1997, which put the brunt of the blame on shared floppy disks. With file sharing now being done primarily through e-mail, it's natural that the Internet has become a replacement for the floppy disk as the carrier of malicious code.

> **NOTE** But viruses aren't just for computers anymore. In August 2000, the first malicious code affecting PDA's (Personal Digital Assistants) was recorded. The program, Liberty Crack, posed as an emulator, but in reality it wiped applications from handheld devices running the Palm OS. And in June of the same year, the Timofonica virus, although executed on computers, was designed to send text messages to all cell phones in Spain—potentially overwhelming the entire cell network.

What Is a Virus?

The precise definition of a virus has been hotly debated for many years. Experts have had difficulty describing the specific traits that characterize a true virus and separate it from other types of programs. To add to the confusion, people tend to lump viruses, worms, Trojan horses, and so on, under the generic umbrella of "virus." This is partly because there is not one industry-acceptable descriptor that includes all of these program types; there continues to be some confusion over the exact definition of what constitutes a virus.

The generally accepted definition of a virus is a program that can be broken up into three functional parts. These parts are

- Replication

- Concealment

- Bomb

The combination of these three attributes makes the collective program a virus.

Replication

A virus must include some method of *replication*, that is, some way to reproduce or duplicate itself. When a virus reproduces itself in a file, this is sometimes referred to as *infection*. Since most people would never knowingly load a virus on their system, replication insures that the virus has some method of spreading.

Replication occurs when the virus has been loaded into memory and has access to CPU cycles. A virus cannot spread by simply existing on a hard disk. This means that an infected file must be executed in order for a virus to become active. "Executed" is a generic term. This could refer to an infected executable file that has been initiated from a command prompt, or it could be an infected Microsoft Word document that has been loaded into a text editor that is capable of processing embedded macros. In either event, there is now some process using CPU cycles that helps to spread the virus code.

File Infection

The method of replication falls into one of two categories. The first is *file infection*. This method of replication relies on the virus's ability to attach itself to a file. In theory, any type of file is vulnerable to attack. Attackers tend to focus, however, on files that will provide some form of access to CPU cycles. This may be through direct execution or by having the code processed by some secondary application.

For example, a Word document does not directly execute any type of commands in memory. The application Microsoft Word, however, is capable of reading macro commands embedded within the Word document and executing them in memory. So while it is the Word *document* that is actually infected, it is the Word *application* that provides the transport for replication.

A similar type of virus was popular many years ago that leveraged vulnerabilities in DOS's ANSI.SYS driver. Any text document can contain embedded ANSI commands. If a user had the ANSI driver loaded, these commands could be parsed from a text file and executed, even if the user was simply viewing the text within the file. There have even been viruses that embed themselves in raw source code files. When the code is eventually compiled, the virus becomes capable of accessing CPU cycles, thus replicating even further.

The most popular type of infection, however, is to infect direct executable files. In the PC world, these are files with a COM, EXE, PE, or BAT file extension. A virus will add a small piece of code to the beginning of the file. This is to insure that when the file is executed, the virus is loaded into memory before the actual application. The virus will then place its remaining code within or at the end of the file.

Once a file becomes infected, the method of replication can take one of two forms. These are referred to as resident and nonresident replication. A *resident* replicating virus, once loaded into memory, waits for other programs to be executed and then infects them when they are. Viruses such as Cabanas have shown that this is even possible on protected-memory systems such as Windows NT. A *nonresident* replicating virus will select one or more executable files on disk and directly infect them without waiting for them to be processed in memory. This will occur every time the infected executable is launched.

Sometimes a virus may take advantage of the extension search order of the operating system in order to facilitate the loading of the virus code without actually infecting the existing file. This type of virus is known as a *companion virus*. A companion virus works by insuring that its executable file is launched before the legitimate one is launched.

For example, let's say you have an accounting program that you initialize by executing the file GL.EXE. If you try to launch your accounting program by simply typing **gl**, an attacker could generate a virus named GL.COM that loads itself into memory and then passes control over to the GL.EXE file. This is possible because when a file extension is not specified, DOS and Windows will first try to execute a file with a COM extension, then an EXE extension, and finally a BAT extension. Once a match is found, the operating system ends the search and executes the program. In our example, the operating system would find the virus file (COM extension) before the real program file (EXE extension) and execute the virus file.

Boot Sector Replication

The second category of replication is *boot sector replication*. These viruses infect the system area of the disk that is read when the disk is initially accessed or booted. This can include the master boot record, the operating system's boot sector, or both.

NOTE   Viruses that use both file and boot sector replication technologies are known as multi-partite.

A virus infecting these areas will typically take the system instructions it finds and move them to some other area on the disk. The virus is then free to place its own code in the boot record. When the system initializes, the virus loads into memory and simply points to the new location for the system instructions. This allows the system to boot in a normal fashion—except the virus is now resident in memory.

NOTE   A boot sector virus does not require you to execute any programs from an infected disk in order to facilitate replication. Simply accessing the disk is sufficient. For example, most PCs will do a systems check on boot up that verifies the operation of the floppy drive. Even this verification process is sufficient to activate a boot sector virus, if one exists on a floppy left in the machine. This can cause the hard drive to become infected, as well.

Boot sector viruses rely on disk-to-disk contact to facilitate replication. Both disks must be attached to the same machine. For example, if you access a shared directory on a system with a boot sector virus, the virus cannot replicate itself to your local machine. This is because the two machines do not share memory or processor cycles.

There are, however, programs known as *droppers* that can augment the distribution of boot sector viruses, even across a network. A dropper is effectively an installation utility for the virus. The dropper is typically coded to hide the virus contained within it and escape detection by anti-virus software. It also poses as some form of useful utility in order to entice a user to execute the program. When the dropper program is executed, it installs the virus on the local system.

NOTE   By using a dropper, an attacker could theoretically infect a system with a boot sector virus even across a network. Once the virus has been dropped, however, disk-to-disk access is required for further replication.

Common Traits of File Infection and Boot Sector Replication

What is common to file and to boot sector replication is that a virus must have some method of detecting itself. This is to avoid potential corruption by performing a double infection. If a corruption does occur, the program may become unusable or the user may suspect that something is wrong. In either event, the replication process may cease. If replication cannot continue, the virus is doomed to die out, just like any living organism.

An Interesting Catch-22

One of the methods used by virus programmers to insure that duplication does not occur can also be used to detect the virus and prevent it from infecting files. Many virus programmers identify a code string that they know is unique to their particular virus. The virus is then programmed to look for this code string before it infects a file. If a match is found, the file is not infected.

Anti-virus software can be programmed to look for this signature code string. This allows the software to quickly identify the existence of the virus. Also, by adding this code string to a file without the actual virus code, the file can be inoculated against infection by the actual virus.

Macro Viruses

Macro viruses are executed by an application, as opposed to an operating system, and therefore are operating system independent. Written in Visual Basic for Applications (VBA) and executed by one of the programs in Microsoft's Office suite (Word, Excel or Access), macro viruses are hidden in documents and spreadsheets and spread by typically infecting other similar documents, although occasionally they can infect, damage, or destroy other files on the system.

According to the ICSA, macro viruses account for 80 percent of all known viruses, and the known number is growing at a rate that is unprecedented in computer history. The danger of macro viruses lies in their ability to infect files at any stage of the application use, whether opening, saving, or editing (or even deleting) a document. And because VBA is easy to learn and program, the technical level of expertise necessary to create a macro virus is very low.

Concealment

In order to facilitate replication, a virus must have one or more methods of masking its existence. If a running virus were to simply show up on your Windows 98 Taskbar, you'd see right away that there was a problem. Viruses employ a number of methods to camouflage their presence.

Small Footprint

Viruses tend to be very small. Even a large virus can be less than 2KB in size. This small footprint makes it far easier for the virus to conceal itself on the local storage media and while it is running in memory. In order to insure that a virus is as small as possible, most viruses are coded using assembly language.

If a virus is small enough, it may even be able to attach itself to a file without noticeably affecting the overall file size. There are viruses known as *cavity viruses* that will look for repetitive character sequences within a file (usually a null value) and overwrite this area for virus storage. This allows the virus to store the bulk of its code within a file without affecting the reported file size.

Attribute Manipulation

In order to protect files from virus infection, early DOS computer users would set their executable file permissions to read-only. The thinking was that if the file could not be modified, a virus would be unable to infect it. Of course, virus programmers responded by adding code to the virus that allowed it to check the file's attributes before infection. If the attributes were set to read-only, the virus would remove the read-only attribute, infect the file, and then set the attributes back to their original values. Needless to say, this method of protection is of little value against modern viruses.

This is not true in a true multi-user environment, however, where the permissions level can be set on a user-by-user basis. If administrator-level privileges are required to change a file's permissions, the virus cannot change these attributes when run from a regular user account.

For example, in a NetWare server environment, regular users are given read-only access to the public directory. If a user's computer contracts a virus, the virus will be unable to spread to other machines by infecting files within the public directory, because the virus will be unable to modify these files. Of course, if the administrator's computer becomes infected, all bets are off—this account does have write access to the public directory. Setting the minimum level of required permissions not only helps to enhance security—it can help to prevent the spread of viruses, as well.

NOTE   Interestingly, this lack of account security is at the root of why viruses have flourished in DOS, Windows 9x, and Mac environments. There have been very few viruses written for UNIX and Windows NT/2000 because the ability to set file permissions hinders the virus's ability to replicate and infect additional files. This is one of the reasons why virus programmers have focused on other platforms.

Along with permission attributes, viruses can also modify the date and time stamps associated with a file. This is to insure that a user is not clued in to a problem by noticing that a file has been modified. Early virus scanners would look for date changes as part of their virus-detection routine. Since most modern viruses will restore the original date and time stamps after infection, this method of detection has become less than effective.

> **NOTE** Windows NT systems running NTFS are particularly vulnerable due to the use of *data streams*. A data stream is a hidden file that can be associated with a regular file. This provides a hidden area for an attacker to hide virus code. Data streams are not visible when you use Explorer or the `DIR` command. You must reference the stream directly (meaning you already know it exists) or by using a tool specifically designed to find data streams, such as LADS (List Alternate Data Streams), freeware that can be downloaded at `www.heysoft.de/nt/ep-lads.htm`.

Stealth

Stealth allows a virus to hide the modifications made to a file or boot sector. When the virus has been loaded into memory, it monitors system calls made to files and disk sectors. When a call is trapped, the virus modifies the information returned to the process making the call so that it sees the original, uninfected information. This aids the virus in avoiding detection.

For example, many boot sector viruses contain stealth ability. If the infected disk is booted (thus loading the virus into memory), programs such as `FDISK` will report a normal boot record. This is because the virus is intercepting sector calls from `FDISK` and returning the original boot sector information. If you boot the system from a clean floppy disk, however, the drive will be inaccessible. If you run `FDISK` again, the program will report a corrupted boot sector on the drive.

Concealment can also be accomplished by modifying the information reported by utilities such as `DIR` and `MEM`. This allows a virus to hide its existence on the local storage medium and in physical memory. To use stealth, however, the virus must be actively running in memory. This means that the stealth portion of the virus is vulnerable to detection by anti-virus software.

Countermeasures

Some viruses include countermeasures to fight back against detection. These viruses will monitor the system for indications of an active virus scan, then take preventive measures to insure that they go undetected. Think of this as stealth ability with an attitude.

For example, some viruses will monitor system activity once they become active in memory. If the virus detects that a virus scan has been initiated, it will attempt to fool the scanner into thinking that some other virus is present on the system. Typically, the reported virus will require some form of destructive cleaning that will trash the system if the virus is not actually present. The virus will then attempt to seed itself within the file system so that if a recovery is attempted, the virus can infect the new configuration.

Like stealth, these countermeasures rely on the virus's being active in memory so the virus can monitor activity. This is why it is so important to boot a system from a boot disk you know to be clean before you attempt any repair. On DOS systems, it is also important to actually power cycle the system: many viruses are capable of trapping the CTRL+ALT+DEL key sequence and creating a false warm boot. This allows the virus to remain active in memory, even though it appears the system has been restarted.

Encryption

Virus programmers have not overlooked the benefits of encryption. Encryption allows the virus programmer to hide telltale system calls and text strings within the program. By encrypting the virus code, virus programmers make the job of detecting the virus much more difficult.

Detection is not impossible, however, as many viruses use a very simple form of encryption and the same key for all virus code. This means that while it may be difficult to retrieve the actual virus code, the decryption sequence will be identical for all infected files. If the decryption key can be broken, it can be used to detect all future instances of the virus. Even if the decryption key is not broken, the cipher string becomes a telltale signature that anti-virus software can use to detect the virus.

The efficiency of this method of detecting encrypted viruses depends on the resulting cipher string. Remember that the anti-virus software has no way of knowing whether it is looking at encrypted or plain text information. If the cipher string can be made to resemble some benign form of code, the anti-virus software will have a difficult time differentiating between infected and non-infected files.

Polymorphic Mutation

A polymorphic virus has the ability to change its virus signature from infected file to infected file while still remaining operational. Many virus scanners detect a virus by searching for telltale signature code. Since a polymorphic virus is able to change its appearance between infections, it is far more difficult to detect.

One way to produce a polymorphic virus is to include a variety of encryption schemes that use different decryption routines. Only one of these routines would be available in any instance of the virus. This means that an anti-virus scanner will be unable to detect all occurrences of the virus unless all the decryption routines are known.

This may be nearly impossible if the virus utilizes a random key or sequence when performing encryption. For example, many viruses include benign or dormant code that can be moved around within the virus before encryption without affecting the virus's operational ability. The cipher string created by the process will vary with each instance of the virus, because the code sequence will vary.

The most efficient method of creating a polymorphic virus is to include hooks into an object module known as a *mutation engine*. Because this engine is modular, it can easily be added to any existing virus code. The mutation engine includes a random-number generator, which helps to scramble the resulting ciphertext even further. Since a random-number generator is used, the resulting ciphertext becomes unpredictable and will vary with every file infected. This can make the virus nearly impossible to detect, even for other instances of the virus itself.

Bomb

Our virus has successfully replicated itself and avoided detection. The question now becomes, "What will the virus do next?" Most viruses are programmed to wait for a specific event. This can be almost anything—including the arrival of a specific date, the infection of a specific number of files, or even the detection of a predetermined activity.

Once this event has occurred, the true purpose of the virus becomes evident. This might be as benign as playing a tune through the computer's speakers, or as destructive as completely wiping out all the information that has been stored on the computer's hard drive.

Most bombs can perform a malicious task because the current DOS and Windows environments provide no clear containment between the operating system and the programs they run. A virus can have direct access to lower-level functions. This functionality is provided because the operating system expects programs to be trustworthy.

For example, DOS and Windows applications are allowed to directly address memory and the interrupt table. While this can help to boost an application's performance by allowing it to circumvent the operating system, it also provides much of the functionality required for a virus to utilize stealth.

There are limits to what a bomb can do, however. While a bomb can render a computer unusable, it cannot cause physical damage to any of the components. This means that in a worst-case scenario you can always completely wipe out all the data on a computer and start from scratch. Not exactly the first option you would want to hear—but at least you know your hardware will remain intact and functional once the virus is eliminated.

Hoaxes

Sometimes referred to as a *socially engineered viruses*, hoaxes can be just as troublesome as the real thing. Social engineering viruses meet all the criteria of a normal virus, except they rely on people to spread the infection, not a computer. A good example of a social engineering virus is the Good Times virus hoax that has circulated the Internet for many years. This e-mail message announces that a dangerous virus is being circulated via e-mail and has the ability to wipe out all the files on your computer. This message even claims that the virus's existence has been confirmed by AOL (who we all know is the world's authority on viruses). People concerned that their friends may be attacked by this virus would then forward the hoax to every person in their address books. How does a social engineering virus meet the criteria that define a true virus?

Replication   These viruses rely on two human traits in order to replicate themselves to other systems: good intentions and gullibility. Since it is human nature to help others, we are more than happy to circulate what appear to be virus warnings, e-mail requests from dying children, and the like, to other computer users. Since it is also human nature to believe what we read—and perhaps to be a bit too lazy to verify information—we might forward the virus along without verification.

Concealment   In order to conceal the threat, the virus will use language that makes the message believable to the average user. For example, the message may claim that a company like AOL, IBM, or Microsoft has verified the existence of the virus mentioned in the alert. Since these are computer-related companies familiar to the average user, the message appears to be authoritative.

Bomb This is the part of social engineering viruses that most people do not even think about. The "bomb" is wasted bandwidth, as well as unnecessary fear. Since the message is a hoax, bandwidth is wasted every time it is circulated. Since the sender has assumed a sense of urgency with the message, the virus is typically sent out en masse. Unnecessary fear comes into play as the message usually includes a warning of disaster if it is ignored (for example, the user's computer becomes infected by the hoax virus or the child with cancer dies because she did not receive enough e-mail to pay for her treatment). This fear will manifest itself as additional stress and worry. Thus the bomb is how these e-mails affect both computer resources and their human operators.

No virus scanner can detect social engineering viruses. Only education and verifying information can keep these viruses from spreading.

NOTE A wonderful resource for social engineering viruses is the Computer Virus Myths home page located at www.vmyths.com.

Worms

A computer worm is an application that can replicate itself via a permanent or dial-up network connection. Unlike a virus, which seeds itself within the computer's hard disk or file system, a worm is a self-supporting program. A typical worm will only maintain a functional copy of itself in active memory; it will not even write itself to disk.

There are actually two different strains of computer worms. The first will operate on only a single computer, just like a typical application. The worm will only use the system's network connection as a communication channel in order to replicate itself to additional systems or to relay information. Depending on the worm design, it may or may not leave a copy of itself running on the initial system once it replicates to a new host.

The second strain of computer worm actually uses the network connection as a nervous system so that it may have different segments of its code running on multiple systems. When there is a central node coordinating the effort of all these segments (a sort of "brain"), the worm is referred to as an *octopus*.

NOTE　The name *worm* is derived from a 1975 story by John Brunner called "The Shockwave Rider." The story's hero uses a program called a "tapeworm" in order to destroy the totalitarian government's computer network. This destruction removes the government's power base, thus freeing the people under its control. Before the publication of this story, there was no universally agreed-upon name to describe these programs (life imitating art, so to speak).

The Vampire Worm

Worms have not always been considered a bad thing. In the 1980s John Shock and Jon Hepps of Xerox were doing some wonderful worm research in order to show just how beneficial these programs could be. To this end, they created a number of worm programs and used them for administration on Xerox's network.

The most effective was the *vampire worm*. This worm would sit idle during the day when system utilization was high. At night, however, the worm would wake up and use idle CPU time in order to complete complex and highly processor-intensive tasks. The next morning the vampire worm would save its work and go back to sleep.

The vampire worm was extremely effective until the day that Xerox employees came into work and found that all the computer systems had crashed from a malfunctioning process. When the systems were restarted, they were immediately crashed by the worm. This led to the worm's removal from all of the network's systems and an end to further testing.

The Great Internet Worm

Worms received little attention until November 3, 1988. This was the day after the great Internet worm had been released onto the Internet. In less than six hours, this 99-line program had effectively crippled all of the 6,000 Sun and VAX systems connected to the Internet.

The program was written by Robert Morris, the son of one of the country's highest-ranking security experts at that time. It has been suggested that the writing of the worm was not a malicious act, but the effort of a son to break out from his father's shadow. This thinking is supported by the actual worm code, as the program does not perform any intentionally destructive functions.

What the worm did do was to start a small process running in the background of every machine it encountered. This experiment would have probably gone completely unnoticed—except for one minor programming flaw. Before infecting a host, the worm did not perform a check to see if the system was already infected. This led to the multiple infection of systems. While one instance of the worm created little processor load, dozens—or possibly hundreds—of instances would bring the system to its knees.

Administrators found themselves in a losing battle. As a system was cleaned and restarted, it would again become quickly infected. When it was discovered that the worm was using Sendmail vulnerabilities in order to move from system to system, many administrators reacted by disconnecting from the Internet or by shutting down their mail systems. This probably did more harm than good, because it effectively isolated the site from updated information on the worm—including information on how to prevent infection.

From all the chaos that ensued from this incident, many good things did arise. It took an episode of this magnitude to change people's thinking regarding system vulnerabilities. At the time, such vulnerabilities were simply considered minor bugs. The Internet worm incident pushed these deficiencies into a class of their own. This incident spawned the creation of the Computer Emergency Response Team (CERT), an organization that is responsible for documenting, and helping to resolve, computer-related security problems.

The WANK Worm

While the Internet worm is probably the best known, it was certainly not the worst worm ever encountered. In October 1989, the WANK (Worms Against Nuclear Killers) worm was released on unsuspecting systems. While highly destructive, this worm was unique in that it only infected DEC systems and only used the DECnet protocol (it was not spread via IP). This worm would

- Send e-mail (presumably to the worm's creator) identifying which systems it penetrated along with the logon names and passwords used

- Change passwords on existing accounts

- Leave additional trapdoor access into the system

- Find users on random nodes and ring them using the phone utility

- Infect local COM files so that the worm could reactivate later if it was cleaned from the system

- Change the announcement banner to indicate the system had been "WANKed"

- Modify the logon script to make it appear that all of a user's files were being deleted

- Hide the user's files after logon so the user would be convinced that the files had been deleted

As you can imagine, this worm ruined more than one system administrator's day. It took quite some time to successfully purge this worm from all the infected systems.

IRC Worms

Hostile worms exist even today One of the more common types are IRC (Internet Relay Chat) worms. These worms affect all users running mIRC communication software. When a user joins a specific IRC channel, the worm infects the user's system. It then sits quiet and waits for one of the IRC channel participants to issue a recognized keyword.

Each keyword is designed to elicit some form of specific action. For example, one keyword is designed for victims running UNIX. When the keyword is issued, the worm sends a copy of the local password file to the IRC user who issued the command (using mIRC's DCC command). Another keyword is designed for Windows 95/98 users and delivers a copy of the Registry. Still another gives the person issuing the command full read and write access to the local hard drives of all infected systems.

Macro Worms

Similar to macro viruses, macro worms use VBA and Microsoft applications as their executing environment. A macro worm typically spreads by sending a copy of itself as an innocuously (but appealingly) named attachment to every e-mail address stored in Outlook or Outlook Express. The worm depends on social engineering, (naming the attachment "I Love You," for example), and the default configuration in Outlook (which hides the filename extensions of attachments) to induce the recipient to execute the worm. Because of the success of these worms, (including the infamous I Love You worm), some programmers have created hybrid programs that are really more virus than worm, deleting files and causing other operating system mischief.

Trojan Horses

A Trojan horse, as the name implies, is an application that hides a nasty surprise within an innocuous or pleasant package. The surprise is a process or function, specifically added by the Trojan horse's programmer, that performs an activity that the user is unaware of—and would probably not approve of. The visible application may or may not do anything that is actually useful. The hidden application is what makes the program a Trojan horse.

Why Trojan Horses Are Not Viruses

Trojan horses (or "Trojans" for short) differ from viruses in that they do not replicate or attach themselves to other files. A Trojan is a stand-alone application that had its bomb included from the original source code. It does not become malicious due to the effects of another application.

For example, there are a number of UNIX Trojans that are made to replace existing network applications. An attacker may replace the telnet server process (`telnetd`) with one of his own creation. While the program will function identically to the standard `telnetd` program, it will quietly record all logon names and passwords that authenticate to the system. Conversely, an attacker could also replace the telnet client application, giving himself valid account information on remote systems. This would allow him to systematically penetrate every server on a network.

Attackers have also created Trojans designed to be immediately destructive. For example, in April 1997, many people fell prey to the `AOL4FREE.COM` Trojan. While users thought they had found a utility that would give them a free account on AOL, what they actually received was a wonderful tool for removing all those pesky files on a system's local hard drive. As soon as the program was launched, it would permanently delete all files located on the C: drive.

The most successful (hence common) Trojan attack targets users who run Windows 95/98 or Windows NT/2000 Dial-Up Networking. This Trojan has been programmed into a number of helpful utilities that are designed to entice the user to download them. When the utility is installed, the Trojan enumerates the user's phone book and grabs a copy of the Windows Dial-Up Networking cache. It then uses a number of Windows API calls in order to e-mail this information to the Trojan's author. Besides potentially yielding access to the local system, the attacker now has valid ISP account information to use in order to attack other systems.

Did I Just Purchase a Trojan Horse?

Of course, not all Trojans have been written by true attackers. For example, some users were extremely surprised to find out that when they joined the Microsoft Network, the software made a complete inventory of system hardware and software. This included Microsoft software and competitors' products. When the user connected to the network, this information was automatically forwarded to Microsoft, which could collect marketing data and check for proper product licensing. While Microsoft claimed that this information was being collected for technical support use only, many people considered it to be a clear invasion of privacy.

There are many other situations in which vendors add functionality at the expense of breaching a customer's security posture. For example, in May 1998, it was made public knowledge that 3COM, as well as a number of other network hardware vendors, were including "back door" accounts for access into their switch and router products. These undocumented accounts are typically invisible to the end user and cannot be deleted or disabled. While vendors again claimed they had created these back doors for technical support reasons (in case an administrator forgets a password, for example), it still leaves the product horribly exposed and the administrator woefully uninformed.

Such activities exist in a gray area between technical support and Trojans. While these undocumented back doors are being added by reputable vendors, they compromise security and fail to make the customer aware of potential exposure. Clearly, back-door access is a feature that many administrators would like to disable—but they have to learn of its existence first.

Preventive Measures

Now that you have seen the implications of these rogue programs, what can you do about them? The only foolproof way to identify a malicious program is to have a knowledgeable programmer review the source code. Since most applications are already in an executable format, this would require a step back to reverse engineer every file on the system. Obviously, doing so is too time-consuming and expensive to be a feasible option for the typical organization.

With this in mind, any other preventive measures will fall short of being 100 percent effective. You are faced with performing a risk analysis in order to determine just how much protection you actually require. There are many different techniques that you can employ in order to prevent infection. Each has its strengths and weaknesses, so a combination of three or more techniques is usually best.

Access Control

Establishing an access control policy is not only a good security measure; it can help to prevent the spread of rogue programs, as well. Access control should not be confused with file attributes (such as read-only or system), which can easily be changed by an infecting program. True access needs to be managed through a multi-user operating system that allows the system administrator to set up file permission levels on a user-by-user basis.

Access control will not remove or even detect the existence of a rogue program. It is simply one method of helping your systems to resist infection. For example, most viruses count on the infected machine having full access to all files (such as the default permissions under Windows NT). If a savvy system administrator has modified these default permissions so that users only have read access to their required executables, a virus will be unable to infect these files.

NOTE This will not work for all executables, however. Some actually require that they modify themselves during execution. Users need write access to these executables, and you can expect the time and date stamps to change on a regular basis. How do you know which executables require write access? Usually you don't. It's a matter of trial and error to see which executables change their date and time stamps or break when write access is not provided. These self-writing executables are rare, however. You should not run into them very often.

Checksum Verification

A *checksum*, or Cyclic Redundancy Check (CRC), is a mathematical verification of the data within a file. This allows the contents of the file to be expressed as a numeric quantity. If a single byte of data within the file changes, the checksum value changes, as well, even if the file size remains constant. Typically, a baseline is first created of a non-infected system. The CRC is then performed at regular intervals in order to look for file changes.

There are a couple of drawbacks to this method. First, a CRC cannot actually detect file infection; it can only look for changes. This means that self-writing executables would fail the checksum verification on a regular basis. Also, even if the change is actually due to a virus, a CRC has no way of cleaning the file. Finally, many viruses have been specifically written to fool a CRC into thinking that the file information has not changed.

> **TIP**
>
> While a CRC is a not the most effective check against viruses, it can be a big help in discovering Trojan horse replacements. A Trojan designed to replace an existing authentication service (such as telnet or FTP client and server software) does not simply modify the existing files; it replaces them. This file replacement would be flagged and reported by a checksum verification. A virus scanner, however, would completely miss this problem, provided that the files did not include any virus-like code. This makes the CRC far more effective at identifying Trojans.

Process Monitoring

Another method of preventing rogue programs from taking hold of a system is *process monitoring*. Process monitoring observes different system activity and intercepts anything that looks suspicious. For example, the BIOS in most modern desktop computers contains an anti-virus setting. When enabled, this setting allows the computer to intercept all write attempts to the master boot record. If a boot sector virus attempts to save itself to this area, the BIOS will interrupt the request and prompt the user for approval.

Again, there are a few problems. The first is that viruses and normal programs share a lot of similar attributes: it can be extremely difficult to distinguish between the two. For example, running the FDISK utility will also trigger the BIOS virus warning just described. Even though FDISK is not a virus (unless you subscribe to the school of thought that all Microsoft programs are viruses), it will still trigger the warning because its activity is considered suspicious. This is referred to as a *false positive*— the BIOS thinks it has detected a virus when in fact it has not.

This brings us to the second problem with process monitoring, which is the requirement of user intervention and proficiency. For example, a user who receives the false positive just mentioned must be computer savvy enough to realize that a true virus was not actually detected, but that the normal operation of FDISK set off the alarm.

Then again, maybe there *is* in fact a boot sector virus on the floppy disk where FDISK is stored. This could cause the user to assume that a false positive has been reported when in fact there is an actual virus. While this would trigger the BIOS virus alert at a different point in the process (when FDISK is loaded rather than when FDISK is closed), the end user needs a high level of skill and computer proficiency just to identify virus problems accurately.

The problem of correctly distinguishing between a virus and a normal application becomes even more apparent when you start trying to monitor other types of activity. Should file deletions be considered suspicious? Certainly a file maintenance utility will be used to delete files from time to time, generating frequent false positives. The same would be true for attempting to monitor file changes, memory swapping, and so on. All of these activities may be performed by a virus—but they may also be performed by a normal application.

About the only useful process monitoring is the BIOS virus warning described earlier. While there is the potential for false positive warnings, it is actually pretty rare for a user to be running FDISK or some other application that will legitimately attempt to write to the boot sector. Typically, this will only occur if the user is installing a new operating system. This means that the frequency of false positives would be minimal.

Virus Scanners

The most popular method of detecting viruses is through the use of virus-scanning software. Virus scanners use *signature files* in order to locate viruses within infected files. A signature file is simply a database that lists all known viruses, along with their specific attributes. These attributes include samples of each virus's code, the type of files it infects, and any other information that might be helpful in locating the virus. By using a separate file to store this information, you can update your software to detect the latest viruses by replacing this single file. You do not have to update the entire program. This is useful because many new viruses are detected each month.

When a scanner checks a file, it looks to see if any of the code within the file matches any of the entries within the signature file. When a match is found, the user is notified that a virus has been detected. Most scanners are then capable of running a separate process that can clean the virus, as well.

The biggest limitation of virus scanners is that they can only detect known viruses. If you happen to run across a newly created virus, a scanner may very well miss it. This is a particularly nasty problem when you are dealing with a polymorphic virus. As mentioned in "Polymorphic Mutation" earlier in this chapter, polymorphic viruses are capable of changing their signature with each infection. In order for a virus scanner to be 100 percent effective against this type of virus, it must have a signature file that lists all possible polymorphic permutations. If even one permutation is missed, the virus scanner may fail to clean an infected file—and the virus can again infect the system.

TIP   When selecting a virus scanner, look for one that not only has the capability of detecting many different viruses, but many different polymorphic strains, as well.

Compressed or encrypted files can also cause problems for a virus scanner. Since both of these processes rearrange the way information is stored, a virus scanner may be unable to detect a virus hidden within the file.

For example, let's say you use PKZIP to compress a number of files in order to transport them on a floppy disk. You then use a virus scanner to check the disk in order to verify that none of the compressed files contains a virus. Unless the virus scanner you are using understands the ZIP file format (many do not), it would be unable to detect a virus hidden within one of the files.

This is even more of a problem with encrypted files. Since a virus scanner has no way to decrypt a manually encrypted file, it will most likely miss any viruses that are present. You must first decrypt the file, and then perform a virus scan, in order to insure that no viruses are present.

Virus Scanner Variations

There are two basic types of virus scanners:

- On demand

- Memory resident

On-demand scanners must be initialized through some manual or automatic process. When an on-demand scanner is started, it will typically search an entire drive or system for viruses. This includes RAM memory and storage devices such as a hard drive or a floppy disk.

Memory-resident virus scanners are programs that run in the background of a system. They are typically initialized at system startup and stay active at all times. Whenever a file is accessed, a memory-resident scanner will intercept the file call and verify that no viruses are present before allowing the file to be loaded into memory.

Each of these methods has its trade-offs. On-demand scanners work after the fact. Unless you always initialize the scanner before accessing any file (an unlikely occurrence unless you are very meticulous or very bored), your system will contract a virus before it is detected. While a memory-resident virus scanner is capable of catching a virus before it infects your system, it does so with a cost in performance. Every file scanned will degrade the system's file access speed, thus slowing down the responsiveness of the system.

The manufacturers of memory-resident virus scanners are well aware that file access speed is important and recognize that many users would opt to disable the scanner rather than take a large performance hit. For this reason, many memory-resident scanners are not quite as thorough as their on-demand counterparts. Better performance can be achieved by only checking for the most likely virus signatures, or by only scanning files that are the most likely to become infected (such as COM files).

TIP   A good security posture will include the use of both on-demand and memory-resident virus scanners.

Problems with Large Environments

All virus scanner vendors periodically release updated signature files to insure that their products can detect as many known viruses as possible. Updating signature files can create a great deal of extra work for system administrators who are responsible for large networking environments. If you are running DOS, Windows, or Macintosh operating systems on the desktop, you will most likely have signature files on each of these systems that will need updating.

Many vendors have taken steps to rectify this problem. For example, Intel's LANDesk Virus Protect uses the concept of *virus domains* in order to group multiple servers and desktop machines. The network administrator can then update signature files, view alerts, and even control scanning parameters from a single console screen. This can dramatically reduce the amount of work required to administer virus protection in a large-scale environment.

A scaleable virus protection solution will not only reduce overall costs, it will help to insure that your environment remains well protected. As mentioned, virus scanning vendors periodically release updated signature files. These signature files are of little use, however, if they are not installed on every system that requires them. A scaleable solution will provide a simple method of distributing these signature files to all systems that require them. A solid enterprise solution will also include some form of advanced alerting function so that the network administrator will be notified of all viruses detected on any system on the network.

Heuristic Scanners

Heuristic scanners perform a statistical analysis in order to determine the likelihood that a file contains program code that may indicate a virus. A heuristic scanner does not compare code to a signature file like a virus scanner; it uses a grading system to determine the probability that the program code being analyzed is a virus. If the program code scores enough points, the heuristic scanner will notify the user that a virus has been detected. Most modern virus scanners include heuristic scanning ability.

One of the biggest benefits of heuristic scanners is that they do not require updating. Since files are graded on a point system, no signature files are required for comparison. This means that a heuristic scanner has a good probability of detecting a virus that no one else has ever seen. This can be extremely useful if you find that you are unable to update signature files on a regular basis.

The biggest drawback to heuristic scanners is their tendency to report false positives. As mentioned, virus code is not all that different from regular program code. This can make it extremely difficult to distinguish between the two. As system administrator, you may find yourself chasing your tail if you deploy a poor heuristic scanner that has a tendency toward reporting nonexistent viruses.

Application-Level Virus Scanners

Application-level virus scanners are a new breed in virus protection. Instead of being responsible for securing a specific system from viruses, an application-level virus scanner is responsible for securing a specific service throughout an organization.

For example, e-mail makes a wonderful transport for propagating viruses through file attachments. Trend Micro manufactures a product called InterScan VirusWall, which can act as an SMTP relay with a twist. Instead of simply receiving inbound mail and forwarding it to the appropriate mail system, InterScan VirusWall can perform a full virus scan of all attachments before relaying them to an internal mail host.

Along with scanning SMTP traffic, InterScan VirusWall can scan FTP and HTTP traffic. This includes raw files, as well as many archive formats such as PKZIP. This helps to insure that all files received from the Internet are free of malicious viruses.

TIP

Many vendors now make products that will directly integrate with existing firewall products. For example, Cheyenne Software makes a virus scanning plug-in for Check Point's FireWall-1 product. This allows virus scanning to be managed on the same system that is responsible for network security. This gives the network administrator a single point of management for both security and virus protection.

Deploying Virus Protection

Now that you have a good idea of how viruses work and what tools are available to prevent infection, let's take a look at some deployment methods to safeguard your network.

NOTE

These suggestions should only be considered a guide; feel free to make modifications that better fit your specific needs.

Look at the network diagram shown in Figure 11.1. It shows a mixed environment that uses a number of different server operating systems. The desktop environment utilizes a mixture of operating systems, as well. Let's assume that you are consulting for the organization that owns this environment and you have been charged with protecting it from viruses, as well as Trojans and worms. You have also been asked to perform this task with a minimal impact on network performance. Take a moment to study the diagram and consider what recommendations you would make.

FIGURE 11.1:

Sample network requiring virus protection

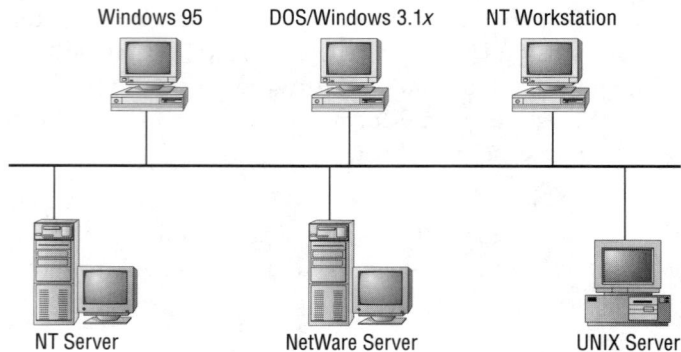

FIGURE 11.1:

Sample network requiring virus protection

Protecting the Desktop Systems

While the desktop environment uses a mixture of operating systems, the hardware platform is consistent (PC compatible). This means that all desktop systems will be susceptible to many of the same types of viruses. You should try to standardize your desktop suggestions as much as possible, despite the fact that there are multiple operating systems in use.

Enable BIOS Boot Sector Protection

One of the most cost-effective suggestions you could make would be to enable boot sector protection through the systems' BIOS. This is a quick yet effective way to insure that the boot sectors of all systems remain secure. You would want to follow this up with some end-user education about what the boot sector warning means and how users should respond to it. Unless a user tries to upgrade his or her operating system, false-positive warnings should not be a problem.

On-Demand Scanning

Each desktop system should utilize an on-demand scanner configured to perform a full virus check of all local drives on a regular basis. This check could be scheduled to run nightly if desktop systems are typically left powered up at night. If nightly virus scans are not an option, scans could be run during some other period of inactivity (such as lunchtime) or weekly as part of a server logon script.

It is important that the on-demand scanner check all local files to insure that a virus has not been planted through a dropper or sneaked in through some file with an obscure file extension. A proper on-demand scanner should include heuristic scanning capability, as well. There should also be some method of reporting all scanning results to a central location so that the data can be reviewed by a system administrator.

Memory-Resident Scanning

Each desktop should also launch a memory-resident scanner during system initialization to weed out viruses before they can be stored on the local file system or executed in memory. In the interest of performance, you may wish to tweak which files are checked by the memory-resident scanner.

Since you will be performing a regular on-demand scan of each desktop system, you have a bit of leeway in how meticulous you need to be in verifying files with your memory-resident scanner. By only checking files that are most commonly infected by viruses, you can reduce the impact of the memory-resident scanner on system performance. While this diminishes your security posture a bit, the gain in system performance may be worth the slightly higher risk.

Your memory-resident scanner should check

- File reads only

- Worms

- Executable files such as COM and EXE files

- Macro-enabled documents, such as Microsoft Word and Excel

You want to check file reads—but not writes, because checking files that are written to disk would be redundant. If a scanner failed to find a virus when the file was read into memory, it is extremely unlikely that the same scanner will detect the virus when it is written to disk. You also want to check for worms because many do not save any information to disk; thus they may go undetected by an on-demand scanner. Finally, you want to configure your memory-resident scanner to check the files most likely to become infected. This includes executable files, as well as files that are capable of saving macro commands.

Options Not Considered

I did not mention setting file attributes or checksum verification because, as you saw earlier, these methods are ineffectual against many strains of viruses. I did not mention other types of process monitoring (besides the BIOS boot sector warning) for the same reason. The suggestions are designed to provide the greatest level of protection with the least amount of labor.

One additional option, however, is to use the file permissions on the NT/2000 workstation in order to prevent the user from having write access to any executable files. While this would decrease the chances of virus infection on these systems, it would also break from the standard configuration used on the other desktop machines. Since DOS and Windows 95/98/Me are not true multi-user operating systems, there is no way to restrict local user access to selective parts of the file system. This means that the NT/2000 workstation configuration would differ from the other desktop machines.

Also, this option does not address the macro viruses, which are the most common forms of virus found in the wild. These viruses hide within document files. Users must have write access to their document storage folders in order to save their files. With this in mind, this option may cause more problems than it solves.

Protecting the NT and NetWare Servers

Since the NT/2000 and NetWare servers are shared resources, they require a slightly different method of protection from the desktop machines. Virus protection on these systems is far more critical, as they can be used as a transport for propagating viruses between the desktop machines. In the case of the NT/2000 server, it can not only be a transport; it can even become infected itself, as well.

On-Demand Scanning

As with the desktop systems, configure on-demand to perform a full scan of all files on a nightly basis. Most server-based virus scanning products include a scheduler for just this purpose. If nightly backups are performed, the on-demand scanner should be set to scan the file system before performing the backup operation. This insures that all archived files are virus-free.

Memory-Resident Scanning

Memory-resident software designed for Windows NT will check the server's memory and files stored to the local file system. Memory-resident scanning operates in a slightly different fashion, however, when run from a NetWare server. This is because the server is incapable of running standard executables. Since the system is simply used for file storage, memory does not need to be checked. It is inbound network traffic that we are most concerned with scanning.

Your server-based memory resident scanner should check

- Local memory for worms and Trojans (NT only)
- Inbound executable files from the network
- Inbound macro-enabled documents from the network

As with the desktop machines, this minimal file checking is done in the interest of improving performance. On the off chance that a virus sneaks through, you would expect the nightly on-demand virus scan to catch it.

TIP   You can gain some additional benefits by using products from different vendors to secure each part of your network from viruses. For example, you could use a product from one vendor on the servers and another on the desktop machines. This is because no two vendors' signature files are identical. By mixing and matching products, you can receive the maximum amount of virus protection.

File Permissions

As mentioned earlier in this chapter, setting user-level file permissions insures that executable files do not become infected. The benefits of this configuration will depend greatly on how applications are stored on the network. If all applications are stored on the local workstation, there will be no executables on the server to protect by setting read-only user-level access. If, however, all applications are launched from one or both of the servers, you can decrease the likelihood of virus infection by setting the minimum level of required permissions.

Options Not Considered

Neither process monitoring nor checksum verification was suggested, because both of these methods are less effective than running virus scanning software. Remember that the objective is to provide the greatest amount of protection while creating the least amount of administrative maintenance. The suggestions made achieve that goal.

Protecting the UNIX System

One important piece of information is missing: what exactly is the UNIX system used for? You have not been told if it is a simple mail relay or a full-blown server accepting a full array of Intranet services. The answer to this question could greatly affect your recommendation. For the purpose of this example, let's assume that this is an engineering system used to compile C code. Users connect to the system via telnet and FTP.

TIP   Always make sure you have enough information to make an informed and logical decision!

File Integrity Checking

One of your biggest concerns with the UNIX system should be the possibility that someone will attempt to load a Trojan on the system in order to capture authentication information. By replacing the telnet server with one of her own creation, an attacker could record logon information from every user who authenticates with the system.

The easiest way to detect this type of activity is to perform a regular file integrity check. This should include a CRC checksum so that changes can be detected even if the current file has the same size and time stamp. You should verify the telnet and FTP servers, as well as any other process that accepts inbound connections. This check should be run as an automated process with the results being analyzed on a different machine. By analyzing the results on a different machine, you are less likely to have the results altered by someone who has compromised the system.

Process Monitoring

Another concern with the UNIX machine is that someone may infiltrate the system with a worm. This would show up as a new process running on the system. As with the integrity check, you should automate this audit and analyze the results on a separate system. By knowing what should be running on the system, you can take action if a new process appears.

File Permissions

By default, only the root user can overwrite software that runs as a server on the system. This means that an attacker would first need to crack the root account or perform a root-level exploit before he could replace any of the server software. This level of file access should be maintained in order to reduce the chance of a system compromise. Regular user accounts should not be granted write access to these files.

Options Not Considered

What about virus-scanning software? UNIX-compatible viruses are extremely rare. Given the described use of this particular system, it is extremely unlikely that a virus infection will occur. Your greater concern is with Trojans and worms.

Summary

In this chapter, we discussed the differences between viruses, Trojans, and worms and how each of them can affect an infected system. You saw what preventive measures are available and the effectiveness of each. You also looked at a mixed-network environment and considered how best to go about protecting it from infection.

In the next chapter, you will learn about backups and disaster recovery. These provide your last line of defense when catastrophic failures occur. From a security perspective, it is always best to plan for the worst.

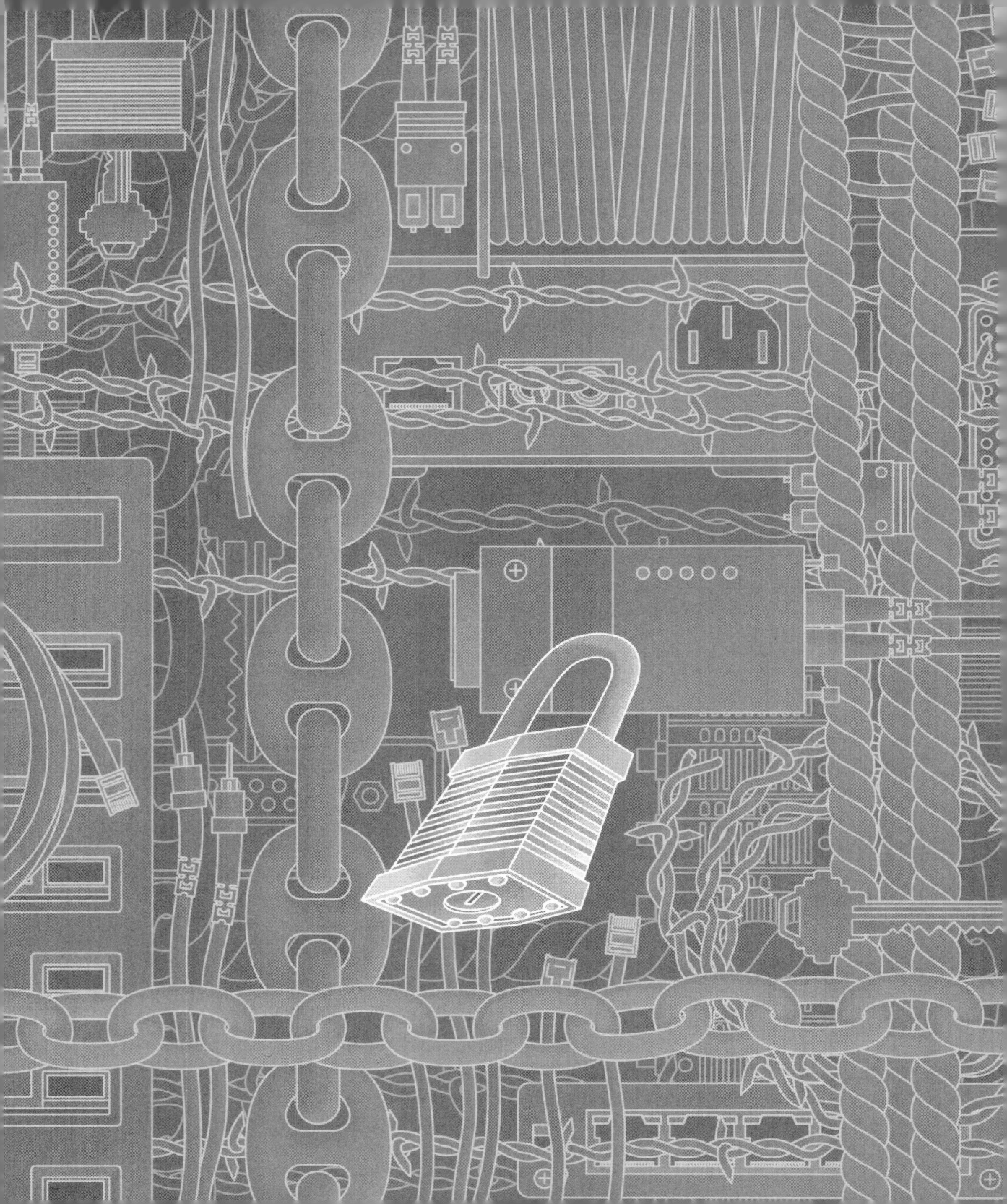

CHAPTER

TWELVE

12

Disaster Prevention and Recovery

Disaster prevention is defined as the precautionary steps you take to insure that any disruption of your organization's resources does not affect your day-to-day operations. Think of disaster prevention as being like insurance: in each case, you invest money in case you may need it—but you hope you never will.

Disaster recovery is all about contingency planning. Despite all the preparations that go into insuring that the worst never happens, you need to have a backup plan that determines what you will do when disaster becomes reality. This is your last line of defense between recovery and complete failure.

In Chapter 2, we discussed risk analysis and the importance of identifying your critical resources. We also stressed placing a dollar value on resource unavailability in order to determine just how much downtime you can live with. In this chapter, we will discuss what options are available to you in keeping those resources accessible.

Disaster Categories

Disaster solutions fall into two categories:

- Maintaining or restoring a service
- Protecting or restoring lost, corrupted, or deleted information

Each category has its place in guarding your assets, and no disaster solution is complete unless it contains elements from both categories.

For example, let's say you have two hard drives installed in a server that are mirrored together. *Mirroring* insures that both disks always contain exactly the same information. When mirroring is used, a single hard drive failure will not bring down the entire server. The remaining hard drive can continue to provide file storage and give users access to previously saved information. Mirroring is considered a disaster recovery *service* solution because it helps to insure that file services remain available.

Now let's assume that a user comes to you and claims that she needs to retrieve a file that she deleted three months ago. Despite the passage of so much time, this information is now critical to performing her job, and the information cannot be re-created.

If mirroring is the only disaster recovery procedure you have in place on this file server, then you are in deep trouble. While mirroring insures that files get saved to both hard drives in the mirrored pair, mirroring also insures that deleted files are removed in both as well. Mirroring provides no way to recover this lost information, making it an ineffective information recovery solution.

TIP   When identifying a full disaster recovery solution, make sure you find methods to recover from service failures as well as to recover lost information. Both are critical to insuring that you have a contingency plan in any disaster situation.

Network Disasters

While network disasters have the ability to shut down communications through an entire organization, they receive very little attention compared to their server counterparts. Most organizations will take great strides to insure that a server remains available. Very few subject the network to the same level of scrutiny, even though it is the network that will get them to this server. Without a functioning network, a server is of little use.

In the next sections, we'll review different network technologies and their potential vulnerabilities that might lead to loss of network functionality. Although this might seem to be a lot of information (and a lot of it is based on common sense), a thorough understanding of these vulnerabilities and characteristics in general contributes greatly to overall troubleshooting—especially when a failure is not readily apparent.

Media

Good disaster recovery procedures start with your network media. While physical cables are still the predominant media for most LANs, wireless is rapidly growing as an option, and must be considered as part of the overall disaster recovery. If you do chose cable, the cabling you choose will go a long way toward specifying how resilient your network will be in case of failure. Whichever media you choose will carry all of your network communications, so a failure at this level can be devastating.

Thinnet and Thicknet

Thinnet and Thicknet cabling date back to the original Ethernet specifications of the '70s. Both cable specifications allow multiple systems to be attached to the same logical segment of cable. This provides a central point of failure, because if any portion of this length of cable becomes faulty, every system attached to it will be unable to communicate.

I can honestly say that out of the 100+ companies I have consulted for over the past two years, not one of them was considering a new network installation that included Thinnet or Thicknet cable. Unfortunately, at least 15 percent of them still used Thinnet to attach workstations and/or servers to the network. Two of them were still using Thicknet.

TIP One of the biggest improvements you can make to network availability is to replace Thinnet and Thicknet cabling with a more modern solution.

Twisted Pair

Category 5 (CAT5) cabling is the current cabling standard for most network installations. While this will eventually be replaced with fiber due to increasing bandwidth requirements, the wide installation base of CAT5 cable will guarantee that it will be included in future topology specifications for at least a few more years. For example, while Gigabit Ethernet is based on fiber, concessions have been made to include CAT5 cabling for short cable runs (50–75 meters).

The problem arises from the amount of category 3 (CAT3) cabling that is still in use, as well as the number of cabling installations that have only been tested for 10Mb operation. CAT5 does not guarantee that 100Mb or faster operation is possible; it only provides the ability to support these speeds. The CAT5 components must be properly assembled and tested to function properly.

It is entirely possible that CAT3 cabling or improperly installed CAT5 cabling will allow you to hook up 100Mb or higher devices and have them communicate with each other. Problems typically do not occur until a heavy load is placed on the network. Of course, a heavy load typically means that you have many users relying on network services. Problems due to poor cabling can take the form of slow network performance, frequent packet retransmissions due to errors, or even disconnection of users from services.

Your best preventive medicine for avoiding twisted-pair cabling problems is to test and certify your cables before use. If this is not possible, or if you have been pressed into using below-grade cabling, consider segmenting these problem areas with one or more switches. A switch has the ability to trap packet errors and to isolate transmissions into multiple collision domains. While this will not fix the errors, it will limit the scope of the effect that your cable problems have on the rest of your network.

Fiber Cabling

Since fiber uses light for transmitting network information, it is immune to the effects of electromagnetic interference (EMI). EMI can cause transmission errors, especially if the cabling is under heavy load. This makes fiber an excellent choice for avoiding EMI failures, thus increasing the availability of services the fiber cable is connecting.

NOTE For a detailed discussion of fiber cable, see Chapter 4.

Excessive Cable Lengths

Every logical topology has specifications that identify the maximum cable lengths you can use. For example, 10Mb and 100Mb Ethernet both specify that twisted-pair cable runs cannot exceed 100 meters. These rules exist to insure that a system at one end of the cable run can properly detect the transmissions of a system located at the opposite end.

Exceeding these topology specifications for cable length can produce intermittent failures due to low signal strength and slow down communications along the entire segment due to an increase in collisions. Since these problems will not be consistent, they can be very difficult to troubleshoot.

TIP A good cable tester is the quickest way to tell if you have exceeded cable-length limitations for your logical topology.

Wireless Technologies

Some organizations are choosing wireless as their media of choice. While wireless technologies have existed for quite some time, slow transfer speeds and lack of open, common standards have limited its market penetration until now. With the adoption of new technologies and standards (802.1b1, in particular), high-speed wireless LAN (WLAN) is now technically feasible.

A WLAN is a transmission system that is designed to be location-independent, allowing network access using radio waves rather than a cable infrastructure. In corporate environments, WLANs are usually used as the final link between an existing wired network and a group of client computers.

However, there are still threats to a wireless infrastructure:

Interference   Although 802.11b, in particular, is the preferred wireless LAN standard, other competing wireless standards still exist (HomeRF and Bluetooth). In the fall of 2000, the FCC ruled that HomeRF could increase its range of frequencies to overlap with that of 802.11b. While HomeRF uses frequency-hopping that allows traffic to move from frequency to frequency in search of the best signal (and avoid other signals), 802.11b does not. As a result, there is a very real possibility that stations running 802.11b protocol could interfere with those running HomeRF.

Installation and configuration   What seems like the advantage of a wireless network can actually be the source of most of its problems. Mobile users have to be handed off from one AP (Access Point) to another, just as a cell phone is handed off from one cell tower to another as the caller moves between cells. If there are not enough APs to cover an area or if they are incorrectly configured, communication with the network can be lost.

It is important to note that wireless technologies can be a positive part of any organization's disaster recovery plan—used as a backup in case there is a failure in the wiring infrastructure of an organization. Also, because WLANs are usually added gradually to an existing wire-based network, the wires themselves become the backup plan in case the WLAN fails.

Topology

The topology you choose can also have a dramatic effect on how resilient your network will be in case of failure. As you will see in the following sections, some topologies do a better job than others of recovering from the day-to-day problems that can happen on any network. Changing your topology may not be an option. If not, then this section will at least point out some of the common problems you may encounter and give you an idea of possible contingency plans.

Ethernet

Ethernet has become the topology of choice for most networking environments. When used with twisted-pair cabling, the topology can be extremely resistant to failure due to cabling problems on any single segment. This helps to isolate problems so that only a single system will be affected. Of course, if this single system happens to be one of your servers, the break in connectivity can still affect multiple users.

The biggest flaw in Ethernet is that a single system is capable of gobbling up all of the available bandwidth. While this is an uncommon occurrence with modern network cards, older network interface cards (NIC) were prone to a problem known as *jabbering*. A jabbering network card was a NIC with a faulty transceiver that would cause it to continually transmit traffic onto the network. This would cause every other system on the network to stop transmitting and wait for the jabbering card to finish transmitting. Since the faulty card would continue to jabber as long as it had power, network communications would grind to a halt.

Due to improvements in technology, jabbering network cards are now rare. The introduction of switching has also made jabbering NICs less of an issue. When a NIC jabbers, the packets it transmits are not legal Ethernet packets. This means that a switch checking for errors will reject these packets and not forward them on to the rest of the network. This isolates the problem system so that it does not affect the operation of other systems on the network.

Token Ring

While *Token Ring* was designed to be fault tolerant, it is not without its problems. Token Ring is a wonderful topology when all systems operate as intended. For example, a NIC attached to a Token Ring network is capable of performing a self-diagnostic check if other NICs on the ring inform it that there may be a problem. Obviously, a faulty NIC may not be able to perform a true diagnostic check. If the NIC thinks that it is OK, it will jump back in the ring and continue to cause problems.

One possible error condition with Token Ring is having a NIC detect, or be pre-programmed with, the wrong ring speed. Since Token Ring requires that each system successively pass the token to the next, a single NIC set to the wrong speed can bring down the entire ring. For example, let's say that every system on a ring is set to 16Mb. If a system joins this ring but has been hard set to 4Mb, all communication will stop. This is because the new system will pass the token too slowly, causing the other systems to think the token has become lost. When the token is passed along, the error condition is clear—but only until the incorrectly configured system grabs the token again. This will cause the ring to flap back and forth between an operational and a dysfunctional state.

A Token Ring switch will mitigate the effect that a single system set to the wrong ring speed will have on the rest of the network. In fact, depending on the switch, this one system may very well be able to operate at 4Mb while the rest of the ring runs at 16Mb. Unfortunately, Token Ring switches are less popular and far more expensive than their Ethernet counterparts. This has severely limited their application in the field.

NOTE   An Ethernet network would not have the same difficulty. If a single system were set to the wrong topology speed, only that one system would be affected. All other systems would continue to communicate as usual.

What happens with Token Ring if two systems have the same media access control (MAC) number? In an Ethernet environment, a duplicate MAC only affects the two systems attempting to use the same number. In Token Ring, however, a duplicate MAC can bring down the entire ring. This is because Token Ring requires that every system keep track of the MAC address used by its upstream neighbor (the previous system on the ring) and its downstream neighbor (the next system on the ring). Duplicate MAC addresses completely confuse the systems on the ring as they attempt to figure out who is located where.

FDDI

Fiber Distributed Data Interface (FDDI) is also a ring topology, but a second ring has been added in order to rectify many of the problems found in Token Ring. This second ring remains dormant until an error condition is detected. When this occurs, the FDDI systems can work together in order to isolate the problem area. FDDI is considered to be a dying technology because no effort has been made to increase speeds beyond 100Mb. The technology is still worth considering, however, due to its fault-tolerant nature.

NOTE   FDDI can be run in *full duplex mode*, which allows both rings to be active at all times. Enabling this feature, however, eliminates the use of the second ring for redundancy.

In an FDDI ring environment, each station is connected to both rings in order to guard against cable or hardware failure. Let's assume that you have a cable failure between two of the routers shown in Figure 12.1. When this cable failure occurs, the system immediately downstream from the failure will quickly realize it is no longer receiving data. It then begins to send out a special maintenance packet called a *beacon*. A beacon is used by token stations to let other systems around the ring know it has detected a problem. A beacon frame is a system's way of saying, "Hey, I think there is a problem between me and my upstream neighbor because I am no longer receiving data from it." The station would then initialize its connection on the secondary ring so that it would now send and receive data on Connector A.

FIGURE 12.1:

Four routers connected to an FDDI ring

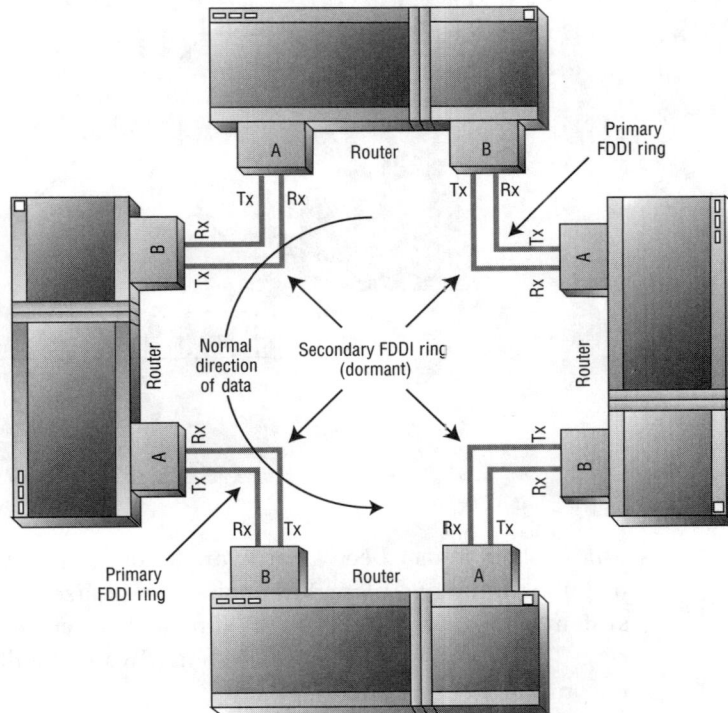

The beacon packet would continue to be forwarded until it reached the beaconing system's upstream neighbor. This upstream neighbor would then initialize its connection to the secondary ring by sending and receiving on Connector B. This, in effect, isolates the problem area and returns normal connectivity. When the beaconing station begins to receive its own beacons, it ceases transmission, and ring operation returns to normal. The final transmission path would resemble the network shown in Figure 12.2. By using beacon frames, the systems on the network can determine the failure area and isolate it by activating the secondary ring.

FIGURE 12.2:

How FDDI stations recover from a cable failure

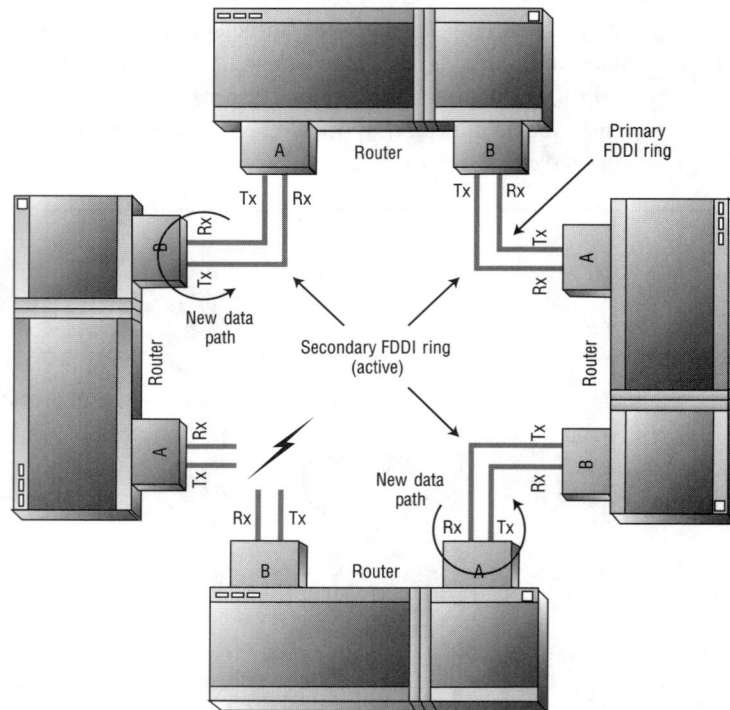

If this had, in fact, been a hardware failure caused by a fault in the upstream neighbor and that system was unable to initialize the secondary ring, the faulty system's upstream neighbor would have detected this and stepped in to close the ring. This would isolate the problem hardware but allow the rest of the network to continue to function.

Each router would continue to monitor the faulty links until connectivity appears to be restored. If the link passes an integrity test, the primary ring returns to full operation, and the secondary ring again goes dormant. This type of network fault tolerance can be deemed critical in environments where connectivity must be maintained seven days a week, 24 hours a day (referred to as 24×7 operation). This functionality is what still makes FDDI the most fault-tolerant networking topology available today for local area networks.

NOTE   FDDI also supports a star topology, which does not provide any redundancy. An FDDI network can consist of both star and ring connections.

802.11b (WLAN)

The 802.11b standard defines two primary players:

Station   Usually, this would be a PC equipped with a wireless NIC.

Access Point (AP)   Acts as a bridge between a wired network and wireless computers. Consisting of a radio, a wired interface (Ethernet), and bridging software, the AP is the base that allows one or more stations to connect to the network.

802.11b also works in two modes:

Infrastructure   Also called a *Basic Service Set (BSS)*, this mode is a wireless network that has at least one access point connected to a wired network and one to a group of one or more wireless stations. Two or more BSSs in a single subnetwork is called *an Extended Service Set* (ESS). Infrastructure mode is the most common for corporate environments.

Ad Hoc   This is known as *Independent BSS (IBSS)* or *peer-to-peer mode*. It consists simply of a group of wireless stations that communicate directly without the bridging services of an AP.

Like Ethernet (802.3), 802.11b forces the sender to listen to the medium before transmitting. In Ethernet, the full access protocol is known as Carrier Sense Multiple Access with Collision Detection (CSMA/CD). In a wireless network, however, collision detection is not possible, because a station cannot transmit and listen at the same time—and therefore cannot "hear" a collision occurring.

To compensate, 802.11b uses a modification called Carrier Sense Multiple Access with Collision Avoidance (CSMA/CA). CSMA/CA works like this: the sender listens, and if no activity is detected it waits an additional random amount of time, and it then transmits. If the packet is received intact, the receiver issues an acknowledgment to the sender, which completes the process. If an acknowledgment isn't received, a collision is assumed, and the packet is retransmitted. Unfortunately, CSMA/CA adds additional overhead, which means that an 802.11 network will be slower than an equivalent speed Ethernet network.

Another potential problem is known as the "hidden node," in which two stations on opposite sides of an access point can both "hear" activity from an access point but not from each other. Fortunately 802.11b has an option called Request to Send/Clear to Send (RTS/CTS). This protocol dictates that a sender transmit an RTS first, and then wait for a CTS from the AP. Since all stations can hear the AP, waiting for the CTS causes them to delay transmitting, eventually allowing each sender to communicate without any chance of a collision. RTS/CTS causes overhead, however, which is another potential negative.

Designing a WLAN with multiple APs avoids having a single point of failure. Although reassociation with a new AP usually occurs because the station has physically moved away from its original AP, it can also occur if there is a change in radio characteristics or high network traffic—essentially providing a load balancing feature.

Leased Line or T1 Connections

Private-circuit WAN topologies, such as leased lines or T1 connections, are good at insuring privacy, but they also introduce a single point of failure. A leased line or T1 circuit is the equivalent of a single, long cable run between two of your geographically separated sites. If any portion of this circuit is interrupted, there is no built-in redundancy to insure that information can still be exchanged between these two sites.

If you will be using a private circuit, consider an analog or ISDN redundancy option, discussed later in this section. This is particularly important if you are following the latest trend of removing servers from field offices and consolidating them in a central location. While this provides a single point of management, it also creates a single point of failure. If a field office that does not have a server loses its private circuit connection to the main office, that field office is without network resources. If the company had also moved to a thin-client architecture, then this field office would be down completely.

Frame Relay

Frame relay is also capable of providing WAN connectivity, but it does so across a shared public network. This network is *packet switched*, meaning that if any segment within the frame relay cloud experiences a failure, traffic can be diverted across operational links. While this may cause a bit of traffic congestion, at least you still have connectivity.

It is not impossible, however, for the entire frame relay network to go down. This has happened recently to both MCI and AT&T. In both cases, all customers experienced downtime. This varied from a few hours to a few days, depending on the client's location. While outages are rare, these failures have shown that they are possible.

TIP   While frame relay does provide better fault tolerance than private circuits, it is not immune to failure. If you have a WAN segment running over frame relay which absolutely must remain operational 24 × 7, consider building in some redundancy to the circuit.

Integrated Services Digital Network (ISDN)

ISDN is a telephone company technology that provides digital service, typically in increments of 64Kbps. ISDN has been available since the early 1980s, but it has only seen broad implementation in the last part of the '90s because of the limitations of analog modems and the rising popularity of the newer packet-switched technologies. ISDN requires that the phone company install services within their phone switches to support digitally switched connections. ISDN was initially stalled by high costs, lack of standards, and low acceptance by consumers.

Because the circuits involved in an ISDN connection are dedicated, any interruption with a single circuit will cause the entire connection to fail. While still a viable option for some organizations, and in some areas the only choice of cheap Internet access, most modern companies find that emerging DSL technology is cheaper and more flexible—although even DSL has been plagued with its own implementation problems. Still, ISDN remains a known technology that has a solid performance history and does not have any recent history of major failures.

Digital Subscriber Line (DSL)

Digital Subscriber Line (DSL) is similar to ISDN in that both use existing copper telephone lines and both require short distances to a central switching office (less than 18,000 feet). DSL is circuit-oriented, but instead of utilizing fixed physical circuits for the entire length of the connection, DSL simply needs a complete circuit to the LECs POP. This dramatically reduces the amount of failure points in any given connection. DSL can also provide a dramatically higher level of speed than ISDN—up to 32Mbps downstream and up to 1Mbps upstream. This speed is not fixed like ISDN or a T1, and this can cause problems for some organizations that require dedicated throughput (in both directions of the connection) for video conferencing or other multimedia uses.

Single Points of Failure

As you may have surmised from the previous section, one of the best ways to eliminate disasters on a network is to identify single points of failure and either build in redundancy or develop a contingency plan. Unknowingly creating a single point of failure is the most common mistake made in a network design.

For example, consider the configuration of the average Internet connection:

- A single firewall
- A single router
- A single CSU/DSU
- A single leased line or T1 connection

This configuration has three electronic devices, as well as a network circuit that is not under your control—all capable of interrupting Internet service. The electronic devices are not exactly components you can replace by running down to the local Radio Shack. The WAN circuit is controlled by your local exchange carrier, so the response time you receive to problems may be directly affected by the business relationship you have with the local exchange carrier. (Translation: "The more money you spend on a monthly basis, the more likely you are to see a service tech by the end of the millennium.")

While these issues may not be a big deal for some organizations, many do rely on Internet connectivity as part of their daily business practices. It is possible that when Internet connectivity was first established, consistent access to Internet services may not have seemed important or been considered a critical business function. Now that Internet access has become a critical business function, no one has gone back to evaluate the impact of the loss of this service.

So you need to go back to your risk analysis and identify your single points of network failure. You also need to evaluate the effect that loss of service will have on your organization. If any point in your network can be considered critical, you need to build in redundancy.

Consolidated Equipment

In the early 1990s, chassis hubs became extremely popular due to their high port density and single point of management. It was not uncommon to have 200 or more systems connected through a single hub. Of course, neither was it uncommon to have 200 or more users who were unable to access network resources because a power supply or a single management board had failed. This is why many organizations have stuck with stackable hubs; although these require more rack space, the failure of a single unit does not bring down an entire network.

There has been a resurgence of interest in consolidated solutions with the release of the Cisco's 5000 series switch, as well as multiple product offerings from Cabletron. Like their chassis hub predecessors, these products claim lower administration costs due to a central point of management. While there is validity in this claim, it does not speak to financial loss due to a catastrophic failure of a single device.

Stackable solutions provide you with more flexibility in recovering from a failure. For example, if you are using six stackable switches instead of a single consolidated unit and one of these switches fails, you will not experience a complete network outage. Although you still have a failed device to deal with, you at least have some breathing space. You can use the remaining five units in order to continue providing services to important users such as your boss (if the outage coincides with your review), the person who cuts the weekly payroll, and that administrative assistant who drops off brownies every holiday.

Taking Advantage of Redundant LAN Routes

As you saw in Chapter 3, dynamic routing can be used to take advantage of multiple paths between network segments. Some routing protocols will even take such metrics as network utilization into account when determining which path is the best route along which to forward your traffic.

While static routes are your best bet when only a single path is available (such as a WAN link) or in areas where you are concerned that an attacker may corrupt the routing table (such as an Internet connection), for the majority of your internal network you should use a dynamic routing protocol such as OSPF. If there is only one connection point between each of your routed segments, consider purchasing another router for redundancy or adding more network cards to one of your servers. Using metrics such as hop count and cost, you can configure your network to only route through the server in case of emergency. This will help to insure that the server does not experience additional load unless the primary router fails.

Dial Backup for WAN Connections

WAN connections are prime candidates for providing a single point of failure. Due to the recurrent costs of maintaining a WAN link, most organizations do not build any type of redundancy into their wide-area network. This is a shame, because you have no real control over this portion of your network. You are at the mercy of your exchange carrier to feel your urgency and rectify the problem as soon as possible.

One potential solution is to configure your border routers to fail over to a backup circuit if the primary line fails. This backup can be an analog dial-up line along with a couple of modems, or you could go for increased bandwidth by utilizing an ISDN solution. In either case, you will have a lot less available bandwidth if the line that fails is a full T1, but you are better off being able to provide a minimal amount of bandwidth between your two locations than no bandwidth at all.

Configuring a router to perform dial backup is not difficult. The following example shows the commands required for a Cisco router to bring up an ISDN connection on bri 0 when the primary circuit on serial 0 fails to respond:

```
interface serial 0
 backup delay 10 120
 backup interface bri 0
 ip address 192.168.5.1 255.255.255.0
!
interface bri 0
 ip address 192.168.5.2 255.255.255.0
 dialer string 5551212
 dialer-group 1
 dialer in-band
 dialer string 5551212
 async dynamic routing
!
dialer-list 1 protocol ip permit
```

This configuration tells the router that if serial 0 fails to respond for 10 seconds, the bri 0 interface should be initiated as an alternate path. Likewise, if the serial 0 circuit returns to operation for a minimum of 120 seconds, the bri 0 line should be torn down. The dialer-list command identifies the type of traffic that can bring up the alternate circuit path. In this case, we have specified that any IP traffic is capable of initiating the circuit.

> **TIP**
>
> If you are using ISDN as a backup solution, and you are using a primary rate ISDN (PRI) interface at your main office in order to accept basic rate ISDN (BRI) connects from multiple field offices, remember that the call will have to be initiated from the BRI side of the circuit.

Saving Configuration Files

All of the network disaster solutions we've discussed until now have dealt with availability of service. As mentioned earlier in this chapter, no disaster recovery solution is complete unless you are able to restore lost information, as well. In this case, we are not talking about your data that is traveling along the network. Protocols do a very good job of insuring that this information does not become lost. The real concern is the configuration files that you use to program routers, switches, and even hubs along your network.

When a network device fails, chances are you will also lose the configuration that has been programmed into it. It is also possible that someone may inadvertently change the configuration to an unusable state. If either of these events occurs, it is a good thing to have a backup of your configuration file so that the original setup can be restored. This is also useful for historic purposes, when you wish to see what changes have been made to your network and when.

Terminal Logging

The easiest way to save your configuration information is *terminal logging*. Most terminal emulation and telnet programs have some method of recording all the information that passes by on the terminal screen. If your networking device has a single command that shows all configuration information, you can use terminal logging to archive this information for later retrieval.

Some devices, such as Cisco routers and switches, will let you paste this information to your terminal screen in order to configure the device. For example, the `write term` command will display all configuration information to the terminal screen. This allows this configuration information to be easily saved. If the device should fail later, simply open a terminal session with the new device and place it in configuration mode. Copy the original configuration of the original device to your Clipboard (using Notepad or WordPad), and paste it into the terminal screen connected to the new device. Save the configuration, and your replacement is ready for action.

The drawback to terminal logging is that it only works for configuration; you cannot save the operating system. Also, if your network device does not provide a single command for displaying all configuration information, the process of recording the full configuration can be tedious.

Trivial File Transfer Protocol (TFTP) Server

Trivial File Transfer Protocol (TFTP) is similar to FTP, except that it uses UDP as a transport and does not use any type of authentication. When a client wishes to retrieve a file from a TFTP server or save a file to a TFTP server, it simply needs to know the file's name and the IP address of the TFTP server. There are no command parameters that allow you to authenticate or even change to a new directory.

Given the lack of authentication, TFTP is not exactly something you want coming through your firewall. Most networking devices, however, support TFTP for saving or retrieving configuration information. A single TFTP server can archive configuration files for every device on your network. If a device on your network fails, simply plug it in, assign an IP address, and use TFTP to retrieve the required configuration file.

TIP

Most vendors use TFTP in order to configure devices with their latest operating system versions. This means that you can keep a known-to-be-stable operating system version on the TFTP server with the required configuration file. When a device needs to be replaced, simply use TFTP to load both the operating system and the configuration file from the TFTP server.

By saving the configuration information from your network devices, you can be assured of recovering from a network disaster as quickly as possible. Few things in life are a greater letdown than having a network device fail and finally receiving the replacement, only to discover that you do not remember the configuration of the original device and you will have to spend the next few hours playing trial-and-error.

Server Disasters

Now that you have seen how to make your network more fault tolerant, it is time to consider your servers. There is a wide range of options available in order to make servers more disaster resistant. The only limiting factors are your budget and, in some cases, your operating system—not all solutions are available for every platform. Disaster prevention on a server is usually viewed as being the most costly, as we can typically only justify the expenditure on a single system.

Uninterruptible Power Supply (UPS)

While all computers need a source of clean and steady power, this is even more important when the computer will act as a server, because multiple users will rely on the system. A good power source is not just one that is free from blackout or brownout conditions; it should be free of surges and spikes, as well.

As little as a 10 percent fluctuation in power can cause an error condition on a computer, even less if it is in the form of a steady stream of noise. While brownouts or blackouts are easy to identify because they will cause the system to reboot, spikes, surges, and noise can cause far more subtle problems, such as the application error just described. Electrical power is like network wiring: we do not think to check it until we have spent time chasing our tails replacing drivers and loading patches.

Tracking Down Power Problems

I was once called in by a client to troubleshoot a problem with some backup software on a NetWare server. The backup software appeared to be hanging the server and causing 100 percent CPU utilization. The problem was not completely consistent: it happened during random stages of the backup process. What was odd, however, was that it only happened on Monday and Thursday nights between 7:30 PM and 8:00 PM, even though the client ran the backup every night. The problem could not be reproduced during regular business hours. Installing all current patches had no effect.

I decided to work late one Thursday night to see if I could diagnose the problem. At 7:00 PM, the cleanup crew came in and started emptying waste baskets and vacuuming the rugs. At approximately 7:40 PM, a member of the cleaning crew plugged a vacuum into an outlet just outside the server room.

All ran fine until the vacuum was powered off. The resulting power spike immediately caused a 100 percent CPU race condition on the server. I asked the employee if the crew vacuumed this office space every night and was told that while the crew emptied wastebaskets every night, they only vacuumed on Mondays and Thursdays. Needless to say, the client had a UPS installed by Monday—and the problem was solved.

TIP   While a good UPS is an excellent idea for any computer system, it should be considered critical equipment for your servers. An intelligent UPS will include software that can shut down the server if power is unavailable for a specific amount of time. This insures that your server does not come crashing down once the battery supply has run dry.

RAID

RAID, or *redundant array of inexpensive disks*, not only provides fault tolerance against hard disk crashes; it can also improve system performance. RAID breaks up or copies the data you wish to save across multiple hard disks. This prevents a system failure due to the crash of a single drive. It also improves performance, as multiple disks can work together in order to save large files simultaneously.

The process of breaking up data across multiple disks is referred to as *striping*. Depending on the level of RAID you are using, the system may also store parity information known as Error Correction Code (ECC). Some RAID systems are *hot swappable*, meaning you can replace drives while the computer is still in use, reducing downtime to zero.

RAID can be implemented as either a hardware or a software solution. With hardware RAID, the RAID controller takes care of all RAID functionality, making the array appear as a single logical disk to the operating system. Software RAID is program code, which is either part of the existing operating system or available as add-on software. Software RAID is usually slower than hardware RAID because it requires more CPU utilization. Regardless of the solution you use, RAID classifications are broken up into different levels: RAID 0–RAID 5.

NOTE   There are classifications for RAID 6–RAID 10, but these are simply variations on the original six specifications.

RAID 0

RAID 0 is used strictly for performance gains and provides no fault tolerance. Instead of saving a file to a single disk, RAID 0 stripes the data across multiple hard drives. This improves performance by letting the drives share the storage load—but it also increases the chance of failure, as any one disk crash will disable the entire array. Because of the lack of fault tolerance, RAID 0 is not widely used.

RAID 1

RAID 1 maintains a full copy of all file information on every disk. This is why RAID 1 is sometimes referred to as *disk mirroring*. If a single disk fails, each of the remaining disks has a full copy of the entire file system. This prevents a system crash due to the failure of any one disk. This also means that disk storage is limited to the size of a single disk. In other words, if you have two 4GB drives mirrored together, you only have 4GB of available storage, not 8GB.

A RAID 1 disk array will actually perform worse than a single disk solution. This is because the disk controller must send a full copy of each file to every single drive. This limits the speed of the array to that of the slowest disk. Novell developed a term for a variation on disk mirroring called *disk duplexing*. Disk duplexing functions in the same way as disk mirroring, except that multiple controller cards are used. This helps to eliminate some of the performance degradation because each controller only needs to communicate with a single drive. Duplexing also helps to increase fault tolerance because the system can survive not only a drive failure, but a controller failure, as well.

RAID 2

RAID 2 is similar to RAID 5, except that data is stored to disk one byte at a time. Error correction is also used to prevent a single drive failure from disabling the array. The block mode data transfer used by other RAID specifications is far more efficient than the byte mode used by RAID 2. This causes RAID 2 to suffer from extremely poor performance, especially when dealing with multiple small files. Due to its poor performance, RAID 2 is not widely used.

RAID 3 and RAID 4

RAID 3 and RAID 4 are identical specifications, except that RAID 3 involves the use of three disks and RAID 4 involves the use of four. These RAID specifications dedicate a single disk to error correction and stripe the data across the remaining disks. In other words, in a RAID 4 array, disks 1–3 will contain striped data, while disk 4 will be dedicated to error correction. This allows the array to remain functional through the loss of a single drive.

The ECC is essentially a mathematical summation of the data stored on all the other hard drives. This ECC value is generated on a block-by-block basis. For example, consider the following math problem:

```
3 + 4 + 2 + 6 = 15
```

Think of all the values to the left of the equals sign as data that is stored to a specific block on each data disk in a RAID 4 array. Think of the total as the value stored to the same block on the parity drive. Now let's assume that disk 3 crashes and a file request is made of this group of blocks. The RAID array is presented with the following problem:

```
3 + 4 + ? + 6 = 15
```

As you can see, it is pretty easy to derive the missing value. While this will require a bit more processing, thus slowing down disk access a bit, the array can reproduce the missing data and return the file information. While this example is greatly simplified, it essentially shows how RAID levels 3–5 recover from a disk failure.

RAID levels 3 and 4 are where you start to see an improvement in performance over using a single disk. You also take less of a storage hit in order to provide fault tolerance. Since data is stored on all the disks but one, the total storage capacity of a RAID 3 or RAID 4 array is the total storage of all the disks, minus the storage of one of them. In other words, if you have four 4GB drives in a RAID 4 configuration, you will have 12GB of available storage.

RAID 5

RAID 5 is similar to RAID 3 and RAID 4, except that all disks are used for both data and ECC storage. This helps to improve speed over RAID 3 and RAID 4, which can suffer from bottlenecks on the parity drive. It also helps to improve capacity, as you can use more than five drives on a RAID 5 array. Like RAID 3 and 4, the total storage capacity is the combined storage of all the disks minus one. RAID 5 is by far the most popular RAID solution after disk mirroring.

Redundant Servers

Server redundancy takes the concept of RAID and applies it to the entire computer. Sometimes referred to as *server fault tolerance*, redundant servers provide one or more entire systems to be available in case the primary one crashes. It does not matter if the crash is due to a drive crash, a memory error, or even a motherboard failure. Once the primary server stops responding to requests, the redundant system steps in to take over.

As shown in Figure 12.3, redundant servers typically share two communication channels. One is their network connection, while the other is a high-speed link between the two systems. Depending on the implementation, this link can be created using proprietary communication cards or possibly 100Mb Ethernet cards. Updates are fed to the secondary via this high-speed link. Depending on the implementation, these updates may simply be disk information or may possibly include memory address information, as well.

NOTE   When memory address information is included, the secondary is capable of stepping in for the primary with no interruption in service.

FIGURE 12.3:

A redundant server configuration

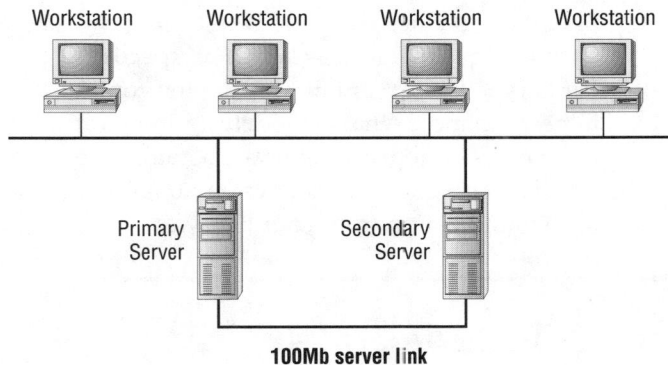

100Mb server link

Not all redundant server solutions include a high-speed link. For example, Octopus, which is discussed at length at the end of this chapter, uses the server's network connection when exchanging information. Octopus does not require a high-speed link between the two systems. The benefit of using the existing network is that the secondary server can be located anywhere, even at a remote facility. Since the secondary server can be safely tucked away in another location that is miles away, the setup is far more fault resilient to facility-wide problems such as fire, lightning strikes, floods, or even cattle stampedes.

If you do not have a link between the two systems, memory information is not shared and the secondary is not capable of stepping in immediately. A client request originally sent to the primary server would have to time out and be reset before it could be serviced by the secondary server. This would add a delay of a minute or two before the secondary is fully utilized. Another drawback is increased network utilization. This is because all information is shared over the network, not over an isolated link between the two systems.

Server redundancy can be implemented at the operating-system level or as an add-on product. Novell's SFT-III and Microsoft's Cluster Server (MSCS) are good examples of support at the operating-system level for running redundant servers. There are also many third-party offerings from companies like Vinca, Network Integrity, and Qualix Group that are capable of adding redundant server support. The option you choose will depend on the features you are looking for. Each product supports redundant servers in a slightly different fashion.

Clustering

Clustering is similar to redundant servers, except that all systems take part in processing service requests. The cluster acts as an intelligent unit in order to balance traffic load. From a client's perspective, a cluster looks like a single, yet very fast server. If a server fails, processing continues but with an obvious degradation in performance. What makes clustering more attractive than server redundancy is that your secondary systems are actually providing processing time; they do not sit idle waiting for another system to fail. This insures that you get the highest level of utilization from your hardware.

Linux Clustering

An excellent example of clustering is the Beowulf project at NASA's Goddard Space Flight Center (GSFC). Back in 1994, NASA's Center of Excellence in Space Data and Information Sciences (CESDIS) clustered 16 Linux systems together. All systems were based on the Intel 486DX4 100MHz chip, and the total cost of the cluster was less than $50,000. All communications between the clustered systems utilized a set of 100Mb Ethernet networks. The goal was an inexpensive alternative to the high-end workstations that were being used for Earth and space science applications.

The resulting cluster had a combined processing speed capable of 1.2 billion floating point operations per second (Gigaflop) and up to eight times the disk I/O bandwidth of a conventional system. This placed the Linux cluster on par with supercomputers costing four to five times more.

Clustering is an excellent solution for boosting both fault tolerance and performance, and is available for UNIX, VMS, and Microsoft NT and 2000.

Data Backup

Keeping a duplicate copy of your data has always been the best way to protect against disaster, corruption, or loss. Although traditional methods rely on tape, newer backup methods are starting to gain the attention of companies—including Internet-based backups that provide for offsite storage and a reduction of in-house maintenance of backup equipment and procedures.

Tape Backup

The mainstay of most network administrators, *tape backups* are the method of choice for protecting or restoring lost, corrupted, or deleted information. All of the server-based options we have discussed so far have focused on maintaining or restoring the server as a service. None is capable of restoring that proverbial marketing file that was deleted over three months ago. Here is where tape backups come in: their strength is in safeguarding the information that actually gets stored on the server.

NOTE   The ability to restore files becomes even more important if you are using UNIX or Windows NT as a file server. Neither of these operating systems includes a utility for restoring deleted network files.

Most backup software supports three methods of selecting which files should be archived to tape. These methods are

- Full backup
- Incremental backup
- Differential backup

Full Backups

As the name implies, a *full backup* is a complete archive of every file on the server. A full backup is your best bet when recovering from a disaster: it contains a complete copy of your entire file system, consolidated to a single tape or set of tapes. The only problem with performing a full backup is that it takes longer to complete than any other backup method. If you need to back up large amounts of information (say 10GB or more), it may not be feasible to perform a full backup every night.

Incremental Backups

Incremental backups only copy to tape files that have been recently added or changed. This helps to expedite the backup process by only archiving files that have changed since the last backup was performed. The typical procedure is to perform a full backup once a week and incremental backups nightly. If you needed to rebuild your server, you would first restore the full backup, and then every incremental backup created since the full backup was performed.

The one flaw in incremental backups is that they do not track deletions. This means you could potentially end up trying to restore more data than you have capacity for. For example, consider Table 12.1. Let's say you have a 12GB drive on which you are storing file information. At the beginning of the day on Monday, you have 10GB of files saved on this disk. In the course of the day, you add 1GB of file information. At the end of the day, you perform a full backup, which writes 11GB of data to tape.

TABLE 12.1:   Storage Problems with Incremental Backups

Day	Storage Used	File Adds	File Deletes	Saved to Tape
Monday	10GB	1GB	0GB	11GB
Tuesday	11GB	1GB	3GB	1GB
Wednesday	9GB	2GB	0GB	2GB
Thursday	11GB	1GB	3GB	1GB

You start the day on Tuesday with 11GB out of the 12GB used for storage. In the course of the day, you add 1GB of files but delete 3GB in order to free up disk space. At the end of the day, you perform an incremental backup and save 1GB of new data to tape.

You start the day on Wednesday with 9GB out of 12GB used for storage. You add 2GB of files and perform an incremental backup, saving 2GB of data to disk. Thursday you save 1GB of data to disk but delete 3GB. You incrementally back up the 1GB of data to tape. At the end of the day on Thursday, you have 9GB out of 12GB used for storage.

Friday morning you walk in and find that someone has performed a bit of housekeeping, deleting all the files from your 12GB drive. You immediately spark up your backup software and restore the full backup performed on Monday. You then load the Tuesday incremental tape and restore that, as well. No sooner does the Tuesday tape finish the restore process than you get an "out of disk space" error from the server. Despite the fact that you still have two tapes with 3GB of data to restore, you have no free space left on your 12GB drive.

The capacity problem in this example is typical of incremental backups. For this reason, most system administrators perform differential backups instead of incremental.

Differential Backups

A *differential backup* differs from an incremental backup in that it backs up all files that have changed since a full backup was last performed. It does not back up files from the time of the last backup. For example, if you perform a full backup on Monday and then a differential backup every other night of the week, the differential backup performed on Thursday night will include all file changes from Tuesday through Thursday. This helps to reduce the chances of the capacity problem you saw in restoring incremental backups. While it is still possible to end up with more data on tape than drive capacity, this problem is far less likely to occur.

Another benefit of performing differentials over incrementals is that you only need to restore two tapes after a server crash. This not only expedites the process but also reduces the chance of failure. For example, look again at Table 12.1. For an incremental backup, you would need to restore four tapes in order to retrieve all of your data. If differentials were performed, you would only have to restore two. This reduces your chances of running across a bad tape.

TIP   Tape backups are fine for tape storage periods of a year or less. If you need to archive information for a longer period of time, consider using some form of optical media or storing your tapes in a climate-controlled environment.

Internet Backups

An alternative or addition to tape backups can be Internet backups. Part of a larger outsourcing movement, Internet backups are typically included in a larger service package of outsourced, remote management. Products such as Connected's Connected TLM will automatically and regularly copy encrypted data from an organization and store it offsite in a secure facility.

The advantages of Internet backups include

Low Administrative Overhead   Because local implementation and maintenance is usually limited to a small software package, Internet-based backups run seamlessly and without intervention or monitoring on behalf of the internal IT staff of an organization. Tapes do not need to be monitored for quality or deterioration, taken offsite, or secured.

Reduced Risk   Because data is always stored offsite, there is never a fear from an onsite disaster permanently destroying data. Because data is not being stored on tape, the risk of losing control of proprietary or confidential data through theft or negligence is more controlled; no one can simply walk off with a backup tape.

There are some significant potential disadvantages with Internet backups, such as:

Speed   Even with a T1 backups can take a significant amount of time. Although there is an increasing trend of greater bandwidth availability, this pales in comparison to the rate of growth of corporate data. As an example, it would take 2–3 hours to back up a 450MB file over a T1 link.

Recoverability   The time it takes to restore data from an Internet backup is greater than that of a local backup, and not just because of the slower speed of the connection. Requesting the backup service, locating the data, and initiating the process adds extra overhead to an already slow transfer rate.

Despite the disadvantages, some organizations are adding Internet backups as part of their overall data recovery solution, using the benefit of offsite storage as an additional guarantee against data loss.

Application Service Providers

Application Service Providers (ASPs) solve the problem of server failure and data loss in a unique way. All data services are outsourced, with only the end-user client application running locally within an organization. All data and services are hosted through the Internet. The ASP is then responsible for ensuring the availability and redundancy not only of the data, but also of the entire application itself.

Although this is still an emerging solution, it has become an ideal one for many smaller organizations that do not have the budget to maintain either an entire IT staff or hardware/software infrastructure. Larger organizations that use one or two primary lines of business applications can also benefit from entering into tight relationships with ASPs.

The drawbacks of utilizing an ASP become obvious. Should the Internet connection fail, no recourse is available for an organization to get access to their applications or to their data. Billing or service disputes with the ASP can mean that data is held hostage, and continued business is stopped until the dispute is resolved.

Also, service alternatives are restricted to a single company. Switching between ASPs can be difficult, and the portability of data can be impossible, leaving an organization without critical assets.

Server Recovery

While tape backups are fine for protecting file information, they are not a very efficient means of recovering a server. Let's assume that you suffer a complete server failure and you need to rebuild the server on a new hardware platform. The steps to perform this task would include

1. Installing the server operating system

2. Installing any required drivers

3. Installing any required service packs

4. Installing any required hotfixes or security patches

5. Installing the backup software

6. Installing any required patches to the backup software

7. Restoring your last full backup tape

8. Restoring any incremental or differential tapes as required

This is obviously a very time-consuming and labor-intensive process. It would be a minor miracle if this server could be put into operation in anything less than a full day, especially if it is used to store a lot of data.

The alternative is to use a package specifically designed for server recovery. Typically, these packages will create a small number of boot disks along with an image of the server. The boot disks allow the system to be started without an operating system. The server recovery software will then access the previously created image and restore all the data to the server. Once the server reboots, it is back in operation.

Some vendors make server recovery products that will integrate directly with a backup solution. For example, the ARCServe product line from Computer Associates includes both a backup program and a server recovery program. If you are using ARCServe for performing your nightly backups, it makes sense to also obtain a copy of the ARCServe disaster recovery option. This is because the recovery option is capable of reading the ARCServe backup tapes. This allows the recovery program to automatically restore your server to the configuration it had during the last full backup. If you purchased a server recovery program from another vendor, you would have to maintain the image file separately to insure that it stays up to date.

The only drawback to a server recovery solution is that it saves the entire system as an image. While this expedites both the backup and the restore process, it also means that you cannot access individual files. Even with a server recovery solution, you still need a regular backup solution to replace that occasional lost file.

Simulating Disasters

By now you should have quite a few ideas about how to make your network more fault resistant and how to recover from failures when they occur. It is not enough to simply implement a disaster solution; you must test and document your solutions, as well. Testing is the only way to insure that the recovery portion of your plan will actually work. Documenting the process is the only way to insure that the correct procedure will be followed when disaster does occur.

Nondestructive Testing

Nondestructive testing allows you to test your disaster prevention and recovery plans without affecting the normal workflow of your operation. This is the preferred method of testing: you do not want to cause a disaster while testing out a potential solution. For example, 9:00 AM on a Monday morning is not the best time to initially test out the hot-swappable capability in your server's drive array.

The Importance of Disaster Simulation

I cannot overemphasize the importance of testing your disaster recovery solution. I once consulted for a company that wanted to implement a facility-wide disaster recovery solution. In other words, the company wanted to insure that if the whole building went up in smoke, it could recover to a remote facility and be back in operation within 96 hours. It was expected that most of the data would be migrated to this other facility via backup tape, as the remote facility was also used for offsite tape storage.

Only when we simulated a disaster did we find one minor flaw. The DEC tape drive sitting on the main production server was incompatible with the tape drive on the replacement server. In fact, the tape drive on the production server was so old, we could not obtain a duplicate drive to read the tapes created by the production system. Had this been an actual failure, recovery would have taken a wee bit longer than 96 hours.

The solution was twofold:

- Replace the tape drive on the production server with an identical model to that of the replacement server.

- Document that any future tape drive upgrades must be duplicated on both systems.

There are a number of ways you can implement nondestructive testing. The most obvious is to use alternative hardware in order to simulate your disaster. For example, you could take another server that is identical to your production server and try to restore your backups to this alternative system.

Not everyone has the luxury of redundant components at their disposal in order to test their recovery plans. If you're not one of the lucky ones, try to plan your testing around plant shutdowns or extended holidays. Although the last thing anyone wants to do is to spend a long weekend simulating network outages, it is far preferable to experiencing an actual disaster. There is nothing worse than a server outage at 9:00 on a workday morning that has been caused by a part that must be special ordered. Simulating your disasters ahead of time helps to insure that you will be capable of a full recovery when an actual disaster does occur.

Document Your Procedures

The only thing worse than spending a long weekend simulating network outages is spending a long weekend simulating network outages and writing documentation.

As networking staff levels continue to drop, it is hard enough to keep up with the day-to-day firefighting, let alone simulate additional disasters and document your findings. We all like to think that we have minds like a steel trap and we will remember every last detail when an actual disaster does occur.

The fact is that the stress of trying to restore a lost service or deleted information can make the best of us a little sloppy. It is far easier to document the process when you can take your time and think things through with a clear head. When you are under pressure, it is far too easy to try a shortcut to get things done more quickly—only to find that your shortcut has made matters worse. Documenting the process when you are not under the gun to restore service allows you to write up a clear set of instructions to follow.

Octopus for Windows 2000 and Windows NT

Legato Octopus provides real-time data protection and server availability for Windows 2000 and Windows NT networks. It captures updates to selected files on source systems and forwards them across LANs and WANs to user-specified target systems. An up-to-date copy of every specified file is always available on the network in the event of data loss or hardware failure at the source location.

When the Octopus target detects that the Octopus source has gone offline, the Octopus target will stand in for it, responding to share requests. In other words, if you have a system named Brooke that is advertising a share named Music, the full Uniform Naming Convention (UNC) name would be \\Brooke\Music. If the server Brooke should happen to crash, the Octopus target would stand in, advertising the share \\Brooke\Music and responding to any file access requests to that share. From an end-user perspective, Brooke is still online and happy. Brooke will even still be listed under Network Neighborhood.

An Octopus Example

This creates some interesting possibilities for backing up your file and share information. For example, examine the network in Figure 12.4. This figure shows a main office network that is connected to two remote field offices. All locations run on a 24×7 schedule, meaning that all servers are expected to be online and responsive during all hours of the day. This, of course, leaves exactly zero downtime for nightly backups. While you could run a backup program during a business shift, the server being backed up would not exactly be considered "responsive." Backup programs eat up a lot of CPU time and disk I/O as they attempt to back up your files as quickly as possible. This would make server response time to user file queries extremely poor.

FIGURE 12.4:

Three 24×7 networks that require backing up and 100-percent availability

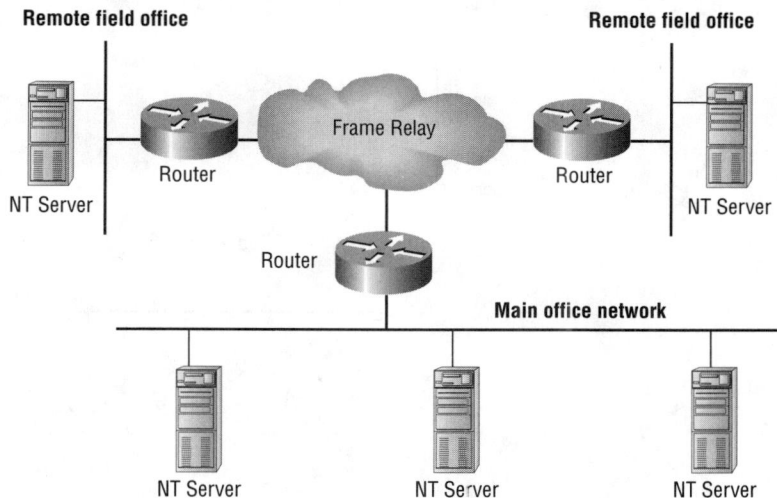

There is also a potential availability problem. Remember that all servers are expected to be available at all hours of the day. Since these three networks are connected through frame relay, each link into the frame relay cloud can be considered a potential single point of failure. We are also vulnerable to server crashes and power outages. If any of these disasters occurs at a specific site, the other two servers will no longer be able to access the server data.

One possible solution is to create a new node off the frame relay cloud, as shown in Figure 12.5. This network has another NT server installed, complete with tape drive caddie. This system is also configured as an Octopus target and all the other NT servers are configured as Octopus sources. This setup allows you to mirror shares from each of your production NT servers, in real time, to a remote location.

Octopus can be used to back up multiple servers to a remote location.

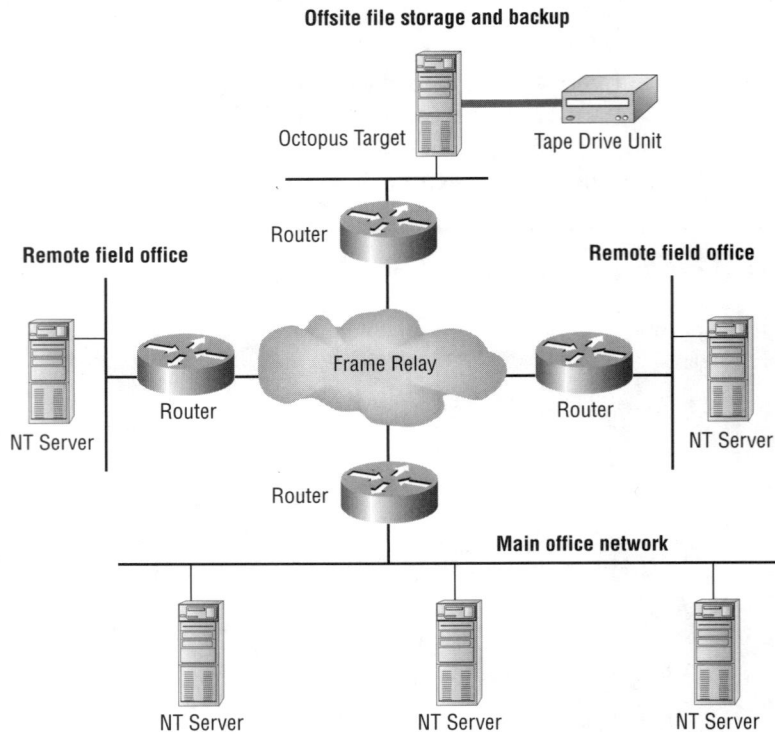

In this example, Octopus has helped to solve a number of problems. First, the data is being mirrored in real time, thus minimizing the effects of a disk crash. If your only disaster solution were to run a tape backup system off the server that contains the data, all changes made on that server since the time the backup process completed would be lost. Since Octopus mirrors the data immediately after a change, the amount of data that could be lost would be minimal. We have also resolved the problem of having a backup system tie up server resources, because the tape backups are now being performed offsite. This means that running a tape backup at any time of the day will have no effect on server responsiveness for your users. Bandwidth contention on the WAN should not be an issue because this back system sits on its own dedicated link.

We have also addressed the availability issue. If any one of your sites should go down, the data normally stored at that site would still be available. This is because the Octopus target would detect the server outage and step in for the missing system.

Any network still functioning would be able to access the mirrored copy of the shares from the target server. In short, an entire facility could be swallowed up by the earth, and from a share access perspective, you would never know the difference.

Installing Octopus

Octopus must be installed on every system that will act as an Octopus target or an Octopus source. To begin the installation process, insert the CD into an NT server and launch the Setup executable. This will produce the Site Select dialog box, shown in Figure 12.6, which prompts you to enter the Microsoft machine name of the system on which you wish to install Octopus. You can type in the server name (as I have done in the figure) or you can click the Get button in order to search the network for NT servers. The Network Sites section of the dialog box allows you to customize the amount of information that is reported during a Get. Once you have entered the correct server name, click Continue.

FIGURE 12.6:

The Octopus Site Select dialog box

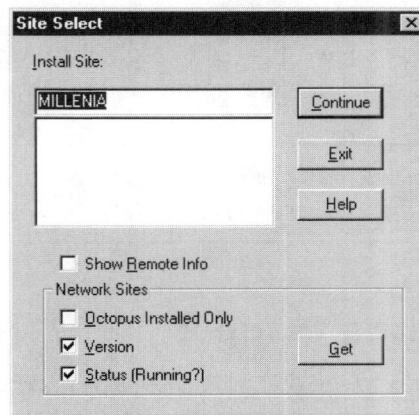

TIP   Using Get to search the network for NT servers is an extremely slow process. You should type in the server name directly whenever possible.

You are next prompted to select a path for the program and data files, as shown in Figure 12.7. These storage locations will only be used by the Octopus software, not your mirrored shares and files. Later, when you identify which shares you wish to mirror, you will be able to select a destination on the target system. Once you have entered the file paths, click the Continue button.

FIGURE 12.7:

The Install Paths dialog box

The final dialog box will prompt you for your license key. You need to visit the Qualix Group Web site (www.octopustech.com) or contact the Qualix Group directly with your product's serial number in order to generate a license key. Once you have entered this key, the program files will be copied to your hard drive and you will be prompted to reboot the NT server.

NOTE   Remember that you must install a copy of Octopus on every server that will be acting as either a source or a target.

Configuring Octopus

When you log on to the 2000 or NT server and launch the Octopus icon, you will be presented with the Octopus console shown in Figure 12.8. All share replication is configured from the Octopus source, so if you are not currently sitting at the source's console, you can connect to the source system by selecting Functions ➤ Attach from the console menu. This will produce the same Site Select dialog box you worked with during the product installation. You can either type in the name of the Octopus source NT server you wish to connect to or use the Get button to search the network for NT servers that have Octopus installed. Once you select the source you wish to work with, the console will become active for that system.

FIGURE 12.8:

The Octopus console screen

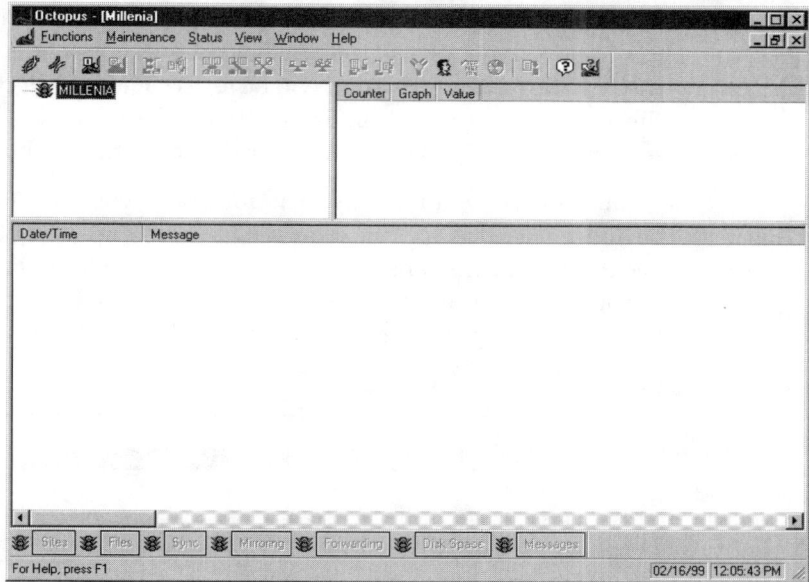

Next you need to add a specification that identifies which information you wish to replicate and to which source. Select Maintenance ➢ Add Specification ➢ Share from the Octopus console menu. This will produce the Mirror Shares screen shown in Figure 12.9. You should first configure your system to replicate all share information.

> **WARNING**
>
> Octopus can only mirror unique share names. This means that two Octopus sources sharing the same target must not have any shares with the same name. If they do, one of the shares will be disabled on the target system in order to avoid conflicts.

FIGURE 12.9:

Replicating shares with the Mirror Shares screen

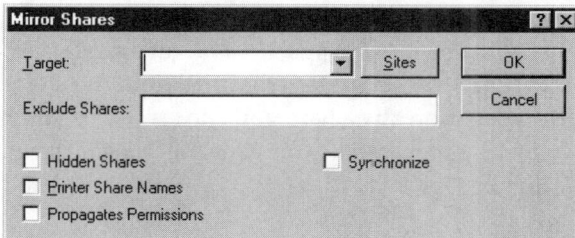

The Exclude Shares field allows you to specify certain shares that you do not wish to replicate. To save all shares except for the administrative shares, leave this option blank. The Target Site field allows you to identify the Octopus target where this share information will be saved. Finally, selecting the Synchronize check box will cause this information to be immediately replicated to the target system. When all of your options are set, click the OK button.

You also need to identify which directories you wish to replicate. This is done by adding another specification, as shown in Figure 12.10. You can only specify one directory path per specification. If you need to replicate multiple directories, simply create additional specifications. Checking the Include Subdirectories box will cause Octopus to replicate all directories located under the specified source directory.

FIGURE 12.10:

Replicating files with the Select Source screen

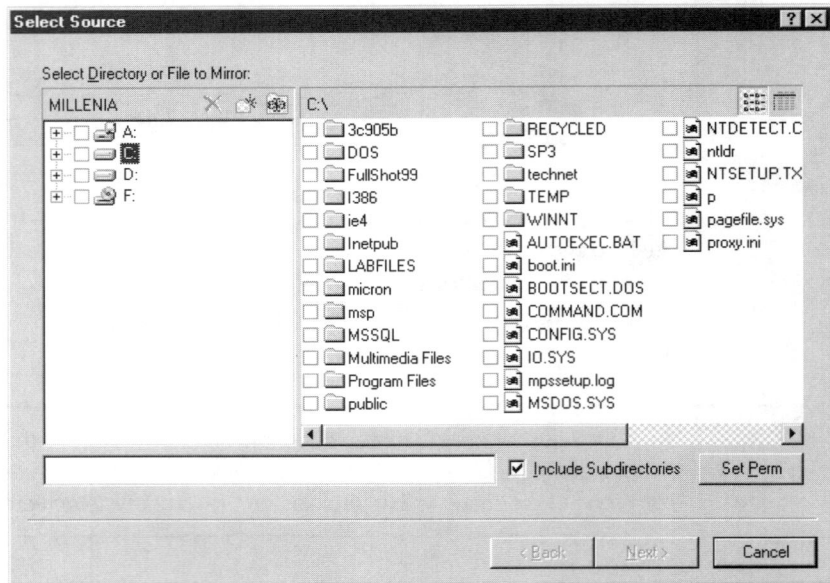

You also need to specify a target system and a target directory. This should be the same target system that will hold the shares, but you can locate the directory information anywhere you choose. Once you have finished, click OK and add shares as required. Your Octopus console screen should now appear similar to Figure 12.11.

FIGURE 12.11:

The Octopus console with directory specifications

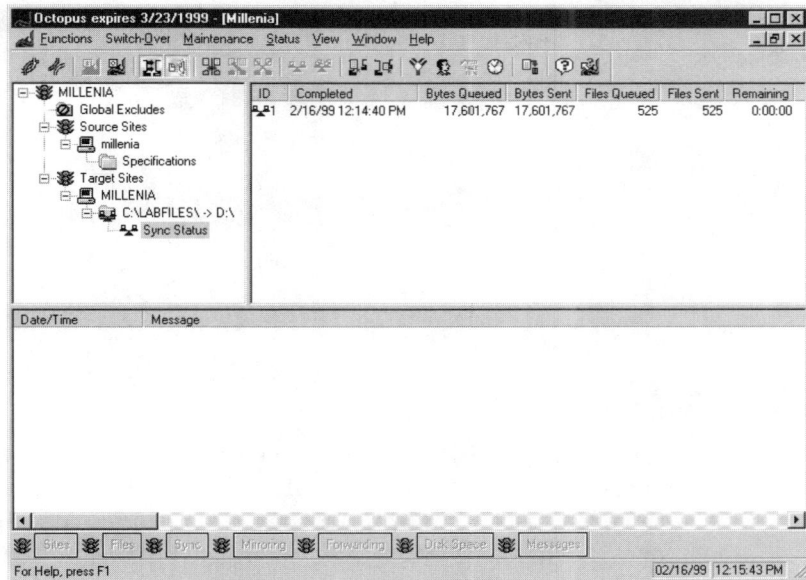

The left windows of the Octopus console show that the Octopus source is set up to replicate to the target system LAB31. The green traffic lights tell you that these systems are still able to communicate with each other. Under the target systems, you can see all the specifications you have configured. In this example, we are replicating the labfiles directory. The right pane shows the current replication status of the specification highlighted in the top pane. In Figure 12.11, you can see that Octopus found and replicated 525 files within the labfiles directory.

Now that your file information is being replicated, you need to tell your Octopus systems how they should respond when a failure occurs. This is done by selecting Switch-Over ➤ Source Options from the Octopus console screen. This displays the Source Options dialog box, as shown in Figure 12.12.

The Timeouts tab allows you to set up communication parameters between the source and the target system. The settings in Figure 12.12 tell the source to transmit a heartbeat every 15 seconds. The target is configured so as not to assume that the source is offline unless 60 seconds pass in which the target receives no heartbeat transmission. These settings help to insure that one or two lost packets do not trigger the fail over process.

FIGURE 12.12:

The Source Options window

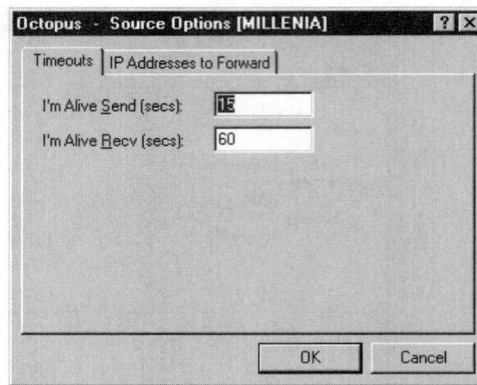

If you click the IP Addresses to Forward tab, you can specify whether the target system should assume the IP address of the source system when it fails. You can even specify multiple network cards. This insures that systems that use DNS or WINS to locate the source system will be directed to the target system after a failure.

> **NOTE**   Remember that the target can only assume the IP address of the source if the two systems are located on the same logical network.

The final tab, Cluster To, allows you to specify the target system. If you have created a specification (as we did earlier in this configuration), this value should be filled in for you and should not need to be changed. Once you have configured your Source Options, you can click OK to save your changes.

Finally, you need to configure the options for your target system. To do this, select Switch-Over ➤ Target Options from the Octopus console screen. This will produce the clustering Target Options dialog box, as shown in Figure 12.13.

The Options tab lets you configure how the target responds when it needs to stand in for another system. You can define executables or batch processes to run when a target stands in, as well as when the source returns to operation. You can also specify whether the target should replace its IP address with that of the source or whether it should use both addresses simultaneously. If you click the Take Over tab, you will see any current sources that this target has taken over.

FIGURE 12.13:

The Target Options window

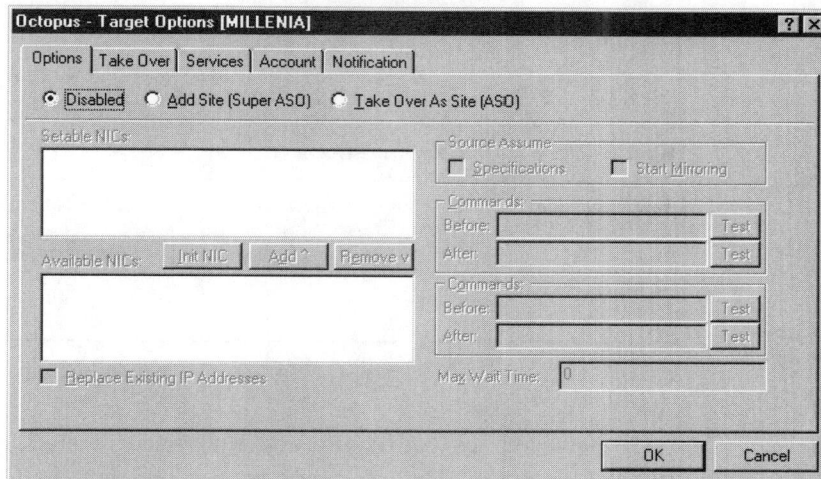

The Services tab allows you to specify which services should be run on the target system once a fail over has taken place. By default, all services on the target system are restarted when the target needs to stand in for a source. This allows the Octopus target to assume machine names and IP addresses as required. You can, however, specify that certain services are not to be restarted and even set certain services to be run only once a fail over takes place.

The Account tab is for entering authentication information. This is only required if the source is a stand-alone server and the target needs to provide a new System ID (SID). If the source is a PDC or a BDC, this information is not required.

The Notification tab allows you to specify who should be notified when the target needs to stand in for the source. An alert can be sent to an e-mail address, to an NT logon name as a pop-up message, or even to an entire domain.

Once you have finished configuring your target options, click OK to save your changes. Your source and target systems are now configured to provide server-level fault tolerance in case of disaster.

Testing Octopus

In order to show you how a fail over would look to the average end user, I have configured three Octopus systems for testing. Two of them (www and holnt200) are

Octopus sources, while the third (lab31) is set up as the Octopus target. Table 12.2 shows the share names being used by each system.

TABLE 12.2:   Share Names Used on the Octopus Test Systems

Host	Configuration	Shares
www	Octopus source	`hotfix`, `labfiles`
holnt200	Octopus source	`accounting`, `marketing`, `last_share`
lab31	Octopus target	`<<none>>`

Once the sources were configured, the systems were allowed to sit until replication was complete. The replication process took less than 10 minutes. Once this process was complete, lab31 had a copy of every share located on the two Octopus sources. A Network Neighborhood view of these shares is shown in Figure 12.14.

FIGURE 12.14:

Lab31 with a copy of all shares

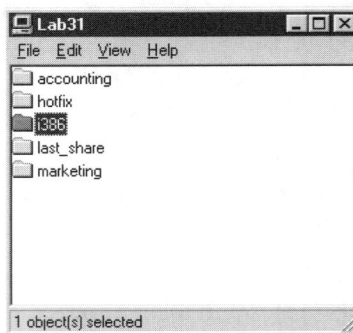

I then pulled the power plug (literally) on servers www and holnt200 and allowed one minute to elapse for the target to figure out that these two source systems were offline (this was the configured stand-in time). At just over a minute, a notification was sent to the domain administrator that these two source systems were no longer responding. Switch-Over ➢ Target Options ➢ Take Over from the Octopus console screen was then checked in order to see if lab31 had in fact stepped in for www and holnt200. As shown in Figure 12.15, this process had already been completed. The Added Names field shows us what source systems the target has stepped in for.

FIGURE 12.15:

The Target Options Take Over tab

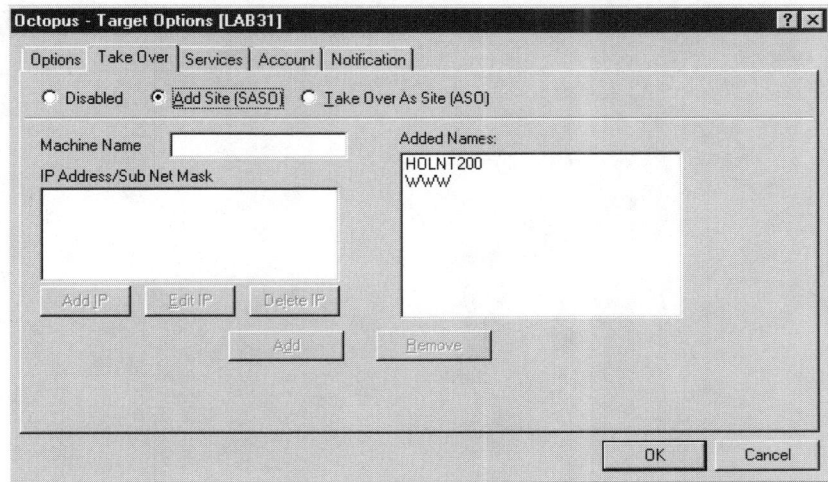

To confirm that the target had stepped in for the source systems, I launched Network Neighborhood from a Windows 95 test system. As shown in Figure 12.16, the client Hellsfarr was fooled into thinking that all the servers were still online and functional. Response time for the Neighborhood search was no longer than when the servers were actually online.

FIGURE 12.16:

Lab31 standing in for www and holnt200

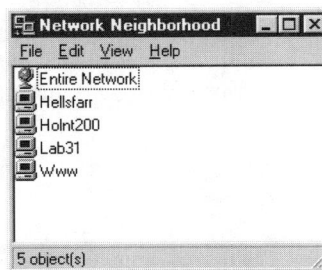

Finally, both www and holnt200 were checked to insure that the correct share names were associated with the correct systems. As shown in Figure 12.17, lab31 associated the correct share names with the system www. Opening up each share produced the expected list of files.

FIGURE 12.17:

Lab31 advertising the correct shares for www

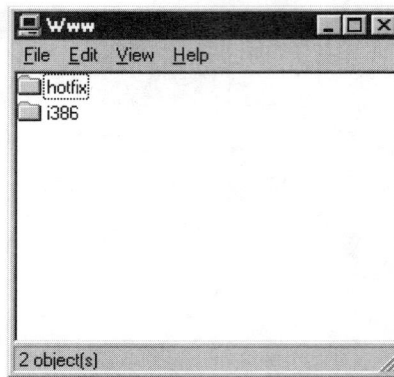

Summary

In this chapter, you saw what disaster prevention and disaster recovery options are available for protecting your network. We discussed network-based disasters and server-based disasters. We also discussed the importance of testing and documenting your disaster recovery procedures. Finally, you took a look at a product designed to provide redundant-server fault tolerance in an NT server environment.

In the next chapter we will discuss Novell NetWare, looking at what insecurities exist in the operating system and what you can do to lock it down.

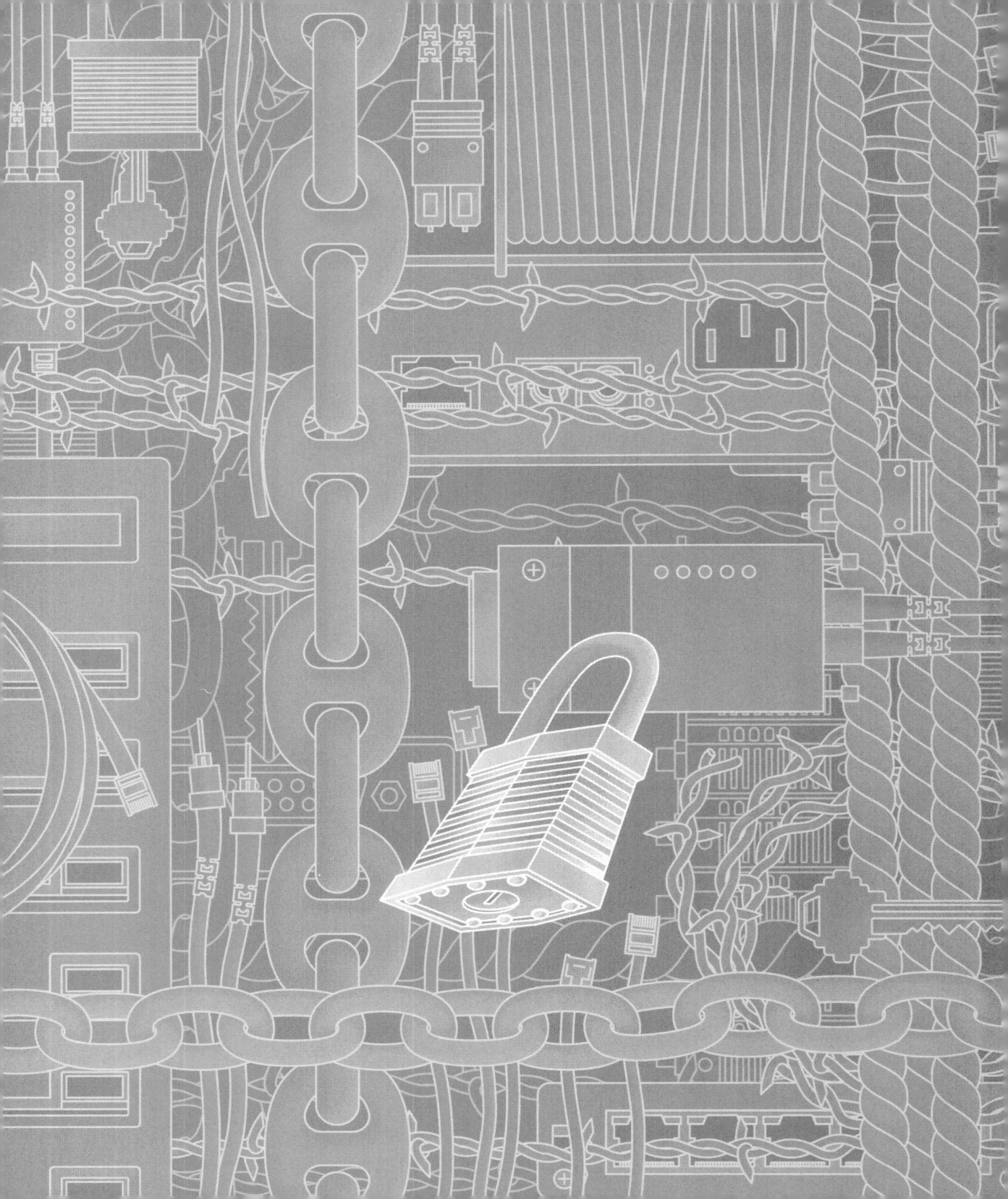

NetWare

## 13

Released in 1983, Novell NetWare has become the mainstay for a majority of networks for providing file and print services. As of version 4.11, Novell has included a number of IP applications that are designed to facilitate the construction of an internal Internet, known as an *intranet*. An intranet provides many of the connectivity options usually associated with the Internet (HTTP, FTP, and so on), except access to these resources is restricted to internal personnel only.

As of version 5.0 (the most current version is 5.1), NetWare includes native support for the IP protocol. While NetWare has supported client communication under IP for a while using NetWareIP, NetWareIP was simply an IP tunnel carrying IPX traffic. NetWare version 5.0 allows you to remove IPX from the picture entirely.

The default security posture of a NetWare server is pretty tight. The file system supports a detailed level of permissions, and users are provided very little access to system resources by default. There are still a few things you can do, however, to increase security.

NetWare Core OS

The core of NetWare is a 32-bit, multitasking, multithreaded kernel. Symmetrical multiprocessor support is included with the core OS. The kernel is designed to be modular. This means that applications and support drivers can be loaded and unloaded on the fly.

TIP   It also means that most of the changes can be made without rebooting the system. Need to change an IP address? This can be done with two commands at the command prompt and takes effect immediately. This can be a lifesaver for environments that cannot afford to reboot a server every time a change has been made.

As of version 5.0, NetWare includes support for Java. The Novell Java Virtual Machine (JVM) allows the server to support the execution of Java scripts. This lets you develop or run Java-based applications directly off the server.

NetWare versions up to 4.x were designed to run completely within the physical memory installed on the server. In other words, swap space or virtual memory was not supported. This means that the total memory available to the operating system is what was physically installed on the server.

NOTE   NetWare version 5.0 added support for virtual memory.

Memory never goes to waste on a NetWare server. Any memory that remains after the core OS, supporting applications, and drivers have been loaded goes to caching frequently accessed files. The more available memory, the more files can be cached. This means that when a user requests a commonly used file, the server can access the information from faster memory instead of disk. When the operating system requires additional memory, it takes that memory from the file-caching pool.

Novell has also improved recovery from critical system errors, called *abnormal ends* or ABENDs. In previous versions of NetWare, an ABEND would cause a server to stop all processing. The only forms of recovery were to restart the server through the online debugger or to hit the power switch.

NetWare also has the ability to restart the server after a predetermined period of time if an ABEND occurs. You can even select what kind of an ABEND causes a server to restart. For example, you can set the server to simply recover from application ABENDs but to perform a system restart if the failure mode is hardware related.

NetWare includes a *garbage collection* setting. While this will not stop by your cubicle and empty your trash, it can recover server memory from unloaded processes.

With earlier versions of NetWare, if a poorly coded application was unloaded from memory, the application might not have returned all the memory it was using to the free memory pool. This is a common problem with applications running on any operating system. The garbage collection process scans for these memory areas that are no longer in use. When it finds them, the pointers are deleted and the space is returned to the free memory pool for use by other applications.

New features have been added to insure that applications do not tie up the processor(s) for an excessive amount of time. NetWare includes a *relinquish control alert* setting that produces an error message when an application refuses to play fair and share the available CPU cycles. There is also a *CPU hog timeout* setting, which allows the system to automatically kill any process monopolizing all of the server's processor time.

C2 Certification

NetWare is the only distributed network operating system to receive C2 certification as a trusted network component from the National Computer Security Center (NCSC). While NT is also C2 certified, at the time of this writing it is not approved as a trusted network, only as an operating system. Even then, it is only certified as a stand-alone workstation with no removable media or network connection. NetWare is also being evaluated for Electronic Data's E2 rating. E2 is the European counterpart to C2. The specifications of each are very similar.

C2 Specifications

In order to be approved as a C2 trusted network component by the NCSC, a product is expected to meet the following specifications:

- The system must be able to uniquely identify every system user.
- The system must be able to selectively track user logons and object changes.
- The system must be able to maintain an audit log.
- The system's audit log must identify the source of all entries (which remote system, terminal, or server console).
- The system administrator must be able to restrict access to the audit log.
- The system must have a method of setting individual and group access control.
- The system administrator must have a method of limiting the propagation of access control rights.
- The system administrator must have a method of validating that the system is functioning correctly.
- The system must include a manual describing all security features.
- The security features must be tested by the NCSC and found to have no obvious flaws.

It is the final specification (no obvious flaws) that seems to trip up most systems submitted for C2 trusted network approval. C2 certification does not guarantee that your system will be impenetrable. It does, however, tell you that the product has been designed with security in mind and that these security precautions have been accepted by a third-party government agency.

NetWare Directory Services

For access control, NetWare uses NetWare Directory Services (NDS), which provides a hierarchical approach to assigning and managing network access rights. This allows an entire networking environment to be managed through a single console. NDS also provides an extremely detailed level of control over user access to network resources. An organization's NDS structure is commonly referred to as the *NDS tree*.

The structure of NDS is similar to the directory structure on a hard drive. Subdirectories known as *Organizational Units* (OU), or *containers*, can be defined off the root. Access rights can be set on each of the containers so that users only have access to the resources they need. You can define more containers to organize user access even further.

> **NOTE**   It is even possible to assign subadministrators who only have supervisor-type privileges for a small portion of the tree. NDS scales extremely well because it allows a large organization to have administrators who can only manage the resources for their specific groups, while allowing full management rights to the people responsible for the entire network. Rights are assigned on a trickle-down basis, meaning a user will assume rights to all subcontainers unless you specifically set the permissions otherwise.

Network access is also centralized. When a user logs in to the network, she authenticates to the entire NDS tree, not just a specific server or portion of the tree. This means that she automatically receives access to all network resources that have been assigned to her—even if that resource exists on a remote portion of the tree (such as a printer in a remote field office).

NDS Design

For an example of how an NDS tree may be configured, take a look at Figure 13.1. The organization Cam has been broken up into five geographic locations: Albuquerque, Boise, Los Angeles, Salt Lake City, and Tampa. Any user assigned access to the geographic containers can be granted access privileges to all resources at that location. If each location has its own IS staff, this is where you would create IS staff accounts. By defining these administrators within the geographic containers, you can give them access to all on-site resources while insuring that they have no access to resources at other locations. Further, you could create a small number of user accounts directly under the Cam container, which would allow these administrators to manage the entire tree.

FIGURE 13.1:

An example NDS tree

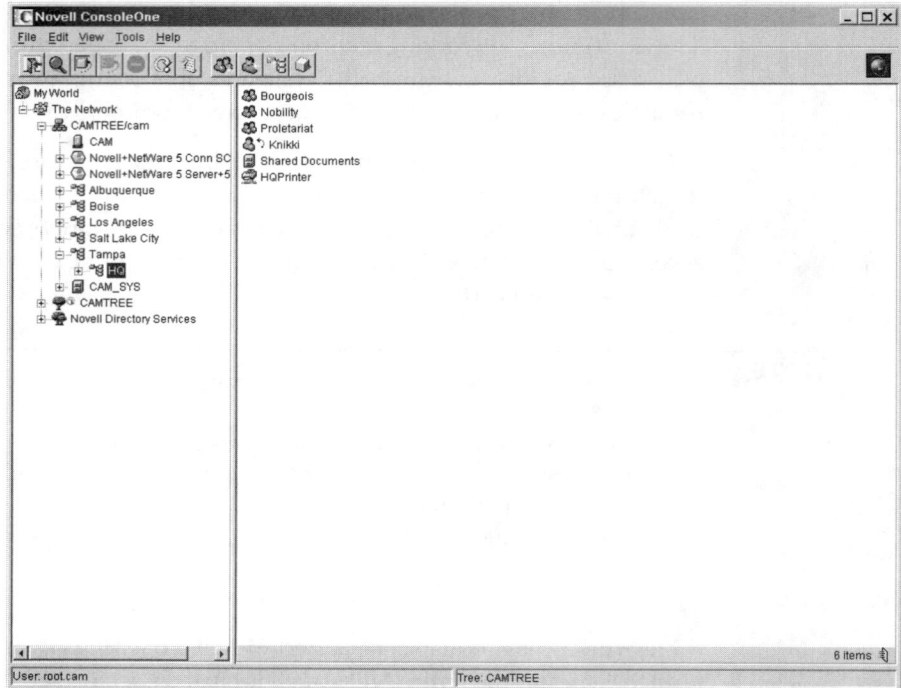

At each geographic location, you could define further containers in order to structure your resources by department. This allows you to organize your network resources beyond geographic location. For example, look at the HQ container (underneath the Tampa organization) in Figure 13.1. Within the HQ container, we have defined a number of user groups as well as the printer, file, and application resources these user groups will need access to. This simplifies security management: you can organize network objects based on their access requirements.

NDS can even deal with specialized cases in which users need access to multiple containers within the tree. For example, let's say that Knikki is the accountant of Cam, Inc., and so requires access to all financial data. You do not wish to grant Knikki access to the entire NDS tree, however, because Knikki has been known to poke around where she does not belong.

In Knikki's case, you could simply create a user object for her under one of the containers (which has been done under Salt Lake City, but is not shown in the figure), then alias her user object within the other containers where she requires access. The Knikki object in Figure 13.1 is simply an alias that points back to the original. This allows you to make access control changes and have them linked to all of the Knikki objects. Using aliased objects allows you to give Knikki access to the resources she needs without giving her access to the entire tree.

Account Management

Starting with NetWare 5.0, user accounts are managed using ConsoleOne, a Java-based utility. NetWare 4.x used NetWare Administrator (nwadmin), and NetWare 3.x used syscon. Because ConsoleOne can run the server itself, it is no longer necessary to have a separate workstation to perform basic account management.

As a result, account management could not be easier. In order to view all security settings for a specific user, simply right-click the user object and select Details. This pulls up a user information screen similar to the one shown in Figure 13.2. As you can see, this single console lets you administer all aspects of this user account, including password restrictions, file access rights, and even the user's logon script. In the next few sections, we will look at some of the security administration you can perform through this console.

FIGURE 13.2:

Managing the user Comodus with ConsoleOne

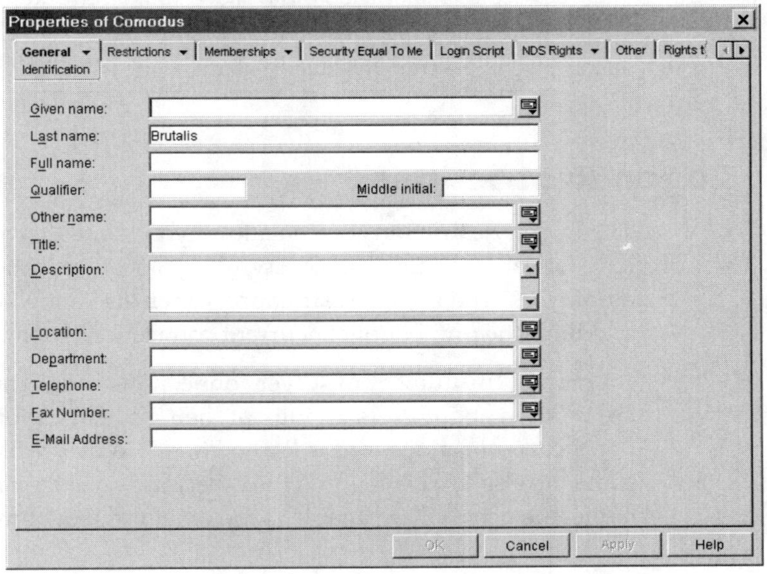

Identification

The Identification button allows you to record information about a user beyond his or her logon name. This information can include

- Full name

- Location

- Department

- Phone number

- Descriptive information, such as the user's direct supervisor

While the ability to record detailed user information may not seem like a security feature on the surface, it can be invaluable if you are tracking down a problem.

Let's say you are reviewing your system and you see some suspicious activity coming from the user account jsmith. It appears that jsmith may be trying to gain access to the payroll database. Using ConsoleOne, you quickly look up jsmith's account information and find out that he reports to Toby Miller at extension 1379. Armed with this information, you quickly give Toby a call to attempt to catch jsmith in the act.

> **TIP** When performing a system audit, it is extremely beneficial to have access to detailed user information. This allows you to correlate logon activity and audit log entries with actual users. In a large environment, it is extremely unlikely that a system administrator will have every user's logon name committed to memory.

Logon Restrictions

The Logon Restrictions button allows you to assign a predetermined expiration date for each account. This is useful if your organization works with temporary employees. The Logon Restrictions screen also allows you to disable an account and limit the number of concurrent connections each user may have.

Limiting the number of server connections a user can have is beneficial if you are worried about users giving out their authentication credentials. If the number of concurrent connections is limited to one, a user will be far less likely to let someone else use his logon. This is because once the other user logs on under his name, the user will be unable to log on at the same time.

Limiting concurrent connections is also a good way to identify stolen accounts. If a user attempts a logon and receives a message that he is logged on from another system, he can inform the administrator, who can then track down the potential attacker.

Password Restrictions

The Password Restrictions button allows you to define password criteria for each user. Here is a list of the parameters you can set on this screen:

- Allow users to change their own passwords.
- Define whether the account is required to use a password.
- Define a minimum number of characters for the password.
- Require that this account always use a unique password.
- Define how often the password must be changed.
- Define the number of incorrect logon attempts before the account becomes locked.
- Change the account's current password.

TIP　Password restrictions under NDS are extremely flexible: you can define parameters on a user-by-user basis. For example, you could require regular users to use a password of at least six characters. Additionally, you could require network administrator accounts to use a 12-character password in order to make these high-level accounts more difficult to crack.

Login Time Restrictions

The Login Time Restrictions screen allows the system administrator to define when a particular user is allowed to authenticate to the NDS tree. Restrictions can be set by the time of day and/or day of the week.

NOTE　NDS does not account for holidays.

For example, in Figure 13.3 the system administrator has limited when the user Comodus can gain access to network resources. Comodus is only allowed to log on from 7:00 AM to 6:00 PM Monday through Friday and from 8:00 AM to noon on Saturdays. During any other time period, Comodus will not be allowed to log on to the system. If he is already authenticated when the time period expires, he will receive a five-minute warning and then be disconnected from the system.

FIGURE 13.3:

The Login Time Restrictions screen

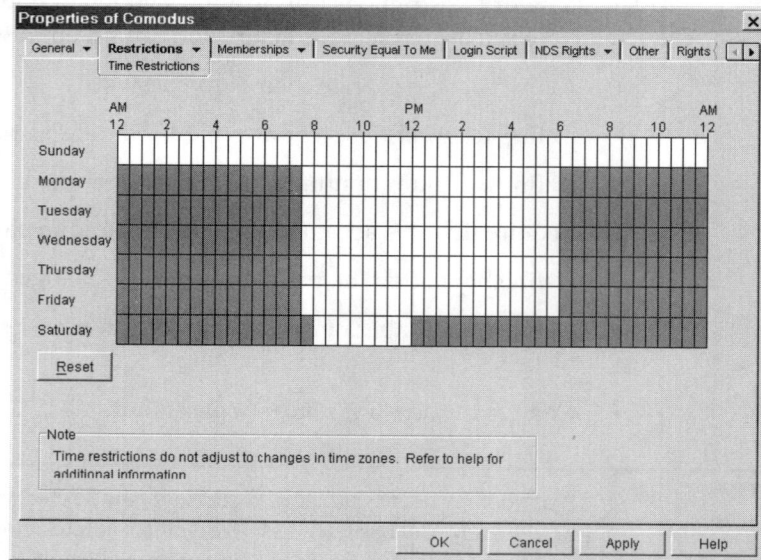

Time restrictions are an excellent way to kick users off a system before running a backup. A user who remains logged on to the system may also have files open. Backup programs are typically unable to back up open files because they need exclusive access to the file information in order to insure a proper backup. By using time restrictions, you can disconnect your users from the network before launching your backup program.

Network Address Restriction

The Network Address Restriction button allows the NDS administrator to identify which systems a user may use when authenticating with the NDS tree. As shown in Figure 13.4, the administrator is allowed to restrict a user by multiple network protocols. This can insure that users are only allowed to gain access to network resources from their assigned workstations.

FIGURE 13.4:

FIGURE 13.4:

The Network Address
Restriction screen

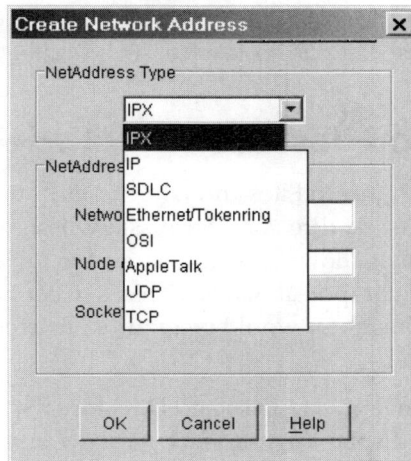

For example, let's say that you have an application that runs on a dedicated system and needs access to certain files on the server. Let's also assume that you would like to have this one account log on without a password, so that if the system is power cycled it will immediately be able to gain access to network resources without waiting at the password prompt.

An account without a password is obviously a security hazard. You can, however, take precautions to insure that this account remains relatively secure. By defining a network address restriction for this account that only allows a logon to be performed from this dedicated system, the account will remain secure—provided that the workstation remains physically secure. This prevents someone from using the account to log on from another location on the network.

Intruder Lockout

The Intruder Lockout button displays a screen that shows statistics regarding failed logon attempts. The system administrator is allowed to view whether the account has been locked out due to too many incorrect password attempts. The administrator can also see how many bad password attempts took place, as well as the host address of the system used. This is extremely valuable information if you are attempting to track an intruder.

NOTE   Failed logon attempts can also be recorded to the audit log.

Even if an account does not become locked, the Intruder Lockout screen displays the number of failed attempts, as well as the amount of time left before the failure count is set to zero.

Rights to Files and Directories

The Rights to Files and Directories button allows the NDS administrator to view all file and directory permissions assigned to a particular user. This is a powerful tool that allows an administrator to review all of a user's assigned file access rights in one graphical display. This is in contrast to Windows NT Explorer, where an administrator would be required to check every directory, on every server, one at a time.

The Rights to Files and Directories screen is shown in Figure 13.5. The top window displays the server volumes where access has been granted. The center window displays the directories on this volume where the user has been granted access. Finally, the bottom of the screen shows the specific rights that have been granted to this user for the highlighted directory. A description of each of the NetWare directory rights is shown in Table 13.1.

T A B L E 1 3 . 1 :   Directory Rights

Right	Description
Supervisor	Provides a combination of all other access rights
Read	Allows a user to view the contents of or execute a file
Write	Allows a user to view and modify the contents of a file
Create	Allows a user to create new files or salvage files that have been deleted
Erase	Allows a user to delete or overwrite a file
Modify	Allows a user to rename a file or change its attributes
File Scan	Allows a user to view the contents of a directory without being able to view the contents of any of the files saved within it
Access Control	Allows a user to change trustee assignments and grant access rights to other users

FIGURE 13.5:

The Rights to Files and Directories screen

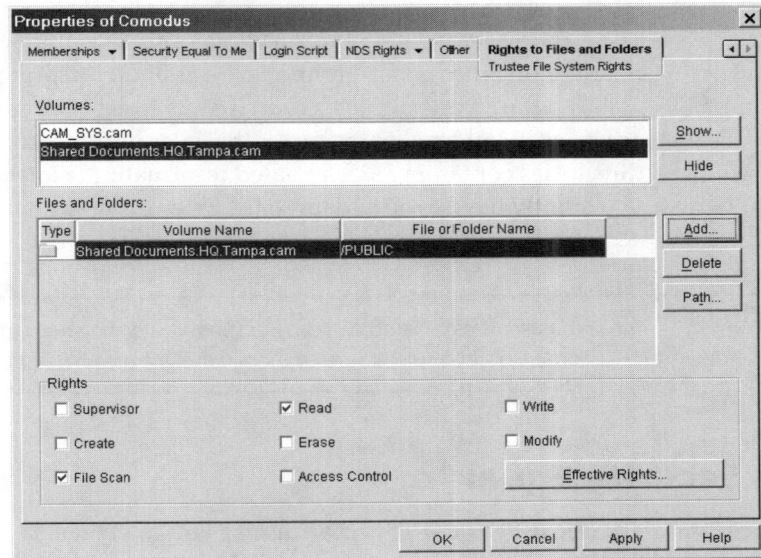

> **NOTE**   Assigning only the Create right would allow users to copy files to a directory but not view or modify those files once they get there.

> **WARNING**   The Supervisor and the Access Control rights are the ones you need to be the most careful with. The Supervisor right not only assigns full permissions, but it cannot be filtered out from subdirectories. The Access Control right allows a user to grant permissions that he himself does not even have.

Let's say you gave the user Charlie File Scan and Access Control rights to a specific directory. Charlie could then use the Access Control right to grant Roscoe Read, Write, and Erase rights to this directory—even though Charlie does not have these permissions himself. In fact, Charlie could grant Roscoe the Access Control right so that Roscoe could then turn around and give Charlie a full set of permissions. The only exception is the Supervisor right, which can only be granted by an administrator equivalent.

Group Membership

The Group Membership button allows you to define which groups this user is a member of. Since access rights can be assigned to groups, it is usually easier to assign permissions to each group first, then add the users who need this level of access as members. For example, the Sales group could be assigned access to all directories containing sales-related information. Now when you create new users, you simply have to add them to the Sales group rather than assigning specific access rights to each required directory.

TIP	If a user is associated with any groups, you will need to review the group's rights in order to get a full picture of the file areas a user has access to.

Security Equal To

The Security Equal To button allows you to view and configure all access rights that have been inherited from another user or group. This screen gives the NDS administrator a central location where all security equivalencies can be viewed.

For example, it is a common practice to make all support staff security equivalent to the NDS Admin. This gives the support staff full control of all NDS objects. While Admin equivalency needs to be reviewed on a per-user basis, having support staff use a different account from the administrator account is an excellent practice. Doing so provides accountability within the audit logs. If all support personnel are using the Admin account to make changes, you have no traceability. By giving support staff their own accounts, you are able to go back through the logs in order to see who has made specific changes.

You should provide support personnel with two accounts: one for making administrative-level changes and the other for performing daily activities. It is far too easy for an administrator to become lax when working on a system. Unfortunately, this laxity can lead to mistakes. Users who have full system access can inadvertently cause major damage ("I deleted all files on the F: drive? Isn't it F for Floppy?").

By using an alternative account for performing administrative functions, the support person has an opportunity to wake up and focus a little more closely on the task at hand. After completing the required task, support personnel can log back off and use their regular user accounts.

File System

As you saw in the last section, most file system access is controlled through nwadmn95. This is to insure that the NDS administrator can quickly identify the access rights that have been granted to each user. NetWare does, however, provide an additional utility called Filer, which allows the administrator to control the flow of access rights recursively through directories. The flow of access rights is controlled using the *inherited rights mask*.

Inherited Rights Mask

File system access can be tuned down to the file level. Normally, file access rights trickle down through directories. This means that if a user is given read access to directories at a certain level, that user will also have read access to any subsequent subdirectories. NetWare provides an inherited rights mask that allows these rights to be masked out so that they will not trickle down to included subdirectories. This allows the system administrator to assign the precise rights required at any directory level.

For example, examine the directory structure in Figure 13.6. We have a directory named Shared located off the root of the CAM_SYS volume. Within the Shared directory are a number of subdirectories that have been broken up by department. We wish to grant users the File Scan right within the Shared directory in order to allow them to see any subdirectories they have access to. We do not, however, want to grant users File Scan rights to all of the subsequent subdirectories located under Shared.

FIGURE 13.6:

An example directory structure

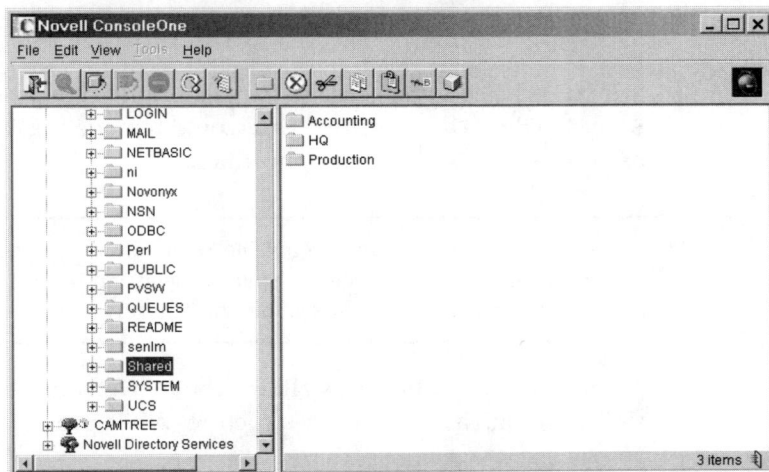

By default, any user who is granted File Scan rights to the Shared directory will automatically receive File Scan rights to the Sales and Marketing directories. This is where the inherited rights mask becomes useful: it allows you to prevent the File Scan right from trickling down to each subdirectory. By filtering out the File Scan right, you can prevent users from seeing what files are located in any directory for which they have not explicitly been granted permissions.

To create an inherited rights mask, right-click on the directory within ConsoleOne, select Properties, then the Inherited Rights Filter tab of the Properties window as seen in Figure 13.7.

FIGURE 13.7:

Navigating directories
with Filer

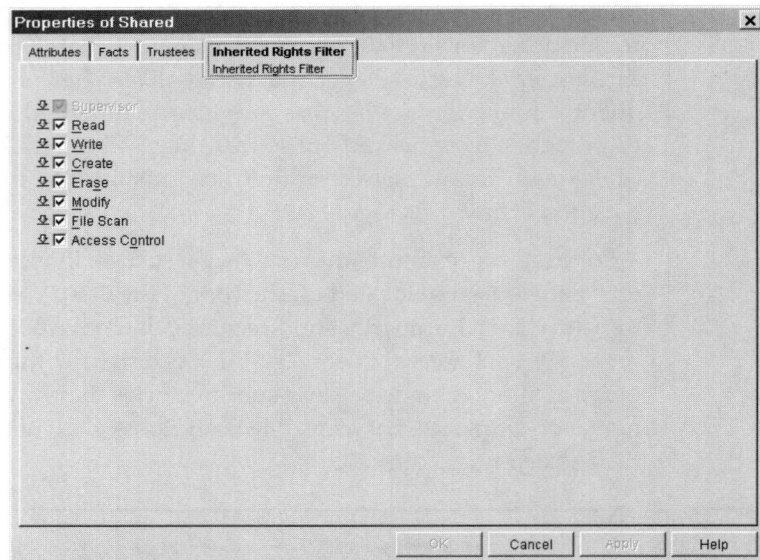

If you wished to prevent the File Scan right from passing through from the Shared to the Sales directory, you would remove the File Scan right from the Sales directory's inherited rights filter.

NOTE   Since you have prevented the File Scan right from propagating down any sub-directories, you will need to specifically assign this right to all users whom you wish to be able to see files within this directory.

The inherited rights mask allows you to overcome the propagation of access rights through a subdirectory structure. While propagation is usually desired, there are times when the administrator needs more granular control in order to specifically assign access rights to every directory. The inherited rights mask gives the administrator this ability.

Logging and Auditing

There are several types of log that can be generated with NetWare server. Of most interest for security is the *console log*, which is created with the utility console.nlm. This utility can create a log that records all console activity and error messages. The second type of log is the audit log. This log is created using the *Auditcon* utility.

> **NOTE** A log of all ABENDS is kept in **abend.log** in the SYSTEM directory on a NetWare server. This log can be useful in determining if a hacker is attempting a DoS (Denial of Service) attack by forcing your system to crash.

Auditcon

NetWare includes Auditcon, Novell's system auditing utility. Auditcon allows the system administrator, or someone designated by the system administrator, to monitor server events. Events range from user logons to password changes to specific file access. Over 70 events can be monitored. The benefit of Auditcon's being a separate utility from nwadmn95 is that the administrator can designate a regular user to monitor events.

> **TIP** Auditcon is an excellent solution for large organizations where the person administering the network is not the same person who is monitoring security. An auditor can be designated to monitor system events without being given any other type of administration privilege.

By launching Auditcon and selecting Audit Directory Services, you are allowed to audit the tree based on specific events or a user's logon name. Figure 13.8 shows the configuration screen for selecting which NDS events you wish to monitor. For example, you could create a log entry every time a new member is added to a group or whenever the security equivalency for an object is changed.

FIGURE 13.8:

The Auditcon Audit by DS Events screen

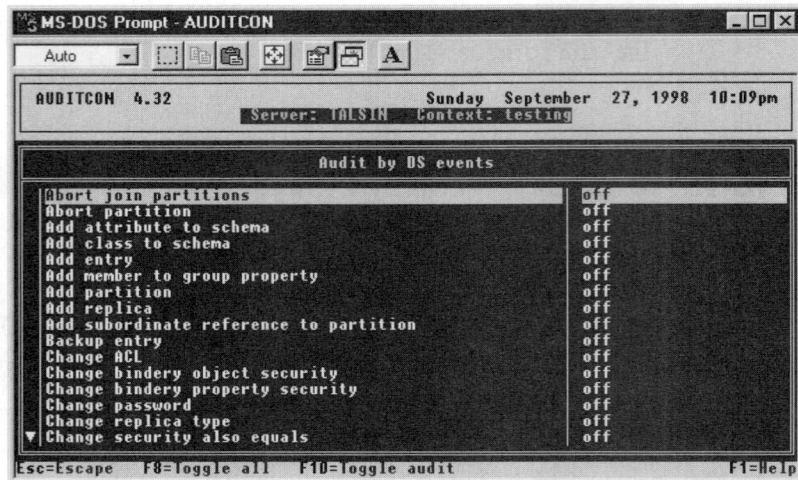

The ability to track a specific user is also very important. For example, you may want to log all activities performed by your administrator-level accounts. This can help you to identify when access privileges are being abused or when a high-level account has been compromised.

Using Auditcon, you can even choose to audit specific file system activities. For example, in Figure 13.9 we have enabled auditing of directory deletions. You could choose to track directory deletions for a specific user or globally for everyone.

FIGURE 13.9:

Auditcon allows you to audit specific file events.

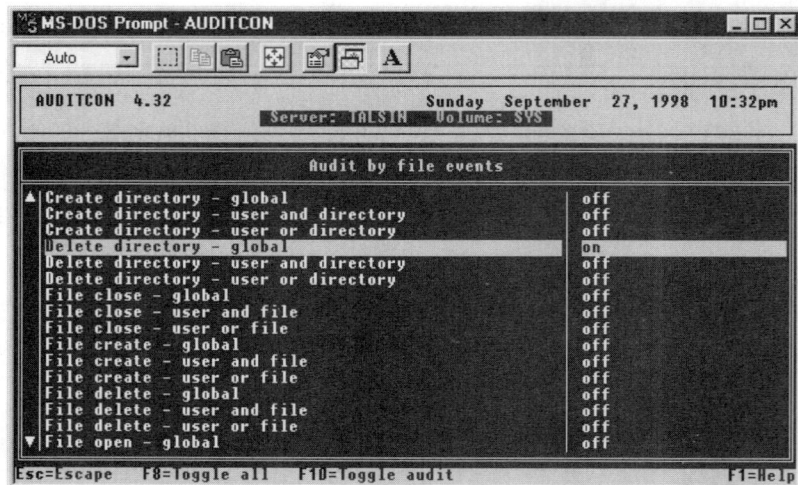

TIP

Tracking file system activities can be extremely useful when you wish to document improper access to sensitive files.

Network Security

NetWare includes a number of methods for securing network communications. Packet signature provides a secure method for communicating with a NetWare server, while the Filtcfg utility allows the system administrator to perform basic packet filtering. Starting with NetWare 5.0, Novell has included additional technologies including Public Key Infrastructure Service (PKIS), the integration of LDAP and SSL into NDS, the Novell International Cryptographic Infrastructure (NICI), and the Novell Modular Authentication Service (NMAS).

Packet Signature

There is a type of system attack, which has been around for a number of years, known as *connection hijacking*. Connection hijacking is when someone on the network sends information to a server and pretends that the data is actually coming from an administrator who is currently logged in. This allows the attacker to send commands to the server that the server will accept, thinking they are coming from the system administrator.

Packet signature is useful in deterring this type of attack. Packet signature requires both the server and the workstation to sign each frame using a shared secret prior to transmission. The signature is determined dynamically and changes from frame to frame. The server will only accept commands from a station that is properly signing frames.

In practice, if an attacker sends commands to the server pretending to be the administrator, the server will reject and log all frames received without a valid signature. Since the correct signature is changing constantly, it is extremely difficult for an attacker to determine what to use for a signature. This feature helps to protect an administrator's connection during daily maintenance.

NOTE

Packet signature can also be enabled for all users.

Setting Packet Signature

Packet signature can be configured to four different security levels. These settings must be configured on both the workstation and the server. Table 13.2 describes each of the available packet signature levels.

TABLE 13.2:   Packet Signature Levels

Signature Level	Description
0	Do not use packet signature.
1	Use packet signature only if the remote system requires it.
2	Use packet signature if the remote system supports it, but signing is not required.
3	Do not communicate with remote systems that do not support packet signature.

By default, NetWare clients and servers are configured to use a packet signature level of 1 (sign only when required). This means that in environments where the default settings have not been changed, packet signature is not being used.

The Nomad Mobile Research Centre (NMRC) has discovered a spoofing vulnerability with packet signature similar to NT's C2MYAZZ. The exploit allows an attacker to fool a workstation and a server into not using packet signature. This exploit is effective at every signature level except for 3. Needless to say, you should insure that all workstations used by your network administrators have a packet signature level of three.

NOTE   The NMRC has documented a number of vulnerabilities with Novell products. You can access its Web site at www.nmrc.org.

Set packet signature to level three on the server by entering the following at the console

```
SET NCP Packet Signature Option=3
```

Set packet signature on the client to level three by right-clicking on the small red N in the System Tray (assuming the client is Windows-based) and selecting Novell Client Properties, then Advanced Settings, then Signature Level, and finally 3.

Filtcfg

The Filtcfg utility allows a NetWare server to act as a static packet filter. You can use packet filtering to control traffic flowing to and from the server. If you have installed two or more network cards, you can also control traffic between different network segments. Filtcfg supports the filtering of IP, IPX, and AppleTalk traffic.

In order to filter traffic, you must enable filtering support through the Inetcfg utility for each protocol you wish to filter. Once you have enabled support, you can initialize the Filtcfg utility by loading it at the server console. This produces the Filter Configuration menu screen shown in Figure 13.10. From this screen you can choose the protocol you wish to filter.

FIGURE 13.10:

The Filter Configuration menu

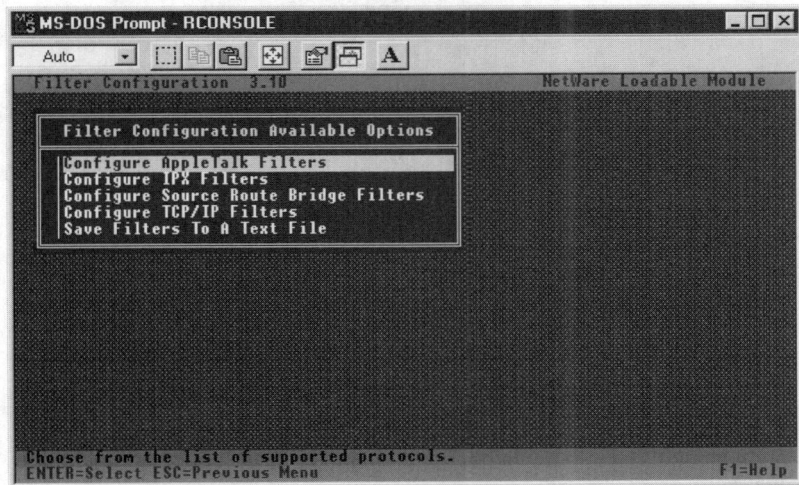

If you select the TCP/IP option, you are first prompted to identify any routing protocols you wish to filter. You are also prompted for the direction of the filter. For example, you can choose to filter out certain outgoing or incoming RIP updates. The difference is whether you want the server itself to receive these routing updates. An incoming filter will drop the update before it is received by the server. An outgoing filter will allow the route to be propagated to the server itself, but the server will not propagate the route information through any of its other network cards.

In addition to filtering routing information, you can also perform static packet filtering. The Packet Forwarding Filters screen is shown in Figure 13.11. Filtcfg provides two methods of defining packet filters. You can specify the packets you wish to permit (the default setting), or you can specify the packets you wish to deny. In either case, you are allowed to define exceptions.

FIGURE 13.11:

The Packet Forwarding
Filters screen

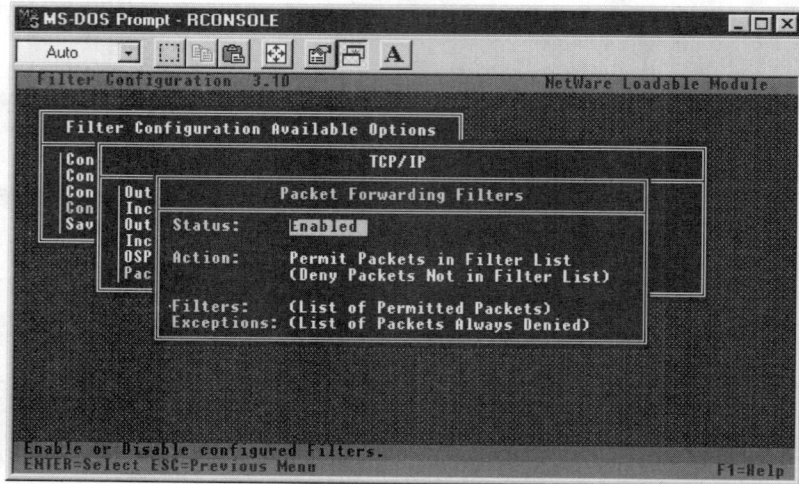

For example, you could choose to configure the packets you wish to permit and specify that all traffic be allowed between the subnets 192.168.1.0 and 192.168.2.0. You could also define an exception that globally denies FTP connection requests in both directions. The combination of filters allows the system administrator to create a very complex access control policy.

If you highlight the Filters option in the Packet Forwarding Filters screen and press Enter, you are presented with a list of currently installed filters. Pressing the Insert key allows you to configure additional filter rules. The Define Filter screen is shown in Figure 13.12.

The Source Interface option lets you associate a filter rule with a specific network card. This is useful when you wish to define spoofing filters. For example, let's assume that you have an internal network address of 192.168.1.0, which is connected to the NetWare server via a 3COM card. Let's also assume that you have an SMC card that connects to a demilitarized zone. In order to prevent spoofed packets, you could define a filter rule stating that all traffic received by the SMC interface with an IP source address of 192.168.1.0 should be dropped.

FIGURE 13.12:

The Define Filter screen

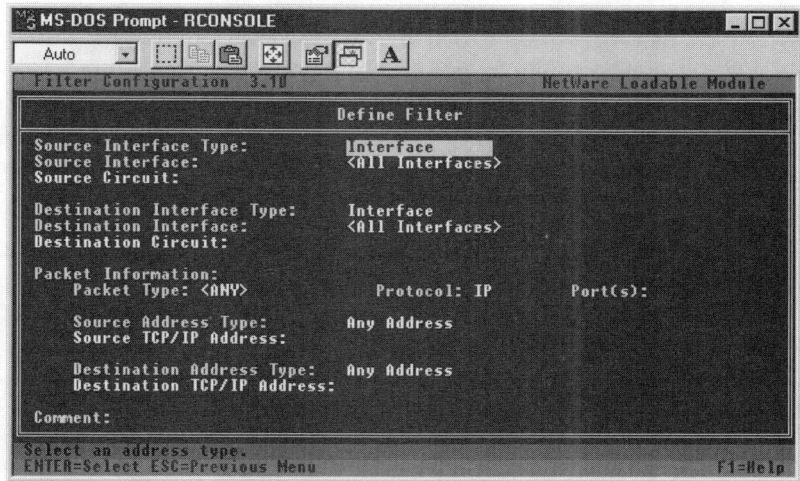

You can also define the source and destination IP address, the destination interface, and the type of IP packet. Highlighting the Packet Type field and pressing Enter produces the screen shown in Figure 13.13. This is a list of predefined IP packet types that you can use for creating your filter rules. If you need to filter a service that is not listed, simply press the Insert key to define a new packet type.

FIGURE 13.13:

Defined TCP/IP Packet Types screen

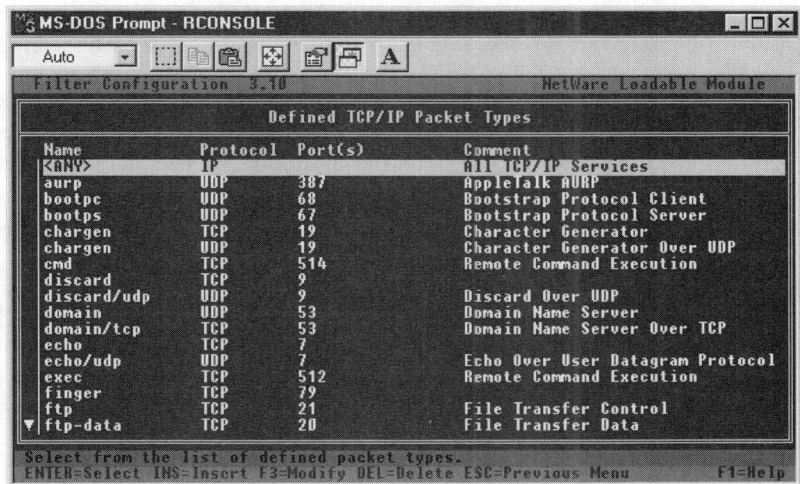

There are a number of limitations when defining your packet filters:

- You cannot distinguish between acknowledgment (ACK=1) and session establishment (SYN=1) packets.

- You cannot define ICMP type codes.

- You cannot define support for services that use dynamic port assignments such as RPC.

NOTE   Obviously, these limitations make Filtcfg a poor choice for securing an Internet connection. Filtcfg's modest packet-filtering ability may be sufficient, however, for providing security between internal network segments.

Once you have defined your filter rules, press the Escape key to exit and save (I know—it's a NetWare thing). You must now reinitialize the system in order to have your filter policy take effect.

Public Key Infrastructure Service (PKIS)

Novell uses PKIS to request, manage, and store certificates and key pairs in NDS. It also creates an Organizational CA (Certificate Authority) specific to a particular NDS tree (and hence, specific to your organization). Several other network security services rely on PKI, including Novell Secure Authentication Service, SSL, and Novell LDAP Services. As a result, NetWare Servers can use authentication and encryption to accept secure logins, verify LDAP requests (remember that LDAP is designed to allow third parties to query a given directory—in this case NDS), and encrypt network communications.

Several components make up Novell PKI, including PKI.NLM (on the NetWare server), PKI_SERVER.DLL (on NT servers), LIBPKISERVEc.S and NPKI (for Sun Solaris servers), and ConsoleOne—the administrative tool for PKI. After installing PKI some of the administrative tasks will be:

Create an Organizational CA.   This consists of a public and private key, along with the certificate, certificate chain (chain of authority) and other configuration information. The private key is encrypted and stored in NDS, and Organizational CA is represented as an object stored in the Security container of NDS.

Create a Server Certificate object.   Multiple Server Certificates can be stored on a single server. A PKI-aware application can be configured to use any of the Server Certificates available on that server.

Request a public key certificate.   At a minimum, public keys hold a public key, a subject and issuer name, a period of validity (the security world's equivalent of freshness dating), a serial number, and a certificate authority's digital signature

Novell Modular Authentication Service (NMAS)

NMAS is designed to incorporate additional authentication technology into Novell's already robust security system. NMAS defines three key components, although the last (graded authentication) is really a combination of the first two: login factors, login methods and sequences, and graded authentication.

Login Factors

Login factors are really unique areas that can be used to authenticate a user. Consider a password; this login factor is really something that you "know." How about a smart card? This is something you "have." And biometrics? That's right—something you "are." Let's look at how NMAS uses all three:

Password Authentication   There are actually several technologies to support passwords. The following three choices allow an administrator to choose a method that best integrates with existing administrative polices or other implemented technologies.

NDS passwords   Username and password information is encrypted before being sent over the wire, which results in a reduction of speed and an increase in processor load, but is considered the most secure option.

Clear-text   Username and password information is sent "in the clear"—in other words, without encryption. This option is available for low-security access (such as an e-mail password) as defined by the administrator.

SHA1/MD5   This technology hashes, or summarizes, information in such a way that the data is altered before being sent across the network, and yet remains relatively easy to compute. This option is considered moderately secure.

Physical Authentication Like our password technologies, there are multiple methods of verifying the physical presence of a user. Again, the technology that you choose will depend on many factors, including policies and existing infrastructure (and, of course, cost).

Smart card This plastic card (the general shape of a credit card, but slightly thicker) contains a microchip that can be programmed to store identification information (including digital certificates).

Token Typically hand-held, tokens are devices that generate a unique password every time they are used (called a "one-time" password). Tokens typically rely on one of two mechanisms:

Challenge-response After a user provides a correct username and password, the server sends a random number to the token. The token returns an encrypted version of the number, utilizing the user's encryption keys stored in the token. The server, which also has a copy of the user's encryption keys, encrypts the random number itself with those keys, and then compares the results. If they match, the user is authenticated.

Time-synchronous The token and server share an algorithm that generates a common number at specific intervals. After the user successfully provides a username and password, the server prompts for the number displayed at that moment on the token. When the server verifies the expected number for that time interval, the user is authenticated.

Biometric Authentication Biometric authentication systems use measurable biological traits to identify and authenticate. Systems consist of some type of sensor, along with the software to identify *match points*—those areas of the data that are unique and specific to any given individual. By requiring multiple match points, biometric systems use an overwhelming statistical proof to authenticate a user. Biometric authentication is grouped into two categories:

Static These systems capture characteristics that don't change over time. Examples include retinas, fingerprints, and facial features.

Dynamic These systems focus on biological behaviors as opposed to set characteristics. Examples include voice or handwriting patterns.

Methods and Sequences

A login method is an implemented login factor. A login sequence is one or more login methods in a specific sequence. Because of the variety of login methods and sequences, NMAS supports graded authentication, which controls access to network resources based on the login method used by a particular user. NMAS provides eight predefined groupings of methods and sequences known as *security clearance labels*:

- Biometric, Password, and Token

- Biometric and Password

- Biometric and Token

- Password and Token

- Biometric

- Password

- Token

- Logged In (provides network access without using an NMAS method)

Administrators assign these labels to NetWare volumes (partitions). When a user has authenticated using NMAS, she is said to have a *session clearance*. If a user has the same clearance level as that of the label of a partition, she can access that partition (to the degree that she has NDS and file system partitions to the volume). If a user has a lower clearance level than that applied to the volume, she has no access.

By providing authentication methods and sequences beyond a simple password, NMAS strengthens the access control already inherent in NetWare and gives an administrator a powerful and flexible platform for controlling access to resources.

Tweaking NetWare Security

Novell provides some security tweaks that allow you to enhance the security of your server even further. These include the SECURE.NCF script, as well as a number of console parameter settings.

The *SECURE.NCF* Script

NetWare includes a script called SECURE.NCF. When run during server startup, it automatically enables many of NetWare's security features, thus enhancing the security of the server. The SECURE.NCF script performs the following:

- Disables support for unencrypted passwords

- Disables the ability to access auditing functions using a general password

- Enables the ability to automatically repair bad volumes during startup

- Rejects bad NCP packets

All of these settings are required if you need to insure that your system meets C2 trusted network specifications. If you are not required to meet C2 standards, you can optionally comment out any setting that you do not wish to use.

Secure Console

When run from the server console, the Secure Console command provides the following security features:

- Only allows the server to load software which is located in the SYS:SYSTEM directory

- Disables the console debugging utility

- Prevents the time and date from being changed by anyone but the console operator

Once the Secure Console command has been invoked, it cannot be disabled without rebooting the server. The secure console features are designed to help protect the server from attacks at the server console.

TIP   In order to improve security even further, use the Lock Server Console option included with the Monitor utility.

Securing Remote Console Access

NetWare can be configured to allow you to remotely access the server console from any network workstation. Access is provided via the Rconsole utilities or any generic telnet program. There are a number of known security issues involved when enabling remote console access. The details of these vulnerabilities are described in the sections that follow.

Securing the Console Password

In NetWare versions 3.2 and earlier, the console password was included in the AUTOEXEC.NCF in a clear text format. This meant that anyone who could gain read access to the file would have been able to see the console password. The syntax used was

```
load remote secretpass
```

where *secretpass* is the password used to gain access to the server console. As of NetWare versions 4.1*x* and higher, remote access can be administered from the Inetcfg utility. By selecting Manage Configuration ➢ Configure Remote Access from the Inetcfg main menu, you can define your remote access parameters, including the remote console password.

The problem with Inetcfg is that it saves the password information in clear text to the file SYS:ETC\Netinfo.cfg. This is extremely bad: if you are running any of the IP services such as Web or NFS, users are provided Read access to this directory. This means that any valid system user could potentially gain access to the server console.

Clearly, some method of encrypting the console password is required. To encrypt the console password, issue the following commands from the server console:

```
load remote <password>
remote encrypt <password>
```

As shown in Figure 13.14, this will create the file SYS:SYSTEM\LDREMOTE.NCF, which contains an encrypted version of your password string. The -E switch tells the remote program that the password has been saved in an encrypted format.

You now have a number of options. You can

- Run the LDREMOTE.NCF file prior to running the INITSYS.NCF script within the AUTOEXEC.NCF file.

- Copy and paste the full command into your AUTOEXEC.NCF file.

- Copy and paste the -E switch, as well as the encrypted password, into the Remote Access Password field of the Inetcfg utility.

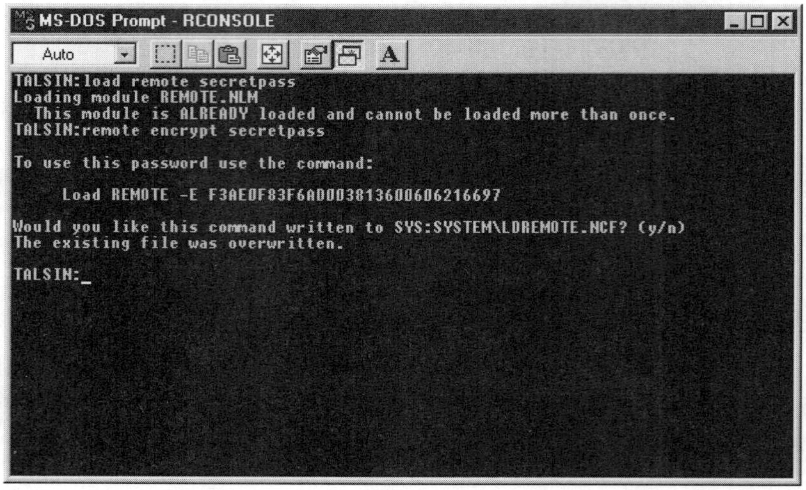

FIGURE 13.14:

Encrypting the remote console password

```
TALSIN:load remote secretpass
Loading module REMOTE.NLM
   This module is ALREADY loaded and cannot be loaded more than once.
TALSIN:remote encrypt secretpass

To use this password use the command:

     Load REMOTE -E F3AE0F83F6AD0D38136D0606216697

Would you like this command written to SYS:SYSTEM\LDREMOTE.NCF? (y/n)
The existing file was overwritten.

TALSIN:_
```

> **TIP**
>
> The choice is yours, but it is probably best to use the LDREMOTE.NCF script. This will save the encrypted password to the SYS:SYSTEM\ directory and keep Inetcfg from importing the commands.

Accessing the Console Using Telnet

Although NetWare allows you to use telnet to access the server console, this does not mean doing so is a good idea. The biggest problem with enabling telnet support to the server is that telnet sessions are not logged. Unlike an Rconsole connection, which generates an entry within the system log, telnet is capable of quietly connecting to the server without leaving a trace.

The other problem with using telnet is that authentication with the server uses clear text passwords. This means that even if you go to all the trouble of encrypting the console password, telnet transmits the password in clear text, so that anyone with a packet sniffer may read it.

> **WARNING**
>
> The Inetcfg utility allows you to selectively enable Rconsole and/or telnet support. It is highly advised that you leave telnet support disabled.

The Pandora Factor

The most successful attack strategy on NetWare servers is known as Pandora. More an ongoing project and tool set as opposed to coordinated attack, Pandora exploits weaknesses in NDS and NetWare Packet Signature in an attempt to gain access to the entire NDS system, not just a sole server.

NOTE   Like most hacker tools, Pandora is a very useful group of tools for legitimate administrators who want to test their own security, especially the strength of user passwords. Visit Pandora at `www.nmrc.org/pandora/index.html`

Defense against Pandora includes some simple actions:

- Pandora only effectively works with passwords up to 16 characters. Passwords with 17 characters or more aren't affected by (the current version) of Pandora. Ensure that your admin password is at least 17 characters long.

- Some of the Pandora tools rely on access to the SYSTEM directory of a NetWare server. Verify that only admin has rights to this directory.

- Because Pandora uses sniffing, keeping all administrative workstations on a separate, switched segment will protect them from any sniffing attack.

- Configure all administrative workstations (and servers) to use packet level 3.

Summary

In this chapter we looked at how to secure a NetWare server environment. NetWare provides a fairly secure environment right out of the box, but there are always a few tweaks you can do to make your networking environment even more secure. To this end, we discussed account management, file access rights, and how to perform NDS audits. We even discussed why it is so important to secure the remote console password.

In the next chapter, we will take a look at Windows NT and how to secure an NT server environment.

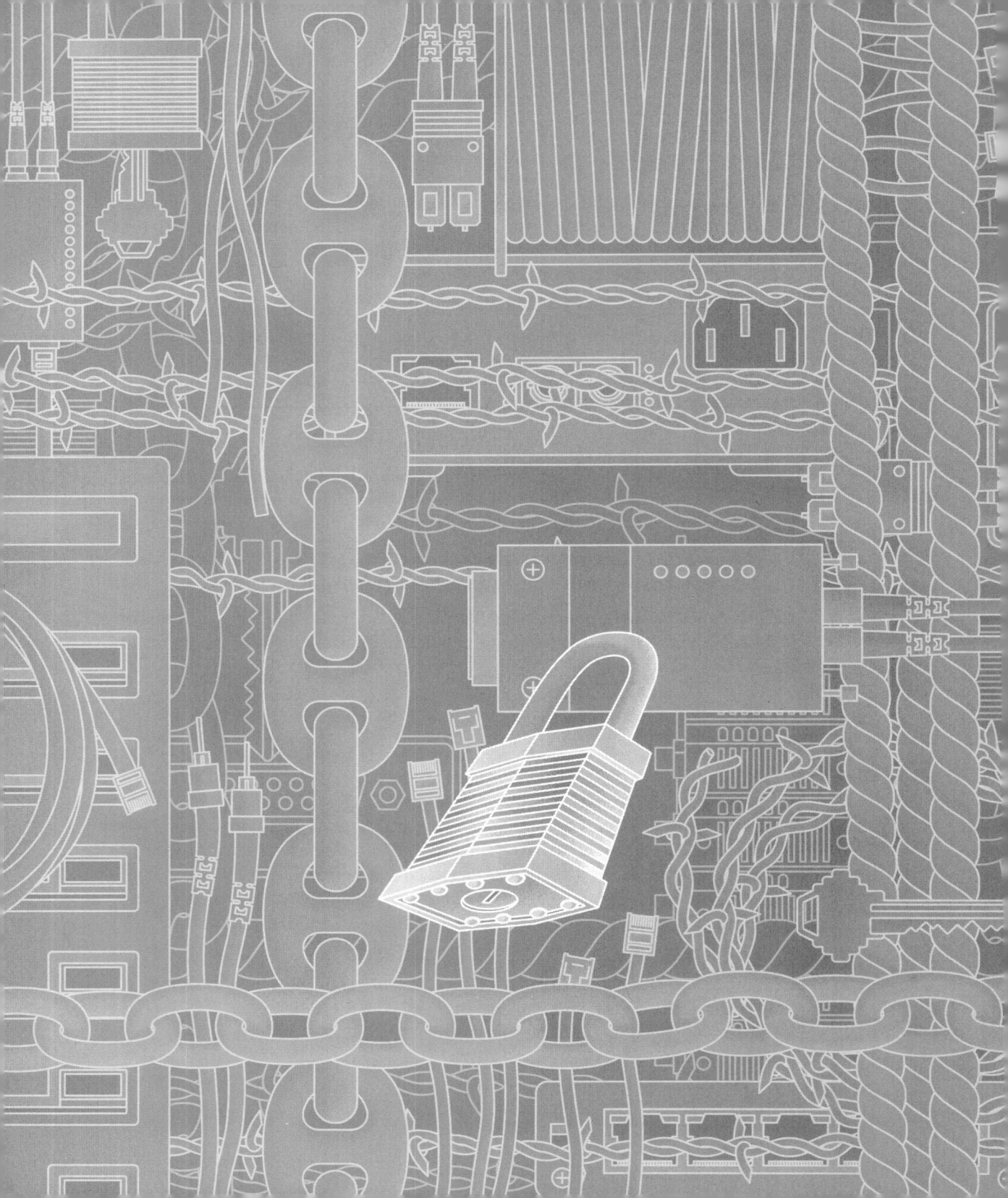

CHAPTER
FOURTEEN

14

NT and Windows 2000

Windows NT Server has proven to be one of the most popular client-server platforms in existence. Windows 2000 is the next version of Microsoft's flagship operating system, and it includes some significant security improvements that, coupled with its ease of use and well-known heritage, provides a powerful (and complex) environment for enforcing security.

The default security posture of an NT server is pretty loose. Windows 2000 is, in some ways, more secure in its default configuration, but still includes some weaknesses. There are a number of procedures you can follow in order to increase security over the default configuration for both systems. We will start with a brief overview of the NT operating system and then jump right into how you can operate a more secure NT environment. We'll follow with a comparison between NT and 2000, and talk about 2000's unique security requirements.

NT Overview

The core operating system of NT Server is 32-bit. While this creates some backward-compatibility problems with 16-bit Windows applications, it helps to ensure that the OS kernel remains stable. NT is both multitasking and multi-threaded. This helps to prevent any single process from monopolizing all available CPU time.

NT Server uses the same Windows-32 application programming interface as NT workstation and Windows 95 and 98. This ensures a familiar programming environment that, in theory, allows a programmer to write a more stable application. For example, a programmer who is familiar with writing Windows Desktop applications will find programming for NT Server very similar as both use the Win32 interface. This is in contrast to the NetWare Loadable Module (NLM) technology used by a NetWare server. A programmer writing code for a NetWare server must be specifically aware of the NLM programming environment.

Because the server uses the same Win32 interface as a Windows workstation, most Desktop applications are supported. This can be a real money saver for small environments that cannot afford to dedicate a system to server activities. Unlike NetWare, which requires you to dedicate a system as a server, NT Server can perform double duty as a user workstation, as well. Server support for Win32 can also be a real time saver for the system administrator. This is because most of the tools that you are used to running from a desktop machine will run from the server, as well.

Unfortunately, NT is missing the remote control features of NetWare's Rconsole or UNIX's telnet (a telnet server is included with Windows 2000 Server). While there are tools available from Microsoft's Web site and from its Resource Kits to manage some server functions remotely, you cannot directly add or remove protocols, launch applications, or access the NT Server Desktop from a remote workstation. Third-party software is required to provide this functionality.

NT uses a database known as the *Registry* in order to save most of the system's configuration information. This can be information regarding user accounts, services, or even system device drivers. Related information is said to be stored under the same hive. For example, the hive HKEY_USERS is used to store information regarding user accounts. Fields within a hive that hold configuration values are known as *keys*.

The benefit of the Registry is that information is stored in a central location, simplifying the process of finding and changing information. While most of NT's settings can be changed through the graphical interface, many settings must be manually changed in the Registry. The tool used for viewing and changing Registry information is known as regedt32.

Out of the box, NT Server provides support for up to four processors. With hardware support, this can be increased to 32. The benefit of additional processors is that more CPU time can be made available to applications running on the server.

Virtual Memory

NT Server supports memory isolation of all applications running on the system. It also supports the use of *virtual memory*. Virtual memory allows the server to utilize more memory space than is physically installed in the system. The benefit is that applications are free to use more memory to add features. The drawback is that virtual memory is stored to disk, which has a slower access time than physical memory by a factor of 100.

It is important to understand that you take a performance hit once you start using a lot of virtual memory. It is true that you can follow Microsoft's minimum memory recommendations by installing 32MB of RAM in a server offering basic file, print, HTTP, WINS, and DHCP services. You may even get the system to boot up and function. Performance on this system would be absolutely dismal, however. For a system with this or a similar configuration, plan on installing at least 96MB–128MB of physical memory.

> **WARNING** Because the Registry contains a majority of the system's configuration information, you should be extremely careful when making changes. Never edit the Registry without first creating an emergency recovery disk, and never make changes without first understanding the effects of the change.

NT Domain Structure

NT Server uses the Windows NT Directory services for user and group management. This is not, as the name implies, a fully hierarchical directory service like NetWare's NDS. It is a flat security structure based upon the use of domains. Active Directory, the replacement to NT directory services in Windows 2000 remedies this problem by allowing a Windows environment to be managed in a hierarchical structure.

A *domain* is a group of workstations and servers associated by a single security policy. A user can perform a single logon and gain access to every server within the domain; there is no need to perform separate logons for each server.

Storing Domain Information

Domain information is stored on *domain controllers*. Each domain has a single Primary Domain Controller (PDC). The PDC contains the master record of all domain information. Any other NT Server can be set up as a Backup Domain Controller (BDC). The BDC receives updates from the PDC, so there is a backup copy of the domain information. A user who logs in can authenticate with the PDC or any one of the BDCs.

This brings a bit of a server-centric dependency to the whole domain model. For example, if the PDC contains a logon script to connect users to network resources, a copy of this logon script must be provided on each BDC. If the logon script on the PDC is changed, the change must be synchronized with each of the BDC servers. The copy of the script on the BDC servers will not be updated automatically.

Do not use the logon script to try to implement a portion of your security policy. This is because all users have the ability to press Ctrl+C and break out of the logon script at any time.

Domain Trusts

To try to emulate a hierarchical structure, domains can be configured to be *trusting*. When a domain trusts another domain, it allows users of that trusted domain to retain the same level of access they have in the trusted domain. For example, Domain A trusts Domain B. This means that everyone who has domain user rights to Domain B (trusted domain) can be permitted access to resources on Domain A (trusting domain). However, since Domain B does not trust Domain A, users in Domain A have no access rights within Domain B. Trusts can be configured to be unidirectional (one domain trusts another) or bi-directional (each domains trusts the other equally). A unidirectional trust is referred to as a *one-way trust,* and a bi-directional trust is referred to as a *two-way trust.*

While domain trusts are fine for a small environment, this model does not scale very well. For example, you cannot administer each domain from a single interface. You must systematically connect to each domain you wish to work with, one at a time. The other problem is, what if you have a few users who require access to multiple domains? With NetWare, you can simply create an alias object in each container where you wish the user to have access. With NT Server, this is not possible without creating multiple trust relationships, even if you only need to accommodate a small group of users.

Finally, you cannot check your trust relationships from a central location. You must go to each primary server in each domain to see what trust relationships have been set up. If it is a large environment, you may have to put pen to paper in order to fully document all of the trust relationships. This is in contrast to NetWare, where a simple scan of the NDS tree will identify who has access and where.

Designing a Trust Architecture

Trusts can be used to enhance security, but the number one rule is to keep it simple. Try to limit the number of trust relationships to only one or two. This will help to ensure that you do not create a web of trust relationships. It will also help to ease administration. So when should domain trusts be used? A good example is shown in Figure 14.1.

FIGURE 14.1:

A network that is a domain trust candidate

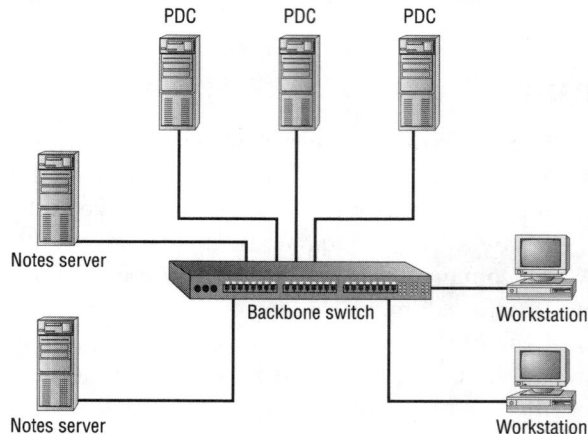

This environment maintains a number of NT PDC and BDC servers. There are also a number of Lotus Notes servers, which are also running on Windows NT. This network is managed by two different support groups. One group is responsible for all Lotus Notes activity (databases, e-mail, and so on), while the other group is responsible for all other network functions.

The problem is that the general support group does not want the Notes group to have administrator access to the entire network. This is understandable—it would grant members of the Notes group access to areas of the network where they do not need to go. The Notes group members claim they must be granted full administrator rights in order to do their jobs effectively. Unless they have full administrator access to the Notes servers, they cannot properly manage the systems.

The solution is to make the two Notes servers a PDC and a BDC of their own domains. This secondary domain can then be configured to trust the primary domains. This is shown in Figure 14.2. The resulting trust relationship allows the Notes group to be granted administrator-level access to the two Notes servers without having administrator-level access to the rest of the network. This trust relationship also allows administrators of the primary domain to retain their level of access in the secondary domain.

FIGURE 14.2:

A trust relationship

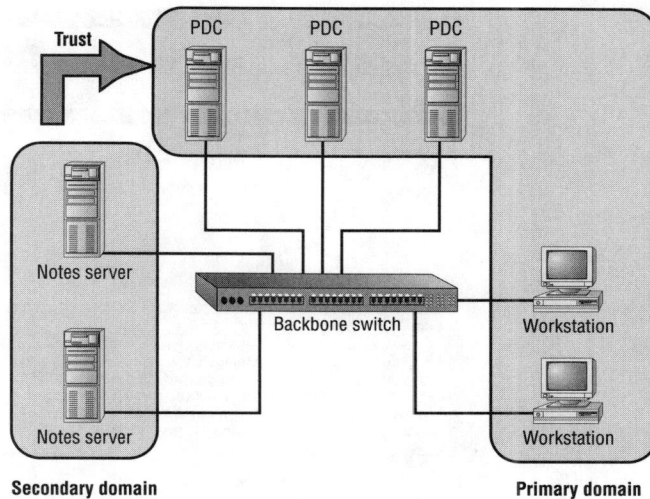

User Accounts

User accounts are managed with the User Manager for Domains utility, which can be accessed from the Administrative Tools program group. The User Manager for Domains utility is shown in Figure 14.3. This tool allows you to add and remove users, assign groups, and define account policies. All user access attributes are managed through this interface except for file, directory, and share permissions. File system permissions are set through Windows NT Explorer.

You can use the User Manager for Domains utility to manage both local and domain accounts. Every NT system, both server and workstation, has local accounts that must be managed outside of the domain. In order to manage local accounts from the NT system itself, you must disconnect from the domain and connect to each system. You can also remotely manage local accounts by selecting User ➢ Select Domain from the User Manager for Domains utility and entering a system name instead of a domain name.

FIGURE 14.3:

The User Manager for
Domains utility

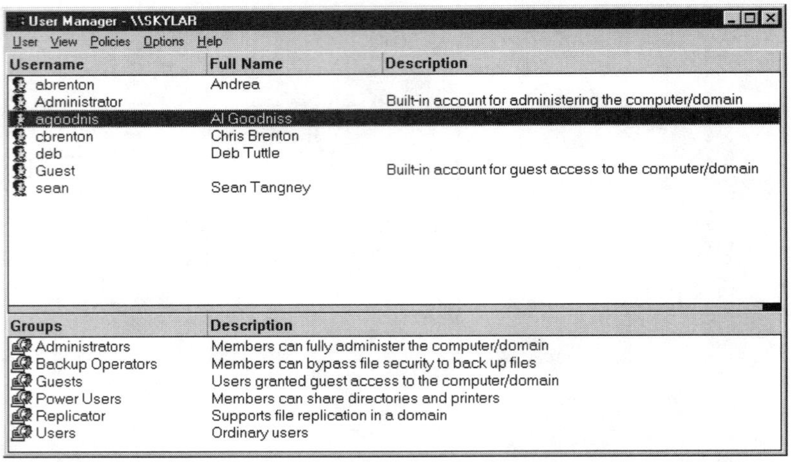

TIP

Updating the local Administrator password on multiple NT systems can be quite a chore. Group23 has made a Perl script available for automating this task. The script can be found at www.emruz.com/g23/.

Working with SIDs

A *Security Identifier*, or SID, is a unique identification number that is assigned to every user and group. The format of a SID is as follows:

```
S-Revision Level-Identifier Authority-Subauthority
```

The initial *S* identifies this number as a SID. For a given domain, all values are identical for every user and group, except for the subauthority. The subauthority provides a unique number to distinguish between different users and groups. There are a number of subauthority numbers that are referred to as *well-known SIDs*. This is because the subauthority number is consistent in every NT domain. For example, the Administrator account will always have a subauthority value of 500. This information can be used by an attacker in order to help target certain accounts for attack.

NOTE

Microsoft Knowledgebase document Q163846 lists all well-known SID numbers, along with their associated accounts.

Exploiting Well Known SIDs

Microsoft, as well as many security consultants, recommends that you rename the NT administrator account. The logic is that if an attacker does not know the logon name being used by the administrator, the attacker will not be able to compromise this account. A set of utilities written by Evgenii Rudnyi, however, shows just how easy it can be to circumvent this attempt at security through obscurity.

Figure 14.4 shows Rudnyi's two utilities in use. The first, user2sid, allows you to input a user or group name and produce the SID for this account. As mentioned, the SID is identical for every account except for the subauthority key. By using the second utility, sid2user, we can substitute the well known SID number we wish to look up (such as 500 for the administrator account). As shown in Figure 14.4, the administrator account has been renamed to Admin_renamed. Through this quick check, we now know which account to target.

FIGURE 14.4:

The user2sid and sid2user utilities

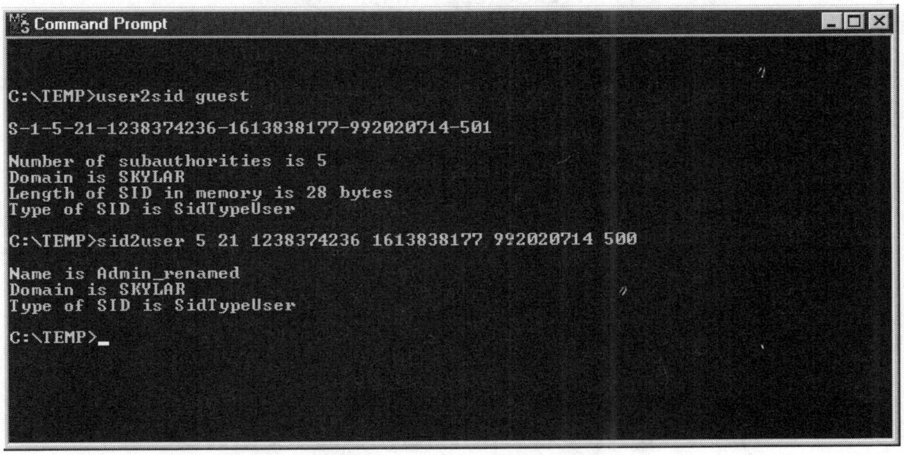

```
C:\TEMP>user2sid guest

S-1-5-21-1238374236-1613838177-992020714-501

Number of subauthorities is 5
Domain is SKYLAR
Length of SID in memory is 28 bytes
Type of SID is SidTypeUser

C:\TEMP>sid2user 5 21 1238374236 1613838177 992020714 500

Name is Admin_renamed
Domain is SKYLAR
Type of SID is SidTypeUser

C:\TEMP>_
```

NOTE   Rudnyi's SID utilities can be downloaded from www.ntbugtraq.com.

TIP   Renaming the administrator account would provide little help in protecting this system. A better tactic would be to ensure that the administrator account is using a strong password and that all failed logon attempts are logged.

The Security Account Manager

The *Security Account Manager (SAM)* is the database where all user account information is stored. This includes each user's logon name, SID, and an encrypted version of each password. The SAM is used by the Local Security Authority (LSA), which is responsible for managing system security. The LSA interfaces with the user and the SAM in order to identify what level of access should be granted.

The SAM is simply a file that is stored in the \WinNT\system32\config directory. Since the operating system always has this file open, it cannot be accessed by users. There are a number of other places where the SAM file can be located, however, that you need to monitor carefully:

\WinNT\repair   This directory contains a backup version of the SAM file stored in compressed format. At a minimum, it will contain entries for the administrator and guest accounts.

Emergency repair disks   When you create an emergency repair disk, a copy of the SAM is saved to floppy.

Backup tape   An NT-aware backup program will be capable of saving the SAM file.

If an attacker can get access to the SAM file from one of these three places, the attacker may be able to compromise the system.

NOTE   In Chapter 16, we will look at how a brute force attack can be launched against the SAM file in order to recover account passwords.

Configuring User Manager Policies

NT provides a number of settings that allow you to define a user access policy. The settings are broken up over two utilities. Account properties and user access rights are set through the User Manager for Domains utility. Desktop customization is enforced through User Manager, but policies are created through the System Policy Editor.

Account Policies

Account policies are set through User Manager by selecting Policies ➤ Account. This produces the Account Policy window shown in Figure 14.5. The Account

Policy window allows you to customize all settings that deal with system authentication. These settings are global, meaning that they affect all system users. A brief explanation of each option follows.

FIGURE 14.5:

The Account Policy window

FIGURE 14.5:

The Account Policy window

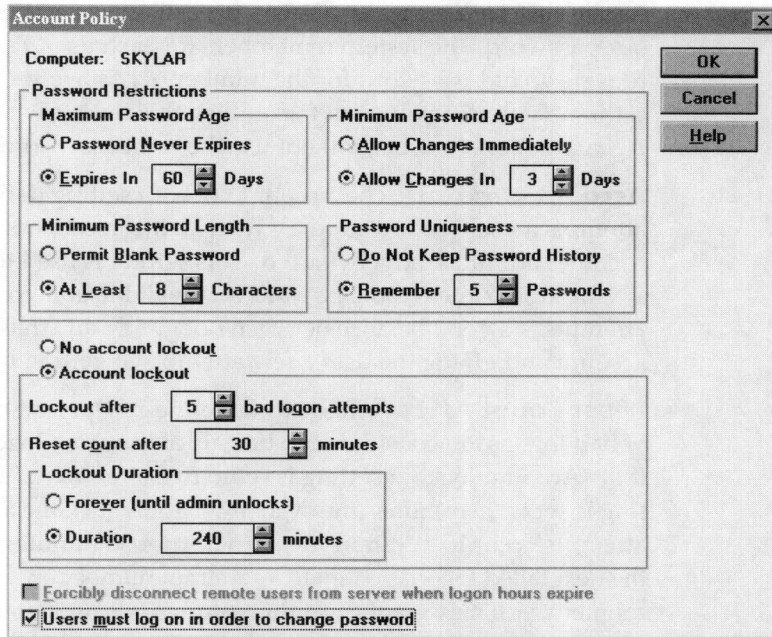

Maximum Password Age   This setting determines the amount of time before a user is forced to change his password. Too long of a period of time can be considered a security risk, while too brief of a period of time may prompt a user to write down his password. Typically, a maximum password age of 30–90 days is considered acceptable.

Minimum Password Age   This setting determines the amount of time that must pass before a user is allowed to change her password. When prompted to change their passwords, some users like to make repetitive password changes in order to cycle past the Password Uniqueness value. This allows the user to exceed the history setting and reset her password back to the current value. By setting a minimum password age, you can prevent users from reusing the same password. A value of three to seven days is usually sufficient to deter this user activity.

Minimum Password Length   This setting determines the smallest acceptable password. Due to vulnerabilities in the LanMan password hash that we will discuss in Chapter 16, it is suggested that you use a minimum value of eight characters for passwords.

Password Uniqueness   This setting allows you to configure how many previous passwords the system remembers for each user. This prevents a user from reusing an old password for the number of password changes recorded in this setting. Typically, you want to combine this setting with the Maximum Password Age value so that users will not use the same password more than once per year.

Account Lockout   The Account Lockout setting defines how many logon attempts a user is allowed to try with an incorrect password before the account becomes administratively locked. This setting is used to prevent attackers from attempting to guess the password for a valid user account. Usually five or six attempts is a good balance between not giving an attacker too many tries at an account and giving the user a few attempts at getting his password right.

Reset Count After   This setting defines the period of time in which a number of bad logons are considered to be part of the same logon attempt. For example, if the Account lockout setting is set to five attempts and the Reset count after setting is set to 30 minutes, the system will only lock the account if five failed logon attempts occur in a 30-minute period. After 30 minutes, the counter is reset and the next failed logon is counted as attempt number one. Depending on your environment, you may want to set this value as low as 30 minutes or as high as one day.

Lockout Duration   If an account does become locked due to an excessive number of logon attempts, the Lockout Duration setting defines how long the account will remain locked. For high-security networks, you should set this value to Forever. This leaves the account locked until it is reset by the system administrator. This allows the administrator to investigate whether the lockout is due to an intruder or to a user who cannot remember her password.

For many environments, a lockout setting that enables the account after a specific period of time is sufficient. This is useful when a user locks her account and the administrator is not available to clear the lockout. It is also useful for preventing DoS attacks. An attacker could purposely attempt multiple logons with a bad password in order to lock out the legitimate user. By setting a duration, the account would be able to clear itself without administrator intervention.

Forcibly Disconnect Remote Users   When time restrictions are used, this setting will disconnect all users who do not log off when the time restriction expires. This is useful to ensure that users do not remain logged on after business hours, thus giving an attacker an active account to work with.

> **TIP**   This setting is also useful to ensure that all document files are closed so that a proper backup can be performed.

Users Must Log On in Order to Change Password   In a Windows environment, users can change their passwords locally and then later update the server with these password changes. This setting means the user can only change his password during an authenticated session with the domain. This ensures that an attacker cannot use a local vulnerability in order to modify a password throughout an NT domain.

Increasing Password Security with *passfilt.dll*

Within Service Pack 2 and later, Microsoft has included the `passfilt.dll` file. This file allows you to increase you password security by challenging a user's password to meet more stringent criteria. The `passfilt.dll` file performs the following checks:

- Passwords must be six characters or greater.
- Passwords must contain a mixture of uppercase, lowercase, numeric, and special characters (at least three of the four categories are required).
- Passwords cannot be a variation of your logon name or full username.

You can use Account Policies to require a longer password, but you cannot specify a shorter one. The domain administrator is able to override these settings on a user-by-user basis. This is done by managing the specific user with User Manager and setting a specific password in the password field. This password will not be subjected to `passfilt.dll`.

To implement `passfilt.dll`, edit the Registry key

```
HKEY_LOCAL_MACHINE\System\CurrentControlSet\Control\LSA\
Notification Packages
```

and add the character string **PASSFILT**. Do not delete the existing key value.

User Rights

User rights are set through the User Manager by selecting Policies ➤ User Rights. This produces the User Rights Policy window shown in Figure 14.6. User rights allow users or groups to perform specific actions on the server. The right is selected from the Right drop-down menu, while the Grant To box identifies which users and groups have been granted this right. Checking Show Advanced User Rights causes the Right drop-down menu to display additional options. Some of the more important rights are described in the sections that follow.

FIGURE 14.6:

The User Rights Policy window

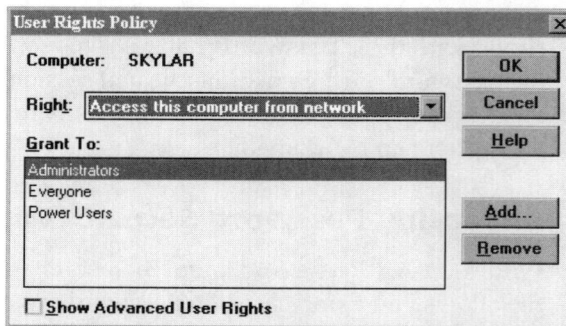

Access This Computer from the Network This right defines which domain users are able to remotely authenticate with each of the servers within the domain. This right applies to all domain servers—not just this specific server, as the name implies.

TIP

Instead of renaming the administrator, create a new account that is an administrator equivalent and use this account for managing the domain. This will allow you to remove the Access this Computer from the Network right from the administrator account. The administrator will still be able to log on from the console, just not over the network. If you also log failed logon attempts, you will be able to see when someone is trying to break in to your domain as administrator.

Backup Files and Directories This right supersedes all file permission settings and allows the users with this right assigned to have read access to the entire file system.

WARNING   Backup Files and Directories is a dangerous right, because it gives the user access to the entire system without being flagged as an administrator equivalent. This right would allow a user to copy the SAM in order to run it through a password cracker.

Bypass Traverse Checking   An advanced user right, Bypass Traverse Checking allows a user to navigate the file system regardless of the permission levels that have been set. File permissions are still enforced; however, the user is free to wander through the directory structure.

Log On Locally   When managing a domain, this right defines who is allowed to log on from the PDC or BDC console. You may wish to limit console access to only administrator-level accounts. This can help to deter (but not completely prevent) physical attacks against the server. Like the Access this Computer from the Network right, you can use failed logon attempts to track whether any of your users have sneaked into the server room and attempted to access the server directly.

Manage Auditing and Security Logs   If file and object auditing has been enabled, this right defines which users are allowed to review security logs and specify which files and objects will be audited.

WARNING   Be careful whom you grant this right to—an attacker can use this right to cover his tracks once he has penetrated a system.

Policies and Profiles

Policies allow you to control the functionality of the user's workstation environment. This can include everything from hiding the Control Panel to disabling the ability to run programs that are not part of the Desktop. Policies can be set up globally for a domain, or they can be applied to specific users or groups.

Profiles allow you to customize the look and feel of a user's Desktop. You do this by authenticating to the domain using a special account and laying out the Desktop environment in exactly the way you want it to appear to your end users. This can include special program groups or even a choice of color schemes and screen savers. There are a number of ways to implement profiles:

Mandatory profile   Absolute enforcement of the Desktop environment. Mandatory profiles are loaded from the server and do not allow any customization. If the user changes her Desktop environment, it will be reset at her next logon.

Local profile   A customizable profile that is stored on the local machine. If the user authenticates from a different workstation, his Desktop environment may appear different.

Network profile   Also referred to as a *roaming profile*. Network profiles allow the user to receive her Desktop settings from any network workstation. Network profiles can be mandatory or customizable.

Policies are useful for deploying a security policy. For example, if your policy states that users are not allowed to load software programs onto the system, policies can remove the tools required to run the Setup program of a new software package. Profiles are more of a management tool, as they allow you to implement a standard Desktop.

Using Policies

Policies are created using the System Policy Editor located within the Administrative Tools program group. The System Policy Editor is shown in Figure 14.7. From the NT server, you can only create policies that will be applied to other NT systems. If you wish to create policies for Windows 95/98 systems, you must copy the Poledit.exe file from the WinNT directory to a Windows 95/98 machine. You must then run the Policy Editor from the Windows 95/98 system.

NOTE   The Policy Editor must be run on the operating system for which you wish to create a policy.

FIGURE 14.7:

The System Policy Editor

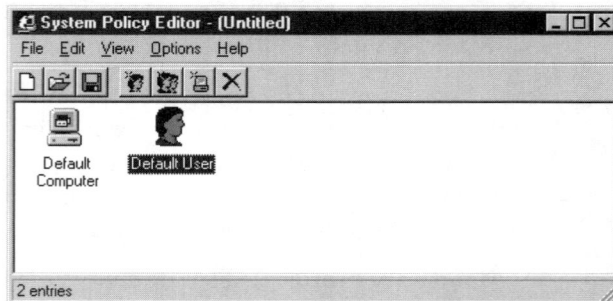

The Policy Editor allows you to control the functionality of the user's workstation environment. This can be done by system, by user, or by groups of users. The default settings for the Policy Editor allow you to create a policy that will be defined for all systems and all users. If you wish to create a more granular environment, you can use the Edit menu to define additional systems, groups, or users.

The policy in Figure 14.8 is made up of four groups:

- Domain Guests

- Domain Admins

- Domain Users

- Power Users

These groups allow you to customize the Desktop based on the level of access granted to each group member. For example, Domain Guests could have their Desktop environment stripped clean, while Domain Admins enjoy access to all Desktop functions. The Domain Users and Power Users groups could be permitted a level of Desktop functionality that falls in between Domain Guests and Domain Admins. This lets you define multiple levels of Desktop access.

FIGURE 14.8:

A sample policy

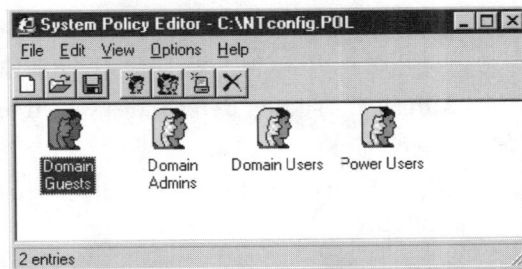

Machine Policies

To configure machine policies, double-click the machine object you wish to manage. This will produce the Computer Properties window shown in Figure 14.9. By navigating the structure, you can enable policy settings that will be enforced either on all machines (if the default policy is modified) or on specific machines (if you select Edit ➢ Add Computer). Some of the more useful machine policy settings you are allowed to configure are listed here.

FIGURE 14.9:

The Computer Properties windows for the default computer policy

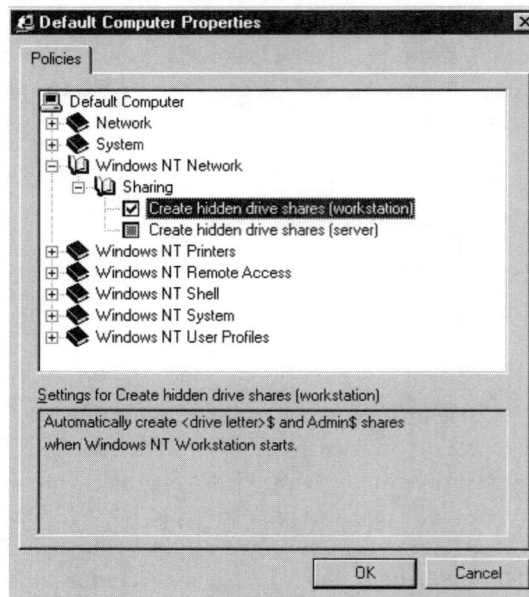

Enable SNMP updates   This setting allows the system to transmit SNMP updates to an SNMP management console.

Run   This setting determines which programs should be run during system startup.

Sharing   This setting determines whether administrative shares should be created.

Custom shared folders   This setting determines whether shared program groups can be created on the system.

Logon Banner   This setting defines a logon banner. This is useful for displaying corporate policies regarding system access.

Shutdown from Authentication Box   This setting determines whether the shutdown option is available from the logon authentication screen. This allows a user to shut down the system without first authenticating with the system. The default is to have this option disabled. Selecting this box enables the shutdown option.

Do not display last logon name   Selecting this option causes the last logon name not to be filled in. By default, Windows remembers the last user who performed a system logon and fills in the logon name field of the authentication window.

User and Group Policies

To configure user or group policies, double-click the object name that you wish to manage. This will produce the Properties window shown in Figure 14.10. Some useful policy settings follow:

FIGURE 14.10:

The Properties window for the default user policy

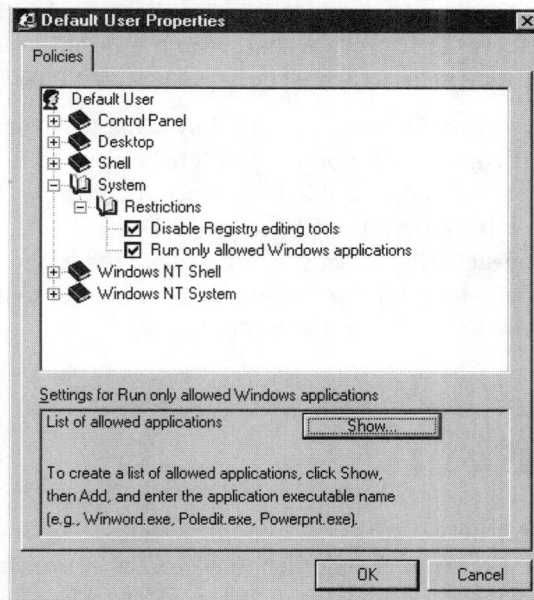

Remove Run command   Prevents a user from selecting Start ➢ Run from the Taskbar

Remove folders from Settings   Prevents a user from selecting Start ➢ Settings in order to modify the system configuration

Remove Find command   Prevents a user from selecting Start ➢ Find, which prevents the user from searching the local drives

Hide drives in My Computer   Prevents a user from browsing local or mapped drives using the My Computer icon

Hide Network Neighborhood   Prevents a user from browsing the network

Disable Registry editing tools   Prevents a user from modifying the Registry keys

Run only allowed Windows applications   Allows the administrator to define which applications can be run by the user

Enabling Policies

Once you have created your policy, enable it by saving the policy to the `NETLOGON` share. The `NETLOGON` share is in the `\WinNT\System32\Repl\Import\Scripts` directory. The policy must be copied to the `NTLOGON` share of every PDC and BDC.

To apply a policy to all NT systems, save the policy under the name `Ntconfig.pol`. If you created a policy that will be applied to Windows 95/98 users, save the policy using the name `Config.pol` and copy this file to the `NETLOGON` share, as well. When a Windows system authenticates with a domain, it looks for these specific files to see if a policy has been enforced. Windows NT systems specifically look for the file `Ntconfig.pol`, while Windows 95/98 systems are configured to look for the file `Config.pol`.

File System

NT Server supports two file systems: FAT and the NT file system (NTFS). While both support long filenames, FAT is optimized for drives up to 500MB, while NTFS is designed for drives of 500MB and larger. NTFS is the preferred file system for storing applications and user files. This is because it supports file and directory-level permissions while FAT does not.

NOTE   Recovering deleted files is only supported under the FAT file system. NT provides no tools for recovering files remotely deleted from an NTFS drive.

Permissions

There are two types of permissions that can be associated with files and directories. These are *share permissions* and *file permissions*. Share permissions are enforced when users remotely attach to a shared file system. When a user attempts to access files through a share, the share permissions are checked to see if the user is allowed access.

File permissions are access rights that are assigned directly to the files and directories. Unlike share permissions, file permissions are enforced regardless of the method used to access the file system. This means that while a user would not be subjected to share permissions if he accessed the file system locally, he would still be challenged by the file-level permissions.

NOTE   This distinction is important when you start setting permissions for services such as your Web server. Access permissions for a Web server are only regulated by file-level permissions. Share permissions have no effect.

When accessing a share over the network, permissions are *cumulative*. This means that a user is subjected to the strictest level of access. For example, if a remote user has Full Control access set as a file permission but only has Read access to a share, that user will only be allowed Read access.

Share Permissions

Share permissions are set through Windows Explorer. Right-click the directory name that you wish to set share permissions on and select the Sharing menu option. This produces the Shared Documents Properties window shown in Figure 14.11.

Notice that there is also a tab marked Security. This is for setting file-level permissions, which we will discuss in the next section.

Selecting the Permissions button in the Shared Documents Properties window produces the Access Through Share Permissions window shown in Figure 14.12. Notice that the default is to give Everyone Full Control access to the share.

TIP   Microsoft file sharing always grants full access to everyone. You should make a habit of reviewing the share permission level and reducing the level of access whenever possible.

FIGURE 14.11:

Sharing properties for
the Shared Documents
directory

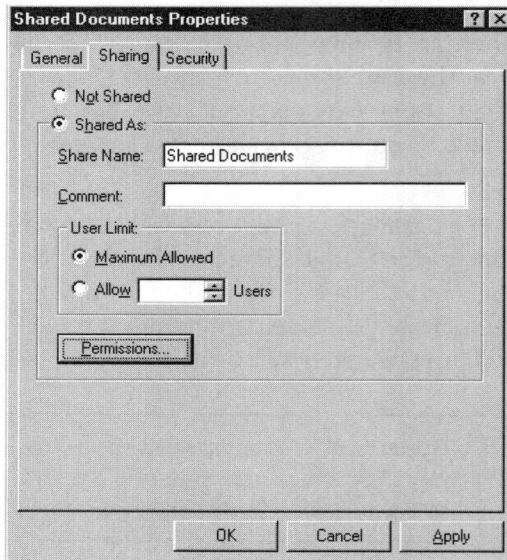

FIGURE 14.12:

The Access Through Share
Permissions window

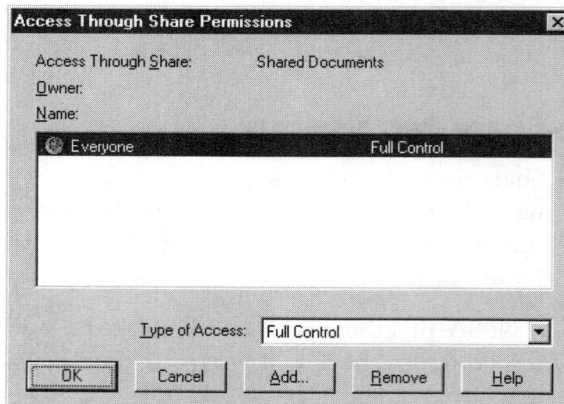

Access levels are set by associating different groups or specific users with certain share permissions. This defines what level of access each user or group will have when attempting to access this specific share. Only four possible share permissions can be assigned:

No Access   No access to the share is permitted.

Read   The user or group may navigate the directory structure, view files, and execute programs.

Change   The user or group has Read permissions and can add or delete files and directories. Permission is also granted to change existing files.

Full Control   The user or group has Change permissions, and can also set file permissions and take ownership of files and directories.

A more appropriate set of share permission than the default setting is shown in Figure 14.13. In this configuration, Everyone has No Access rights by default, because they are not listed on the Access Control List. A user who is part of the Domain Users group is allowed Change-level access. Finally, Domain Admins are allowed Full Control of the share. This allows the Domain Admins to perform any required administrative functions.

FIGURE 14.13:

Some suggested share permissions

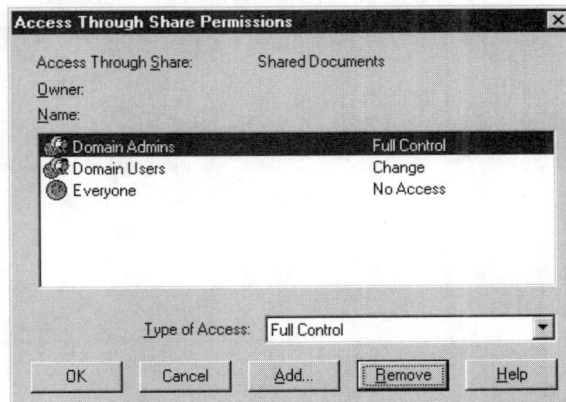

TIP   When modifying share permissions, always add permissions for the Domain Admins first. It is possible to configure a share so that the domain administrators have no access rights!

Once you have configured your share permissions, click OK to save your changes. Make a habit of checking these permission levels twice before leaving this screen. Share permissions take effect immediately and will affect any future users who try to access the share.

File Security

File permissions are also set by right-clicking a directory name within Explorer and opening the Properties window. This time, however, you want to select the Security tab. This produces the window shown in Figure 14.14. This window has three buttons thats allow you to work with file permissions, auditing, or file ownership.

FIGURE 14.14:

The Security tab of the
Shared Documents directory

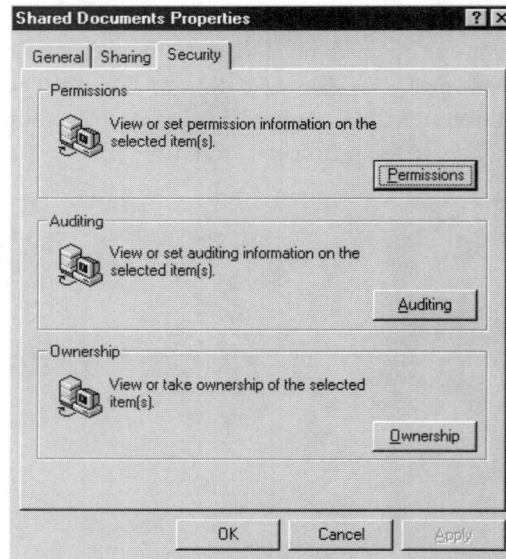

The Permissions Button

File and directory permissions are modified by selecting the Permissions button from the Security tab. This produces the Directory Permissions window shown in Figure 14.15. As you can see from this screen, working with file and directory permissions is very similar to working with share permissions. The only difference is that you have a few more options here.

There are two checkboxes at the top of the screen. Since you are working with a directory instead of a share, the system realizes that you may wish to apply your security changes to all objects within the directory. If only the Replace Permissions on Existing Files option is checked, the permissions are applied to files within this directory only. The Replace Permissions on Subdirectories option allows this permission change to be recursively applied to all files and directories located below the current location. If neither box is checked, the permissions are applied to the directory only and no other directories or files are updated.

FIGURE 14.15:

The Directory Permissions window

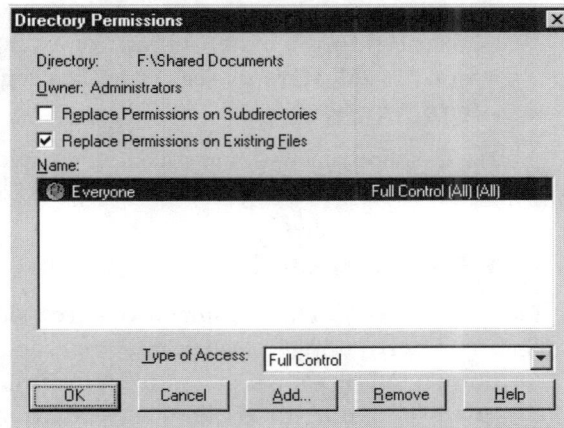

Like share permissions, file or directory permissions are set by associating a user or group with a specific level of access. When working with directory permissions, you have seven permission levels available. This allows a bit more granularity when setting access permissions. The permission settings are

No Access No access to the directory is permitted.

List The user or group may navigate the directory structure and see listed files. This setting does not provide the user or group any file access beyond seeing the file's name.

Read The user or group has List permissions, can view files, and can execute programs.

Add The user or group has List permissions and can add files and directories. Files cannot be viewed or executed.

Add & Read This setting combines the permissions of Read and Add, so that files can be viewed and added but not deleted or changed.

Change The user or group has Add and Read permissions and can delete files and directories. Existing files can also be changed.

Full Control   The user or group has Change permissions and can set file permissions and take ownership of files and directories.

Special Access   This setting allows you to specify the exact right assigned to files or directories. Options are Read, Write, Execute, Delete, Change Permissions, or Take Ownership. This is useful for those unique cases when the generic groups will not suffice. For example, setting the Execute permission for a file will allow a user to run the program without having access to view the directory.

As with share permissions, you should decide on the minimum level of access required by each user or group and set permissions accordingly.

The Auditing Button

Auditing allows you to monitor who is accessing each of the files on your server. Clicking the Auditing button in the Properties window produces the Directory Auditing window shown in Figure 14.16. From this window, you can select specific users and groups and define the activity you wish to record. For example, in Figure 14.16 we are auditing the directory for ownership and permission changes.

FIGURE 14.16:

The Directory Auditing window

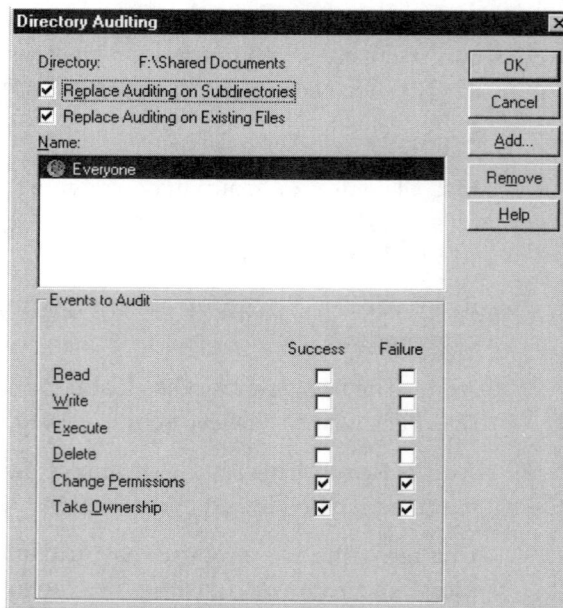

In order to use this feature, you must also launch the User Manager and select Policies ➤ Audit. Auditing must be enabled and the File and Object Access option must be selected. All audit entries will be reported to the Security log in Event Viewer.

NOTE   Auditing is discussed in greater detail in the "Logging" section of this chapter.

The Ownership Button

Clicking the Ownership button from the Properties window allows you to take ownership of a file or directory structure. Domain administrators are always allowed to take ownership (provided they have full control of the file or directory). If full control is enabled for domain users, they can designate other domain users who can take ownership of files or directories they own.

Logging

All NT events are reported through Event Viewer. Access Event Viewer through the Administrative Tools program group. By default, only system and application messages are logged. You can, however, enable auditing, which provides feedback on a number of security-related events. This provides a greater level of detail about what is taking place on the system.

Configuring Event Viewer

There are a few settings within Event Viewer that you may wish to change. From the Event Viewer main menu, select Log ➤ Log Settings. This will produce the Event Log Settings window shown in Figure 14.17. The Change Settings for drop-down menu allows you to configure the System, Application, and Security logs separately. You can also set the maximum size of the log as well as specify what Event Viewer should do if the log grows too large.

FIGURE 14.17:

The Event Log Settings window

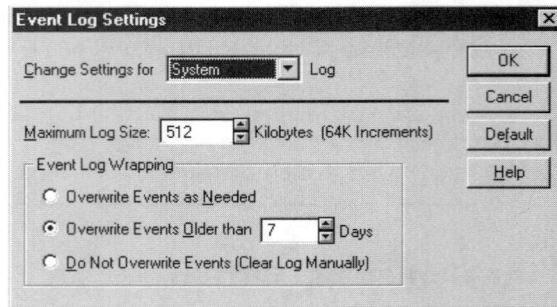

> **TIP**
>
> Given the price of disk space, the default log size setting of 512KB is far too small. Event Viewer keeps track of important events. You want to make sure that you provide enough space to record them. Increase the log size of all three logs to 4098KB. This will use a maximum of 12MB of disk space for log entries—a small price to pay for keeping tabs on your system's health.

The default setting for Event Log Wrapping is also a problem. What happens if you find out that your system was compromised at some time over the last 60 days? If you are overwriting events after seven days, you have no real history to go through in order to track what has happened. Change this setting to Do Not Overwrite Events for all three logs. This will produce a console error if the log file should become full, but it is better than losing your log history.

Reviewing the Event Viewer Logs

You should plan on reviewing your logs on a regular basis. This is one of your best tools for determining whether someone has infiltrated your system. The logs show you what has gone on with your system when you were not there to watch it. Depending on your setup, you can choose from a number of manual and automated methods for reviewing log entries.

Manual Log Review

One of the simplest methods of reviewing your logs is to simply log on to each system from the console and review the log entries. If you have only one or two servers, this may be sufficient. Logs can be archived by simply selecting Log ≻ Save As from the Event Viewer window and saving each log to file. You may wish to save the logs as a .TXT file so that they can be imported into another program, such as Excel or Access, for further review. If you will be transporting the files via floppy disk, consider compressing them first. You can easily fit 12MB worth of logs onto a floppy in PKZIP format.

If you are managing 10 or more NT systems, it may not be practical to walk around to every system. When this is the case, you can select Log ≻ Select Computer from the Event Viewer main menu. This produces the Select Computer dialog box shown in Figure 14.18. From this screen you can select any Windows NT system and remotely view the Event Viewer log. This is extremely useful because it allows you to monitor all of your logs from a central location. It even allows you to save the logs locally, making log archiving a single-step process.

FIGURE 14.18:

The Select Computer dialog box

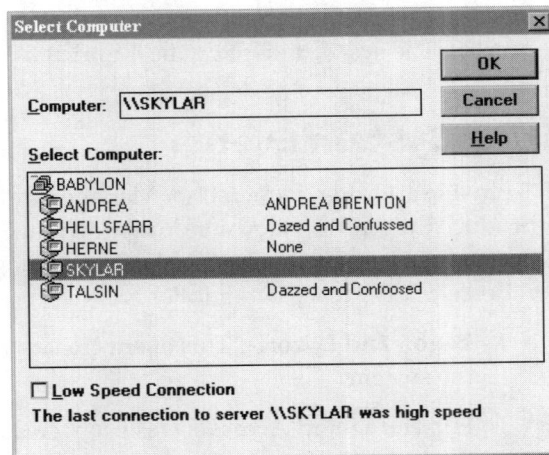

TIP

If your desktop system is Windows 95/98, you can still view Event Viewer log entries remotely. You simply need to acquire the NT Administration tools for Windows 95/98. This is a self-extracting executable named **nexus.exe** that includes Event Viewer, User Manager, and Server Manager for Windows 95/98. All of these tools can be used to manage an NT domain from a Windows 95/98 system. The **nexus.exe** archive can be found on the Microsoft Web site.

Automated Log Review

If you have hundreds or thousands of NT systems to monitor, manually reviewing all of the Event Viewer logs is out of the question. If you have many systems to review, you need to automate the process. Automating the log review process allows you to search the Event Viewer logs in order to see if anything interesting has happened on the system. If an interesting entry is found, the log can be flagged so that the system administrator knows that the log is in need of further review. Automating the log review process can drastically reduce the amount of human work required to locate critical events.

The safest way to automate the review process is to transmit the log entries to a remote system. While this places log information out on the wire, it also prevents attackers from being able to modify log entries on the compromised system in order to cover their tracks. Elmar Haag has written a program that allows an NT system to forward its log entries to any UNIX system running `syslogd`. This consolidates the logs in a central location, where they can be reviewed by an automated process. The `syslogd` client can be found at `www.centaur.de/~haag/logger_NT/`.

Auditing System Events

To enable auditing, launch User Manager and select Policies ➤ Audit. This will produce the Audit Policy window shown in Figure 14.19. For each of the listed events, you can select whether you wish to log event successes, failures, or both. A description of each event follows:

Logon and Logoff   This event creates a log entry as users log on and log off the system.

File and Object Access   This event creates a log entry when files or objects flagged as audited are accessed. Auditing was discussed earlier in this chapter.

Use of User Rights   This event creates a log entry whenever user rights are verified. Selecting this event can create very large log files.

User and Group Management   This event creates a log entry when user and group entries are added, deleted, or modified.

Security Policy Changes   This event creates a log entry when security policies, such as group rights or audited events, are modified.

Restart, Shutdown, and System   This event creates a log entry when the system is restarted or shut down, or when the Security log settings are changed.

Process Tracking   This event tracks application and service calls. Selecting this event can create very large log files.

FIGURE 14.19:

The Audit Policy window

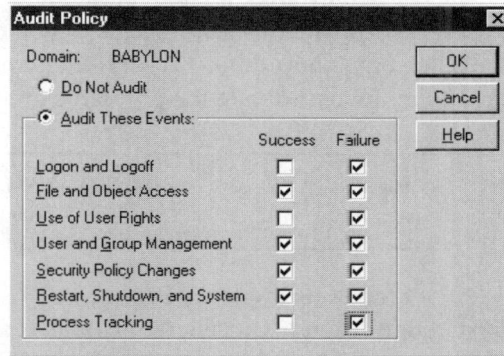

Deciding What to Audit

Given the auditing choices available to you, you must now select which events you wish to monitor. The knee-jerk reaction is to monitor everything; however, this may not be practical. You need to balance the amount of detail collected with the amount of time and resources you are willing to invest in reviewing the logs. If the logs will be reviewed automatically, this may not be a problem. If you will be reviewing the logs manually, having Event Viewer generate 20MB worth of log entries on a daily basis will not help you track what is going on with your system.

The key is to only track events that you deem critical to your environment's security policy. For example, you may not wish to sift through all of the successful logon events. Auditing this information may only help to create additional log entries for you to filter through. You should, however, be interested in logon failures, as this may be an attacker's first attempt at gaining system access.

TIP

The bottom line is to keep your log size manageable. It does absolutely no good to collect all this information if you are not going to review it to check for problems.

Security Patches

NT has suffered from a number of security vulnerabilities over the past few years. It is not uncommon to see two or three major security flaws exposed on a monthly basis. For this reason, it is important that you apply all security-related patches once they are known to be stable. Stability is usually determined within a few weeks. During this testing period, you may wish to consider testing the security patch on a nonproduction server. Microsoft has needed to recall security patches in the past due to the problems they have created.

WARNING   Do not apply a new security patch to a production server until you know it will not cause a problem.

At the time of this writing, Service Pack 6a is the latest major patch release. SP6a is significant because it finally allowed NT 4.0 to be C2 certified. C2 certification is established through the National Computer Security Center (NCSC), a branch of the National Security Agency (NSA). C2 certification requires the following security features:

Mandatory user identification and authentication   The ability of the system to identify authorized users and to allow only them to access system resources.

Discretionary access control   Users can protect information as they see fit.

Auditing and Accountability   Tracking and logging of all user resource access.

Object Reuse   The capability of the operating system to block user access to previously utilized resources.

In order to achieve C2 certification the NSA used these procedures:

- Examination of source code

- Examination of detailed design documentation

- Retesting to ensure that any errors identified during the evaluation have been corrected

> If you will be running Internet Information Server (IIS), there are a number of other security patches you will want to install, as well. See the Microsoft Web site for the latest list of available security patches.

Available IP Services

This section lists available IP services that come with NT Server, along with a brief description of each. Figure 14.20 shows the menu for adding more services. This menu can be accessed through the Network Properties screen. The listed services are those that ship with NT Server. The Have Disk option can be used for adding IP services created by third-party developers.

FIGURE 14.20:

The menu for adding services to the NT Server

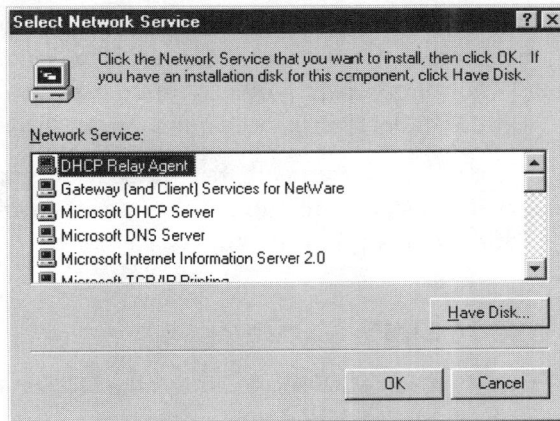

Computer Browser

When NetBIOS over IP is used, the computer browser creates and maintains a list of system names on the network. It also provides this list to applications running on the system, such as the Network Neighborhood. The computer browser properties allow you to add additional domains to be checked for system names.

DHCP Relay Agent

When a DHCP client and server exist on two separate network segments, the *DHCP relay agent* acts as a proxy between the two systems.

The DHCP relay agent ensures that the client's DHCP requests are passed along to the segment where the DHCP server resides. In turn, it also ensures that the replies sent by the server make it back to the client. The benefit of a DHCP relay agent is that it removes the necessity of having a separate DHCP server on each logical network. The relay agent can be located on the same network segment as the client or at the border between the client's and the DHCP server's network segments (acting as a router).

The DHCP relay agent requires that the IP protocol be installed. It also requires the IP address of at least one DHCP server.

Microsoft DHCP Server

The DHCP server allows the NT Server to automatically provide IP address information to network clients. When a client sends out a DHCP request, it can receive all information required to communicate on an IP network, including an IP address, subnet mask, domain name, and DNS server.

The DHCP server requires that the IP protocol be installed. When the DHCP server is installed, it automatically adds a menu option for DHCP Manager to the Administrative Tools menu.

Microsoft DNS Server

The Microsoft DNS server allows the NT Server to respond to clients and other DNS servers with IP domain name information. When the DNS server is configured to use WINS resolution, host name information is provided by WINS, based on NetBIOS system names.

A DNS server normally requires that host name information be manually maintained in a set of text files. If a machine changes its IP address, the DNS tables must be updated to reflect this change. If DHCP is used to provide IP address information, DNS has no way of knowing which host names will be assigned to which IP address.

By using WINS resolution, the DNS server can query the WINS server for host information. The DNS server passes the query along to WINS, which uses its NetBIOS table to match an IP address to a host name. The WINS server then returns this information to the DNS server. To a client querying a DNS server, the transaction is transparent. As far as the client is concerned, the DNS server is solely responsible for responding to the request. The two services do not need to be configured on the same NT Server.

The DNS server requires that the IP protocol be installed. When DNS server is installed, it automatically adds a menu option for DNS Manager to the Administrative Tools menu.

Microsoft Internet Information Server (IIS)

The Microsoft Internet Information Server adds Web, FTP, and Gopher functionality to the NT Server. Once installed, clients can access HTML pages, transfer files via FTP, and perform Gopher searches for files. Installing Service Pack 3 will upgrade IIS to version 3.0. At the time of this writing, IIS 4.0 is the latest release for NT4.0. To get IIS 5.0 you have to upgrade to Windows 2000.

By default, the IIS installation creates the directory InetPub, and places four directories inside it. The first three are the root directories for each of the three servers. All files and directories for each of the three services are to be placed under their respective root directory.

The fourth directory is for scripts. Web applications developed with CGI, WINCGI, Visual Basic, or Perl can be stored in this directory. It also contains some sample scripts and a few development tools.

NOTE   There have been quite a few vulnerabilities found with IIS—probably more than with the NT operating system itself. Make sure you have installed all available and stable security hotfixes. You should also review the IIS directory structure and set appropriate permission levels.

IIS requires that IP be installed. During IIS installation, a menu folder called Microsoft Internet Server is created for the management tools required for these services.

Microsoft TCP/IP Printing

Microsoft's TCP/IP printing allows an NT Server to support UNIX printing, referred to as *line printer daemon* (lpd). TCP/IP printing allows the NT Server to print to a print server that supports lpd, or to a UNIX system that has a directly connected printer.

IP printing also allows the NT Server to act as a printing gateway for Microsoft clients. The NT Server connects to lpd via IP and can advertise this printer as a shared resource on NetBEUI. Microsoft clients using only NetBEUI can send print jobs to this advertised share. The NT Server then forwards these jobs on to the lpd printer.

Microsoft TCP/IP printing requires that the IP protocol be installed. During installation, it adds a new printer port type called LPR, as shown in Figure 14.21. LPR is *Line Printer Remote*, which provides remote access to lpd printers.

FIGURE 14.21:

Installing IP printing adds an additional printer port, called the LPR port, through which an NT server can access UNIX printers.

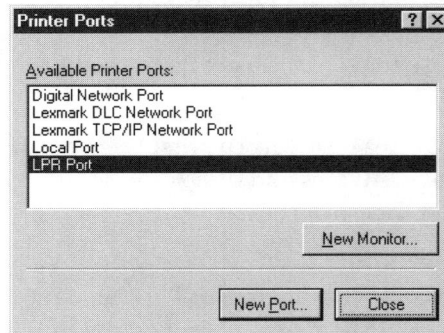

Network Monitor Agent

The Network Monitor Agent allows the NT Server to be remotely accessed and monitored by systems running the NT Server Network Monitoring Tools.

Network Monitor Tools and Agent

The Network Monitor Tool installs a network analyzer similar to Novell's LANAlyzer or Network General's Sniffer, except that it can only capture broadcast frames or traffic traveling to and from the NT server. The Network Monitor

Tool allows the server to capture and decode network frames for the purpose of analysis. Figure 14.22 shows a typical packet capture with the Network Monitor Tool. The tool displays the source and destination address of each system, as well as the protocol in use.

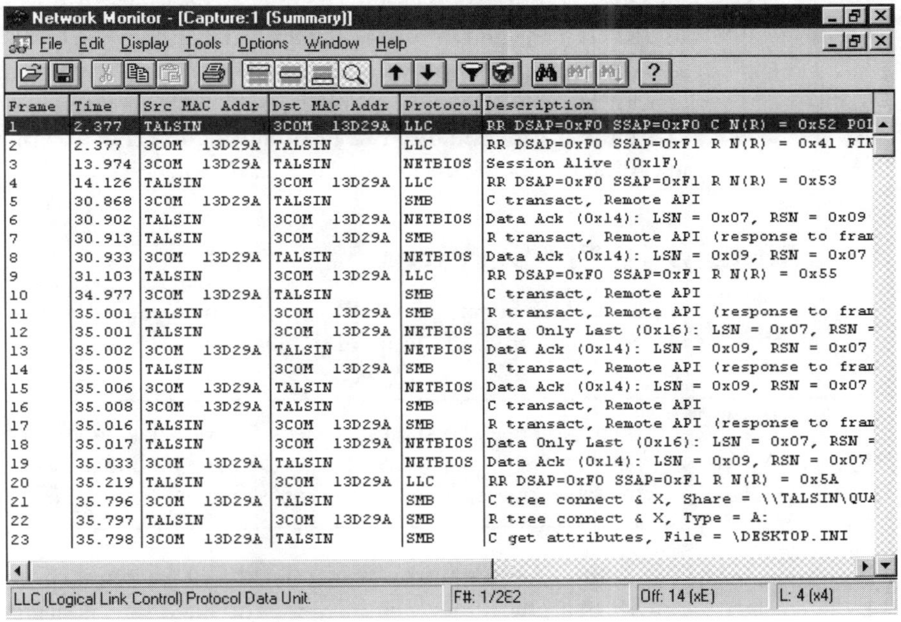
Network Monitor - [Capture:1 (Summary)]
File Edit Display Tools Options Window Help
Frame Time Src MAC Addr Dst MAC Addr Protocol Description
1 2.377 TALSIN 3COM 13D29A LLC RR DSAP=0xF0 SSAP=0xF0 C N(R) = 0x52 POI
2 2.377 3COM 13D29A TALSIN LLC RR DSAP=0xF0 SSAP=0xF1 R N(R) = 0x41 FIN
3 13.974 3COM 13D29A TALSIN NETBIOS Session Alive (0x1F)
4 14.126 TALSIN 3COM 13D29A LLC RR DSAP=0xF0 SSAP=0xF1 R N(R) = 0x53
5 30.868 3COM 13D29A TALSIN SMB C transact, Remote API
6 30.902 TALSIN 3COM 13D29A NETBIOS Data Ack (0x14): LSN = 0x07, RSN = 0x09
7 30.913 TALSIN 3COM 13D29A SMB R transact, Remote API (response to fram
8 30.933 3COM 13D29A TALSIN NETBIOS Data Ack (0x14): LSN = 0x09, RSN = 0x07
9 31.103 TALSIN 3COM 13D29A LLC RR DSAP=0xF0 SSAP=0xF1 R N(R) = 0x55
10 34.977 3COM 13D29A TALSIN SMB C transact, Remote API
11 35.001 TALSIN 3COM 13D29A SMB R transact, Remote API (response to fram
12 35.001 TALSIN 3COM 13D29A NETBIOS Data Only Last (0x16): LSN = 0x07, RSN =
13 35.002 3COM 13D29A TALSIN NETBIOS Data Ack (0x14): LSN = 0x09, RSN = 0x07
14 35.005 TALSIN 3COM 13D29A SMB R transact, Remote API (response to fram
15 35.006 3COM 13D29A TALSIN NETBIOS Data Ack (0x14): LSN = 0x09, RSN = 0x07
16 35.008 3COM 13D29A TALSIN SMB C transact, Remote API
17 35.016 TALSIN 3COM 13D29A SMB R transact, Remote API (response to fram
18 35.017 TALSIN 3COM 13D29A NETBIOS Data Only Last (0x16): LSN = 0x07, RSN =
19 35.033 3COM 13D29A TALSIN NETBIOS Data Ack (0x14): LSN = 0x09, RSN = 0x07
20 35.219 TALSIN 3COM 13D29A LLC RR DSAP=0xF0 SSAP=0xF1 R N(R) = 0x5A
21 35.796 3COM 13D29A TALSIN SMB C tree connect & X, Share = \\TALSIN\QUA
22 35.797 TALSIN 3COM 13D29A SMB R tree connect & X, Type = A:
23 35.798 3COM 13D29A TALSIN SMB C get attributes, File = \DESKTOP.INI
LLC (Logical Link Control) Protocol Data Unit.
F#: 1/2E2
Off: 14 (xE)
L: 4 (x4)

FIGURE 14.22:

The Network Monitor Tool can capture network traffic so that it can be decoded and analyzed.

WARNING Network Monitor is a great tool for monitoring traffic headed to and from the server. It can also be a major security problem if an attacker is able to access the Network Monitor data through a remote agent. Network Monitor can be a useful trouble-shooting tool, but you should not leave it active unless you are using it.

RIP for Internet Protocol

The RIP for Internet Protocol service allows the NT Server to use and propagate routing information broadcasts for the IP protocol. RIP is the only dynamic routing protocol supported for IP by the base NT installation. You can, however, download a copy of RRAS from the Microsoft Web site, which adds support for the OSPF routing protocol.

RPC Configuration

The RPC Configuration service enables NT Server support for Remote Procedure Call (RPC). RPC allows an application running on the local system to request services from another application that is running on a remote system. In order for the application to function correctly, both systems must support RPC. RPC provides similar functionality to a normal function call, except that RPC supports the calling of a subroutine located on a remote system.

Simple TCP/IP Services

Simple TCP/IP Services installs support for some little-used IP applications such as Echo, Chargen, and Quote of the Day.

WARNING   Unless you really need these services, Simple TCP/IP should not be installed. This is because the Echo and Chargen ports can be used to launch a DoS attack against the server or even an entire network segment.

When the Chargen port is transmitted a character, it responds by returning a full set of alphanumeric characters. The Echo port is designed to reflect back all the traffic that has been transmitted to it. There is a DoS exploit that spoofs a packet in order to get two systems communicating between these two ports or even to get a single server speaking to itself. The result is that for every character the Echo port reflects back to the Chargen port, the Chargen port responds with a full set of alphanumeric characters. The result is that network utilization can reach 100 percent, preventing legitimate traffic from reaching its destination.

SNMP Service

The SNMP service allows the NT Server to be monitored by an SNMP management station. It also allows the performance monitor on the NT Server to monitor IP statistics and statistics for IP applications (DNS, WINS, and so on).

When the SNMP service is installed, the NT Server can send configuration and performance information to an SNMP management station such as Hewlett-Packard's HP Openview. This allows the status of the NT Server, as well as other

SNMP devices, to be monitored from a central location. Monitoring can be performed over the IP or IPX protocol.

The SNMP service also adds functionality to the NT Performance Monitor. For example, it allows you to monitor the number of IP packets with errors or the number of WINS queries the server has received. Both SNMP and the applicable service must be installed for these features to be added to Performance Monitor.

Windows Internet Name Service (WINS)

A WINS server allows NetBIOS systems to communicate across a router using IP encapsulation of NetBIOS. The WINS server acts as a NetBIOS Name Server (NBNS) for p-node and h-node systems located on the NT Server's local subnet. WINS stores the system's NetBIOS name, as well as its IP address.

Each WINS server on the network periodically updates the other WINS servers with a copy of its table. The result is a dynamic list, mapping NetBIOS names to IP addresses for every system on the network. A copy of the list is then stored on each WINS server.

When a p-node system needs the address of another NetBIOS system, it sends a discovery packet to its local WINS server. If the system in question happens to be located on a remote subnet, the WINS server returns the remote system's IP address. This allows the remote system to be discovered without propagating broadcast frames throughout the network. When h-nodes are used, the functionality is identical to the p-node, except that an h-node can fall back to broadcast discovery if the WINS server does not have an entry for a specific host.

WINS requires that the IP protocol be installed. During WINS installation, a menu option for WINS Manager is added to the Administrative Tools menu.

Packet Filtering with Windows NT

Windows NT supports static packet filtering of IP traffic. While the capabilities of this filtering are somewhat rudimentary, they can be useful for providing some additional security. Since NT uses static packet filters, it is not capable of maintaining state. This means that NT's filters are unable to distinguish between legitimate acknowledgment traffic and possible attacks.

See Chapter 5 for an in-depth discussion of static packet filtering versus dynamic packet filtering.

NOTE

Windows NT does not allow you to specify the direction of traffic when applying your packet filters. All filtering is done on inbound SYN=1 traffic only. This means that if someone is able to compromise your system, NT's packet filters will be unable to prevent the attacker from relaying information off the system. Finally, NT does not allow you to filter on IP address. This means that any access control policy you create will be applied to all systems equally. In other words, you could not create an access control policy that only allows access from a specific subnet.

Enabling Packet Filtering

To enable packet filtering, go to Network Properties ➢ Protocols and double-click the TCP/IP protocol. This will produce the Microsoft TCP/IP Properties screen. With the IP Address tab selected, click the Advanced button located at the bottom right side of the window. This will produce the Advanced IP Addressing screen shown in Figure 14.23.

FIGURE 14.23:

The Advanced IP Addressing screen

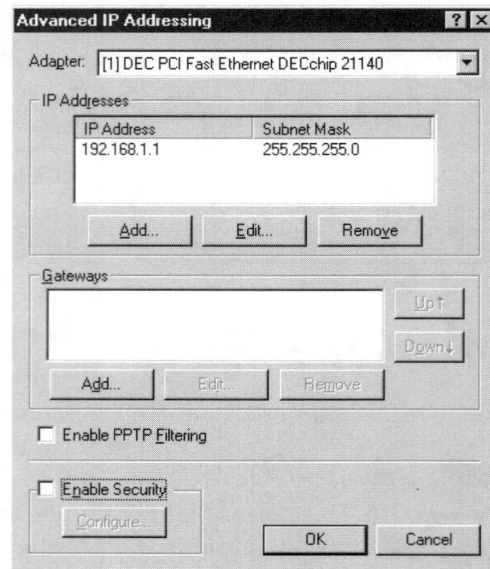

From the Advanced IP Addressing screen, click Enable Security so that the box is checked. This will activate the Configure button located just below it. Clicking the Configure button will produce the TCP/IP Security screen shown in Figure 14.24. The TCP/IP Security screen is used to configure all packet filtering access control policies that will be implemented on the system.

FIGURE 14.24:

The TCP/IP Security screen

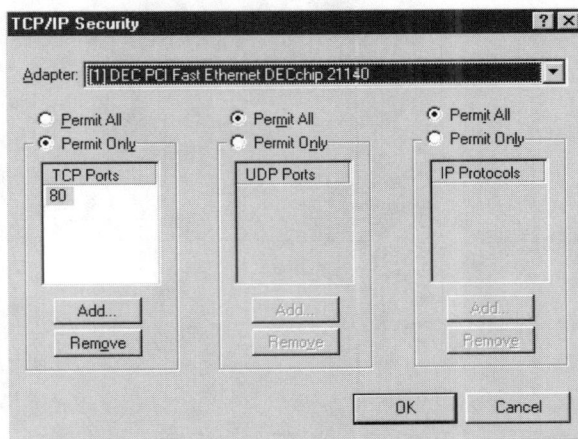

Configuring Packet Filtering

The topmost field on the TCP/IP Security screen is labeled Adapter. This allows you to scroll through all the network adapter cards installed in the system, so that you can assign a different access control policy to each one. This is useful if you have a multi-homed server that connects to two different subnets and you wish to provide different services to each. For example, you could leave all services enabled on one network card while limiting hosts on the other subnet to only accessing HTTP (TCP port 80).

The TCP/IP Security screen also lets you define which services can be accessed through the selected network card. For example, in Figure 14.24 we have specified that all users located off the DEC PCI network card should only be allowed access to services on TCP port 80. This access rule applies to the subnet directly connected to the DEC PCI card, as well as any other subnets that may be sitting behind this one on the other side of another router.

To understand the effects of the packet filter setting, take a look at Figure 14.25. This figure is the result of an IP port scan performed on an NT Server. Notice that the scan has detected a number of open ports on this server.

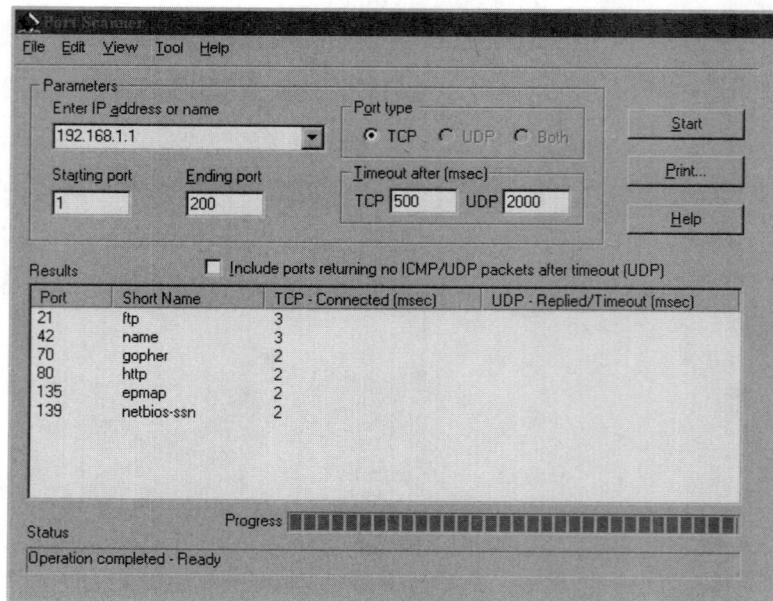

Figure 14.26 is a port scan of the same NT Server after it has been configured with the access control policy shown in Figure 14.24. Notice that the only port still responding to service requests is port 80 (HTTP). If this were a multi-homed system, we could continue to offer all services off another network card, while hosts connecting through this network would only have access to Web services.

Returning to the TCP/IP Security screen shown in Figure 14.24, you have three different options for controlling IP traffic. The first box, labeled TCP Ports, allows you to specify which inbound ports should be active on the system. You can choose Permit All, which will allow all TCP traffic, or you can choose Permit Only, which allows you to specify inbound access to only certain ports. To add a new port, simply click the Add button and type in the number of the port you wish to leave open. These filter settings will only affect TCP packets with the flag setting SYN=1. If traffic is received for a specific port but the SYN flag is not set, the packet filters will not block the traffic.

FIGURE 14.26:

A port scan performed against an NT Server using packet filtering

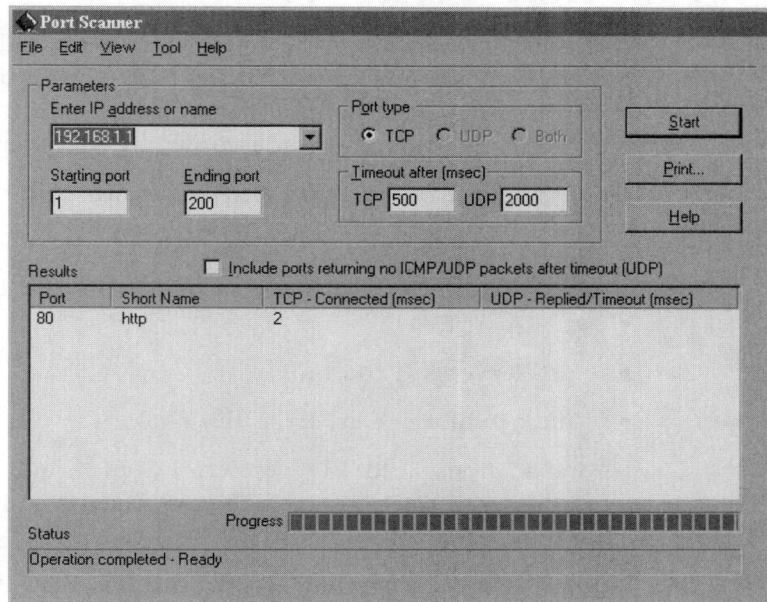

Remember that NT's packet filters only filter in an inbound direction. This means that you are not required to open upper port numbers in order to allow acknowledgments back to the requesting host.

Along with filtering TCP traffic, NT's packet filters allow you to filter on UDP, as well. Remember that NT's packet filters are static, not dynamic. This means that NT may not be as effective at filtering UDP traffic as a real firewall. With TCP traffic, NT can make filtering decisions based on the value of the SYN flag. Since UDP does not use flags, this is not an option. Finally, the TCP/IP Security screen also allows you to filter traffic based on transport. Within the IP Protocols box, you are allowed to click the Add button and specify only certain transports by name.

Once you have configured your packet filter settings, click the OK button from each of the four open screens. You will need to reboot the system for your filters to take effect.

A Final Word on NT Ports

NT does not report conflicts caused by two or more applications acting on a specific port. This means that any ports that are blocked by the packet filters will not produce an error message in Event Viewer. This also means that you need to inspect your system very carefully in order to identify which services are running.

For example, review the port scan we performed in Figure 14.25. The server appears to be running the following services:

- WINS (port 42)

- RPC (port 135)

- NetBIOS over IP (port 139)

- Internet Information Server (IIS)

IIS includes port 21 for FTP, port 70 for Gopher, and port 80 for HTTP. In other words, this looks like a normal NT Server. There is nothing in this port scan that would raise a network administrator's suspicions.

The fact is, this server is hiding a surprise. If you telnet to port 70 of this system, you are presented with a command prompt, as shown in Figure 14.27. You are not prompted for a password, and you are able to gain immediate access to the file system. Obviously, this is not the type of response you would expect from a Gopher server.

How did this happen? The NT Server in question is running a copy of L0pht's Netcat for NT. Netcat is an all-purpose utility that can act as a client as well as a server. It also has the ability to bind itself over another service listening on the same port number. Thus Netcat is able to accept and process inbound service requests before the Gopher service is able to detect the traffic. This means that the network administrator would have to actually attempt a connection with every active port in order to ensure that the correct service is listening.

Since NT does not report conflicts between multiple applications that attempt to bind to the same listening port, Netcat produces no telltale error messages. In fact, it is even possible to launch Netcat so that it would listen for inbound service requests on a port that is supposed to be blocked by your packet filter policy. In other words, it is possible to have applications accept inbound connection requests before the request is subjected to the filters. Again, this type of activity generates no error log messages.

FIGURE 14.27:

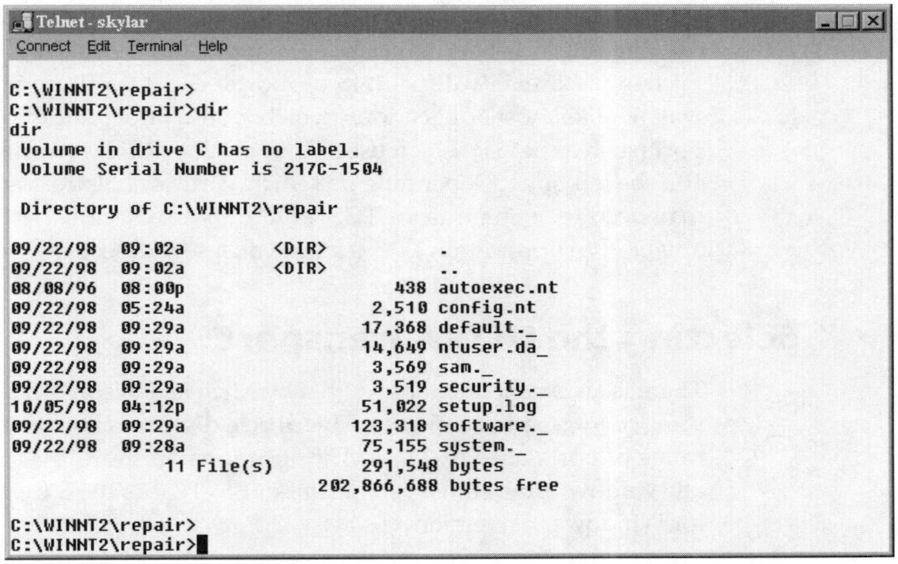

A command session with what appears to be a normal NT Server

```
Telnet - skylar                                                    _ □ ×
Connect  Edit  Terminal  Help

C:\WINNT2\repair>
C:\WINNT2\repair>dir
dir
 Volume in drive C has no label.
 Volume Serial Number is 217C-1504

 Directory of C:\WINNT2\repair

09/22/98  09:02a       <DIR>          .
09/22/98  09:02a       <DIR>          ..
08/08/96  08:00p                  438 autoexec.nt
09/22/98  05:24a                2,510 config.nt
09/22/98  09:29a               17,368 default._
09/22/98  09:29a               14,649 ntuser.da_
09/22/98  09:29a                3,569 sam._
09/22/98  09:29a                3,519 security._
10/05/98  04:12p               51,022 setup.log
09/22/98  09:29a              123,318 software._
09/22/98  09:28a               75,155 system._
              11 File(s)        291,548 bytes
                            202,866,688 bytes free

C:\WINNT2\repair>
C:\WINNT2\repair>█
```

TIP   The moral of this story is that even if you think you have locked a system down tight, it is always a good idea to perform a system review on a regular basis. This review should include a check of which processes are running in memory, as well as what type of response you receive when connecting to each of the active ports.

Securing DCOM

The *Distributed Component Object Model* (DCOM) is an object-oriented approach to making Remote Procedure Calls (RPC). Thus DCOM is sometimes referred to as Object RPC. DCOM is designed to replace Microsoft's original specification called Object Linking and Embedding (OLE) remote automation. The benefit of DCOM over OLE is that DCOM is designed to support multiple flavors of operating systems.

A DCOM client will initially connect to the DCOM server using a fixed port number of UDP 135 (NT RPC). The DCOM server then assigns the ports it will use dynamically. This makes DCOM applications such as NetMeeting and Exchange extremely difficult to support if client traffic must pass through a firewall. Unlike most applications, which would only require you to open a single port (such as SMTP, which uses TCP port 25), DCOM requires that all ports above 1023 be left open. Depending on which Windows platforms you are using, you may need to open ports for TCP, UDP, or both. Obviously, this makes supporting any DCOM application across a firewall a severe security threat.

Selecting the DCOM Transport

There is an excellent paper written by Michael Nelson located at www.microsoft.com/com/wpaper/dcomfw.asp. This article discusses how to go about limiting the range of ports used by DCOM applications. In short, the article mentions that all Windows operating systems default to TCP as the DCOM transport, except for Windows NT version 4.0.

> **TIP**
>
> One of the best ways to begin limiting the number of ports used by DCOM is to ensure that all of your systems are using the same transport.

To change your NT 4.0 systems to use TCP as their default DCOM transport, launch regedt32 and find the following key:

```
HKEY_LOCAL_MACHINE\Software\Microsoft\Rpc
```

This will produce the Registry Editor screen shown in Figure 14.28. The left pane shows the hive objects we needed to navigate in order to find this specific key. The right pane shows the actual key value. This key defines the protocol search order to be used by DCOM. Notice that the first protocol that DCOM is set to use is UDP/IP, which is defined by the ncadg_ip_udp key value.

Once you locate this key, double-click the values in the right pane. This will produce the Multi-String Editor window shown in Figure 14.29. From top to bottom, each line defines the protocol search order for DCOM to use. For example, if DCOM attempts to connect to a remote system using UDP/IP and that connection fails, this window defines that DCOM should then attempt a connection using IPX.

FIGURE 14.28:

Using Registry Editor to change the DCOM default protocol

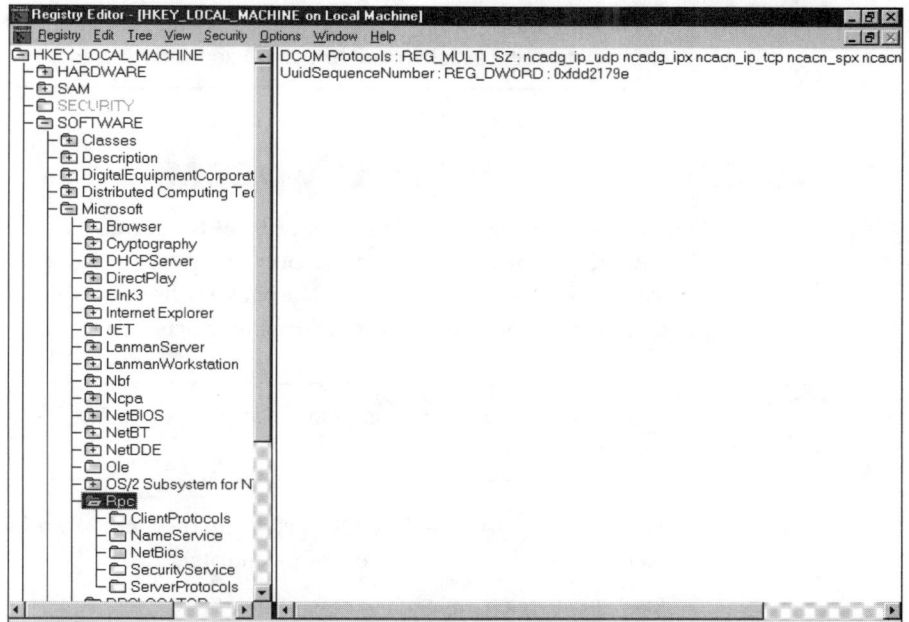

FIGURE 14.29:

The Multi-String Editor showing DCOM's protocol search order

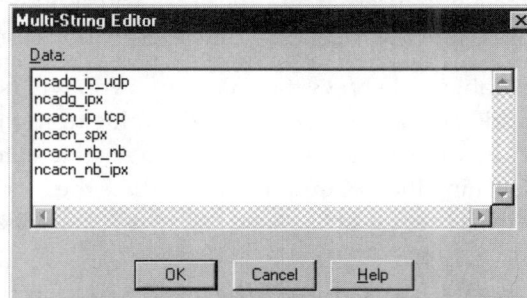

To change the default search order so that the TCP/IP connections are attempted first, use Cut and Paste to move the ncacn_ip_tcp from being the third listed item to being the first. Once this is complete, click the OK button and exit Registry Editor. You will need to reboot the system for your changes take effect.

TIP   Since the Multi-String Editor does not have an Edit menu option, you must use Ctrl+X to cut the highlighted text string and Ctrl+V to paste it.

Limiting the Ports Used by DCOM

Nelson's paper also describes how to limit the range of ports used by DCOM, forcing DCOM applications to use only the ports you specify. This eases the burden of supporting DCOM through a packet filter or a firewall by limiting the ports used to a select few—rather than all ports above 1023.

NOTE   This does not limit which applications try to use DCOM; it simply limits the ports used by DCOM itself.

To define the ports used by DCOM, launch `regedt32` and go back to the key you were editing in the last section of this chapter:

```
HKEY_LOCAL_MACHINE\Software\Microsoft\Rpc
```

With this key highlighted, select Edit ➤ Add Key from the Registry Editor menu. This will produce the Add Key dialog box. In the Key Name field, type in the name **Internet** and click OK. You should now see a key value named Internet appear below Rpc. Click the Internet object so that the entry becomes highlighted.

Table 14.1 shows the values that you will need to add to this key. Values are added by selecting Edit ➤ Add Value from the Registry Editor menu. When the Add Value window appears, you need to enter the value name and data type. Clicking the OK button will produce the String Editor. In the String Editor window, enter the string value shown in Table 14.1.

TABLE 14.1:   Required Key Changes to Make DCOM Use Fixed Port Numbers

Value Name	Data Type	String Value
Ports	REG_MULTI_SZ	57100-57120
57131		
PortsInternetAvailable	REG_SZ	Y
UseInternetPorts	REG_SZ	Y

The Ports string value defines which ports may be used by DCOM. Each line may specify a specific port number or a range. For example, in Table 14.1 ports 57100–57120 have been defined as ports that DCOM can use. An additional port, 57131, has also been defined. If you will be supporting DCOM through a firewall, the string values you associate with the Ports key are the inbound port numbers you will need to open from the Internet to your server.

NOTE   When assigning DCOM ports, it is a good idea to never statically assign the ports 1–49151, as these may be in use by another service or may be dynamically assigned by the system before the DCOM application is activated. When statically assigning ports, use only private port numbers that range from 49152 through 65535. For more information, see: `ftp://ftp.isi.edu/in-notes/iana/assignments/port-numbers`.

DCOM and NAT

One of the caveats about DCOM is that raw IP address information is passed between systems. This means that network address translation cannot be used. NAT is typically used to translate private IP address space into legal IP address space for the purpose of communicating on the Internet. If the DCOM server is sitting behind a device performing NAT, DCOM will not work. This is because the client will attempt to reach the system using the IP address information embedded in the data stream. If you need to support DCOM applications over the Internet, you cannot use NAT to translate IP address information.

TIP   You can use DCOM applications across the Internet using private address space if the data stream will be traveling along a VPN tunnel. This is because a tunnel supports the use of private address space without performing NAT. See Chapter 10 for more details.

Ports Used by Windows Services

Microsoft uses a number of ports and services that are unique to the NT operating system. While the port numbers used by services such as SMTP, FTP, and HTTP are documented in Request For Comment (RFC) 1700, many of the ports used for Windows-specific services, such as WINS or remote event viewing, are not as well documented. This can make supporting Microsoft services extremely difficult across subnets where firewalls or packet filters are being used.

Table 14.2 lists a number of common Windows services along with the transport and port numbers they use.

TABLE 14.2:   Transport and Port Numbers for Common Windows Services

Name	Transport/Port Number
b-node browsing	UDP/137, UDP/138
p-node WINS registration	TCP/139
p-node WINS query	TCP/139
WINS replication	TCP/42
Logon	UDP/137, UDP/138, TCP/139
File share access	TCP/139
Printer share access	TCP/139
Event Viewer	TCP/139
Server Manager	TCP/139
User Manager	TCP/139
Performance Monitor	TCP/139
Registry Editor	TCP/139

NOTE   Keep in mind that in some cases you may need to open more than just the port number listed in Table 14.2. For example, Event Viewer needs to know the IP address used by the remote NT system. If you are not using a local LMHOSTS file, you may need to enable the ports used by WINS, as well.

Table 14.3 lists a number of Windows applications that rely on DCOM. This means that the service will use one or more fixed ports, as well as random ports above 1023, unless you have made the Registry changes documented in the last section. Also, RPC 135 will default to UDP (as shown in the table below) unless you have modified the Registry to use TCP.

TABLE 14.3:   Windows Applications That Use DCOM

Name	Transport/Port Number
Domain Trusts	UDP/135, UDP/137, UDP/138, TCP/139
DHCP Manager	UDP/135
WINS Manager	UDP/135
Message Queue	UDP/135, TCP&UDP/1801, TCP/2101, TCP/2103, TCP/2105
Exchange Client	UDP/135
Exchange replication	UDP/135

NOTE   There are a number of additional Registry key changes you must make to an Exchange server in order to support client communications through a firewall. For more information, see Microsoft's Knowledgebase articles Q148732 and Q155831.

Additional Registry Key Changes

A review of Microsoft's Web site reveals a number of other Registry keys that may be modified in order to enhance security. All key entries should be changed using the `regedt32` utility. The predecessor to this utility, `regedit`, does not have some of the advanced functionality of `regedt32`, such as support for multi-part keys.

NOTE   As mentioned earlier in this chapter, make sure you generate an emergency recovery disk before attempting to edit the Registry.

Logon Banner

By modifying certain Registry keys, it is possible to change the Windows NT logon process so that pressing Ctrl+Alt+Del produces a logon banner. This banner is a dialog box that can be used to display a legal notice or system usage policy. Before users can authenticate to the system, they must click OK or press Enter to make the actual logon screen appear.

To add a logon banner, launch `regedt32` and find the key:

`HKEY_LOCAL_MACHINE\Software\Microsoft\Windows NT\Current Version\Winlogon`

Within this key you will find two key values, one named `LegalNoticeCaption` and the other named `LegalNoticeText`. Click either of these two objects in order to modify the value. The `LegalNoticeCaption` value is the text that will appear in the title area of the dialog box. The `LegalNoticeText` value is the actual text that will appear within the dialog box itself. Once you have made your changes, exit `regedt32` and reboot the system.

Hiding the Last Logon Name

As a convenience, Windows NT retains the logon name of the last user to log on to the system locally. This allows the system to fill in the logon name field the next time someone attempts to authenticate to the system by pressing Ctrl+Alt+Del. For a high-security environment, this may not be considered acceptable because it can provide anyone passing by the system with a valid logon name.

In order to prevent Windows NT from presenting the name of the last user to log on to the system, find the following Registry key:

`HKEY_LOCAL_MACHINE\Software\Microsoft\Windows NT\Current Version\Winlogon`

Highlight the `Winlogon` key and select Edit ➤ Add Value from the Registry Editor menu. When the Add Value window appears add a value name of **DontDisplayLastUserName** with a data type of `REG_SZ`. When you click the OK button, the String Editor window will appear. Enter a string value of **1**.

Once you have entered the string value, click OK, and exit the `regedt32` utility. You will need to reboot the system before the changes will take effect.

Securing the Registry on Windows NT Workstation

You can edit the Registry on a Windows NT system across the network, as well as from the local machine. On a Windows NT Server, remote Registry access is restricted to administrator-level accounts. On a Windows NT Workstation, however, no such restriction exists.

In order to restrict Registry access to administrators on NT Workstation, find the following Registry key:

```
HKEY_LOCAL_MACHINE\SYSTEM\CurrentcontrolSet\Control\SecurePipeServers
```

You will first need to create a key named **winreg** beneath this object. This is performed by highlighting SecurePipeServers and selecting Edit ➤ Add Key from the Registry Editor menu. Once this key has been created, you should highlight it and select Edit ➤ Add Value from the Registry Editor menu. When the Add Value window appears, add a value name of **REG_DWORD** with a data type of REG_SZ. When you click the OK button, the String Editor window will appear. Enter a string value of 1.

Once you have entered the string value, select OK, and exit the regedt32 utility. You will need to reboot the workstation before the changes will take effect.

Securing Access to Event Viewer

By default, Windows NT allows guests and null users access to entries in the Event Viewer System and Application logs. This information can be used by an attacker in order to identify further vulnerabilities on the system. The Security log is exempt from this setting because access is controlled by the Manage Audit Log settings in User Manager. To ensure that the System and Application logs are only accessed by administrator-level accounts, find the following keys:

```
HKEY_LOCAL_MACHINE\System\CurrentControlSet\Services\EventLog\Application
HKEY_LOCAL_MACHINE\System\CurrentControlSet\Services\EventLog\System
```

Highlight the Application key and select Edit ➤ Add Value from the Registry Editor menu. When the Add Value window appears, type in a value name of **RestrictGuestAccess** with a data type of REG_DWORD. When you click the OK button, the String Editor window will appear. Enter a string value of **1**. Once you have entered the string value, click OK and highlight the System key.

Repeat these steps for the System key, as well.

Cleaning the Page File

The *page file* is the area of the hard disk used by Windows NT as virtual memory. As part of memory management, Windows NT will move inactive information from physical memory to the page file so that more physical memory will be available for active programs. When the Windows NT system is shut down, there is no guarantee that this information will be completely removed. Thus an attacker who is able to boot the system to an alternate operating system may be able to read information that was stored in this file.

To ensure that the contents of the page file are purged during shutdown, locate the following key:

```
HKEY_LOCAL_MACHINE\SYSTEM\CurrentControlSet\Control\Session
Manager\Memory Management
```

Highlight the Memory Management key and select Edit ➤ Add Value from the Registry Editor menu. When the Add Value window appears, type in a value name of **ClearPageFileAtShutdown** with a data type of REG_DWORD. When you click the OK button, the String Editor window will appear. Enter a string value of **1**.

Once you have entered the string value, click OK, and exit the regedt32 utility.

NOTE   The system will require two reboots before the page file is wiped.

Windows 2000

Windows 2000 includes many new security features, including

- Active Directory, which is designed to replace the flat security structure of the current domain architecture
- Encrypting File System
- Kerberos version 5
- Public key certificate services
- IPSEC support
- Support for smart cards

Active Directory

While NT 4.0 provided a flat, non-extensible directory service Active Directory provides a very flexible, hierarchical, and expandable directory service.

There are three ways of looking at Active Directory:

As a Store   Active Directory stores information about network objects hierarchically, and makes this information available to users, applications, and services.

As a Structure   All network objects and services are stored as objects within Active Directory. Constructs such as domains, trees, forests, trust relationships, organizational units, and sites are included.

As a Team Player   Active Directory uses standard directory access protocols and can communicate with other directory services and applications.

Other features of Active Directory include the following:

DNS integration   All Active Directory services utilize DNS to advertise, locate, and connect to all network services.

Extensibility   The schema (or structure) of the Active Directory is extensible, meaning that new classes of objects and new attributes of existing classes can be added by administrators or applications.

Object-based policies   Also known as Group Policies, these settings determine user access to resources and how these resources can be used.

Scalability   Active Directory uses one ore more domains, each with one or more domain controllers. Multiple domains can be combined into a domain tree and multiple domain trees can be combined into a forest. A single domain network is still a single tree and single forest.

Multimaster replication   All domain controllers are created equal in the sense that a change to the directory can occur on any domain controller, which in turn updates all the other domain controllers. If one domain controller fails, the others can take over its load.

Centralized security   AD authorizes each user's access to the network. In addition, access control can be defined not only on each object in the directory, but also on each property of each object.

Interoperability   LDAP (Lightweight Directory Access Protocol) allows AD to share object information with applications and other directory services.

Encrypting File System (EFS)

In NT 4.0, user access to files is controlled by Access Control Lists (ACLs). But what if physical control of a computer system is lost? What happens if a laptop is stolen? There are many tools available to a hacker that would permit them to boot the machine in a different operating system that didn't respect ACLs, and sensitive information could be read.

To overcome this problem, Microsoft integrated the Encrypting File System (EFS) into Windows 2000. EFS is based on public-key encryption, taking advantage of the CryptoAPI architecture in Windows. Each file is encrypted using a randomly generated key, called the file encryption key. File encryption uses symmetric encryption algorithms, but future releases will allow other schemes.

EFS is integrated with the NT File System (NTFS). When temporary files are created, the attributes from the original file may be copied to temporary fields as long as all files are on the NTFS volume. If the original file is encrypted, EFS encrypts its temporary copies when attributes are transferred during file creation. EFS resides in the Windows 2000 kernel and uses the non-paged pool to store file encryption keys, ensuring that they never make it to the paging file.

Other characteristics of EFS include:

User interaction   By default, no administrator action is necessary to enable encryption. Encryption and decryption are handled transparently on a per-file or per-directory basis.

Data recovery   W2K allows EFS only when the system is configured with one or more recovery keys. Data recovery is intended for business environments where the organization expects to be able to recover data encrypted by an employee after an employee leaves or when encryption keys are lost.

Command-line   The Cipher utility lets users encrypt and decrypt files and folders from a command line (or an administrative script).

Kerberos Version 5

Prior to W2K, Microsoft relied on the NTLM protocol for user authentication. Starting with W2K, Microsoft has integrated an open, industry-standard protocol developed by MIT, called *Kerberos*. Now in its fifth version, Kerberos is a mature and robust protocol that provides many advantages over NTLM, including:

More efficient authentication to servers   With NTLM, an application server must connect to a domain controller in order to authenticate each client. With Kerberos, the server authenticates the client by examining credentials presented by the client. Credentials are reusable throughout the entire session.

Mutual authentication   NTLM allows servers to verify the identities of their clients. It does not allow clients to verify server's identity, or one server to verify the identity of another. Kerberos assumes nothing—parties at both ends of a connection can know that the party on the other is who it claims to be.

Delegated authentication   Windows services impersonate clients when accessing resources on their behalf. Some distributed applications are designed so that a front-end service must impersonate clients. The Kerberos protocol has a proxy mechanism that allows a service to impersonate its client when connecting to their services. No equivalent is available with NTLM.

Simplified trust management   One of the benefits of Kerberos is that trust between the security authorities for Windows 2000 domains is two-way and transitive (by default). Credentials issued by the security authority for any domain are accepted everywhere in the tree.

Interoperability   Microsoft follows the Kerberos standards as specified by the Internet Engineering Task Force (IETF), which allows W2K to play nice with other networks using Kerberos for authentication.

Public Key Certificate Services

Prior to W2K, encryption was implemented in a fragmented and isolated fashion. With the growth of the Internet and distributed, interoperating networking systems, authenticating the participants of a data session and then encrypting the subsequent session have become minimum standards of data processing.

Public-key cryptography provides three capabilities that are critical for modern networks:

Privacy   Encrypting all network communication, including e-mail, voice, and instant messaging.

Authentication   Verifying the identity of all participants of a session—for the full duration of the session.

Non-repudiation   Creating a binding record of all transactions performed by all parties during a session.

Traditional cryptography relies on secret keys, wherein two parties share a single secret key that is used to both encrypt and decrypt data. Loss or compromise of the secret key makes the data it encrypts vulnerable. Public-key systems, on the other hand, use two keys: a public key that is shared, and a private key that is closely held. These keys are complementary in the sense that if you encrypt something with the public key it can only be decrypted with the corresponding private key, and vice versa.

For example, if Bob wants to send Alice some private data, he uses her public key to encrypt, then sends it to her. Upon receiving the encrypted data, Alice uses her private key to decrypt it. The important concept here is that Alice can freely distribute her public key in order to allow anyone in the world to encrypt data that only she can decrypt. If Bob and Chuck both have copies of her public key, and Chuck intercepts an encrypted message from Bob to Alice, he will not be able to decrypt it; only Alice's private key can that, and she is the only person who holds it.

The previous example takes care of privacy, but what about authentication and non-repudiation? For this we turn to the concept of signing. Signing also uses encryption, but the goal is to prove the origin of the data. If Alice wants the world to know that she is the author of a message, she encrypts it using her private key and posts the message publicly. The only way this message can be decrypted is to use Alice's freely available public key—thus verifying the source of the message as Alice.

Used together, encryption and signing provide for privacy, authentication, and non-repudiation. The framework that provides these services is known as Public Key Infrastructure (PKI). PKI is the operating system and services that make it easy to implement and manage public keys, and it provides features including

Key Management   PKI makes it easy to issue, review, and revoke keys, as well as manage the trust level attached to keys.

Publish Keys   PKI offers an easy format for users to locate and retrieve public keys (including determining whether they are valid or not).

Use Keys   PKI provides integration with third-party applications to easily select which combination of services (encryption and signing) to perform.

While public keys are the objects that PKI uses (private keys are always stored privately), they are usually packaged as digital certificates. The certificate contains the public key and a set of identifying details like the key-holder's name. The binding between attributes and the public key is present because the certificate is digitally signed by the entity that issues it; the issuer's signature on the certificate vouches for its authenticity and correctness.

The problem is, of course, in determining the validity of the entity that issues a certificate in the first place. The answer lies in the concept of a certificate hierarchy. In a hierarchy, each issuer (known as a certificate authority) signs each certificate that it issues (with its private key). The public half of the CA's key-pair is itself packaged in a certificate—one that was issued by a higher-level CA. This pattern can continue through as many levels as possible, but eventually there must be a top-level CA. This CA, known as the *root certificate authority*, signs its own certificate. Obviously, an end user has to trust that the root certificate is who it says it is.

Well-known commercial CAs like Thawte and Verisign issue certificates to millions of users. W2K includes its own PKI, which can be used to issue certificates but also provides services to manage and use them. The primary components of W2K PKI are

Certificate Services   This central PKI service allows organizations to act as their own CAs, giving them the ability to issue and manage digital certificates.

Active Directory   As a directory service, AD serves as the publication service for PKI.

PKI-enabled applications   Internet Explorer, Microsoft Money, Internet Information Server, Outlook, and Outlook Express, as well as many other third-party applications can use W2K PKI.

Exchange Key Management Service (KMS)   This component of Microsoft Exchange archives and retrieves keys used to encrypt and sign e-mail.

Microsoft has made an effort to follow open PKI standards. Some of these are shown in Table 14.4:

T A B L E 1 4 . 4 :   PKI Standards Supported by W2K

Standard	What it does
X.509	Controls format and content of digital certificates
CRL ver. 2	Controls format and content of certificate revocation lists
PKCS family	Controls format and behavior for public-key exchange and distribution
SSL ver. 3	Provides encryption for Web sessions
SGC	Provides SSL-like security without export complications
IPSec	Provides encryption for network sessions using IP
PKINIT	Is the emerging standard for using public keys to log on to networks that use Kerberos
PC/SC	Is a smart card standard

IPSec

NT 4.0 did not provide robust and routine network data encryption—a critical weakness in today's environment of mixed networks and global information exchange. W2K includes IP Security Protocol (IPSec) which ensures that data traffic is safe on two basic levels:

Modification   Data is protected en route.

Interception   Data cannot be viewed or copied en route

IPSec is an open standard designed by the IETF for IP, and it supports network-level authentication, data integrity, and encryption. Because IPSec in W2K is deployed below the transport level of the OSI model, application-specific configuration is no longer necessary. This also dramatically simplifies VPNs. Additional IPSec services provided by W2K include:

Data integrity   IP authentication headers ensure data integrity during communications.

Dynamic rekeying   Regenerating keys at variable intervals during a session dramatically improves protection against attacks.

Centralized management   W2K administrators can set security policies and filters to define granular security based on user, work group, or other criteria.

Flexibility   IPSec policies can be applied to a single workstation, user, group, or enterprise-wide data communications.

IPSec provides for privacy, authentication, and non-repudiation by using an authentication header (AH) and encapsulated security payload (ESP). The AH provides source authentication and integrity. The ESP provides confidentiality (along with authentication and integrity). With IPSec, only the sender and the recipient know the security key. If the authentication data is valid, the receiver knows that the data comes from the purported sender and has not been altered in transit.

Microsoft has included these industry-standard technologies in their implementation of IPSec:

Diffie-Hellman   The preferred method of sharing keys, Diffie-Hellman starts with the two participants exchanging public information. Then, each entity combines the other's public information along with its own secret information to generate a shared-secret value.

Hash Message Authentication Code (HMAC)   Used to verify data integrity, HMAC produces a digital signature for each packet. If the contents of the packet change, the resulting discrepancy is calculated from the encrypted digital signature and the packet is discarded.

Data Encryption Standard (DES)   Used to enforce confidentiality, DES uses a secret key algorithm known as cipher block chaining (CBC) to generate a random number that is used with the secret key to encrypt data.

Other security protocols that support IPSec in W2K are:

Internet Security Association and Key Management Protocol (ISAKMP)
These protocols define a common framework to support the establishment of security associations (SA). An SA is a set of parameters that define the mechanisms (such as keys) for secure communication between two computers.

Oakley Key Determination   Oakley uses Perfect Forward Secrecy (PFS) to make sure that only data directly encrypted by a key can be compromised if the key encryption is broken. It never reuses a key to compute additional keys and never uses the original key-generation material to compute another key.

Because IPSec has been integrated into W2K, it can take advantage of W2K's PKI services including AD, Group Policies, and Certificate Services. This provides a powerful security advantage to W2K—allowing centralized management of all security services.

Smart Cards

NT 4.0 user authentication methods were limited to passwords, unless third-party products were installed. Passwords provide numerous problems including management overhead and personnel issues (users setting weak or easily guessed passwords, or frustration with high password turnover). The security industry as a whole has turned to more secure and easily managed ways of verifying identity. One of the most popular of these methods that strikes a balance between cost and functionality is the smart card.

A smart card is a credit card–sized device that uses an integrated circuit to store information, including certificates, private keys, and any other personal information. Smart cards are used to gain access to computer systems with smart card readers. Typically, a user will swipe (or inset) their smart card through a smart card reader. They are then prompted to enter some additional unique and private information such as a PIN (Personal Identification Number)—similar to the concept of an ATM card. Smart cards, however, store their information not in an unencrypted magnetic strip, but in an encrypted format on the integrated circuit.

Smart cards are very attractive from a security perspective because they enhance software-only solutions such as client authentication, logon, and secure e-mail. Smart cards really exist at the center of several of PKI because they

- Provide tamper-resistant storage for protecting private keys along with personal information.

- Isolate sensitive security operations (such as authentication, digital signatures, and key exchanges) from other parts of the system that do not have a need to know.

- Provide portability to credentials and private information between computers at any geographical location (work, home, on the road, etc.).

Traditionally smart cards have had limited success because of non-standardization. The International Standards Organization (ISO) developed ISO 7816 in an attempt to centralize smart card development. In 1996, Europay, MasterCard, and VISA (EMV) defined a specification that adopted ISO 7816 standards and added additional ones to support the financial services industry. The European telecommunications industry split the standards process by creating their own variant of the ISO 7816 for their Global System for Mobile Communications (GSM) specification to enable identification and authentication of mobile phone users.

None of these specifications met the needs of the computer industry, so in 1997 the PC/SC (Personal Computer/Smart Card) Workgroup (formed by several industry leaders including Microsoft) released the PC/SC specifications. Also based on ISO 7816, these standards include issues relating directly to information systems. Microsoft implemented the standards using the following technology:

CryptoAPI   This component allows for any Smart Card Service Provider (SCSP) to take advantage of cryptographic features integrated into W2K, without having to know cryptography.

SCard COM   A noncryptographic interface, SCard COM allows applications to gain access to generic smart card services.

Because of their integration with W2K services, smart cards can be used as the primary contributor to the PKI of an organization, simultaneously providing a high degree of management and risk-avoidance.

Summary

In this chapter we discussed how to go about securing an NT server environment. You saw how to manage user accounts, as well as how to set file permissions. We also discussed the importance of installing security patches. Finally, we looked at the new technologies included with Windows 2000 that provide a very powerful, centrally managed infrastructure for network security.

In the next chapter, we will discuss how to secure a UNIX system. Since many environments still use UNIX for mission-critical applications, the operating system is a strategic component of many networking environments.

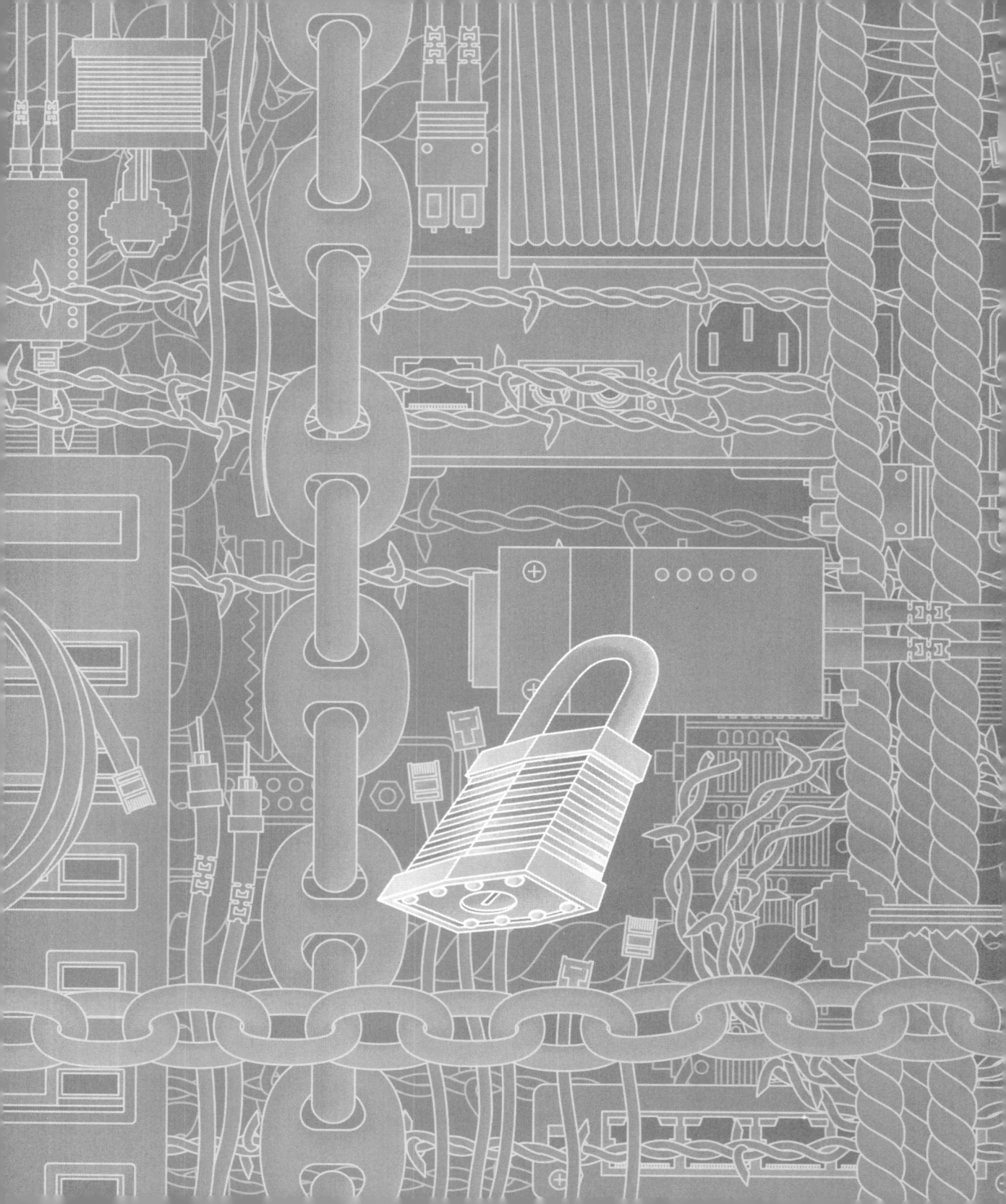

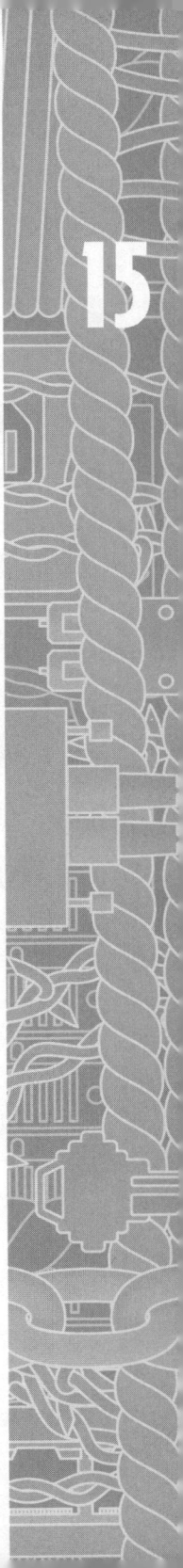

CHAPTER
FIFTEEN

15

UNIX

In order to secure a system running UNIX, you must have a firm handle on how the operating system works. While most UNIX systems come with some type of GUI, these usually won't walk you through the process, nor are there extensive Help buttons to click that will describe a particular setting and when it should be used. UNIX systems are predominantly managed from the command line, although some utilities have been ported to X-Windows. This makes securing a UNIX system extremely difficult for those who are not versed in the operating system.

The reward to learning UNIX is the ability to manage a system that still controls a majority of the world's critical data. While UNIX has lost market share in the small markets, it is still the major player in supporting mission-critical applications. It also has the ability to become an extremely secure application server. For example, while an NT server running Internet Information Server (ISS) requires that the RPC (135) and all NetBIOS ports (137–139) be left open and vulnerable, a UNIX system running Apache only requires you to open the ports you actually want to offer services on (such as port 80 for Web). With fewer open ports, it is less likely an attacker will find an entry point into your system.

UNIX History

Developed in 1969 at Bell Labs, UNIX is by far the oldest distributed NOS in use today. Its creation is credited to Ken Thompson, who was working at that time for Bell Labs on the Multiplex Information Computing System (MULTICS) for a General Electric mainframe. Bell Labs eventually dropped the project, and with it went a very important piece of software: a game called Space Travel.

It is rumored that Thompson set out to create a new operating system to which the game could be ported. MULTICS assembly code was rewritten for an available DEC PDP-7, and the new operating system was named UNICS.

Bell Labs eventually took interest in UNICS, as additional functionality beyond the game Space Travel was added, which gave the operating system some commercial appeal. By 1972, it was named UNIX and had an install base of 10 computers. In 1973, Thompson and Dennis Ritchie rewrote the kernel in C, making the operating system much more portable.

In 1974, the IP protocol was developed and integrated into the UNIX operating system. No longer were multiple terminals required to access a single UNIX system.

A shared media called Ethernet could be used to access the system. UNIX had become a true NOS.

In the mid-'70s Bell Labs started releasing UNIX to universities. Since Ma Bell was still regulated at the time, it was not allowed to profit from UNIX's sales. For this reason, only a minimal fee was charged for the UNIX source code, which helped to make it widely available.

Once UNIX hit the universities, its development expanded from the injection of fresh blood. Students began improving the code and adding features. So dramatic were these changes at the University of California at Berkeley that the university began distributing its own flavor of UNIX: the Berkeley Software Distribution (BSD). The UNIX version that continued to be developed by Bell Labs is known as System V (pronounced "five").

Because UNIX could meet so many needs (and could run on so many platforms), many versions proliferated in the early 1980s. AT&T contributed to this diversity because of its licensing policy at the time; it retained the UNIX name, allowing any other distributor to name their own version of UNIX—with results like Solaris (Sun) and HP-UX (Hewlett-Packard). Even Microsoft released a version of UNIX called XENIX.

Finally, in 1987, AT&T along with Sun Microsystems and Microsoft agreed to combine the major versions of UNIX into a single distribution. Called System V Release 4 (abbreviated to SVR4), this version combined the best features of XENIX, BSD, and System V Release 3—and as a result became a de facto standard well into the 1990s. In 1993, six other vendors created a standard called COSE (Common Open Software Environment) including Hewlett-Packard, SCO (The Santa Cruz Operation), Sun-Soft, Univel, and UNIX System Laboratories. That same year, AT&T sold UNIX to Novell, which in turn sold it to SCO in 1995. Despite the repeated (and occasional) efforts to standardize UNIX, it is still a fragmented, but respected operating system.

The beginning of the 1990s saw another trend—non-commercial clones of the UNIX operating system, most notably FreeBSD and Linux.

FreeBSD

FreeBSD was born from a tumultuous legal battle involving Novell and U.C. Berkeley in the early 1990s. Originally developed as patch for an existing i386 version of BSD, then re-created from the bits of the 4.4BSD-Lite2 version of UNIX remaining after the settlement of the lawsuit between Novell and U.C. Berkeley,

FreeBSD has used a controlled development model to create an exceptionally stable (and secure) but free operating system.

So how does FreeBSD differ from Linux—in that they both employ an open model when it concerns their source code and price? For starters, FreeBSD is not dependent on any one person—unlike Linux, which is ultimately controlled by Linus Torvalds. And because FreeBSD inherited so much technology from an earlier, mature version of UNIX (BSD), its networking traditionally has been much more robust and has performed better than Linux (although that is rapidly changing). A third reason is that Linux takes after the other main family of UNIX, SVR4, in terms of file system layout, boot process, and executable standard. And finally, there is the issue of licensing; while Linux depends on the GNU CopyLeft license (which severely limits the commercial advantages to investing in Linux development), FreeBSD has its own license that permits much more commercial investment.

In the end, the decision to run FreeBSD over Linux (or even a mainstream version of UNIX) comes down to many personal preferences. One negative, FreeBSD does not support the same extensive range of hardware (such as obscure video cards) that Linux does. However, FreeBSD is dramatically easier to update and maintain "in sync" with the latest releases. Some organizations (such as Yahoo!) have decided to overcome the quandary by installing both, taking advantage of the numerous similarities as opposed to the few differences.

Linux

There is a myth (and it is only a myth) that Linux was created to compete against Microsoft. The truth, however, is much more humble, and, to make a play on an old saying—dissatisfaction is the mother of invention.

In 1991, Linus Torvalds, a student at the University of Helsinki in Finland, was frustrated with his choice of operating systems that would run on the Intel 386 processor. Not inclined to DOS, and unable to afford the more expensive UNIX versions, he decided to create his own UNIX clone based on a very limited PC clone called Minix. Linus then made two decisions that set the stage for the entire culture of open development that has grown with the OS itself: he released (and publicized) the source code on the Internet, and he asked for volunteers to help him further develop the OS.

Linux had two assets that immediately gave his new OS life: an FTP site at the University of Helsinki (where anyone could download the latest—and previous—

versions), and a variety of experienced volunteers who added device drivers, compilers, and code libraries. These elements formed a cohesive whole that allowed anyone to download a relatively complete operating system (albeit, initially, one without a full feature set).

Over time, the open source efforts have given Linux a full range of capabilities that are required for the success of any NOS—multitasking, memory management, and especially, networking. The open approach to software (with critical changes to the kernel still controlled by Torvalds) has created some hesitation in the business community (although it wholly embraces the fact that Linux is technically free of purchasing or licensing costs), simply because there is no single organization that ensures the commercial orientation or timeline of traditional operating systems.

However, in spite of the reservations that Linux might suffer the same "fragmentation" suffered by UNIX, there has been a dramatic growth in the past few years of corporations that are adopting Linux in core business applications, not just for peripheral network services like DNS, DHCP, and HTTP. Combined with the broad hardware and platform support, Linux has gained significant commercial support. This includes a 1.15 billion dollar investment into Linux by IBM (which, along with Compaq and Dell offer Linux pre-installed on their flagship server products) and major application vendors (including Oracle and Informix) porting their products to the Linux platform.

UNIX File System

Most UNIX operating systems are POSIX-compliant file systems that accept filenames up to 254 characters. Names are case sensitive, so `Myfile.txt` and `myfile.txt` would be considered two separate files. *POSIX* is a high-performance file system that helps to reduce the amount of file fragmentation.

UNIX uses *mount points* instead of drive letters when disks are added. A mount point is simply a point in the directory structure when the storage of the new disk has been added. This provides a cleaner feel to the file structure and helps to consolidate information.

For example, let's assume that you are setting up a UNIX machine and that you have two physical hard drives that you wish to use. You want to dedicate the first drive to the operating system, while utilizing the second drive for your users' home directories.

Instead of installing the OS on C: and putting the users' home directories on D:, you would simply assign the second drive for storage of all files under the /home directory. This would store all files on the primary drive, except for those located under the home directory.

There are a few benefits to this. First, it allows the addition of extra drives to be transparent. If you are looking for a file and have no idea where it is located, you can simply go to the root and perform a single search. You are not required to repeat the search for each additional drive, because they have been woven into the fabric of the directory structure.

Using mount points also helps to reduce system-wide failures due to a crashed drive. For example, if your second disk were to fail, you would lose only the users' home directories, not the entire system. This is in contrast to NetWare, which requires you to span the entire volume structure over both disks. If one of those drives fails, none of the files on the volume can be accessed.

Understanding UID and GID

UNIX uses two numbers as part of associating file permissions with their correct user and group. The *User ID* (UID) is a unique number assigned to each logon name on a system. The *Group ID* (GID) is used to uniquely identify each group. When a file is saved to the system, the user's UID and GID are saved along with it. This allows the UNIX system to enforce access restrictions to the file. For example, if your UID is 501, this information is recorded with every file you write to the system so that you can be properly identified as the file's owner.

Two files are used to store the UID and GID information. These are

passwd   Identifies the UID for each user and the GID of the user's primary group

group   Identifies the GID for each group and lists secondary groups for each user

We will discuss the passwd (password) file and the group file in greater detail later in this chapter. For now, just be aware that every user is associated with a unique UID and that every group is associated with a unique GID.

File Permissions

If UNIX has one major security weakness, it is its file permission settings. Permissions are set by three distinctive classes—owner, group, and everyone. I can set specific permissions for when I access a file, for when anyone in my group accesses a file, or for when anyone else on the system accesses the file. Permission settings are limited to read, write, and execute. UNIX does not support some of the more granular permission settings such as change, modify, and delete.

For example, let's assume you have a file called serverpasswords.txt in your home directory (a bad idea, I know, but this is only an example). Let's also assume that you are part of a group called admin. You can set permissions on this file so that you can read and write to it, members of the admin group have read-only access, and everyone else on the system has no access.

There are a few problems with this setup. First of all, even though "everyone else" has no access, they will still see that the file exists unless you remove all read permissions for the entire directory. Seeing a file may prompt others to take further steps and try to access the file, now that they know it is there. While removing all access to a directory may be acceptable in some cases, it may not be possible to do this in every situation, such as when you're working with shared file areas.

Another problem is that permissions are too general. You cannot say, "Give read and write access for this file to Sean and Deb from the admin group, but give all other members read-only access." UNIX was spawned in a much simpler time, when complicated file access was not required. In fact, for many years the focus was on making system access easier, not more difficult.

NOTE   The administrator account called *root* always has full access to all system files. This attribute cannot be removed.

Viewing File Permissions

You can receive a listing of directory files by using the ls (list) command. When combined with the -l (long) switch, file permission information is displayed. It is also useful to include the -a (all) switch, as this will show hidden files, as well. A sample output from the ls command is as follows:

```
[granite:~]$ ls -al
drwx------       3 cbrenton   user        512 Aug 25 18:15 .
drwxr-xr-x    5400 root       wheel     95744 Aug 28 17:01 ..
-rw-r--r--       1 cbrenton   user          0 Oct 31  1997 .addressbook
-rw-r--r--       1 cbrenton   user       1088 May  6  1997 .cshrc
```

```
-rw-r--r--    1 cbrenton   user       258 May   6  1997 .login
-rw-r--r--    1 cbrenton   user       176 May   6  1997 .mailrc
-rw-------    1 cbrenton   user      7881 Aug  25 18:15 .pine-debug1
-rw-------    1 cbrenton   user      8410 Aug  25 16:30 .pine-debug2
-rw-------    1 cbrenton   user      7942 Aug  25 15:08 .pine-debug3
-rw-------    1 cbrenton   user      8605 Aug  25 14:49 .pine-debug4
-rw-r--r--    1 cbrenton   user     11796 Aug  25 18:15 .pinerc
-rw-r--r--    1 cbrenton   user      1824 May   6  1997 .profile
-rw-r--r--    1 cbrenton   user        52 May   6  1997 .profile.locale
-rw-r--r--    1 cbrenton   user       749 May   6  1997 .shellrc
-rw-------    1 cbrenton   user      2035 Jul  13 14:33 dead.letter
drwx------    2 cbrenton   user       512 Aug  25 16:29 mail
```

The first column holds permission information. This output is a string of 10 characters that describes the type of entry, as well as the permissions assigned to the entry. Any entry beginning with a dash (-) is identified as a regular file. Table 15.1 contains a list of valid first characters and the type of entry each describes.

TABLE 15.1:   UNIX File Types

First Character Entry	Description
–	File
d	Directory entry
l	Symbolic link to a file in a remote directory
b	Block device (used for accessing peripherals such as tape drives)
c	Character device (used for accessing peripherals such as terminals)

The remaining nine characters are broken up into three groups of three characters each. The first group of three describes the permissions assigned to the file's owner. In the sample directory listing, all of the files are owned by the user cbrenton. The second group of three characters describes the permissions assigned to the file owner's group. In the sample directory listing, cbrenton is a part of the group user; therefore the second group of permissions is applied to that group. Finally, the third group of three characters describes the permissions granted to everyone else with a valid logon account to the system. Table 15.2 describes the possible permissions.

TABLE 15.2:   UNIX Permission Settings

Character Entry	Description
r	Entry can be viewed or accessed in read-only mode.
w	Entry can be modified or deleted. If assigned to a directory, new files can be created, as well.
x	If the entry is a file, it can be executed. If the entry is a directory, it can be searched.

For example, the file .login in the sample output would be interpreted as follows:

- This is a regular file (- is the first character).
- The owner of the file can read it (r is the second character).
- The owner of the file can write to it (w is the third character).
- The owner of the file cannot execute it (x is not the fourth character).
- The owner's group can read it (r is the fifth character).
- The owner's group cannot write to it (w is not the sixth character).
- The owner's group cannot execute it (x is not the seventh character).
- Everyone else can read it (r is the eighth character).
- Everyone else cannot write to it (w is not the ninth character).
- Everyone else cannot execute it (x is not the tenth character).

For a final example, review the last entry, which is for the directory named mail. The owner (cbrenton) has permission to read, write, and even search this directory. Everyone else on the system (including the group user) has no permissions to this directory. Anyone else who tries to access this directory will receive a "permission denied" error.

Changing File Permissions

The chmod utility can be used to change the permissions assigned to a file or directory. While there are a number of variations on the switches you can use, most users find the numeric system easiest to work with. The numeric system assigns an integer value to the read, write, and execute permissions. The assigned values are as follows:

- r (read): 4
- w (write): 2
- x (execute): 1
- No permissions: 0

By combining the numeric values, you can assign a specific level of access. For example, a numeric value of 6 indicates that the read and write permissions should be assigned, but not the execute permission. A numeric value of 5 would assign read and execute, but not write.

When working with chmod, permissions are set using a three-digit number. The first digit assigns the permission level for the owner. The second digit assigns the permission level for the group. Finally, the third digit assigns the permission level for all other users on the system. For example, executing the command

```
chmod 640 resume.txt
```

assigns

- Read and write access for the owner of resume.txt (6)
- Read-only access for the owner's group (4)
- No access for all other system users (0)

As with any multi-user operating system, you should restrict access permissions as much as possible, while still allowing users to perform their jobs. Most UNIX operating systems default to a pretty loose level of permissions, so you should review the file system and tighten up restrictions before allowing users access. Unfortunately, users do require at least read access to many of the system files. This can be a problem because it allows them to snoop around the system—and perhaps find a vulnerability that will provide a higher level of access.

Changing File Ownership and Groups

Two other utilities for maintaining access control are chown and chgrp. The chown command allows you to change the ownership of a file. This is useful if you need to move or create files and directories. The syntax of the command is

```
chown <switches> <new owner><file or directory name>
```

The most useful switch is -R, which allows you to change ownership through a directory structure recursively. For example, the command

```
chown -R lynn *
```

would give Lynn ownership of all files in the current directory as well as any subdirectories located below the current location. Lynn would be unable to take ownership of these files by running the chown command herself; the root user would have to run the command for her.

NOTE   Remember: UNIX is case sensitive, so the *R* must be capitalized.

The chgrp command allows you to change the group associated with a file. This is useful if you wish to associate a file with a different group than your primary group. For example, let's say that the passwd file defines your primary group as users. Let's assume that you are also a member of the group admin. When you create a file, the file is automatically associated with the group users. If you wish instead to associate this file with the admin group, you would need to run the command:

```
chgrp admin file_name
```

This would change the group association of the file to the admin group. Any group permissions that have been set will now be associated with admin, not users. As with the chown command, you can use the -R switch to recursively change the group association of every file in an entire directory structure.

Account Administration

UNIX systems can be self-sufficient when it comes to administering users and groups. This means that if you have multiple UNIX systems, account information can be administered separately on each. Many UNIX flavors can also be centrally managed through Network Information Services Plus (NIS+), an updated version of NIS (formerly known as Yellow Pages).

NIS+ is a hierarchical database system designed to share user and group information across multiple systems. A collection of systems sharing NIS information is called a *domain*. To give a user access to the domain, an administrator simply needs to add that user's account to the master NIS server. If the user attempts to access a system within the domain, that system will contact the master in order to validate the user's logon. This allows the user to gain access to the system, even though there is no local account defined.

The Password File

All user authentication requests are verified against the password file named passwd. Here is a sample passwd file:

```
[cbrenton@thor /etc]$ cat passwd
root:Y2YeCL6KFw10E:0:0:root:/root:/bin/bash
bin:*:1:1:bin:/bin:
daemon:*:2:2:daemon:/sbin:
adm:*:3:4:adm:/var/adm:
lp:*:4:7:lp:/var/spool/lpd:
sync:*:5:0:sync:/sbin:/bin/sync
shutdown:*:6:0:shutdown:/sbin:/sbin/shutdown
halt:*:7:0:halt:/sbin:/sbin/halt
mail:*:8:12:mail:/var/spool/mail:
news:*:9:13:news:/var/spool/news:
ftp:*:14:50:FTP User:/home/ftp:
nobody:*:99:99:Nobody:/:
cbrenton:7aQNEpErvB/v.:500:100:Chris Brenton:/home/cbrenton:/bin/bash
deb:gH/BbcG8yxnDE:501:101:Deb Tuttle:/home/deb:/bin/bash
dtuttle:zVKShMTFQU4dc:502:102:Deb Tuttle(2):/home/dtuttle:/bin/csh
toby:PpSifL4sf5lMc:503:103:Toby Miller:/home/toby:/bin/bash
```

Each row indicates authentication information for a single user. Entry fields are separated by a colon (:). From left to right, the fields are identified as

- The logon name

- The encrypted password

- The User ID

- The primary GID

- The description for this logon name (usually the user's full name)

- The location of the user's home directory

- The shell or command line interpreter for this user

The root user always has a UID and GID of 0. Processes such as FTP are also assigned a unique UID and GID so that these processes do not have to run on the system as root. This limits the amount of damage an attacker can cause by compromising one of these services.

Any password field that has a value of an asterisk (*) is a *locked account*. You cannot authenticate to the system using a locked account. Locked accounts are useful for disabling user access or for securing processes that will be running on the machine.

TIP   Any account that has a blank or invalid shell entry will be unable to telnet to the system or log on from the console. This is useful if you wish to offer services such as POP and IMAP but do not want to allow people to gain shell access to the system via telnet.

The Password Field

As you can see from the sample output of our passwd file, the ciphertext of each encrypted password is clearly visible. This is required because users need read access to the passwd file in order to authenticate with the system. This can also be a major security problem: any user with legitimate access to the system can copy the passwd file to another machine and attempt to crack user passwords using a brute force attack.

UNIX uses a very strong encryption algorithm when encrypting user passwords. UNIX uses a twist on 56-bit DES, where the plain text is all zeros and the encryption key is the user's password. The resulting ciphertext is then encrypted again, using the user's password as the key. This process is repeated a total of 25 times.

To make the final ciphertext even more difficult to crack, a second key is introduced known as a *grain of salt*. This salt is based on the time of day and is a value between 0 and 4,095. This insures that if two users have identical passwords, the resulting ciphertexts will not be identical. For example, look again at the output of the passwd file. One user, Deb Tuttle, has two separate accounts. Even though both accounts use the exact same password, you would never be able to tell from the resulting ciphertext.

The salt value used to encrypt the password is the first two characters of the ciphertext. So when the password for deb was created, the salt used was gH, while the salt used for the dtuttle password was zV. When a user authenticates with the system, the salt is extracted from the ciphertext and used to encrypt the password entered by the user. If the two ciphertext values match, the user is validated and permitted access to the system.

Cracking UNIX Passwords

UNIX is said to use *one-way encryption* when creating ciphertext for the passwd file. This is because it is not practical to try to directly crack a file that has been encrypted 25 times. Also, it is not the data an attacker is trying to read; this is a known value of all zeros. An attacker would be trying to find the actual password value, which is also the key. Of course, in order to decrypt the ciphertext you need the key—but if you have the key you already have the user's password.

So how does one go about cracking UNIX passwords? By applying the same process that the system does to authenticate a user. When Woolly Attacker tries to crack a password, he pulls the salt from the ciphertext entry within the passwd file. He then systematically encrypts a number of words, trying to produce a matching ciphertext string. When a match is found, Woolly knows he has the correct password.

NOTE   The file that contains the list of words used for cracking purposes is known as a dictionary file.

An attacker cannot reverse-engineer the ciphertext, but he can attempt to guess the right value using a brute force attack. This is why it is so important not to use common words or variations on server names and user names for passwords. These are typically the first words an attacker will try.

Shadow Passwords

One way to resolve the problem of users' viewing the encrypted passwords within the passwd file is to locate the ciphertext somewhere else. This is the purpose of the *shadow password* suite: it allows you to locate the ciphertext within a file that is only accessible to the root user. This prevents all users on the system from having access to this information.

When shadow passwords are used, the password field within the passwd file contains only the character x. This tells the system that it needs to look in the file named shadow for the password ciphertext. The format of the shadow file is identical to the passwd file in that all fields are separated by a colon (:). At a minimum, each line of the shadow file contains the user's logon name and password. You can optionally include password aging information, such as the minimum and maximum allowable time before forcing a user to change her password.

WARNING If you decide to use shadow passwords, make sure that any other authentication system you are using is compatible with the shadow format. For example, many older versions of NIS (but not NIS+) expect the password information to be stored within the `passwd` file. If you install the shadow password suite on one of these systems, NIS will break—and it is possible that you will no longer be able to gain access to the system.

The Group File

As mentioned earlier in this section, the group file is used to identify the GID associated with each group, as well as the group's members. Most UNIX versions will allow users to be a member of more than one group. A sample group file is shown here:

```
disk::6:root
lp::7:daemon,lp
mem::8:
kmem::9:
wheel::10:cbrenton
mail::12:mail
news::13:news
ftp::50:
nobody::99:
users::100:cbrenton,deb,dtuttle,toby
cbrenton::500:cbrenton
deb::501:deb
dtuttle::502:dtuttle
toby::503:toby
```

Notice that the users cbrenton, deb, dtuttle, and toby are all members of a unique group that shares their logon name, as well as members of the group users. If you refer back to the passwd file, you will see that the primary group for each of these users is the group that matches his or her logon name. This is a security feature because it helps to prevent users from unintentionally providing more access to a file than was intended.

When a user creates a file, the system provides read and write access for the file's owner as well as the owner's group. This means that if I create a file called resume.txt, everyone in my primary group has write access to this file. This is rather a loose set of permissions to have assigned by default; the user may forget or may not know enough to go back and use the chmod command.

To resolve this file permission problem, every user is assigned to a unique group. This means that, by default, all other users are viewed as "everyone else" and provided only a minimum level of file access (usually read-only). If, however, I want to allow other users to have a higher level of access to the file, I can use the chgrp command. This means I have to think about what I am doing before I can grant further access to the file.

For example, let's say the user cbrenton creates a file named smtp.txt. A list of the file would produce the following:

```
[cbrenton@thor cbrenton]$ ls -al smtp.txt
-rw-rw-r--   1 cbrenton cbrenton      499 Feb  5  1997 smtp.txt
```

Since the user cbrenton is in a unique group named cbrenton, all other users on the system will have read-only access to the file. If cbrenton wishes to allow deb, dtuttle, and toby to have write access, he can use the chgrp command to associate this file with the group users. The syntax of the command would be

```
chgrp users smtp.txt
```

After running this command, a new listing of the file smtp.txt would appear as follows:

```
[cbrenton@thor cbrenton]$ ls -al smtp.txt
-rw-rw-r--   1 cbrenton users       499 Feb  5  1997 smtp.txt
```

Now all members of the group users (deb, dtuttle, and toby) would have read and write access to the file smtp.txt. Any user on the system who is not part of the group users still has just read-only access to the file.

The Wheel Group

On a UNIX system, users are allowed to assume the identity of another user using the su command. If no logon name is specified with the su command, su defaults to the root account and prompts you for the root user password. Here is an example of using the su command:

```
[cbrenton@thor cbrenton]$ whoami
cbrenton
[cbrenton@thor cbrenton]$ su
Password:
[root@thor cbrenton]# whoami
root
```

```
[root@thor cbrenton]# who am i
thor.foobar.com!cbrenton ttyp0     Aug 30 23:34 (192.168.1.25)
[root@thor cbrenton]#
```

First, I verify my current logon name. As you can see from the output of the whoami command, the system identifies me as cbrenton. I then type in **su** with no switches, and the system prompts me for the root user's password. Once I have entered the password, a repeat of the whoami command identifies me as now being the root user. Notice that if I use the who am i command, the system still knows my true identity.

This is extremely useful for tracking who has assumed administrator privileges. If I check the final entry in the /var/log/messages file, I find the following entry:

```
Aug 30 23:34:56 thor su: cbrenton on /dev/ttyp0
```

This tells me who assumed root-level privileges and at what time the event occurred. If I am worried that a user improperly assuming root may attempt to delete this entry in order to cover his tracks, I can use syslog in order to export all log entries to a remote system.

One way to reduce the number of people capable of assuming root-level privileges is through the use of the wheel group entry within the group file. Only members of the wheel group are allowed to assume root-level privileges. If you review the group file in this section, you will see that only the user cbrenton is allowed to su to root. This means that even if the user deb knows the root-level password, she cannot assume root from her account. She must either log on to the system directly as the root user or by first breaking into the account cbrenton. This makes it far more difficult to compromise the root-level account.

Limit Root Logon to the Local Console

As mentioned in the last section, if Deb knows the root-level password she can circumvent the wheel group security by logging on to the system directly as root. This is a bad thing, because we now lose the ability to log these sessions. Clearly, it would be beneficial to be able to limit the types of connections that the root user can make with the system.

For example, you could limit the root account so that logon is only permitted from the local console. This means that someone must gain physical access to the machine in order to directly log on as the root user. This also means that any users connecting to the system remotely (with a program such as telnet) will be forced to first log on as themselves and then su to root. This would allow you to enforce the wheel group restrictions for all remote users.

Most flavors of UNIX allow you to limit root's ability to access the system. Typically, this is done by creating entries in the /etc/securetty file. A sample securetty file would be

```
[root@thor /etc]# cat securetty
tty1
tty2
tty3
tty4
```

The entries within the securetty file identify which interfaces root is allowed to use when accessing the system. Direct terminal sessions with the system are identified as tty. This file identifies that root can only gain system access from the first four local consoles. All other connection attempts are rejected. This means that if Deb tries to telnet to the system as root, the logon will be rejected even if she knows the correct password. An example of such a session would be

```
Trying 192.168.1.200 (thor) ...
Connected to thor.foobar.com
login: root
Password:
Login incorrect
login: root
Password:
Login incorrect
login:
```

As you can see, there is no visible indication that root is not allowed to access the system via telnet. As far as an attacker is concerned, the root password could have been changed. This helps to keep Woolly Attacker from trying to come at the system from a different console.

Optimizing the UNIX Kernel

Removing kernel support for any unneeded services is a great way to further lock down your system. Not only does this help to optimize system performance, it can improve security, as well. For example, if you will be using your UNIX system as a router or a firewall, you may wish to disable support for source-routed packets. This prevents an attacker from using source routing for spoofing or to circumvent the routing table.

Configuring a UNIX kernel varies slightly with each implementation. Which options you can configure when rebuilding the kernel depend on which options are included by the manufacturer. For the purpose of demonstration, we will be working with Red Hat's version of Linux. Red Hat supports a number of graphical utilities that can be used when rebuilding a UNIX kernel, something that is not available with every platform.

NOTE   Linux by far supports the largest number of configurable options. If you are rebuilding the kernel on another UNIX flavor, chances are you will see fewer configurable settings.

Running Make

The stock Linux kernel is designed to support the lowest common denominators. While this allows it to run on the widest range of systems, it is probably not optimized for your specific configuration.

TIP   Most distributions install a kernel that is configured to support a 386 processor. Recompiling the kernel to match your unique hardware requirements can greatly optimize your system's performance.

There are several commands used in reconfiguring the kernel on a Red Hat Linux system. They are

- `make clean` or `make mrproper`
- `make config`, `make menuconfig`, or `make xconfig`
- `make dep`
- `make zImage` or `make bzImage`
- `make modules`
- `make modules_install`
- `make zlilo` or `make bzlilo`

You only need to use one of the three commands listed in the first bullet. The differences are explained below. The make clean command is no longer required, but it will not hurt to run it. All commands should be executed from the /usr/src/linux directory.

Configuring the Kernel

Always back up your kernel before you start. That way, if something embarrassing happens, you can always fall back on your original configuration. The kernel file is /vmlinuz. Simply copy—do not move!—the file to /vmlinuz.old. There are three command choices when it comes to selecting the configuration parameters of the kernel. They are

- make config

- make menuconfig

- make xconfig

The make config command is the oldest and the most familiar command to administrators who are old salts with Linux. The make config interface is completely command-line driven. While not very pretty, the make config interface provides default settings that should be fine if left alone. If you do not understand a prompt, do not change it. You can access online Help by typing a question mark in the prompt answer field. The biggest drawback is that you pretty much have to walk through each and every prompt. With the menu utilities, you can jump in and just change what you need to. Figure 15.1 shows the typical output when a make config is performed.

Typing **make menuconfig** enables the ASCII character interface shown in Figure 15.2. Using the arrow keys, you can navigate between menu options. Selecting **y** for a highlighted option enables support; pressing **n** disables support. Some menu items allow you to select **m** for *modular support*. This allows the driver to be loaded or unloaded as required while the system is running. Pressing **h** brings up a brief Help menu.

The make xconfig command is intended to be run from a shell within X-Windows. It is similar to menuconfig, but it's a lot prettier. It is also a bit easier to navigate. Figure 15.3 shows the network section of the xconfig utility.

FIGURE 15.1:

Output of a make config

```
[root@toby linux]# make config
rm -f include/asm
( cd include ; ln -sf asm-i386 asm)
/bin/sh scripts/Configure arch/i386/config.in
#
# Using defaults found in arch/i386/defconfig
#
*
* Code maturity level options
*
Prompt for development and/or incomplete code/drivers (CONFIG_EXPERIMENTAL) [N/y/?]
*
* Loadable module support
*
Enable loadable module support (CONFIG_MODULES) [Y/n/?]
Set version information on all symbols for modules (CONFIG_MODVERSIONS) [Y/n/?]
Kernel daemon support (e.g. autoload of modules) (CONFIG_KERNELD) [Y/n/?]
*
* General setup
*
Kernel math emulation (CONFIG_MATH_EMULATION) [Y/n/?]
Networking support (CONFIG_NET) [Y/n/?]
```

FIGURE 15.2:

The menu-based kernel
configuration screen

```
Linux Kernel v2.0.27 Configuration
----------------------------------------------------------------------------
+------------------------------ Networking options ------------------------------+
| Arrow keys navigate the menu.  <Enter> selects submenus --->.  Highlighted letters are |
| hotkeys.  Pressing <Y> includes, <N> excludes, <M> modularizes features.  Press <Esc><Esc> |
| to exit, <?> for Help.  Legend: [*] built-in  [ ] excluded  <M> module  < > module capable |
|                                                                              |
| +--------------------------------------------------------------------------+ |
| |       [*] Network firewalls                                             | |
| |       [*] Network aliasing                                             | |
| |       [*] TCP/IP networking                                           | |
| |       [*] IP: forwarding/gatewaying                                   | |
| |       [ ] IP: multicasting                                            | |
| |       [*] IP: firewalling                                             | |
| |       [ ] IP: firewall packet logging                                 | |
| |       [*] IP: accounting                                              | |
| |       [ ] IP: optimize as router not host                             | |
| |       <M> IP: tunneling                                               | |
| |       <M> IP: aliasing support                                        | |
| |       --- (it is safe to leave these untouched)                       | |
| |       [ ] IP: PC/TCP compatibility mode                               | |
| |       <M> IP: Reverse ARP                                             | |
| +-----------v(+)----------------------------------------------------------+ |
| A------------------------------------------------------------------------- |
|                  <Select>    < Exit >    < Help >                          |
+----------------------------------------------------------------------------+
```

FIGURE 15.3:

The X-Windows–based kernel configuration screen

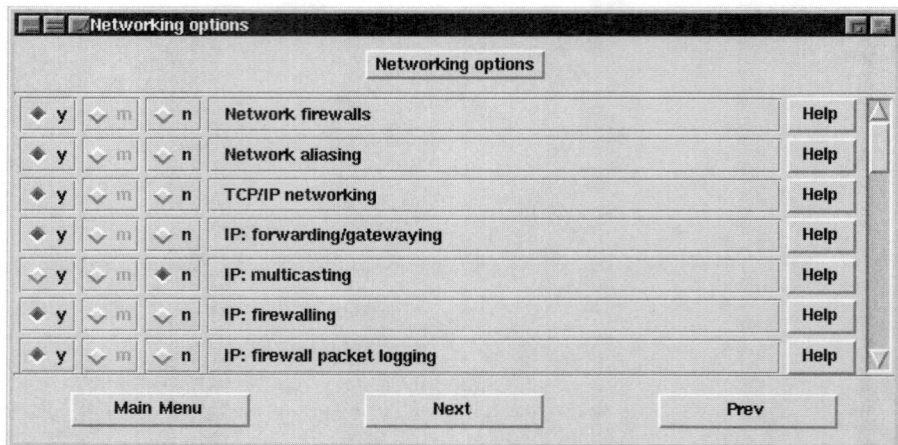

Configuration Options

Regardless of the method you choose, you will need to select which features you wish to enable or disable. Brief descriptions of features related to networking are listed here.

TIP   For a more complete list see the online Help and How-To files.

Networking Support?   This enables networking. If you do not answer yes to this prompt, you will not receive any of the other networking prompts. The default is yes.

Limit Memory to Low 16MB?   This is provided for older systems that have trouble addressing memory above 16MB. Most systems do not need this support. The default is no.

PCI BIOS Support?   This provides support for systems with one or more PCI bus slots. Most newer systems support PCI. The default is yes.

Network Firewall?   This allows the Linux system to act as a firewall. This option enables firewalling in general, although firewalling for IP is the only protocol supported at this time. This option also needs to be enabled if you wish to do IP masquerading. The default is yes.

Network Aliasing?   This allows multiple network addresses to be assigned to the same interface. Currently, the only supported protocol is IP. This is useful if you need to route two logical networks on the same physical segment. This option should be enabled if you plan to use the Apache Web server in a multihomed capacity. Apache can use the different IP addresses assigned to the interface to direct HTTP requests to different Web sites running on the machine. The default is yes.

TCP/IP Networking?   This enables or disables IP networking. If you wish to use IP to communicate, you should enable this option. The default is yes.

IP: Forwarding/Gateway?   This allows the Linux system to forward IP traffic from one interface to another acting as a router. This can be LAN to LAN or LAN to WAN. If the Linux box will be providing firewall services, you should disable this option. If you will be using IP masquerading (even if the system will be a firewall as well), you should enable this option. The default is yes.

IP: Multicasting?   If you will be using IP multicasting or transmitting routing updates using OSPF, this option should be enabled. The default is no.

IP: Firewalling?   This option enables firewall support for the IP protocol. This option should also be enabled if you wish to do IP masquerading or traffic accounting, or to use the transparent proxy. The default answer is yes.

IP: Firewall Packet Logging?   When the system is used as a firewall, this option creates a file that logs all passing traffic. It also records what the firewall did with each packet (accept, deny). Logging is a good way to keep an eye on who may be knocking at the front door. I usually enable this option. That way, if you do not need the information you can simply clean it out from time to time. The default is no.

IP: Accounting?   When the system acts as a firewall or gateway, this option logs all passing traffic. If Linux will be routing on the internal network, you may want to disable this option because the log can get quite large. If Linux will be routing to or firewalling a WAN connection, you may want to enable this option if you wish to keep track of WAN utilization. The default is yes.

IP: Optimize as Router Not Host?   If the Linux box will be acting strictly as a router, firewall, or proxy, you should enable this option. If the system will be hosting a HTTP, FTP, DNS, or any other type of service, this option should be disabled. The default is no.

IP: Tunneling? This enables support for IP encapsulation of IP packets, which is useful for amateur radio or mobile IP. The default is modular support, which means you can load it while the system is active if you need it.

IP: Aliasing Support? This option allows you to assign two or more IP addresses to the same interface. Network Aliasing must also be enabled. The default is modular support.

IP: PC/TCP Compatibility Mode? PC/TCP is a DOS-based IP protocol stack. There are some compatibility issues: older versions do not quite follow the same set of communication rules as everyone else. If you have trouble connecting to a Linux system from a host running PC/TCP, enable this option. Otherwise, you should disable this option. The default is no.

IP: Reverse ARP? This option is typically used by diskless workstations to discover their IP addresses. Enabling this option allows the Linux system to reply to these requests. If you plan to run bootp services, you may want to enable this option in case you need it (either now or later). If the Linux system will not be providing bootp or DHCP services, this option can be disabled. The default is modular support.

IP: Disable Path MTU Discovery? Maximum Transfer Unit (MTU) allows a system to discover the largest packet size it may use when communicating with a remote machine. When MTU is disabled, the system assumes it must always use the smallest packet size for a given transmission. Because this option can greatly affect communication speed, use MTU unless you run into a compatibility problem. The default is no, which enables MTU discovery.

IP: Drop Source Routed Frames? Source routing allows a transmitting station to specify the network path along which replies should be sent. This forces the system replying to the request to transmit along the specified path instead of the one defined by the local routing table.

NOTE

There is a type of attack where a potential attacker can use source-routed frames to pretend to be communicating from a host inside your network when the attacker is actually located out on the Internet. Source routing is used to direct the frame back out to the Internet, instead of toward the network where the host claims to be located. When source routing is used for this purpose, it is called IP spoofing.

Some network topologies, such as Token Ring and FDDI, use source routing as part of their regular communications. If the Linux box is connected to one of these token-based topologies, source routing should be enabled. If you are not using these topologies to communicate, this option should be disabled to increase security. The default is yes, which will drop all source-routed frames.

IP: Allow Large Windows?   This option increases the transmission buffer pool to allow a greater number of frames to be in transit without a reply. This is useful when the Linux box is directly connected to a high-speed WAN link (multiple T1s or faster) that connects two sites separated by an extremely large distance (for example, a coast-to-coast connection). The additional buffer space does require additional memory, so this option should only be enabled on systems that meet this criterion and have at least 16MB of physical memory. The default is yes.

The IPX Protocol?   This option enables support for the IPX protocol. You must answer yes to this prompt in order to configure any IPX services. The default is modular support.

Full Internal IPX Network?   NetWare servers use an internal IPX network to communicate between the core OS and different subsystems. This option takes this concept one step further by making the internal IPX network a regular network capable of supporting virtual hosts. This option is more for development than anything else right now, as it allows a single Linux system to appear to be multiple NetWare servers. Unless you are doing development work, this option should be disabled. The default is no.

AppleTalk DDP?   This option enables support for the AppleTalk protocol. When used with the netalk package (Linux support for AppleTalk), the Linux system can provide file and printer services to Mac clients. The default is modular support.

Amateur Radio AX.25 Level 2?   This option is used to support amateur radio communications. These communications can be either point to point or through IP encapsulation of IP. The default is no.

Kernel/User Network Link Driver?   This option enables communications between the kernel and user processes designed to support it. As of this writing, the driver is still experimental and is not required on a production server. The default is no.

Network Device Support?   This option enables driver-level support for network communications. You must answer yes to this prompt to enable support for network cards and WAN communications. The default is yes.

Dummy Net Driver Support?   This option enables the use of a loopback address. Most IP systems understand that transmitting to the IP address 127.0.0.1 will direct the traffic flow back at the system itself. This option should be enabled because some applications do use the loopback address. The default is modular support.

EQL (Serial Line Load Balancing) Support?   This option allows Linux to balance the network load over two dial-up links. For example, you may be able to call your ISP on two separate lines, doubling your available bandwidth. The default is modular support.

PLIP (Parallel Port) Support?   This option enables support for communication between two systems using a null printer cable. Both systems must use bi-directional parallel ports for communications to be successful. This is similar to connecting two systems via the serial ports with a null modem cable, except it supports faster communications. The default is modular support.

PPP (Point-to-Point) Support?   This option allows the Linux system to create or accept PPP WAN connections. This should be enabled if you plan to use your Linux system to create dial-up connections. The default is modular support.

SLIP (Serial Line) Support?   SLIP is the predecessor to PPP. It provides IP connectivity between two systems. Its most popular use is for transferring mail. Because of the additional features provided by PPP, SLIP is used very little. The default is to provide modular support.

Radio Network Interfaces?   This option allows the Linux system to support spread-spectrum communications. Spread spectrum is most commonly used for wireless LAN communications. You must answer yes to this prompt in order to receive prompts to configure the radio interface. The default is no.

Ethernet (10 or 100Mbit)?   This option allows the Linux system to communicate using Ethernet network cards. You must answer yes to this prompt to select an Ethernet driver later. The default answer is yes.

3COM Cards?   This option allows you to select from a list of supported 3COM network cards. If you answer no, you will not be prompted with any

3COM card options. If you select yes, you will receive further prompts allowing you to selectively enable support for each 3COM card that is supported by Linux.

Upon startup, Linux will attempt to find and auto-detect the setting used on each network card. The accuracy rate is pretty good, although it does sometimes miss on some ISA cards. When you reboot the system, watch the configuration parameters it selects for the card. If these are correct, you're all set. If they are wrong, you will need to change either the card settings or the configuration parameters. The card is set through the configuration utility that ships with it. The startup settings can be changed through the Red Hat control panel's Kernel Daemon Configuration option. The default for this prompt is yes.

AMD LANCE and PCnet (AT1500 and NE2100)?   This is similar to the 3COM prompt, except this option will enable support for AMD and PCnet network cards. The default is yes.

Western Digital/SMC Cards?   This is similar to the 3COM prompt, except this option will enable support for Western Digital and SMC network cards. The default is yes.

Other ISA Cards?   This is similar to the 3COM prompt, except this option enables support for some of the more obscure network cards, such as Cabletron's E21 series or HP's 100VG PCLAN. If you select yes, you will receive further prompts allowing you to selectively enable support for a variety of network cards that are supported by Linux. The default is yes.

NE2000/NE1000 Support?   This is the generic Ethernet network card support. If your card has not been specifically listed in any of the previous prompts, enable this option. The default is modular support.

Most Ethernet network cards are NE2000 compatible, so this prompt is a bit of a catchall.

EISA, VLB, PCI and on Board Controllers?   There are a number of network cards built directly into the motherboard. If you select yes, you will receive further prompts allowing you to selectively enable support for a variety of built-in network cards that are supported by Linux. The default answer is yes.

Pocket and Portable Adapters?   Linux also supports parallel port network adapters. If you select yes, you will receive further prompts allowing you to selectively enable support for a variety of parallel port network adapters supported by Linux. The default answer is yes.

Token Ring Driver Support?   Linux supports a collection of Token Ring network adapters. If you select yes, you will receive further prompts allowing you to selectively enable support for a variety of Token Ring network adapters supported by Linux. The default answer is yes.

FDDI Driver Support?   Linux supports a few FDDI network adapters. If you select yes, you will receive further prompts allowing you to selectively enable support for different FDDI network cards supported by Linux. The default answer is no.

ARCnet Support?   ARCnet is an old token-based network topology that is used very little today. If you select yes, you will receive further prompts allowing you to selectively enable support for different ARCnet network cards supported by Linux. The default support is modular.

ISDN Support?   This option enables support for ISDN WAN cards. If you plan to use ISDN, you should also enable the PPP support listed previously. The default support is modular.

Support Synchronous PPP?   This option provides support for synchronous communications over an ISDN line. Some ISDN hardware requires this to be enabled and will negotiate its use during connection. If you plan to use ISDN, you should enable this option in case you need it. The default is yes.

Use VJ-Compression with Synchronous PPP?   This option enables header compression when synchronous PPP is used. The default is yes.

Support Generic MP (RFC 1717)?   When synchronous PPP is used, this option allows communications to take place over multiple ISDN lines. Since this is a new specification and not yet widely supported, the default answer is no.

Support Audio via ISDN?   When supported by the ISDN card, this option allows the Linux system to accept incoming voice calls and act as an answering machine. The default answer is no.

NFS Filesystem Support?   This option enables support for mounting and exporting file systems using NFS. NFS is most frequently used when sharing files between UNIX systems; however, it is supported by other platforms, as well. The default answer is yes.

SMB Filesystem Support?   This option enables support for NetBIOS/ NetBEUI shares. This is most frequently used between Microsoft Windows systems for sharing files and printers. The default answer is yes.

SMB Win95 Bug Workaround?   This option fixes some connectivity problems when the Linux system attempts to retrieve directory information from a Windows 95 system that is sharing files. The default is no.

If you use file sharing for Windows 95, you should enable the SMB Win95 Bug Workaround.

NCP Filesystem Support?   This option allows the Linux system to connect to NetWare servers. Once connected, the Linux system can mount file systems located on the NetWare server. The default support is modular.

Dependencies Check

Once you have finished the configuration, it is now time to run `make dep`. This command performs a dependencies check to insure that all required files are present before compiling the kernel. Depending on your system speed, this command could take 1–15 minutes to run. While it is not quite as thrilling as watching grass grow, you should keep an eye on the dependencies check to make sure that there are no errors.

TIP   Errors are usually in the form of missing files. If you note what is missing, you can go back and see where you may have lost it.

Cleaning Up the Work Space

Next you can run a `make clean` to insure that any object files get removed. This is typically not required with the latest revision kernels, but it does not hurt to run it just in case. This command usually takes less than one minute to execute.

Compiling the Kernel

Until now we have not changed the active system. All our changes have been to configuration files. The next command, `make zImage`, will create a kernel with the configuration parameters you selected and replace the one you are currently using. If you receive errors that the kernel is too large (which is common with kernel versions greater than 2.2.*x*), try `make bzImage`, which creates a compressed image of the kernel.

Make sure you type a capital I in **zImage** or **bzImage**. This is important because UNIX commands are case sensitive.

How long this command will take to run depends on your processor speed and the amount of physical memory that is installed in the system. A 400MHz Pentium with 128MB of RAM should take 10–20 minutes to create a new kernel.

Configuring the Boot Manager

The last step is to tell Linux's boot manager LILO that it needs to set pointers for a new image. This is done with the command make zlilo, make bzlilo, or by copying the kernel image to the /boot directory and editing /etc/lilo.conf by hand and adding an entry for the new kernel, and rerunning the lilo command.

You can now reboot the system and boot off of the new kernel. You should not notice any new errors during system startup. If you do, or if the system refuses to boot altogether, you can use the emergency recovery disk to boot the system and restore the backup kernel we discussed in the "Configuring the Kernel" section of this chapter. This will allow you to restart the system so you can figure out what went wrong.

Changing the Network Driver Settings

You may need to change the network driver settings if auto-probe fails to configure them properly. This can be done through the Red Hat Control Panel using the Kernel Daemon Configuration option. Figure 15.4 shows the Kernel Configurator window, in which you can add, remove, or change the settings of device drivers.

FIGURE 15.4:

The Kernel Configurator

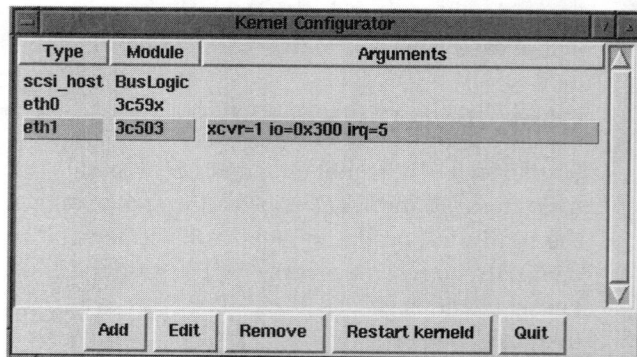

When you highlight a specific driver and select Edit, you will see the Set Module Options dialog box, shown in Figure 15.5. This allows you to change the configuration parameters that Linux uses to initialize your network card. Once the changes are complete, you can restart the kernel to have these changes take effect.

FIGURE 15.5:

The Set Module Options window allows you to change the startup parameters for a specific driver.

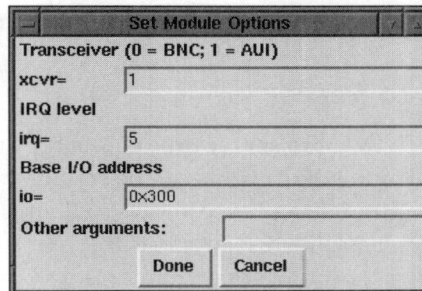

You should now have an optimized kernel, which only includes support for the options you wish to utilize. This will prevent an attacker from accessing any of these services, because support has been removed from the kernel itself. To add support back in, an attacker would have to rebuild the system kernel. Most likely, such an event would not go unnoticed.

TIP   Once the kernel has been optimized, you should remove any unneeded IP services from the machine, as well.

IP Service Administration

UNIX has evolved into a system that is capable of supporting many IP services. This is excellent from a functionality perspective—but not so good for security. Service-rich systems are easier to exploit because the chances of finding a vulnerability are greater. For example, someone wishing to attack your UNIX system may find that you have done a good job of locking down HTTP, FTP, and SMTP services but that there is a Finger exploit you have missed.

In the next few sections we will look at the IP services available on most flavors of UNIX and how you can disable the ones you do not need.

IP Services

There are a large number of IP services available for UNIX. The specific flavor of UNIX that you are using will determine which services are enabled by default. Under each service description, I have noted which services are commonly enabled. You will need to check your specific configuration, however, to see which services you are running and which ones you are not.

bootp Server

The UNIX bootp server provides bootp and DHCP services to network clients. DHCP and bootp clients can be serviced independently or in a mixed environment. The bootp service allows a client to dynamically obtain its IP address and subnet mask. DHCP supports these configuration settings and many others, such as default route, domain name, and so on. Most flavors of UNIX do not ship with a bootp server running.

DNS Server

The domain name server of choice for the UNIX platform is the Berkeley Internet Name Domain (BIND) server. BIND is the original, and still the most popular, utility used to exchange domain name information on the Internet. A BIND server can be configured to provide primary, secondary, or caching-only domain name services.

Most UNIX operating systems ship with a local DNS server running. BIND is configured to act as a caching name server by default, unless you specifically configure the system to act as a primary or secondary. As a cache-only name server, BIND is still capable of responding to queries on TCP and UDP ports 53. BIND runs as its own separate process called named.

BIND is infamous for the way in which hackers have exploited it over the years in order to gain access to UNIX systems. Verify that you have the latest version of BIND, and check with CERT (www.cert.org) for the latest security information regarding this critical network service.

Finger Server

Finger is one of those services that is typically overlooked but can provide a major security hole. UNIX provides both client and server Finger services, which allow you to finger an account by name in order to collect information about that user. A sample output from a Finger request would be as follows:

```
[cbrenton@thor cbrenton]$ finger root@loki.foobar.com
Login: root                          Name: root
Directory: /root                     Shell: /bin/bash
Last login Sun Aug 30 17:43 (EDT) on ttyp0 from 192.168.1.25
New mail received Mon Aug 31 02:41 1998 (EDT)
    Unread since Mon Aug 31 01:03 1998 (EDT)
No Plan.
[cbrenton@thor cbrenton]$
```

There are a couple of points worth noting about this output. First, I am running the Finger client from the system Thor in order to query a user on a remote machine named Loki. Finger is not just for local access but is designed for use over the network. Finger will work on any user within the passwd file, which includes the root user.

I now know that root has not checked on the system since Sunday, when the root user connected via a telnet session (ttyp0) from 192.168.1.25. If I were considering an attack on this system, I'd now have some great information to work with:

- I can watch how often root checks the system, in order to maximize my chances of avoiding detection.

- I can monitor telnet sessions between Loki and 192.168.1.25 in order to try to capture the root logon password.

- Once I obtain root's password, I know I will not need physical access to the machine because root is allowed to authenticate via telnet.

This is a pretty hefty amount of information to achieve by simply running a single command. Had the root user actually been connected to the system, the output would have appeared similar to the following:

```
[cbrenton@thor /etc]$ finger deb
Login: deb                           Name: Deb Tuttle
Directory: /home/deb                 Shell: /bin/bash
On since Mon Aug 31 13:15 (EDT) on ttyp3 from 192.168.1.32
    16 minutes 46 seconds idle
No mail.
No Plan.
```

As you can see, Deb had an active telnet session from 192.168.1.32 but has not done anything for the last 16 minutes and 46 seconds. If I have physical access to Deb's computer, I may take the long period of inactivity to mean that she is away from her desk. This might be a great opportunity for me to walk over and see if there is anything interesting in her files.

Finger runs as a process under inetd, which is discussed later in this chapter. Most flavors of UNIX have Finger enabled by default.

FTP Server

UNIX provides FTP services, including the ability to service anonymous FTP requests. When someone uses FTP to connect to the system and she uses a valid logon name and password, she is dropped into her home directory and has her normal level of access to the file system. If, however, someone authenticates using the logon name anonymous, she is dropped into a sub-directory (typically /home/ftp) and is not allowed to navigate the system above this point. As far as anonymous FTP users are concerned, /home/ftp is the root-level directory.

> **NOTE**   Subdirectories set up under /home/ftp can allow anonymous users to receive read-only or read-write access to files. This is called *anonymous FTP access*, and it prevents people from gaining access to the complete file system without proper authentication.

FTP runs as a process under inetd. While most versions of UNIX ship with the FTP server enabled, not all support anonymous FTP access. The most popular version of FTP, wu-ftp, is also notorious for weaknesses that have allowed hackers to penetrate systems. Like DNS (above) make sure you have the latest secure version, and verify with CERT that there are no known issues with the version you are running.

HTTP Server

Many UNIX systems ship with a Web server called Apache (the most popular Web server to date). Apache predominates among UNIX-based Web servers because it supports advanced features such as Java scripting and *multihoming*. Multihoming is the ability to host multiple domain names on the same Web server. Apache looks at the destination Web server address and directs the query to the appropriate directory structure for that domain.

HTTP can be a particularly nasty process to leave running because vulnerabilities have been found with some of the older, stock CGI scripts. If you are actively maintaining your server, you have probably updated many of these older scripts already. The situation you should avoid is an HTTP process that has been loaded on the system and forgotten about. Web services run as their own separate process called `httpd`.

IMAP and POP3 Servers

UNIX supports remote mail retrieval using both POP3 and IMAP. POP3 is the older standard and is supported by most remote mail clients. IMAP has more features than POP3, but IMAP is just starting to become popular. IMAP has some known vulnerabilities, so make sure that you are running the most current version.

Most UNIX flavors ship with both POP3 and IMAP services active. Both run as a process under `inetd`.

NOTE   For more information on POP3 and IMAP, see Chapter 3.

---

login and *exec*

These two daemons—`login` and `exec`—are referred to as the *trusted hosts* daemons. This is because they allow remote users to access the system without requiring password authentication. The commands that use these daemons are `rcp` (copy a file to a remote system), `rlogin` (log on to a remote system), and `rsh` (execute a command on a remote system). Collectively, these are known as the *R commands*.

Trust is based on security equivalency. When one system trusts another, it believes that all users will be properly authenticated and that an attack will never originate from the trusted system. Unfortunately, this can create a domino effect. All an attacker needs to do is compromise one UNIX machine and then use the trusted host equivalency to compromise additional systems.

Trusted hosts are determined by the contents of the `/etc/hosts.equiv` file. This file contains a list of trusted systems, as you can see in the following example:

```
loki.foobar.com
skylar.foobar.com
pheonix.foobar.com
```

If this `host.equiv` file is located on the system named `thor.foobar.com`, then Thor will accept `login` and `exec` service requests from each of these systems without requiring password authentication. If any other system attempts to gain access, the connection request is rejected.

WARNING   It is far too easy to exploit the minor level of security provided by the R commands. An attacker can launch a spoof attack or possibly corrupt DNS in order to exploit the lack of password security. Both `login` and `exec` run as daemons under `inetd`. It is highly recommended that you disable these services. Using `ssh` (secure shell) will provide the same functionality but with authenticated and encrypted communications.

Mail Server

Most flavors of UNIX include Sendmail for processing SMTP traffic. While there are a few other SMTP programs available for UNIX, Sendmail is by far the most popular. At the time of this writing, the current version of Sendmail is 8.11.2x. Older versions of Sendmail (especially versions prior to 8.0) have many known exploits. If you are running an older version, you should seriously consider updating.

WARNING   Unfortunately, many UNIX vendors do not stay up to date on Sendmail releases, so it is entirely possible that you will install a new OS version, only to find that Sendmail is one or two years old.

Most versions of UNIX ship with Sendmail installed and running. Sendmail runs as its own separate process. The name of the daemon is `sendmail`.

News Server

The most popular UNIX news server is the InterNetNews daemon (INND). When a UNIX news server is provided with an appropriate feed, remote users can connect to the server to read and post news articles. If no feed is available, the server can be used for intranet discussion groups.

News is not included with most UNIX packages. This is mostly due to the amount of resources the typical news server uses. Besides gobs of disk space (8GB to store a few weeks' worth of articles is not uncommon), an active news server will bring a low-grade processor to its knees.

TIP   If you decide to run news, it is a good idea to dedicate a system to the task.

NFS Server

UNIX can use NFS to export portions of the server's file system to NFS clients, or to act as an NFS client itself and mount remote file systems. Functionality is similar to NetWare (where you would map a drive letter to a section of the remote file system) or to NT server (where you would map to a share). The difference is that the remote NFS file system can be mounted to any point in UNIX client's file system.

Most flavors of UNIX that ship with NFS support NFS version 1. The original version of NFS was pretty insecure, mostly because it used UDP as a transport. NFS version 2 supports TCP, which helps to make the protocol easier to control with static packet filtering. Many UNIX operating systems ship with the NFS server active. Unless you specifically configure it otherwise, no file systems are exported by default.

Using NFS is still considered to be a risky venture because packet filtering is easily exploited and overcome by any skilled hacker. Consider using NFS only if necessary, and then only behind firewalls.

SAMBA

SAMBA is a suite of tools that allow a UNIX machine to act as a session message block (SMB) client or server. This is the same protocol used by Windows systems, which means that a UNIX system running SAMBA is capable of participating in a Windows workgroup or domain (although it cannot act as a PDC or BDC). This allows the UNIX machine to share files or printers with Windows systems.

Most UNIX flavors do not ship with SAMBA pre-installed. The exception to this is Linux. SAMBA is available for free, however, and supports many flavors of UNIX. SAMBA runs its own set of daemons, which are not controlled by inetd. These daemons are smbd and nmbd.

Talk

UNIX supports Talk, which is similar to Internet Relay Chat (IRC). Talk does not require a dedicated server, because a session is created directly between two UNIX machines. You establish a connection by typing **talk user@host.domain**.

The recipient of a Talk request accepts or rejects the connection. Once a connection is established, the screen is split so that users can type messages simultaneously. Most flavors of UNIX ship with Talk installed and activated. Talk is run as a process under inetd.

Because modern security philosophy is minimalist, only activate Talk if it is absolutely necessary. Using Talk-like clients (thus avoiding the activation of daemons) can achieve the same communication capability. Some examples include IRC, ICQ, and America Online's Instant Messenger (AIM).

Time Server

UNIX can use the network time protocol (NTP) to both send and receive time synchronization updates. Typically, one system on the network is set up as a *time reference server*. This server syncs its time with one of the many available time servers on the Internet. Other systems on the network then check with the reference time server to insure that their system time remains accurate.

Most flavors of UNIX ship with NTP installed and active. NTP is run as a process under inetd. NTP 3, the most current version, can use certificates to verify the identity of reference servers on the network, thereby eliminating unknown servers from posing as reference servers.

NOTE Although there are no known direct exploits against NTP, it is possible that an attacker may attempt to propagate bogus time information if you have a security policy that is looser during certain parts of the day.

Telnet Server

UNIX can accept telnet requests to provide remote console access to the server. Clients connecting to the system through telnet have the same abilities as they would have if they were sitting in front of the server console.

NOTE This is a powerful feature, so you should plan to take additional steps to limit who has telnet access to your UNIX machines.

Telnet is supported by all modern versions of UNIX. By default, the telnet server is active. Telnet runs as a process under inetd.

Additional steps taken to secure telnet include limiting the administrative functions that can be performed in a telnet session (including logging in as root), or replacing telnet with ssh (secure shell)—which provides the same functionality but encrypts the communication (in telnet the username and password are sent over the network media in clear text).

inetd

inetd is the super server that is responsible for monitoring service ports on a UNIX system (starting in Red Hat Linux 7 this has been replaced with xinetd, an improved version that provides better security and management). It is also responsible for launching the appropriate daemon when a service request is received. inetd uses two files in order to determine how to handle service requests:

services   Identifies the service associated with each port

inetd.conf   Identifies the daemon associated with each service

The Services File

The services file was discussed at length in Chapter 3, so I will only briefly mention it here. The services file contains a single line entry, which identifies each port that inetd is expected to monitor. For example, the line entry for telnet appears as follows:

```
telnet          23/tcp              #Provide remote terminal access
```

This tells inetd that any request using TCP as a transport that is received on port 23 is attempting to access the service telnet. Once inetd identifies that a remote user is trying to access telnet, inetd references the inetd.conf file to determine how to handle the request.

inetd.conf

The inetd.conf file tells inetd which daemon to launch for a given service request. Here is an example of an inetd.conf file:

```
# These are standard services.
#
ftp     stream  tcp    nowait   root   /usr/sbin/tcpd   in.ftpd -l -a
telnet  stream  tcp    nowait   root   /usr/sbin/tcpd   in.telnetd
gopher  stream  tcp    nowait   root   /usr/sbin/tcpd   gn
#smtp   stream  tcp    nowait   root   /usr/bin/smtpd   smtpd
#nntp   stream  tcp    nowait   root   /usr/sbin/tcpd   in.nntpd
#
# Shell, login, exec and talk are BSD protocols.
#
shell   stream  tcp    nowait   root   /usr/sbin/tcpd   in.rshd
login   stream  tcp    nowait   root   /usr/sbin/tcpd   in.rlogind
```

```
#exec    stream  tcp     nowait  root    /usr/sbin/tcpd  in.rexecd
talk     dgram   udp     wait    root    /usr/sbin/tcpd  in.talkd
ntalk    dgram   udp     wait    root    /usr/sbin/tcpd  in.ntalkd
#dtalk   stream  tcp     waut    nobody  /usr/sbin/tcpd  in.dtalkd
#
# Pop and imap mail services et al
#
pop-2    stream  tcp     nowait  root    /usr/sbin/tcpd  ipop2d
pop-3    stream  tcp     nowait  root    /usr/sbin/tcpd  ipop3d
imap     stream  tcp     nowait  root    /usr/sbin/tcpd  imapd
#
# Tftp service is provided primarily for booting.  Most sites
# run this only on machines acting as "boot servers." Do not uncomment
# this unless you *need* it.
#
#tftp    dgram   udp     wait    root    /usr/sbin/tcpd  in.tftpd
#bootps  dgram   udp     wait    root    /usr/sbin/tcpd  bootpd
#
# Finger, systat and netstat give out user information which may be
# valuable to potential "system crackers."  Many sites choose to
disable
# some or all of these services to improve security.
#
# cfinger is for GNU finger, which is currently not in use in RHS Linux
#
finger   stream  tcp     nowait  root    /usr/sbin/tcpd  in.fingerd
#cfinger stream  tcp     nowait  root    /usr/sbin/tcpd  in.cfingerd
#systat  stream  tcp     nowait  guest   /usr/sbin/tcpd  /bin/ps -auwwx
#netstat stream  tcp     nowait  guest   /usr/sbin/tcpd  /bin/netstat -f
inet
#
# Time service is used for clock synchronization.
#
time     stream  tcp     nowait  nobody  /usr/sbin/tcpd  in.timed
time     dgram   udp     wait    nobody  /usr/sbin/tcpd  in.timed
#
# Authentication
#
auth     stream  tcp     nowait  nobody  /usr/sbin/in.identd in.identd
-l -e -o
#
# End of inetd.conf
```

From left to right, each line entry includes

- The service, as identified in the services file
- The socket type
- The transport
- The flags to use at initialization
- The user account that provides privileges for this daemon
- The name of the daemon, including any required switches

Once inetd has checked the services file and identified a service request as looking for telnet, inetd will access the inetd.conf file and reference the following line:

```
telnet  stream  tcp     nowait  root    /usr/sbin/tcpd  in.telnetd
```

This tells inetd to go to the /usr/sbin directory and run the tcpd daemon using in.telnetd as a switch while using root-level privileges.

WARNING   You should be very careful with any service that runs under root-level privileges, because such services are prime targets for attack. An attacker who can compromise a root-level service may be able to steal information or install a back door to provide future access. This is why many services run as *guest* or *nobody*—compromising the service will provide very little access.

Disabling Services Called by *inetd*

One of the best ways to secure a UNIX system is to shut down all unneeded services. The more services running on the system, the easier it is for an attacker to find an exploit that will allow access to the system.

TIP   Disabling unneeded services is also an easy way to boost system performance. The fewer processes you have enabled, the more resources you will have available for the services you need to run.

To disable services running under inetd, simply add a pound sign (#) to the beginning of the entry within the inetd.conf file. For example, to disable telnet access to the system, simply change the entry to

```
#telnet  stream  tcp     nowait  root    /usr/sbin/tcpd  in.telnetd
```

Once you have commented out all the services you do not wish to run, you simply need to restart the `inetd` process. Do this by identifying the process ID being used by the service and sending that process ID a restart request. To find the process ID for `inetd`, type the following:

```
[root@thor /etc]# ps -ax|grep inetd
  151  ?   SW    0:00 (inetd)
 7177  p0  S     0:00 grep inetd
[root@thor /etc]# kill -HUP 151
[root@thor /etc]#
```

The `ps -ax` portion of the first command lists all running processes. Instead of letting this output scroll past the top of the screen, we have piped (|) it to the `grep` command. We are telling `grep` to filter through the output produced by `ps -ax` and only show us the entries that include the keyword `inetd`. The first entry (process ID 151) is the actual `inetd` process running on the UNIX system. The second listing (process ID 7177) is our `grep` command performing its search.

Now that you know the process ID being used by `inetd`, you can signal to the process that you want it to restart. This is done with the second command: `kill -HUP 151`.

NOTE   Remember that with UNIX case is important, so you must type in the command exactly.

Once you have restarted `inetd`, it should ignore service requests that you have commented out. You can test this by using telnet and pointing it to the service port in question. For example,

```
telnet thor 110
```

will create a connection with the POP3 service port (110). If you have commented out the POP3 service, you should immediately receive a Connection Refused error.

Working with Other Services

Not all services are called by `inetd`. BIND, Sendmail, and SAMBA, for example, each commonly runs as its own process. HTTP is another service that is commonly run as its own process and is not called by `inetd`. This is done for performance reasons: the service can respond to requests faster if it does not have to wait for inetd to wake it up. On an extremely busy system, this can provide a noticeable improvement in performance.

Disabling Stand-Alone Services

To disable a stand-alone service, you need to disable the initialization of that service during system startup. Many services will look for key files before they initialize. If this key file is not found, the service is not started. This is done to prevent errors. For example, BIND will look for the file /etc/named.boot during startup. Sendmail checks for a file named sendmail.cf before it will initialize. If these files are not found, the process fails to start.

One of the methods you can use to disable a process from starting is to delete or rename the process's key file. For example, the command

```
mv named.boot named.boot.old
```

will rename the named.boot file named.boot.old. This will prevent BIND from being able to locate its key file, thus causing initialization to fail.

You can also disable a stand-alone service by renaming its initialization script or by commenting it out. For example, in the Linux world, all process initialization scripts are stored under /etc/rc.d/init.d. These initialization files bear the names of the processes that they start. For example, the Sendmail initialization script is named sendmail.init. By renaming this file to sendmail.init.old, you can prevent Sendmail from being called during system initialization.

Once you have changed your initialization files so that all unnecessary daemons will not be started, you can restart the system or simply kill the current process. To kill a running process, use the ps and grep commands, as we did in the inetd example. You would then issue the kill command without any switches. The output of these commands would appear similar to this:

```
[root@thor /root]# ps -ax|grep sendmail
  187  ?   S     0:00 (sendmail)
  258  p0  S     0:00 grep sendmail
[root@thor /root]# kill 187
[root@thor /root]# ps -ax|grep sendmail
  263  p0  S     0:00 grep sendmail
[root@thor /root]#
```

Once you have reduced the number of services running on your UNIX system, you can use *TCP Wrapper* to limit who can access these services.

TCP Wrapper

TCP Wrapper allows you to specify which hosts are allowed to access each service managed by `inetd`. Most modern versions of UNIX ship with TCP Wrapper pre-installed.

NOTE   Despite its name, TCP Wrapper can be used with services that require either TCP or UDP as a transport.

TCP Wrapper is activated by having `inetd` call the TCP Wrapper daemon instead of the actual service daemon. Let's refer back to our telnet example:

```
telnet  stream  tcp    nowait  root    /usr/sbin/tcpd  in.telnetd
```

`inetd` is actually calling the TCP Wrapper daemon (`tcpd`), not the telnet daemon (`in.telnetd`). Once `tcpd` is called, the service request is compared to a set of access rules. If the connection is acceptable, it is allowed to pass through to the `in.telnetd` daemon. If the connection request fails access control, the connection is rejected.

Access control is managed using two files:

`hosts.allow`   Defines which systems will be permitted access to each service

`hosts.deny`   Defines which service requests will be rejected

When verifying access from a remote system, `tcpd` first checks the `hosts.allow` file. If no matching entry is found, `tcpd` then checks the `hosts.deny` file. The syntax of both files is as follows:

```
<comma separated list of services>:<comma separated list of hosts>
```

Valid services can only be those services managed by `inetd`. Valid hosts can be listed by host name, domain, or IP address. For example, consider the following output:

```
[root@thor /etc]# cat hosts.allow
pop-3, imap: ALL
ftp: .foobar.com
telnet: 192.168.1
finger: 192.168.1.25
[root@thor /etc]# cat hosts.deny
ANY: ANY
```

The hosts.allow file states that all hosts with connectivity to the system are permitted to access POP3 and IMAP services. FTP, however, is limited to hosts within the foobar.com domain. We have also limited telnet access to source IP addresses on the 192.168.1.0 network. Finally, only the host at IP address 192.168.1.25 is allowed to finger the system.

The hosts.deny entry allows us to define the security stance "that which is not expressly permitted is denied." If a service request is received and a match is not found in the hosts.allow file, this catchall rule specifies that we do not wish to allow the remote system access to our UNIX server.

TCP Wrapper is an excellent way to fine tune access to your system. Even if all your UNIX systems are sitting behind a firewall, it cannot hurt to take preventive measures to lock them down further. This helps to insure that anyone who manages to sneak past the firewall will still be denied access to your UNIX system.

Summary

In this chapter you saw how to go about locking down your UNIX (or UNIX-based system, like Linux and FreeBSD) system. We discussed file permissions and how they can be tuned to restrict access to sensitive files. You also looked at how the UNIX system deals with authentication and why it is so important to lock down the root user account. Finally, you looked at IP services and how you can limit which hosts have access to them.

The next chapter will look at some common exploits, describing how each vulnerability is exploited and what you can do to protect your network.

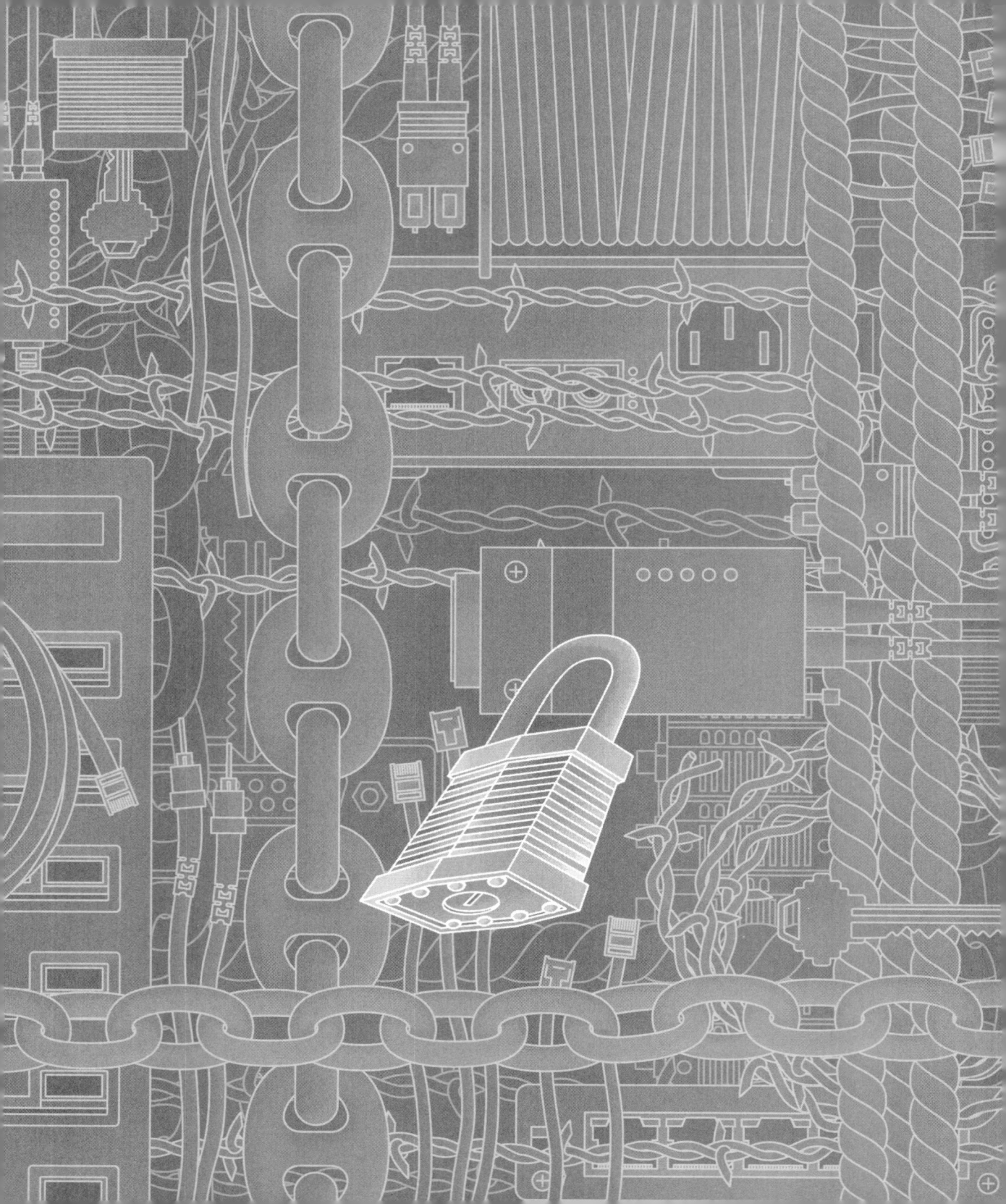

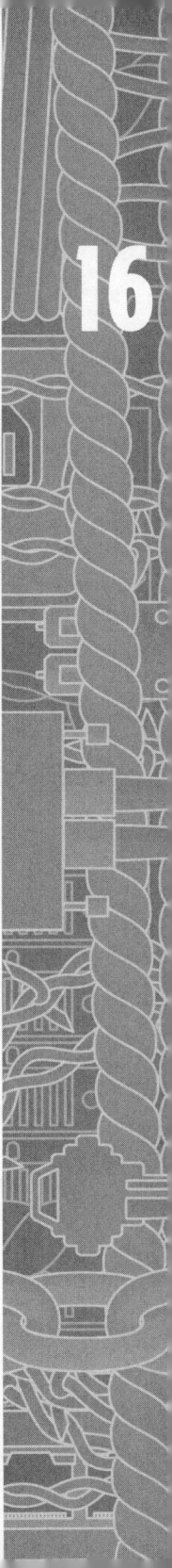

The Anatomy of an Attack

In this chapter, we will look at some of the common tricks and tools that an attacker may use in order to compromise your assets. This is not intended to be a how-to on attacking a network. Rather, it is intended to show you, the network administrator, how an attacker is likely to go about finding the points of vulnerability within your network. Here, we will focus on how you can identify the signs of an attack and what you can do to prevent it.

The initial discussions will assume that the attacker is someone outside of your network perimeter who is trying to break in. This is done simply to show what additional steps an attacker must take when working with limited information. A regular user on your network, who already has an insider's view of your network, would be able to skip many of these steps. As you saw in Chapter 1, an overwhelming majority of network attacks originate from inside the network. This means that the precautionary steps you take to secure your network resources cannot concentrate solely on the network perimeter.

Collecting Information

Woolly Attacker has seen one of your TV ads and decided that your political views do not match his own. He decides his best recourse is to attack your network. The question is, where to begin? At this point, Woolly does not even know your domain name. In order to attack your network, he has to do some investigative work.

The *whois* Command

The first thing Woolly can try is a whois query at the InterNIC. The InterNIC maintains a publicly accessible database of all registered domain names. This database can be searched using the whois utility. By querying for the name of the organization, Woolly will be able to find out if it has a registered domain name. For example, searching for an organization named CameronHunt.com would produce something that looks like the following:

```
[granite:~]$ whois CameronHunt.com
Registrant:
Cameron Hunt (CAMERONHUNT-DOM)
     392 E. 12300 So. Ste A.
     Draper, UT 84020
     US
```

```
Domain Name: CAMERONHUNT.COM
Administrative Contact, Technical Contact, Billing Contact:
    Hunt, Cameron (CHL150)  cam@cameronhunt.com
    10312 Bay Club Ct.
    Tampa, FL 33607
    (813) 207-0363

Record last updated on 05-Apr-2000.
Record expires on 19-Jan-2002.
Record created on 19-Jan-2000.
Database last updated on 12-Feb-2001 16:21:38 EST.

Domain servers in listed order:

DNS.CAMERONHUNT.COM        64.36.56.58
DNS.COPPERKNOB.COM         64.36.56.59
```

By running this simple command, we now have some interesting information to work with. So far we know

- The organization's domain name

- The organization's location

- The organization's administrative contact

- The phone number and fax number for the administrator

- A valid subnet address within the organization (64.36.56.0)

Domain Name

The organization's domain name is important because it will be used to collect further information. Any host or users associated with this organization will also be associated with this domain name. This gives Woolly a keyword to use when forming future queries. In the next section, we will use the domain name discovered here to produce some additional information.

Physical Location

Woolly also knows where this organization is located. If he is truly intent on damaging this network or stealing information, he may now attempt to apply for a temporary job or even better, offer his consulting services. This would allow him to be granted a certain level of access to network resources in order to continue his investigation or possibly to install backdoor access into the network. While this would require quite a bit of legwork, the easiest way to breach a network perimeter is to be invited inside it.

The address also tells Woolly where to go if he wishes to do a bit of dumpster diving. Dumpster diving is when an attacker rummages through a dumpster in an effort to find company private information. This can be valid account names, passwords, or even financial information. Over the years, this process has been simplified because many organizations separate their paper trash from the rest for recycling. This makes finding useful information far easier and a lot cleaner.

Administrative Contact

The administrative contact is typically an individual who is responsible for maintaining the organization's network. In some cases, a technical contact, who is subordinate to the administrative contact, will be listed as well. This can be extremely useful information if Woolly wants to attempt a social engineering attack. For example, he could now call an end user and state, "Hi, I'm Sean, who has just been hired on the help desk. Tom Smith asked me to call you because there is a problem with your account on one of the servers. What's your password?" If Woolly gets lucky, he will end up with a valid logon name and password, which will provide at least minimal access to network resources. This minimal access is all that is required to get a foothold and go after full administrator access.

Phone Numbers

Phone numbers may seem like a strange piece of information to go after, but they can actually be quite useful. Most organizations utilize a phone service called *Direct Inward Dial* (DID). DID allows someone to call a seven-digit phone number and directly reach the desk of an employee without going through an operator. The numbers are usually issued in blocks. For example, 555-0500 through 555-0699 may be a block of DID numbers assigned to a specific organization. DID makes it very easy for an attacker to discover every phone number your organization uses.

So Woolly may try calling phone numbers that are just a few numbers off from the listed contact. This may allow him to reach other employees on whom to attempt his previously described social engineering attack. Woolly may also set up a *war dialer* in order to test consecutive phone numbers. A war dialer is simply a piece of software that dials a series of phone numbers. The war dialer will then identify which phone numbers were answered by a computer. This allows Woolly to review the lists and attempt to infiltrate any phone number that was answered by a computer. If his social engineering attack was successful, he even has a valid account to try.

Valid Subnet

One of the last pieces of information produced by the whois command is an IP address entry for DNS.CAMERONHUNT.com. Since this host is part of our target domain, we can assume that the subnet it sits on is also part of this same domain. Woolly does not know whether the host is inside or outside the firewall, but he now knows one valid subnet to use once he decides to launch his attack.

The *nslookup* Command

Now that the whois command has given Woolly a starting reference point, he can use the nslookup command to collect even more information. The nslookup command allows you to query DNS servers in order to collect host and IP address information. If Woolly wishes to attack the network, he must find out what hosts are available as targets. The nslookup utility does an excellent job of supplying this information.

What a War Dialer Can Find

It is not uncommon for organizations to overlook security on their dial-in devices. For example, in the spring of 1998, Peter Shipley (who designed a very well known vulnerability analysis tool known as SATAN) used a war dialer to systematically call phone numbers within the San Francisco Bay area. He found multiple systems that granted full access without any type of authentication. These included

- A firewall that protected a financial services organization

- A hospital system that allowed patient records to be viewed or modified

- A fire department system allowing fire engines to be dispatched

While these are extreme examples, it is not uncommon for organizations to allow their users to have modems on their desktops. This, in effect, puts the employee in charge of security for that modem line, something many employees may not be qualified to handle.

When Woolly launches the `nslookup` utility, he is informed of the current DNS that `nslookup` will use, as shown in the following output:

```
[granite:~]$ nslookup
Default Server:  granite.sover.net
Address:  209.198.87.33
>
```

This output tells us that `nslookup` will use the server `granite.sover.net` when making DNS queries. Since Woolly wants to find out information about `CAMERONHUNT.com`, he would change the default DNS server to one of the two systems listed in the `whois` output. This is shown in the following output:

```
> server DNS.CAMERONHUNT.COM
Default Server:  DNS.CAMERONHUNT.COM
Address:  64.36.56.58

>
```

The `nslookup` utility is now pointed at `DNS`, one of CameronHunt's DNS servers. All queries will now be directed to this system instead of to `granite`. The first thing that Woolly will want to try is to perform a *zone transfer*. A zone transfer will allow Woolly to collect all host and IP address information with a single command. This is shown in the following output:

```
> ls -d CAMERONHUNT.COM > hosts.1st
[DNS.CAMERONHUNT.COM]
Received 20 answers (0 records).
> exit
```

The first command attempts to get the DNS server to list all valid host information for the `CAMERONHUNT.com` domain and output this to a file called `hosts.1st`. The fact that he received 20 answers to his query tells Woolly that the command was successful, and he now has a valid list of all hosts registered with the DNS. Of course, newer DNS systems (like Windows 2000 DNS, which stores its zone files within Active Directory) will refuse such a request unless the transfer is initially authenticated. But many administrators (as evaluated by security experts and demonstrated by the many number of DNS hacks—even at Microsoft) do not activate this simple security procedure. At this point, Woolly exits the `nslookup` utility because he was able to gather quickly all the information he required.

TIP   You can limit who can perform zone transfers from your name servers by using the `xfers` command (if your DNS system supports the `named.boot` file). This command is placed in the `named.boot` file and precedes a list of IP addresses that are the only systems allowed to perform zone transfers with the name server.

Had Woolly received a "Can't list domain" error message, this would have been an indication that zone transfers from this name server were limited to only specific hosts. Woolly would now be forced to systematically try some common names such as `mail`, `ftp`, `www`, and so on, in order to discover additional subnets within the CameronHunt network. There is no guarantee that Woolly would have been able to identify every valid name using this method, because this process would become a guessing game. The zone transfer was successful, however, as shown by the contents of the `hosts.1st` file:

```
[DNS.CAMERONHUNT.COM]
$ORIGIN CAMERONHUNT.COM.
@                       1H IN SOA     DNS postmaster (
                                      5            ; serial
                                      1H           ; refresh
                                      10M          ; retry
                                      1D           ; expiry
                                      1H )         ; minimum
                        1H IN NS      dns
                        1H IN NS      206.79.230.10
                        1H IN MX      5 mail
cam                     1H IN CNAME   mail
ftp                     1H IN CNAME   web
web                     1H IN A       64.36.56.58
honeypot                1H IN A       64.36.55.57
www                     1H IN A       web
```

This file has produced some very useful information. Woolly may have two valid IP subnets at which he can direct his attacks instead of just one (64.36.56.0 and 64.36.55.0). The 206.79.230.0 subnet is not a target because the `whois` information lists this host as being part of another domain (exodus.net).

Woolly also knows that `mail` is the mail system for the domain because of the MX record entry. In addition, he knows that `mail` is the only mail system, so if he can disable this one host he can interrupt mail services for the entire domain. Finally, this file shows that the Web server is also acting as the FTP server. It may be possible for Woolly to use the FTP service in order to compromise the Web server and corrupt Web pages. This would allow him to penetrate potentially sensitive information.

Search Engines

Search engines can be an excellent method of collecting additional information about an organization's internal network. If you have not done so already, try searching for hits on your organization's domain name. You will be amazed at the amount of information that accrues once an organization has been online for a while. This can include mail messages, newsgroup posts, and pages from internal Web servers (if they are visible from the Internet).

For example, look closely at Figure 16.1. The domain bofh.org has a mail relay named thor.bofh.org that is responsible for sending and receiving all e-mail. As far as the outside world is concerned, Thor is bofh.org's only mail system. If you look closely at this mail header, however, you will see that there is another mail system hiding behind Thor named mailgw.bofh.org.

FIGURE 16.1:

A search engine hit that displays an e-mail header

```
Book   Instant Message   Vulnerability   Book Stuff   Personal   Lookup   games   Security   Jobs

From firewalls-owner@GreatCircle.COM  Sat Jun 15 00:54:47 1997
Received: from relay2.UU.NET (relay2.UU.NET [192.48.96.7]) by ns.ams.nexial.nl
        (8.7.4/8.7.3) with ESMTP id AAA23790 for <firewalls@ams.nexial.nl>;
        Sat, 15 Jun 1997 00:54:46 +0200 (MET DST)
Received: from miles.greatcircle.com by relay2.UU.NET with ESMTP
        (peer crosschecked as: miles.greatcircle.com [198.102.244.34])
        id QQaucy06065; Fri, 14 Jun 1997 19:08:14 -0400 (EDT)
Received: (majordom@localhost) by miles.greatcircle.com (8.7.1-lists/Lists-960417-1)
        id NAA19655 for firewalls-outgoing; Fri, 14 Jun 1997 13:24:27 -0700 (PDT)
Received: (mcb@localhost) by miles.greatcircle.com (8.7.4/Miles-951221-1) id NAA19645
        for firewalls@greatcircle.com; Fri, 14 Jun 1997 13:24:21 -0700 (PDT)
Received: from thor.bofh.org (thor.bofh.org [201.15.48.10]) by miles.greatcircle.com
        (8.7.4/Miles-951221-1) with ESMTP id FAA18598 for <firewalls@greatcircle.com>;
        Tue, 11 Jun 1997 05:12:57 -0700 (PDT)
Received: from mailgw.bofh.org (mailgw.bofh.org [201.15.50.11]) by thor.bofh.org (8.7.1/8.7.1)
        with SMTP id IAA03757; Tue, 11 Jun 1997 08:05:49 -0400
Received: from Microsoft Mail (PU Serial #1654)
From: CBrenton@bofh.org (Brenton, Chris)
To: Woolly_Attacker@hacksRus.org (Woolly)
Message-ID: <1997Jun11.081300.1654.28425@mailgw.bofh.org>
X-Mailer: Microsoft Mail via PostalUnion/SMTP for Windows NT
Mime-Version: 1.0
Content-Type: text/plain; charset="US-ASCII"
Date: Tue, 11 Jun 1997 08:12:58 -0400
Subject: RE: Attack?
Sender: firewalls-owner@GreatCircle.COM

Document: Done
```

This mail header reveals quite a bit of information that could be used to attack the internal network. The information within the mail header tells us

- The mail relay Thor is a UNIX machine running Sendmail (version 8.7.1 at the time of this posting).

- The mail relay is on IP subnet 201.15.48.0.

- There is a second mail system hiding behind Thor named mailgw.bofh.org.

- The mailgw host is on IP subnet 201.15.50.0.

- The mailgw host is an NT server running Postal Union's gateway software.

- The internal mail system is Microsoft Mail.

Not bad for a single search engine hit.

TIP	The way to avoid this problem is to have the mail relay strip all previous outbound mail header information. This will make it appear as though all mail originates from the relay itself, thus preventing any information about your internal network from leaking out.

Probing the Network

Now that Woolly has collected some general information about the target, it is time for him to begin probing and prodding to see what other systems or services might be available on the network. Woolly would do this even if he has already found his way inside the firewall through some other means, such as a contract job or dial-in access. Probing gives an attacker a road map of the network, as well as a list of available services.

The *traceroute* Command

The traceroute command is used to trace the network path from one host to another. This is useful when you wish to document the network segments between two hosts. An example of the output created by traceroute is shown in Figure 16.2.

FIGURE 16.2:

Output from the traceroute command

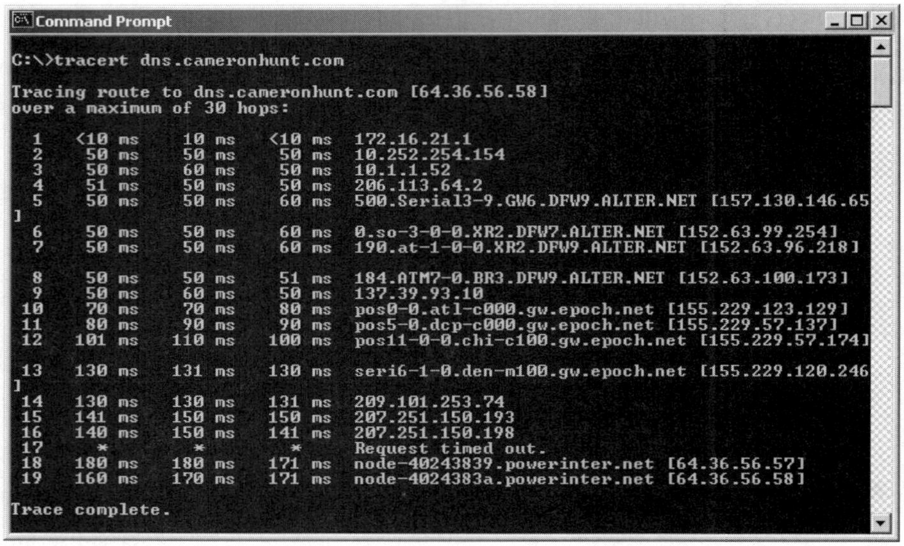

```
Command Prompt                                                      _ □ ×

C:\>tracert dns.cameronhunt.com

Tracing route to dns.cameronhunt.com [64.36.56.58]
over a maximum of 30 hops:

  1   <10 ms    10 ms   <10 ms   172.16.21.1
  2    50 ms    50 ms    50 ms   10.252.254.154
  3    50 ms    60 ms    50 ms   10.1.1.52
  4    51 ms    50 ms    50 ms   206.113.64.2
  5    50 ms    50 ms    60 ms   500.Serial3-9.GW6.DFW9.ALTER.NET [157.130.146.65
]
  6    50 ms    50 ms    60 ms   0.so-3-0-0.XR2.DFW7.ALTER.NET [152.63.99.254]
  7    50 ms    50 ms    60 ms   190.at-1-0-0.XR2.DFW9.ALTER.NET [152.63.96.218]

  8    50 ms    50 ms    51 ms   184.ATM7-0.BR3.DFW9.ALTER.NET [152.63.100.173]
  9    50 ms    60 ms    50 ms   137.39.93.10
 10    70 ms    70 ms    80 ms   pos0-0.atl-c000.gw.epoch.net [155.229.123.129]
 11    80 ms    90 ms    90 ms   pos5-0.dcp-c000.gw.epoch.net [155.229.57.137]
 12   101 ms   110 ms   100 ms   pos11-0-0.chi-c100.gw.epoch.net [155.229.57.174]

 13   130 ms   131 ms   130 ms   seri6-1-0.den-m100.gw.epoch.net [155.229.120.246
]
 14   130 ms   130 ms   131 ms   209.101.253.74
 15   141 ms   150 ms   150 ms   207.251.150.193
 16   140 ms   150 ms   141 ms   207.251.150.198
 17     *         *         *    Request timed out.
 18   180 ms   180 ms   171 ms   node-40243839.powerinter.net [64.36.56.57]
 19   160 ms   170 ms   171 ms   node-4024383a.powerinter.net [64.36.56.58]

Trace complete.
```

NOTE In the Windows world, the command name is truncated to `tracert` in order to accommodate an eight-character filename.

The output in Figure 16.2 shows us the host name and IP address of each router that must be crossed between the source and destination systems. The three preceding columns identify the amount of time it takes to cross the previous network segment.

Just before reaching DNS, we crossed a few network segments on powerinternet .net. Notice also that several hops timed out and failed to respond to a traceroute query. This could be because of a slow link speed or possibly because the device is filtering out these requests.

Returning to our nslookup information, Woolly still needs to verify whether the honeypot address is located within the CameronHunt.com domain or that the Web site is hosted at an alternate location. To find out, he can rerun the traceroute command, only this time using honeypot.CameronHunt.com as a target system. The output of this test is shown in Figure 16.3. As you can see, the trace terminates on an unknown network. This verifies that honeypot is a host that doesn't exist and that Woolly has only the 64.36.56.0 subnet to use when targeting attacks.

FIGURE 16.3:

Woolly verifies that
honeypot isn't a
valid host.

```
Command Prompt                                                    _|□|×
C:\>tracert honeypot.cameronhunt.com

Tracing route to honeypot.cameronhunt.com [207.108.246.6]
over a maximum of 30 hops:

  1    <10 ms   <10 ms    10 ms  172.16.21.1
  2     50 ms    51 ms    50 ms  10.252.254.154
  3     50 ms    50 ms    50 ms  10.1.1.52
  4     50 ms    50 ms    50 ms  206.113.64.2
  5     50 ms    60 ms    50 ms  500.Serial3-9.GW6.DFW9.ALTER.NET [157.130.146.65
]
  6     50 ms    70 ms    50 ms  0.so-3-0-0.XR2.DFW7.ALTER.NET [152.63.99.254]
  7     50 ms    60 ms    60 ms  190.at-1-0-0.TR2.HOU7.ALTER.NET [152.63.99.90]
  8     90 ms   100 ms    90 ms  132.at-6-1-0.TR2.LAX9.ALTER.NET [152.63.4.218]
  9    101 ms   100 ms   100 ms  196.ATM6-0.XR2.LAX2.ALTER.NET [152.63.112.153]
 10    111 ms   110 ms   110 ms  194.ATM10-0-0.GW1.PHX1.ALTER.NET [146.188.249.13
3]
 11    141 ms   150 ms   150 ms  uswest-albq-gw.customer.ALTER.NET [157.130.227.1
18]
 12    141 ms   160 ms   150 ms  20.fa6-0-0.albq-cust.albq.uswest.net [207.108.24
0.221]
 13    150 ms   160 ms   161 ms  207.108.243.86
 14     *         *         *     Request timed out.
 15     *         *         *     Request timed out.
 16     *         *         *     Request timed out.
 17     *         *         *     Request timed out.
 18     *         *         *     Request timed out.
 19     *         *         *     Request timed out.
 20     *         *         *     Request timed out.
 21     *         *         *     Request timed out.
 22     *         *         *     Request timed out.
 23     *         *         *     Request timed out.
 24     *         *         *     Request timed out.
 25     *         *         *     Request timed out.
 26     *         *         *     Request timed out.
 27     *         *         *     Request timed out.
 28     *         *         *     Request timed out.
 29     *         *         *     Request timed out.
 30     *         *         *     Request timed out.

Trace complete.

C:\>
```

NOTE   If Woolly had taken a contract job with CameronHunt.com or found his way into
the network by some other means, the `traceroute` command would be able to
produce even more information; it would document each of the internal IP subnets, as well as which routers connect them. By choosing a few selective hosts,
Woolly would be able to generate a full network diagram.

Host and Service Scanning

Host and service scanning allows you to document what systems are active on the
network and which ports are open on each system. This is the next step in identifying which systems may be vulnerable to attack. The steps to perform are

1. Find every system on the network.

2. Find every service running on each system.

3. Find out which exploits each service is vulnerable to.

These steps can be performed individually, or you can locate a tool that will perform all of them at once. For the sake of completeness, we will look at each of these steps one at a time.

Ping Scanning

A Ping scanner simply sends an ICMP request to each sequential IP address on a subnet and waits for a reply. If a reply is received, the scanner assumes that there is an active host at this address. The scanner will then create a log entry of the systems that respond and possibly attempt to resolve the IP address to a host name. A simple batch or script file can be used to create a homespun Ping scanner. You can also find a number of graphical utilities such as WildPackets' (formerly AG Group) iNetTools, shown in Figure 16.4.

FIGURE 16.4:

The Ping scanner included in the iNetTools utility

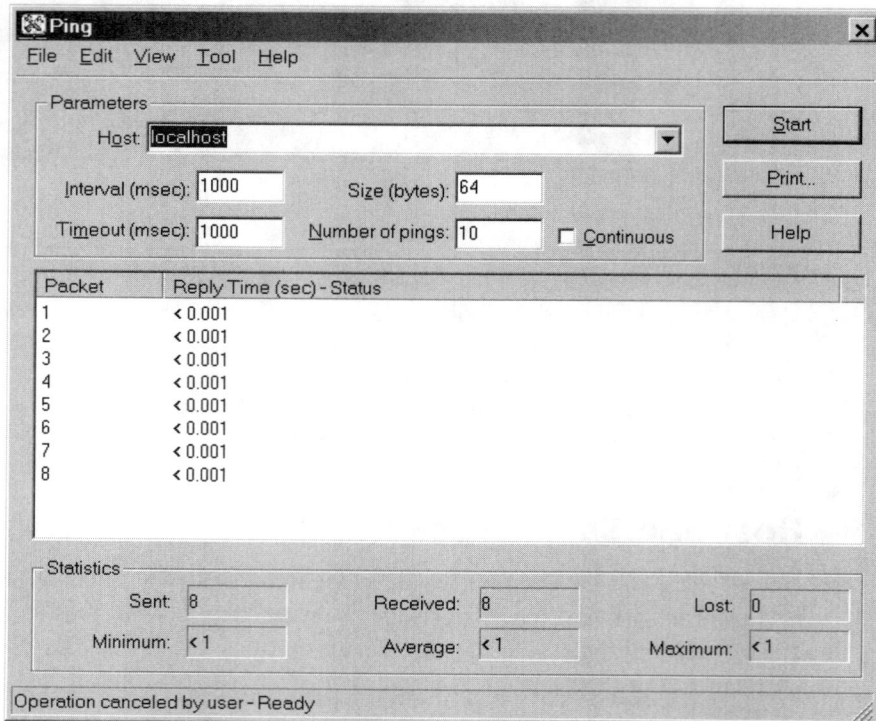

An additional feature of the iNetTools utility is that if the tool cannot resolve the IP address to a DNS host name, it will attempt to look up the system's NetBIOS name instead. This is helpful if you are scanning a network with many Windows desktop systems that may not have entries on the DNS server.

Port Scanning

A port scanner allows you to sequentially probe a number of ports on a target system in order to see if there is a service that is listening. Think of a burglar walking through an apartment building and jiggling all the doorknobs to see if one is unlocked, and you will get the idea. A port scanner simply identifies which well-known services are listening and waits for connection requests.

Figure 16.5 shows the results of a scan against the system 64.36.56.59 using iNetTools. As you can see, iNetTools has identified a number of open ports on this system. Notice that the information about which ports are open reveals the functionality of a system, which in this case is acting as an FTP, mail, DNS, and Web server.

FIGURE 16.5:

A port scan of a system

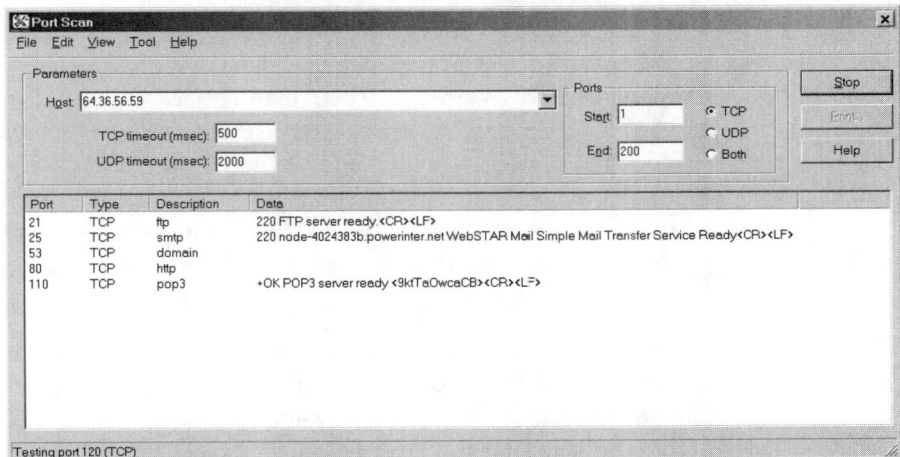

Exactly how does a port scanner work? This is shown in Figure 16.6. If you look at packet 35, the port scanner initiates a TCP three-packet handshake with a machine named Thor. The port scanner transmits a packet with a flag setting of

SYN=1 with a destination port of 23 (telnet). In packet 36, Thor replies by transmitting a response of SYN=1, ACK=1. Because of this response by Thor, the port scanner knows that there is a service listening at the telnet port. In packet 37, the scanner completes the three-packet handshake by transmitting ACK=1. The scanner then immediately ends the session in packet 38 by transmitting ACK=1, FIN=1. In packet 39, Thor acknowledges this request by transmitting ACK=1.

FIGURE 16.6:

An analyzer trace of a TCP port scan

No.	Source	Destination	Layer	Summary	Error	Size	Interpacket Time	Absolute Time	Relative Time
35	Scanner	Thor	tcp	Port:1546 ---> TELNET SYN		64	68 ms	11:31:02 PM	2 s
36	Thor	Scanner	tcp	Port:TELNET ---> 1546 ACK SYN		64	1 ms	11:31:02 PM	2 s
37	Scanner	Thor	tcp	Port:1546 ---> TELNET ACK		64	367 µs	11:31:02 PM	2 s
38	Scanner	Thor	tcp	Port:1546 ---> TELNET ACK FIN		64	710 µs	11:31:02 PM	2 s
39	Thor	Scanner	tcp	Port:TELNET ---> 1546 ACK		64	681 µs	11:31:02 PM	2 s
40	Scanner	Thor	tcp	Port:1547 ---> 24 SYN		64	9 ms	11:31:02 PM	2 s
41	Thor	Scanner	tcp	Port:24 ---> 1547 ACK RESET		64	642 µs	11:31:02 PM	2 s
42	Scanner	Thor	tcp	Port:1545 ---> 22 SYN		64	450 ms	11:31:02 PM	3 s
43	Scanner	Thor	tcp	Port:1543 ---> FTP-DATA SYN		64	136 µs	11:31:02 PM	3 s
44	Scanner	Thor	tcp	Port:1547 ---> 24 SYN		64	69 µs	11:31:02 PM	3 s
45	Thor	Scanner	tcp	Port:22 ---> 1545 ACK RESET		64	687 µs	11:31:02 PM	3 s
46	Thor	Scanner	tcp	Port:FTP-DATA ---> 1543 ACK RESET		64	405 µs	11:31:02 PM	3 s
47	Thor	Scanner	tcp	Port:24 ---> 1547 ACK RESET		64	412 µs	11:31:02 PM	3 s
48	Scanner	Thor	tcp	Port:1548 ---> SMTP SYN		64	68 ms	11:31:02 PM	3 s
49	Thor	Scanner	tcp	Port:SMTP ---> 1548 ACK SYN		64	1 ms	11:31:02 PM	3 s
50	Scanner	Thor	tcp	Port:1548 ---> SMTP ACK		64	356 µs	11:31:02 PM	3 s
51	Scanner	Thor	tcp	Port:1548 ---> SMTP ACK FIN		64	715 µs	11:31:02 PM	3 s
52	Thor	Scanner	tcp	Port:SMTP ---> 1548 ACK		64	691 µs	11:31:02 PM	3 s
53	Scanner	Thor	tcp	Port:1549 ---> 26 SYN		64	9 ms	11:31:02 PM	3 s
54	Thor	Scanner	tcp	Port:26 ---> 1549 ACK RESET		64	653 µs	11:31:02 PM	3 s
55	Scanner	Thor	tcp	Port:1545 ---> 22 SYN		64	450 ms	11:31:03 PM	3 s
56	Scanner	Thor	tcp	Port:1549 ---> 26 SYN		64	165 µs	11:31:03 PM	3 s
57	Scanner	Thor	tcp	Port:1547 ---> 24 SYN		64	24 µs	11:31:03 PM	3 s
58	Thor	Scanner	tcp	Port:22 ---> 1545 ACK RESET		64	761 µs	11:31:03 PM	3 s
59	Thor	Scanner	tcp	Port:26 ---> 1549 ACK RESET		64	413 µs	11:31:03 PM	3 s
60	Thor	Scanner	tcp	Port:24 ---> 1547 ACK RESET		64	389 µs	11:31:03 PM	3 s

The scanner knew that Thor was listening on port 23 because it was able to complete a full TCP three-packet handshake with the system. To find out what happens when a service is not active, refer back to Figure 16.6, but this time look at packets 55, 56, and 57. In these three transmissions, the scanner is probing Thor at ports 22, 26, and 24, respectively, to see if a service is listening. In packets 58, 59, and 60, Thor replies by transmitting ACK=1, RST=1. This is a target system's way of letting the source know that there is no service available on that port. By sorting through the different responses, a port scanner can accurately log which ports have active services.

Port scanning has a few shortcomings. The first is that the connection attempt will most certainly be logged by the target system. This would provide the system administrator on the target system with a record that a port scan has taken place. The second is that port scanning can easily be filtered out by any packet filter or firewall. This is because the port scanner relies on the initial connection packet with SYN=1.

TCP Half Scanning

TCP half scanning was developed in order to get past the logging issue. A TCP half scan does not try to establish a full TCP connection. The half scanner transmits only the initial SYN=1 packet. If the target system responds with a SYN=1, ACK=1, then the half scanner knows that the port is listening and immediately transmits an RST=1 in order to tear down the connection. Since a full connection is never actually established, most (but not all) systems would not log this scan. Since a TCP half scan still relies on the initial SYN=1 packet, it can be blocked by a packet filter or firewall, just like a full scanner.

FIN Scanning

The final type of scanner is known as a FIN scanner. A FIN scanner does not transmit a SYN=1 packet in an attempt to establish a connection. Rather, a FIN scanner transmits a packet with ACK=1, FIN=1. If you refer back to packet 38 in Figure 16.6, you will remember that these are the flags we used in order to tear down our TCP connection. In effect, the FIN scanner is telling the target system that it wishes to tear down a connection, even though no connection exists.

NOTE   How the target system responds is actually kind of interesting (to a bit weenie, anyway). If the target port does not have a service listening, the system will respond with the standard ACK=1, RST=1. If there is a service listening, however, the target system will simply ignore the request. This is because there is no connection for the target system to tear down. By sorting through which ports elicit a response and which do not, a FIN scanner can determine which ports are active on the target system.

What makes this type of scanner even more lethal is that neither a static packet filter nor many firewalls will block this type of scan. This allows an attacker to identify systems even if they are on the other side of a firewall.

FIN scanning does not work on every type of system. For example, a Microsoft TCP stack will respond with an ACK=1, RST=1 even if the port is active. This means that while Microsoft's TCP stack does not comply with RFC 973, you cannot use a FIN scanner against a Windows systems in order to identify active ports because it will appear that none of the system's ports has active services. The ACK=1, RST=1 will still inform the attacker that a system is present, however, and that it is some form of Microsoft operating system.

Passive Monitoring

In order to collect more information about your network, an attacker may attempt to monitor traffic. This can be accomplished by directly installing an analyzer onto your network or, more subversively, by identifying internal systems. You have seen what an attacker can learn by installing a network analyzer on your network to monitor traffic flow. In this section, we will look at one of the more subtle methods an attacker can use to collect information about your internal systems.

For example, review the packet capture in Figure 16.7. This is a standard HTTP data request that a client sends to a Web server. If Woolly Attacker is able to get some of your internal users to connect to his Web site (perhaps through an enticing e-mail), he has the possibility of collecting a wealth of information. Starting at about halfway through the packet capture, our Web client is telling the remote Web server several things:

- The preferred language is English.

- The system is running at 800 × 600 resolution.

- The video card supports 16 million colors.

- The operating system is Windows 95.

- The system uses an *x*86 processor.

- The browser is Microsoft Internet Explorer version 3.0.

The last three pieces of information are the most interesting. Woolly now knows that if he wishes to attack this system, he needs to focus on exploits that apply to an *x*86 system running Windows 95 and Internet Explorer 3.0. As you will see later in this chapter, many of these can be launched simply by having an IE user download a Web page.

One of the reasons that proxy firewalls are so popular is that most of them filter out information regarding operating system and browser type. This puts an attacker in a hit-or-miss position: the exploit may or may not work on the target system.

NOTE   The less information you unknowingly hand out about your network, the harder it will be for an attacker to compromise your resources.

FIGURE 16.7:

An HTTP data request

FIGURE 16.7:

An HTTP data request

No.	Source	Destination	Layer	Summary	Error	Size	Interpacket Time	Absolute Time	Relative Time
6	0060973A6A08	00805FE2D09A	tcp	Port:1048 ---> 80 ACK		64	2 ms	1:18:18 PM	3 ms
7	0060973A6A08	00805FE2D09A	tcp	Port:1048 ---> 80 ACK PUSH		452	647 µs	1:18:18 PM	3 ms
8	00805FE2D09A	0060973A6A08	tcp	Port:80 ---> 1048 ACK PUSH		130	3 ms	1:18:18 PM	7 ms

```
   0:  00 80 5F E2 D0 9A 00 60 97 3A 6A 08 08 00 45 00    ..._....`.:j...E.
  10:  01 B2 C6 01 40 00 20 06 71 E8 C6 70 CA 5E C6 70    ....@. .q..p.^.p
  20:  CA 1C 04 18 00 50 00 1E F8 64 00 90 EA 63 50 18    .....P...d...cP.
  30:  80 00 DB 8F 00 00 47 45 54 20 2F 61 75 2E 69 63    ......GET /au.ic
  40:  61 20 48 54 54 50 2F 31 2E 30 0D 0A 41 63 63 65    a HTTP/1.0..Acce
  50:  70 74 3A 20 69 6D 61 67 65 2F 67 69 66 2C 20 69    pt: image/gif, i
  60:  6D 61 67 65 2F 78 2D 78 62 69 74 6D 61 70 2C 20    mage/x-xbitmap,
  70:  69 6D 61 67 65 2F 6A 70 65 67 2C 20 69 6D 61 67    image/jpeg, imag
  80:  65 2F 70 6A 70 65 67 2C 20 2A 2F 2A 0D 0A 52 65    e/pjpeg, */*..Re
  90:  66 65 72 65 72 3A 20 68 74 74 70 3A 2F 2F 31 39    ferer: http://19
  A0:  38 2E 31 31 32 2E 32 30 32 2E 32 38 2F 64 65 66    8.112.202.28/def
  B0:  61 75 6C 74 2E 68 74 6D 0D 0A 41 63 63 65 70 74    ault.htm..Accept
  C0:  2D 4C 61 6E 67 75 61 67 65 3A 20 65 6E 0D 0A 55    -Language: en..U
  D0:  41 2D 70 69 78 65 6C 73 3A 20 38 30 30 78 36 30    A-pixels: 800x60
  E0:  30 0D 0A 55 41 2D 63 6F 6C 6F 72 3A 20 63 6F 6C    0..UA-color: col
  F0:  6F 72 31 36 0D 0A 55 41 2D 4F 53 3A 20 57 69 6E    or16..UA-OS: Win
 100:  64 6F 77 73 20 39 35 0D 0A 55 41 2D 43 50 55 3A    dows 95..UA-CPU:
 110:  20 78 38 36 0D 0A 49 66 2D 4D 6F 64 69 66 69 65     x86..If-Modifie
 120:  64 2D 53 69 6E 63 65 3A 20 54 75 65 2C 20 32 35    d-Since: Tue, 25
 130:  20 41 75 67 20 31 39 39 38 20 31 34 3A 30 36 3A     Aug 1998 14:06:
 140:  31 30 20 47 4D 54 3B 20 6C 65 6E 67 74 68 3D 32    10 GMT; length=2
 150:  39 38 0D 0A 55 55 73 65 72 2D 41 67 65 6E 74 3A 20  98 .User-Agent:
 160:  4D 6F 7A 69 6C 6C 61 2F 32 2E 30 20 28 63 6F 6F    Mozilla/2.0 (com
 170:  70 61 74 69 62 6C 65 3B 20 4D 53 49 45 20 33 2E    patible; MSIE 3.
 180:  30 3B 20 57 69 6E 64 6F 77 73 20 39 35 29 0D 0A    0; Windows 95)..
 190:  48 6F 73 74 3A 20 31 39 38 2E 31 31 32 2E 32 30    Host: 198.112.20
 1A0:  32 2E 32 38 0D 0A 43 6F 6E 6E 65 63 74 69 6F 6E    2.28..Connection
 1B0:  3A 20 4B 65 65 70 2D 41 6C 69 76 65 0D 0A 0D 0A    : Keep-Alive....
```

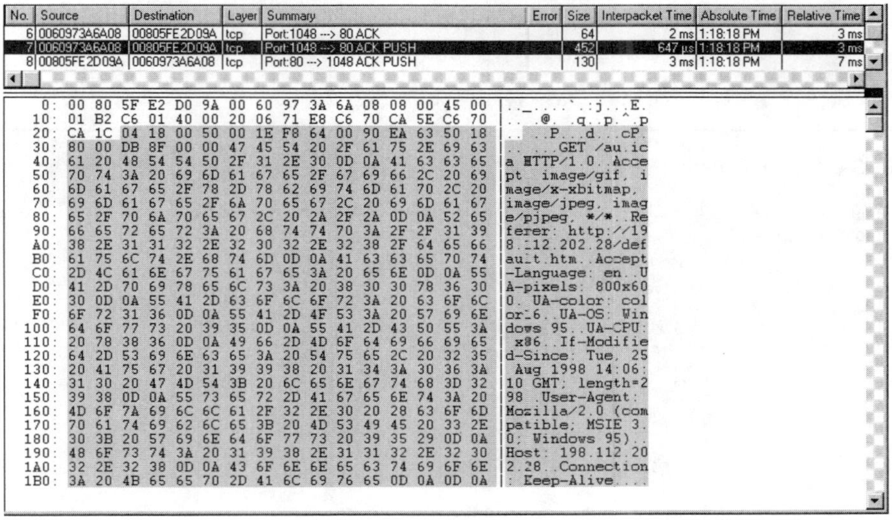

Checking for Vulnerabilities

Now that Woolly has an inventory of all systems on the network and he knows what services are running on each, he can turn his attention to finding out what vulnerabilities can be exploited. This can be accomplished in a hit-or-miss fashion by simply launching the exploit to see what happens. A dangerous attacker, however, will take the time required to know that an exploit will work before trying it. This helps to insure that the attacker does not set off some kind of alarm while bumping around in the dark. Vulnerability checks can be performed manually or automatically through some form of software product.

Manual Vulnerability Checks

Manual vulnerability checks are performed by using a tool, such as telnet, to connect to a remote service and see what is listening. Most services do a pretty good job of identifying themselves when a remote host connects to them. While this is done for troubleshooting purposes, it can provide an attacker with more information than you intended to give out.

For example, take a look at Figure 16.8. We have opened a telnet session to the SMTP port on `mailsys.foobar.org`. This was accomplished by typing the following command at a system prompt:

```
telnet mailsys.foobar.org 25
```

FIGURE 16.8:

Using telnet to connect to a remote mail server

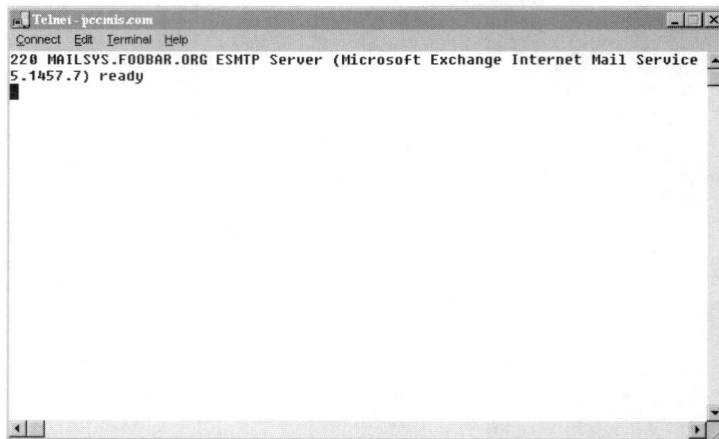

The trailing 25 tells telnet not to connect to the default port of 23; rather, it should connect to port 25, which is the well known port for SMTP. As you can see, this mail server is more than happy to let us know that it is running Microsoft Exchange (thus the OS is Windows NT) and that the software version is 5.0. The build number of 1457.7 tells us that there are no Exchange service packs installed. This build is the original 5.0 version. An attacker looking to disable this system now knows to look for vulnerabilities that pertain to Exchange 5.0. Table 16.1 shows a number of commands you can use when connecting to a service port via telnet.

Figure 16.9 shows telnet being used to connect to a remote server named Thor that is running IMAP4. Notice that IMAP4, like many of the other services we discussed, sends passwords in the clear (`2secret2` is the password for the user `cbrenton`). Also notice that IMAP 4 expects each command from the client to be preceded by a line identifier (such as 1,2,3 as used in the figure). As with Figure 16.8, we now know what software is answering queries on this port. This helps us to identify which exploits may be effective against this system.

TABLE 16.1:   Service Port Commands When Using Telnet

Service	Port	Commands	Comments
FTP	21	user, pass, stat, quit	This provides a command session only. You cannot transfer a file.
SMTP	25	helo, mail from:, rcpt to:, data, quit	E-mail can be forged using these commands.
HTTP	80	get	You will receive a page error, but you will at least know the service is active.
POP3	110	user, pass, stat, list, retr, quit	Mail can be viewed by connecting to the POP3 port.
IMAP4	143	login, capability, examine, expunge, logout	All commands must be preceded by a unique line identifier.

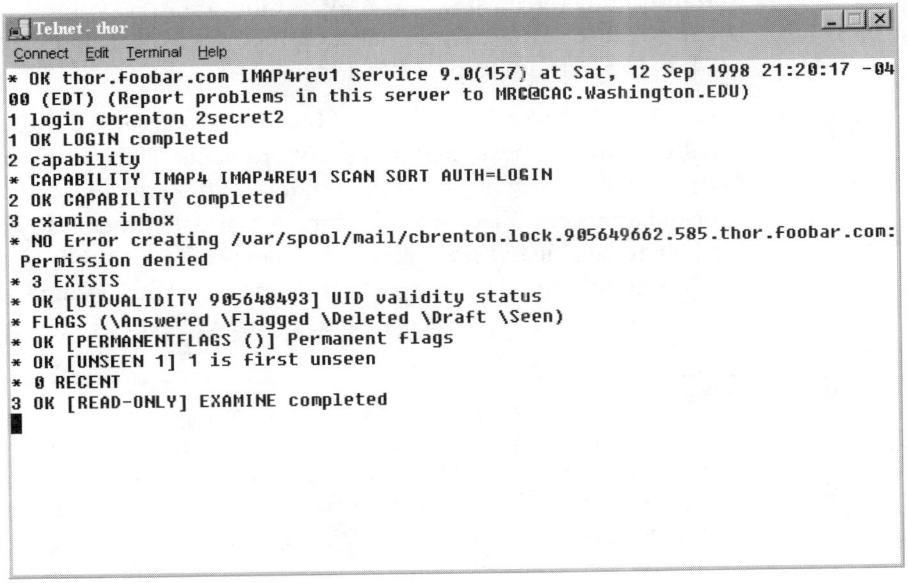

FIGURE 16.9:

Using telnet to connect to a remote IMAP4 server

```
Telnet - thor
Connect  Edit  Terminal  Help
* OK thor.foobar.com IMAP4rev1 Service 9.0(157) at Sat, 12 Sep 1998 21:20:17 -04
00 (EDT) (Report problems in this server to MRC@CAC.Washington.EDU)
1 login cbrenton 2secret2
1 OK LOGIN completed
2 capability
* CAPABILITY IMAP4 IMAP4REV1 SCAN SORT AUTH=LOGIN
2 OK CAPABILITY completed
3 examine inbox
* NO Error creating /var/spool/mail/cbrenton.lock.905649662.585.thor.foobar.com:
 Permission denied
* 3 EXISTS
* OK [UIDVALIDITY 905648493] UID validity status
* FLAGS (\Answered \Flagged \Deleted \Draft \Seen)
* OK [PERMANENTFLAGS ()] Permanent flags
* OK [UNSEEN 1] 1 is first unseen
* 0 RECENT
3 OK [READ-ONLY] EXAMINE completed
```

Clearly, manual vulnerability-checking takes a bit of work. It is time-consuming because it requires manual intervention in order to verify the target service. Manual vulnerability-checking also requires that attackers have at least half a clue about what they are doing. Knowing which service is running on the target system is of little help to an attacker who cannot figure out how to exploit this information.

Automated Vulnerability Scanners

An *automated vulnerability scanner* is simply a software program that automatically performs all the probing and scanning steps that an attacker would normally do manually. These scanners can be directed at a single system or at entire IP subnets. The scanner will first go out and identify potential targets. It will then perform a port scan and probe all active ports for known vulnerabilities. These vulnerabilities are then reported back to the user. Depending on the program, the vulnerability scanner may even include tools to actually exploit the vulnerabilities that it finds.

For example, Figure 16.10 is a screen capture of the Security Analyzer from WebTrends. By defining an IP subnet range, this scanner will go out and find all active systems on that subnet. It will then perform a port scan and report any vulnerabilities that may exist. The program even includes an Ethernet sniffer so that traffic along the local subnet may be monitored. As you can see from the screen capture, Security Analyzer has identified some potential vulnerabilities on ports 21 and 25 of the system at IP address 192.168.1.200.

Vulnerability scanners are not some mystical piece of software that can magically infiltrate a system and identify problems. They simply take the manual process of identifying potential vulnerabilities and automate it. In fact, an experienced attacker or hacker performing a manual vulnerability check is far more likely to be able to find potential problems because she is in a better position to adapt to the characteristics of each specific system. A vulnerability scanner is no better at performing a security audit than whoever programmed it.

WARNING   Beware of security experts who make their living by strictly running automated vulnerability software. Most will provide the canned reports created by the software package and little extra value. I've run into more than one so-called expert who did not even understand the output of the reports they were producing. Ask for references before contracting with anyone to perform a security audit.

FIGURE 16.10:

FIGURE 16.10:

The Security Analyzer from WebTrends

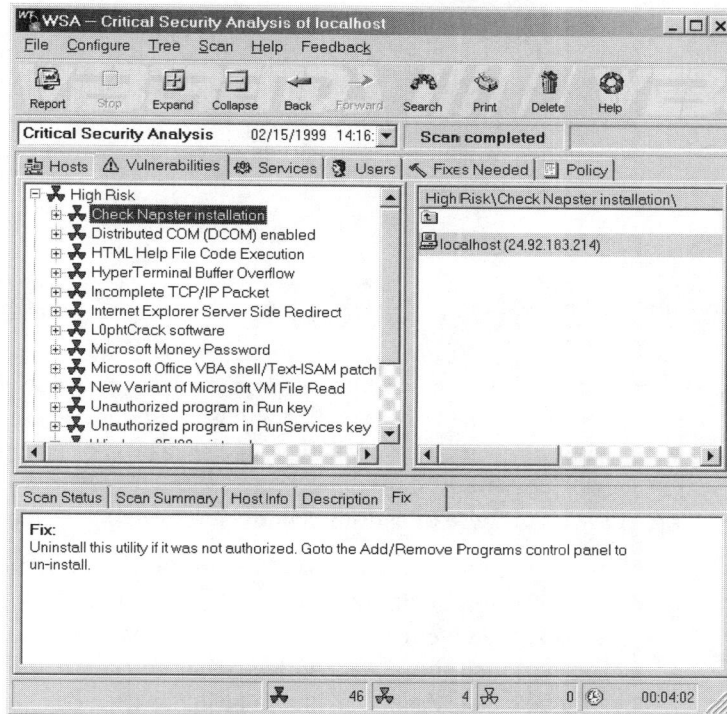

It is impossible for a remote vulnerability scanner to identify all exploits without actually launching them against the remote system. For example, you cannot tell whether a remote system is susceptible to a teardrop attack without actually launching the attack to see if the system survives. This means that you should not assume that a system has a clean bill of health just because a remote vulnerability scanner does not identify any specific problems.

It is possible for a vulnerability scanner to identify exploits without having to launch them when the software is running on the system that you wish to check or when it has full access to the file system. A software program running locally has the benefit of being able to check application and driver dates and compare these to a list of known fixes. For example, a vulnerability scanner running on an NT server that you wish to check would be able to verify that the tcpip.sys is dated 1/9/98 or later. This would indicate a patched driver, which is not susceptible to any known Teardrop attacks.

Vulnerability scanners are simply a tool; they are not a magic bullet for finding all known security problems. While vulnerability scanners are fine for providing some initial direction about which system may be in the most need of attention, they should not be considered a final authority on which systems are secure and which ones are not. There is no tool that can replace an experienced administrator who stays informed of security issues and has an intimate understanding of the systems he manages.

Launching the Attack

Once Woolly Attacker knows your weak spots, he is ready to launch an attack. The type of attack he launches will greatly depend on his final objectives. Is he after one specific resource, or does he want to go after all systems on the network? Does he wish to penetrate a system or will a denial of service suffice? The answers to these questions will decide his next course of action.

In this section, we will look at a number of different exploits. The intent is not to give a listing of all known exploits—any such list would be out of date before this book even went to print. Rather, the goal is to show you a selective sampling of the exploits found in the wild so that you can better understand what can and cannot be done when attacking a target system or network. The idea is to make you aware of the types of attacks that can be launched—so that you will be better able to determine whether a particular resource is safe.

NOTE   Some exploits that were briefly described earlier in this book have been included here for completeness.

Hidden Accounts

While not an exploit *per se*, hidden user accounts can completely circumvent a security policy. For example, let's say you have a border router that is protecting your network by providing packet filtering. Imagine the security breach of having that device contain a hidden, administrator-level account that has a password that cannot be changed. Far-fetched, you say? Try telling that to 3COM.

In the spring of 1998, it came to light that 3COM was configuring layer-2 and -3 switches within its CoreBuilder and SuperStack II product line with hidden administrator accounts. The authentication pair used for most of these devices was a logon name of debug with a password of synnet. This administrator-level account could not be changed or deleted and was not visible from the management software. This meant that you could take all the right steps to secure your network hardware—only to have an attacker come in through the back door.

In 3COM's defense, it was not the first vendor nor will it probably be the last to hide accounts within its firmware. A number of other hardware vendors have done the same, citing support issues as the primary motivating force. These firms reason that, by including a hidden administrator account, a technical-support person would be able to help a user who has forgotten the administrator password on the visible account. Many vendors, such as Cisco, have taken a more secure approach to handling such problems. For example, if you forget the password to your Cisco router, it can still be recovered, but you need physical access to the device and you must take it offline during the recovery process. This provides a far more secure method of password recovery.

TIP   Unless a vendor has made a statement to the contrary, it is impossible to know which network devices have hidden administrator accounts. This means that you should not rely solely on password authentication; rather, you should take additional measures in order to secure these devices. For example, you may wish to consider disabling remote management of the device altogether or limiting management access to only certain IP addresses.

Man in the Middle

The classic *man-in-the-middle* exploit is to have an attacker sitting between the client and the server with a packet analyzer. This is the variation that most people think of when they hear the term "man in the middle." There are, in fact, many other forms of man-in-the-middle attacks, which exploit the fact that most network communications do not use a strong form of authentication. Unless both ends of the session frequently verify whom they are talking to, they may very well be communicating with an attacker, not the intended system.

Stepping in on a conversation is typically referred to as *session hijacking*. An attacker waits for two systems to begin a legitimate communication session and then injects commands into this data stream, pretending to be one of the communicating systems. Session hijacking tools have been available for NetWare for some time. There are tools that allow any user to hijack the supervisor's communication session and promote his or her own logon ID to a supervisor equivalent. In the summer of 1997, a similar tool was released for Windows NT environments, called C2MYAZZ.

C2MYAZZ

The C2MYAZZ utility is an excellent example of using spoofing in order to hijack a communication session. When Windows 95 and NT were originally introduced, they included two methods of authenticating with a Session Message Block (SMB) system. The default was to authenticate using an encrypted password. This was the preferred method for authenticating with a Windows NT domain. LanMan authentication was also included, however, for backwards compatibility with SMB LanMan servers. LanMan authentication requires that the logon name and password be sent in the clear.

When C2MYAZZ is run, it passively waits for a client to authenticate to the NT server. When a logon is detected, C2MYAZZ transmits a single packet back to the client, requesting that LanMan authentication be used instead. The client, trusting that the server is sending the request, happily obliges and retransmits the credentials in the clear. The C2MYAZZ utility would then capture and display the logon name and password combination. C2MYAZZ causes no disruption in the client's session, because the user can still log on and gain system access.

A packet capture of C2MYAZZ in action is shown in Figure 16.11. A client establishes a connection with an NT domain controller named FirstFoo by initializing a TCP three-packet handshake. In packet 6, the client informs the server that it wishes to authenticate to the domain. Packet 7 is where things start to get interesting. Notice that C2MYAZZ has transmitted a packet back to the client. The source IP address used by C2MYAZZ (192.168.1.1) is that of the server FirstFoo. All acknowledgment and sequence numbers are spoofed, as well, so that the client assumes that it has received this packet from the server FirstFoo. The bottom window is the data being transmitted by C2MYAZZ that tells the client to use clear text authentication.

In packet 8, the domain controller FirstFoo responds, telling the client that encryption is supported—but at this point it is too late. The client has already received the spoofed packet from C2MYAZZ, so the client assumes that the real transmission from FirstFoo must be a duplicate and discards the information. The client then proceeds to use clear text authentication. The C2MYAZZ utility is then free to document the logon name and password, as both have been transmitted in the clear.

FIGURE 16.11:

A packet capture of
C2MYAZZ telling a client to
use clear text passwords

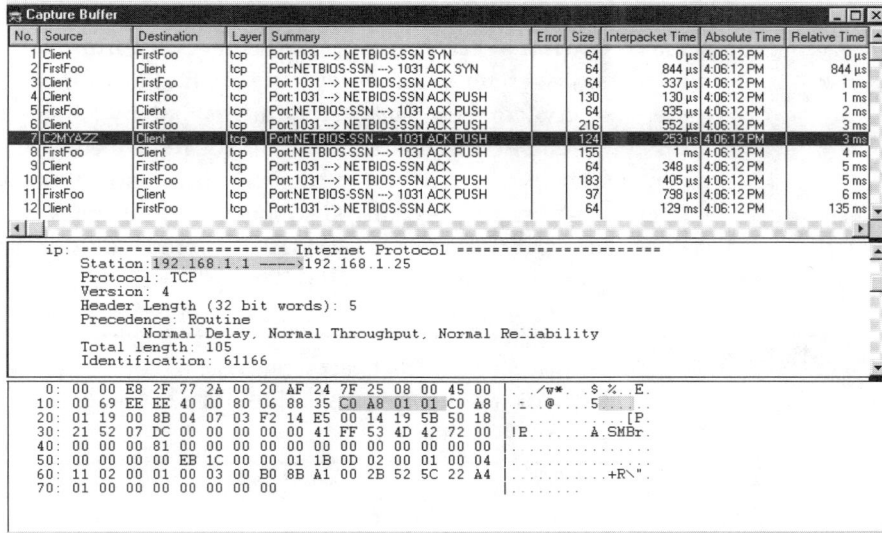

NOTE   What is interesting about this exploit is that if both the server and the client are
unpatched, there is no interruption in connectivity. The client authenticates to the
server and receives access to network resources. Microsoft has made two patches
available for this exploit: one of the patches gets loaded on all clients and the other
gets loaded on the server. If you load the client patch, the client will refuse to send
logon information in the clear. If the server patch is loaded, the server will not accept
clear text logons. The client may still transmit clear text authentication information,
but the server will not accept clear text credentials. This means that unless you patch
every single system, C2MYAZZ now becomes an effective tool for causing a denial
of service because clients will no longer be able to authenticate with the domain.

The reason that C2MYAZZ is so effective is that neither the client nor the server
makes any effort to authenticate the remote system. Since the client accepts the
spoofed packet as legitimate, C2MYAZZ is free to hijack the session. The Microsoft
response to this problem—which is to stop using clear text authentication information—is simply a patch, not a true fix. Since this patch does not include authentication, the SMB session is still vulnerable to hijacking attacks. As mentioned, this
attack is a variation of an old NetWare attack that allowed users to hijack a supervisor's session and promote themselves to a supervisor equivalent. This is what
prompted Novell to create *packet signature*.

Packet signature is an authentication process that allows the NetWare server and client to validate each other's identity during the course of a communication session. When the server receives a packet of data from the client, the signature information is referenced in order to insure that the transmission source is legitimate. The problem with packet signature is that, by default, clients and servers are configured not to use it unless signing is requested by the other system. This means that packet signature as a method of authentication is not used by default. Even if a client setting is changed so that it requests packet signature, it is far too easy to use a utility similar to C2MYAZZ, which would inform the client that packet signature is not supported.

TIP

The only way to insure that packet signature is used is to set packet signing to the highest setting. This prevents the client from talking to any server that does not support packet signature.

Buffer Overflows

When a programmer writes an application, she must create memory pools, referred to as *buffers*, in order to accept input from users or other applications. For example, a login application must allocate memory space in order to allow the user to input a logon name and password. In order to allocate enough memory space for this information, the programmer must make an assumption about how much data will be received for each variable. For example, the programmer may decide that users will not need to enter a logon name larger than 16 characters and that passwords will never be larger than 10 characters. A *buffer overflow* is when more data is received by a process than the programmer ever expected the process to see, and no contingency exists for when the process has to deal with an excessive amount of data.

An Example of a Buffer Overflow

For an example of how buffer overflows are used as exploits, let's return to our example in Figure 16.8, where we had established a session with an Exchange server using telnet. If we take a quick trip to www.rootshell.com and do a search for known vulnerabilities of Exchange, we find that this version of Exchange is susceptible to a buffer overflow attack.

For example, if you use an LDAP bind request (consisting of a username, password, and binding method) and pad the bind method with more than 256 characters, the LDAP service will crash, and a hacker could execute code. This is because when the LDAP connector was coded, the programmers assumed that allocating enough memory space to handle a binding method containing 254 characters was more than sufficient. While it seems safe to assume that a binding method that is greater than 254 characters would ever exist, the problem is that the programmers never told the application what to do if it ever did actually receive a 255-character binding method.

Instead of truncating the data or outright rejecting it, the LDAP connector will still attempt to copy this long address into a memory space that can only handle 254 characters. The result is that the characters after character number 254 will overwrite other memory areas or get passed off to the core OS for processing. If you are lucky, this causes the server to crash. If you are not so lucky, the remaining characters can be interpreted as instructions for the operating system and will be executed with the level of permissions granted to that service. This is why running services as root or administrator is considered so dangerous. If Woolly Attacker can cause a buffer overflow, he may be able to execute any command he wants on the target system.

Other Buffer Overflow Attacks

Buffer overflows have become the most popular way to cause a denial of service or to attempt to execute commands on a remote system. There are many exploits that rely on sending a process too much information in order to attack the target system. Some of the more popular buffer overflow attacks over the last few years have been

- Sending oversized ICMP request packets (Ping of death)

- Sending an IIS 3.0 server a 4,048-byte URL request

- Sending e-mail messages with 256-character filename attachments to Netscape and Microsoft mail clients

- Sending an SMB logon request to an NT server with the data size incorrectly identified

- Sending a Pine user an e-mail with a from address in excess of 256 characters

- Connecting to WinGate's POP3 port and entering a username with 256 characters

As you can see, buffer overflow problems exist over a wide range of applications and affect every operating system. The only way to know for sure if an application is susceptible to buffer overflows is to review the source code.

NOTE

You may be able to find a buffer overflow problem through trial and error, but failing to produce a buffer overflow does not mean that the software is secure. You simply might not have tried enough characters. The only surefire method of verifying that a program is not susceptible to buffer overflows is to review the original source code.

SYN Attack

A *SYN attack* exploits the use of a small buffer space during the TCP three-packet handshake in order to prevent a server from accepting inbound TCP connections. When the server receives the first SYN=1 packet, it stores this connection request in a small "in-process" queue. Since sessions tend to be established rather quickly, this queue is small and only able to store a relatively low number of connection requests. This was done for memory optimization, in the belief that the session would be moved to the larger queue rather quickly, thus making room for more connection requests.

A SYN attack floods this smaller queue with connection requests. When the destination system issues a reply, the attacking system does not respond. This leaves the connection request in the smaller queue until the timer expires and the entry is purged. By filling up this queue with bogus connection requests, the attacking system can prevent the system from accepting legitimate connection requests. Thus a SYN attack is considered a denial of service.

Since the use of two memory spaces is a standard TCP function, there is no way to actually fix this problem. Your two options are

- To increase the size of the in-process queue
- To decrease the amount of time before stale entries are purged from the in-process queue

Increasing the queue size provides additional space so that additional connection requests can be queued, but you would need an extremely large buffer to insure that systems connected to a 100Mb or 1Gb network would not be vulnerable to a SYN attack. For systems connected to slower network connections, this use of memory would be a complete waste. As for decreasing the time before connection requests are purged, a timer value that is set too low would prevent busy systems or systems connected by a slow network link to be refused a connection.

Tuning a system so that it cannot fall prey to a SYN attack becomes a balancing act. You want to increase the in-process queue in order to handle a reasonable number of concurrent connection requests without making the buffer so large that you are wasting memory. You also want a purge time that is low enough to remove stale entries but not so low that you start preventing legitimate systems from establishing a connection. Unfortunately, most operating systems do not allow you to tune these values. You must rely on the operating system vendor to pick appropriate settings.

Teardrop Attacks

In order to understand how a *teardrop attack* is used against a system, you must first understand the purpose of the fragmentation offset field and the length field within the IP header. The fragmentation offset field is typically used by routers. If a router receives a packet that is too large for the next segment, the router will need to fragment the data before passing it along. The fragmentation offset field is used along with the length field so that the receiving system can reassemble the datagram in the correct order. When a fragmentation offset value of 0 is received, the receiving system assumes either that this is the first packet of fragmented information or that fragmentation has not been used.

If fragmentation has occurred, the receiving system will use the offset to determine where the data within each packet should be placed when rebuilding the datagram. For an analogy, think of a child's set of numbered building blocks. As long as the child follows the numbering plan and puts the blocks together in the right order, he can build a house, a car, or even a plane. In fact, he does not even need to know what he is trying to build. He simply has to assemble the blocks in the specified order.

The IP fragmentation offset works in much the same manner. The offset tells the receiving system how far away from the front of the datagram the included payload should be placed. If all goes well, this schema allows the datagram to be reassembled in the correct order. The length field is used as a verification check to insure that there is no overlap and that data has not been corrupted in transit. For example, if you place fragments 1 and 3 within the datagram and then try to place fragment 2, but you find that fragment 2 is too large and will overwrite some of fragment 3, you know you have a problem.

At this point, the system will try to realign the datagrams to see if it can make them fit. If it cannot, the receiving system will send out a request that the data be resent. Most IP stacks are capable of dealing with overlaps or payloads that are too large for their segment.

Launching a Teardrop Attack

A teardrop attack starts by sending a normal packet of data with a normal-size payload and a fragmentation offset of 0. From the initial packet of data, a teardrop attack is indistinguishable from a normal data transfer. Subsequent packets, however, have modified fragmentation offset and length fields. This ensuing traffic is responsible for crashing the target system.

When the second packet of data is received, the fragmentation offset is consulted to see where within the datagram this information should be placed. In a teardrop attack, the offset on the second packet claims that this information should be placed somewhere within the first fragment. When the payload field is checked, the receiving system finds that this data is not even large enough to extend past the end of the first fragment. In other words, this second fragment does not overlap the first fragment; it is actually fully contained inside of it. Since this was not an error condition that anyone expected, there is no routine to handle it and this information causes a buffer overflow—crashing the receiving system. For some operating systems, only one malformed packet is required. Others will not crash unless multiple malformed packets are received.

Smurf

Named after the original program that would launch this attack, *Smurf* uses a combination of IP spoofing and ICMP replies in order to saturate a host with traffic, causing a denial of service. The attack goes like this: Woolly Attacker sends a spoofed Ping packet (echo request) to the broadcast address of a network with a large number of hosts and a high-bandwidth Internet connection. This network is known as the bounce site. The spoofed Ping packet has a source address of the system Woolly wishes to attack.

The premise of the attack is that when a router receives a packet sent to an IP broadcast address (such as 206.121.73.255), it recognizes this as a network broadcast and will map the address to an Ethernet broadcast address of FF:FF:FF:FF:FF:FF. So when our router receives this packet from the Internet, it will broadcast it to all hosts on the local segment.

I'm sure you can see what happens next. All the hosts on that segment respond with an echo-reply to the spoofed IP address. If this is a large Ethernet segment, there may be 500 or more hosts responding to each echo request they receive.

Since most systems try to handle ICMP traffic as quickly as possible, the target system whose address Woolly Attacker spoofed quickly becomes saturated with echo replies. This can easily prevent the system from being able to handle any other traffic, thus causing a denial of service.

This not only affects the target system, but the organization's Internet link, as well. If the bounce site has a T3 link (45Mbps) but the target system's organization is hooked up to a leased line (56Kbps), all communication to and from the organization will grind to a halt.

So how can you prevent this type of attack? You can take steps at the source site, bounce site, and target site to help limit the effects of a Smurf attack.

Blocking Smurf at the Source

Smurf relies on the attacker's ability to transmit an echo request with a spoofed source address. You can stop this attack at its source by using router access lists, which insure that all traffic originating from your network does in fact have a proper source address. This prevents the spoofed packet from ever making it to the bounce site.

Blocking Smurf at the Bounce Site

In order to block Smurf at the bounce site, you have two options. The first is to simply block all inbound echo requests. This will prevent these packets from ever reaching your network.

If blocking all inbound echo requests is not an option, then you need to stop your routers from mapping traffic destined for the network broadcast address to the LAN broadcast address. By preventing this mapping, your systems will no longer receive these echo requests.

To prevent a Cisco router from mapping network broadcasts to LAN broadcasts, enter configuration mode for the LAN interface and enter the command

```
no ip directed-broadcast
```

NOTE   This must be performed on every LAN interface on every router. This command will not be effective if it is performed only on your perimeter router.

Blocking Smurf at the Target Site

Unless your ISP is willing to help you out, there is little you can do to prevent the effects of Smurf on your WAN link. While you can block this traffic at the network perimeter, this is too late to prevent the attack from eating up all of your WAN bandwidth.

You can, however, minimize the effects of Smurf by at least blocking it at the perimeter. By using dynamic packet filtering or some form of firewall that can maintain state, you can prevent these packets from entering your network. Since your state table would be aware that the attack session did not originate on the local network (it would not have a table entry showing the original echo request), this attack would be handled like any other spoof attack and promptly dropped.

Brute Force Attacks

A *brute force attack* is simply an attempt to try all possible values when attempting to authenticate with a system or crack the crypto key used to create ciphertext. For example, an attacker may attempt to log on to your server as administrator using a list of dictionary words as possible passwords. There is no finesse involved; the attacker is simply going to try every potential word or phase to come up with a possible password.

One of the most popular ways to perform a brute force attack is with a *password cracker*, and no program displays how effective these programs can be like Security Software Technologies' L0phtCrack (developed by L0pht, which later became @stake). L0phtCrack uses both a dictionary file and a brute force guessing attack in order to discover user passwords. Figure 16.12 is a screen capture of L0phtCrack attempting to crack a number of user passwords. This particular session has just been started. Notice that several passwords have already been cracked.

Encrypted NT passwords are saved in the \WinNT\system32\config directory in a file named SAM. L0phtCrack provides three ways to access this information:

- By directly importing them into L0phtCrack if the software is running on the NT server

- By reading a backup version of the SAM file saved to tape, an emergency recovery disk, or the \WinNT\repair directory

- By sniffing them off the network using the included readsmb.exe utility

FIGURE 16.12:

L0pht's L0phtCrack utility

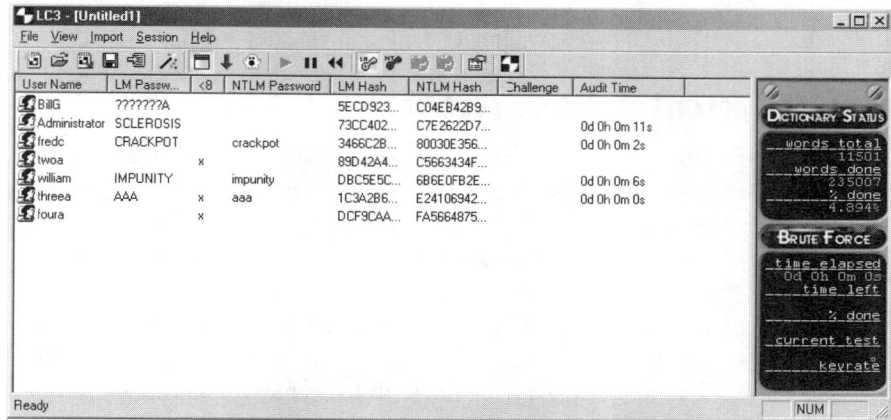

Once the authentication information has been collected, it is imported into the L0phtCrack utility. Unlike some password crackers that attempt to crack the entire ciphertext, L0phtCrack takes a few shortcuts in order to reduce the time required to crack passwords. For example, if you look at Figure 16.12, the <8 column indicates accounts with a password of fewer than eight characters. This is determined by looking at the ciphertext in the LanMan hash. Any password that contains fewer than eight characters will always have the string AAD3B435B51404EE appended to the end for padding. This allows L0phtCrack to quickly determine that the password string contains fewer than eight characters.

The passwords are first checked against a dictionary file with thousands of words. This dictionary file can be edited with any text editor if the user wishes to add more words. Dictionary checking is extremely fast—checking the accounts shown in Figure 16.12 took less than 10 seconds. Any passwords that are not cracked by the dictionary search are then subjected to a brute force attack, which is capable of testing both alphanumeric and special characters. The amount of time it takes to brute force the password depends on the number of characters in the password. For example, the account cbrenton in Figure 16.12 has a 10-character password. Had this password been seven characters or less, the search time would have been reduced by roughly one-third.

As system administrator, you simply cannot control the use of password crackers: password crackers are available for every platform. While you may be able to prevent an attacker from running a password cracker directly on your server, she can always run the cracking software on some other machine. This means your only true defense is to protect any files that include password information, as well as prevent sniffing on your network through the use of routers and switches.

Physical Access Attacks

With all the attention given to network-based attacks, many people forget that the most straightforward way to compromise a network is by gaining physical access to one or more network systems. Systems that are kept in secluded or locked areas are the most vulnerable, as this provides the attacker with the necessary privacy to compromise a system. As I have emphasized, an overwhelming majority of attacks originate from within an organization. This provides an attacker with a certain level of legitimate access to network resources. With physical access to a system, it is not very difficult to increase this access to that of an administrator.

For example, let's assume that you have an NT workstation environment for all of your client systems. Profiles are mandatory and users are provided with minimal access to both the local system and network resources. All service packs have been installed, as have all security hotfixes. Every NT workstation has full auditing enabled so that every event is recorded and sent off to a remote process that looks for suspicious activity and archives the logs for future review.

This certainly sounds like a secure client environment, doesn't it? If Woolly Attacker has private physical access to the machine, he can easily perform the following steps:

- Pop the cover on the computer and disconnect the battery in order to clear the CMOS password.

- Boot the system off a floppy in order to gain access to the local file system.

- Copy the SAM file so that password information can be run through a password cracker.

- Remove the local administrator password so that he has full access to the local NT operating system.

- Reboot the system with the NIC disconnected so that he can log on locally as administrator without tripping any alarms.

- Change the logging level so that suspicious activity is not reported.

- Install sniffing software so that other network communications can be monitored.

- Use the compromised passwords in order to attack other network systems.

In short, a savvy attacker can completely circumvent the security of this environment in less than half an hour. The greatest delays would be in waiting for NT to boot or shut down. If you are managing security for a large environment, you should not plan on being able to fully secure any of your client systems. As you can see from this scenario, they are far too easy to compromise.

NOTE   The exception would be a thin client environment such as WinFrame or MetaFrame. This is because the local workstations are little more than terminals; all security is managed on the server itself.

Summary

In this chapter we discussed some of the ways an attacker might go about attacking your network. We started by looking at the ways an attacker can collect information about your network with little more than your organization's name. We then discussed how an attacker could go about collecting even more information about your specific network environment in order to determine what vulnerabilities may be exploitable. Finally, we looked at some of the assault methods available to an attacker who wishes to compromise your resources.

In the next chapter, we will discuss how to stay ahead of these attacks. We will look at how to stay informed of the exploits that have been found—and how to find your vulnerabilities before an attacker does.

CHAPTER

SEVENTEEN

17

Staying Ahead of Attacks

Thanks to the complexities of modern software, it is safe to say that security vulnerabilities will be with us for many years to come. While public discussion of those vulnerabilities goes a long way toward insuring that current software is purged of exploitable code, this makes no guarantee that future releases will be free from the same problems. For example, buffer overflows have plagued programmers since the early '70s and are still very much a problem today.

In order to maintain a secure environment, you need to stay abreast of these exploits as they are discovered. Gone are the days when you could wait for a product upgrade or a service pack in order to fix a security problem. For example, Microsoft releases security-related hotfixes constantly. Clearly, you would not want to leave security holes simply because you were waiting for a patch from a vendor.

Information from the Vendor

Vendor channels are your best bet for finding the latest security patches. While most vendors will also issue security advisories, you can usually find out about specific exploits much sooner through third-party sources. You are also far more likely to get an accurate description of the exploit that is free from marketing spin. For example, a Microsoft press release regarding Back Orifice (a famous Trojan horse) stated:

> "Back Orifice" does not expose or exploit any security issue in Windows, Windows NT, or the Microsoft BackOffice suite of products. As far as demonstrating an inherent security vulnerability in the Windows platform, this is simply not true.

Obviously, this is a great public relations spin, but it is not very helpful to the system administrator who is trying to determine how much of a threat this vulnerability poses to her local networking environment. So, while the vendor may be willing to tell you that the vulnerability exists, you might have to look elsewhere for the full scoop.

3COM

3COM makes a wide variety of networking products, including network cards, switches, and routers. The company also has a popular handheld computer line called the Palm. 3COM has made a name for itself by supplying reasonably priced products that provide above-average performance. The 3COM Web site can be found at www.3com.com.

Technical Information

The 3COM Web site contains a wealth of technical papers and briefs. While the inventory is not quite as extensive as the one maintained by Cisco, the 3COM site has papers on topics ranging from ATM to network management to security. Some of these papers are product specific; for example, one of the security papers specifically deals with using a 3COM NetBuilder as a firewall. There are many papers, however, that simply deal with a specific technology. These papers can be found through the link www.3com.com/technology/tech_net/white_papers/index.html.

You can also find a decent amount of product support on 3COM's Web site. There is no knowledge base, but there are support tips and release notes for each of its products. Product documentation is also available online.

NOTE   In order to get access to 3COM's knowledge base, you must purchase a support contract. This gives you access to a wider range of problems, such as known bugs.

The generic support can be found at http://infodeli.3com.com/index.htm.

3COM has made improvements in the past few years in issuing security advisories for their products. This is in sharp contrast to previous years. Unfortunately, 3COM does not have a mailing list dedicated to security issues, something other vendors have implemented to improve timely notification of product vulnerabilities.

Patches and Updates

3COM makes patches and updates available free to all its customers. You do not need a service contract simply to receive patch updates. This is extremely useful; you are not required to purchase a service contract simply to fix known bugs. There is also some helpful third-party software on 3COM's support site, such as a Windows-based TFTP server. A TFTP server is required if you wish to update the firmware on a 3COM router or switch. You can access 3COM patch files through this link to their software library: http://support.3com.com/infodeli/swlib/index.htm.

Cisco

Cisco specializes in infrastructure hardware. It has a diverse product line, which includes switches, routers, firewalls, and even intrusion detection systems. Seeing as most of the Internet runs on Cisco hardware, Cisco is obviously a major player in the network connectivity field. You can find the Cisco Web site at www.cisco.com.

Technical Information

Cisco provides one of the best sites on the Internet if you are looking for network-related advice. Along with product-specific documentation, there is a wealth of technology information. Looking to implement BGP or OSPF in your environment? The Cisco site contains a number of white papers, as well as tutorials that explain the technology and how to implement it.

The Cisco Web site has a large number of security-related documents geared toward helping the network administrator lock down his environment. You can literally perform a search on just about any vulnerability (such as teardrop, Smurf, and so on) to receive information that describes the exploit and what you can do to protect your internal systems. To make life even easier, all documents can be retrieved directly from the search engine on the main page.

Cisco does an excellent job of publicizing vulnerabilities once these are discovered and resolved. Cisco announces these patches through CERT, as well as through its own distribution channels. As a major Internet player, Cisco has set the standard for commercial vendors in acknowledging vulnerabilities when they are found and issuing patches in a timely manner.

Patches and Updates

If Cisco falls short in any area, it would have to be in making new patches publicly available. Cisco does not issue hotfixes in order to patch its routers or switches. Rather, the company releases a new revision of the device's operating system. Because these updates may include product enhancements, as well, Cisco does not make them available via publicly accessible areas such as its Web or FTP sites. You need to have a Cisco support contract to receive these updates.

To its credit, Cisco will provide free updates when a major security hole is found. For example, when it was found that the Cisco 700 series routers were vulnerable to a buffer overflow attack if a user entered an extremely long password string, Cisco made updates freely available to all Cisco 700 series customers, regardless of whether or not the customer had a support contract.

Linux

While the core Linux operating system is not considered a commercial product, it is actively produced and supported by a large number of volunteers, as well as the different organizations that distribute it. Linux has established itself as a robust operating system that is capable of handling mission-critical operations. It can act as an application server, a router, or even a firewall. Most Linux-related information is linked to the main Web site at `www.linux.org`.

Technical Information

The Linux Web site is host to a plethora of documents created by the Linux Documentation Project (LDP). There are FAQs, HOWTOs, and mini-HOWTOs on literally every function or service supported by Linux. No matter what you are trying to do with your Linux operating system, chances are there is documentation to walk you through the process. These documents even include many of the caveats you need to watch out for while performing your installation. Links to documentation can be found at `www.linux.org/docs/index.html`.

This page even includes links to many Linux-related mailing lists and newsgroups. The list is literally too extensive to include in this chapter. Mailing lists provide an excellent way to get real-time help when a Linux problem has you completely stumped. If phone support is more to your liking, a number of vendors will provide this service for a fee. A list of vendors can be found at `www.linux.org/vendors/index.html`.

The Linux development team actively propagates security-related vulnerabilities and patch information as these are discovered. This information is circulated through CERT and through a number of Linux discussion channels. The team is also extremely responsive in issuing patches.

Patches and Updates

As a noncommercial operating system, Linux can be received free of charge. This is also true for security-related patches and fixes. There are a number of locations where Linux source code can be downloaded. Some of the more popular include

- `ftp://ftp.cc.gatech.edu/pub/linux/`
- `ftp://sunsite.unc.edu`
- `ftp://ftp.caldera.com/pub/`
- `ftp://ftp.redhat.com/redhat`

Microsoft

Microsoft has come under heavy fire over the last few years for the large number of security vulnerabilities found in its software products. While Microsoft was initially somewhat unresponsive when security exploits were identified, the company has picked up the pace recently. It is not uncommon for Microsoft to release a security patch within hours of the vulnerability's being reported. You will find the Microsoft Web site at www.microsoft.com.

Technical Information

While Microsoft's Web site contains an acceptable amount of technical information, most of it is labeled "premium content." While there is no charge for accessing premium content, you are forced to fill out a marketing questionnaire and configure your browser to accept cookies. The questionnaire requires the typical information: who you are, where you work, and what your e-mail address is. You are also prompted to accept future e-mails from Microsoft, which contain marketing and promotional information.

The requirement that your browser must accept cookies is probably the biggest problem. A *cookie* is a text file, which is saved to your local system, that allows a Web site to identify who you are and where you have been. Predominantly, this is used by companies like Double-Click.net in order to determine which banner ads have proved to be most effective against you in the past. What is really frightening is that cookies can be used to track your movements throughout the Internet and document which Web sites you have visited. You can read the first cookie specification at www.netscape.com/newsref/std/cookie_spec.html.

If you do not have your browser configured to accept cookies, you will be faced with the error screen shown in Figure 17.1. Notice that Microsoft also uses this opportunity to try to get you to use its own browser.

Microsoft does post security-related bulletins to its Web site. These alerts can be found at www.microsoft.com/security/.

Patches and Updates

Microsoft makes all security fixes freely available via its Web site. Microsoft has also made their updates known through the Critical Update Notification program. This utility runs in the background on Windows systems and periodically connects to Microsoft's network to determine if there is any recently released patches. The user is notified and given the opportunity to download any fixes as soon as they are released. As mentioned earlier in this section, Microsoft has become extremely responsive in issuing security-related patches. These patches can be retrieved from the FTP site `ftp://ftp.microsoft.com`.

FIGURE 17.1:

You must accept cookies before viewing technical documents.

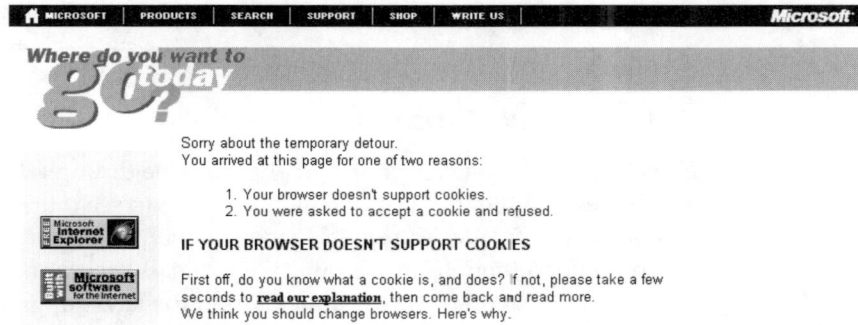

Novell

Novell makes a wide range of networking products that are focused on its Net-Ware operating system. Novell has a pretty good track record with regard to security. Novell's Web site is located at `www.novell.com`.

Technical Information

The Novell Web site contains a number of white papers; however, all are specific to Novell product offerings. There is very little general information if you are looking to find out about a specific technology. Novell offers a documentation site that contains online manuals for its product offerings. The documentation site is located at `www.novell.com/documentation`.

Novell also maintains a knowledge base that you can search in order to find resolutions to known problems. The knowledge base is extensive and documents support calls handled by Novell's technical support staff. Here you can find answers to just about any Novell-related issue. The problem is that the search engine does not do a very good job of helping you locate documents. For example, entering the phrase **security AND alert** brings up product information on WordPerfect, NetWare Connect, and NetView as the closest matches. These documents are not exactly what you may be looking for if you are searching to find out about any recent vulnerabilities. You can find the Novell support site at `http://support.novell.com`.

NOTE   Novell does not participate in CERT advisories and does not dedicate space on its Web site to announcing security-related problems. You may be able to find security issues within the knowledge base, but you must already know what you are looking for in order to find it. This means that you must rely completely on third-party channels for vulnerability information regarding NetWare products.

Patches and Updates

Novell makes all patch updates freely available through its support Web site. There is even a file find utility that allows you to see if there is patch update available for a specific file. You can also view Novell's suggested minimum patches and download them from the same page. Finally, recent patches can all be viewed from a single page, so you can quickly find the latest upgrades.

Sun Microsystems

Sun manufactures one of the most popular lines of UNIX operating systems. These boxes have found homes as engineering workstations and high-end application servers. Sun is known for pushing the performance envelope with its UltraSPARC product line, which is already using 64-bit processors running at speeds of 900MHz.

Technical Information

Sun has made a tremendous improvement to its support infrastructure, and most patches and support information can be found (for free) on their Web site, www.sun.com. This is in sharp contrast to several years ago when even patches had to be purchased.

NOTE   Sun also actively participates in CERT advisories and has posted a number of vendor bulletins.

Sun also maintains a section of its Web site for updating clients on security-related information. This page can be accessed through the link http://sunsolve.sun.com/pub-cgi/show.pl?target=security/sec.

Third-Party Channels

There are a number of third-party resources you can use in order to stay informed of the latest security-related exploits. Typically, these resources are established by helpful netizens or organizations that specialize in network security. All of the resources listed here are free, meaning that there is no entry fee required in order to access security-related information. Some resources do post advertisements, however, in order to defray the cost of maintaining the resource.

Third-party security resources include vulnerability databases, Web sites, mailing lists, and newsgroups. Each has its own drawbacks and benefits:

Vulnerability database   Provides search capability for finding exploits but no feedback if you have additional questions

Web site   May have direct links to patch information, as well as a more detailed description, but you will have a harder time finding a specific exploit

Mailing list   Provides immediate notification of exploits as they are found, but some lists can bury your mailbox with 50+ messages a day

Newsgroup   Offers more detailed discussions regarding specific exploits, but you may have to sift through lots of messages to find the information you are looking for

---

TIP   Generally, it is best to subscribe to only one or two mailing lists in order to be informed of exploits as they are found. You can then use the vulnerability databases and Web sites when you wish to research a specific issue.

Vulnerability Databases

Vulnerability databases allow you to search for an exploit based on specific criteria. For example, you may be able to search for exploits that affect a specific operating system (NT, Linux, and so on), meet a specific attack signature (denial of service, cracking, and so on), or even exploits that have been discovered over a specific range of dates.

ISS's X-Force Database

Internet Security System's X-Force database can be searched by platform or by keyword. There are seven different flavors of UNIX to choose from, depending on your taste, as well as all Windows operating systems, which are grouped into a single category. The database only lists operating system exploits; there are no entries for networking hardware such as 3COM or Cisco devices. You can choose to display a month's worth of exploits or all entries for a specific platform. You can also select to have hits displayed with a short summary or all on one page.

A unique feature of the X-Force database is that each entry is assigned a level of risk. If your query produces multiple entries, you can quickly scan through the list in order to find the worst of the bunch. The database entries are sufficiently descriptive, although not always 100 percent accurate. For example, if you look up the Exchange exploit, which we discussed in the last chapter, the record states:

> This action will cause the Exchange Server to crash. This attack does not result in loss of data or unauthorized access to data held in Exchange Server. The Exchange Server could also be vulnerable to stack overwriting attempts by allowing an attacker to insert code as part of the address and have it executed.

As you can see, there are some inconsistencies in this entry. If the exploit causes the server to crash, at a minimum you are going to lose any data that is still in RAM and has not yet been written to disk. Also, this record contradicts itself by first stating that this exploit cannot be used for unauthorized access, but then goes on to say that it could be used to execute code.

The X-Force database can be found at this URL, `http://xforce.iss.net`.

Packet Storm

Packet Storm bills itself as "the largest and most updated library of information security information in the world." It is indeed one of the most comprehensive search and reporting engines on all aspects of information security, and covers not just the weaknesses of a given system but also provides a news service covering the latest happenings in the information security realm.

Packet Storm provides a unique feature called Storm Watch, which reports on the topics searched most often on their database. A printout of the top 20 searches is shown in Table 17.1.

Packet storm can be found at the URL, `http://packetstorm.securify.com/`.

TABLE 17.1:   Top 20 Requested Areas of Security Interest

Query	Date
apache	Sun Feb 18 10:52:22 PST 2001
named	Sun Feb 18 10:52:20 PST 2001
firewall software windows	Sun Feb 18 10:52:18 PST 2001
linux 2.0.35	Sun Feb 18 10:52:18 PST 2001
ssi exec	Sun Feb 18 10:52:15 PST 2001
pimp.c	Sun Feb 18 10:52:13 PST 2001
unix keylogger	Sun Feb 18 10:52:05 PST 2001
epmap	Sun Feb 18 10:52:04 PST 2001
proftpd 1.2.0pre2	Sun Feb 18 10:52:03 PST 2001
exec cmd	Sun Feb 18 10:52:01 PST 2001
NT 4.0	Sun Feb 18 10:51:49 PST 2001
apache exploit	Sun Feb 18 10:51:48 PST 2001
root shell	Sun Feb 18 10:51:28 PST 2001
mail	Sun Feb 18 10:51:25 PST 2001
uin sniffer	Sun Feb 18 10:51:24 PST 2001
windows 98	Sun Feb 18 10:51:23 PST 2001
php	Sun Feb 18 10:51:12 PST 2001
+apache +exploit	Sun Feb 18 10:51:10 PST 2001
solaris	Sun Feb 18 10:51:08 PST 2001
windows 98	Sun Feb 18 10:51:08 PST 2001

Security Bugware

More of a listing than a true database, the Security Bugware site probably contains the most complete listing of exploits and vulnerabilities of any site on the Internet. The amount of information is staggering. The Windows section alone contains more than 250 entries. Some of these are somewhat repetitive. For example, there are five entries for Ping, but three of these are different implementations of the

Ping of death. This repetition is actually a good thing, because it gives you a more complete picture of how a vulnerability can be exploited.

There is no search capability for the entries. You must select one of 12 operating system categories and wade through the results. The entries are listed in alphabetical order, so searching the page is not too difficult. You can also use the Find function within your Web browser in order to have some limited search capabilities.

NOTE   The vulnerability listings are also complete in terms of diversity of the listed products. Not only are major operating systems listed; you can also find vulnerability entries for networking hardware and network applications. If you link to only a single vulnerability database, this is the one to pick.

The site can be accessed through the URL http://161.53.42.3/~crv/security/bugs/list.html.

Web Sites

Third-party Web sites can contain a wealth of information about all forms of security-related issues. There are sites that can give you pointers on securing your environment, as well as sites that provide the same tools an attacker would use against your network. There are obviously too many security-related sites to list them all here, so I have chosen a few of my favorites.

AntiOnline

AntiOnline is one of those sites with a little bit of everything. The main page has a listing of current news events that pertain to network security. There is also a "Quick Tips" section, which provides some excellent hints on dealing with some of the day-to-day security issues a network administrator faces, such as tracking spoofed addresses or dealing with spam. Another link brings you to an online library with papers on a wide range of security topics. There is even a file archive containing a large number of security tools, both positive and negative in functionality. You can access Antionline at www.antionline.com/.

The CERT Home Page

The Computer Emergency Response Team (CERT) maintains the site responsible for collecting Internet-based exploits and works with vendors to get vulnerabilities resolved. CERT also issues public bulletins on known vulnerabilities.

While CERT primarily focuses on UNIX vulnerabilities, it does issue Windows bulletins, as well.

The site also contains helpful pointers for securing your environment. The URL for CERT is `www.cert.org/`.

Guide to (Mostly) Harmless Hacking

Despite its name, this is actually a very useful (although a little dated) site if you are looking to protect yourself against attack. While there are many examples of how to launch attacks, there are just as many that discuss how to prevent them. There are even some helpful tips on writing shell scripts and batch files. All examples assume that the reader has very little computer experience, making the tutorials easy to follow. The guide can be found at `www.spaziopiu.it/elettrici/gtmhh/`.

L0pht and @stake

L0pht started out as a group of hackers working out of the Boston area who specialized in system security and cryptography. Their site was a wealth of security-related information, including advisories and tools. Some of the best-known vulnerabilities were discovered in L0pht's test lab. This means that most of L0pht's advisories are based on firsthand information.

In January of 2000, L0pht joined a newly formed company called @stake (created by former executives of Compaq, Forrester Research, and Cambridge Technology Partners). Because the former members of L0pht now run the research lab at @stake, the Web site continues to be one of the best sources of security advisories. Many of the tools pioneered by L0pht (like L0phtcrack and Antisniff) are now distributed by Security Software Technologies and can be found at `www.securitysoftwaretech.com/`.

Newer tools developed by the research lab are still hosted to the local Web site. The entire research lab can be found at `www.atstake.com/research/index.html`.

The National Security Institute

The National Security Institute (NSI) home page goes beyond the network and publishes security-related information on a variety of topics. Along with computer security, the site covers personal security, terrorism, security legislation, and even travel advisories. The information on the site is extremely diverse. You can even read papers on the psychological effects of implementing an information security policy. This site is an excellent resource if you are looking to expand your knowledge of the security field. The NSI home page can be accessed at `http://nsi.org/`.

Phrack Magazine Home Page

Phrack magazine is one of the longest-running electronic periodicals dealing with system vulnerabilities. Quite a few exploits have been made known to the public through the pages of *Phrack*. While most of the articles are written from the perspective of how to perform an exploit, the articles do an excellent job of describing all the gory details of why an exploit is effective. This is just the information you need in order to insure that you do not fall prey to attack. Phrack is not published on any set schedule. The most recent issue, #56, was released in May of 2000. Phrack does not have its own Web site, but archives can be found at `http://packetstorm.securify.com/mag/phrack/`.

Robert Malmgren's NT Security FAQ

As the name implies, this site is NT specific (no Windows 2000 information), but it contains everything you would ever want to know about securing an NT server. Every aspect of an NT server is covered in great detail, including account administration, the Registry, and the file system. There is even a section on NT-compatible firewall and authentication options. If you need to secure an NT server, this site is well worth the visit. The NT Security FAQ can be accessed at `www.it.kth.se/~rom/ntsec.html`.

Mailing Lists

Mailing lists are an extremely useful tool for staying informed of security vulnerabilities. They provide you with immediate notification when vulnerabilities are released to the public. They also supply a forum where the fine points of a particular exploit can be discussed in detail. A mailing list can provide you with far more information regarding a specific exploit than a vulnerability database, because most mailing lists are interactive. If the list is an open forum, you are free to ask questions.

NOTE To join a mailing list, you must send an e-mail message to the mailing list server. This message must include some form of keyword or words in the body of the message (not the subject line) such as **subscribe**. To be removed from a list, you typically repeat the process using the word **unsubscribe**.

Bugtraq

The mother of all vulnerability discussion lists, Bugtraq is a moderated mailing list for the discussion of exploits. Many vulnerabilities are announced publicly for the first time on this list. The mailing list focuses on what exploits have been found, as well as what can be done to fix them. This is the one list you can subscribe to that will guarantee that you hear about any exploits that are discovered. While traffic volume is a bit high, the information collected through this list is well worth the price of hitting your Delete key a few extra times a day.

Security Focus hosts the Bugtraq archive and the subscription form at `www.securityfocus.com/about/feedback/subscribe.html`.

Firewall-Wizards

The Firewall-Wizards mailing list is for the discussion of all topics related to firewalls and perimeter security. The list is moderated by Marcus Ranum, who helps to insure that all posts stay on topic and that all spam is filtered. Traffic levels tend to be fairly low, with peaks when something exciting is going on within the firewall industry. The list has some extremely knowledgeable members, making it a great place to pick up firewalling tips.

To get more details and to join the list, go to `www.nfr.com/mailman/listinfo/firewall-wizards`.

InfoSec News

The InfoSec News mailing list disseminates security-related news articles. These include excerpts from newspapers, magazines, and online references. The mailing list is closed, meaning that only the moderator is allowed to post. You can, however, contribute by sending the moderator security-related news articles. The list does not discuss vulnerabilities so much as what is going on in the security field. For details on how to join the list, go to `www.c4i.org/isn.html`.

ISS's X-Force IDS Discussion List

ISS hosts a number of discussion lists under the X-Force branch of its Web site; one of the more popular is the intrusion detection system mailing list. This is an unmoderated list with a focus on any topic related to intrusion detection systems. The list is an open discussion forum, meaning that anyone is free to post questions or comments. To join the list, point your browser to `http://xforce.iss.net/maillists/`.

The NTBugtraq Mailing List

The NTBugtraq mailing list focuses solely on Microsoft Windows exploits and vulnerabilities. Despite the list's name, it discusses all Microsoft operating systems and applications. The list is very heavily moderated, keeping postings to an absolute minimum. In fact, most of the postings originate from the list moderator or from the Microsoft programming staff. If you are strictly interested in Windows, this may be a good list to join.

> **NOTE**
> Windows-related vulnerabilities that originate on the Bugtraq mailing list eventually find their way to this list, as well.

For more NTBugtraq information and to join the list, go to `www.ntbugtraq.com`.

Newsgroups

If newsgroups are more your style, there are a number of groups that deal with security-related topics. Newsgroups are useful in that you do not have to worry about filling up your Inbox. Messages are posted to newsgroup servers, which you can review at your leisure. The only problem with newsgroups is that they tend to have a very high signal-to-noise ratio. This is because newsgroup forums are unmoderated.

> **NOTE**
> A high signal-to-noise ratio means that you may have to filter through a lot of postings in order to find the information that interests you.

I have listed some newsgroups that may be of interest here, but I have not included a complete description. This is because the newsgroup name is typically descriptive:

- `comp.os.ms-windows.nt.admin.security`

- `comp.os.netware.security`

- `comp.security`

- `comp.security.firewalls`

- `comp.security.ssh`

- `comp.security.unix`

- `comp.security.misc`

- `microsoft.public.access.security`

Auditing Your Environment

The task of securing a network environment can be daunting, especially if you have multiple servers to deal with. It can be tough enough to handle the day-to-day firefighting, let alone figure out how to best lock down your systems. For the network administrator with many jobs to do, security can get put on the back burner in order to free time for other activities.

Many times the problem is not knowing what to look for. Most network administrators can change settings or load patches as required—but it would be nice to have some guidance about what needs to be done. The most obvious option is to hire a security consultant; however, this may be beyond your budget.

If you need to fix exploits, the vulnerability scanners covered in Chapter 16 are a good place to start. Products from Internet Security Systems (ISS) and WebTrends do an excellent job of documenting known exploits. Sometimes, however, what you are looking for is some guidance on how to create a more secure computing environment. When this is the case, consider using a *security auditing program*.

A security auditing package does not look for bugs or known vulnerabilities. Rather, it allows you to verify that all systems on your network comply with your security policy. For example, if your policy states that all user accounts should be forced to change their passwords every 90 days, an auditing package will check each of your servers in order to verify that this is the case.

Kane Security Analyst

Intrusion Detection's Kane Security Analyst (KSA) is a server auditing package. It does not perform vulnerability checks, but it will assess the security policy compliance level of each of your servers. KSA is capable of auditing Windows NT, NetWare (both bindery and NDS), UNIX, and even Lotus Notes servers. As part of KSA's assessment, it will check user accounts, the file system, logging, and even the Registry on NT/2000 systems. You enter the criteria for your organization's security policy, and KSA reports which network servers are noncompliant.

For an example, we will take a look at KSA's auditing ability when dealing with Windows 2000.

> **NOTE**
> The auditing process and reports generated against Windows NT/2000 are similar to each of the other platforms. The only big difference with Windows NT/2000 is that KSA can check Registry permissions and verify which drives are using NTFS.

You can download the latest 30-day evaluation copy of KSA from www .intrusion.com.

Installing KSA

The KSA installation could not be simpler. Simply download the latest version from KSA's Web site, run the self-extracting executable (pointing the contents to a temporary directory), and run the setup.exe file. After it prompts you for a directory location, the Setup program will install all the required files. If you decide later to remove KSA, you can do so by clicking the Add/Remove Programs icon within Control Panel.

> **NOTE**
> KSA must be run from a Windows server or workstation, version 3.51 or higher. While the program will successfully install on Windows 95/98, it will not run.

You can install the software on any NT/2000 system and audit servers remotely. You do not need to install the software on every system. Once the software installation is complete, simply go to the Kane Security Analyst program group and click the Kane Security Analyst icon.

Using KSA

The KSA main screen is shown in Figure 17.2. In order to perform a compliance audit, you need to follow three simple steps:

1. Set a security standard.

2. Run a security audit.

3. Display the analysis of a security audit.

Each of these steps is progressively numbered as a different button along the bottom of the screen. The fourth button can be used to review compliance history. Once an audit has been performed, you can quickly select to view a single portion of the audit using the icons at the top of the screen. This allows you to hone in on a specific portion of the audit.

FIGURE 17.2:

The KSA main screen

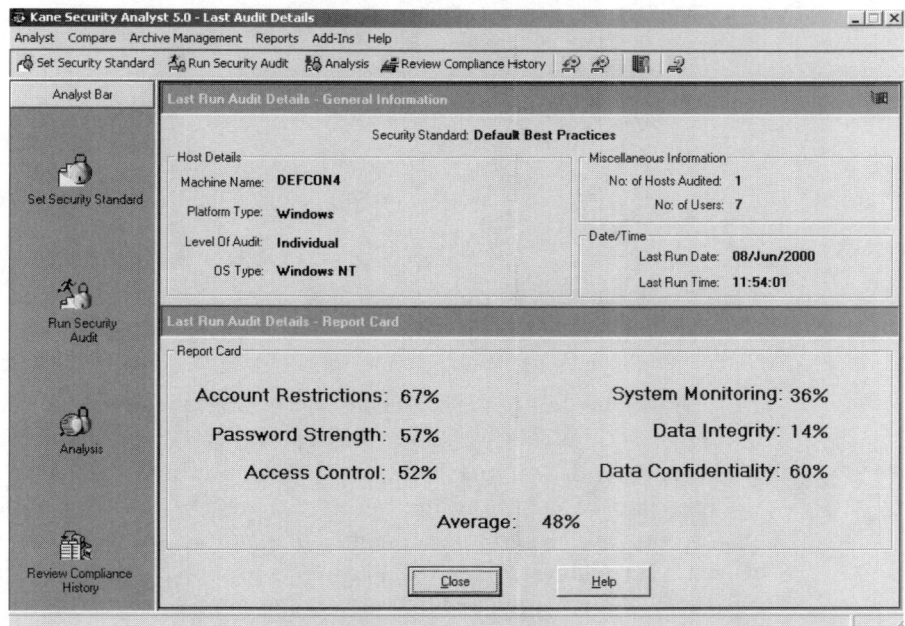

Defining a Security Policy

In order to input your security policy, click the Set Security Standard button. This produces the screen shown in Figure 17.3. The buttons along the left side of the screen allow you to select different aspects of your security policy. For example, Account Restrictions is selected by default. This button allows you to define whether KSA should check to see if station and time restrictions are being used. You can also tell KSA to check for disabled or dormant accounts.

FIGURE 17.3:

Setting security policy account restrictions

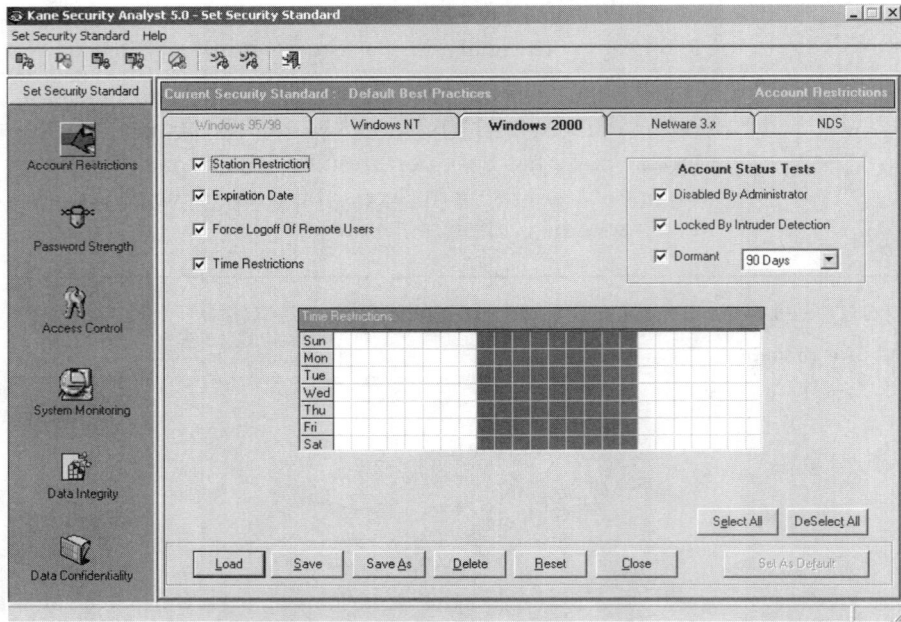

Along the top of the screen are some tabs labeled for different operating systems. Each tab allows you to select parameters for the applicable operating systems on your network. You must purchase additional licenses in order to activate these tabs. The buttons on the left and the tabs at the top allow you to navigate through all the audit parameters. For example, selecting System Monitoring along with the NetWare 4 tab will allow you to set which logging options should be checked on all of your NetWare 4.*x* servers.

Performing an Audit

In order to run an audit, select the Run Security Audit button from the KSA main screen. This will produce the Run Security Audit window shown in Figure 17.4. From this screen you tell KSA whether you wish to update a previous audit or perform a new one from scratch. You must also select which systems or domain you would like to have checked during the audit.

FIGURE 17.4:

The Run Security Audit window

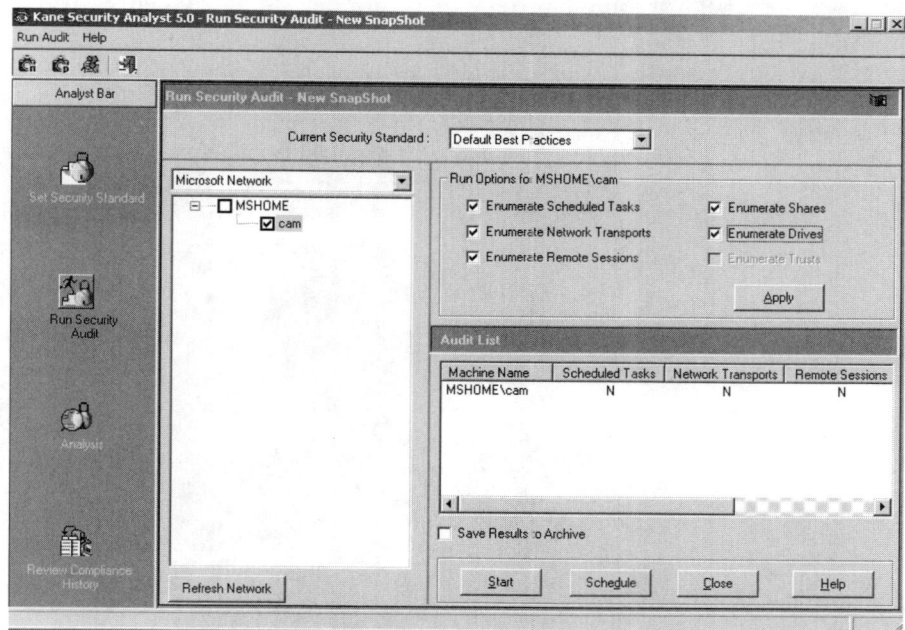

The Schedule button allows you to run the audit on a schedule. This is useful if you would prefer to have the audit run during off hours or on the weekend, but you do not want to be there in order to initiate it.

You can even have the scheduler run the audit on a regular basis so that you can compare different audits to see if any of your policy settings have changed.

Once you have selected the audit parameters, simply click the Start icon in the lower right portion of the screen. The amount of time it takes to perform the audit will vary based on the speed of the machine performing the audit and how many systems you have instructed KSA to check. Once the audit is complete, you can review the results.

Reviewing the Audit Results

You can review a graphical summary of the audit results by selecting the Survey Risk Analysis button from the KSA main screen. This produces the Risk Analysis Survey window shown in Figure 17.5. As you can see, the graphic does an excellent job of illustrating which portions of the system configuration meet your security policy guidelines and which ones do not. A score of 100 percent is full compliance. Anything less indicates that the system needs some tuning. You can use the percentage of compliance as a metric for determining where to focus your attention first.

FIGURE 17.5:

The Risk Analysis Survey window

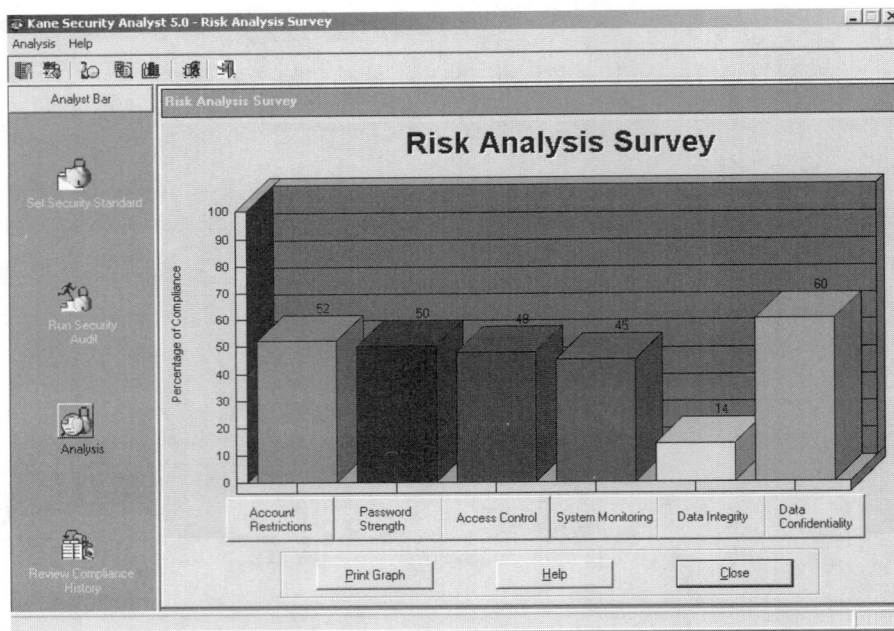

If you select the System Monitoring button in the Risk Analysis Survey window, you can retrieve detailed information about why System Monitoring scored so poorly. This will produce the System Monitoring screen shown in Figure 17.6. DEFCON4 scored so poorly on the System Monitoring test because event logs and retention time have been incorrectly configured. Since our policy stated that all servers should utilize these features, KSA has flunked this system. If you look in the lower right corner of the figure, you will see that the Security Log Size is too small and that log entries are not being retained long enough. This information is extremely useful, because you now know exactly what settings need to be modified in order to bring this system into compliance.

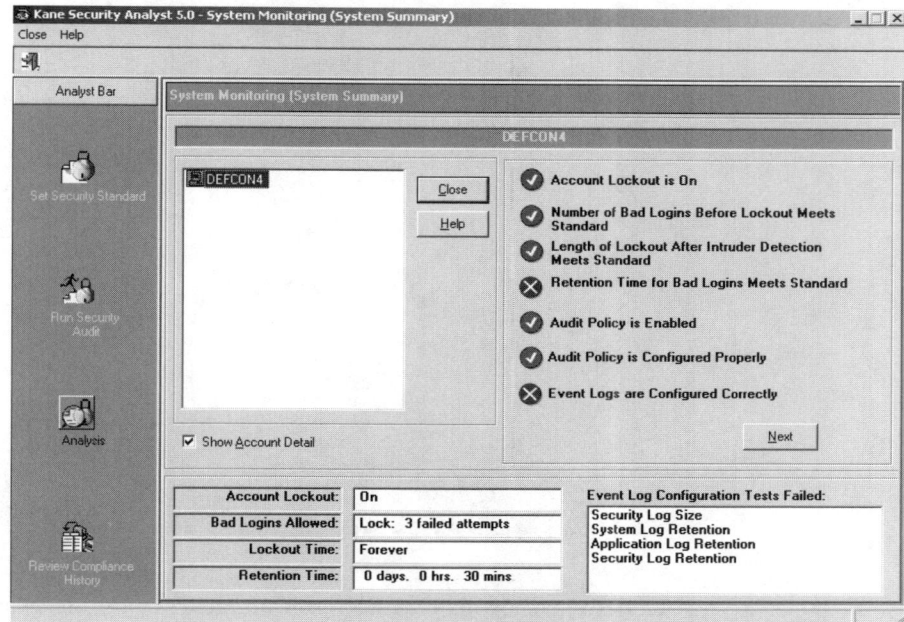

Now that we have run an audit, we can investigate some of the other KSA features. For example, clicking the Registry Rights icon on the main KSA screen produces the Registry Rights window shown in Figure 17.7. From this window you can browse the access rights assigned to each user or group. The left pane allows you to navigate the Registry, while the right pane shows you who has been assigned access and what level of permissions has been granted. The Add button allows you to flag this Registry key as a favorite.

It can be extremely time-consuming to navigate the entire Registry tree in order to check permissions. Typically, there are only a few Registry keys that you will want to check on a regular basis, such as the SAM key. The Favorite Keys tab allows you to indicate which keys you find most interesting. You can then select the Favorite Keys tab to view all your favorite keys in a single area. This saves you from having to search the Registry every time you wish to check their permission settings.

FIGURE 17.7:

The Registry Rights window

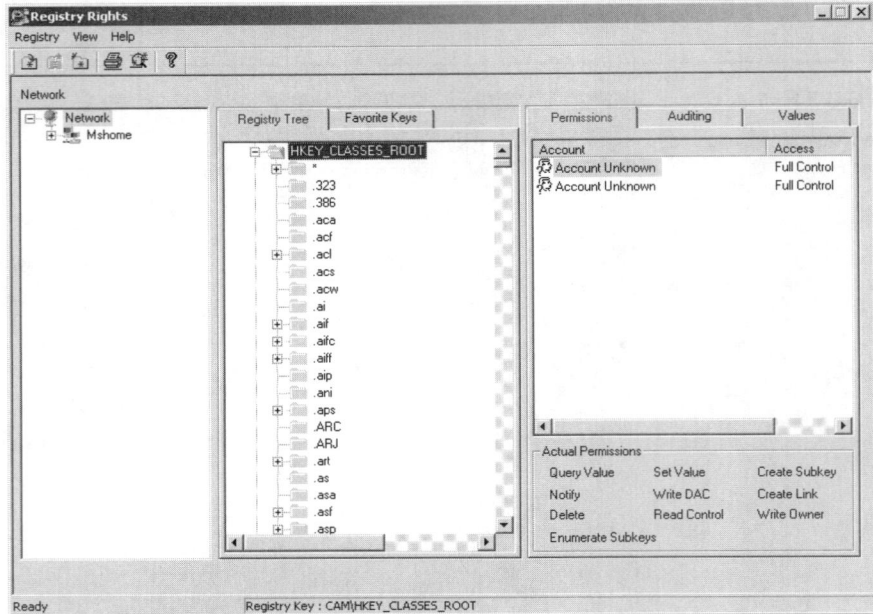

Another useful icon is the Report Manager. The Report Manager allows you to create custom reports and selectively choose which information is reported in each. For example, you could create a single report that identifies all the services running on every server, as well as error log entries. This allows you to quickly verify the health of all your network services.

Putting the Results to Use

Once you have your audit, it is now time to focus on your problem areas and get them resolved. KSA is an excellent tool because it does not give you a false sense of security. Systems are verified based on the security policy you input into the software. This means that you are not checking your systems against some arbitrary standard. You are verifying which systems are in compliance with your security policy and which ones are not. This allows the tool to be molded for any networking environment.

Summary

In this chapter we discussed how you can stay better informed of exploits as they are found. We discussed what vendor and third-party resources are available for investigating vulnerabilities and where to find patches. We also discussed which mailing lists and newsgroups are available if you need to find out more information. Finally, we looked at how to perform a security audit on your network and what tools are available to aid you in this task.

APPENDIX

A

About the CD-ROM

This CD-ROM contains security software products that will enable you to identify vulnerable points in your network and secure your business against malicious attack. Sybex provides these products for its readers through exclusive partnerships with the software companies involved. Installation information is presented below; where indicated, review the readme files that accompany each product for more information.

> **NOTE**   You will need Windows NT 4 to install these products on your machine.

FireWall-1

Included on the CD is a fully functioning, 30-day evaluation copy of the industry-leading firewall and security suite, FireWall-1, from Check Point Software Technologies, Ltd. FireWall-1 is available for the following operating systems:

- Windows NT 4
- Windows 2000
- Red Hat Linux 6.1
- Sun Solaris 2.6, 7
- HP-UX 10.20, 11.0
- AIX 4.2.1, 4.3.2, 4.3.3

> **NOTE**   For security reasons, you cannot install or activate your fully functioning evaluation copy of FireWall-1 until you have received a certification key from Check Point. E-mail sales@checkpoint.com to receive this key.

Check Point has included complete documentation on FireWall-1, available in PDF format for Acrobat Reader. These user manuals are located in the FireWall-1/Docs/Userguid folder on the CD-ROM. To begin, open the gs.pdf file and read "Getting Started with Check Point FireWall-1."

NOTE If you don't have Acrobat Reader, you can install it directly from the CD-ROM. The setup files are located in the `FireWall-1/Docs/Pdfread` folder; choose the appropriate setup for your operating system.

To install FireWall-1 on Windows NT 4, simply double-click the setup.exe file in the FireWall-1 folder on the CD and the Installshield Wizard will guide you through the installation process.

WARNING Do not install firewall demo products on production servers! They can restrict service to the machines so that you will not be able to log in correctly or use the machines for any other purpose.

Guardian

Included on the CD is a fully functioning, 30-day evaluation copy of the award-winning Guardian firewall from NetGuard, Inc. Double-click the `setup.exe` file in the NetGuard folder on the CD to install the program. If you have any questions about Guardian's installation or operation, you can skim through the 158-page *User's Manual* that is included on the CD in PDF format

WARNING Do not install firewall demo products on production servers! They can restrict service to the machines so that you will not be able to log in correctly or use the machines for any other purpose.

If you have any questions about the installation or operation of the Guardian firewall, contact NetGuard, Inc. at

NetGuard, Inc.
2445 Midway Road
Building 2
Carrollton, Texas 75006
972-738-6900
sales@netguard.com
www.netguard.com

Internet Scanner

Internet Security Systems, Inc. (ISS) has provided an evaluation copy of Internet Scanner, its complete network security vulnerability detection system. Double-click the `setup.exe` file located in the ISS folder on the CD.

NOTE   For security purposes and due to the powerful nature of ISS' Internet Scanner, the company requires that in order to fully evaluate the product, you utilize an encrypted license key. To obtain an extended evaluation key from Internet Security Systems (ISS), you can e-mail the company with your request at `sales@iss.net`. In the e-mail, please include your name, mailing and e-mail addresses, phone number, and the IP address range of your network. A license key will be e-mailed to you as soon as possible. You can also contact ISS by phone at (888) 901-7477.

Network Monitoring Suite (NMS)

Included on the CD is a fully functioning, 30-day evaluation copy of Lanware, Inc's Network Monitoring Suite (NMS). NMS is a software package designed to monitor the performance of critical elements of your network including routers, hubs, Windows NT Workstations, and Windows NT and UNIX servers. You must fill out the form at `www.lanware.net/download/eval/nms_registration.asp` in order to request and receive a 30-day license for NMS.

Double-click the `setup.exe` file located in the Lanware folder on the CD to install the program. If you have any questions about the installation or operation of NMS, contact Lanware, Inc. at

Lanware, Inc.
`sales@lanware.net`
`www.lanware.net`

WinZip

WinZip Computing (formerly Nico Mak Computing, Inc.) has provided a shareware evaluation copy of WinZip, its popular compression/decompression program. To install this product, locate the `setup.exe` file in the WinZip folder on the CD and double-click it.

> **NOTE**   You will need WinZip to install some of the other products included on this CD.

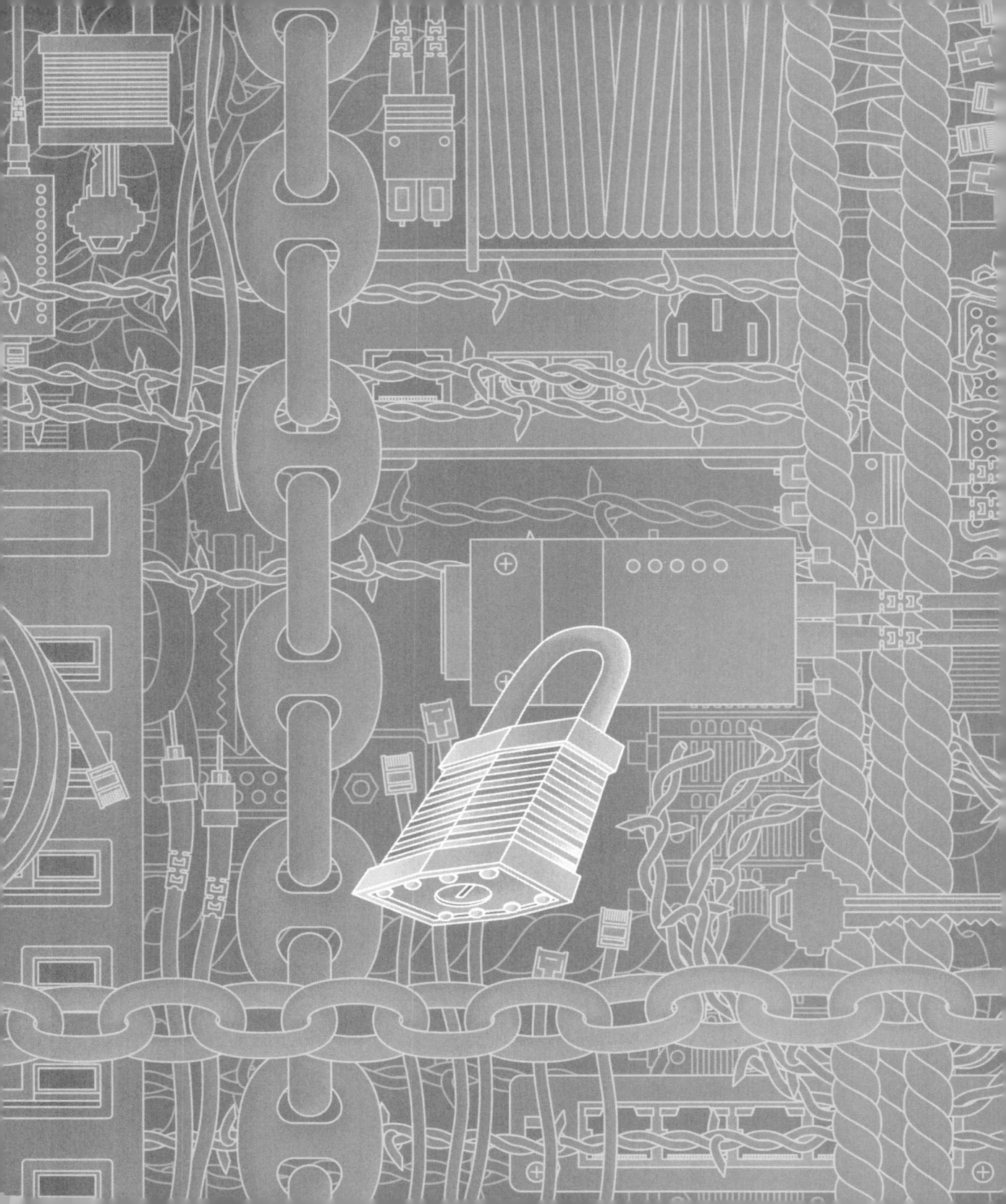

APPENDIX

B

Sample Network Usage Policy

While this appendix has been included in order to provide you with a sample network usage policy, ideally usage policies are process-driven and usually go through several steps which are part of a never-ending cycle as business needs and technology change.

NOTE   The following links are two examples of actual usage policies. The first is corporate, the second is for an educational institution:
www.oit.gatech.edu/security/policy/usage/contents.html
www.dmtnet.com/Internetpolicy/policy.pdf

Principles behind an Effective Network Usage Policy

There are two principles traditionally used to justify network usage policies:

Total Cost of Ownership (TCO)

TCO includes measuring employee productivity versus resource utilization.

Employee Productivity   Networks exist to ease the transfer of information, thereby making workers more productive. Ideally this productivity can be measured, which allows management to tie appropriate network usage to productivity goals.

Resource Utilization   The utilization of resources within a company must be suitably justified. Network activities that do not contribute to the bottom line simply cannot be justified from a cost perspective. Usage policies help define which activities are a justifiable use of resources—all other activities are automatically prohibited.

Risk Mitigation

Policies reduce the threat of information activity by defining those network activities that unjustifiably compromise company liability, threaten sensitive information, or open the organization to negative publicity:

Liability   Traditionally considered the domain of discrimination or sexual harassment, liability issues have expanded to include any communication that would result in the company being held liable.

Sensitive Information   Any information that would provide an advantage to a competitor—it is often the subject of intense scrutiny from rivals.

Negative Publicity   Any communication or use of resources that would lead to a negative image of an organization, negative publicity often has a direct impact to the revenue flow of an organization due to lost sales and stock revenue

The Developmental Process

The process of fine-tuning the for a specific organization goes through many phases:

Discovery   This first step is ideally performed with input from all levels of an organization that use the network. This not only provides a comprehensive policy, but eases employee support and education efforts. Typical questions are:

- What company roles (or individuals) need access?
- Which specific network services do they need?
- What are the current methods of access (including time and location)?
- Which core business applications are internet-integrated?
- What constitutes sensitive data?
- What are the measurable productivity goals, and how do network resources achieve those goals?
- What risks to network (and information) resources exist? (i.e. corporate espionage, liability, and negative publicity)
- What are the legal issues surrounding employee monitoring vs. privacy?

Definition   The second step synthesizes the collected information from the first step to create the policy. Topics include the following:

- Definitions of acceptable use as they fit into overall company vision/ mission, core business process/applications, and individual/collective roles

- Definitions and examples of sensitive data, processes, and resources

- Risks to data including corporate espionage, liability, and negative publicity

- Declaration of intent to monitor employee communication along with definition and examples of appropriate private communication and employee consent procedures

- Consequences of policy violation, including penalty and appeal process

- Procedures for complaint and/or modification of the policy

- Methods of disseminating the policy

Implement   The third step is to implement the policy. Implementation fundamentally consists of two steps:

- Disseminate the policy and educate the employees

- Enforce the policy

Review   The final step is to review the effectiveness of the policy against the two principles underlying the policy, namely (and in review): Total Cost of Ownership and risk mitigation. If the policy is not effective in satisfying these principles, the process is run again.

This sample policy that follows has been developed for Fubar Corporation. Fubar makes a wide range of desktop applications including FuMeeting, which is its premier meeting scheduler, and FuHR, which is an employee database system. There is a main office in New York, as well as a small sales office located in San Diego. The sales office is connected to the main office via a 128K Frame Relay connection. The corporate office also has a T1 connection to the Internet.

There are more than 200 employees working out of the corporate office; about half of them are programmers. Fubar has a very modern telecommuting policy and allows each programmer to work from home one day a week. In addition, Fubar's sales personnel spend a lot of time on the road doing presentations and making sales calls. Because so many employees spend time working away from the office, Fubar has deployed two remote-access solutions. Remote access is provided via a dial-in modem pool, as well as over the Internet using special VPN software.

The sensitivity of the information entering the network via remote connections is considered moderate. Since the programmers are working on the latest program code, Fubar could lose its business edge if this information were to fall into the hands of a competitor. Additionally, the sales information is considered sensitive because this data could give a competitor clues about new product releases.

Scope

The scope of this document is to define the company policies on proper network usage. The corporate network is a substantial investment toward profitability. It exists in order to improve employee productivity and to increase workflow efficiency. The components of the network are considered to be

- All cabling used for carrying voice and electronic information
- All devices used for controlling the flow of said voice and electronic information
- All computer components including (but not limited to) monitors, cases, storage devices, modems, network cards, memory chips, keyboards, mice network cards, and cables
- All computer software
- All output devices including printers and fax machines

Disciplinary action for failure to comply with any of the policy guidelines described in this document will be rendered on a per-incident basis. The company reserves the right to seek legal action when local, state, or federal laws have been broken or when financial loss has been incurred.

Network Management

All network maintenance, including configuration changes to desktop systems, are to be made solely by the operations staff. Employees or contractors who are not members of the operations staff are not allowed to make system modifications, even to the workstations issued to them by the company. Any of the following activities would be considered a modification to the system:

- Patching a system's network drop to a new location

- Using a system's floppy drive to boot an alternative operating system

- Removing a system's case or cover

- Installing any software package, including software downloaded from the Internet

Hardware management is restricted in order to insure that warranties are not inadvertently voided and that security precautions are not circumvented. Software installation is restricted in order to insure that the company remains in compliance with software licensing laws. It also insures that proper support for the software can be provided by the internal operations staff and that software incompatibilities are avoided.

Password Requirements

Each employee will be issued a unique logon name in order to gain access to network resources. Every logon name will also have an associated password. The password provides verification that only the authorized user may access network resources using this unique logon name. It is the responsibility of every employee to insure that his or her password remains secret. Passwords are to be used under the following guidelines:

- Passwords are to be a minimum of six alphanumeric characters.

- Passwords cannot consist of common words or variations on the employee's name, logon name, server name, or company name.

- The employee will be required to change his or her password every 60 days. If the employee does not do so, his or her account will be disabled. In order to reactivate a disabled account, the employee must have his or her direct supervisor contact the network operations staff.

- During authentication, the employee will have three attempts at entering his or her password correctly. If all three attempts fail, the account will be disabled. In order to reactivate the account, the employee must have his or her direct supervisor contact the network operations staff.

- Every company computer is required to use a screen saver that activates after 15 minutes of inactivity. Once the screen saver becomes active, it should require that the user again authenticate with the system before gaining access.

- For accessing the network remotely, either through the dial-in modem pool or through an Internet-based Virtual Private Network (VPN), the employee will be issued a security token which will produce a new password every 60 seconds. The password generated by the security token is to be used when the employee is accessing the network remotely.

- Passwords are to be kept private. The employee is expected to not write down his or her password or share it with other individuals. The exception is that an employee will surrender his or her password if requested to do so in the presence of his or her direct supervisor and a member of human resources.

- When accessing resources outside of the corporate network, the employee is required to use a different password from the one used for internal systems. This is to insure that critical password strings are not transmitted over public networks. Any questions about which systems are internal to the corporate network should be directed to the employee's direct supervisor or a member of the network operations staff.

- The company reserves the right to hold the employee liable for damages caused by the employee's failure to protect the confidentially of his or her password in accordance with the above guidelines.

A strong password policy insures that all network resources remain secure.

Virus Prevention Policy

All computer resources are to be protected by anti-virus software. It is the responsibility of the employee to insure that the virus software running on his or her system is not disabled or circumvented. If the employee receives any type of warning from the anti-virus software running on the system, he or she is to immediately cease using the system and contact a member of the network operations staff or his or her direct supervisor.

It is the responsibility of the network operations staff to keep all anti-virus software up to date. This will be performed through an automated process while the employee is connected to network resources. Employees who suspect that their anti-virus software has not been updated in the last 60 days should contact a member of the network operations staff.

Workstation Backup Policy

On a weekly basis, the network operations staff will perform a backup of documents stored on each employee's workstation. Every employee is assigned a day of the week during which he or she must leave his or her system powered up at the end of the day. The employee is to log off of the system, but the system must remain powered up. It is the responsibility of the employee to insure that his or her system remains powered up on the correct day. Employees should contact their direct supervisor to find out which day they have been assigned.

When an employee's workstation is backed up, only documents within the

```
C:\My Documents
```

directory will be saved. Documents stored in any other directory will be ignored. The employee bears responsibility for insuring that he or she saves all documents to this directory. All company-issued applications are designed to save file information to this directory by default.

Remote Network Access

The company provides both a dial-in modem pool and Internet-based VPN access in order to remotely connect to network resources. These are the only sanctioned methods of remote network access. Connecting a modem and a phone line to any part of the network (including desktop systems) is strictly prohibited and can be considered grounds for immediate dismissal.

Remote network access is provided on an as-needed basis. Any employee who requires remote access to network resources must have his or her direct supervisor submit a request form to the network operations department. The employee will then be issued the following:

- A security token for accessing network resources

- A list of modem pool phone numbers
- Required software for creating an encrypted VPN session over the Internet
- Directions for installing the VPN software
- Directions for accessing the network remotely

The company holds no responsibility for supporting the system that the employee plans to use for remote access. The employee agrees that by accepting the software, he or she is responsible for any and all upgrades required to support remote access. This includes (but is not limited to)

- A phone line
- A modem
- A faster processor
- Additional disk drive space

In addition, support for remote access will be provided by the network operations staff only for the internal network up to and including the network perimeter. The employee is responsible for providing his or her own support for connectivity problems outside of this scope.

The employee agrees to keep all information regarding remote network access confidential. The employee will not disclose password information or make copies of the VPN software, even for other employees. Propagating remote access details is considered a security breach and grounds for immediate dismissal.

General Internet Access Policy

Company network resources, including those used to gain access to Internet-based sites, are only to be used for the express purpose of performing work-related duties. This policy is to insure the effective use of networking resources and shall apply equally to all employees. Direct supervisors may approve the use of network resources beyond the scope of this limited access policy when said use meets the following conditions:

- The intended use of network resources is incidental.
- The intended use of network resources does not interfere with the employee's regular duties.

- The intended use of network resources serves a legitimate company interest.

- The intended use of network resources is for educational purposes and within the scope of the employee's job function.

- The intended use of network resources does not break any local, state, or federal laws.

- The intended use of network resources will not overburden the network.

Internet Web Site Access Policy

When accessing an Internet-based Web site, employees are to use a Web browser that meets the corporate standard. This standard requires the use of Internet Explorer 5.5 with the following configuration:

- There are no additional plug-ins.

- Java, JavaScript, and ActiveX have been disabled.

- Cookies have been disabled.

These settings are to insure that the employee does not inadvertently load a malicious application while browsing Internet Web sites. Failure to comply with these security settings can result in the loss of Internet access privileges. Web browser software should only be installed by network operations personnel. In order to maintain proper software licensing, employees are prohibited from retrieving browser software or upgrades from any other source. Any employee who is unsure whether his or her browser meets these company standards should contact network operations.

Internet Mail and Newsgroup Access Policy

Inbound and outbound Internet mail messages are limited to a maximum size of 8MB. Any employee who needs to transfer a file that exceeds this requirement should contact the network operations group for access to the corporate FTP server. This limitation is enforced in order to insure that one oversized e-mail message does not affect the flow of all corporate messages.

All messages transmitted to Internet-based mailing lists or newsgroups should include a company disclaimer as part of each message. The required disclaimer is "The opinions expressed in this message do not reflect the views of my employer."

The company reserves the right to monitor these transmissions and discard any messages that do not include this disclaimer.

Personal Internet-Based Accounts

Company network resources may not be used to access personal Internet-based accounts. These include (but are not limited to)

- Personal e-mail accounts
- Personal shell accounts
- Personal accounts with a service provider such as AOL or CompuServe

Personal accounts on online services should not be accessed from company systems. This does not include company-based accounts or subscriptions that may exist on Internet-based systems. Access to corporate accounts is considered acceptable, provided that access falls within an employee's job duties.

Privacy and Logging

It is the position of the company that all corporate network resources are owned solely by the company itself. This includes (but is not limited to) e-mail messages, stored files, and network transmissions. The company reserves the right to monitor and/or log all network-based activity. The employee is responsible for surrendering all passwords, files, and/or other required resources if requested to do so in the presence of his or her direct supervisor and a member of human resources.

Additional Information

All queries regarding information within this document, as well as issues that have not been specifically covered, should be directed to the employee's immediate supervisor. The immediate supervisor is responsible for relaying all queries to network operations or human resources, whichever is more appropriate.

INDEX

Note to the reader: Throughout this index **boldfaced** page numbers indicate primary discussions of a topic. *Italicized* page numbers indicate illustrations and tables.

B

C

D

F

G

H

O

P

R

S

T

W

X

Z

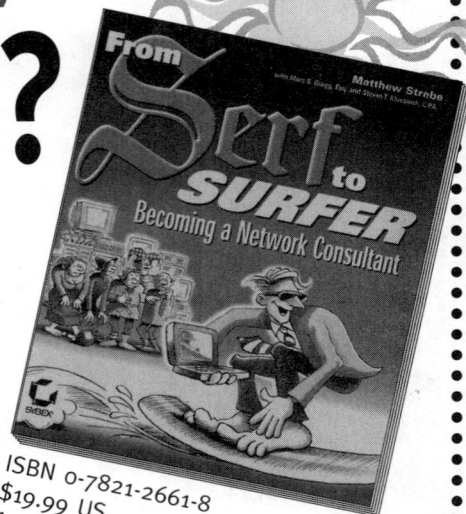